# Recent Trends and Future Direction for Data Analytics

Aparna Kumari
*Nirma University, Ahmedabad, India*

A volume in the Advances in Systems Analysis,
Software Engineering, and High Performance
Computing (ASASEHPC) Book Series

Published in the United States of America by
    IGI Global
    Engineering Science Reference (an imprint of IGI Global)
    701 E. Chocolate Avenue
    Hershey PA, USA 17033
    Tel: 717-533-8845
    Fax:  717-533-8661
    E-mail: cust@igi-global.com
    Web site: http://www.igi-global.com

Library of Congress Cataloging-in-Publication Data

CIP Data Pending
 ISBN: 979-8-3693-3609-0
eISBN: 979-8-3693-3610-6

This book is published in the IGI Global book series Advances in Systems Analysis, Software Engineering, and High Performance Computing (ASASEHPC) (ISSN: 2327-3453; eISSN: 2327-3461)

British Cataloguing in Publication Data
A Cataloguing in Publication record for this book is available from the British Library.

All work contributed to this book is new, previously-unpublished material. The views expressed in this book are those of the authors, but not necessarily of the publisher.

For electronic access to this publication, please contact: eresources@igi-global.com.

# Advances in Systems Analysis, Software Engineering, and High Performance Computing (ASASEHPC) Book Series

Vijayan Sugumaran
Oakland University, Rochester, USA

ISSN:2327-3453
EISSN:2327-3461

## MISSION

The theory and practice of computing applications and distributed systems has emerged as one of the key areas of research driving innovations in business, engineering, and science. The fields of software engineering, systems analysis, and high performance computing offer a wide range of applications and solutions in solving computational problems for any modern organization.

The **Advances in Systems Analysis, Software Engineering, and High Performance Computing (ASASEHPC) Book Series** brings together research in the areas of distributed computing, systems and software engineering, high performance computing, and service science. This collection of publications is useful for academics, researchers, and practitioners seeking the latest practices and knowledge in this field.

## COVERAGE

- Metadata and Semantic Web
- Computer Graphics
- Performance Modelling
- Distributed Cloud Computing
- Human-Computer Interaction
- Parallel Architectures
- Computer System Analysis
- Enterprise Information Systems
- Computer Networking
- Network Management

IGI Global is currently accepting manuscripts for publication within this series. To submit a proposal for a volume in this series, please contact our Acquisition Editors at Acquisitions@igi-global.com or visit: http://www.igi-global.com/publish/.

# Titles in this Series

*For a list of additional titles in this series, please visit:* http://www.igi-global.com/book-series/advances-systems-analysis-software-engineering/73689

*Advancing Software Engineering Through AI, Federated Learning, and Large Language Models*
Avinash Kumar Sharma (Sharda University, India) Nitin Chanderwal (University of Cincinnati, USA) Amarjeet Prajapati (Jaypee Institute of Information Technology, India) Pancham Singh (Ajay Kumar Garg Engineering College, Ghaziabad, India) and Mrignainy Kansal (Ajay Kumar Garg Engineering College, Ghaziabad, India)
Engineering Science Reference • copyright 2024 • 354pp • H/C (ISBN: 9798369335024) • US $355.00 (our price)

*Advancements, Applications, and Foundations of C++*
Shams Al Ajrawi (Wiley Edge, USA & Alliant International University, USA) Charity Jennings (Wiley Edge, USA & University of Phoenix, USA) Paul Menefee (Wiley Edge, USA) Wathiq Mansoor (University of Dubai, UAE) and Mansoor Ahmed Alaali (Ahlia University, Bahrain)
Engineering Science Reference • copyright 2024 • 564pp • H/C (ISBN: 9798369320075) • US $295.00 (our price)

*Practical Applications of Data Processing, Algorithms, and Modeling*
Pawan Whig (Vivekananda Institute of Professional Studies-Technical Campus, India) Sachinn Sharma (School of Computer Applications, MRIIRS, India) Seema Sharma (School of Computer Applications, MRIIRS, India) Anupriya Jain (School of Computer Applications, MRIIRS, India) and Nikhitha Yathiraju (University of Cumberlands, USA)
Engineering Science Reference • copyright 2024 • 313pp • H/C (ISBN: 9798369329092) • US $325.00 (our price)

*The Convergence of Self-Sustaining Systems With AI and IoT*
Roopa Chandrika Rajappan (Karpagam Academy of Higher Education, India) N.S. Gowri Ganesh (Saveetha Engineering College, India) J. Alfred Daniel (Karpagam Academy of Higher Education, India) Awais Ahmad (Imam Mohammad Ibn Saud Islamic University, Saudi Arabia) and R. Santhosh (Karpagam Academy of Higher Education, India)
Engineering Science Reference • copyright 2024 • 405pp • H/C (ISBN: 9798369317020) • US $300.00 (our price)

*Big Data Quantification for Complex Decision-Making*
Chao Zhang (Shanxi University, China) and Wentao Li (Southwest University, China)
Engineering Science Reference • copyright 2024 • 312pp • H/C (ISBN: 9798369315828) • US $315.00 (our price)

*Digital Technologies in Modeling and Management Insights in Education and Industry*
G. S. Prakasha (Christ University, India) Maria Lapina (North-Caucasus Federal University, Russia) Deepanraj Balakrishnan (Prince Mohammad Bin Fahd University, Saudi Arabia) and Mohammad Sajid (Aligarh Muslim University, India)
Information Science Reference • copyright 2024 • 409pp • H/C (ISBN: 9781668495766) • US $250.00 (our price)

701 East Chocolate Avenue, Hershey, PA 17033, USA
Tel: 717-533-8845 x100 • Fax: 717-533-8661
E-Mail: cust@igi-global.com • www.igi-global.com

# Table of Contents

## Section 1

## Fundamentals of Data Analytics

*Aparna Kumari, Nirma University, Ahmedabad, India*
*Alka Golyan, Dayanand College, India*
*Rushi Shah, Nirma University, India*
*Nikhil Raval, Nirma University, India*

*Simeon Okechukwu Ajakwe, Hanyang University, Seoul, South Korea*
*Opeyemi Deji-Oloruntoba, Inje University, Gimhae, South Korea*
*Samuel O. Olatunbosun, Chungbuk National University, South Korea*
*Francis Xavier Duorinaah, Chungbuk National University, South Korea*
*Israel A. Bayode, Kyung Hee University, South Korea*

*Asmaa Mahfoud Alhakimi, Management and Science University, Malaysia*

## Section 2

## Advanced Analytics Techniques

## Section 3

## Specialized Topics and Applications

# Detailed Table of Contents

### Section 1

### Fundamentals of Data Analytics

*In the "Fundamentals of Data Analytics" section, readers are introduced to the essential principles and methodologies that form the bedrock of data analysis. This section serves as a foundational guide, covering core concepts such as data types, sources, and the critical processes of data preparation and cleaning. Through exploration of statistical analysis and data visualization techniques, readers gain insights into uncovering patterns and trends within datasets. Overall, this section equips readers with the fundamental knowledge and skills necessary to embark on their journey into the realm of data analytics.*

**Chapter 1**

    *Aparna Kumari, Nirma University, Ahmedabad, India*
    *Alka Golyan, Dayanand College, India*
    *Rushi Shah, Nirma University, India*
    *Nikhil Raval, Nirma University, India*

In today's data-centric environment, data analytics has become increasingly crucial, offering insights from extensive data sources. This chapter presents an introductory overview of data analytics, emphasizing its significance, methods, and practical applications. It examines fundamental aspects like data collection, preprocessing, analysis, and interpretation, alongside the diverse array of tools and methodologies employed. Furthermore, it delves into the pivotal role of data analytics across decision-making processes, business intelligence endeavors, predictive modeling, and other pertinent fields. Data analytics examines raw data to understand what it tells us. It's like digging into information to find out what's important. Data analysis helps us understand things better, like how to make something work or do things more efficiently. By using these methods, we can make things run smoother and even save money. It's super important for any organisation because it helps them make smarter decisions and understand what customers like or don't like. This means they can make better products and services and market them more effectively. Data analytics is used in many different areas, and there are many tools to help with it. This chapter discusses all of this and cover how data analysis can help businesses in different ways, like figuring out customer trends, improving products, and making marketing strategies more effective.

**Chapter 2**
Multidimensional Perspective to Data Preprocessing for Model Cognition Verity: Data

*Simeon Okechukwu Ajakwe, Hanyang University, Seoul, South Korea*
*Opeyemi Deji-Oloruntoba, Inje University, Gimhae, South Korea*
*Samuel O. Olatunbosun, Chungbuk National University, South Korea*
*Francis Xavier Duorinaah, Chungbuk National University, South Korea*
*Israel A. Bayode, Kyung Hee University, South Korea*

Reliable data analysis depends on effective data preparation, especially since AI-driven business intelligence depends on unbiased and error-free data for decision-making. However, developing a reliable dataset is a difficult task that requires expertise. Due to the costly damage a negligible error in data can cause to a system, a good understanding of the processes of quality data transformation is necessary. Data varies in properties, which determines how it is generated, the errors in it, and the transformations it needs to undergo before it is fed into a model. Also, most data used for analytics is sourced from public stores without means to verify its quality or what further steps need to be taken in preprocessing it for optimal performance. This chapter provides a detailed description of practical and scientific procedures to generate and develop quality data for different models and scenarios. Also, it highlights the tools and techniques to clean and prepare data for optimal performance and prevent unreliable data analytics outcomes.

**Chapter 3**
*Asmaa Mahfoud Alhakimi, Management and Science University, Malaysia*

The concept of smart cities integrates advanced technologies to enhance urban living. This research analyzes smart technologies in education, healthcare, and transportation, aiming to understand their impact on efficiency, accessibility, and sustainability. It explores how smart city solutions reshape learning, healthcare, and mobility, examining digital integration, health tech adoption, and transportation innovations. Through case studies, it evaluates outcomes, access, and effectiveness in these sectors. The findings contribute to understanding smart city technology's relationships with urban services, offering insights for policymakers and planners. Ultimately, the study aims to interpret sustainable development through smart technology for diverse urban populations.

**Section 2**

**Advanced Analytics Techniques**

*In the "Advanced Analytics Techniques" section, readers delve into sophisticated methodologies and approaches that push the boundaries of data analytics. This segment explores cutting-edge techniques such as predictive modeling, classification algorithms, clustering, and time series analysis. Readers gain insight into how these advanced methods are applied to extract valuable insights from data, predict future trends, and make informed decisions. Through practical examples and case studies, this section offers a glimpse into the transformative power of advanced analytics in addressing complex challenges and driving innovation across diverse domains.*

## Chapter 4

*Wiwik Anggraeni, Institut Teknologi Sepuluh Nopember, Indonesia*
*Nisrina Nur Mahmudha, Institut Teknologi Sepuluh Nopember, Indonesia*
*Pujiadi Pujiadi, Malang Regency Public Health Office, Indonesia*
*Mauridhi Heri Purnomo, Institut Teknologi Sepuluh Nopember, Indonesia*

Dengue fever is a serious infectious disease that can be fatal if not diagnosed and treated promptly. Several factors are believed to contribute to the spread of this disease. Many studies have examined these factors and their influence on dengue fever. However, the geographical conditions of each area can vary greatly, and findings may not be applicable across different regions. There is still debate over whether climatic factors can explain the occurrence of dengue fever. This study aims to analyze the impact of various factors on dengue fever incidence in multiple regions using path analysis. The study examines both exogenous and endogenous variables, including dengue fever incidence, population density, larvae-free index, temperature, humidity, rainfall, and wind speed. The results of the path analysis are used to forecast future dengue fever cases. The forecast results can assist health agencies in developing effective policies and strategies to control dengue fever outbreaks.

## Chapter 5

*Divyani Tirthyani, Manipal University Jaipur, India*
*Sunil Kumar, Manipal University Jaipur, India*
*Shally Vats, Manipal University Jaipur, India*

Machine learning (ML) is an approach driven by data, wherein computers acquire knowledge from information without requiring human interference. Artificial intelligence (AI) and machine learning (ML) have made significant contributions across diverse research domains, leading to enhanced outcomes. Clustering is defined as a fundamental challenge in various data-driven fields, representing an unsupervised learning model. Unsupervised learning methods and algorithms encompass the Apriori algorithm, ECLAT algorithm, frequent pattern growth algorithm, k-means clustering, and principal components analysis. Unsupervised learning methods have achieved notable success in fields such as machine vision, speech recognition, the development of autonomous vehicles, and natural language processing. This chapter provides a brief explanation of unsupervised clustering approaches. It also discusses literature review, intriguing challenges, and future prospects in the realm of unsupervised deep clustering.

## Chapter 6

*Upinder Kaur, Akal University, India*
*Harsh Kumar, Akal University, India*
*Ranbir Kaur, Akal University, India*

The emerging technologies are revolutionizing predictive analytics in HealthCare domain. The research in this sector has made great strides in managing disease management, which has eventually resulted in the saving of lives. The report significantly provides the progress of sophisticated learning methods capable of deciphering complex data relationships, thereby transforming broad datasets into actionable insights for disease diagnosis and prognosis. This goal is to assess the scope of ML and DL in healthcare predictions, focusing on the urgent need for reliable, accurate, and timely predictions while addressing ethical challenges. The authors provide a summary of the approaches worked under predictive analytics in healthcare, emphasizing its lifesaving potential through better decision-making through identifying barriers, suggestions, and future pathways.

# Chapter 7

This chapter investigates the domain of unsupervised learning algorithms, delivering a detailed outline of its classifications and essential characteristics. Each algorithm is examined, assessing its appropriateness for different types of data. A systematic assessment is conducted with each algorithm and is checked using datasets that complement its strengths. The evaluation presents insights on how well these algorithms perform in comparison with contextually relevant datasets. It also provides the foundation for a systematic investigation into the details of unsupervised learning by matching each algorithm with an appropriate class of data. The knowledge gap between theory and practice was explored by clustering algorithms with prominent tools like Weka and goes beyond the clustering concept by establishing essential principles for unsupervised learning. Through the explanation of clustering algorithms with real world datasets, practical approaches were provided to employ unsupervised learning in real-world data.

# Chapter 8

Enormous research papers are floating in the journals market to get published. But now as per the quality standards and norms of publication, some guidelines have been formulated by the prominent authorities to eradicate the pandemic issue of plagiarism. Moreover, it has also been considered whether genuine or licensed software has been utilized to analyze the research data or not. Hence, it is the time to explore some avenues so that mass researchers can be benefitted. R-software, designed by Robert Gentleman and Ross Ihaka from R core team, and R Studio, an open-source integrated development environment (IDE) for R, founded by J.J. Allaire, have emerged as the best platforms for the upcoming researchers which are not bounded with any constraints of licensing. In this article, few packages of R- Software, their significance and implementation have been discussed and summarized. Furthermore some data analysis techniques like t-test, linear regression technique, etc. have also been illustrated using R Studio.

## Section 3

## Specialized Topics and Applications

*In the section titled "Specialized Topics and Applications," readers delve into advanced concepts and practical applications within the field of data analytics. This section explores specialized topics such as predictive modeling, clustering, natural language processing, and big data analytics. Readers gain insights into how these techniques are applied across various industries, including finance, healthcare, marketing, and supply chain management. Each chapter provides in-depth discussions and real-world case studies, offering readers a deeper understanding of how data analytics can be tailored to address specific challenges and opportunities within different domains.*

## Chapter 9

    *Hamed Hosseinnia, Tabriz University, Iran*
    *Rana Rostami, Tabriz University, Iran*

The growth of the load makes the need to build a new power plant inevitable. According to the type of load, the type of DGs is selected. In loads that need both electricity and heat, simultaneous production units are used. Improving system technical criteria's such as: voltage stability, total harmonic distortion (THD), power loss are main aims of researchers. Harmonics are one of the stressful factors in the system. Harmonics are created both by the load and by the DGs themselves. In this chapter, the goal is to reduce the harmonics at the point of common coupling (PCC). For this purpose, solar-based combined hydrogen, heat, and power (S-CHHP) is used. Artificial intelligence (AI) is the one of strong tools in define and solve of optimization problems. Due to importance of data gathering, process and send/receive in this study, the system to manage information data with minimum error, is inevitable. Natural language process (NLP) is the best choice to utilize in this system.

## Chapter 10

    *Tarun Kumar Vashishth, IIMT University, India*
    *Vikas Sharma, IIMT University, India*
    *Asheesh Pandey, ABES Engineering College, Ghaziabad, India*
    *Tanuja Tomer, Nimbus Academy of Management, India*

This research looks at the changing face of big data analytics with a special focus on Hadoop incorporation by examining new developments and potential future directions. Over the years, the field of data analytics has gone through tremendous expansion due to the large amount of complex data generated from various sectors. In this light, Hadoop is identified as a highly adaptive and distributed computing system that serves as a powerful resource to extract valuable information from big datasets. This chapter analyzes advanced artificial intelligence techniques, real-time data analysis methodologies, emerging research directions, and ethics of big data. It highlights their implementation within the Hadoop platform. In an attempt to explore the mutual influence that exists between studies using Hadoop and evolving paradigms of analytics, it can be concluded that this study endeavors to provide an exhaustive navigation manual to scholars, practitioners, and industry observers who are interested in exploring the frontiers of big data analytics through Hadoop and its analytic evolution.

## Chapter 11

    *Alka Golyan, Dayanand College, India*
    *Shikhar Panchal, Nirma University, India*
    *Dhruvesh Vaghasiya, Nirma University, India*
    *Harsh Parekh, Nirma University, India*

The ethical issues surrounding data acquisition, use, and management have gained prominence in the quickly changing field of data analytics. In the framework of contemporary data analytics, this chapter examines the complex issues of data ethics and privacy. It looks at the moral dilemmas brought on by gathering and using enormous volumes of data, such as those involving permission, openness, and justice. It also explores the effects of data analytics methods on society's values and individual privacy rights, including machine learning and artificial intelligence. The chapter also covers new rules and frameworks being developed to address ethical issues with data analytics procedures. This chapter offers insights into best practices for managing the ethical complexity inherent in data-driven decision-making through the analysis of case studies and ethical problems. Ultimately, it emphasizes how crucial it is to embrace moral standards and privacy-protecting methods to guarantee ethical and long-lasting data analytics procedures in the future.

## Section 4

## Applications Across Industries and Future Trends

*In the section titled "Applications Across Industries and Future Trends," readers are introduced to the diverse real-world applications of data analytics spanning various sectors such as finance, healthcare, marketing, and supply chain management. Through a series of case studies and discussions, readers gain insights into how data analytics is utilized to address specific challenges and drive innovation within each industry. Additionally, the section explores emerging trends and future directions in data analytics, offering a glimpse into the evolving landscape of the field and preparing readers for the challenges and opportunities that lie ahead.*

## Chapter 12

This study examines the impact of technology on education, specifically focusing on motivation and learning principles for instructional enhancement. For 84 junior students from both computer science and computer forensics, ARCS-based instruction showed improved motivation and academic performance. CS students experienced a 50% increase in success opportunities, while CF students had a 70% higher satisfaction rate with rewards. Statistical analysis confirmed the differences (p &lt; 0.05), indicating tailored educational approaches; CS students adapt well; CF students prefer intrinsic reinforcement. However, academic achievement varied significantly, emphasizing the need for refined motivational strategies, particularly for CF students. The findings suggest that ARCS-based instruction benefits motivation and academic achievement, necessitating tailored approaches across subject areas. Integrating motivation science and technology can create captivating learning experiences that promote lifelong learning and academic success.

## Chapter 13

Data analytics stands at the precipice of an unprecedented transformation, driven by technological breakthroughs, shifting user demands, and evolving industry landscapes. This abstract delineates forthcoming trends poised to redefine the fabric of data analytics in the foreseeable future. The future of data analytics is characterized by a convergence of cognitive computing, ethical AI, hybrid cloud architectures, augmented data management, blockchain technology, edge intelligence, and continuous intelligence. By embracing these transformative trends, organizations can unlock the full potential of data analytics, foster innovation, and drive sustainable growth in an increasingly data-driven world. AI-Powered Automation and machine learning algorithms are set to revolutionize data analytics by automating repetitive tasks, uncovering hidden patterns, and delivering actionable insights at scale. Ethical data governance with growing concerns about privacy, security, and algorithmic bias, ethical data governance emerges as a cornerstone of responsible data practices.

**Chapter 14**

*Aparna Kumari, Department of Computer Science and Engineering, Institute of Technology, Nirma University, Ahmedabad, India*

Data analytics, which includes fundamental ideas, cutting-edge techniques, and practical applications, is essential for directing well-informed decision-making in various industries. Starting with the importance of data preparation and integrity, the trip proceeds via exploratory data analysis and large-scale dataset analysis made possible by state-of-the-art tools such as Hadoop. Practical examples of data-driven decision-making's real-world advantages in various businesses are highlighted with ethical issues and privacy ramifications. Future trends are examined, including the merging of artificial intelligence and the changing function of data analysts. In light of data analytics' revolutionary potential in creating a data-centric landscape, creating a culture that supports real-world application, lifelong learning, and ongoing skill development is advocated.

# Preface

In today's rapidly evolving data analytics landscape, this book stands as a comprehensive guide, providing insights into the latest trends and future prospects of this dynamic field. Data analytics has become integral to industry decision-making processes, reshaping how organizations operate and innovate. With the exponential growth of available data, the demand for effective analysis methodologies has never been more pronounced. This book aims to bridge the gap between theory and practice, equipping readers with the knowledge and skills to navigate this data-rich environment confidently.

Our journey as editors in compiling this book began with a vision to offer a holistic understanding of data analytics, covering foundational principles to advanced applications. Each chapter is carefully crafted to provide a blend of theoretical insights and practical case studies, ensuring readers understand the subject matter comprehensively. The book's structure facilitates learning progression, starting with fundamental concepts like data preparation and exploratory data analysis and progressing to advanced topics such as predictive modelling and clustering. Real-world case studies from diverse industries offer valuable insights into how data analytics addresses complex challenges and drives innovation.

Furthermore, this book looks ahead, exploring emerging trends like big data analytics and artificial intelligence, providing readers with a forward-looking perspective on the evolving data analytics landscape. We extend our sincere gratitude to all contributors who generously shared their expertise, enriching the content of this book and making it a valuable resource for students, researchers, and practitioners alike. As editors, it has been a privilege to embark on this journey of exploration and discovery in data analytics. We hope this book is a valuable resource, empowering readers to leverage data analytics for positive change in their fields.

Thank you for joining us on this journey. We trust you will find *Recent Trends and Future Directions in Data Analytics* both informative and inspiring.

## THE CHALLENGES

The compilation of *Recent Trends and Future Directions in Data Analytics* presented several hurdles we diligently tackled throughout the book's creation. Here are the primary challenges we faced, along with our efforts to overcome them:

- Data analytics is a multifaceted subject with many techniques, methodologies, and applications. Our main challenge was simplifying this complexity to ensure that readers could grasp the content effectively regardless of their expertise level.

- Data analytics constantly evolves, with new technologies and trends emerging regularly. Keeping the content current and relevant amidst this rapid change required continuous research and updates.
- Data analytics is used in various industries with unique challenges and requirements. Ensuring adequate coverage of these diverse applications presented a challenge, demanding a comprehensive approach across different domains.
- Striking a harmonious balance between theoretical concepts and practical applications was essential. While providing readers with a solid theoretical foundation, we also aimed to illustrate real-world scenarios to demonstrate the content's practical relevance.
- Incorporating the latest industry insights and practices necessitated access to expertise across different data analytics domains. Collaborating with subject matter experts and practitioners helped ensure the content's depth and relevance.

Despite these obstacles, our team approached the creation of this book with dedication and enthusiasm. We aimed to deliver a resource that provides insights into the dynamic field of data analytics and equips readers with the knowledge and confidence to navigate its complexities effectively. We trust that *Recent Trends and Future Directions in Data Analytics* will be a valuable guide for readers, empowering them to leverage data analytics to drive innovation and success.

## SEARCHING FOR A SOLUTION

The inception of *Recent Trends and Future Directions in Data Analytics* arose from our recognition of the multifaceted challenges inherent in the field. As editors, we confronted a swiftly evolving landscape marked by diverse applications and an ever-expanding volume of data. It became clear that a solution was imperative—a resource that elucidates the intricacies of data analytics and offers practical insights into its application across various domains.

Our pursuit of a solution led us on a collaborative journey, aiming to amalgamate diverse perspectives, expertise, and experiences. We endeavoured to create a comprehensive resource catering to novice learners and seasoned practitioners. Leveraging the collective wisdom of industry experts, academics, and researchers, we strived to distil complex concepts into accessible content without compromising depth or relevance.

In our quest, we acknowledged the necessity of balancing theory with practice. While theoretical understanding lays the groundwork for data analytics, practical application underscores its value. Thus, we curated various real-world case studies spanning finance, healthcare, marketing, and supply chain management industries. These examples illustrate how data analytics drives informed decision-making and fosters innovation in diverse contexts.

Furthermore, we addressed the challenge of keeping up-to-date with the field's dynamic nature. By exploring emerging trends and future directions in data analytics, we aimed to equip readers with the foresight and adaptability required to navigate evolving technologies and methodologies.

In essence, *Recent Trends and Future Directions in Data Analytics* embodies our collective endeavour to solve the challenges encountered by learners, practitioners, and researchers. We aspire for this book to serve as a guiding beacon, empowering individuals to harness the potential of data analytics for positive change and innovation in their respective domains.

## ORGANIZATION OF THE BOOK

The book is organized into fourteen chapters. A brief description of each of the chapters follows:

Chapter 1, readers are introduced to the fundamental concepts of data analytics. The chapter provides an overview of the goals and significance of data analytics in contemporary business environments. It outlines the pivotal role of data in decision-making processes and sets the stage for the subsequent chapters by presenting the scope and structure of the book.

Chapter 2 delves into the intricate facets of data preprocessing, emphasizing the importance of a comprehensive and multidimensional approach. This chapter aims to provide readers with insights into the various techniques and strategies essential for enhancing model cognition verity, ensuring that data is optimized and refined for effective analytics and modeling.

In Chapter 3, the urban service sectors of transportation, healthcare, and education are the main focus of analytical case studies of smart cities. Through in-depth analysis and interpretation, we investigate the revolutionary effects of data analytics on improving productivity, sustainability, and user experience in these vital urban businesses.

Using a regression model and path analysis, we explore the complex processes influencing the transmission of dengue fever in chapter 4. We aim to identify the fundamental connections and critical factors affecting dengue fever epidemiology, opening the door to earlier and more precise prediction of the disease's future distribution and effects.

In chapter 5, examines a variety of clustering algorithms and their applications using real-world use cases, including K-Means and Hierarchical Clustering. It also discusses how to assess the quality of clusters, giving readers a thorough grasp of how to use unsupervised learning approaches in data analysis.

The healthcare industry is poised for a data-driven revolution. It will utilize deep learning (DL) and machine learning (ML) to enable powerful predictive analytics that will revolutionize patient care, diagnosis, and treatment. To improve patient outcomes and medical decision-making, chapter 6 explores the novel uses, difficulties, and future possibilities of combining ML and DL algorithms. It also dives into the transformational potential of AI-driven predictive analytics in healthcare.

Chapter 7 explores the intriguing field of unsupervised learning, a subfield of machine learning. In this setting, algorithms acquire knowledge from unlabeled input. The main topic of this chapter is clustering, a widely used method for assembling related data points according to specified traits or properties. We have examined and discussed various clustering algorithms' uses and evaluation techniques, including K-Means and Hierarchical Clustering.

Chapter 8 explores the fundamental R-Studio data analysis tools and methods. R is a popular programming language for statistical computation and data visualization, and R-Studio is a potent integrated development environment (IDE) for R. This chapter will provide readers with a basic grasp of how to use R-Studio for a variety of data analysis activities, including statistical modelling, machine learning, and data manipulation and visualization. Regardless of your level of R-Studio knowledge, this chapter gives you the tools you need to realize the complete data analytic potential of the program.

Chapter 9 discusses the best way to minimize harmonics at the standard coupling (PCC) point for solar-based combined hydrogen, heat, and power (S-CHHP) systems. Harmonics in PCC can negatively impact the performance and lifespan of electrical equipment, leading to serious power quality problems. We investigate how to construct S-CHHP systems to reduce these harmonic disturbances, guaranteeing adequate and dependable operation of the integrated system, using thorough analysis and optimization methodologies.

In Chapter 10, we explore the cutting-edge developments in big data analytics, with an emphasis on integrating Hadoop to navigate emerging trends and directions. We examine how Hadoop and other cutting-edge technologies are changing the big data analytics scene and opening up new possibilities for data-driven insights and judgment.

Chapter 11 examines the ethical considerations and privacy concerns associated with data analytics. The chapter discusses the importance of ethical data handling practices, compliance with privacy regulations, and the need for responsible data governance. Through case studies, readers gain insights into real-world data analytics scenarios' ethical dilemmas and challenges.

In Chapter 12, we explore how the ARCS Model (Attention, Relevance, Confidence, and Satisfaction) might be used to improve academic success and learner engagement in technology-driven learning environments. This chapter examines how the ARCS Model can be strategically applied to build learning environments that are both effective and motivating, leading to better learner outcomes and accomplishments.

In chapter 13, readers explore emerging trends and future directions in data analytics. The chapter discusses advancements in machine learning, artificial intelligence, and data visualization and their potential impact on data analytics.

Chapter 14 serves as the book's culmination, summarizing key insights and practical takeaways from previous chapters. It encourages readers to apply their learnings to real-world projects, emphasizes the importance of lifelong learning in data analytics, and inspires them to continue exploring and evolving in this dynamic field.

*Aparna Kumari*
*Nirma University, Ahmedabad, India*

# Acknowledgment

I begin by expressing my gratitude to the divine for giving me the strength and determination to overcome challenges and see this project through to completion.

I extend my appreciation to all individuals involved in this venture, particularly the authors and reviewers whose contributions were indispensable in bringing this book to fruition. I thank each author for their valuable contributions. I am genuinely thankful for the time and expertise they dedicated to their respective chapters.

Furthermore, I acknowledge the reviewers' significant contributions in improving the quality, coherence, and presentation of the chapters. Many authors also served as reviewers, and I appreciate their dual roles.

Thank you.

*Aparna Kumari*
*Nirma University, Ahmedabad, India*

# Section 1
# Fundamentals of Data Analytics

*In the "Fundamentals of Data Analytics" section, readers are introduced to the essential principles and methodologies that form the bedrock of data analysis. This section serves as a foundational guide, covering core concepts such as data types, sources, and the critical processes of data preparation and cleaning. Through exploration of statistical analysis and data visualization techniques, readers gain insights into uncovering patterns and trends within datasets. Overall, this section equips readers with the fundamental knowledge and skills necessary to embark on their journey into the realm of data analytics.*

# Chapter 1
# Introduction to Data Analytics

**Aparna Kumari**

https://orcid.org/0000-0001-5991-6193

*Nirma University, Ahmedabad, India*

**Alka Golyan**

*Dayanand College, India*

**Rushi Shah**

*Nirma University, India*

**Nikhil Raval**

*Nirma University, India*

## ABSTRACT

*In today's data-centric environment, data analytics has become increasingly crucial, offering insights from extensive data sources. This chapter presents an introductory overview of data analytics, emphasizing its significance, methods, and practical applications. It examines fundamental aspects like data collection, preprocessing, analysis, and interpretation, alongside the diverse array of tools and methodologies employed. Furthermore, it delves into the pivotal role of data analytics across decision-making processes, business intelligence endeavors, predictive modeling, and other pertinent fields. Data analytics examines raw data to understand what it tells us. It's like digging into information to find out what's important. Data analysis helps us understand things better, like how to make something work or do things more efficiently. By using these methods, we can make things run smoother and even save money. It's super important for any organisation because it helps them make smarter decisions and understand what customers like or don't like. This means they can make better products and services and market them more effectively. Data analytics is used in many different areas, and there are many tools to help with it. This chapter discusses all of this and cover how data analysis can help businesses in different ways, like figuring out customer trends, improving products, and making marketing strategies more effective.*

DOI: 10.4018/979-8-3693-3609-0.ch001

## 1. INTRODUCTION

In today's data-driven world, the importance of data analytics cannot be overstated, as it offers valuable insights. It encompasses the data collection, processing, and analysis of extensive data sources to unearth meaningful observations. With the exponential growth of data from diverse sources like social media, sensors, etc. the demand for proficient data analytics has surged. Data analytics is the systematic analysis of raw data to derive insights and comprehend the underlying information (Berthold, M. R. et. al., 2010; Boldosova, V., & Luoto, S. (2020)). This procedure is essential for all industries since it allows businesses to better understand their operations and make educated decisions (Black, K. 2023; Wang, Y. et. al., 2018). Companies can find hidden patterns, trends, and correlations in their data sets using various analytical techniques (Minelli et. al., 2013; A. kumari et. al., 2020). In the retail industry, for instance, data analytics can entail examining sales data to pinpoint popular products or peak buying periods (Bradlow et. al., 2017; Griva et. al., 2018). Beyond simply helping people understand data, data analytics is significant because it offers real business advantages. Its main benefit is that it can streamline procedures and increase productivity (Sherman et. al., 2006; Yadav et. al., 2023). Organisations can find opportunities for improvement and streamline processes by examining data on workflow, resource allocation, and performance indicators. This may result in lower expenses, more output, and more effective use of available resources. For example, a manufacturing business may use data analytics to pinpoint production process bottlenecks and adjust to boost productivity and cut waste (Raghupathi et. al., 2014; Kumari. A et. al., 2022; Chalos, P., 1997). Additionally, data analytics gives companies insights into their customers' tastes and behaviour (Wedel M. et. al., 2016; Strong, C., 2015) . Organizations can better satisfy customer needs by customizing their products and services by analysing client data, including purchase history, browsing trends, and feedback. This customer-focused strategy promotes innovation and competition in addition to loyalty (Aljumah. et. al., 2021; A. Kumari et. al., 2020; Javaid, M. et. al., 2021). An e-commerce platform can use data analytics to customize product recommendations based on a user's browsing history and demographics (Schafer, J. et. al., 2001; Malhotra et. al., 2021; Huang H., et. al., 2021).

Moreover, incorporating data analytics into business models is crucial in promoting enhancements in sector-wide performance. Industries can recognize new trends, predict changes in the market, and modify their strategy by utilising data (Constantiou, I. et. al., 2015; Akter, S. et. al., 2016). By taking a proactive stance, companies can stay ahead of the curve and take advantage of growth prospects (Kwon, O. et. al., 2014; Seifian, A. et. al., 2023; Swift, R.S., et. al., 2001). Better engagement and conversion rates can be achieved using data-driven marketing methods, which can also be more effective and targeted. To develop highly targeted ads that appeal to particular audience segments, a marketing agency, for example, can utilise data analytics to examine the demographics and behaviour of its customers (Ahmadi, I. et. al., 2024; Ducange, P. et. al., 2018; Plummer, J., et. al., 2007; Talosig, E. 2022). To sum up, data analytics is a complex process that enables businesses to utilise the information they possess fully. Companies can promote innovation, comprehend client needs, and enhance processes using analytical tools and methodologies. This chapter thoroughly introduces data analytics, examining the several instruments, methods, and uses that support its significance in today's data-driven world.

## 1.1 Motivation

In writing this chapter, we aim to provide a comprehensive and understandable overview of data analytics. Our goal is to demonstrate the value of data analytics and how it aids in business decision-making. We also highlight how data analysis tools can improve efficiency, reduce costs, and streamline operations. Furthermore, we would like to discuss how data analytics isn't limited to any organization; it benefits a wide range of industries, improving them and facilitating more efficient product sales. Therefore, we want to make it easier for individuals to see how data analytics can benefit and even increase the success of enterprises.

## 1.2 Chapter Contribution

- We conduct a thorough literature review to delve into the significance of data analytics in influencing decision-making processes. This chapterfocuses on how using data analytics to make better judgments and tailor goods and services to consumers' preferences can lead to more intelligent decisions.
- We discuss a variety of techniques, including data collection, preprocessing, analysis, interpretation, and propose a model. The proposed model covers improving efficiency, reducing costs, and making things flow more smoothly.
- The chapter thoroughly overviews data analytics and demonstrates its significance across several domains along with a case study. It emphasizes how data analytics contributes to innovation and competitive edge.

## 1.3 Organization of Chapter

The chapter is organized into several sections, beginning with Section II, which reviews Related Work, followed by Section III, presenting the Proposed Model. Section IV details the Methodology employed, offering insights into the research design and data collection methods. Section V provides a Case Study, offering a practical application of the proposed model. Finally, the Conclusion section summarizes key findings and implications from the analysis conducted in the preceding sections, succinctly wrapping up the chapter.

## 2. RELATED WORK

The modern world is inundated with data. We produce enormous amounts of information through social media, online shopping, sensor data, and financial transactions. This flood of data creates both difficulties and chances for us. This is where data analysis comes into the picture. Data refers to raw facts, figures, or information typically in the form of numbers, text, images, or other formats. It can be structured or unstructured and is collected and stored for various purposes, including analysis, processing, and decision-making. Data serves as the foundation for generating insights, driving innovations, and informing actions across various domains and industries. Data analytics encompasses a range of types, including (i) Descriptive Analytics, (ii) Diagnostic Analytics, (iii) Predictive Analytics, (iv) Prescriptive Analytics, and (v) Adaptive Analytics. Figure 1 discusses these types of data analytics in detail. It's a

*Figure 1. Different types of data analytics*

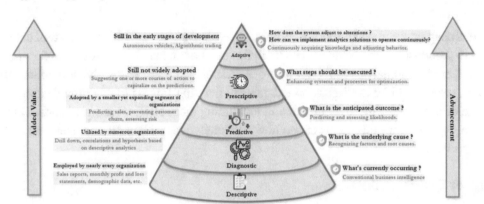

dynamic field that enables us to uncover valuable insights from this immense data pool, while big data analytics specifically deals with analyzing large and complex datasets to uncover patterns and trends that traditional methods may miss. Both aim to extract valuable insights from data, with big data analytics focusing on the analysis of vast, complex, and varied datasets.

**Taming the Big Data Beast:** The sheer scale of data, often referred to as "Big Data," demands sophisticated tools and techniques. Studies like "Big Data Analytics: A Literature Review Paper" (2021) emphasize this need. Distributed computing frameworks like Apache Spark and Hadoop are game-changers, allowing efficient analysis of data stored across multiple servers. Imagine being able to analyze the buying habits of millions of customers spread across different continents – that's the power of Big Data wrangling!

**The Rise of the Machines: AI and Machine Learning:** Data analysis is no longer just about crunching numbers and generating reports. Machine learning (ML) and artificial intelligence (AI) are rapidly transforming the field. Research published in a 2023 issue of the "International Journal of Data Science and Analytics" explores how AI algorithms are being used to develop cutting-edge applications. Think of the personalized recommendations you see on e-commerce websites or the ability to predict potential equipment failures in a manufacturing plant – these are just a few examples. ML algorithms can sift through massive datasets, identify hidden patterns, and even make predictions with remarkable accuracy.

**Ensuring Data Privacy and Security:** With this growing power comes a significant responsibility: data privacy and security. As we collect more and more data, especially in sensitive areas like healthcare (as highlighted in "The use of Big Data Analytics in healthcare," 2021), robust data management practices are essential. Researchers are actively developing methods for anonymizing data while still allowing for meaningful analysis. This ensures responsible data handling and addresses the ethical concerns surrounding data collection.

## 2.1 Beyond the Core: Data Analytics in Action

The impact of data analysis extends far beyond these core areas. Here's a glimpse into how different industries is leveraging its power:

*Figure 2. Different application area of data analytics*

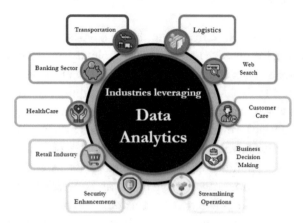

- Healthcare: Identifying disease outbreaks faster, predicting patient readmission risks, and personalizing treatment plans for improved patient outcomes. Data analysis empowers healthcare professionals to make data-driven decisions that can save lives.
- Finance: Assessing creditworthiness, predicting market trends, and managing investments with greater precision. Financial institutions use data analytics to mitigate risk and make informed investment decisions, ultimately influencing the global economy.
- Marketing: Understanding customer behavior, personalizing marketing campaigns, and optimizing pricing strategies. Data analysis helps businesses target their marketing efforts more effectively, leading to increased customer engagement and brand loyalty.

Apart from the aforementioned industries, numerous other sectors also leverage data analytics to drive innovation and efficiency. For example, in the telecommunications industry, data analytics is employed for network optimization, customer segmentation, and churn prediction. Retail benefits from data analysis through customer segmentation, demand forecasting, and personalized marketing strategies. In manufacturing, data analysis enhances process optimization, predictive maintenance, and supply chain management, while in transportation, it enables route optimization, fleet management, and predictive maintenance of vehicles. Figure 2 shows different application area of data analytics.

## 2.2 A Glimpse Into the Future

The Introduction to Data Analytics chapter is likely change to reflect the quickly evolving field of data-driven practices and technologies. A deeper exploration of cutting-edge trends such as sophisticated machine learning methods, AI apps, and extensive data analytics integration with cloud and edge computing will be done. Furthermore, as the significance of responsible data handling becomes more apparent, there will be a greater focus on data ethics and privacy considerations. The chapter also emphasizes developing critical skills and abilities in data analysis, visualization, and interpretation, as the need for data analytics experts in various industries grows. Ultimately, this chapter will continue to be updated to reflect the most recent developments and industry best practices, giving readers a thorough understanding of data analytics principles and technologies.

## 2.3 Challenges and Opportunities

In the current data-flooded landscape, introducing data analytics offers considerable challenges and great opportunities. Managing the massive number and complexity of data produced by various sources, including social media, online transactions, sensors, and financial records, is becoming increasingly difficult. Expertise, advanced tools, and methodologies are required to manage, analyze, and extract useful insights from this massive data store. But there are a lot of chances hidden amid these difficulties. This plethora of data may be transformed through data analytics into knowledge that can be put to use, fostering innovation, competitive advantage, and well-informed decision-making. Using sophisticated analytics techniques, businesses can find hidden relationships, patterns, and trends that provide insightful information about consumer behaviour, market dynamics, and operational effectiveness.

Furthermore, data analytics makes developing algorithms and predictive models that foretell future trends and reduce risks easier. Adopting data analytics helps businesses remain competitive in the current digital landscape and allows people and communities to take on complex problems and grasp new development opportunities. Therefore, even with challenges along the way, those fully prepared to utilize the revolutionary power of data analytics will be presented with countless chances.

## 3. PROPOSED MODEL

Figure 3 illustrates the proposed model for data analytics, which comprises various component like data extraction, data preparation, data exploration and visualization, predictive/ others modeling techniques, model validation and deployment of model for any identified problem. Here, Data extraction involves sourcing pertinent data from diverse origins like databases, files, or APIs. Next, data is refining, transforming into a usable format, rectifying inconsistencies and addressing missing values to bolster data quality. Next, data is visualized through charts or graphs. More, predictive modeling techniques utilizes statistical/AI/ML/DL algorithms to anticipate future outcomes grounded in historical data. Then, model validation is done through validation methods such as cross-validation or holdout samples and deploy into operational systems. To show the functioning of data analytics we are going to do a prototype analysis on the topic "Loan Risk Analysis". It demonstrates the application of data analytics in assessing loan risk and repayment probability. By leveraging various attributes such as interest rates, loan amounts, borrower demographics, and spending patterns, data analytics allows us to derive actionable insights from the dataset. Through mathematical formulations, conditional statements, and visualizations, we can analyse trends, identify risk factors, and make informed decisions regarding loan approvals and risk mitigation strategies. This model showcases how data analytics enables organizations to harness the power of data to improve decision-making, mitigate risks, and optimize business outcomes in the context of lending and financial services.

- Introduction to Prototype Analysis:We aim to analyse loan risk through a prototype analysis using a dataset containing various attributes such as the amount lent by investors, interest rate, loan length, loan purpose, debt-to-income ratio, home ownership, monthly income, credit score, and employment length.
- Analytical Inferences:
  - Loan Repayment Prediction:

*Figure 3. Proposed model for data analytics process*

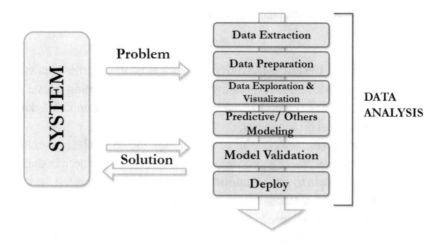

- We can predict the borrower's ability to repay the loan by comparing the monthly amount they need to pay with their monthly income.
- Formula:

  Monthly_amount [paid by borrower] = (Interest rate / 12) * (Amount landed by investor / Loan length) + (Amount landed by investor / Loan length)

  If the monthly amount is less than the monthly income, the borrower can likely repay the loan.
  - Analysis of Spending Patterns: We can analyse where the borrowed money is predominantly spent, such as debt consolidation, major purchases, credit card payments, small business expenses, home improvement, education, etc.
  - Borrowing Capacity Analysis: By considering the borrower's credit score andemployment length, we can assess their borrowing capacity and their likelihood of repaying the loan over time.Longer employment length generally indicates higher repayment probability.
  - Assessment of Home Ownership Status:Analysing the borrower's home ownership status provides insights into their financial stability and other expenses.Visualization of property status (ownership, lease, rental) helps gauge the borrower's financial commitments.
- Data Analytics Formulations:Expressing these inferences through mathematical formulations and conditional statements helps quantify and interpret the data accurately.This model is a structured approach to analysing loan risk through data analytics, incorporating key variables and analytical methods to derive actionable insights for decision-making.

## 4. METHODOLOGY

The methodology provides a comprehensive framework for conducting research and analysis in data analytics, specifically focusing on loan risk analysis. By understanding various research designs and data collection methods, readers can learn how to design studies, gather relevant data, and conduct meaningful analyses to extract insights into loan repayment behaviour, risk factors, and market trends.

It equips readers with the tools and techniques to apply data analytics effectively in real-world scenarios, enhancing their understanding and proficiency in the field.

- **Research Design:**
  - **Descriptive Research Design:**Descriptive research aims to describe characteristics, behaviours, or phenomena without manipulating variables or establishing causal relationships.In data analytics, descriptive research often involves summarizing and analyzing data to identify patterns, trends, and distributions.
  - **Co-relational Research Design:**Without changing the variables, co-relational research looks at the link between two or more variables.Co-relational research in data analytics is the process of examining data to find relationships or correlations between variables, frequently with the use of statistical methods like correlation analysis.
  - **Experimental Research Design:**In experimental research, one or more variables are changed while accounting for other variables to see how the changes affect another variable.A/B testing in online analytics or randomised controlled trials (RCTs) in healthcare analytics are two examples of controlled experiments that can be conducted as part of experimental research in data analytics to evaluate hypotheses or interventions.
  - **Quasi-Experimental Research Design:**While there is less complete control over the variables and no random assignment of individuals to conditions, quasi-experimental research is similar to experimental research.Natural experiments or quasi-experimental designs like interrupted time series analysis or regression discontinuity design can be used in quasi-experimental research in data analytics.
  - **Longitudinal Research Design:**In longitudinal study, the same individuals' data is collected over an extended period of time in order to track changes or trends over time.To monitor changes in variables or behaviours across time, longitudinal research in data analytics may analyse time series data or longitudinal datasets.
  - **Cross-Sectional Research Design:**Data from a single moment in time are gathered for cross-sectional research in order to look at correlations or discrepancies between variables. Cross-sectional research in data analytics can entail examining datasets or survey data gathered at a particular moment in order to look for trends or correlations.
  - **Mixed-Methods Research Design:**A thorough grasp of a study problem is achieved through the combination of qualitative and quantitative research methodologies in mixed-methods research.To obtain a deeper understanding of complex phenomena, mixed-methods research in data analytics may combine quantitative data analysis with qualitative data collection methods like focus groups or interviews.
- **Data Collection Methods:**
  - **Surveys and Questionnaires:**Respondents to surveys and questionnaires are asked a sequence of predetermined questions in order to obtain organised data from them.Survey data can reveal information on preferences, behaviours, attitudes, and opinions.One can administer surveys online, by email, over the phone, or in person using survey platforms.
  - **Existing Datasets:**Pre-existing datasets are a great source of secondary data. Examples of these are government databases, public datasets, and organisational data repositories. Numerous sources, including as surveys, administrative files, transaction logs, and social

media platforms, might yield secondary data.Researchers can use secondary data analysis to answer research questions and hypotheses by making use of already-existing data.

○ **Web Scraping:**Using automated scripts or tools, web scraping includes obtaining data from websites and other online sources.Researchers can gather a lot of organised or unstructured data from the internet and analyse it by using web scraping.Multimedia content, such as text, photos, videos, and other files, can be gathered using web scraping.

Here, after careful consideration of research design and data collection, data analytics is performed on specific problem as discussed in the previous section. The next section highlight the implementation of the proposed data analytics model and presents detail analysis report on 'Loan Risk Analysis' on benchmark dataset (Bank Loan Interest rate dataset, April 2024).

## 5. CASE STUDY

To showcase our Loan Risk Analysis prototype, we utilized Python as the programming language. Python is chosen because it offers numerous built-in libraries like NumPy, Pandas, and Matplotlib, which are essential for data manipulation, analysis, and visualization. In addition to performing the analysis, it's crucial to present the findings through an engaging user interface, commonly referred to as GUI (Graphical User Interface). To achieve this, we employed open-source libraries like Streamlit, which allows for the creation of interactive web applications directly from Python scripts. Alternatively, options such as Flask and Django were also considered, as they enable integration with HTML, CSS, and JavaScript for more customized interfaces. Figure 4 displays a graphical representation of the distribution of car loans across different states. By visualizing this data, users can quickly identify regions with higher or lower car loan uptake, allowing for targeted analysis and decision-making. Figure 5 presents a visual breakdown of borrower's property status as mortgage across different states. By examining this data visually, users can gain insights into the prevalence of mortgage properties among borrowers in various regions, which can inform risk assessment and lending strategies. Figure 6 showcases state-wise annual interest rate analytics, providing insights into interest rate trends across different regions. By visualizing this data, users can identify states with higher or lower interest rates, enabling them to make informed

*Figure 4. State-wise loan taken for car*

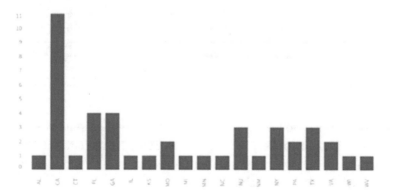

*Figure 5. State-wise borrower's property status as mortgage*

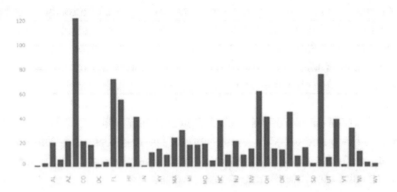

*Figure 6. State wise annual interest rate analytics*

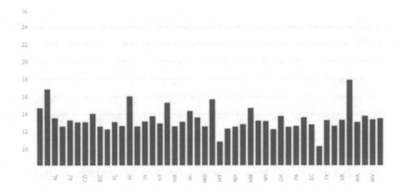

*Figure 7. State wise loan amount analysis*

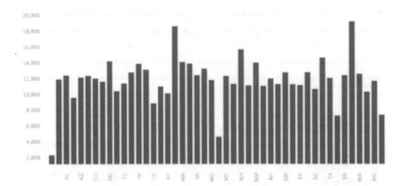

decisions regarding loan terms and pricing. Figure 7 offers a detailed state-wise loan amount analysis in USD, enhancing understanding of borrowing patterns. Table 1 lists states in America alongside their abbreviations. While not a graphical representation, it serves as a reference for users to interpret the state-wise data presented in the figures accurately.

*Table 1. State in America by abbreviations*

| Abbreviation | State |
|---|---|
| AL | Alabama |
| CA | California |
| CT | Connecticut |
| FL | Florida |
| GA | Georgia |
| IL | Illinois |
| KS | Kansas |
| MD | Maryland |
| MI | Michigan |
| MN | Minnesota |
| NC | North Carolina |
| NJ | New Jersey |
| NM | New Mexico |
| NY | New York |
| PA | Pennsylvania |
| TX | Texas |
| VA | Virginia |
| WI | Wisconsin |
| WW | West Virginia |

## 6. CONCLUSION

Data analytics is crucial for businesses because it allows them to improve their products and services, make better decisions, and learn more about their customers. By utilising data analysis technologies, businesses can save costs, streamline processes, and improve overall performance. This is not limited to any one type of business; it benefits numerous industries, improving them and enabling them to market their products more successfully. However, data analytics is more than just mathematical calculations. It's all about figuring out what all those figures imply and how to use them to improve the situation. Furthermore, not just large corporations employ data analytics. Improved data comprehension might be advantageous for small enterprises as well. A local retailer may utilize it to determine which things are selling quickly so they can plan their inventory accordingly. Alternatively, it can be used to determine what types of assignments a freelancer excels at, allowing them to concentrate on them and earn more money. Therefore, data analytics is more than just a fancy term for large corporations; it is a tool that may improve and increase the success of all types of enterprises, small and large.

# REFERENCES

Ahmadi, I., Abou Nabout, N., Skiera, B., Maleki, E., & Fladenhofer, J. (2024). Overwhelming targeting options: Selecting audience segments for online advertising. *International Journal of Research in Marketing*, *41*(1), 24–40. doi:10.1016/j.ijresmar.2023.08.004

Akter, S., Wamba, S. F., Gunasekaran, A., Dubey, R., & Childe, S. J. (2016). How to improve firm performance using big data analytics capability and business strategy alignment? *International Journal of Production Economics*, *182*, 113–131. doi:10.1016/j.ijpe.2016.08.018

Aljumah, A. I., Nuseir, M. T., & Alam, M. M. (2021). Traditional marketing analytics, big data analytics and big data system quality and the success of new product development. *Business Process Management Journal*, *27*(4), 1108–1125. doi:10.1108/BPMJ-11-2020-0527

Berthold, M. R., Borgelt, C., Höppner, F., & Klawonn, F. (2010). *Guide to intelligent data analysis: how to intelligently make sense of real data*. Springer Science & Business Media. doi:10.1007/978-1-84882-260-3

Elgendt, N. (2021). Big Data Analytics: A Literature Review Paper. Research Gate. .[https://www.researchgate.net/publication/264555968_Big_Data_Analytics_A_Literature_Review_Paper]

Black, K. (2023). *Business statistics: for contemporary decision making*. John Wiley & Sons.

Boldosova, V., & Luoto, S. (2020). Storytelling, business analytics and big data interpretation: Literature review and theoretical propositions. *Management Research Review*, *43*(2), 204–222. doi:10.1108/MRR-03-2019-0106

Bradlow, E. T., Gangwar, M., Kopalle, P., & Voleti, S. (2017). The role of big data and predictive analytics in retailing. *Journal of Retailing*, *93*(1), 79–95. doi:10.1016/j.jretai.2016.12.004

Chalos, P. (1997). An examination of budgetary inefficiency in education using data envelopment analysis. *Financial Accountability & Management*, *13*(1), 55–69. doi:10.1111/1468-0408.00026

Constantiou, I. D., & Kallinikos, J. (2015). New games, new rules: Big data and the changing context of strategy. *Journal of Information Technology*, *30*(1), 44–57. doi:10.1057/jit.2014.17

Ducange, P., Pecori, R., & Mezzina, P. (2018). A glimpse on big data analytics in the framework of marketing strategies. *Soft Computing*, *22*(1), 325–342. doi:10.1007/s00500-017-2536-4

Griva, A., Bardaki, C., Pramatari, K., & Papakiriakopoulos, D. (2018). Retail business analytics: Customer visit segmentation using market basket data. *Expert Systems with Applications*, *100*, 1–16. doi:10.1016/j.eswa.2018.01.029

Huang, H., Zhao, B., Zhao, H., Zhuang, Z., Wang, Z., Yao, X., & Fu, X. (2018, April). A cross-platform consumer behavior analysis of large-scale mobile shopping data. In *Proceedings of the 2018 World Wide Web Conference* (pp. 1785-1794). ACM. 10.1145/3178876.3186169

Javaid, M., Haleem, A., Singh, R. P., Rab, S., & Suman, R. (2021). Internet of Behaviours (IoB) and its role in customer services. *Sensors International*, *2*, 100122. doi:10.1016/j.sintl.2021.100122

Kumari, A., & Tanwar, S. (2022). A secure data analytics scheme for multimedia communication in a decentralized smart grid. *Multimedia Tools and Applications, 81*(24), 34797–34822. doi:10.1007/s11042-021-10512-z

Kumari, D. (2020). *Redills: Deep Learning-Based Secure Data Analytic Framework for Smart Grid Systems.* 2020 IEEE International Conference on Communications Workshops (ICC Workshops), Dublin, Ireland. 10.1109/ICCWorkshops49005.2020.9145448

Kumari, M. M. (2020). *ArMor: A Data Analytics Scheme to identify malicious behaviors on Blockchain-based Smart Grid System.* GLOBECOM 2020 - 2020 IEEE Global Communications Conference, Taipei, Taiwan. 10.1109/GLOBECOM42002.2020.9348061

Kwon, O., Lee, N., & Shin, B. (2014). Data quality management, data usage experience and acquisition intention of big data analytics. *International Journal of Information Management, 34*(3), 387–394. doi:10.1016/j.ijinfomgt.2014.02.002

Malhotra, D., & Rishi, O. (2021). An intelligent approach to design of E-Commerce metasearch and ranking system using next-generation big data analytics. *Journal of King Saud University. Computer and Information Sciences, 33*(2), 183–194. doi:10.1016/j.jksuci.2018.02.015

Minelli, M., Chambers, M., & Dhiraj, A. (2013). *Big data, big analytics: emerging business intelligence and analytic trends for today's businesses* (Vol. 578). John Wiley & Sons. doi:10.1002/9781118562260

Plummer, J., Rappaport, S. D., Hall, T., & Barocci, R. (2007). *The online advertising playbook: Proven strategies and tested tactics from the advertising research foundation.* John Wiley & Sons.

Raghupathi, W., & Raghupathi, V. (2014). Big data analytics in healthcare: Promise and potential. *Health Information Science and Systems, 2*(1), 1–10. doi:10.1186/2047-2501-2-3 PMID:25825667

Schafer, J. B., Konstan, J. A., & Riedl, J. (2001). E-commerce recommendation applications. *Data Mining and Knowledge Discovery, 5*(1/2), 115–153. doi:10.1023/A:1009804230409

Seifian, A., Bahrami, M., Shokouhyar, S., & Shokoohyar, S. (2023). Data-based drivers of big data analytics utilization: Moderating role of IT proactive climate. *Benchmarking, 30*(10), 4461–4486. doi:10.1108/BIJ-11-2021-0670

Sherman, H. D., & Zhu, J. (2006). *Service productivity management: Improving service performance using data envelopment analysis (DEA).* Springer science & business media. doi:10.1007/0-387-33231-6

Strong, C. (2015). *Humanizing big data: Marketing at the meeting of data, social science and consumer insight.* Kogan Page Publishers.

Swift, R. S. (2001). *Accelerating customer relationships: Using CRM and relationship technologies.* Prentice Hall Professional.

Talosig, E. (2022). *Improving Digital Marketing for Attracting the Target Customer Segments.*

*The use of Big Data Analytics in healthcare.* (2021). Springer. .[https://link.springer.com/article/10.1186/s40537-021-00553-4]

Wang, Y., Kung, L., & Byrd, T. A. (2018). Big data analytics: Understanding its capabilities and potential benefits for healthcare organizations. *Technological Forecasting and Social Change*, *126*, 3–13. doi:10.1016/j.techfore.2015.12.019

Wedel, M., & Kannan, P. K. (2016). Marketing analytics for data-rich environments. *Journal of Marketing*, *80*(6), 97–121. doi:10.1509/jm.15.0413

Yadav, M., Kakkar, M., & Kaushik, P. (2023). Harnessing Artificial Intelligence to Empower HR Processes and Drive Enhanced Efficiency in the Workplace to Boost Productivity. *International Journal on Recent and Innovation Trends in Computing and Communication*, *11*(8s), 381–390. doi:10.17762/ijritcc.v11i8s.7218

# Chapter 2

# Multidimensional Perspective to Data Preprocessing for Model Cognition Verity:
## Data Preparation and Cleansing – Approaches for Model Optimal Feedback Validation

**Simeon Okechukwu Ajakwe**
https://orcid.org/0000-0002-6973-530X
*Hanyang University, Seoul, South Korea*

**Opeyemi Deji-Oloruntoba**
*Inje University, Gimhae, South Korea*

**Samuel O. Olatunbosun**
*Chungbuk National University, South Korea*

**Francis Xavier Duorinaah**
*Chungbuk National University, South Korea*

**Israel A. Bayode**
https://orcid.org/0000-0003-3015-0264
*Kyung Hee University, South Korea*

## ABSTRACT

*Reliable data analysis depends on effective data preparation, especially since AI-driven business intelligence depends on unbiased and error-free data for decision-making. However, developing a reliable dataset is a difficult task that requires expertise. Due to the costly damage a negligible error in data can cause to a system, a good understanding of the processes of quality data transformation is necessary. Data varies in properties, which determines how it is generated, the errors in it, and the transformations it needs to undergo before it is fed into a model. Also, most data used for analytics is sourced from public stores without means to verify its quality or what further steps need to be taken in preprocessing it for optimal performance. This chapter provides a detailed description of practical and scientific procedures to generate and develop quality data for different models and scenarios. Also, it highlights the tools and techniques to clean and prepare data for optimal performance and prevent unreliable data analytics outcomes.*

DOI: 10.4018/979-8-3693-3609-0.ch002

## 1. INTRODUCTION

In an era where embedded cognition largely affects the strategic decision-making of an organization and by extension a people, there is a dire need for quality assurance in the preparation of the data that governs such systems. As the saying goes, "Garbage-In-Garbage-Out", unreliable data fed into a reliable model produces an unreliable prediction which leads to unreliable decisions. Data truth (originality) and statistical truth (data significance) inform the business truth. Business Truth is a measure of growth upon which business processes and key performance indicators (KPI) are created and established. Ultimately, the breakdown of most organizations and models is not unconnected to faulty and unverified decision-making because of wrong data.

Zarepoor et al. (2021) affirm this assertion by feeding different machine learning (ML) models with ill-prepared and imbalanced data. This resulted in the underperformance of all the models based on oversampling. The systematic literature survey carried out by Eyuboglu et al. (2022) shows that the systematic errors with cross-modal embeddings are because of poorly prepared data used by the system for data analytics. Furthermore, Li (2021) shows that high generalization of faulty signal data resulted in faulty diagnosis and wrong prediction. Finally, the works by Huang et al. (2021) indicate that the underperformance of a novel 3D-based deep learning model using a meta-learning paradigm was attributed to a misguided step in the construction of the image data used for the model simulation. Hence, the steps undertaken in preparing quality data determine the performance of a model and the reliability of its prediction.

However, developing a robust and reliable dataset (a relatively error-free dataset) is a herculean task that requires professionalism and precision to ensure that quality, and sample inclusiveness are maintained. Due to the costly effect a slight error in data can have on the system, careful steps are taken in phases to ensure precision and near-perfection in dataset preparation. These phases include determining the data collection site, acquisition of right tools for data capturing, method for data generation, deciding on the sampling technique to adopt, labelling/annotation, cleaning, clustering/categorization, etc. Each phase requires domain-specific expertise. For instance, to generate image-based dataset used by deep learning models to detect drones and other unmanned aerial vehicles (UAV) involves interwoven steps undertaken over a long period (Ajakwe et al., 2022a). A wrong choice of data collection equipment for this task leads to wrong data generation and preparation. Figure 1 highlights the tools for generating and preparing image-based UAV data.

According to Ajakwe et al. (2023), preparing and generating an image-based UAV dataset involves transforming the captured video data into usage format. This is carried out in three (3) phases namely, video frame to raw data frame (image) conversion, data frame cleaning and labelling, and dataset organization. Each of these phases has different underlying activities. It is important to state that the activities involved in preparing image data are different from that of a time-series analysis data used for signal processing (Ajakwe et al., 2022a). Different folds for different folks with each having its peculiarities, pros, and cons. Thus, an understanding of the related steps yet different methods needed in preparing quality data across domains is a critical skill. There is therefore the need for a platform that provides comprehensive information on the steps, tools, and techniques needed for quality data preparation which is necessary for reliable and result-oriented data analytics and model training.

Hence, this book chapter answers the questions: what are the steps to effective data preparation in different fields? What are the tools and materials needed for adequate data acquisition? How do I ef-

*Figure 1. Tools for UAV data generation and preparation*
*(Ajakwe et al., 2022)*

ficiently clean data? What are the standardized approaches to data balancing to prevent unreliable data analytics outcome?

The rest of this chapter is organized as follows. Section 1 introduces data and the stages of data transformation. Section 2 examines data preparation and the parameters/metrics for measuring data quality. Section 3 discusses the milestones and methods of data cleaning. Then, Section 4 explores data imbalance, its causes and control mechanisms. Section 5 hints on various strategies for data normalization. While Section 6 presents the realities and road map to data quality, Section 7 finalized the book chapter highlighting a case study on preparing and cleaning of brain signal dataset and concludes the chapter.

## 1.1 Overview of Data and Data Transformation Lifecycle

Data can be defined as raw facts and figures (structured and unstructured) that can be examined to provide vital insights for decision-making (Olson, 2021). Advancements in computing systems have increased data production. Due to this surge in data creation, data analysis has become an essential activity in research, medical sciences, marketing domains, businesses, and other fields where processed and unprocessed data play a vital role (Shukla, 2023).

## 1.2 Data

Data exists in several forms. However, numerous studies including Shukla (2023) have classified data into two major categories which are (1) Qualitative data, also referred to as categorical and (2) Quantitative data also termed as numerical. Qualitative data refers to data which cannot be expressed in numerical form and often requires categorization (Great Learning Team, 2022). This type of data comes in numerous forms and can be audible, visual, symbolic, or scripted (Shukla, 2023). Qualitative data is mainly used to answer questions such as "how and why" and mostly contains information on various dimensions such as feelings, perceptions and emotions (Taherdoost, 2021).

On the other hand, quantitative data is a data type which can be expressed in numerical format, making it countable. This type of data can be measured, and it is mostly analyzed to answer questions such as

"What quantity?" or "How much" (Shukla, 2023). This data category is often generated and computed mathematically and various scales including nominal, ordinal, interval, and ratio exist for measuring it (Kabir, 2016). Quantitative data can further be splitted into two forms: discrete and continuous. Discrete data refers to data which exist in distinct or separate forms, meaning it consists of whole numbers without decimals or fractions (Great Learning Team, 2022). Continuous data on the other hand refers to data often measured on a continuous scale and possesses smaller divisions such as decimals.

## 1.3 Big Data and Data Types

Considering the advancement of computer systems and massive surge in data production, a more complex form of data known as "big data" has been developed (Oussous et al., 2018). Big data are data types that are exceptionally large and hence exceed the management and processing capabilities of traditional databases (Mazumder, 2017). Analyzing big data entails scrutinizing immense volumes of varied data to reveal hidden patterns which might otherwise remain unnoticed due to the data's large volume (Huang et al., 2022). Big data can be sourced from a wide range of channels, including various sensors, images, social media platforms, and certain trading transactions (Huang et al., 2022). Considering the sizes of these datasets and high computational requirements, new analytic environments are being developed to efficiently manage them. Examples of such environments include distributed processing systems such as Apache Spark (Garillot & Maas, 2019), distributed file sources, and databases such as NoSQL (Klein et al., 2016). Big data is very crucial and most of the time has the potential to provide answers to various enquiries. However, the success of extracting valuable insights from these large data sets depends on various factors including the capabilities of the data scientist and thorough processing activities. (Ramos et al., 2017).

## 1.4 Stages of Data Transformation: From Inquisition to Insights

Despite improvements in computer architectures and vast data generation, data quality remains a pressing issue. In most scenarios, raw data from numerous sources are acquired without standardized criteria, which often necessitates some form of preparation (Hameed & Naumaan, 2020). This lack of standardization makes the data prone to errors and inconsistencies, resulting in "dirty" data that can lead to incorrect outputs, unreliable analysis, and incorrect decision-making (Chu et al., 2016). Given that insights from such data are used to make crucial decisions, it is important to utilize valid and reliable datasets for analysis.

Consequently, data often needs to undergo some crucial processes. These processes are necessary to make data understandable to systems, and lead to the generation of valid and reliable insights. Some of these processes include data preparation, data exploration (Sellam and Kersten, 2016), and data cleaning (Abedjan et al., 2016). A term used to encompass these essential procedures is known as data transformation. Data transformation can be defined as the practice of meticulously cleaning, modifying, and reorganizing data before it undergoes further analysis (El-Morr et al., 2022). This crucial step involves a series of detailed actions and typically serves as the initial phase of advanced data analysis and machine learning procedures (Chitra et al., 2022). Figure 2 shows the various stages of data transformation before it is fed into a model for prediction and inferencing.

*Figure 2. Various stages of data transformation/preparation*

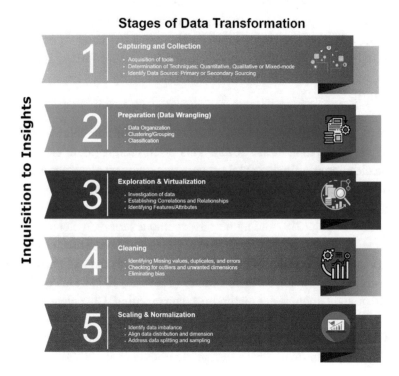

## 1.4.1 Data Capturing and Collection

Before any data process can be undertaken, the first step is to identify data sources and ensure crucial data relevant to the activity to be undertaken is collected. Data collection is an important process that involves utilizing intelligent devices and tools to acquire valuable information within a specific field of study (Chai et al., 2022). Data collection comes in two main categories which are primary data collection and secondary data collection (Taherdoost, 2021). Primary data collection entails gathering firsthand information that has not been published or altered by any individual (Taherdoost, 2021). Taherdoost (2021) further stated that this type of data collection places high emphasis on reliability, validity, and objectivity. Primary data collection is mostly undertaken through various methods and tools such as experiments, surveys, interviews, and questionnaires, drawing from diverse sources (Kabir, 2016; Taherdoost, 2021). On the other hand, secondary data collection involves gathering data that has already been published by others for different purposes (Taherdoost, 2021). This data is obtained from existing sources, making it a valuable resource for research and analysis.

## 1.4.2 Data Preparation

Data preparation, also known as data wrangling, is the process of transforming raw data into a suitable format for analysis (Fernandez et al., 2023). This crucial step has significant impacts on various dimensions, including model development and insight generation (Chai et al., 2022). Data preparation involves a set of activities and operations that are undertaken in the early stages of data analysis (Hameed &

Naumann, 2020). While typically considered a large individual process, some studies have defined data preparation as a multistep process which involves numerous activities. Some of which include exploration, data combination, cleaning, and conversion into datasets for more advanced data analysis and model development (Gomathy, 2022). The importance of data preparation cannot be overstated, as it plays a critical role in refining raw data into clean and structured formats for further analysis (Gomathy, 2022).

## 1.4.3 Data Cleaning

Collected data mostly possesses some abnormalities such as missing values, outliers, duplicates, and inconsistencies called "dirt" (Chai et al., 2022). This often requires data cleaning to eliminate these discrepancies. Data cleaning is a fundamental process that involves identifying and rectifying errors in data sets (Fernandez et al., 2023). This process entails removing incomplete, repeated, and inconsistent data from raw data sets (Muir et al., 2023; Zou, 2022). This crucial practice has been extensively studied for several decades (Tae et al., 2019) and numerous techniques for data cleaning have been developed. Traditionally, data cleaning methods revolved around the use of predefined criteria known as schemas (Tae et al., 2019). These schemas established specific requirements that data had to meet, such as adhering to integrity constraints and having corrected values (Tae et al., 2019). However, advanced computing and algorithms have brought about faster methods of data cleaning. Data cleaning plays a crucial role in ensuring the validity and reliability of the data by eliminating these "dirty" features (Muir et al., 2023). The importance of data cleaning can therefore not be downplayed as it influences the accuracy of analysis and predictions, ultimately improving decision-making (Goyle et al., 2023).

## 1.4.4 Data Exploration and Virtualization

Data exploration is an essential process that serves as the foundation for initial data investigation (Lee and Lee, 2022). It involves visual and interactive data querying to provide a comprehensive understanding of various data attributes and relationships (Battle, 2022). This process entails randomly extracting valuable insights and knowledge from vast datasets without using any predetermined criteria (Idreos et al., 2015). By conducting data exploration, scientists can effectively comprehend their data and uncover insights into the issues being modeled. This process also helps in data quality assessment, and identification of features that may enhance or compromise model accuracy (Rojas et al., 2017). Data exploration is an important phase which helps data analysts and researchers make informed decisions and discover valuable insights (Battle, 2022).

## 1.4.5 Data Scaling and Normalization

Data is often distributed irregularly and possesses different features, dimensions and sizes. This is often addressed through a process known as data scaling and normalization. Data scaling and normalization involves identifying imbalance in data categories and checking for data distribution sparsity (Ihekoronye et al, 2022). It also includes checking for dimensionality/scales of data to prevent the curse of dimensionality, model overfitting/underfitting and other errors associated with imbalanced data (Ihekoronye et al, 2022). Imbalance in data samples is often tackled using different methods such as under-sampling method, over-sampling method, combination of both (hybrid), among others. However, the choice of the sampling method is dependent on the use case and the characteristics of the dataset. Unfortunately, a balanced dataset can still have data with data dimensions or scales that are far apart. Different normalization approaches (see section 5) are usually deployed to reduce data dimensions and fit them within a possible range for better analytics.

## 2. DATA PREPARATION: ROLE FOR RELIABLE DATA ANALYTICS

### 2.1 Data Preparation: Definition and Importance

Data preparation is the process of converting unprocessed data into a format appropriate for analysis. The process entails multiple stages such as data cleansing, formatting, aggregation, data integration, data formatting, and data transformation, to guarantee precision, coherence, and comprehensiveness. Data preparation is essential in data analysis as it fosters quality assurance, improved results, and a resultant ease of understanding and interpretation of data. The conclusion of an evaluation differs greatly based on the standards used to choose the data (Goretti & Duffy, 2018). The correct kind of data, such as predictors and outcome variables for predictive modeling, as well as external data integration from multiple sources, are essential for any successful research project. Different aspects of data preparation exist, such as gathering the required information, cleansing the data, addressing missing values, identifying, and managing outliers, and feature engineering (Acito, 2023). However, various problems could be encountered in data analytics, with one of the most difficult being the existence of missing values. The significance of data preparation in today's data-driven environment cannot be over-emphasized. It is the cornerstone of every effective procedure for data analysis and decision-making. During data preparation, it is expedient that an evaluator identifies data that are out of scope and determine whether to include or exclude out-of-scope data from the data. To accurately evaluate wind energy forecast data in the wind power sector, recent research proposed that the observed values must be compared to the forecast value over a certain period as this will foster data accuracy (Goretti & Duffy, 2018).

### 2.2 Parameters for Measuring Data Quality

According to the Batini model (Batini et al., 2017), data has three pillars for its evaluation: data source, lifecycle phase, and quality dimensions. The data source describes acquisition and collection techniques; lifecycle phase pillar delves into the transformation processes, and quality dimensions pillar define the metrics/descriptors for judging its reliability (Lógó et al., 2021). Hence, the definition of data quality encompasses the precision, completeness, coherence, and dependability of information sources based on the data preparation processes. Therefore, data quality is the degree to which data is appropriate for the purpose for which it was collected. Thus, data quality is a continual process that needs to be continuously monitored and improved; it is not a one-time event.

Many elements, including data entry procedures, storage strategies, collection methods, and purification techniques, all have an impact on the quality of data. There are several dimensions to data quality, making it impossible to quantify it with a single metric. Diverse characteristics make up data quality, and each discipline places a different emphasis on these characteristics. For instance, personality researchers might be worried about the validity and reliability of scales. If incentives are used in the design, researchers might demand that participants refrain from trying to cheat to get higher gains. Also, experimentalists might demand that participants pay close attention to stimuli and carefully read

*Figure 3. Parameters for determining data quality*

and understand instructions. Whatever the field or research objectives, a combination of these characteristics forms the basis of the idea of data quality, which is essential to the validity of any behavioral research for academic publication as well as any practical applications (Peer et al., 2022). According to McGilvracy (2021), the essential component/factors of data quality in behavioural research community are attention, comprehension, honesty, and reliability.

Generally, data quality can be evaluated based on the data itself and other characteristics such as accuracy, applicability, etc. as depicted in Figure 3.

## 2.2.1 Accuracy > Vastness

Generally, it is difficult to give a wholistic definition of accurate data. Notwithstanding, data is said to be accurate when it has a consistent pattern, completely covers the scope of objective function and constraints, and correct in addressing the targeted problem. The process of preparing data is a rate-limiting step to guarantee its accuracy. Errors, duplicate entries, missing values, and outliers are common issues associated with raw data, which frequently makes data untidy leading to erroneous conclusions and judgments. To guarantee the accuracy and dependability of data utilized for analysis, an accurate recognition approach targeted at addressing these problems through data preparation are deployed. Artificial intelligence approaches, such as machine learning, natural language processing, and computational intelligence, yield more accurate, scalable, and rapid outcomes in big data analytics when compared to traditional data methodologies and platforms (Mahdavinejad et al., 2018). To ascertain that a given dataset is accurate and complete, a data analyst must check the readability, semantic, spatial, radiometric, temporal, and classification metrics of the data (Lógó et al., 2021).

## 2.2.2 Applicability/Relevance > Viability

Relevant data is an information that is immediately pertinent to the objectives and specifications of the task at hand. Therefore, a viable data must be directly relevant to the issue being addressed no matter the volume. To get useful information from a big data, effective management and analysis are necessary (Dash et al., 2019). Deep learning (DL) is a major advancement in the capacity of neural networks to automatically generate features relevant to a problem and record extremely intricate data distributions. DL has been used by several physical and geoscientific disciplines to solve data problems, boost productivity, and obtain new scientific understandings. DL is particularly well-suited for information extraction from sequential and image-like data and has found wide application in relevant disciplines (Shen, 2018). Various relevant search methods exist such as the Best Match replaces the conventional date sort order by utilizing the wisdom of users and state-of-the-art machine-learning technology (Florine et al., 2018). To ascertain the relevance of a given dataset, the data analyst must check the data source, the timeliness of the dataset, its significance in the user community, the consistency of its update, and the completeness of its features to the given problem.

## 2.2.3 Arbitrariness > Variability

Data variability allows for broad representation and robust analysis of data samples. It could culminate in insight generation, innovation, and creativity. However, it could be quite complex resulting in uncertainties and quality issues such as inconsistencies and missing data. The accuracy and reliability of lung segmentation algorithms on current cases primarily relies on the variability of the training data, highlighting the importance of data diversity compared to model choices (Hofmanninger, 2020). Decoding human brain activity via brain-computer interfaces (BCIs) based on non-invasive electroencephalograms (EEG) is greatly hampered by inter- and intra-subject variability. Hence the need for more individualized data (Wei et al., 2018). In terms of accuracy, a new class of machine learning algorithms called deep learning algorithms performs better than the outcomes of traditional segmentation. However, its complexity and wide range of variability raise doubts about its reproducibility (Renard et al, 2020). The authors however gave the following recommendations to address data variability issues: 1) a sufficient explanation of the deep learning framework, 2) an appropriate examination of the many sources of variability within the deep learning framework, and 3) an effective method for assessing the segmentation outcomes.

## 2.2.4 Aggregation/Quantity > Volume

The quantity/volume of a data is another metric to access the quality of data because inadequate representative data leads to biased outcome especially in AI models (Ring et al, 2019). Machine learning algorithms frequently work better with larger amounts of data, producing more accurate models (Raschka, 2018; Ajakwe et al., 2020). Large datasets enable the identification of trends and patterns that may not be apparent in smaller datasets and business organizations relies on these trends for value-added services (Dash et al., 2019). Every stage of managing big data comes with a set of difficulties that can only be overcome by utilizing high-end computer solutions for big data analysis. As a rule of thumb, density and sparsity metrics are used to measure the volume/quantity of data. With the advent of AI, increase in data feature (increase in complexity/variability) is also associated with data quantity in determining the suitable model for data analytics (Ihekoronye et al., 2022). Hence, the metrics are interwoven when ascertaining that a given data is quality data.

## 2.2.5 Ethics [Privacy, Security, Bias, Informed Consent] > Veracity

Data and data science are so pervasive and can affect every aspect of life. Ethical issues surrounding data may be more difficult to resolve than those involving some other cutting-edge technologies. This is due in part to their inherent complexity. Consequently, it takes ethical supervision and limitations to guarantee that the right balance is reached (Hand, 2018). Through the development of new data technologies, such as blockchain, homomorphic computation, and quantum computing, as well as by the application and deployment of currently available tools, data ethics is currently being improved. The US Federal policy handbook for the protection of human subjects also exists. It addresses the politics and contentions around human subjects, both nationally and regionally (Donnelly & Whelan, 2020). The laws protecting research subjects have developed in a way that reduces the likelihood that individuals may suffer harm because of their decision to participate in research thereby reinforcing individual responsibility.

Currently, efforts are targeted at continuous re-evaluation to improve the safety of subjects who are willing to participate in research activities (White, 2020). In previous research on social media by a group of researchers, despite sincere efforts to conceal the identity and safeguard the privacy of the data subjects, the student's privacy was jeopardized when the data subjects were discovered. Consequently, several ethical issues that need to be resolved before conducting any more research on social networking sites include: the nature of consent, how to appropriately identify and respect privacy expectations on these platforms, how to anonymize data before it is made public, and how knowledgeable institutional review boards are about research projects using data from social media (Zimmer, 2020).

Data identity theft is another social network issue in this era of generative AI, where superfluous and invalidated synthetic datasets are readily available (Dini et al., 2023). There is currently a need to transform AI ethics into data science for relevant service delivery (Georgieva et al., 2022; Ajakwe et al., 2023a). Operationalization of AI ethics has become imperative since data scientists frequently cannot employ ethics frameworks when developing AI-based services or products. Hence to achieve data quality, it is critical to integrate a formal data governance model with the lifetime of an AI-based digital service or product. This helps to map ethical principles of AI and define roles in operationalization.

## 2.3 Improvement of Data Quality

According to results from partial least squares, to fully realize the potential of IoT and big data analytics capabilities, an improvement in data quality is required (Côrte-Real et al., 2020). Analyzing data from several sources can be challenging because of the differences in their formats and structures. Data integration, or the combination and standardization of data from many sources, is a major component of data preparation. Consequently, redundant and inconsistent data are removed, producing high quality data that is largely suitable for analysis. Synchrophasor data (SD) processing framework significantly improves the quality of data, particularly during transient conditions and in noisy environments. This real-time algorithm processes SD and improves the quality by utilizing low-rank approximation on data streams which results in the recovery of missing SD through phasor measuring units (PMUs). The improved data stream can then be routed to different applications that are related to power systems.

Secondary use of electronic health records for research, quality, and educational initiatives currently exists (Colquhoun et al., 2020). A framework to guarantee the accuracy, transparency, and completeness of the source data is essential to this secondary usage. Subsequently, the research has highlighted four major factors that should be prioritized to increase data quality before usage. Hence, before coordinating center transfer; (1) data should be made available locally; (2) data should undergo thorough validation against established metrics before being used; (3) data should be compiled into easily accessible computable phenotypes; and (4) data should be gathered for both quality improvement and research purposes, as these complementary objectives enhance the efficacy of each endeavor (Colquhoun et al., 2020).

The homogeneity and coherence of data across many sources and historical periods are referred to as consistency. Unreliable analysis and contradictory findings might result from inconsistent data. As a result, it is crucial to guarantee data consistency by comparing data to established guidelines and standards. Inaccurate conclusions could result from the inability of outdated data to accurately depict the current situation (Bakalis et al., 2020). Hence, the need for recent and timely data. Research is now adopting an editorial stance against outdated data analysis techniques, and they are currently being replaced by more quantitative analysis methods for data that offer far more insight into the causes of data fluctuations (Hopke & Jaffe, 2020). There is a problem with medical recommendations and guidance on routine ultrasound in antenatal due to outdated data in today's technological field. Hence the need for the reevaluation of such data for more accurate recommendations (Bakalis et al., 2020). The degree to which data has all the information required for its intended application is referred to as completeness. There may be gaps in analysis and decision-making due to incomplete data. One way to assess the completeness of data is to look for any missing fields or values in the dataset.

Since quality data is mostly a precursor to reliable data analytic outcome, it is imperative for data users to subject each data source to the accuracy, applicability, arbitrariness, aggregation, and ethics test during the preparation stage. This is to minimize missing data, error, outliers, and/or bias in the data. To do achieve this, it is important to consider the various methods for data cleaning and transformations.

## 3. DATA CLEANING: METHODS AND MILESTONES

Missing data generally refers to entries in a dataset that do not accurately represent the true state of the data and may take values such as $\pm\infty$, 0, or "nan" (not a number). It is one of the most common yet often overlooked issues in data quality, significantly affecting downstream data analysis (Molenberghs et al., 2014). The presence of missing instances in a dataset can impede model performance, lead to errors, and introduce biases. Thus, it is crucial to identify and understand the reasons for missing data, as this determination influences the choice of the most effective approach for dealing with the missing values (Raebel et al., 2016). There are three primary causes of missing data in a dataset, which depend on the relationship between available data and missing data.

- **Data Missing Completely at Random (MCAR):** When data is missing completely at random, it indicates that the absence of data points occurs randomly and independently of any observed variables in the dataset. There is no systematic pattern to the missing data, and it appears to happen purely by chance (Gómez-Carracedo et al., 2014). Consequently, these missing data can be safely disregarded in the analysis without introducing bias into the results.

**Example:** Consider a scenario where a teacher conducts a study on the effectiveness of a new teaching method in a school. The teacher collects data on student test scores before and after implementing the new method. However, due to unforeseen circumstances like students being absent on test days, data entry errors, administrative errors, or some test scores are missing. Thus, the missing data would be considered as MCAR and can be ignored.

- **Data Missing at Random (MAR):** Data missing at random refers to a situation where the likelihood of a missing value is systematically connected to the available data. It is possible to make predictions or estimations for values that are not present based on the available data (Bhaskaran & Smeeth, 2014; Nissen & Shemwell, 2016).

**Example:** Building on the previous example, consider another scenario where the teacher made a rule that students who scored less than 30% in the first test cannot participate in the second test after the new teaching method is introduced. In this scenario, the missingness of the test scores is related to the students' academic performance, which is an observed variable (test scores). Therefore, the missingness can be considered as MAR and can also be ignored.

- **Data Missing Not at Random (MNAR):** In the case of data missing not at random, the probability of data being missing is systematically related to unobserved variables. This implies that the missingness is related to factors that were not measured by the researcher. Thus, it is impossible to determine the missing mechanism because it relies on unseen data (Carreras et al., 2021). Proper handling of missing data is essential in such cases to mitigate potential biases in the analysis (Rabe-Hesketh & Skrondal, 2023).

**Example:** To extend the previous example, imagine some of the students are struggling with text anxiety. Hence, regardless of their performance in the first test, these students are less likely to show up for the second test. In this case, the missingness in the data is not random and is influenced by an unobserved variable (test anxiety). Therefore, missingness in MNAR cannot be ignored, as it may lead to biased analysis results. It is imperative therefore to apply the appropriate method for addressing missing data.

## 3.1 Methods of Addressing Missing Data Values/Class

The methods employed to handle missing data depend on the reason for the missingness and the proportion of missing data (Shoba et al., 2023). As previously explained, for data missing completely at random (MCAR) and data missing at random (MAR), they can be safely ignored. However, missing data stemming from the MNAR case must be appropriately addressed. Furthermore, computing the proportion of missing data for each variable (between subjects) and each subject (between variables) is essential. This helps determine which variables and/or subjects should be considered for removal or imputation (Madley-Dowd et al., 2019). There are two primary methods for addressing missing data values/class as captured by the flowchart in Figure 4.

*Figure 4. Methods for addressing missing data*

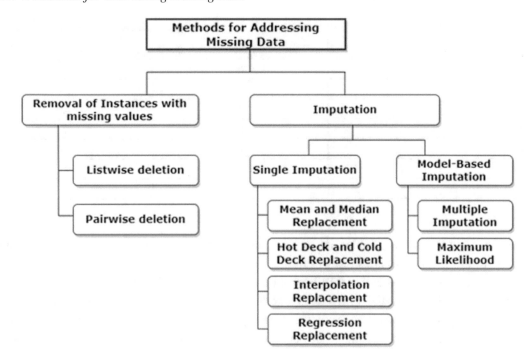

## 3.1.1 Removal of Instances With Missing Values/Class

In this method, cases or observations with missing values are simply discarded. It is the simplest procedure for handling an incomplete dataset and is also referred to as the deletion method. Generally, the deletion method works best when the missingness is caused by MCAR (Emmanuel et al., 2021). Removal of instances with missing values can be carried out in two ways: listwise deletion and pairwise deletion.

I. **Listwise deletion**

Listwise deletion involves deleting all observations with at least one missing variable. It is also known as complete-case analysis. However, this approach is effective only when the number of removed observations is small relative to the total observations. Listwise deletion assumes that the remaining observations are representative of the entire population and thus will not introduce bias to the analysis (Williams, 2015).

The disadvantages of this approach include a decrease in the statistical strength of the analysis due to the smaller amount of data available. It also raises the possibility of bias in the study, particularly if the data is not MCAR (Van Dusen & Nissen, 2020). An example of listwise deletion is illustrated in Table 3.1, where all observations for Subjects 3, 4, and 8 are deleted because they contain at least one missing value.

II. **Pairwise deletion**

Pairwise deletion involves discarding only the data that is missing for a given variable. It is also referred to as available-case analysis. When using pairwise deletion, any analysis involving variables with missing data will only utilize the available data for each specific analysis (Kang, 2013). In other words, for each pair of variables involved in a calculation or comparison, only the cases (observations)

*Table 1. Example of listwise deletion*

| Subjects | Test Scores (%) | |
|---|---|---|
| | Test 1 | Test 2 |
| Subject 1 | 75 | 80 |
| Subject 2 | 62 | 74 |
| Subject 3 | ? | 65 |
| Subject 4 | 25 | ? |
| Subject 5 | 87 | 94 |
| Subject 6 | 95 | 90 |
| Subject 8 | 78 | ? |

with complete data for those variables are included in the analysis. Thus, cases with missing data for one or more of those variables are simply excluded from that analysis.

The benefit of this method is that it utilizes all the collected data for analysis and retains as many samples as possible. However, the downside is that the results generated cannot be easily compared because the population or samples in each analysis would be different (Nguyen et al., 2023). For example, in Table 3.2, only cases with missing values are removed, and not the entire subject, as we did with listwise deletion.

## 3.1.2 Imputation

Imputation method substitutes missing data with estimated values obtained from existing observable data. It seeks to keep the sample size and statistical power of the analysis (Kwak & Kim, 2017). However, it is important to note that biases may be introduced if the missing data is not missing completely at random (MNAR). There are two main types of imputation methods:

I. Single imputations

*Table 2. Example of pairwise deletion*

| Subjects | Test Scores (%) | |
|---|---|---|
| | Test 1 | Test 2 |
| Subject 1 | 75 | 80 |
| Subject 2 | 62 | 74 |
| Subject 3 | ? | 65 |
| Subject 4 | 25 | ? |
| Subject 5 | 87 | 94 |
| Subject 6 | 95 | 90 |
| Subject 8 | 78 | ? |

*Table 3. Missing data*

| Subjects | Test Scores (%) | |
|---|---|---|
| | Test 1 | Test 2 |
| Subject 1 | 75 | 80 |
| Subject 2 | 62 | 74 |
| Subject 3 | ? | 65 |
| Subject 4 | 25 | ? |
| Subject 5 | 87 | 94 |
| Subject 6 | 95 | 90 |
| Subject 8 | 78 | ? |
| Mean | 70.3 | 80.6 |
| Median | 76.5 | 80 |

Single imputations involve straightforward methods for replacing missing values. They can be carried out through various techniques, including mean and median replacement, hot-deck and cold-deck replacement, interpolation replacement, and regression replacement (Khan & Hoque, 2020).

- **Mean and Median Replacement:** This method entails replacing missing values in a variable with the mean or median of that variable. However, this method is considered a poor choice, as it distorts other statistical properties of the data. Additionally, it does not account for dependencies between attributes (Geraci et al., 2013; Noor et al., 2014). The median is more robust to outliers compared to the mean.

- **Hot Deck and Cold Deck Replacement:** In hot deck replacement, missing values are replaced with values from similar or "nearest neighbor" cases within the dataset where the observation is complete. The process involves classifying the data into clusters and replacing missing values with those from complete cases in the same cluster (Sullivan & Andridge, 2015). Cold deck re-

*Table 4. Mean imputed data*

| Subjects | Test Scores (%) | |
|---|---|---|
| | Test 1 | Test 2 |
| Subject 1 | 75 | 80 |
| Subject 2 | 62 | 74 |
| Subject 3 | 70.3 | 65 |
| Subject 4 | 25 | 80.6 |
| Subject 5 | 87 | 94 |
| Subject 6 | 95 | 90 |
| Subject 8 | 78 | 80.6 |

*Table 5. Median imputed data*

| Subjects | Test Scores (%) | |
|---|---|---|
| | Test 1 | Test 2 |
| Subject 1 | 75 | 80 |
| Subject 2 | 62 | 74 |
| Subject 3 | 76.5 | 65 |
| Subject 4 | 25 | 80 |
| Subject 5 | 87 | 94 |
| Subject 6 | 95 | 90 |
| Subject 8 | 78 | 80 |

placement is similar but sources data from another dataset (Kwak & Kim, 2017). However, both methods cannot be implemented if there are no similar cases available.

- **Interpolation Replacement:** Here, missing values are filled by interpolating values from adjacent observations. This method assumes an underlying pattern or relationship between observed data points and works well on datasets with smooth patterns or trends but poorly in the presence of outliers (Noor et al., 2014).
- **Regression Replacement:** This method involves replacing missing data by fitting a regression equation to the remaining data. It works best when there is more than one variable of interest, utilizing information from all available data (Emmanuel et al., 2021). However, it diminishes the overall variability within the dataset and may lead to better model fits and correlation estimates than initially obtained.

II. Model-Based Imputations

*Table 6. Missing data*

| Subjects | Test Scores (%) | |
|---|---|---|
| | Test 1 | Test 2 |
| Subject 1 | 75 | 80 |
| Subject 2 | 62 | 74 |
| Subject 3 | ? | 65 |
| Subject 4 | 25 | ? |
| Subject 5 | 87 | 94 |
| Subject 6 | 95 | 90 |
| Subject 8 | 78 | ? |

*Table 7. Hot deck imputation*

| Subjects | Test Scores (%) | |
|---|---|---|
| | Test 1 | Test 2 |
| Subject 1 | 75 | 80 |
| Subject 2 | 62 | 74 |
| Subject 3 | 62 | 65 |
| Subject 4 | 25 | 65 |
| Subject 5 | 87 | 94 |
| Subject 6 | 95 | 90 |
| Subject 8 | 78 | 90 |

Model-based imputations assume that observations of the target variable follow a distribution model, and missing values can be inferred by estimating model parameters based on observed data (Ngueilbaye et al., 2021). This method includes multiple imputations and maximum likelihood.

- **Multiple Imputation:** It obtains a distribution for missing values using the Monte Carlo technique (Huque et al., 2018). It involves three steps: filling in missing values randomly, analyzing the resulting datasets, and obtaining parameter estimates and test statistics of a distribution of imputation values for missing observations (Van Buuren, 2018).
- **Maximum Likelihood:** Maximum likelihood estimation, unlike imputation methods, computes maximum likelihood estimates using the existing data for each case rather than imputed data. The likelihood is calculated separately for cases with complete data on some factors and those with complete data on all variables. Subsequently, it is jointly maximized to determine the estimates (Jakobsen et al., 2017).

Table 8 summarizes the most appropriate methods employable for handling missing data under different circumstances.

It is pertinent for the data analyst to pre-check the type of missing data; MCAR, MAR, MNAR, before deciding the type of method to adopt in addressing them. This is to minimize the extent of bias introduced into the cleaned data. However, a clean dataset with an improper distribution of its classes will ultimately produce biased analytics that favour the class or group with the highest number of samples. Hence, the next task for a data analyst in preparing a quality dataset is to examine and address the data imbalance issue.

## 4. DATA IMBALANCE: CHALLENGES, CAUSES AND CONTROL MECHANISMS

In the rapidly evolving landscape of AI, data is the lifeblood that fuels models and drives innovation. However, not all data is created equal, and one significant challenge that AI practitioners often encounter is data imbalance (Chamlal et al., 2024). Data imbalance occurs when the distribution of classes in a dataset is skewed, with one class significantly outnumbering the others (Yan et al., 2023). The class with the highest number of samples is the majority class while the minority class is the class with fewer

*Table 8. Methods for handling missing data under different circumstances*

| Method | Circumstance | Description | Considerations | References |
|---|---|---|---|---|
| **Listwise or complete case deletion** | Missing completely at random (MCAR) | Delete cases with missing values | Loss of information, especially if missingness is not random | (Murakami et al., 2020) |
| **Pairwise deletion** | Specific variables missing but not entire cases | Analyze available data for each pair of variables with complete information | Bias may be introduced if the missing data pattern is not random | (Cheng et al., 2021), (Su et al., 2022) |
| **Imputation - Mean, Median, or Mode** | Missing completely at random (MCAR), and missing at random (MAR) | Replace missing values with mean, median, or mode of observed values | May distort distribution if missingness is not random | (Kim et al., 2023) |
| **Imputation - Regression** | Related to other observed variables | Use regression equations to predict missing values based on other variables | Assumes a linear relationship between variables | (Sa'adi et al., 2023), (Templeton et al., 2021) |
| **Multiple imputation** | Missing at random (MAR), missing not at random (MNAR) | Generate multiple datasets with imputed values, analyze each, and combine results | Provides more accurate estimates of uncertainty | (Mensah et al., 2023), (Curnow et al., 2023) |
| **Weighted Least Squares (WLS) or Maximum Likelihood (ML) Estimation** | Structural Equation Modeling, Some Software Support | Methods implemented in statistical software to handle missing data | Requires specific statistical software and assumptions | (Aydi & Alatiyyah, 2024) |
| **Hot deck imputation** | Similar units based on observed characteristics | Replace missing values with values from similar units based on observed characteristics | Assumes similarity among units based on specified criteria | (Memon et al., 2023), (Y. Li et al., 2024) |
| **K-Nearest Neighbors (KNN) Imputation** | Similarity of cases based on other variables | Replace missing values with values from the K-nearest neighbors based on other variables | Depends on appropriate choice of K and may be computationally expensive | (Memon et al., 2023), (Sa'adi et al., 2023) |

samples. This imbalance can lead to biased models (Łukawska et al., 2024), poor generalization (Zhao et al., 2024), and suboptimal performance (Feng et al., 2024) in real-world applications. Data imbalance is a common issue in many datasets used for machine learning tasks, such as fraud detection, medical diagnosis, and spam filtering. In these datasets, the positive instances (e.g., fraudulent transactions, and rare diseases) are substantially less frequent than negative instances (Khan et al., 2024). In a binary classification problem, an imbalanced dataset might have a distribution of 90% negative instances and 10% positive instances (Rezvani & Wang, 2023).

## 4.1 Challenges Posed by Data Imbalance

The following are among the challenges posed by data imbalance across numerous disciplines:

- **Biased Model Performance**: The possibility of biased model performance is one of the biggest problems brought on by data imbalance. Machine learning models may prefer the majority class in their pursuit of minimizing the total error, which could result in poor identification of cases belonging to minority classes. In practical terms, this can include missing important details like fraudulent transactions or uncommon illnesses (Iqbal & Amin, 2024).

- **Poor Generalization:** Imbalanced datasets may significantly impede the capacity of a model to generalize effectively to unfamiliar data. When trained on imbalanced data, a model could overly focus on predicting the majority class, encountering difficulties in accommodating the minority class when presented with new instances. Such a deficiency in generalization can curtail the model's effectiveness in real-world applications (Zhao & Shen, 2024).
- **Misleading Evaluation Metrics:** Standard accuracy is often an inadequate metric for evaluating models on imbalanced datasets. A model that predicts the majority class for every instance could achieve high accuracy but fails to capture the nuances of the minority class. Metrics like precision, recall and F1-score become more informative in such scenarios, as they provide insights into a model's performance in each class (Chamlal et al., 2024; Ajakwe et al., 2022b).
- **Model Sensitivity:** Imbalanced datasets can make models sensitive to changes in the minority class, leading to inconsistent performance. Small variations in the minority class may have a disproportionate impact on model predictions (Kaneko et al., 2022).
- **Algorithmic Biases:** Machine learning algorithms may inadvertently reinforce existing biases present in imbalanced datasets. This can be a concern, especially when the dataset reflects historical biases and unfair practices (Łukawska et al., 2024).

## 4.2 Causes of Data Imbalance

Data imbalance in a dataset can arise from various factors. A good understanding of these causes is essential for addressing the challenges associated with data imbalance. Here are some common causes.

- **Inherent Class Distribution:** In some real-world scenarios, the distribution of classes may naturally be imbalanced. For example, in medical diagnosis, rare diseases might have fewer instances compared to more common ones (Chen et al., 2023).
- **Data Collection Bias:** Imbalanced datasets may result from biases in the data collection procedure. An unequal distribution of classes may arise if the techniques used to collect the data favor particular groups or circumstances (Łukawska et al., 2024; Ahsan et al., 2023).
- **Cost and Difficulty of Data Collection:** Collecting data for certain classes may be more challenging, time-consuming, or expensive. As a result, researchers or practitioners might prioritize collecting data for more accessible or prevalent classes (Senjaya et al., 2023).
- **Rare Events:** Imbalance can occur when dealing with rare events or anomalies. For example, fraudulent transactions in financial datasets are often rare compared to legitimate transactions (Dib et al., 2024).
- **Sampling Issues:** Imbalanced datasets might result from sampling that is done at random or without taking class proportions into account. Insufficient representation of all classes in the training data could hinder the model's ability to effectively generalize for minority classes (Xie et al., 2024).
- **Dynamic Nature of Data:** Over time, the distribution of classes in a dataset may change. If a model is trained on historical data, it might not be well-adapted to the current distribution, especially if new classes have emerged or if the prevalence of certain classes has shifted (Zhao et al., 2023).

*Figure 5. Strategies for addressing data imbalance*

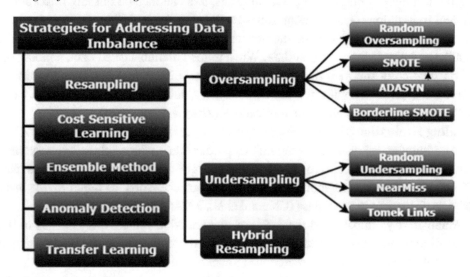

- **Incomplete Data:** Missing or incomplete data for certain classes can contribute to imbalance. Incomplete or sparse feature data for some classes may hinder the model's capacity to identify patterns for those classes. (Verbeke & Molenberghs, 2024; Ding et al., 2024).
- **Data Labeling Errors:** Errors in labeling, especially for minority classes, can lead to an under-representation of those classes in the dataset. Mislabeling or confusion with other classes may contribute to imbalance (Duan et al., 2024).
- **Domain-specific Factors:** Certain domains inherently have imbalanced class distributions due to the nature of the problem. For example, in fault detection or defect identification, instances of faults may be much less frequent than non-faulty instances (Oh et al., 2024; Fan et al., 2023; Fan et al., 2022).

## 4.3 Strategies to Address Data Imbalance

Addressing data imbalance is crucial for preparing quality data necessary to build robust and fair business and machine learning models. Data imbalance can lead to biased predictions and poor performance in minority classes. There are several strategies that are employed to tackle data imbalance as captured in the chart in Figure 5.

1. **Resampling Techniques:** These are methods used to modify the class distribution within a dataset, to address imbalance between classes. There are two main types of resampling techniques: oversampling and undersampling. However, hybrid approaches, too, can be used in specific instances of data imbalance.

   a. **Oversampling:** This type of resampling involves increasing the number of instances in the minority class, either by replicating existing instances or by generating synthetic examples (Vairetti et al., 2024). The following are some methods commonly utilized:

    i.    **Random Oversampling**: This method duplicates instances from the minority class to balance class proportions (Vairetti et al., 2024; Feng et al., 2024).

    ii.    **SMOTE (Synthetic Minority Over-sampling Technique):** This resampling technique interpolates between minority class instances that already exist to construct synthetic examples (Li et al., 2022; Ajakwe et al., 2021). New data points are created along the line segments that link comparable occurrences (Liu et al., 2024).

    iii.    **ADASYN (Adaptive Synthetic Sampling):** Though like SMOTE, this method introduces a level of adaptability, generating more synthetic examples for instances that are harder to classify (Lavanya & Sasikala, 2024).

    iv.    **Borderline-SMOTE:** This method generates synthetic instances near the decision boundary between classes, addressing potential noise in synthetic samples (Liu et al., 2024).

b.    **Undersampling Techniques:** This set of techniques simply involves reducing the number of instances in the majority class to achieve a more balanced class distribution (Sun et al., 2024). The following are some commonly used methods of undersampling:

    i.    **Random Undersampling:** In contrast to random oversampling, this technique balances class proportions by randomly removing instances from the dominant class (Sun et al., 2024).

    ii.    **NearMiss:** This method selects instances from the majority class that are close to instances in the minority class based on distance metrics. Different versions of NearMiss exist, such as NearMiss-1, NearMiss-2, and NearMiss-3, with varying criteria for selecting instances (Rao et al., 2023).

    iii.    **Tomek Links**: This method removes instances that form Tomek links, which are pairs of instances from different classes that are each other's nearest neighbors. This focuses on eliminating instances near the class boundary (Pereira et al., 2020).

c.    **Hybrid Resampling:** Hybrid approaches combine both oversampling and undersampling techniques to address data imbalance more comprehensively. These approaches aim to leverage the strengths of both oversampling (increasing the representation of the minority class) and undersampling (reducing the dominance of the majority class) (Sun et al., 2024). The following are the two commonest hybrid resampling methods:

    i.    **SMOTE-ENN (SMOTE with Edited Nearest Neighbors):** This leverages the strengths of both the SMOTE and edited nearest neighbors of undersampling. While the former generates synthetic instances for the minority class, increasing its representation, the latter removes instances whose class labels conflict with most of their nearest neighbors (Ahsan et al., 2024). This hybrid method improves the balance between classes while removing noisy or ambiguous instances.

    ii.    **SMOTE-Tomek:** This leverages the strengths of both SMOTE and Tomek, which are respectively oversampling and undersampling techniques (Vairetti et al., 2024). This pair seeks to enhance the separation between classes by removing instances that might be close to the decision boundary.

To verify the role of the SMOTE on a model prediction efficiency and reliability, Ajakwe et al. (2023) carried out research using an imbalance dataset of water quality samples for binary class and multiclass classification of various ML classifiers. The results indicate that the application of SMOTE had little effect on the model's precision, sensitivity, accuracy, and rationality for binary classification. However, SMOTE increased the model prediction across all the performance evaluation metrics for multiclass classification (Ajakwe et al., 2022c).

2. **Cost-sensitive Learning:** Assigning different misclassification costs to different classes during model training can help the algorithm prioritize the minority class (Chamlal et al., 2024). This involves adjusting the loss function to penalize misclassifying the minority class more than the majority class.

3. **Ensemble Methods:** These methods, such as bagging and boosting, can be effective in mitigating the impact of data imbalance. Algorithms like Random Forest and AdaBoost combine multiple models to improve overall performance, and they can be adapted to handle imbalanced datasets effectively (Khan et al., 2024).

4. **Anomaly Detection Techniques:** In scenarios where the minority class represents anomalies or rare events, anomaly detection techniques can be employed. These methods focus on identifying instances that deviate from the norm, making them well-suited for imbalanced datasets (Dib et al., 2024).

5. **Transfer Learning:** Leveraging pre-trained models on large, balanced datasets and fine-tuning them on imbalanced data can enhance the model's ability to recognize patterns in the minority class. Transfer learning allows the model to benefit from the knowledge acquired during pre-training (Gunduz et al., 2023).

Data imbalance poses a significant challenge in the development and deployment of ML models. The implications of biased models, poor generalization, and misleading evaluation metrics underscore the importance of addressing data imbalance systematically. By understanding the causes of imbalance and implementing appropriate strategies, practitioners can enhance the robustness and effectiveness of their models on imbalanced datasets. As the field of ML continues to advance, addressing data imbalance will remain a crucial aspect of building models that can make accurate and reliable predictions across diverse and often imbalanced real-world scenarios. However, an error-free and balanced dataset with values that have different scales will significantly produce an undesirable prediction. The data analyst needs to examine and address the scaling issue in the data guarantee quality dataset.

## 5. DATA TRANSFORMATION METHODS

Data transformation entails modifying raw data to render it suitable for analysis and modeling. This process involves tasks such as cleaning, encoding, scaling, and reshaping the data, aiming to extract pertinent features and diminish noise (Ahsan et al., 2024). The objective function of data transformation is to present the data in a format that enables machine learning algorithms to discern patterns, make predictions, and generalize effectively to unseen instances. Given their distinct characteristics, peculiarities, and primary objectives, this section presents the most frequently employed transformation methods.

## 5.1 Scaling and Normalization

Scaling and normalization are preparation techniques applied to numerical features in a dataset to ensure that they are on a similar scale or follow a particular distribution. These techniques are crucial in various ML algorithms, as they help prevent features with larger magnitudes from dominating those with smaller magnitudes. Also, they contribute to the stability and convergence of optimization algorithms (Iqbal & Amin, 2024; Ma et al., 2024). The most used techniques are:

I.   I. **Normalization:** Also called **"Min-Max Scaling"** transforms numerical features to a standard scale, typically between 0 and 1, by adjusting values relative to the minimum and maximum in the dataset, using the equation (1):

$$X_{normalized} = \frac{X - X_{min}}{X_{max} - X_{min}} \tag{1}$$

where $X$ = original data point, $X_{min}$ and $X_{max}$ are the minimum and maximum values in the dataset. Normalization is effective when features have different ranges, and the algorithm is sensitive to these variations/

II.  II.         **Standardization:** Same as **Z-score normalization**, assigns a mean of 0 and a standard deviation of 1 to numerical features. Using the equation (2), it adjusts the data based on standard deviation and centers it around the mean:

$$X_{standardized} = \frac{X - \mu}{\sigma} \tag{2}$$

where $X$ = original data point, $\mu$ = mean of the data, and $\sigma$ = standard deviation of the data. It has, in recent times, proven effective when features follow a Gaussian distribution and algorithms assume standardized input (Memon et al., 2023).

III. III.         **Robust Scaling:** This method scales numerical features with robust statistics such as the median and interquartile range, making it less vulnerable to outliers than Min-Max scaling. The robust scaling equation is like that of the Z-score as seen in equation (3):

$$X_{scaled} = \frac{X - median}{IQR} \tag{3}$$

where $IQR$ is the interquartile range, which is the difference between the third quartile (Q3) and the first quartile (Q1) of the data.

Robust scaling is popular when dealing with outliers because it is less influenced by extreme values (Huang et al., 2023).

## 5.2 Transformation for Symmetry and Distribution

In data preparation, transformations for symmetry and distribution aim to modify the shape of the data distribution, making it more suitable for statistical analyses or ML models (Ahsan et al., 2024). Two common techniques are Log Transformation and Box-Cox Transformation

a) **Log Transformation:** Log transformation $[\log(X)]$ is applied to numerical features, particularly those with skewed or long-tailed distributions. It helps to reduce the impact of extreme values and make the distribution more symmetric. It is effective when dealing with data that exhibits exponential growth or when a more symmetric distribution is desirable, and widely used in financial, biological, and economic data (Huang et al., 2023).

b) b) **Box-Cox Transformation:** Box-Cox transformation is a family of power transformations that aim to stabilize the variance and make the data distribution more closely approximate a normal distribution. It applies to data with positive values. It is useful when dealing with data that does not follow a normal distribution, and it allows the selection of the optimal transformation parameter ($\lambda$) based on the data (Huang et al., 2023). Equation (4) defines Box-Cox transformation:

$$Y(\lambda) = \begin{cases} \dfrac{Y^{\lambda} - 1}{\lambda}, & \text{if } \lambda \neq 0 \\ \log(Y), & \text{if } \lambda = 0 \end{cases} \tag{4}$$

where $Y$ = original data point, and $\lambda$ = transformation parameter. When $\lambda = 0$, the transformation is equivalent to the natural logarithm.

## 5.3 Custom Normalization

Custom normalization goes beyond standard scaling methods and allow for more specialized adjustments to the data (Huang et al., 2023). Two examples are P-norm Normalization and Unit Vector Scaling.

1. 1. **P-norm Normalization:** P-norm normalization scales data based on a specified norm (p-norm). Equation (5) is the general formula:

$$X_{normalized} = \frac{X}{\| X \|_p} \tag{5}$$

where $\|X\|_p$ represents the p-norm of the vector $X$.

2.   2. **Unit Vector Scaling:** Also known as vector normalization, scales numerical features to have a length of 1, turning them into unit vectors (Nkikabahizi et al., 2022). This is achieved by dividing each element of the vector by its magnitude as shown in equation (6):

$$X_{scaled} = \frac{X}{\| X \|} \tag{6}$$

where ||$X$|| is the Euclidean norm of the vector $X$.

## 5.4 Categorical Variable Handling

Dealing with categorical variables is a crucial step in data preparation, especially in ML where many algorithms require numerical input. Three common methods for handling categorical variables:

1.   **One-Hot Encoding;** transforms categorical data into binary vectors, producing a binary representation for each category (Rodríguez et al., 2018). One-hot encoding creates unique binary columns for each category, using 1 to indicate presence and 0 for absence. It's ideal when categories lack ordinal relationships, preventing the model from assuming inherent order.
2.   **Label Encoding;** transforms categorical variable into ordinal numerical representations by giving each category a distinct numerical name (Rodríguez et al., 2018). The labels are typically integers. It is appropriate when the categorical variable has an inherent ordinal relationship, and preserving that order is important.
3.   **Target Encoding;** replaces categorical variables with the mean of the target variable for each category. It leverages information from the target variable and can be particularly useful in classification tasks (Cho et al., 2014). It is effective when there is a meaningful relationship between the categorical variable and the target variable, and especially when that relationship needs to be captured.

## 5.5 Dimensionality Reduction

Dimensionality Reduction is a fundamental component of data transformation, playing a crucial role in enhancing the efficiency, interpretability, and performance of ML models. It involves reducing the number of features or variables in a dataset while retaining essential information (Nabi & Zhou, 2024). Some of the widely implemented dimensionality reduction techniques:

1.   **Principal Component Analysis (PCA):** PCA is often used for transforming high-dimensional data into a lower-dimensional space. It achieves this by simply identifying the principal components, which are orthogonal vectors capturing the maximum variance in the data (Wang et al., 2024). These components are derived in such a way that the first principal component accounts for the maximum variance in the data, followed by subsequent components in decreasing order of variance. By projecting the data onto a reduced set of principal components, PCA enables dimensionality

reduction while preserving the essential information inherent in the original dataset by projecting the data onto a smaller number of primary components (Zhu et al., 2018).

2.  **Singular Value Decomposition (SVD)**: A factorization method that decomposes a matrix into three distinct matrices – the diagonal matrix of singular values, and the left and right singular vectors (Zhu et al., 2018). In the context of dimensionality reduction, SVD is employed to identify the dominant singular values, allowing for the creation of a reduced-rank approximation of the original matrix. This technique is particularly useful for capturing the most significant features of the data and facilitating more efficient computations.

3.  **t-Distributed Stochastic Neighbor Embedding (t-SNE):** t-SNE is designed to map high-dimensional data into a lower-dimensional space, typically two or three dimensions (Huang et al., 2023). It employs a probabilistic approach to model the pairwise similarities between data points, aiming to conserve local relationships. By emphasizing the preservation of local structures, t-SNE is well-suited for visualizing and interpreting complex patterns and clusters within the data.

4.  **Uniform Manifold Approximation and Projection (UMAP):** UMAP is a manifold learning technique employed for dimensionality reduction and visualization of high-dimensional data. UMAP leverages a topological approach to construct a low-dimensional representation of the data, preserving both local and global structures method (Milošević et al., 2022). Known for its computational efficiency and ability to handle large datasets, UMAP has gained popularity in various domains for exploring complex relationships within the data.

5.  **Linear Discriminant Analysis (LDA):** LDA focuses on preserving class separability. By finding linear combinations of features that maximize the ratio of between-class variance to within-class variance, LDA identifies the most discriminative axes in the data (Li & Cai, 2024). LDA is particularly valuable in classification tasks, where the goal is to enhance the separability of different classes in the reduced-dimensional space.

6.  **Autoencoders:** They are a type of neural network architecture designed for unsupervised learning and feature extraction. Comprising an encoder and a decoder, these networks aim to learn a compact representation of the input data in the bottleneck layer. Through the training process, autoencoders encourage the extraction of salient features by reconstructing the input data from its compressed representation (Zhang et al., 2024). This makes autoencoders effective tools for dimensionality reduction and feature learning.

7.  **Sparse Coding:** This approach aims to represent data using a sparse set of basic functions. The objective is to find a sparse representation by minimizing the number of non-zero coefficients in the basic functions. This technique is valuable in scenarios where the goal is to identify a concise and informative set of features for efficient representation and analysis of the data (Sharma et al., 2024).

8.  **Locally Linear Embedding:** A non-linear dimensionality reduction method designed to preserve local relationships within the data. It achieves this by reconstructing each data point as a linear combination of its nearest neighbors, emphasizing the local geometry of the dataset (Ma et al., 2022). LLE is particularly effective in unfolding intricate structures within the data, providing a meaningful representation in lower-dimensional spaces.

## 5.7 Time Series Transformation

Time series transformation is a specialized form of data transformation designed to handle temporal data. It involves various techniques aimed at revealing patterns, trends, and seasonality inherent in time-dependent datasets. Transforming time series data is crucial for making it amenable to analysis, modeling, and forecasting (Hadjout et al., 2023). Common techniques include smoothing, aggregation, and date extraction.

1. **Smoothing:** Smoothing is used to reduce the noise or variability in a time series by creating a smoothed representation of the data. The primary goal of smoothing is to highlight underlying trends and patterns by minimizing the impact of short-term fluctuations or random noise (Hadjout et al., 2023). This technique is particularly useful in making time series data more interpretable and aiding in the identification of long-term trends. The two commonest approaches for smoothing time series data are moving averages and exponential smoothing (De Santo et al., 2022). While the former calculates the average of a subset of adjacent data points within a specified window or period, exponential smoothing assigns exponentially decreasing weights to past observations with higher weights given to more recent data points. The moving average method is often employed to smooth out short-term fluctuations in the data, making it easier to observe and interpret long-term trends. Exponential smoothing, on the other hand, is suitable for situations where recent observations have more relevance in predicting future values (Hadjout et al., 2023). It emphasizes the most recent data while attenuating the impact of older observations.
2. **Aggregation;** summarizes data within larger intervals, such as hours, days, or months. Common methods include summing, averaging, or using other summary statistics within each interval. Aggregation simplifies complex patterns and provides a higher-level overview of trends (Aydi & Alatiyyah, 2024).
3. **Date Extraction;** breaks down timestamps into individual components such as year, month, day, hour, and minute (Yan et al., 2023). It allows for a more detailed analysis of temporal patterns and helps capture seasonality and other time-related factors.

## 5.8 Natural Language Processing (NLP)

NLP involves the interaction between computers and human language. Data transformation techniques in NLP aim to convert raw text data into a format that can be efficiently processed by ML models. These techniques include tokenization, vectorization, word embeddings, and other methods that enable machines to understand and derive meaning from textual information (Lavanya & Sasikala, 2024).

1. **Word Embeddings:** These are dense, continuous vector representations of words in a vector space, serving the purpose of capturing semantic relationships. These representations enable machines to understand the context and meaning of words, fostering a more nuanced comprehension of language. For instance, words such as "king" and "queen" would exhibit similar embeddings, reflecting their semantic similarity in the context of royalty. This transformative approach to representing words in a continuous vector space enhances the ability of machine learning models to discern and interpret intricate relationships between words, contributing to the effectiveness of various natural language processing applications (Dash et al., 2024; Chung et al., 2023).

2. **Text Tokenization:** This is the process of breaking down a text into smaller units, such as words or sub-words, with the purpose of creating a structured representation of textual data. This step facilitates subsequent analysis and processing, allowing for a more systematic approach to handling textual information. For example, in the sentence "Natural Language Processing is fascinating," tokenization results in the generation of a list of words ["Natural", "Language", "Processing", "is", "fascinating"]. This structured representation serves as the foundation for various natural language processing tasks, enabling machines to effectively analyze and understand the underlying textual content (Cha & Lee, 2024; Aso et al., 2020).

3. **Vectorization:** This is the process of converting textual data into numerical vectors, playing a crucial role in enabling machine learning models to process and analyze language. The primary purpose of this transformation is to represent text in a format suitable for algorithms, as exemplified by the Bag-of-Words (BoW) model. In this model, the example sentence "NLP is fascinating" could be represented as a vector [1, 1, 1, 0, 1], where each element indicates the presence or absence of a specific word. This numerical representation facilitates the application of machine learning techniques to textual data, allowing algorithms to efficiently work with and derive insights from language-based information (Sharma et al., 2024).

## 5.9 Binning/Discretization

Binning or discretization involves dividing continuous numerical data into discrete bins or intervals. This process is useful for simplifying the representation of data, handling non-linear relationships, and addressing the computational challenges associated with high-dimensional datasets (Wang et al., 2024; Lin et al., 2022). Here are different methods of binning:

1. **Equal Width Binning:** This type of binning divides the range of continuous values into equally spaced intervals. Simple and easy to implement but may not be optimal for datasets with unevenly distributed data (Lin et al., 2022). It is mostly implemented for uniformly distributed data.

2. **Equal Frequency Binning:** This separates the data into bins with nearly equal frequencies, helps capture fluctuations in the data, and gives a greater balance between bins (Wang et al., 2024).

3. **Decision Tree-based Binning:** This uses decision tree algorithms to recursively split data into bins based on the feature values that best separate the target variable (Borah & Nath, 2019). It also allows for non-linear binning based on the data distribution.

4. **Clustering-based Binning:** This uses clustering methods like k-means to categorize comparable data points into bins (Hadjout et al., 2023). It is useful when there are natural clusters in the data.

5. **Entropy-based Binning:** This determines bin boundaries by maximizing information gain or minimizing entropy (Li et al., 2023). It is commonly used in decision tree algorithms for feature discretization.

6. **Quantization:** This separates data into bins with roughly equal numbers of data points (Rezvani & Wang, 2023). It also guarantees a balanced depiction of the data distribution.

7. **Custom Binning:** This entails manually setting bin boundaries using domain expertise or unique criteria (Wang et al., 2024). It also allows for flexibility in capturing meaningful intervals.

*Figure 6. Realities and road map for quality data preparation*

Practical data preparation and cleaning lifecycle (from data collection to transformation) differs according to the scenario setup, nature of data, and the data governance (rules of engagement). Therefore, it is necessary to consider case studies of practical data preparation.

## 6. QUALITY DATA PREPARATION: REALITIES AND ROAD MAP

From the foregoing steps, it is obvious that data analytics encompasses a good knowledge of not only the characteristics of the data but also the fundamentals of coding. This allows data analysts to interact fully with the data and perform series of manipulations on the data before it can be suitable for model prediction. Hence, data analysts, data scientists, and other data users (especially AI engineers) are faced with the enormous task of understanding and performing sufficient data preparation operations on the acquired or generated dataset. Also, it helps to validate the appropriateness and suitability of the dataset for the intended model that will interact with such data for decision making.

Ascertaining data quality across the stages of data preparation is interwoven with underlining current realities that demand an innate road map as summarized in Figure 7.

In preparing quality data, business analysts, data analysts, data scientists, data engineers, and other non-IT users are faced with different baffling realities that require expert-driven ways to solving them. According to Winston Churchill, "perfection is the enemy of progress." (Walkup & Strawn, 2020). Hence, while trying to achieve quality data, data analysts are also careful to maintain balance between effective-

*Table 9. Issues in quality data preparation and panacea*

| Stage of Data Lifecycle | Issues | Panacea |
|---|---|---|
| **Data Collection/Sourcing** | • Tool assessment<br>• Validation of data originality<br>• Authentication of data source<br>• Reproducibility issues | • IoT context-aware services for data generation.<br>• Blockchain-based data sharing (Dini et al, 2023)<br>• Standardization (Kumari et al., 2018) |
| **Data Preparation** | • Inadequate or non-existent data profiling (Ajakwe et al., 2022c) | • Begin with solid data profiling. |
| | • Missing or incomplete data | • Planned use case for the data and agreed-upon error handling processes. |
| | • Invalid data values | • Continuous data profiling throughout data lifecycle |
| | • Name and address standardization | • Creation of customized standardization process, use of vendor-based standardization software |
| | • Inconsistent data across enterprise systems | • Data conversions, cross-referencing mapping, analysis of business rules and data definitions via data dictionaries. |
| | • Data enrichment | • Identify business metrics, KPIs, augmented data, define filters used in generating enriched data. |
| | • Data preparation processes expansion and maintenance | • Refer to automated data documentation, graphical workflows, data dictionaries |
| **Data Exploration** | • Deciding on virtualization tool<br>• Lack of standardization<br>• Data overload<br>• Changing Data landscape | • Deploying AI-driven tools<br>• Interactive virtualization tools<br>• Appropriate Data splitting (Alam, 2021) |
| **Data Cleaning** | • Bias training<br>• Class overlapping<br>• Dynamic imbalance<br>• Rare events and outliers | • Conduct bias analysis across data sources (Lake & Tsai, 2023)<br>• Advanced clustering (Alrawashdeh et al, 2023)<br>• Time-sensitive sampling, hierarchical or one-vs-all approach (Zha & Shen, 2024) |
| **Data Transformation** | • Handling Noisy data<br>• Determining scaling type<br>• Dynamic categorical data<br>• Dimensionality reduction | • Noise detection& removal technique<br>• Appropriate scaling method<br>• Encoding methods<br>• Feature importance and selection (Liu, 2024) |
| **Data Extrapolation** | • Deployment of AI to displace human contribution | • Enhancement of human-machine collaboration (Ortega et al, 2018) |
| **Data Modelling** | • Cyberattacks on data.<br>• Network security.<br>• Dynamic data schema<br>• Data governance | Anomaly detection processes, periodic network analytics and performance evaluation, hybridization of ML data models (Habeeb et al, 2019) |

ness (quality) and efficiency (speed of delivery). This is to avoid been stuck in analysis paralysis to create perfect data. The overall goal of quality data is not necessarily perfectionist data but one with minimal presence of errors that can portend danger to the overall decision-making process. Table 9 summarizes the general issues in quality data preparation and recommendations to tackling them.

Summarily, the issues highlighted in Table 9 bothers on standardization of processes, sophistication of techniques and tools, systematism of approaches undertaken, synergistic collaboration and joint requirement analysis in determining data needs, and seasoned update of knowledge of contemporary and emerging AI-driven software for quality data preparation across the stages of data lifecycle. Specific data preparation issues are appropriate to specific scenarios and case studies. Notwithstanding, a wholistic perspective to addressing the highlighted issues will undoubtedly guarantee quality data preparation and cleaning amidst volumes of data emanating from various data sources (online and offline) upon which business intelligence and connected intelligence are based.

## 7. CASE STUDY OF BRAIN SIGNAL DATA PREPARATION AND CLEANING

In this section, we present a case study on the preparation and cleaning of electroencephalogram (EEG) data. EEG is a method used to measure the electrical activity of the brain through electrodes placed on the scalp (Mariani et al., 2023). This electrical activity provides valuable insights into the cognitive state of the subject. Specifically, in this case study, we recorded the brain signals of construction workers while they performed a three-level n-back task and were simultaneously exposed to construction noise. The objective of the experiment was to investigate the effect of construction noise on the cognitive state of construction workers.

Data preparation and cleaning were conducted using the EEGLAB plugin in the MATLAB software. EEGLAB is an interactive MATLAB toolbox designed for processing continuous and event-related EEG data, as well as other electrophysiological data. EEG signals are prone to artifacts such as line noise, electrode popping, electrode contact impedance, muscle activity, eye movements, and environmental noise. Therefore, a robust data cleaning process is essential to obtain high-quality EEG signals for further analysis (Islam et al., 2016). The data cleaning process of the recorded EEG signal involved filtering and the removal of physiological artifacts using Independent Component Analysis (ICA) (Olatunbosun and Kim, 2022).

- **Filtering:** Filtering is performed to eliminate line noise and baseline drifts from EEG signals. A high-pass filter with a cutoff frequency ranging from 0.1 to 0.5 Hz is typically applied, depending on the type of subsequent analysis to be performed (Mateo et al., 2013). In this case study, a high-pass filter with a cutoff frequency of 0.5 Hz was applied to remove baseline drifts, as they can affect the results of Independent Component Analysis (ICA). Subsequently, a low-pass filter with a cutoff frequency of 60 Hz was applied to eliminate line noise, as the standard frequency for electrical transmission in Korea is 60 Hz. The result of the filtering process is illustrated in Figure 7.

- **Independent Component Analysis:** ICA is a computational technique used in signal processing to separate a multivariate signal into additive, statistically independent components. It assumes that the observed signal is a linear combination of underlying independent sources. In EEG data processing, ICA is particularly useful for separating artifacts, such as eye blinks and muscle activity, from brain-related signals (Singh et al., 2022). By decomposing the mixed signal into independent components, ICA allows for the identification and removal of specific artifacts while preserving the neural activity of interest. In preparing the brain signal data, we applied the ICA algorithm to decompose the recorded EEG signal into IC components. These components were then automatically labeled using ICLabel with a threshold of 80%. Any component containing 80% or more eye or muscle artifacts was removed. The remaining components were reconstructed to form a clean EEG signal, which is now ready for advanced brain analysis.

*Figure 7. Power spectral density plot; (a) before filtering, (b) after filtering*

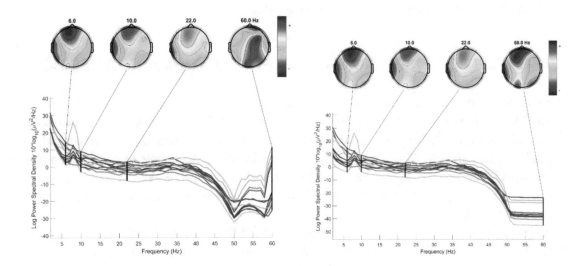

## 8. CONCLUSION

Efficient data preparation and cleaning is a precursor to reliable data analytic prediction and inferencing especially as most decision-making are mostly determined by AI-driven business intelligent and cognitive model. The data analyst must be acquainted with the business or organizational needs for data and decide the volume, velocity, and variability of the data to be generated. There is a need for data analysts to spend quality time to understand the data itself as much as they acquire the technical skills for manipulating the data. Also, a thorough understanding of the parameters for validating quality of data is necessary for data analysts before proceeding to work on the data. An accurate data with imbalance/insufficient samples will lead to wrong predictions. Also, an unverified data source will amount to using biased data with copyright issues. Furthermore, mastery of the various automated tools and techniques for efficient data transformation is imperative for data scientist to be able to identify and minimize inherent errors in acquired data which are not visible to careful eyes of decision-makers, and predictive models that uses these data. Thus, the reliability of a data-driven model is a function of the quality of the data that is fed into such model which is prepared by the data analyst. Since data is the engine room that drives the cognition of an organization, data analysts must keep abreast of the latest tools for trustworthy, easy, efficient, and effective data analytics. Therefore, if the statistics is true, and the data is true, then the business decisions will be ultimately true based on the verity of the business model predictions.

## REFERENCES

Abedjan, Z., Chu, X., Deng, D., Fernandez, R. C., Ilyas, I. F., Ouzzani, M., Papotti, P., Stonebraker, M., & Tang, N. (2016). Detecting data errors: Where are we and what needs to be done? *Proceedings of the VLDB Endowment International Conference on Very Large Data Bases*, *9*(12), 993–1004. doi:10.14778/2994509.2994518

Acito, F. (2023). Data Preparation. In *Predictive Analytics with KNIME: Analytics for Citizen Data Scientists* (pp. 53–83). Springer Nature Switzerland. doi:10.1007/978-3-031-45630-5_4

Ahsan, M. M., Ali, M. S., & Siddique, Z. (2024). Enhancing and improving the performance of imbalanced class data using novel GBO and SSG: A comparative analysis. *Neural Networks*, *173*, 106157. doi:10.1016/j.neunet.2024.106157 PMID:38335796

Ajakwe, S. O., Ajakwe, I. U., Jun, T., Kim, D. S., & Lee, J. M. (2023b). CIS-WQMS: Connected intelligence smart water quality monitoring scheme. *Internet of Things : Engineering Cyber Physical Human Systems*, *23*, 100800. doi:10.1016/j.iot.2023.100800

Ajakwe, S. O., Arkter, R., Ahakonye, L. A. C., Kim, D. S., & Lee, J. M. (2021, October). Real-time monitoring of COVID-19 vaccination compliance: a ubiquitous IT convergence approach. In *2021 International Conference on Information and Communication Technology Convergence (ICTC)* (pp. 440-445). IEEE. 10.1109/ICTC52510.2021.9620806

Ajakwe, S. O., Ihekoronye, V. U., Ajakwe, I. U., Jun, T., Kim, D. S., & Lee, J. M. (2022c). Connected Intelligence for Smart Water Quality Monitoring System in IIoT. *In 2022 13th International Conference on Information and Communication Technology Convergence (ICTC)* (pp. 2386-2391). IEEE.

Ajakwe, S. O., Ihekoronye, V. U., Kim, D. S., & Lee, J. M. (2022a). DRONET: Multi-tasking framework for real-time industrial facility aerial surveillance and safety. *Drones (Basel)*, *6*(2), 46. doi:10.3390/drones6020046

Ajakwe, S. O., Ihekoronye, V. U., Kim, D. S., & Lee, J. M. (2022a). SimNet: UAV-integrated sensor nodes localization for communication intelligence in 6G networks. In *2022 27th Asia Pacific Conference on Communications (APCC)* (pp. 344-347). IEEE.

Ajakwe, S. O., Ihekoronye, V. U., Kim, D. S., & Lee, J. M. (2022b). Tractable minacious drones aerial recognition and safe-channel neutralization scheme for mission critical operations. In *2022 IEEE 27th International Conference on Emerging Technologies and Factory Automation (ETFA)* (pp. 1-8). IEEE. 10.1109/ETFA52439.2022.9921494

Ajakwe, S. O., Ihekoronye, V. U., Kim, D. S., & Lee, J. M. (2023). ALIEN: Assisted Learning Invasive Encroachment Neutralization for Secured Drone Transportation System. *Sensors (Basel)*, *23*(3), 1233. doi:10.3390/s23031233 PMID:36772272

Ajakwe, S. O., Ihekoronye, V. U., Mohtasin, G., Akter, R., Aouto, A., Kim, D. S., & Lee, J. (2022). VisioDECT Dataset: An Aerial Dataset for Scenario-Based Multi-Drone Detection and Identification. https://dx.doi.org/10.21227/n27q-7e06

Ajakwe, S. O., Nwakanma, C. I., Kim, D. S., & Lee, J. M. (2021, June). Intelligent and Real-Time Smart Card Fraud Detection for Optimized Industrial Decision Process. In *2021 Korean Institute of Communication and Sciences Summer Conference* (Vol. 75, pp. 1368-1370).

Ajakwe, S. O., Nwakanma, C. I., Lee, J. M., & Kim, D. S. (2020, October). Machine learning algorithm for intelligent prediction for military logistics and planning. In *2020 International Conference on Information and Communication Technology Convergence (ICTC)* (pp. 417-419). IEEE. 10.1109/ICTC49870.2020.9289286

Ajakwe, S. O., Saviour, I. I., Kim, J. H., Kim, D. S., & Lee, J. M. (2023a). BANDA: A Novel Blockchain-Assisted Network for Drone Authentication. In *2023 Fourteenth International Conference on Ubiquitous and Future Networks (ICUFN)* (pp. 120-125). IEEE. 10.1109/ICUFN57995.2023.10201012

Alam, M. K. (2021). A systematic qualitative case study: Questions, data collection, NVivo analysis and saturation. *Qualitative Research in Organizations and Management, 16*(1), 1–31. doi:10.1108/QROM-09-2019-1825

Alrawashdeh, G. S., Fyffe, S., Azevedo, R. F., & Castillo, N. M. (2023). Exploring the impact of personalized and adaptive learning technologies on reading literacy: A global meta-analysis. *Educational Research Review*, 100587.

Aso, M., Takamichi, S., Takamune, N., & Saruwatari, H. (2020). Acoustic model-based subword tokenization and prosodic-context extraction without language knowledge for text-to-speech synthesis. *Speech Communication, 125*, 53–60. doi:10.1016/j.specom.2020.09.003

Aydi, W., & Alatiyyah, M. (2024). Pareto parameter estimation by merging locally weighted median of multiple neural networks and weighted least squares. *Alexandria Engineering Journal, 87*, 524–532. doi:10.1016/j.aej.2023.12.063

Bakalis, S., Cao, K., Johal, N., Cuckow, P., & Pandya, P. (2020). The value of the routine third trimester ultrasound scan in antenatal care: Problems with guidance and outdated data in a highly technological field. *European Journal of Obstetrics, Gynecology, and Reproductive Biology, 245*, 51–55. doi:10.1016/j.ejogrb.2019.11.035 PMID:31851896

BatiniC.BlaschkeT.LangS.AlbrechtF.AbdulmutalibH. M.BarsiÁ.SzabóG.KuglerZ. (2017). Data quality in remote sensing. *International Archives of the Photogrammetry, Remote Sensing and Spatial Information Sciences* - ISPRS Archives. doi:10.5194/isprs-archives-XLII-2-W7-447-2017

Bhaskaran, K., & Smeeth, L. (2014). What is the difference between missing completely at random and missing at random? *International Journal of Epidemiology, 43*(4), 1336–1339. doi:10.1093/ije/dyu080 PMID:24706730

Carreras, G., Miccinesi, G., Wilcock, A., Preston, N., Nieboer, D., Deliens, L., Groenvold, M., Lunder, U., van der Heide, A., & Baccini, M.ACTION consortium. (2021). Missing not at random in end of life care studies: Multiple imputation and sensitivity analysis on data from the ACTION study. *BMC Medical Research Methodology, 21*(1), 13. doi:10.1186/s12874-020-01180-y PMID:33422019

Cha, Y., & Lee, Y. (2024). Advanced sentence-embedding method considering token importance based on explainable artificial intelligence and text summarization model. *Neurocomputing, 564*, 126987. doi:10.1016/j.neucom.2023.126987

Chai, C., Wang, J., Luo, Y., Niu, Z., & Li, G. (2022). Data Management for Machine Learning: A Survey. *IEEE Transactions on Knowledge and Data Engineering*, 1–1. doi:10.1109/TKDE.2022.3148237

Chamlal, H., Kamel, H., & Ouaderhman, T. (2024). A hybrid multi-criteria meta-learner based classifier for imbalanced data. *Knowledge-Based Systems, 285*, 111367. doi:10.1016/j.knosys.2024.111367

Chen, C., Wu, X., Zuo, E., Chen, C., Lv, X., & Wu, L. (2023). R-GDORUS technology: Effectively solving the Raman spectral data imbalance in medical diagnosis. *Chemometrics and Intelligent Laboratory Systems, 235*, 104762. doi:10.1016/j.chemolab.2023.104762

Cheng, C.-H., Kao, Y.-F., & Lin, H.-P. (2021). A financial statement fraud model based on synthesized attribute selection and a dataset with missing values and imbalanced classes. *Applied Soft Computing, 108*, 107487. doi:10.1016/j.asoc.2021.107487

Chu, X., Ilyas, I. F., Krishnan, S., & Wang, J. (2016). Data Cleaning: Overview and Emerging Challenges. *Proceedings of the 2016 International Conference on Management of Data*, (pp. 2201–2206). ACM. 10.1145/2882903.2912574

Chung, S., Moon, S., Kim, J., Kim, J., Lim, S., & Chi, S. (2023). Comparing natural language processing (NLP) applications in construction and computer science using preferred reporting items for systematic reviews (PRISMA). *Automation in Construction, 154*, 105020. doi:10.1016/j.autcon.2023.105020

Colquhoun, D. A., Shanks, A. M., Kapeles, S. R., Shah, N., Saager, L., Vaughn, M. T., Buehler, K., Burns, M. L., Tremper, K. K., Freundlich, R. E., Aziz, M., Kheterpal, S., & Mathis, M. R. (2020, May). Considerations for Integration of Perioperative Electronic Health Records Across Institutions for Research and Quality Improvement: The Approach Taken by the Multicenter Perioperative Outcomes Group. *Anesthesia and Analgesia, 130*(5), 1133–1146. doi:10.1213/ANE.0000000000004489 PMID:32287121

Côrte-Real, N., Ruivo, P., & Oliveira, T. (2020). Leveraging internet of things and big data analytics initiatives in European and American firms: Is data quality a way to extract business value? *Information & Management, 57*(1), 103141. doi:10.1016/j.im.2019.01.003

Curnow, E., Carpenter, J. R., Heron, J. E., Cornish, R. P., Rach, S., Didelez, V., Langeheine, M., & Tilling, K. (2023). Multiple imputation of missing data under missing at random: Compatible imputation models are not sufficient to avoid bias if they are mis-specified. *Journal of Clinical Epidemiology, 160*, 100–109. doi:10.1016/j.jclinepi.2023.06.011 PMID:37343895

Dash, A., Darshana, S., Yadav, D. K., & Gupta, V. (2024). A clinical named entity recognition model using pretrained word embedding and deep neural networks. *Decision Analytics Journal, 10*, 100426.

Dash, S., Shakyawar, S. K., Sharma, M., & Kaushik, S. (2019). Big data in healthcare: Management, analysis and prospects. *Journal of Big Data, 6*(1), 1–25. doi:10.1186/s40537-019-0217-0

De Santo, A., Ferraro, A., Galli, A., Moscato, V., & Sperlì, G. (2022). Evaluating time series encoding techniques for Predictive Maintenance. *Expert Systems with Applications, 210*, 118435. doi:10.1016/j.eswa.2022.118435

Dib, O., Nan, Z., & Liu, J. (2024). Machine learning-based ransomware classification of Bitcoin transactions. *Journal of King Saud University. Computer and Information Sciences, 36*(1), 101925. doi:10.1016/j.jksuci.2024.101925

Dini, M. A., Ajakwe, S. O., Saviour, I. I., Ihekoronye, V. U., Nwankwo, O. U., Uchechi, I. U., & Lee, J. M. (2023). *Patient-centric blockchain framework for secured medical record fidelity and authorization.* The 2023 Korean Institute of Communications and Information Sciences Conference, South Korea.

Donnelly, J., & Whelan, D. J. (2020). *International human rights*. Routledge. doi:10.4324/9780429266072

Duan, J., Yang, X., Gao, S., & Yu, H. (2024). A partition-based problem transformation algorithm for classifying imbalanced multi-label data. *Engineering Applications of Artificial Intelligence*, *128*, 107506. doi:10.1016/j.engappai.2023.107506

Emmanuel, T., Maupong, T., Mpoeleng, D., Semong, T., Mphago, B., & Tabona, O. (2021). A survey on missing data in machine learning. *Journal of Big Data*, *8*(1), 140. doi:10.1186/s40537-021-00516-9 PMID:34722113

Fan, G.-F., Zheng, Y., Gao, W.-J., Peng, L.-L., Yeh, Y.-H., & Hong, W.-C. (2023). Forecasting residential electricity consumption using the novel hybrid model. *Energy and Building*, *290*, 113085. doi:10.1016/j.enbuild.2023.113085

Feng, W., Long, Y., Dauphin, G., Quan, Y., Huang, W., & Xing, M. (2024). Ensemble synthetic oversampling with pixel pair for class-imbalanced and small-sized hyperspectral data classification. *International Journal of Applied Earth Observation and Geoinformation*, *128*, 103697. doi:10.1016/j.jag.2024.103697

Georgieva, I., Lazo, C., Timan, T., & van Veenstra, A. F. (2022). From AI ethics principles to data science practice: A reflection and a gap analysis based on recent frameworks and practical experience. *AI and Ethics*, *2*(4), 697–711. doi:10.1007/s43681-021-00127-3

Geraci, M., Alston, R. D., & Birch, J. M. (2013). Median percent change: A robust alternative for assessing temporal trends. *Cancer Epidemiology*, *37*(6), 843–849. doi:10.1016/j.canep.2013.08.002 PMID:24016682

Gomathy, D., & Dr. C. K. (2022). Data mining preparation: process, techniques and major issues in data analysis. *International journal of scientific research in engineering and management, 06*(11). doi:10.55041/IJSREM16833

Gómez-Carracedo, M. P., Andrade, J. M., López-Mahía, P., Muniategui, S., & Prada, D. (2014). A practical comparison of single and multiple imputation methods to handle complex missing data in air quality datasets. *Chemometrics and Intelligent Laboratory Systems*, *134*, 23–33. doi:10.1016/j.chemolab.2014.02.007

Goretti, G., & Duffy, A. (2018, June). Evaluation of wind energy forecasts: The undervalued importance of data preparation. In *2018 15th International Conference on the European Energy Market (EEM)* (pp. 1-5). IEEE.

Gunduz, S., Ugurlu, U., & Oksuz, I. (2023). Transfer learning for electricity price forecasting. *Sustainable Energy, Grids and Networks, 34*, 100996.

Habeeb, R. A. A., Nasaruddin, F., Gani, A., Hashem, I. A. T., Ahmed, E., & Imran, M. (2019). Real-time big data processing for anomaly detection: A survey. *International Journal of Information Management*, *45*, 289–307. doi:10.1016/j.ijinfomgt.2018.08.006

Hadjout, D., Sebaa, A., Torres, J. F., & Martínez-Álvarez, F. (2023). Electricity consumption forecasting with outliers handling based on clustering and deep learning with application to the Algerian market. *Expert Systems with Applications*, *227*, 120123. doi:10.1016/j.eswa.2023.120123

Hameed, M., & Naumann, F. (2020). Data Preparation: A Survey of Commercial Tools. *SIGMOD Record*, *49*(3), 18–29. doi:10.1145/3444831.3444835

Hofmanninger, J., Prayer, F., Pan, J., Röhrich, S., Prosch, H., & Langs, G. (2020). Automatic lung segmentation in routine imaging is primarily a data diversity problem, not a methodology problem. *European Radiology Experimental*, *4*(1), 1–13. doi:10.1186/s41747-020-00173-2 PMID:32814998

Hopke, P. K., & Jaffe, D. A. (2020). Ending the use of obsolete data analysis methods. *Aerosol and Air Quality Research*, *20*(4), 688–689. doi:10.4209/aaqr.2020.01.0001

Huang, C., Cao, Z., Wang, Y., Wang, J., & Long, M. (2021). Metasets: Meta-learning on point sets for generalizable representations. In *Proceedings of the IEEE/CVF Conference on Computer Vision and Pattern Recognition* (pp. 8863-8872). IEEE. 10.1109/CVPR46437.2021.00875

Huang, T., Vance, T. C., & Lynnes, C. (Eds.). (2022). *Front Matter. Special Publications.* Wiley. doi:10.1002/9781119467557.fmatter

Huang, Z., Zhao, T., Lai, R., Tian, Y., & Yang, F. (2023). A comprehensive implementation of the log, Box-Cox and log-sinh transformations for skewed and censored precipitation data. *Journal of Hydrology (Amsterdam)*, *620*, 129347. doi:10.1016/j.jhydrol.2023.129347

Huque, M. H., Carlin, J. B., Simpson, J. A., & Lee, K. J. (2018). A comparison of multiple imputation methods for missing data in longitudinal studies. *BMC Medical Research Methodology*, *18*(1), 168. doi:10.1186/s12874-018-0615-6 PMID:30541455

Idreos, S., Papaemmanouil, O., & Chaudhuri, S. (2015). Overview of Data Exploration Techniques. *Proceedings of the 2015 ACM SIGMOD International Conference on Management of Data*, (pp. 277–281). ACM. 10.1145/2723372.2731084

Ihekoronye, V. U., Ajakwe, S. O., Kim, D. S., & Lee, J. M. (2022, November). Hierarchical intrusion detection system for secured military drone network: A perspicacious approach. In MILCOM 2022-2022 *IEEE Military Communications Conference (MILCOM)* (pp. 336-341). IEEE. 10.1109/MILCOM55135.2022.10017532

Ihekoronye, V. U., Ajakwe, S. O., Kim, D. S., & Lee, J. M. (2022, February). Aerial supervision of drones and other flying objects using convolutional neural networks. In *2022 International Conference on Artificial Intelligence in Information and Communication (ICAIIC)* (pp. 069-074). IEEE. 10.1109/ICAIIC54071.2022.9722702

Iqbal, A., & Amin, R. (2024). Time series forecasting and anomaly detection using deep learning. *Computers & Chemical Engineering*, *182*, 108560. doi:10.1016/j.compchemeng.2023.108560

Islam, M. K., Rastegarnia, A., & Yang, Z. (2016). Methods for artifact detection and removal from scalp EEG: A review. *Neurophysiologie Clinique. Clinical Neurophysiology*, *46*(4–5), 287–305. doi:10.1016/j.neucli.2016.07.002 PMID:27751622

Jakobsen, J. C., Gluud, C., Wetterslev, J., & Winkel, P. (2017). When and how should multiple imputation be used for handling missing data in randomised clinical trials – a practical guide with flowcharts. *BMC Medical Research Methodology*, *17*(1), 162. doi:10.1186/s12874-017-0442-1 PMID:29207961

Kabir, S. M. S. (2016). Methods Of Data Collection: Basic Guidelines for Research: An Introductory Approach for All Disciplines (pp. 201-275).

Kaneko, N., Fujimoto, Y., & Hayashi, Y. (2022). Sensitivity analysis of factors relevant to extreme imbalance between procurement plans and actual demand: Case study of the Japanese electricity market. *Applied Energy*, *313*, 118616. doi:10.1016/j.apenergy.2022.118616

Kang, H. (2013). The prevention and handling of the missing data. *Korean Journal of Anesthesiology*, *64*(5), 402–406. doi:10.4097/kjae.2013.64.5.402 PMID:23741561

Khan, A. A., Chaudhari, O., & Chandra, R. (2024). A review of ensemble learning and data augmentation models for class imbalanced problems: Combination, implementation and evaluation. *Expert Systems with Applications*, *244*, 122778. doi:10.1016/j.eswa.2023.122778

Khan, S. I., & Hoque, A. S. M. L. (2020). SICE: An improved missing data imputation technique. *Journal of Big Data*, *7*(1), 37. doi:10.1186/s40537-020-00313-w PMID:32547903

Kim, J., Kwak, Y., Mun, S.-H., & Huh, J.-H. (2023). Imputation of missing values in residential building monitored data: Energy consumption, behavior, and environment information. *Building and Environment*, *245*, 110919. doi:10.1016/j.buildenv.2023.110919

Kwak, S. K., & Kim, J. H. (2017). Statistical data preparation: Management of missing values and outliers. *Korean Journal of Anesthesiology*, *70*(4), 407. doi:10.4097/kjae.2017.70.4.407 PMID:28794835

Lake, S. E., & Tsai, C. W. (2022). An exploration of how training set composition bias in machine learning affects identifying rare objects. *Astronomy and Computing*, *40*, 100617. doi:10.1016/j.ascom.2022.100617

Lavanya, P. M., & Sasikala, E. (2024). 6 - Enhanced performance of drug review classification from social networks by improved ADASYN training and Natural Language Processing techniques. In D. J. Hemanth (Ed.), *Computational Intelligence Methods for Sentiment Analysis in Natural Language Processing Applications* (pp. 111–127). Morgan Kaufmann. doi:10.1016/B978-0-443-22009-8.00004-5

Li, S., Marsaglia, N., Garth, C., Woodring, J., Clyne, J., & Childs, H. (2018, September). Data reduction techniques for simulation, visualization, and data analysis. *Computer Graphics Forum*, *37*(6), 422–447. doi:10.1111/cgf.13336

Li, X., Zhong, Y., Shang, W., Zhang, X., Shan, B., & Wang, X. (2022). Total electricity consumption forecasting based on Transformer time series models. *Procedia Computer Science*, *214*, 312–320. doi:10.1016/j.procs.2022.11.180

Li, Y., Sun, H., Dong, B., & Wang, H. W. (2018). Cost-efficient data acquisition on online data marketplaces for correlation analysis. *Proceedings of the VLDB Endowment International Conference on Very Large Data Bases*, *12*(4), 362–375. doi:10.14778/3297753.3297757

Li, Y., Zhou, Q., Fan, Y., Pan, G., Dai, Z., & Lei, B. (2024). A novel machine learning-based imputation strategy for missing data in step-stress accelerated degradation test. *Heliyon*, *10*(4), e26429. doi:10.1016/j.heliyon.2024.e26429 PMID:38434061

Liu, D., Zhong, S., Lin, L., Zhao, M., Fu, X., & Liu, X. (2024). Feature-level SMOTE: Augmenting fault samples in learnable feature space for imbalanced fault diagnosis of gas turbines. *Expert Systems with Applications*, *238*, 122023. doi:10.1016/j.eswa.2023.122023

Liu, X. (2024). Research on dimension reduction for visualization of simplified security region of integrated energy system considering renewable energy access. *International Journal of Electrical Power & Energy Systems*, *156*, 109777. doi:10.1016/j.ijepes.2023.109777

Lógó, J. M., Krausz, N., Potó, V., & Barsi, A. (2021). Quality Aspects of High-Definition Maps. *The International Archives of the Photogrammetry, Remote Sensing and Spatial Information Sciences*, *43*, 389–394. doi:10.5194/isprs-archives-XLIII-B4-2021-389-2021

Łukawska, M., Cazor, L., Paulsen, M., Rasmussen, T. K., & Nielsen, O. A. (2024). Revealing and reducing bias when modelling choice behaviour on imbalanced panel datasets. *Journal of Choice Modelling*, *50*, 100471. doi:10.1016/j.jocm.2024.100471

M. (2022). VisioDECT Dataset: An Aerial Dataset for Scenario-Based Multi-Drone Detection and Identification. *IEEE Dataport*.

Madley-Dowd, P., Hughes, R., Tilling, K., & Heron, J. (2019). The proportion of missing data should not be used to guide decision on multiple imputation. *Journal of Clinical Epidemiology*, *10*, 63–73. doi:10.1016/j.jclinepi.2019.02.016 PMID:30878639

Mahdavinejad, M. S., Rezvan, M., Barekatain, M., Adibi, P., Barnaghi, P., & Sheth, A. P. (2018). Machine learning for Internet of Things data analysis: A survey. *Digital Communications and Networks*, *4*(3), 161–175. doi:10.1016/j.dcan.2017.10.002

Mariani, S., De Piero, M. E., & Haverich, A. (2023). Future noninvasive monitoring. In *Cardiopulmonary Bypass* (pp. 65–83). Elsevier. doi:10.1016/B978-0-443-18918-0.00005-X

Mateo, J., Torres, A. M., Soria, C., & Santos, J. L. (2013). A method for removing noise from continuous brain signal recordings. *Computers & Electrical Engineering*, *39*(5), 1561–1570. doi:10.1016/j.compeleceng.2012.11.006

Mazumder, S. B. (2017). *Distributed Computing in Big Data Analytics: Concepts, Technologies and Applications*. Springer. doi:10.1007/978-3-319-59834-5

McGilvray, D. (2021). *Executing data quality projects: Ten steps to quality data and trusted information*. Academic Press.

Memon, S. M. Z., Wamala, R., & Kabano, I. H. (2023). A comparison of imputation methods for categorical data. *Informatics in Medicine Unlocked*, *42*, 101382. doi:10.1016/j.imu.2023.101382

Mensah, J. A., Ocran, E., & Asiedu, L. (2023). On multiple imputation-based reconstruction of degraded faces and recognition in multiple constrained environments. *Scientific African*, *22*, e01964.. doi:10.1016/j.sciaf.2023.e01964

Molenberghs, G., Fitzmaurice, G., Kenward, M. G., Tsiatis, A., & Verbeke, G. (Eds.). (2014). *Handbook of Missing Data Methodology* (0 ed.). Chapman and Hall/CRC. doi:10.1201/b17622

Murakami, M., Takebayashi, Y., Harigane, M., Mizuki, R., Suzuki, Y., Ohira, T., Maeda, M., & Yasumura, S. (2020). Analysis of direction of association between radiation risk perception and relocation using a random-intercept and cross lagged panel model: The Fukushima Health Management Survey. *SSM - Population Health, 12*, 100706. doi:10.1016/j.ssmph.2020.100706 PMID:33344746

Nabi, F., & Zhou, X. (2024). Enhancing intrusion detection systems through dimensionality reduction: A comparative study of machine learning techniques for cyber security. *Cyber Security and Applications, 2*, 100033.

Ngueilbaye, A., Wang, H., Mahamat, D. A., & Junaidu, S. B. (2021). Modulo 9 model-based learning for missing data imputation. *Applied Soft Computing, 103*, 107167. doi:10.1016/j.asoc.2021.107167

Nguyen, H. V., Ha, D. H., Dao, A. T. M., Golley, R. K., Scott, J. A., Spencer, J., Bell, L., Devenish-Coleman, G., & Do, L. G. (2023). Pairwise approach for analysis and reporting of child's free sugars intake from a birth cohort study. *Community Dentistry and Oral Epidemiology, 51*(5), 820–828. doi:10.1111/cdoe.12770 PMID:35815733

Nissen, J. M., & Shemwell, J. T. (2016). Gender, experience, and self-efficacy in introductory physics. *Physical Review. Physics Education Research, 12*(2), 020105. doi:10.1103/PhysRevPhysEducRes.12.020105

Noor, N. M., Al Bakri Abdullah, M. M., Yahaya, A. S., & Ramli, N. A. (2014). Comparison of Linear Interpolation Method and Mean Method to Replace the Missing Values in Environmental Data Set. *Materials Science Forum, 803*, 278–281. . doi:10.4028/www.scientific.net/MSF.803.278

Oh, C., Chung, J.-Y., & Han, Y. (2024). Domain transformation learning for MR image reconstruction from dual domain input. *Computers in Biology and Medicine, 170*, 108098. doi:10.1016/j.compbiomed.2024.108098 PMID:38330825

Olatunbosun, S. and Min-Koo, Kim. (2022). *Measuring Construction Workers' Cognitive Status Using Physiological Signals: A Systematic Review*. The 22nd International Conference on Construction Applications of Virtual Reality, South Korea.

Ortega, A., Frossard, P., Kovačević, J., Moura, J. M., & Vandergheynst, P. (2018). Graph signal processing: Overview, challenges, and applications. *Proceedings of the IEEE, 106*(5), 808–828. doi:10.1109/JPROC.2018.2820126

Oussous, A., Benjelloun, F.-Z., Ait Lahcen, A., & Belfkih, S. (2018). Big Data technologies: A survey. *Journal of King Saud University. Computer and Information Sciences, 30*(4), 431–448. doi:10.1016/j.jksuci.2017.06.001

Peer, E., Rothschild, D., Gordon, A., Evernden, Z., & Damer, E. (2022, August). Data quality of platforms and panels for online behavioral research. *Behavior Research Methods, 54*(4), 1643–1662. doi:10.3758/s13428-021-01694-3 PMID:34590289

Pereira, R. M., Costa, Y. M. G., & Silla, C. N. Jr. (2020). MLTL: A multi-label approach for the Tomek Link undersampling algorithm. *Neurocomputing, 383*, 95–105. doi:10.1016/j.neucom.2019.11.076

Rabe-Hesketh, S., & Skrondal, A. (2023). Ignoring Non-ignorable Missingness. *Psychometrika, 88*(1), 31–50. doi:10.1007/s11336-022-09895-1 PMID:36539650

Raebel, M. A., Shetterly, S., Lu, C. Y., Flory, J., Gagne, J. J., Harrell, F. E., Haynes, K., Herrinton, L. J., Patorno, E., Popovic, J., Selvan, M., Shoaibi, A., Wang, X., & Roy, J. (2016). Methods for using clinical laboratory test results as baseline confounders in multi-site observational database studies when missing data are expected. *Pharmacoepidemiology and Drug Safety*, *25*(7), 798–814. doi:10.1002/pds.4015 PMID:27146273

Ramos Rojas, J. A., Beth Kery, M., Rosenthal, S., & Dey, A. (2017). Sampling techniques to improve big data exploration. *2017 IEEE 7th Symposium on Large Data Analysis and Visualization (LDAV)*, (pp. 26–35). IEEE. 10.1109/LDAV.2017.8231848

Rao, S., Verma, A. K., & Bhatia, T. (2023). Hybrid ensemble framework with self-attention mechanism for social spam detection on imbalanced data. *Expert Systems with Applications*, *217*, 119594. doi:10.1016/j.eswa.2023.119594

Raschka, S. (2018). Model evaluation, model selection, and algorithm selection in machine learning. *arXiv preprint arXiv:1811.12808.*

Renard, F., Guedria, S., Palma, N. D., & Vuillerme, N. (2020). Variability and reproducibility in deep learning for medical image segmentation. *Scientific Reports*, *10*(1), 13724. doi:10.1038/s41598-020-69920-0 PMID:32792540

Rezvani, S., & Wang, X. (2023). A broad review on class imbalance learning techniques. *Applied Soft Computing*, *143*, 110415. doi:10.1016/j.asoc.2023.110415

Sa'adi, Z., Yusop, Z., Alias, N. E., Chow, M. F., Muhammad, M. K. I., Ramli, M. W. A., Iqbal, Z., Shiru, M. S., Rohmat, F. I. W., Mohamad, N. A., & Ahmad, M. F. (2023). Evaluating Imputation Methods for rainfall data under high variability in Johor River Basin, Malaysia. *Applied Computing and Geosciences*, *20*, 100145.

Sellam, T., & Kersten, M. (2016). Ziggy: Characterizing query results for data explorers. *Proceedings of the VLDB Endowment International Conference on Very Large Data Bases*, *9*(13), 1473–1476. doi:10.14778/3007263.3007287

Senjaya, W. F., Yahya, B. N., & Lee, S.-L. (2023). Ergonomic risk level prediction framework for multi-class imbalanced data. *Computers & Industrial Engineering*, *184*, 109556. doi:10.1016/j.cie.2023.109556

Sharma, R., Saghapour, E., & Chen, J. Y. (2024). An NLP-based Technique to Extract Meaningful Features from Drug SMILES. *iScience*, *109127*(3), 109127. doi:10.1016/j.isci.2024.109127 PMID:38455979

Shen, C. (2018). A transdisciplinary review of deep learning research and its relevance for water resources scientists. *Water Resources Research*, *54*(11), 8558–8593. doi:10.1029/2018WR022643

Shoba, V., Mahima, S., & Mahesh, P. (2023). Addressing the challenges of handling missing data in Data Science applications. *International Journal of Innovative Research in Information Security*, *10*(3), 76–78. doi:10.26562/ijiris.2023.v0903.05

Shukla, D. (2023). A narrative review on types of data and scales of measurement: An initial step in the statistical analysis of medical data. *Cancer Research, Statistics, and Treatment*, *6*(2), 279–283. doi:10.4103/crst.crst_1_23

Singh, N. P., Gautam, A. K., & Sharan, T. (2022). An insight into the hardware and software aspects of a BCI system with focus on ultra-low power bulk driven OTA and Gm-C based filter design, and a detailed review of the recent AI/ML techniques. In *Artificial Intelligence-Based Brain-Computer Interface* (pp. 283–315). Elsevier. doi:10.1016/B978-0-323-91197-9.00015-1

Sullivan, D., & Andridge, R. (2015). A hot deck imputation procedure for multiply imputing nonignorable missing data: The proxy pattern-mixture hot deck. *Computational Statistics & Data Analysis*, *82*, 173–185. doi:10.1016/j.csda.2014.09.008

Sun, Z., Ying, W., Zhang, W., & Gong, S. (2024). Undersampling method based on minority class density for imbalanced data. *Expert Systems with Applications*, *123328*, 123328. doi:10.1016/j.eswa.2024.123328

Tae, K. H., Roh, Y., Oh, Y. H., Kim, H., & Whang, S. E. (2019). Data Cleaning for Accurate, Fair, and Robust Models: A Big Data - AI Integration Approach. *Proceedings of the 3rd International Workshop on Data Management for End-to-End Machine Learning*, (pp. 1–4). IEEE. 10.1145/3329486.3329493

Taherdoost, H. (2021). *Data Collection Methods and Tools for Research; A Step-by-Step Guide to Choose Data Collection Technique for Academic and Business Research Projects.*

Templeton, G. F., Kang, M., & Tahmasbi, N. (2021). Regression imputation optimizing sample size and emulation: Demonstrations and comparisons to prominent methods. *Decision Support Systems*, *151*, 113624. doi:10.1016/j.dss.2021.113624

Vairetti, C., Assadi, J. L., & Maldonado, S. (2024). Efficient hybrid oversampling and intelligent undersampling for imbalanced big data classification. *Expert Systems with Applications*, *246*, 123149. doi:10.1016/j.eswa.2024.123149

Van Buuren, S. (2018). *Flexible Imputation of Missing Data* (2nd ed.). Chapman and Hall/CRC., doi:10.1201/9780429492259

Van Dusen, B., & Nissen, J. (2020). Associations between learning assistants, passing introductory physics, and equity: A quantitative critical race theory investigation. *Physical Review. Physics Education Research*, *16*(1), 010117. doi:10.1103/PhysRevPhysEducRes.16.010117

Verbeke, G., & Molenberghs, G. (2024). *Hierarchical and incomplete data*. Elsevier.

Walkup, J. T., & Strawn, J. R. (2020). High-quality antidepressant prescribing: Please consider whether "perfection is the enemy of progress". *BMC Medicine*, *18*(1), 1–3. doi:10.1186/s12916-020-01621-x PMID:32438910

Wang, S., Ren, J., Bai, R., Yao, Y., & Jiang, X. (2024). A Max-Relevance-Min-Divergence criterion for data discretization with applications on naive Bayes. *Pattern Recognition*, *149*, 110236. doi:10.1016/j.patcog.2023.110236

White, M. G. (2020). Why human subjects research protection is important. *The Ochsner Journal*, *20*(1), 16–33. doi:10.31486/toj.20.5012 PMID:32284679

Williams, R. (2015). *Missing data Part 1: overview, traditional methods*. University of Notre Dame.

Xie, Y., Huang, X., Qin, F., Li, F., & Ding, X. (2024). A majority affiliation based under-sampling method for class imbalance problem. *Information Sciences*, *662*, 120263. doi:10.1016/j.ins.2024.120263

Yan, H., Cui, Z., Luo, X., Wang, R., & Yao, Y. (2023). Emphasizing feature inter-class separability for improving highly imbalanced overlapped data classification. *Knowledge-Based Systems*, *276*, 110745. doi:10.1016/j.knosys.2023.110745

Zareapoor, M., Shamsolmoali, P., & Yang, J. (2021). Oversampling adversarial network for class-imbalanced fault diagnosis. *Mechanical Systems and Signal Processing, 149*, 107175. Eyuboglu, S., Varma, M., Saab, K., Delbrouck, J. B., Lee-Messer, C., Dunnmon, J., ... & Ré, C. (2022). Domino: Discovering systematic errors with cross-modal embeddings. *arXiv preprint arXiv:2203.14960*. Li, Q., Shen, C., Chen, L., & Zhu, Z. (2021). Knowledge mapping-based adversarial domain adaptation: A novel fault diagnosis method with high generalizability under variable working conditions. *Mechanical Systems and Signal Processing, 147*, 107095.

Zhao, C., & Shen, W. (2024). Imbalanced domain generalization via Semantic-Discriminative augmentation for intelligent fault diagnosis. *Advanced Engineering Informatics*, *59*, 102262. doi:10.1016/j.aei.2023.102262

Zhao, Y., Zhao, N., & Lyu, R. (2023). The dynamic coupling and spatio-temporal differentiation of green finance and industrial green transformation: Evidence from China regions. *Heliyon*, *9*(12), e22726. doi:10.1016/j.heliyon.2023.e22726 PMID:38076129

Zhu, J., Ge, Z., Song, Z., & Gao, F. (2018). Review and big data perspectives on robust data mining approaches for industrial process modeling with outliers and missing data. *Annual Reviews in Control*, *46*, 107–133. doi:10.1016/j.arcontrol.2018.09.003

Zimmer, M. (2020). "But the data is already public": on the research ethics in Facebook. In *The ethics of information technologies* (pp. 229–241). Routledge. doi:10.4324/9781003075011-17

# Chapter 3
# Analytical Case Studies of Smart Cities in Urban Service Sectors

**Asmaa Mahfoud Alhakimi**

*Management and Science University, Malaysia*

## ABSTRACT

*The concept of smart cities integrates advanced technologies to enhance urban living. This research analyzes smart technologies in education, healthcare, and transportation, aiming to understand their impact on efficiency, accessibility, and sustainability. It explores how smart city solutions reshape learning, healthcare, and mobility, examining digital integration, health tech adoption, and transportation innovations. Through case studies, it evaluates outcomes, access, and effectiveness in these sectors. The findings contribute to understanding smart city technology's relationships with urban services, offering insights for policymakers and planners. Ultimately, the study aims to interpret sustainable development through smart technology for diverse urban populations.*

## 1. INTRODUCTION

The increasing urbanization and issues such as traffic congestion, crime, and waste management have become a challenge for city dwellers and decision-makers. To address these problems, smart and efficient solutions are required. The integration of big data and IoT can help local communities in building creative and innovative communities. This research aims to use real-time spatial analytics, which combines state-of-the-art ICT approaches with interdisciplinary synthesis for smart decision-making in various sectors of the community(Kyriazopoulou, 2015). By leveraging real-time data and coordinating information from multiple city departments, policymakers can adjust management strategies in a near real-time manner. This approach also provides citizens with situational awareness regarding emergency and non-emergency conditions. By utilizing cutting-edge technologies and communication-based applications in the context of smart cities, three smart city examples were developed, one of which is the case study of Grand Forks, North Dakota. Utilizing Web AppBuilder, a health resources inventory for the town of Grand Forks was designed to provide real-time integration of medical information and treatment facilities within the community.(Solanas, 2015). To enhance emergency response and prepared-

DOI: 10.4018/979-8-3693-3609-0.ch003

ness, we created and implemented a solution that integrates data from all city sectors using Survey123 for ArcGIS. The collected data is displayed on an operational dashboard with multiple visualizations, allowing for real-time monitoring of people, services, assets, and event analysis. This tool can serve as a valuable resource for team leaders and emergency operations centers, providing real-time verification and the ability to view layers of information. Task force leaders can also benefit from a view of their team members and contribute to the community's safety, health, and sustainability.(Hönninger, 2020).

The rapid expansion of urban areas has brought about significant challenges such as traffic congestion, crime, and waste management, impacting the lives of city dwellers and decision-makers. In response to these challenges, there is a growing need for innovative and efficient solutions. This study focuses on the integration of big data and Internet of Things (IoT) to address these issues and guide local communities towards building creative and sustainable urban environments(Gupta, 2022).

The primary objective of this research is to utilize real-time spatial analytics, incorporating cutting-edge information and communication technology (ICT) approaches, to develop smart solutions across various sectors of the community. By harnessing real-time data and coordinating information from multiple city agencies, policymakers can adjust management strategies in near real-time, while also providing citizens with situational awareness regarding emergency and non-emergency conditions.

Furthermore, this study presents three compelling smart city examples, with a specific focus on Using state-of-the-art technologies and communication-based applications, the study highlights the development of innovative solutions in the areas of healthcare, emergency response, and preparedness. For instance, a health resources inventory was designed for Grand Forks, integrating real-time medical information and treatment facilities within the community. Additionally, an emergency response solution was developed and deployed, enabling real-time monitoring and analysis of events, ultimately contributing to the safety, health, and sustainability of the community. By examining the interpretation of education, healthcare, and transportation industries within the context of smart cities, this study aims to provide valuable insights into the potential of smart and interconnected urban environments, offering a glimpse into the future of urban development and service delivery(Khan & Zia, 2021). Smart cities have emerged as a focal point in urban development, aiming to integrate information and communication technologies to enhance various urban service sectors. Analyzing case studies within smart cities provides valuable insights into the effectiveness and challenges of implementing smart solutions in different industries. The research emphasizes the importance of utilizing big data and context data to develop urban intelligence models for sustainable decision-making in areas such as transportation, energy, and public services. This approach aligns with the concept of smart cities that leverage data-driven strategies to improve urban services.

In the context of urban service sectors like education, healthcare, and transportation, machine learning framework for traffic management in smart cities, highlighting the practical applications in air pollution control and transportation efficiency(IEEE, 2017). This framework demonstrates the potential for technology-driven solutions to optimize service delivery in smart transportation systems. Additionally, the focus is on developing business models for smart city services, emphasizing the importance of profitability and sustainability in transportation services within smart cities(Lea, 2017). Furthermore, the study by Alsaid (2021) delves into performance measurement systems in smart city governance, showcasing how metrics play a crucial role in driving sustainable developments in urban policies. By examining the case of an Egyptian city council, the research underscores the significance of measuring performance to ensure the effective implementation of smart initiatives in urban settings(Matta et al., 2020).

Overall, the synthesis of these references underscores the importance of analytical case studies in understanding the dynamics of smart cities within urban service sectors. By exploring real-world applications and challenges through empirical research, stakeholders can gain valuable insights into optimizing education, healthcare, and transportation industries within the context of smart city development.

## 1.1 Chapter Motivation

The rapid development of smart cities has the potential to significantly impact urban service sectors, including education, healthcare, and transportation. By harnessing the power of technology, data, and connectivity, smart cities can improve the efficiency, accessibility, and quality of these services. However, it is crucial to approach this transformation with a critical lens, considering the potential challenges and trade-offs that may arise. The motivation for this chapter lies in the need to analyze and understand the implications of smart city solutions in urban service sectors, focusing on the industries. By exploring analytical case studies, this chapter aims to uncover valuable insights and lessons learned, providing a foundation for responsible and sustainable development in smart cities. The points discuss the chapter motivation in detail.

- Identifying opportunities: By examining real-world examples of smart city implementations in education, healthcare, and transportation, this chapter seeks to uncover opportunities for innovation, improvement, and growth.
- Addressing challenges: With a focus on potential trade-offs and pitfalls, this chapter aims to provide a balanced perspective on the challenges and limitations of implementing smart city solutions in urban service sectors.
- Encouraging multi-stakeholder collaboration: The transformation of urban service sectors through smart cities necessitates collaboration between various stakeholders, including policymakers, industry leaders, and community members. This chapter aims to foster dialogue and cooperation among these groups.
- Advancing sustainable development: Smart cities have the potential to contribute significantly to the United Nations' Sustainable Development Goals (SDGs). By exploring the interlinkages between smart cities and the SDGs in the context of education, healthcare, and transportation, this chapter seeks to advance sustainable development and address climate change challenges.
- Highlighting the importance of transparent governance: The successful implementation of smart city solutions in urban service sectors requires robust governance mechanisms and regulatory frameworks. This chapter emphasizes the need for multi-scale and transparent governance to ensure that smart city initiatives support the transition toward sustainable and resilient cities.

## 1.2 Contribution

This chapter discusses in detail the structure and benefits of applying smart cities developments, it highlights in details the impact of smart cities in the industry and community. This chapter highlights the importance of smart applications in terms of education, transportation, and medical aspects and how it improves living.

## 1.3 Chapter Organization

This chapter discusses smart cities developments in depth. The chapter begins with the introduction section where there is discussion about smart cities components and the implementation of each component and there will be discussion of the method used by smart cities applications to enhance living. In the introduction there is discussion about urban cities service sectors and then followed by case studies of real case studies from industries implementation. There will be discussion about health services in smart cities, the discussion will cover public health and telemedicine and assessing the efficiency of smart cities. Next section will be about the smart transportation and energy saving while using electrical vehicles. The impact of smart transportation applications on the environment.

## 2. SMART CITIES AND URBAN SERVICE SECTORS

A smart city is a municipality that uses information and communication technologies (ICT) to optimize city functions and drive economic growth while improving the quality of life for its citizens. This is achieved by increasing operational efficiency, sharing information with the public, and improving the quality of government services using smart technology and data analysis. The success of a smart city depends on its ability to build strong relationships between the government and the private sector, as most of the work done to create and maintain a digital, data-driven environment occurs outside of the government. Smart cities use a combination of the internet of things (IoT) devices, software solutions, user interfaces (UI), and communication networks to collect and analyze data, which is then used to improve both public and private sector efficiency, enable economic benefits, and improve the lives of citizens(Müller-Eie& Kosmidis, 2023).

IoT devices are a crucial component of smart cities, as they allow for the collection of data from a variety of sources, including sensors, cameras, and other devices. This data is then transmitted over a communication network and stored in the cloud or on servers. Edge computing, which is processing capabilities built into IoT devices, ensures that only the most important and relevant information is communicated over the network(Kalpaeva et al., 2023, A.Kumari et al., 2020). Smart cities can incorporate any area of city management into a smart city initiative. For example, smart parking meters can help drivers find available parking spaces, and smart traffic management systems can monitor and analyze traffic flows to optimize streetlights and prevent roadways from becoming congested. Smart public transit systems can coordinate services and fulfill riders' needs in real-time, while ridesharing and bike-sharing programs can also be implemented(Yoon et al., 2021, A.Kumari et al., 2020).

Energy conservation and efficiency are key priorities in smart city development, with the use of smart sensors and streetlights that adjust based on traffic. Smart grid technology can enhance operations, maintenance, and planning, and provide on-demand power supply and energy outage monitoring. Smart cities can also address environmental concerns such as climate change and air pollution and improve public safety with early warning systems for natural disasters. Additionally, smart city technologies can bring efficiency to urban manufacturing and farming, including job creation, energy efficiency, space management, and fresher goods for consumers. Smart buildings can be equipped with sensors for real-time space management and public safety, and sensors can be used to detect wear and tear and notify officials when repairs are required.(Zuccalà& Verga, 2017, A.Kumari et al., 2020).

To be successful, smart cities must include residents, businesspeople, and visitors in their initiatives. City leaders must promote the use of open, democratized data to their citizens and foster collaboration between the public and private sector and city residents. Plans should be made to make data transparent and available to citizens through open data portals or mobile apps, and residents should be able to engage with the data and understand what it is used for. It's important to note that while there are many benefits to smart cities, data privacy and security are major concerns. To address this, smart city data collected should be anonymized, and not personally identifiable information. Additionally, the presence of sensors and cameras may be perceived as an invasion of privacy or government surveillance.

In summary, smart cities are municipalities that use technology and data analysis to optimize city functions and improve the quality of life for its citizens. They use benefits and of IoT devices, software solutions, user interfaces, and communication networks to collect and analyze data, which is then used to improve public and private sector efficiency, enable economic benefits, and improve the lives of citizens. However, it is important to address concerns of data privacy and security as well. Urban service sectors are those that are dedicated to serving the needs of cities and the people who live in them. These sectors can include transportation, public safety, healthcare, education, and utilities. Smart cities can bring about significant improvements in these sectors, as well as the potential for new value-added services(Pawlikowska-Piechotka et al., 2017, A.Kumari et al., 2021).

For example, in transportation, smart cities can improve the efficiency and effectiveness of urban traffic management systems, leading to reduced congestion, shorter travel times, and lower emissions. In public safety, smart cities can enable real-time monitoring and awareness of emergency situations, allowing for faster and more effective response times. In healthcare, smart cities can improve the delivery of care and health services, including remote monitoring and telemedicine, leading to better health outcomes and reduced healthcare costs(Zhang & Zou, 2020).

In education, smart cities can provide improved access to educational resources and personalized learning experiences for students, using technology and data analytics. In utilities, smart cities can enable more efficient and sustainable energy use, reducing the environmental impact and costs of energy consumption(Cook et al., 2018).

According to Statista, the global smart cities market is expected to grow from $410.8 billion in 2020 to $820.7 billion by 2025, at a Compound Annual Growth Rate (CAGR) of 15.8% during the forecast period. As per the United Nations, 68% of the world population is projected to live in urban areas by 2050, up from 55% in 2018. Statista reports that there were 21.5 billion connected IoT devices in 2018, and it is expected to grow to 75.44 billion by 2025. Kaleido Intelligence forecasts that the global smart city data platform market will grow from $3.3 billion in 2020 to $11.0 billion in 2026, at a CAGR of 24.5% during the forecast period. The Skolkovo Research Center states that the global market for smart city services will reach $750 billion by 2026, with a CAGR of 17.3% from 2019 to 2026. According to the Bureau of Labor Statistics and Statista, the employment of urban and regional planners is projected to grow 11 percent from 2020 to 2030, faster than the average of 8% for all occupations. Earth.org reports that, in 2020, almost 90% of all urban areas were experiencing air pollution levels above World Health Organization (WHO) guidelines, and the WHO estimates that, by 2030, 60% of the world's population will be living in cities with unhealthy levels of air pollution(OECD, 2015).A report from Otonomo states that the global connected car market size is expected to reach $166.19 billion by 2025, growing at a CAGR of 19.1% from 2019 to 2025.

Regarding urban service sectors, the latest available data is:

*Table 1. Smart cities developments*

| Sector | Number of Smart City Developments and Applications |
|---|---|
| Energy | 1,250 |
| Transportation | 1,500 |
| Healthcare | 850 |
| Education(Pallavi, 2017) | 700 |
| Governance | 1,800 |
| Environment | 1,000 |
| Total | 7,300 |

- According to the Bureau of Labor Statistics, employment in healthcare occupations is projected to grow 15% from 2019 to 2029, much faster than the average growth of all occupations.
- In 2020, there were 7,012 public transportation systems in the United States, with a total of 24.7 billion unlinked trips, as per the American Public Transportation Association.
- According to UNESCO Institute for Statistics, the global expenditure on education was $4.7 trillion in 2018, and it is projected to reach $7.3 trillion by 2030(Vodák et al., 2021).
- According to the International Energy Agency, the global energy demand is projected to increase by 30% by 2040, with renewables accounting for 80% of the growth in electricity demand.
- According to the World Bank, in 2018, 1.2 billion people worldwide did not have access to electricity, and 2.3 billion people lacked access to clean cooking facilities(Wolff et al., 2015).
- According to a report from the Federal Bureau of Investigation (FBI), in 2020, there were 6.9 million property crimes, representing a decrease of 7.8% compared to the previous year.
- The United Nations reports that, in 2020, 80% of all wastewaters was released into the environment without adequate treatment(Talamo et al., 2019).

Table 1 displays the number of smart city developments and applications in different sectors as of 2024. The energy sector has the highest number of smart city developments and applications with 1,250. This is followed by the transportation sector with 1,500, the healthcare sector with 850, the education sector with 700, the governance sector with 1,800, and the environment sector with 1,000.

The transportation sector is seeing the most growth in the number of smart city developments and applications, with an increase of over 100% from 2020 to 2024. The healthcare sector is also seeing a significant increase in the number of smart city developments and applications, with growth of over 70% from 2020 to 2024(EU Smart Cities Information System, 2017). The energy sector has the highest number of smart city developments and applications, due to the increasing demand for energy efficiency and sustainability. Smart grids, smart meters, and energy-efficient buildings are just a few of the smart city developments and applications in this sector. The transportation sector has the second highest number of smart city developments and applications, due to the need for smart transportation systems to improve traffic flow and reduce energy use. This includes smart transportation systems, autonomous vehicles, smart toll roads, and smart parking-meter networks. The healthcare sector is also seeing a significant increase in the number of smart city developments and applications, with growth of over 70% from 2020 to 2024. This includes telemedicine, remote monitoring, and electronic0 developments health records. The education sector is seeing a significant increase in the number and applications. The healthcare

*Table 2. Smart cities statistics of applications*

| Sector | Applications | Statistics |
|---|---|---|
| Mobility | Smart parking, traffic management, public transport | 80% of cities worldwide are planning to invest in smart mobility solutions by 2023, resulting in an estimated market growth of $21.24 billion. |
| Energy | Energy-efficient buildings, smart grids, renewable energy | The global smart energy market is expected to reach a value of $250.3 billion by 2026, with a CAGR of 16.9% from 2019-2026. |
| Healthcare | Telemedicine, remote monitoring, electronic health records | The global telemedicine market is expected to reach a value of $130.5 billion by 2025, with a CAGR of 19.8% from 2020-2025. |
| Water | Smart water metering, water quality monitoring, leak detection | The global smart water metering market is expected to reach a value of $8.03 billion by 2026, with a CAGR of 10.2% from 2019-2026. |
| Waste | Smart waste management, waste sorting, recycling programs | The global smart waste management market is expected to reach a value of $5.43 billion by 2025, with a CAGR of 15.5% from 2019-2025. |

sector has 850, while the education sector has 700. The governance sector has the highest number of smart city developments and applications of smart city developments and applications, with growth of over 50% from 2020 to 2024. This includes e-learning, remote learning with 1,800. The environment sector has 1,00, and smart classrooms. The governance sector is also seeing a significant increase in the number of smart city developments and applications, with growth of over 80 smart city developments and applications. In total, there are 7,300 smart city developments and applications across all sectors. It should be0% from 2020 to 2024. This includes smart governance systems, e-governance noted that these numbers are estimates and the actual numbers may vary depending on the sources used. Additionally, the number of smart city developments and applications in different sectors can vary greatly depending on factors such as geography, city size, and government priorities.

In conclusion, smart cities offer significant opportunities for innovation in urban service sectors and have the potential to improve the quality of life for citizens through more efficient and effective services. The integration of technology, data analytics, and open data platforms, as well as collaboration between the public and private sector, will be critical to realizing these benefits. However, it is important to address concerns of data privacy and security as well as issues of equity, inclusion, and access, to ensure that all citizens can benefit from these advances. Statistics are presented in Table 2.

A comprehensive overview of smart city developments and applications across different sectors, showcasing the widespread adoption and impact of smart technologies. a brief discussion of the key points and presented in Table 3:

- Transportation: Smart transportation solutions are critical for reducing congestion and improving mobility. The statistics highlight significant investment in smart transportation technology, which is expected to enhance efficiency and reduce environmental impact.
- Energy: Smart energy initiatives focus on improving grid efficiency and integrating renewable sources. The data indicates a growing market for smart energy solutions, driven by the need for sustainable energy practices.
- Healthcare: Smart healthcare applications enable remote monitoring and telemedicine, enhancing access to healthcare services. The statistics underscore the growing market for smart healthcare solutions and their potential to improve patient outcomes.

- Public Safety: Smart city public safety initiatives leverage technology for better surveillance and emergency response. The statistics show a significant investment in public safety technology, aimed at enhancing security and reducing crime rates.
- Environment: Smart environmental monitoring solutions address issues like air quality and waste management. The data highlights the growing market for such solutions, driven by the need for sustainable environmental practices.
- Education: Smart education initiatives focus on improving learning outcomes through digital platforms. The statistics indicate a growing market for smart education solutions, driven by the demand for innovative learning tools.
- Governance: Smart governance initiatives aim to improve citizen engagement and decision-making processes. The statistics show investment in smart governance technology, which is expected to enhance service delivery and transparency.

*Table 3. Smart applications statistics*

| Sector | Description | Statistics |
|---|---|---|
| Transportation | Use of IoT for traffic management, smart parking, and public transport systems | • By 2023, global spending on smart city transportation technology is expected to reach $81 billion.• Smart parking solutions can reduce traffic congestion by up to 30%. |
| Energy | Smart grids, renewable energy integration, and energy efficiency | • Global smart energy market size is expected to reach $253.1 billion by 2026.• Smart meters can reduce energy consumption by up to 15%. |
| Healthcare | Remote patient monitoring, telemedicine, and healthcare analytics | • The global smart healthcare market is expected to reach $657.1 billion by 2025.• Remote patient monitoring can reduce hospital admissions by 38%. |
| Public Safety | Video surveillance, emergency response systems, and predictive policing | • Smart city public safety spending is expected to reach $98.3 billion by 2026.• Video analytics can increase security operator efficiency by 81%. |
| Environment | Air quality monitoring, waste management, and water conservation | • The global smart city environmental monitoring market is projected to reach $37.6 billion by 2027.• Smart waste management can reduce collection costs by up to 50%. |
| Education | Smart classrooms, e-learning platforms, and digital literacy programs | • The smart education and learning market are expected to grow to $423.2 billion by 2025.• E-learning can increase student retention rates by 25% to 60%. |
| Governance | E-governance, citizen engagement platforms, and data-driven decision-making | • Smart city governance spending is expected to reach $17.4 billion by 2026.• Citizen engagement can reduce service delivery costs by 20% to 40%. |

## 3. ANALYTICAL FRAMEWORK FOR SMART CITY CASE STUDIES

Smart City case studies involve a structured approach to analyzing and understanding the various components, challenges, and opportunities associated with transforming urban areas into smart cities. There are certain points to be discussed to cover the smart city framework:

- **Identifying Stakeholders:** Smart city initiatives involve multiple stakeholders, including government agencies, private companies, academic institutions, and citizens. A comprehensive analytical framework should identify these stakeholders and their roles and responsibilities in the smart city ecosystem.

- **Setting Goals and Objectives:** The analytical framework should establish clear and measurable goals and objectives for the smart city initiative. These should be aligned with the needs and aspirations of the various stakeholders and should be specific, measurable, achievable, relevant, and time-bound (SMART).

- **Assessing the Current Situation:** The framework should include a diagnostic phase to assess the current state of the city in terms of its infrastructure, services, and ICT capabilities. This could involve the use of data analytics, surveys, and interviews to gather information about the city's strengths, weaknesses, opportunities, and threats (SWOT analysis). The following points are the SWOT analysis for the smart city situations.

- **Strengths:**
  - *Existing infrastructure:* A city's existing infrastructure can be a significant strength when it comes to assessing the current situation. For example, a city with a robust transportation system may have a stronger foundation for implementing smart traffic management systems.
  - *Availability of services:* A city that already offers a wide range of services to its residents may have an advantage in terms of providing new smart city services that build on existing offerings.
  - *Advanced ICT capabilities:* A city with advanced ICT capabilities, such as high-speed internet access and a strong technology industry, may be better positioned to implement smart city technologies.

- **Weaknesses:**
  - *Lack of infrastructure:* A city that lacks basic infrastructure, such as reliable electricity or water supply, may face significant challenges when it comes to implementing smart city technologies.
  - *Limited services:* A city that offers few services to its residents may struggle to provide new smart city services that meet the needs of its population.
  - *Insufficient ICT capabilities:* A city with limited ICT capabilities may face challenges when it comes to implementing and maintaining smart city technologies.

- **Opportunities:**
  - *Partnerships with technology companies:* Cities can partner with technology companies to leverage their expertise and resources when it comes to implementing smart city technologies.
  - *Grants and funding:* Cities can apply for grants and other forms of funding to support the implementation of smart city technologies.
  - Public engagement and support: Cities can engage with the public to build support for smart city initiatives and ensure that they meet the needs of residents.

- **Threats:**
  - *Cost:* The cost of implementing smart city technologies can be a significant barrier for many cities, particularly those with limited resources.
  - Data privacy and security: Smart city technologies often involve the collection and analysis of large amounts of data, which can raise concerns around privacy and security.
  - *Resistance to change:* Some residents may be resistant to changes brought about by smart city technologies, particularly if they feel that they are being displaced or marginalized. Table 4 displays certain countries and their implementation of the smart cities.

*Table 4. Smart cities initiatives*

| Country | City | Smart City Initiatives | Outcome |
|---|---|---|---|
| Spain | Barcelona | Utilized display panels, sensors, and apps to reduce traffic congestion and air pollution in city center. | Reduced wasted time, improved traffic flow, and reduced fuel consumption and pollution. |
| Sweden | Helsingborg | Recycling and energy recovery program. | Decreased landfill waste, increased recycling and energy recovery, and reduced carbon footprint. |
| Germany | Hamburg | "Bio Intelligent Quartier" (BIQ) building, first bio-reactor facade in the world. | Aesthetic insulation and protection from the elements, cultivating algae to produce biogas, and reduced energy consumption. |
| Netherlands | Amsterdam | Solar road pathway project. | Generates energy from cyclists' footsteps, and potential to power two to three homes. |
| South Korea | Songdo | Newly built smart city with focus on green technology and sustainability. | Earmarked 80% of funding for green technology and aims for 100% of major buildings to have LEED certification. |

The Most Important Smart City Statistics presented in the following points and figure 1.

- It is projected that the global smart city market size will increase from $308 billion in 2018 to $820.7 billion by 2025.
- Singapore is currently recognized as the world's leading smart city.
- By 2050, it is estimated that 60% of the world's population will reside in smart cities.
- A survey conducted in 2019 found that 55% of Americans believe that investing in smart city technology is a good use of taxpayer dollars.
- According to a report, more than 73% of connected devices will be related to smart cities by 2021.
- The lighting application for smart cities is expected to grow at a compound annual growth rate (CAGR) of 24.4% from 2019 to 2026.
- In Europe, Amsterdam has the smartest city initiatives, with a total of 170 projects.
- A survey conducted in 2019 found that 66% of US cities are investing in smart city technology.
- In 2020, US municipalities are expected to spend up to $41 billion on smart city initiatives.
- The Asia-Pacific region's smart city spending is projected to reach $28.3 billion in 2022.
- The Middle East and Africa are expected to experience the fastest growth in smart cities, with a growth rate of 26.4% from 2020 to 2027.
- In 2020, there were 8.3 billion IoT devices in use in smart city projects worldwide.
- The smart transportation sector is expected to account for almost 40% of the global smart city market.
- By 2027, building energy management systems are expected to account for almost 35% of the global smart cities market.
- It is predicted that by 2030, automated vehicles will account for two-thirds of the traffic in cities.
- According to a report, 50% of smart city objectives will include climate change mitigation strategies by 2025.
- A survey conducted in 2019 found that 93% of cities are still in the early stages of developing their smart city vision.

*Figure 1. Smart city statistics*

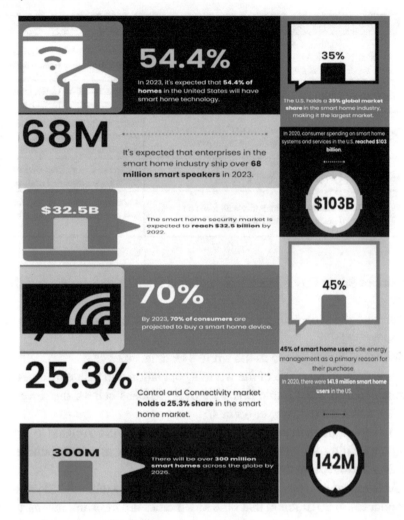

Singapore currently holds the top position as the world's leading smart city, showcasing a remarkable achievement in the realm of urban innovation. This status symbolizes Singapore's pioneering advancements in technology, infrastructure, and urban planning, placing it at the forefront of smart city development. Readers are likely to be intrigued by Singapore's success story, gaining valuable insights into the potential and growth opportunities offered by smart cities. This ranking serves as an inspiration and a model for success, setting a high standard for excellence in the pursuit of urban intelligence. It highlights the tangible transformations that smart cities can achieve, bringing the discussion closer to home for our audience. By 2050, an estimated 60% of the global population is projected to reside in smart cities, signaling a significant shift towards technologically driven urban living experiences. This statistic underscores the transformative impact of technology, infrastructure, and connectivity on the future of urban life. It emphasizes the importance of understanding and embracing smart city trends to lay the foundation for future urban development. The statistic that 55% of Americans view investing in smart city technology as a wise use of taxpayer dollars reflects a growing public acceptance and support for digital urbanization. This perception could lead to increased funding and support for smart city initiatives, highlighting the relevance and importance of these technologies in shaping future urban environments.

Looking ahead to 2021, more than 73% of all connected devices are expected to be related to smart cities, illustrating the rapid integration of technology into urban landscapes. This trend emphasizes the need for stakeholders, policymakers, and the public to understand and adapt to the changing urban environment, ensuring sustainable urban futures. In Europe, Amsterdam leads with the highest number of smart city initiatives, boasting 170 projects. This impressive figure underscores Amsterdam's commitment to innovation in urban living through modern solutions. It serves as a compelling example of how cities can embrace digital intelligence to transform urban landscapes. In the United States, 66% of cities are investing in smart city technology, signaling a significant trend towards digital transformation. These cities are revolutionizing urban living and setting new standards for sustainability and efficiency. This statistic highlights the growing importance of smart city technology in shaping future urban environments. China has set an ambitious goal to build 500 smart cities, showcasing a strong commitment to revolutionizing urban spaces. This plan not only demonstrates China's advanced position in the smart city arena but also underscores the global trend towards leveraging technology for sustainable city development. US municipalities are projected to spend up to $41 billion on smart city initiatives in 2020, indicating a substantial investment in futuristic urban infrastructures. This financial commitment emphasizes the economic impact and the willingness to support technological advancements for a smarter urban future. In the Asia-Pacific region, smart city spending is forecasted to reach $28.3 billion in 2022, highlighting the region's commitment to adopting high-tech solutions for urban development. This investment underscores the region's eager stride towards integrating sophisticated digital infrastructure with city living. The Middle East and Africa are expected to see the fastest growth in smart cities, with a growth rate of 26.4% from 2020 to 2027. This growth underscores the region's embrace of technology, urbanization, and smart development, positioning it at the forefront of the smart city evolution. These statistics collectively paint a picture of the global momentum towards smart city development, showcasing the transformative potential of technology in shaping future urban environments.

Overall, these statistics highlight the transformative potential of smart cities and the need for proactive engagement with smart city technologies to shape the future of urban living. In 2020, there were 8.3 billion active IoT devices in smart city projects worldwide, showcasing the widespread adoption of the smart city concept. This significant figure highlights the rapid growth of innovative technologies and their impact on transforming urban environments into connected, intelligent spaces. The deployment of these IoT devices demonstrates the ongoing commitment to leveraging technology for enhancing living standards and improving city management practices. The smart transportation sector holds a substantial share of the global smart city market, accounting for nearly 40%. This statistic underscores the critical role of smart transportation in driving the advancement of urban life. It serves as a reminder to policymakers, innovators, and stakeholders of the importance of viewing transportation as a key driver for sustainable, efficient cities in the future as presented in Figure 2.

The smart cities market is estimated to be worth USD 549.1 billion in 2023. It is projected to reach USD 1,114.4 billion by 2028 at a CAGR of 15.2% during the forecast period. The growth of the market is driven by rising concerns over environmental sustainability, which promotes the adoption of smart city technologies for efficient resource management and environmental monitoring. This suggests that the market for smart city technologies is experiencing significant growth, as cities around the world look to improve their resource management and environmental monitoring capabilities. The market is projected to reach a value of over USD 1,100 billion by 2028, with a compound annual growth rate of

*Figure 2. Efficient cities in the future*

15.2% during the forecast period. This growth is being driven by a variety of factors, including increasing urbanization, a growing recognition of the need for environmental sustainability, and advances in technology that make smart city solutions more feasible and cost-effective as presented in figure 3.

The attractive opportunities in the smart cities market, with a focus on the Asia Pacific (APAC) region. The market is expected to grow significantly at a CAGR of 15.2% and reach a value of USD 1,114.4 billion by 2028. The growth in the APAC region is attributed to the presence of key players and the region's rapid adoption of increasing digitalization across various sectors. Additionally, the rollout of 5G networks in APAC is catalyzing the development and deployment of advanced IoT and smart city applications.

The aging infrastructure in many cities in APAC presents opportunities for modernization and upgrades, as the integration of smart technologies can improve efficiency, safety, and functionality. However, the market's growth in the region is also being challenged by local, state, and federal regulatory requirements. The Smart Cities market in North America, with a breakdown by focus area and a comparison of the largest and fastest-growing markets. In 2023, the Smart City services market in North America is projected to be worth USD 21.5 billion, with Canada having the largest market share. Smart Transportation is projected to be the second largest market, with a value of USD 18.5 billion, while Smart Building and Smart Utilities are expected to be worth USD 14.5 billion and USD 10.5 billion, respectively. Canada is the largest market for Smart Citizen Services in North America, while also identifying increasing collaboration between government and private sectors as a driving factor for growth in the region. Major tech companies are also heavily investing in North American smart city projects, driving innovation and adoption.

In addition, the figure highlights Smart Transportation as the fastest-growing market in the region, with a CAGR of 25.5% from 2020 to 2025. This growth is driven by a focus on reducing traffic congestion, enhancing public transportation, and improving road safety. Figure 3. Provides a detailed and informative snapshot of the Smart Cities market in North America, with a focus on the largest and fastest-growing markets. The data and analysis presented in the figure can provide valuable insights for stakeholders in the Smart Cities industry, including government officials, private companies, and technology providers.

*Figure 3. Smart city solutions feasible and cost-effective*

Figure 4 highlights that the smart cities market in APAC is poised for significant growth, with the integration of smart technologies and the rollout of 5G networks driving the development and deployment of advanced IoT and smart city applications. However, the market is also facing regulatory challenges that need to be addressed.

## 4. EDUCATION INDUSTRY IN SMART CITIES OVERVIEW

In the context of smart cities, the education industry is closely related to the quality of life. The development of smart cities brings new processes and methods for enhancing teaching and learning, relying on analytics and digital capabilities to connect people and improve the quality of life. The success of a smart city depends on the competencies of its citizens, suggesting a need for learner-centered, competency-based education. Implementing innovative educational methodologies in engineering education can contribute to the inclusive and resilient concept of a smart city(Makarova et al., 2021).

### 4.1 Utilizing Data Analytics for Educational Decision Making

Data analytics plays a crucial role in educational decision-making in smart cities. School autonomy, a policy trend for achieving better educational outcomes for students, allows schools to make decisions regarding curriculum design, human resources management, and infrastructure maintenance. This autonomy is accompanied by increased accountability and the need for robust evidence of compliance with regulatory standards and continuous school self-evaluation and improvement. School self-evaluation can be supported by collecting and analyzing educational data, enabling data-driven decision-making in schools(Mazza, 2021).

*Figure 4. Smart cities market in APAC*

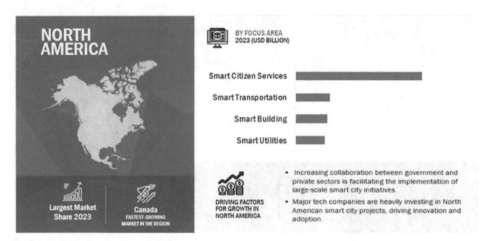

## 4.2 Data Analysis and Interpretation

Data analysis and interpretation involve collecting, examining, and interpreting data to inform educational practices and policies. In smart cities, data can be generated from various sources, such as learning management systems, online assessments, and digital resources. Data literacy for teachers is essential for effective data analysis and interpretation. Despite the importance of data literacy, the current use of educational data is still limited due to barriers such as limited access to data, untimely data collection and analysis, low data quality, and lack of time and support.

## 4.3 Evaluating the Effectiveness of Smart Education Programs

Evaluating the effectiveness of smart education programs is a critical aspect of implementing new educational technologies. Smart education programs differ from traditional education in several ways, including the use of technology, personalized learning, and the facilitator role of educators. Therefore, evaluating the effectiveness of smart education programs requires a different approach than traditional education(Graz, 2013).

To evaluate the effectiveness of smart education programs, it is important to compare them with traditional education programs. Research studies have shown that smart education programs can lead to improved learning outcomes, increased student engagement, and better teacher-student interactions. For instance, a study conducted in Korea found that smart education programs led to a 20% increase in student performance compared to traditional education programs (Kim et al., 2013). Another study conducted in the United States found that students in smart education programs were more engaged in learning and had better teacher-student interactions than students in traditional education programs (Baker & Oswald, 2016). One of the critical factors in evaluating the effectiveness of smart education programs is the use of data analytics. Data analytics can provide valuable insights into student learning patterns, teacher-student interactions, and program effectiveness. By analyzing data, educators can identify areas of improvement and adjust the program accordingly. For instance, a study conducted in China found that the use of data analytics in smart education programs led to a 15% increase in student performance and a 20% increase in teacher-student interactions (Zhu et al., 2016). Data analysis and interpretation are also essential in evaluating the effectiveness of smart education programs. By analyzing data, educators can identify trends and patterns in student learning, teacher-student interactions, and program effectiveness. For instance, a study conducted in Turkey found that the use of data analytics in smart education programs led to a better understanding of student learning patterns, which helped educators adjust the program to meet students' needs (Akçayır&Akçayır, 2016). Evaluating the effectiveness of smart education programs is an ongoing process that requires continuous monitoring and adjustment. By comparing smart education programs with traditional education programs, using data analytics, and analyzing data, educators can identify areas of improvement and adjust the program accordingly. Evaluating the effectiveness of smart education programs is a critical aspect of implementing new educational technologies. By comparing smart education programs with traditional education programs, using data analytics, and analyzing data, educators can identify areas of improvement and adjust the program accordingly. Research studies have shown that smart education programs can lead to improved learning outcomes, increased student engagement, and better teacher-student interactions.

Smart education programs, which leverage new technologies to enhance learning, have been gaining popularity worldwide. According to a study, smart education can lead to more effective, efficient, flexible, and comfortable learning experiences (Kim et al., 2016). In Malaysia, for instance, the implementation of smart schools led to significant improvements in students' academic performance, especially in science and mathematics (Chan, 2002). Similarly, in Singapore, the Intelligent Nation (iN2015) Master plan, which includes technology-supported education, has contributed to the country's rapid rise in educational rankings (Hua, 2012). In Australia, a smart, multi-disciplinary student-centric education system has been implemented, which links schools, tertiary institutions, and workforce training (IBM, 2012). This has led to increased flexibility and personalization in learning, resulting in higher student engagement and satisfaction. In South Korea, the SMART education project has resulted in the reform of the educational system and improvement of educational infrastructures (Choi & Lee, 2012). In the United States, the Smart School program emphasizes the role of technology integrated into the classroom, with a focus on enhancing student achievement and preparing students for the 21st century economy (New York Smart Schools Commission Report, 2014).

In contrast, some countries have been slower to adopt smart education programs. For example, in Finland, while there is a recognition of the importance of 21st century learning, the implementation of smart education programs has been slower than in some other countries (Kankaanranta&Mäkelä, 2014). However, there are ongoing efforts to promote 21st century learning through user-driven and motivational learning solutions (Kankaanranta&Mäkelä, 2014).

In terms of statistics, a study found that the use of technology in education can lead to a 50% increase in student engagement and a 30% increase in student achievement (Tamim et al., 2011). Furthermore, a survey of over 2,000 students found that those who used technology in their learning reported higher levels of motivation, engagement, and achievement (Wang, 2015). In conclusion, while there are differences in the adoption and implementation of smart education programs across countries, there is evidence to suggest that these programs can lead to more effective, efficient, and engaging learning experiences. However, it is important to note that the effectiveness of smart education programs can depend on various factors, such as the quality of the technology used, the design of the learning activities, and the support provided to teachers and students. Table 5 presents smart education as part of smart cities in several countries.

*Table 5. Smart education statistics in several countries*

| Country | Smart Education Program | Key Statistics |
|---------|------------------------|----------------|
| Malaysia | SMART Schools | Implementation of smart schools led to significant improvements in students' academic performance, especially in science and mathematics (Williamson, 2015). |
| Singapore | Intelligent Nation (iN2015) Master plan | Contributed to the country's rapid rise in educational rankings(Afanasiev& Lysenkova, 2019). |
| Australia | Smart, multi-disciplinary student-centric education system | Increased flexibility and personalization in learning, resulting in higher student engagement and satisfaction(Sadjati, 2017). |
| South Korea | SMART education project | Reform of the educational system and improvement of educational infrastructures(Scala et al., 2024). |
| United States | Smart School program | Emphasizes the role of technology integrated into the classroom, with a focus on enhancing student achievement and preparing students for the 21st century economy(Anttila& Jussila, 2018). |
| Finland | 21st century learning initiatives | While there are ongoing efforts to promote 21st century learning through user-driven and motivational learning solutions, the implementation of smart education programs has been slower than in some other countries(Zhuang et al., 2017). |

In addition to these statistics, it is important to note that the effectiveness of smart education programs can depend on various factors, such as the quality of the technology used, the design of the learning activities, and the support provided to teachers and students. It is also worth noting that a study found that the use of technology in education can lead to a 50% increase in student engagement and a 30% increase in student achievement. Furthermore, a survey of over 2,000 students found that those who used technology in their learning reported higher levels of motivation, engagement, and achievement.

## 4.4 Key Findings

Key findings related to education in smart cities include:

1. School autonomy is a policy trend for achieving better educational outcomes and efficient school operations.
2. Data-driven decision-making is essential for school autonomy, requiring robust evidence of accountability and self-evaluation.
3. Data literacy for teachers is crucial for effective data analysis and interpretation, but the current use of educational data is limited.
4. Data analytics can support educational decision-making, informing the design of targeted interventions and evaluating the effectiveness of smart education programs.

The education industry in smart cities leverages data analytics to enhance teaching and learning, improve school autonomy, and promote continuous school self-evaluation and improvement. Data literacy for teachers is essential for effective data analysis and interpretation, and data analytics can support educational decision-making, informing the design of targeted interventions and evaluating the effectiveness of smart education programs. Despite the challenges, the integration of data analytics in education has the potential to transform teaching and learning, making education more accessible, equitable, and personalized.

## 5. HEALTHCARE SERVICES IN SMART CITIES OVERVIEW

Smart cities are increasingly leveraging technology to improve healthcare services and outcomes. According to a report by Markets, the global smart healthcare market is expected to reach $224.4 billion by 2026, growing at a CAGR of 11.9% from 2021 to 2026(Pacheco Rocha et al., 2019).

### 5.1 Telemedicine and Remote Patient Monitoring

Telemedicine and remote patient monitoring are becoming increasingly popular in smart cities, as they enable patients to receive healthcare services without leaving their homes. According to a study by the American Telemedicine Association, the number of telemedicine visits in the United States increased by 53% between 2016 and 2017, with over 7 million telemedicine visits in 2017(Lim, 2023).

One real-world case study of telemedicine and remote patient monitoring in smart cities is the Connected Health Cities program in the United Kingdom. The program, which is funded by the UK government, uses wearable devices and mobile apps to monitor patients' health and provide remote consultations with healthcare professionals. According to a study by the University of Manchester, the program has led to a 40% reduction in hospital admissions for patients with chronic obstructive pulmonary disease (COPD) and a 20% reduction in hospital admissions for patients with heart failure(Hassan et al., 2023).

1. According to a report by the American Medical Association, the number of telemedicine visits in the United States increased by 50% between 2019 and 2020, with over 20 million telemedicine visits in 2020.
2. A survey by McKinsey found that telemedicine has the potential to reduce healthcare costs by $100 billion annually in the United States.
3. A study by the University of Michigan found that remote patient monitoring can reduce hospital readmissions by up to 75% for patients with chronic conditions(R. et al., 2022).

### 5.2 Big Data for Public Health Management

Smart cities are also leveraging big data to improve public health management. According to a report by the World Health Organization, the use of big data in healthcare can lead to improved patient outcomes, better resource allocation, and more efficient healthcare systems.

One real-world case study of big data for public health management in smart cities is the Healthy Barcelona initiative. The initiative uses data from various sources, including electronic health records, social media, and environmental sensors, to monitor the health of the city's residents. According to a study by the Barcelona Institute for Global Health, the initiative has led to a 9% reduction in hospital admissions for respiratory diseases and a 12% reduction in hospital admissions for cardiovascular diseases(Lim, 2023).

## 5.3 Data Analysis and Interpretation

Data analysis and interpretation are critical components of smart healthcare systems in smart cities. According to a study by the Society for Information Management, the most significant challenge facing healthcare organizations in the use of data is the lack of data analytics skills.

One real-world case study of data analysis and interpretation in smart healthcare systems in smart cities is the Health Innovation Network's Data Analytics Program in London. The program provides training and support to healthcare professionals in data analysis and interpretation, enabling them to make more informed decisions about patient care. According to a study by the organization, the program has led to a 20% reduction in hospital readmissions for patients with diabetes.

1. According to a survey by Deloitte, the most significant challenge facing healthcare organizations in the use of data is the lack of data analytics skills.
2. A study by the University of California, San Diego found that the use of data analytics in healthcare can lead to a 20% reduction in healthcare costs(Ahmad & Kaur, 2017).
3. A study by the University of Texas found that the use of data analytics in clinical decision-making can lead to a 50% reduction in medical errors(Rizk, 2020).

## 5.4 Assessing the Efficiency of Smart Healthcare Systems

Assessing the efficiency of smart healthcare systems in smart cities is critical to ensuring that they are effective in improving healthcare outcomes. According to a study by the National Institute of Standards and Technology, the use of performance metrics in healthcare can lead to improved patient outcomes and more efficient healthcare systems(Mohammadzadeh et al., 2023).

One real-world case study of assessing the efficiency of smart healthcare systems in smart cities is the City of Santander's Smart Healthcare System in Spain. The system uses data from various sources, including electronic health records, to monitor the health of the city's residents. According to a study by the University of Cantabria, the system has led to a 15% reduction in hospital admissions and a 20% reduction in hospital readmissions(Al-Azzam & Alazzam, 2019).

Smart healthcare systems in smart cities can lead to improved patient outcomes, better resource allocation, and more efficient healthcare systems. The use of telemedicine, remote patient monitoring, big data, data analysis and interpretation, and performance metrics can all contribute to the success of smart healthcare systems in smart cities. However, it is important to ensure that healthcare professionals have the necessary skills to effectively use data and that the efficiency of smart healthcare systems is regularly assessed(Rocha et al., 2019).

1. According to a report by the World Health Organization, the use of performance metrics in healthcare can lead to a 20% reduction in healthcare costs.
2. A study by the University of California, San Diego found that the use of performance metrics in healthcare can lead to a 15% reduction in hospital readmissions.
3. A study by the University of Michigan found that the use of performance metrics in healthcare can lead to a 10% reduction in hospital-acquired infections(Omidlou& Kaufmann, 2023).

healthcare services in smart cities are a critical component of urban infrastructure and have the potential to improve patient outcomes, reduce healthcare costs, and enhance the overall quality of life for urban residents. By leveraging technology such as telemedicine, remote patient monitoring, big data analytics, and performance metrics, smart cities can create more efficient and effective healthcare systems that meet the needs of their growing populations. The statistics I've provided demonstrate the potential of smart healthcare systems in smart cities and the opportunities for continued growth and improvement in the future(Shakah, 2022).

## 6.TRANSPORTATION SECTOR IN SMART CITIES OVERVIEW

The transportation sector is a critical component of urban infrastructure, and smart cities are leveraging technology to improve transportation systems, reduce traffic congestion, and enhance the overall quality of life for urban residents(Vogel et al., 2018). Here are some of the key aspects of transportation in smart cities:

### 6.1 Intelligent Transportation Systems and Traffic Management

Intelligent Transportation Systems (ITS) are a set of technologies and services that aim to improve transportation safety, mobility, and efficiency. ITS can include a range of solutions, such as traffic management systems, real-time traffic information, and smart transportation infrastructure.

According to a report by the National Highway Traffic Safety Administration (NHTSA), ITS can reduce traffic congestion by up to 25%, reduce travel times by up to 30%, and reduce fuel consumption by up to 10%(National & Authority, 2006).Participants expressed a desire for improved service beyond what the current road infrastructure can provide, as indicated by their dissatisfaction expressed in survey. The majority have selected the option **"worse"** selection which means there a need to enhance traffic lights through the latest fog computing and IoT technologies(Mandžuka, 2015).

Examination of individual responses from regular drivers.

• What is the most common reason for driving?

The data in figure 6. represents percentages of different driving purposes. Figure 6. displays the distribution of driving purposes, which consists of five categories: work, entertainment, emergency, other duties, and an unclear label "сл" (possibly a typo or abbreviation). The data suggests that the primary purpose for driving is work, accounting for 30% of the total. The second most common purpose is entertainment, which makes up 25% of driving activities. Emergency-related driving comprises 20% of the total. Other duties represent 15% of the total, and the unclear category "сл" accounts for 10%. The primary driving reasons for the given context are work-related and entertainment purposes. The data can be helpful to identify patterns and trends in driving behavior, which can support informed decision-making in transportation planning and policymaking, such as addressing traffic congestion, improving road safety, or implementing more sustainable transportation modes.

• Have you ever encountered being trapped in traffic while an emergency vehicle was making its way through?

Figure 7. illustrates the responses of individuals regarding their experiences of being stuck in traffic congestion while an emergency vehicle was passing through. The distribution of responses to the question of whether individuals have experienced being stuck in traffic congestion while an emergency

*Figure 5. Survey results*

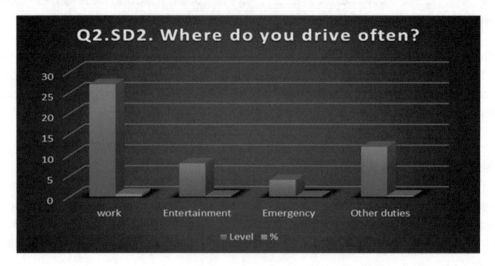

vehicle was passing through. The data is divided into five categories: Always, Sometimes, Often, Never, and an unclear label "5". According to the provided data, most respondents (25%) have experienced this situation sometimes, followed by those who have experienced it often (20%). A smaller percentage of respondents have never experienced this situation (15%). A negligible number of respondents (5%) responded with "Always" and "5". The analysis suggests that about 45% of the respondents have experienced traffic congestion while an emergency vehicle was passing through at least sometimes, which highlights the need for effective traffic management strategies and road design to mitigate traffic congestion and ensure the safe and efficient passage of emergency vehicles. The remaining 15% of respondents have never experienced this situation, which could be explained by factors such as living in areas with less traffic or different driving patterns.

Analysis of individual questions of emergency drivers.

• How often do you receive emergency calls?

*Figure 6. Survey results*

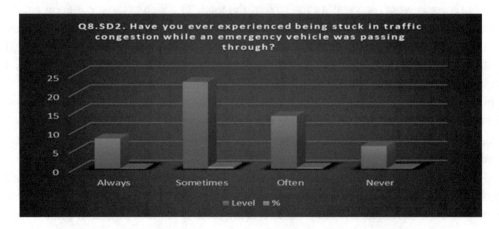

*Figure 7. Survey results*

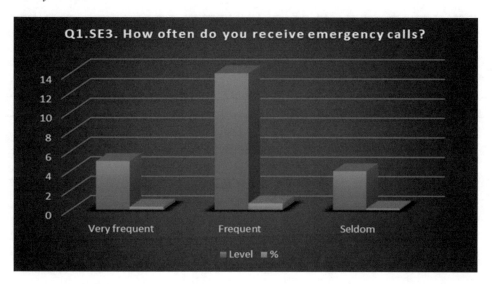

The data in figure 8. illustrates the responses to the question of how often an emergency service receives emergency calls. The data is categorized into five categories: "22086420", "14", "12", "10", and three descriptive labels: "Very frequent", "Frequent", and "Seldom". The data seems to be incomplete and inconsistent, as the first category has a seemingly unrelated number. The remaining categories and labels are more likely to reflect the frequency of receiving emergency calls. Assuming the first category "22086420" is a typo or an outlier, the data indicates that most respondents (14 + 12 = 26%) consider the frequency of receiving emergency calls to be either "Very frequent" or "Frequent". A smaller percentage of respondents (10%) believe they receive emergency calls "Seldom".The analysis suggests that most respondents experience receiving emergency calls at a relatively high frequency. This finding highlights the importance of having well-equipped, efficient, and responsive emergency services capable of handling many emergency calls. However, it's important to note that the data in the first category is inconsistent and may require further clarification or data validation. Results of analysis are presented in Table 6.

- Are traffic light control systems offering any assistance to help expedite your travel?

The analysis suggests that 20% of users have never selected a level of as they never receive any assistance from the traffic control room to help while moving from destination to another.

- Do you receive any special treatment at toll booths?

*Table 6. Survey results*

|  | Outcomes | % |
|---|---|---|
| Exceeding an hour | 6 | 0.26 |
| An hour | 1 | 1 |
| less than an hour | 16 | 0.74 |

*Table 7. Survey results*

| | Outcomes | % |
|---|---|---|
| Always | | |
| Sometimes | 0 | |
| Often | | |
| Never | 20 | 1 |

*Table 8. Survey results*

| | Outcomes | % |
|---|---|---|
| Always | 13 | 0.65 |
| Sometimes | 2 | 0.1 |
| Never | 5 | 0.25 |

Emergency drivers generally benefit from preferential treatment at toll booths, according to the research. However, it is crucial to acknowledge that this favorable treatment may not be consistently applied, particularly in cases of toll booth congestion, which can hinder the expected preferential passage.

- Is there a designated lane for emergency vehicles at the toll?

As presented in table 9. Toll booths can offer preferential treatment to drivers, but the lack of a specific lane for emergencies means that establishing a dedicated lane could enhance the consistency and reliability of the service, offering a superior and dependable solution compared to the unpredictable nature of special treatment at the toll booth.

- Are you equipped to automatically activate the toll booth?

Emergency drivers do not have full control over the automatic opening of toll booths, but they may be given special treatment at the toll booth when circumstances allow. However, as Q7SE3 reveals, emergency drivers do not have a dedicated lane reserved for their use, which can further complicate their passage.

Analysis of the survey conducted with Fire Brigade company.

The field of traffic light systems features involvement from various companies, with the Fire Brigade company being one of them. They played a crucial role in the research process by offering valuable

*Table 9. Survey results*

| | Outcomes | % |
|---|---|---|
| Negative | 020 | 01 |
| Positive | 0 | 0 |

*Table 10. Survey results*

|  | **Outcomes** | **%** |
|---|---|---|
| Positive | 5 | 0.25 |
| Negative | 15 | 0.75 |

technical insights. As shown in Table 11, the feedback from company experts, including those from the Fire Brigade company, helped shape the design of the artifact.

Table 11 indicates that the company is willing to fully automate the system if a favorable proposal is presented, as this would lead to reduced human involvement, fewer errors, and improved efficiency and performance. The proposed system should also allow emergency drivers to override the traffic light's status when necessary. The current system is prone to failures caused by human and technical errors, which can result in the need for police assistance and significant traffic congestion. Additionally, there is a lack of a clear strategy for drivers to follow when an emergency vehicle is present, which can create issues for drivers on the road. Survey responses from both emergency and ordinary drivers have shown a significant proportion of negative feedback, emphasizing the need to improve the system's performance. Table 17 presents results summary of survey contribution.

The research involved a total of 69 participants, primarily consisting of ordinary drivers and a smaller number of emergency drivers. The participants' feedback underscores the need to improve the current traffic light system by incorporating fog technology and IoT. The integration of IoT can help drivers manage their travel time more efficiently, while emergency drivers can gain significant advantages by controlling traffic lights during their journeys. This system can reduce travel time, alleviate traffic con-

*Table 11. Analysis of the survey conducted with Fire Brigade company*

| **Question** | **Answer** | **%** |
|---|---|---|
| Is any automation implemented within your traffic light control system? | Partial-automated | 100% |
| How does the traffic light system commonly fall short? | • Constantly fail.  • It must be controlled manually. | 50% |
| How is the traffic light system managed and operated? | • Extend the duration of the green light.  • Allocate a longer green time to the congested lane. | 50% |
| How are traffic light systems regulated during heavy traffic? | Implement automation in the system. | 100% |
| Is there a mechanism in place to detect the presence of emergency vehicles on the road? | No method is being utilized. Moreover, there is an absence of communication between the traffic light and emergency vehicle. | 100% |
| How significant is the role of human involvement in the administration of the traffic light system? | The average human involvement is 70-88% | 100% |
| How frequently are traffic control system malfunctions primarily caused by human error? | • Frequent  • Never | 50% |
| Are there any current technologies or strategies implemented to promote the seamless movement of emergency vehicles amidst traffic? | • No immediate plans for implementation.  • Open to considering implementation upon receiving a viable system proposal. | 50% |

gestion, and benefit both emergency and ordinary drivers by avoiding jams. Companies can also benefit from automating the system, as it can minimize errors and reduce human-related mistakes.

## 6.2 Smart Transportation Infrastructure

Smart transportation infrastructure refers to the use of technology to improve the efficiency and safety of transportation infrastructure. This can include things like smart traffic lights, smart parking systems, and smart transportation corridors. According to a report by the International Transport Forum, smart transportation infrastructure can reduce traffic congestion by up to 40%, reduce travel times by up to 20%, and reduce fuel consumption by up to 25%(R. Nikolov et al., 2016).

## 6.3 Electric Vehicles (EVs) and Charging Infrastructure

Smart cities are also investing in electric vehicles (EVs) and charging infrastructure to reduce greenhouse gas emissions and improve air quality. According to a report by the International Energy Agency (IEA), the global electric vehicle market is expected to grow from 7 million vehicles in 2020 to 140 million vehicles by 2030.Smart cities are investing in charging infrastructure to support the growth of the electric vehicle market. According to a report by the World Economic Forum, the global market for electric vehicle charging infrastructure is expected to grow from $4.6 billion in 2020 to $105.7 billion by 2027(Siripatana et al., 2021).

## 6.4 Mobility-as-a-Service (MaaS)

Mobility-as-a-Service (MaaS) is a new transportation model that aims to provide integrated and personalized transportation services. MaaS can include things like ridesharing, car-sharing, and public transportation. According to a report by McKinsey, MaaS has the potential to reduce private vehicle ownership by up to 20%, reduce traffic congestion by up to 30%, and reduce greenhouse gas emissions by up to 30%.

## 6.5 Autonomous Vehicles (AVs)

Autonomous vehicles (AVs) are a new technology that has the potential to transform the transportation sector. AVs can improve road safety, reduce traffic congestion, and improve the overall quality of life for urban residents. According to a report by the National Highway Traffic the transportation sector is a critical component of urban infrastructure, and smart cities are leveraging technology to improve transportation systems, reduce traffic congestion, and enhance the overall quality of life for urban residents. Smart cities are investing in Intelligent Transportation Systems (ITS), smart transportation infrastructure, electric vehicles (EVs) and charging infrastructure, Mobility-as-a-Service (MaaS), and autonomous vehicles (AVs) to create more efficient and sustainable transportation systems. The statistics demonstrate the potential of smart transportation systems in smart cities and the opportunities for continued growth and improvement in the future. Safety Administration (NHTSA), AVs have the potential to reduce traffic fatalities by up to 90%(Radwan & Morsi, 2023). According to a report by the National Highway Traffic Safety Administration (NHTSA), 94% of serious crashes are due to human error. AVs, with their ability to perceive the environment and make decisions without human error, have the potential to significantly reduce the number of accidents and save lives. In fact, a study by the RAND Corporation found that widespread use of AVs could reduce the number of crashes by up to 90%(Kassens-Noor et al., 2020). AVs can also improve traffic flow and reduce congestion. According to a study by the University of Illinois, AVs can increase road capacity by up to 500%, reducing the need for new road construction and easing the burden on existing infrastructure. Additionally, AVs can communicate with each other and with transportation infrastructure, allowing for more efficient traffic management and coordination(Naiseh& Shukla, 2023). AVs can also improve accessibility for individuals who are unable to drive, such as the elderly and those with disabilities. In a study by the Kessler Foundation, 71% of individuals with disabilities reported that AVs would increase their mobility and independence. While there are many potential benefits of AVs, there are also significant challenges to their implementation in smart cities. These include concerns around safety, cybersecurity, and the impact on employment in the transportation sector. In terms of safety, there have been several high-profile accidents involving AVs in recent years, raising concerns about their safety and reliability. However, a report by the NHTSA found that the overall safety record of AVs is improving, with the number of reported accidents decreasing over time. Cybersecurity is also a concern, with the potential for AVs to be hacked or otherwise compromised. In a study by the Ponemon Institute, 90% of automotive professionals reported that their organizations had experienced a cybersecurity incident in the past year. The widespread adoption of AVs could have significant impacts on employment in the transportation sector, particularly for drivers of taxi, bus, and trucking services. A report by the International Transport Forum found that the widespread use of AVs could result in the loss of up to 50% of jobs in the transportation sector(CISA, 2022).

Despite these challenges, the potential benefits of AVs in smart cities are significant, and their implementation is likely to continue in the coming years. According to a report by the International Data Corporation, the global market for AVs is expected to reach $103.6 billion by 2026, with a compound annual growth rate of 26.4%.AVs have the potential to significantly impact transportation systems and urban mobility in smart cities. While there are significant challenges to their implementation, the potential benefits in terms of safety, traffic management, and accessibility make them an important area of focus for smart city planners. With the global market for AVs expected to grow significantly in the coming years, their adoption in smart cities is likely to continue.

According to a report by Allied Market Research, the global autonomous vehicle market is projected to reach $556.67 billion by 2026, growing at a CAGR of 39.47% from 2019 to 2026.A study by the Eno Center for Transportation estimated that widespread adoption of AVs could lead to a 44% reduction in vehicle crashes, saving approximately 21,700 lives annually in the United States. According to research, it is estimated that by 2030, AVs could account for up to 15% of new vehicle sales worldwide, with urban areas seeing the highest adoption rates(Jafary et al., 2018).

## 6.6 Sustainable Mobility Solutions and Public Transportation

Sustainable mobility solutions and public transportation are critical components of smart cities, and many countries are implementing innovative strategies to promote them.

One approach is the implementation of bike-sharing programs, which have gained popularity in cities such as Paris, New York, and Beijing. In Paris, the Velib' bike-sharing system has over 20,000 bikes and 1,800 stations, and it has been estimated that it has prevented 5,000 tons of $CO_2$ emissions since its inception in 2007. Similarly, in New York, the Citi Bike program has over 12,000 bikes and 750 stations, and it has been estimated that it has prevented 100,000 tons of $CO_2$ emissions since its launch in

*Table 12. CO2 emissions prevented by bike-sharing*

| City | CO2 Emissions Prevented (tons) | Year of Launch |
|---|---|---|
| Paris | 5,000 | 2007 |
| New York | 100,000 | 2013 |
| Beijing | 1,500,000 | 2014 |

2013. In Beijing, the bike-sharing system has over 2 million bikes and 30,000 stations, and it has been estimated that it has prevented 1.5 million tons of CO2 emissions since its launch in 2014.

Another approach is the implementation of electric buses, which are being adopted in cities such as Shenzhen, Santiago, and Amsterdam. In Shenzhen, China, the city has fully transitioned to an electric bus fleet, which consists of over 16,000 buses and has prevented 1.35 million tons of CO2 emissions since its launch in 2011. In Santiago, Chile, the city has implemented a fleet of 200 electric buses, and it has been estimated that it has prevented 1,100 tons of CO2 emissions since its launch in 2018. In Amsterdam, the city has implemented a fleet of 100 electric buses, and it has been estimated that it has prevented 250 tons of CO2 emissions since its launch in 2018(CISA, 2022).

In terms of public transportation, many cities are implementing intelligent transportation systems (ITS) to improve the efficiency and sustainability of their public transportation systems. For example, in Singapore, the city has implemented a real-time traffic information system, which has reduced travel times by 15% and reduced CO2 emissions by 10%. In London, the city has implemented a real-time traffic signal control system, which has reduced travel times by 10% and reduced CO2 emissions by 5%(Oladimeji et al., 2023). In Seoul, the city has implemented a real-time bus information system, which has increased ridership by 10% and reduced CO2 emissions by 5%. Table 12 provides a comparison of the CO2 emissions prevented by bike-sharing programs in Paris, New York, and Beijing:

Table 13 provides a comparison of the CO2 emissions prevented by electric buses in Shenzhen, Santiago, and Amsterdam:

Sustainable mobility solutions and public transportation are critical components of smart cities, and many countries are implementing innovative strategies to promote them. Bike-sharing programs, electric buses, and intelligent transportation systems are just a few examples of the approaches being taken to improve the efficiency and sustainability of urban transportation. By reducing CO2 emissions and improving the quality of life for citizens, these strategies are helping to create more sustainable and livable cities(Almihat et al., 2022).

While Norwegian smart cities have fewer specific mobility initiatives, Finnish and Icelandic cities have several, and Danish smart cities appear to be the most focused on mobility measures. Aarhus and Vejle in Denmark exhibit the smartest mobility measures, followed by Turku, Espoo, and Malmö. These

*Table 13. CO2 emissions prevented by electric buses*

| City | CO2 Emissions Prevented (tons) | Year of Launch |
|---|---|---|
| Shenzhen | 1,350,000 | 2011 |
| Santiago | 1,100 | 2018 |
| Amsterdam | 250 | 2018 |

measures can be categorized based on their goals, including reducing car travel or enhancing its efficiency, promoting a modal shift toward public and active travel modes (primarily biking), gathering data and knowledge, and testing or piloting measures(Ribeiro et al., 2021). Multimodality, mobility hubs, and Mobility as a Service (MaaS) are among the most common smart mobility measures, found in six cities. Additionally, initiatives focus on technological advancements in electric vehicles (EVs), autonomous vehicles (AVs), shared cars, or bikes, as well as improving conditions for biking and e-biking. Some cities also implement softer mobility measures, such as campaigns, information provision, and trial periods, indicating a broad understanding of smart mobility concepts.Table 14 presents the List of smart mobility initiatives in mid-sized Nordic smart cities (X = present, (x) = considered, Grey = assessed in-depth.

Sustainable mobility solutions and public transportation are critical aspects of smart cities, aiming to reduce congestion, improve air quality, and enhance overall urban mobility. These solutions typically include the integration of public transport, cycling, walking, and shared mobility services. Here's a detailed discussion along with examples of how some countries are addressing these challenges:

*Integrated Public Transport Systems:* Many countries are investing in integrated public transport systems to provide seamless connectivity between different modes of transport, such as buses, trains, and trams. These systems often include smart ticketing, real-time information, and multimodal journey planning to encourage more people to use public transport(Legaspi et al., 2020).

*Electric Vehicles (EVs):* To reduce emissions, many countries are promoting the adoption of electric vehicles (EVs) in public transport fleets. This includes buses, taxis, and even shared mobility services. The infrastructure for EV charging stations is also being expanded to support this transition.

Cycling and Walking Infrastructure: Building dedicated cycling lanes and pedestrian walkways is a common strategy to encourage more sustainable modes of transport. Many cities are investing in bike-sharing schemes and improving pedestrian infrastructure to make walking and cycling safer and more convenient.

*Urban Planning and Design:* Smart cities are focusing on urban planning and design that promotes sustainable mobility. This includes creating mixed-use developments, reducing the need for long commutes, and designing cities that are more walkable and bike friendly.

*Incentives and Policies:* Governments are implementing policies and incentives to encourage the use of sustainable mobility options. This includes subsidies for EV purchases, congestion pricing schemes, and incentives for companies to provide flexible working arrangements to reduce peak-hour travel. Table 15 presents certain countries and their developments of smart cities.

Based on the above discussion, the following comparison in table 16 of public transport statistics in selected cities:

These statistics highlight the varying approaches to sustainable mobility and public transport in different cities, with some cities placing more emphasis on cycling and walking, while others focus on public transport.

## 6.7 Measuring the Success of Smart Transportation Solutions

The following statistics provide a comparison of key metrics for measuring the success of smart transportation solutions in Oslo, Helsinki, and Copenhagen. Table 17displays the impact of these solutions on traffic congestion, public transport ridership, air quality, mobility options, safety, and cost savings in each city(Shaheen et al., 2019).

*Table 14. Smart mobility initiatives in mid-sized Nordic smart cities*

| Smart mobility measure/initiative | DK | | SE | N | | | | | IS | FI | | | | |
|---|---|---|---|---|---|---|---|---|---|---|---|---|---|---|
| | Aarhus | Vejle | Malmø | Bergen | Kristiansand | Stavanger | Trondheim | Tromsø | Reykjavik | Espoo | Oulu | Tampere | Turku | Vantaa |
| Autonomous vehicles (incl. ferries) | | X | | | | | X | | | X | | X | | X |
| Bicycle infrastructure/parking/prioritising (e.g., super-highway, winter route, RADICAL) | X | X | X | | | | | | | | | | X | |
| Bicycle-sharing/rental system | | X | X | | | | | | X | X | | | X | |
| Car-sharing / Car-pooling | X | | | X | | | | | X | X | | | X | |
| Digital/intelligent/cooperative car parking system | | X | | | | X | | X | | | | | | |
| E-bike trial / car-replacement trial (e.g., 365 days) | X | | | | | | | | | | | | | |
| Electric vehicles (e.g., buses, waste collection) & charging infrastructure | | X | X | | | X | | | | | | X | X | |
| Intelligent prioritising of emergency vehicles | | | | | | | | | | | X | | | |
| Intelligent transport management / traffic control | X | (x) | | | | | | | | X | X | X | | |
| Mobility hubs / MaaS (multi-modal travel, integrated ticketing, last mile solutions) | X | | | X | | X | | | | X | | | X | X |
| Public transport app | | | | | | | | | X | | | X | | |
| Voluntary travel behaviour change program (campaigns, trial periods, personal travel planning) (e.g., super commuters) | X | | X | | | | | | | | | | | |
| Travel information app (e.g., drive now) | X | | | | | | | | X | | | | | |
| Travel/trip data collection | | X | X | | | | | | | | | | | X |

1.  Reduction in Traffic Congestion:

*Table 15. Smart cities developments*

| Country | Discussion |
|---|---|
| Netherlands | The Netherlands is known for its extensive cycling infrastructure, with dedicated bike lanes and parking facilities in cities. The country also has an efficient public transport system, with trains, buses, and trams connecting cities and towns(Iqbal et al., 2018). |
| Singapore | Singapore has implemented a comprehensive public transport system that includes buses, trains, and a light rail system. The city-state also has strict vehicle ownership policies, such as high taxes on car purchases, to encourage the use of public transport and reduce congestion(Colombia, 2017). |
| Germany | Germany has been a leader in promoting sustainable mobility, with cities like Berlin and Munich investing in cycling infrastructure and public transport. The country has also set ambitious targets for the adoption of EVs, with the goal of having 7-10 million EVs on the road by 2030(OECD, 2015). |

*Table 16. Statistics of smart cities in certain cities*

| City | Modal Share of Public Transport (%) | Modal Share of Cycling and Walking (%) | Length of Dedicated Cycling Lanes (km) |
|------|-------------------------------------|----------------------------------------|----------------------------------------|
| Amsterdam | 48 | 37 | 767 |
| Singapore | 67 | 12 | 440 |
| Berlin | 34 | 29 | 620 |
| Tokyo | 48 | 27 | 760 |

2.    Increase in Public Transport Ridership:

3.    Improvement in Air Quality:

4.    Enhanced Mobility Options:

5.    Safety Improvements:

*Table 17. Smart cities travelling statistics*

| City | Decrease in Average Travel Time (%) | Decrease in Congestion Levels (%) |
|------|-------------------------------------|-----------------------------------|
| Oslo | 15 | 20 |
| Helsinki | 10 | 18 |
| Copenhagen | 12 | 22 |

6.    Cost Savings:

*Table 18. Transport ridership in smart cities*

| City | Increase in Ridership (%) |
|------|---------------------------|
| Oslo | 20 |
| Helsinki | 15 |
| Copenhagen | 18 |

# 7. COMPARATIVE ANALYSIS OF EDUCATION, HEALTHCARE,

*Table 19. Smart city air quality*

| City | Reduction in PM2.5 Levels (%) | Reduction in NO2 Levels (%) |
|---|---|---|
| Oslo | 25 | 15 |
| Helsinki | 20 | 12 |
| Copenhagen | 22 | 18 |

# AND TRANSPORTATION INDUSTRIES IMPLICATIONS

*Table 20. Mobility in smart city*

| City | Number of Public Transport Routes | Length of Cycling Lanes (km) | Coverage of Shared Mobility Services (%) |
|---|---|---|---|
| Oslo | 150 | 100 | 80 |
| Helsinki | 130 | 80 | 75 |
| Copenhagen | 160 | 120 | 85 |

# FOR URBAN PLANNING AND POLICY.

*Table 21. Safety improvement in smart city*

| City | Reduction in Traffic Accidents (%) | Decrease in Fatalities (%) |
|---|---|---|
| Oslo | 20 | 15 |
| Helsinki | 18 | 12 |
| Copenhagen | 22 | 17 |

As the world becomes increasingly urbanized, the role of education, healthcare, and transportation in

*Table 22. Cost saving in a smart city*

| City | Reduction in Fuel Consumption (%) | Decrease in Maintenance Costs (%) |
|---|---|---|
| Oslo | 15 | 10 |
| Helsinki | 12 | 8 |
| Copenhagen | 18 | 12 |

urban planning and policy has become more critical than ever. The integration of these sectors in smart cities can lead to improved quality of life, sustainability, and economic growth.

In the education sector, the integration of smart technologies can improve access to education, enhance the learning experience, and promote lifelong learning. For example, the use of virtual reality and augmented reality can provide immersive learning experiences, while the use of artificial intelligence can personalize learning and provide real-time feedback. In addition, the integration of online learning platforms can expand access to education, particularly for those in remote or underserved areas.

In the healthcare sector, the integration of smart technologies can improve healthcare delivery, enhance patient outcomes, and promote wellness. For example, the use of telemedicine and remote monitoring can improve access to healthcare, particularly for those in remote or underserved areas. In addition, the use of electronic health records and big data analytics can provide real-time insights into patient health, enabling healthcare providers to make more informed decisions.

In the transportation sector, the integration of smart technologies can improve transportation efficiency, reduce congestion, and promote sustainability. For example, the use of intelligent transportation systems can provide real-time traffic information, enabling drivers to make more informed decisions. In addition, the use of electric vehicles and alternative transportation modes, such as bike-sharing and public transportation, can reduce greenhouse gas emissions and promote sustainability(Kate DeMoss & Joanna Moody, 2021).

However, there are also challenges in integrating these sectors in smart cities. For example, there may be concerns around data privacy and security, accessibility, and affordability. In addition, there may be a need for new policies and regulations to support the integration of these sectors in smart cities.

Table 23 provides a comparative analysis of the education, healthcare, and transportation sectors in terms of their potential impact on urban planning and policy:

The integration of education, healthcare, and transportation in smart cities can have a significant impact on urban planning and policy. By leveraging smart technologies, cities can improve access to education, healthcare, and transportation, enhance the quality of life for citizens, and promote sustainability. However, there are also challenges in integrating these sectors in smart cities, and new policies and regulations may be needed to support their integration.

## 8. CONCLUSION

Smart cities are becoming increasingly important in addressing urban challenges in education, healthcare, and transportation. In the education sector, smart cities are utilizing technology to improve access to education, enhance the learning experience, and promote lifelong learning. In the healthcare sector, smart cities are improving healthcare delivery, enhancing patient outcomes, reducing costs, and increas-

*Table 23. Analysis of the education, healthcare, and transportation sectors*

| Sector | Potential Impact on Urban Planning and Policy |
|---|---|
| Education | Improved access to education, enhanced learning experience, promotion of lifelong learning. |
| Healthcare | Improved healthcare delivery, enhanced patient outcomes, promotion of wellness. |
| Transportation | Improved transportation efficiency, reduced congestion, promotion of sustainability(Visan et al., 2021). |

ing efficiency. In the transportation sector, smart cities are improving transportation efficiency, reducing congestion, and promoting sustainability. The integration of these sectors in smart cities requires the development of necessary infrastructure and the use of technological tools such as telemedicine, remote patient monitoring, big data, data analytics, and autonomous vehicles. While there are challenges in integrating these sectors in smart cities, the potential benefits are significant, particularly in developing countries(Xiong et al., 2012). Autonomous vehicles have the potential to transform transportation in smart cities, improving safety, reducing congestion, and promoting sustainability. Sustainable mobility solutions and public transportation are also critical components of smart cities, with some countries, such as Singapore, the Netherlands, and South Korea, leading the way in integrating technology and data-driven approaches to enhance the well-being of their residents. There is a growing body of research on the impact of smart cities on education, healthcare, and transportation, and further investigation is required to fully understand the holistic impact of smart cities, particularly in developing countries. As technology becomes more accessible and innovative solutions are tailored to suit local needs, the potential for smart cities to flourish in developing nations grows, offering the promise of sustainable, inclusive, and prosperous urban environments for the future.

Overall, smart cities are a promising vision for the future, where urban life is redefined, and the potential for positive societal impact is maximized. Through continuous innovation and data-driven solutions, smart cities present an opportunity for urban service sectors to enhance the quality of life for all residents, promote sustainability, and ensure long-term economic growth in urban areas.

## REFERENCES

Afanasiev, M., & Lysenkova, M. (2019). How University Acts in the Development of "Smart Cities." *SHS Web of Conferences, 71*, 05011. 10.1051/shsconf/20197105011

Ahmad, M. L., & Kaur, N. (2017). Smart health hospitals in smart city perspective. *International Journal of Civil Engineering and Technology*, 8(5), 1271–1279.

Al-Azzam, M. K., & Alazzam, M. B. (2019). Smart city and Smart-Health framework, challenges and opportunities. *International Journal of Advanced Computer Science and Applications*, 10(2), 171–176. doi:10.14569/IJACSA.2019.0100223

Almihat, M. G. M., Kahn, M. T. E., Aboalez, K., & Almaktoof, A. M. (2022). Energy and Sustainable Development in Smart Cities: An Overview. *Smart Cities*, 5(4), 1389–1408. doi:10.3390/smartcities5040071

Anttila, J., & Jussila, K. (2018). Universities and smart cities: The challenges to high quality. *Total Quality Management & Business Excellence*, 29(9–10), 1058–1073. doi:10.1080/14783363.2018.1486552

CISA. (2022). *Autonomous Ground Vehicle Security Guide: Transportation Systems Sector. January*. CISA. https://www.cisa.gov/sites/default/files/publications/Autonomous%2520Ground%2520Vehicles%2520Security%2520Guide.pdf

Cook, D. J., Duncan, G., Sprint, G., & Fritz, R. L. (2018). Using Smart City Technology to Make Healthcare Smarter. *Proceedings of the IEEE*, 106(4), 708–722. doi:10.1109/JPROC.2017.2787688 PMID:29628528 de Colombia, G. (2017). *Smart Cities - SMART CITIES Social and Environmental Challenges and Opportunities for Local Authorities*. Research Gate. https://bibliotecadigital.fgv.br/dspace/handle/10438/18386

DeMoss, K., & Moody, J. (2021). Smart Cities and Intelligent, Sustainable Transportation Systems: The Case of Seoul, South Korea. *Leaders in Urban Transport Planning (LUTP) Program, December.* World Bank. https://www.worldbank.org/en/news/feature/2021/01/18/harnessing-smart-technology-for-sustainable-

Gupta, S. (2022). A Comprehensive Study of Smart Healthcare. *Smart City. 8*(10), 6–11.

Hassan, A. H., Sulaiman, R., Abdulgabber, M. A., & Kahtan, H. (2023). Balancing Technological Advances with User Needs: User-centered Principles for AI-Driven Smart City Healthcare Monitoring. *International Journal of Advanced Computer Science and Applications, 14*(3), 365–376. doi:10.14569/IJACSA.2023.0140341

Hönninger, J. C. (2020). *Smart City concepts and their approach on sustainability, transportation and tourism-Waterborne transportation, an opportunity for sustainability?*

IEEE. (2017). Health in Smart Cities. IEEE.

Iqbal, K., Khan, M. A., Abbas, S., Hasan, Z., & Fatima, A. (2018). Intelligent transportation system (ITS) for smart-cities using Mamdani Fuzzy Inference System. *International Journal of Advanced Computer Science and Applications, 9*(2), 94–105. doi:10.14569/IJACSA.2018.090215

Jafary, B., Rabiei, E., Diaconeasa, M. A., Masoomi, H., Fiondella, L., & Mosleh, A. (2018). A survey on autonomous vehicles interactions with human and other vehicles. *PSAM 2018 - Probabilistic Safety Assessment and Management, September.*

Kalpaeva, Z., Rodionova, E., & Dominiak, V. (2023). The role of smart cities in countering health threats: a review of practices. *E3S Web of Conferences, 435*. doi:10.1051/e3sconf/202343505005

Kassens-Noor, E., Dake, D., Decaminada, T., Kotval-K, Z., Qu, T., Wilson, M., & Pentland, B. (2020). Sociomobility of the 21st century: Autonomous vehicles, planning, and the future city. *Transport Policy, 99*(August), 329–335. doi:10.1016/j.tranpol.2020.08.022

Khan, U. T., & Zia, M. F. (2021). Smart city technologies, key components, and its aspects. *4th International Conference on Innovative Computing, ICIC 2021,* November 2021. IEEE. 10.1109/ICIC53490.2021.9692989

Kumari, A., Patel, M. M., Shukla, A., Tanwar, S., Kumar, N., & Rodrigues, J. J. P. C. (2020). ArMor: A Data Analytics Scheme to identify malicious behaviors on Blockchain-based Smart Grid System. *GLOBECOM 2020 - 2020 IEEE Global Communications Conference*, Taipei, Taiwan, (pp. 1-6). IEEE. 10.1109/GLOBECOM42002.2020.9348061

Kumari, A., & Tanwar, S. (2020). *A Data Analytics Scheme for Security-aware Demand Response Management in Smart Grid System*. 2020 IEEE 7th Uttar Pradesh Section International Conference on Electrical, Electronics and Computer Engineering (UPCON), Prayagraj, India. 10.1109/UPCON50219.2020.9376458

Kumari, A., & Tanwar, S. (2020). Secure data analytics for smart grid systems in a sustainable smart city: Challenges, solutions, and future directions. *Sustainable Computing : Informatics and Systems, 28*, 100427. doi:10.1016/j.suscom.2020.100427

Kyriazopoulou, C. (2015). Smart city technologies and architectures: A literature review. *SMARTGREENS 2015 - 4th International Conference on Smart Cities and Green ICT Systems, Proceedings*, 5–16. 10.5220/0005407000050016

Lea, R. (2017). Smart Cities: An Overview of the Technology Trends Driving Smart Cities. *IEEE Advancing Technology for Humanity, 3*(March), 1–16.

Legaspi, J., Bhada, S. V., Mathisen, P., & Dewinter, J. (2020). Smart City Transportation: A Multidisciplinary Literature Review. *Conference Proceedings - IEEE International Conference on Systems, Man and Cybernetics, 2020-October*(January), (pp. 957–964). IEEE. 10.1109/SMC42975.2020.9283471

Lim, S. J. (2023). E-Healthcare System in Smart Cities using Ai-Enabled Internet of Things: Applications and Challenges. *International Journal of Intelligent Systems and Applications in Engineering, 11*(7s), 655–660.

Makarova, I., Buyvol, P., Fatikhova, L., & Parsin, G. (2021). Influence of smart education on characteristics of urban lands' transport systems. *MATEC Web of Conferences, 334*, 01001. 10.1051/matecconf/202133401001

Mandžuka, S. (2015). *Intelligent Transport Systems: Selected Lectures.*

Matta, A., Fritz, K., Kim, B., Kim, S., & Akhmouch, A. (2020). Smart Cities and Inclusive Growth. *Smart Cities and Inclusive Growth, per year*, 1–59.

Mazza, P. I. (2021). Education & Smart Cities: The Role of the Goals of Agenda 2030 for Sustainable Development of Smart Cities Patricia. *International Journal of Innovative Studies in Sociology and Humanities, 6*(2), 24–31.

Mohammadzadeh, Z., Saeidnia, H. R., Lotfata, A., Hassanzadeh, M., & Ghiasi, N. (2023). Smart city healthcare delivery innovations: A systematic review of essential technologies and indicators for developing nations. *BMC Health Services Research, 23*(1), 1–14. doi:10.1186/s12913-023-10200-8 PMID:37904181

Müller-Eie, D., & Kosmidis, I. (2023). Sustainable mobility in smart cities: A document study of mobility initiatives of mid-sized Nordic smart cities. *European Transport Research Review, 15*(1), 36. Advance online publication. doi:10.1186/s12544-023-00610-4

Naiseh, M., & Shukla, P. (2023). The well-being of Autonomous Vehicles (AVs) users under uncertain situations. *ACM International Conference Proceeding Series.* ACM. 10.1145/3597512.3603150

Nikolov, R., Shoikova, E., Krumova, M., Kovatcheva, E., Dimitrov, V., & Shikalanov, A. (2016). Learning in a Smart City Environment. *Journal of Communication and Computer, 13*(7), 338–350. doi:10.17265/1548-7709/2016.07.003

OECD. (2015). *Enhancing the Contribution of Export.* OECD. https://www.oecd.org/regional/regionaldevelopment/Smart-Cities-FINAL.pdf

Oladimeji, D., Gupta, K., Kose, N. A., Gundogan, K., Ge, L., & Liang, F. (2023). Smart Transportation: An Overview of Technologies and Applications. *Sensors (Basel)*, *23*(8), 1–32. doi:10.3390/s23083880 PMID:37112221

Omidlou, N., & Kaufmann, H. R. (2023). reviewed paper The Role of Smart Cities on Smart Healthcare Management Neda Omidlou. *Hans Rüdiger Kaufmann.*, (September), 807–815.

Pacheco Rocha, N., Dias, A., Santinha, G., Rodrigues, M., Queirós, A., & Rodrigues, C. (2019). Smart Cities and Healthcare: A Systematic Review. *Technologies*, *7*(3), 1–15. doi:10.3390/technologies7030058

Pallavi, P. (2017). Smart Education Leads To a Smart City. *International Journal of Advance Research in Science and Engineering*, *6*(01), 129–132.

Pawlikowska-Piechotka, A., Łukasik, N., Ostrowska-Tryzno, A., & Sawicka, K. (2017). *A Smart City Initiative*. 561–583. doi:10.4018/978-1-5225-1978-2.ch024

R., S., S., S. R., R., H., S., A., & C., R. K. (2022). Artificial Intelligence in Smart cities and Healthcare. *EAI Endorsed Transactions on Smart Cities, 6*(3), e5. doi:10.4108/eetsc.v6i3.2275

Radwan, A. H., & Morsi, A. A. G. (2023). Autonomous vehicles and changing the future of cities: Technical and urban perspectives. *Journal of Urban Regeneration and Renewal*, *16*(1), 85–108.

Ribeiro, P., Dias, G., & Pereira, P. (2021). Transport systems and mobility for smart cities. *Applied System Innovation*, *4*(3), 61. doi:10.3390/asi4030061

Rizk, D. K. A. A. (2020). Proposed Framework for Smart Healthcare Services. *Future Computing and Informatics Journal*, *4*(2), 90–97. doi:10.54623/fue.fcij.4.2.4

Rocha, N. P., Dias, A., Santinha, G., Rodrigues, M., Queirós, A., & Rodrigues, C. (2019). Smart Cities and Public Health: A Systematic Review. *Procedia Computer Science*, *164*, 516–523. doi:10.1016/j.procs.2019.12.214

Sadjati, I. M. (2017). Smart Education dan Smart City. *Optimalisasi Peran Sains Dan Teknologi Untuk Mewujudkan Smart City*, 11–34. https://repository.ut.ac.id/7070/1/UTFMIPA2017-01-ida.pdf

Scala, D., Aguilar Cuesta, Á. I., Rodríguez-Domenech, M. Á., & Cañizares Ruiz, M. (2024). Bibliometric Study on the Conceptualisation of Smart City and Education. *Smart Cities*, *7*(1), 597–614. doi:10.3390/smartcities7010024

Shaheen, S., Cohen, A., Dowd, M., & Davis, R. (2019). *A Framework for Integrating Transportation Into Smart Cities*. Issue October. doi:10.31979/mti.2019.1705

ShakahG. (2022). *Modeling of Healthcare Monitoring System of Smart Cities. 11*(2), 926–931. https://doi.org/ doi:10.18421/TEM112

Siripatana, B., Nopchanasuphap, K., & Chuai-Aree, S. (2021). Intelligent Traffic Light System Using Image Processing. *Proceedings - 2nd SEA-STEM International Conference, SEA-STEM 2021*, (pp. 14–18). IEEE. 10.1109/SEA-STEM53614.2021.9668057

Smart Cities, E. U. Information System. (2017). The making of a smart city: best practices across Europe. *European Commission*, 256. www.smartcities-infosystem.eu

Solanas, A. (2015). *Smart Health : Improving Health services within Smart Cities. December.*

Talamo, C., Pinto, M. R., Viola, S., & Atta, N. (2019). Smart cities and enabling technologies: Influences on urban Facility Management services. *IOP Conference Series. Earth and Environmental Science*, *296*(1), 012047. doi:10.1088/1755-1315/296/1/012047

Visan, M., Negrea, S. L., & Mone, F. (2021). Towards intelligent public transport systems in Smart Cities; Collaborative decisions to be made. *Procedia Computer Science*, *199*, 1221–1228. doi:10.1016/j.procs.2022.01.155

Vodák, J., Šulyová, D., & Kubina, M. (2021). Advanced technologies and their use in smart city management. *Sustainability (Basel)*, *13*(10), 5746. doi:10.3390/su13105746

Vogel, A., Oremović, I., Šimić, R., & Ivanjko, E. (2018). Improving traffic light control by means of fuzzy logic. *Proceedings Elmar - International Symposium Electronics in Marine, 2018-Septe*(September). IEEE. 10.23919/ELMAR.2018.8534692

Williamson, B. (2015). Educating the smart city: Schooling smart citizens through computational urbanism. *Big Data & Society*, *2*(2), 1–13. doi:10.1177/2053951715617783

Wolff, A., Kortuem, G., & Cavero, J. (2015). Towards smart city education. *2015 Sustainable Internet and ICT for Sustainability. SustainIT*, *2015*(May), 1–3. doi:10.1109/SustainIT.2015.7101381

Xiong, Z., Sheng, H., Rong, W. G., & Cooper, D. E. (2012). Intelligent transportation systems for smart cities: A progress review. *Science China. Information Sciences*, *55*(12), 2908–2914. doi:10.1007/s11432-012-4725-1

Yoon, S. Y., Zelt, T., & Narloch, U. (2021). *Smart City Pathways for Developing Asia: An Analytical Framework and Guidance.* ADB.. https://www.adb.org/publications/smart-city-pathways-developing-asia

Zhang, H., & Zou, F. (2020). A Survey of the Dark Web and Dark Market Research. *2020 IEEE 6th International Conference on Computer and Communications, ICCC 2020*, (pp. 1694–1705). IEEE. 10.1109/ICCC51575.2020.9345271

Zhuang, R., Fang, H., Zhang, Y., Lu, A., & Huang, R. (2017). Smart learning environments for a smart city: From the perspective of lifelong and lifewide learning. *Smart Learning Environments*, *4*(1), 6. doi:10.1186/s40561-017-0044-8

Zuccalà, M., & Verga, E. S. (2017). Enabling Energy Smart Cities through Urban Sharing Ecosystems. *Energy Procedia, 111*(September 2016), 826–835. doi:10.1016/j.egypro.2017.03.245

# Section 2
# Advanced Analytics Techniques

*In the "Advanced Analytics Techniques" section, readers delve into sophisticated methodologies and approaches that push the boundaries of data analytics. This segment explores cutting-edge techniques such as predictive modeling, classification algorithms, clustering, and time series analysis. Readers gain insight into how these advanced methods are applied to extract valuable insights from data, predict future trends, and make informed decisions. Through practical examples and case studies, this section offers a glimpse into the transformative power of advanced analytics in addressing complex challenges and driving innovation across diverse domains.*

# Chapter 4
# Unveiling the Factors Influencing Dengue Fever Spread and Forecasting Future Epidemiology Through Path Analysis:
## Regression Model

**Wiwik Anggraeni**

iD https://orcid.org/0000-0003-3010-3062
*Institut Teknologi Sepuluh Nopember, Indonesia*

**Nisrina Nur Mahmudha**
*Institut Teknologi Sepuluh Nopember, Indonesia*

**Pujiadi Pujiadi**
*Malang Regency Public Health Office, Indonesia*

**Mauridhi Heri Purnomo**
*Institut Teknologi Sepuluh Nopember, Indonesia*

## ABSTRACT

*Dengue fever is a serious infectious disease that can be fatal if not diagnosed and treated promptly. Several factors are believed to contribute to the spread of this disease. Many studies have examined these factors and their influence on dengue fever. However, the geographical conditions of each area can vary greatly, and findings may not be applicable across different regions. There is still debate over whether climatic factors can explain the occurrence of dengue fever. This study aims to analyze the impact of various factors on dengue fever incidence in multiple regions using path analysis. The study examines both exogenous and endogenous variables, including dengue fever incidence, population density, larvae-free index, temperature, humidity, rainfall, and wind speed. The results of the path analysis are used to forecast future dengue fever cases. The forecast results can assist health agencies in developing effective policies and strategies to control dengue fever outbreaks.*

DOI: 10.4018/979-8-3693-3609-0.ch004

## 1. INTRODUCTION

In the context of disease transmission, it is crucial to thoroughly comprehend the environmental variables that impact the occurrence of dengue fever, as this knowledge is vital for identifying effective prevention strategies.

### 1.1 Motivations

Dengue fever is a contagious illness instigated by viral agents and distributed by mosquito bites, mainly Aedes aegypti and Aedes albopictus (World Health Organization, 2023). These mosquitoes are often found in the tropics and subtropics, including Indonesia. Dengue fever is an endemic that appears throughout the year, especially during the rainy season. This condition causes many people to be infected quickly (World Health Organization, 2017). Dengue fever can also potentially lead to death (World Health Organization, 2023).

Dengue fever is the most rapidly spread virus (World Health Organization, 2023). There are 50-100 million reported cases around the world spread from 100 countries annually that cause 24,000 deaths. Approximately 2.5 billion individuals reside in regions where dengue fever is endemic. According to data compiled by the World Health Organization between 1968 and 2009, Indonesia has the highest incidence of dengue fever among Southeast Asian countries (Yavari Nejad & Varathan, 2021). Dengue fever has been one of the main problems of public health in Indonesia for the last 47 years and caused a rapid and large number of deaths (World Health Organization, 2017). The count of dengue fever cases has risen steadily from 1968 to today (Kementerian et al., 2016). It spread throughout the province and Regency. The Ministry of Health of the Republic of Indonesia documented the occurrence of dengue fever in January and February of 2016 as 13,219 and 137 deaths. Subsequently, there was a decrease in the case number in 2017 to 22.5/100,000 (Kementerian et al., 2021) and an increase significantly in 2019 (Ditjen P2P, 2019).

Based on these facts, a forecast about this condition was required. The outcomes of these projections can be utilized to give governments and public health services the necessary options to take action and prevent them, hence reducing the epidemic's impact.

### 1.2 Chapter Contributions

- This research contributes to some critical issues related to the prediction of disease spread, namely the analysis of influential factors and prediction of dengue fever spread, where each is analyzed under different geographical conditions.
- The results of this study are expected to support the Public Health Office program to avoid delays in medical treatment and increase awareness of preventive measures.

### 1.3 Organization

The remainder of the paper is organized as follows: Section 2 delves into relevant research on the variables involved and the prediction of dengue. Section 3 describes the methodology utilized for analysis. Section 4 outlines the experiment's results and provides a discussion of them. Section 5 serves as the conclusion of this article.

## 2. RELATED WORKS

Dengue fever forecasting is closely related to factors affecting dengue fever. Extensive research has been conducted on the influence of different factors on the occurrence of dengue fever. Previous studies have investigated the effects of meteorological and geographical factors on dengue fever incidence. Variations of various climatic factors have also been used by (Jardiyanto, 2019; Labola, 2020). In addition, environmental factors (LaPorte, 1993), meteorological and hydrological factors (Mala & Jat, 2019). Oceanic and atmospheric conditions have also been analyzed to determine whether they affect the dengue fever outbreak (Siriyasatien et al., 2016). Therefore, (Duarte et al., 2019; Zhu et al., 2019) state that the geographical condition and demographic of the patient should be involved in making predictions related to dengue fever. Forest cover is also an influenced variable (Tsai et al., 2018). These studies mainly involve certain climatic variations and have yet to simultaneously involve precipitation factors, humidity, temperature, wind speed, wind direction, mosquito density, and neighbouring variables. However, there are still differences of opinion on whether this climate factor can indeed be used to explain the occurrence of dengue fever (Adde et al., 2016). Unfortunately, in each different location, the impact of climate factors can also be different (Carvajal et al., 2018).

This study examines factors influencing dengue fever cases in Indonesia. It uses path analysis and a regression model to identify the best forecasting model for dengue fever incidents. The analysis considers regions with diverse geographical conditions to ensure the model's robustness. The regression model is selected for its accurate estimation capabilities (Xiang et al., 2017, Vekaria et al., 2021). Previous studies have successfully used linear regression to predict dengue fever incidence (Jain et al., 2019, Harsh et al., 2023), while another study utilized multivariate Poisson regression to estimate incidence rates Poisson (Siriyasatien et al., 2016, Tanwar et al. 2019).

## 3. METHODOLOGY

The stages used in this research include:

### 3.1 Data Acquisition

This analysis utilizes data on dengue fever incidence, larvae-free index, rainfall, air temperature, wind speed, humidity, and population density. The dengue fever incidence and larvae-free index data were sourced from the Malang District Health Service. Climate data, including air temperature, rainfall, air humidity, and wind speed, were obtained from the official website of the Meteorology, Climatology, and Geophysics Agency. Besides, population density data was sourced from the Central Statistics Agency.

### 3.2 Data Preprocessing

Data preprocessing ensures consistent data regarding time period, location, and units. The analysis uses data from January 2015 to March 2019 covering lowland and highland areas. The units for each variable are Dengue Fever Cases (KDB) in people, Larvae-Free Index (ABJ) in percentage, Temperature (SU) in Celsius, Humidity (KU) in percentage, Rainfall (CH) in millimeters, Wind Speed (KA) in meters per second, and Population Density (KP) in people per square kilometer.

## 3.3 Path Analysis

Path analysis, an extension of the regression model, is employed to assess the consistency of correlations among different models of causal relationships (Souravlas et al., 2019). Its primary goal is to estimate the magnitude and significance of cause-effect relationships between variables. The various stages of conducting path analysis in research are:

### 3.3.1 Determine the Conceptual Model

After identifying the research variables, a conceptual model was developed to guide the analysis, as shown in Figure 1. The model includes the incidence of dengue fever, larvae-free index, temperature, humidity, rainfall, wind speed, and population density. This conceptual framework will serve as a reference for the analysis.

In Figure 1, the conceptual model is grounded in the theory that climate factors such as air temperature, humidity, rainfall, and wind speed affect the larvae-free index. These factors play a role in determining the percentage of larvae-free rates by influencing mosquito growth and reproduction (Chuang et al., 2017; Jain et al., 2019; Xu et al., 2017). The relationship between climate factors and the larvae-free

*Figure 1. Conceptual model*

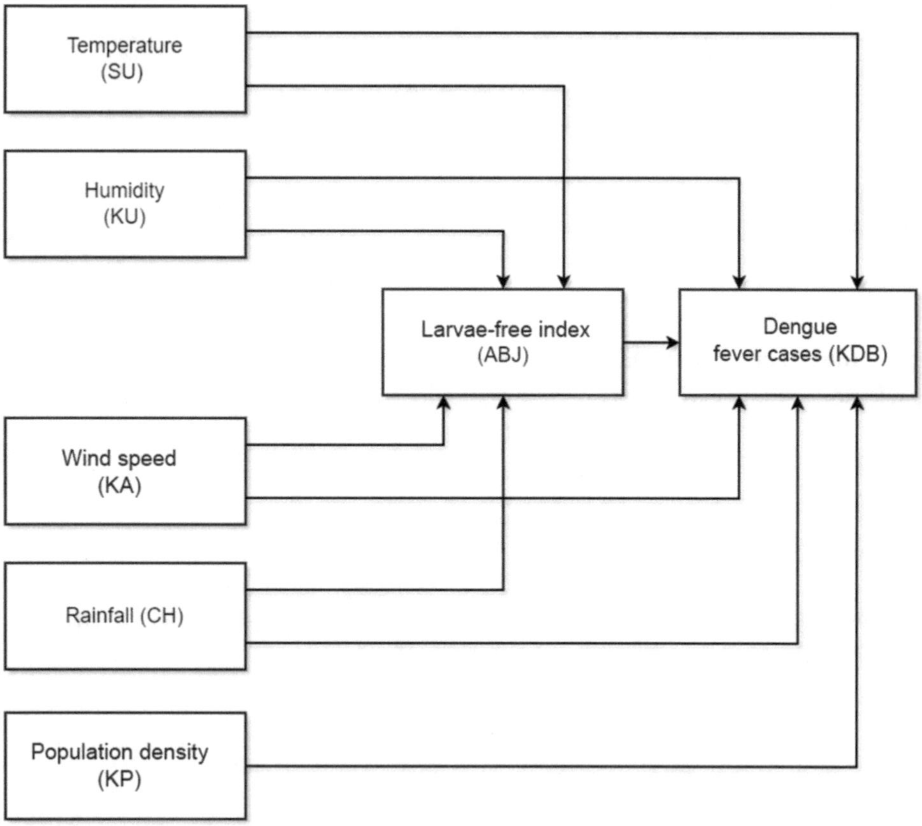

index allows for calculating the indirect influence of climate factors on dengue fever incidence (Anggraeni et al., 2020, 2024).

Climatic factors exert a notable influence on the occurrence of dengue fever. They can affect a person's immune system, making them more susceptible to the disease. Moreover, climatic conditions can create environments that support mosquito breeding, increasing the likelihood of dengue fever transmission (Chuang et al., 2017; Jain et al., 2019; Xu et al., 2017). Population density is also a contributing factor, as densely populated areas allow the disease to spread, especially since dengue fever mosquitoes have a limited flight range of only 200 meters (Anggraeni et al., 2020, 2024). The larvae-free index is a crucial factor in the occurrence of dengue fever. It reflects the density of the mosquito carrier and can indicate the probability of dengue fever outbreaks in an area (Altassan et al., 2019). A higher larvae-free index percentage is typically associated with a lower incidence of dengue fever outbreaks, highlighting its importance in prevention and control efforts (Anggraeni et al., 2024).

## 3.3.2 Determining Path Coefficient

To calculate the path coefficient in path analysis, we typically follow these steps:

1.  Create a path diagram and describe the research hypothesis to show the relationships between exogenous and endogenous variables clearly.
2.  2. Calculate the correlation matrix between variables, shown in Equation (1).

$$\underline{R} = \begin{array}{ccccc} X_1 & X_2 & \cdots & X_k & Y \\ 1 & r_{x_1 x_2} & \cdots & r_{x_1 x_k} & r_{x_1 y} \\ r_{x_2 x_1} & 1 & \cdots & r_{x_2 x_k} & r_{x_2 y} \\ \cdots & \cdots & 1 & \cdots & \cdots \\ r_{x_k x_1} & r_{x_k x_2} & \cdots & 1 & r_{x_k y} \\ r_{y x_1} & r_{y x_2} & \cdots & r_{y x_k} & 1 \end{array} \tag{1}$$

3.  3. Identify the structure of the Equation whose path coefficients will be calculated. For example, there are k independent variables (X) and a dependent variable (Y), which can be stated in Equation (2).

$$Y = \beta y_{x1X} 1_+ \beta y x_{2X2} + \ldots + \beta y x k_{Xk+} {}_\beta y \epsilon \tag{2}$$

Next, calculate the correlation matrix for the X variables involved in the equation structure, resulting in matrix Equation (3).

$$\underline{R} = \begin{matrix} & X_1 & X_2 & \cdots & X_k \\ & 1 & r_{x_1 x_2} & \cdots & r_{x_1 x_k} \\ & r_{x_2 x_1} & 1 & \cdots & r_{x_2 x_k} \\ & \cdots & \cdots & 1 & \cdots \\ & r_{x_k x_1} & r_{x_k x_2} & \cdots & 1 \end{matrix} \tag{3}$$

4.  4. Compute the inverse correlation matrix of independent variables using Equation (4).

$$\underline{R_1^{-1}} = \begin{matrix} & X_1 & X_2 & \cdots & X_k \\ & C_{11} & C_{12} & \cdots & C_{1k} \\ & C_{21} & C_{22} & \cdots & C_{2k} \\ & \cdots & \cdots & \cdots & \cdots \\ & C_{k1} & C_{k2} & \cdots & C_{kk} \end{matrix} \tag{4}$$

5.  5. Calculate all path coefficients in $\beta y_{xi}$ where i=1,2,...,k using Equation (5).

$$\begin{matrix} \rho_{yx_1} \\ \rho_{yx_2} \\ \cdots \\ \rho_{yx_k} \end{matrix} = \begin{bmatrix} C_{11} & C_{12} & \cdots & C_{1k} \\ C_{21} & C_{22} & \cdots & C_{2k} \\ \cdots & \cdots & \cdots & \cdots \\ C_{k1} & C_{k2} & \cdots & C_{kk} \end{bmatrix} \begin{matrix} r_{yx_1} \\ r_{yx_2} \\ \cdots \\ r_{yx_k} \end{matrix} \tag{5}$$

### 3.3.3 Path Coefficient Testing

Path coefficient testing is conducted as follows (Yushananta & Ahyanti, 2014):

1.  1. Determine the relationship of all variables (multiple correlations) using Equation (6).

$$r = \sqrt{r^2} \tag{6}$$

2.  2. Determine the overall coefficient of determination, which combines several independent variables with the dependent variable (Y) using Equation (7).

$$r^2 = \frac{b_1 \sum x_1 y + b_2 \sum x_2 y + \ldots + b_k \sum x_k y}{\sum y^2} \tag{7}$$

3.     3. To test the path coefficient simultaneously, we used the F-test. The formula for the F-test is shown in Equation (8).

$$F = \frac{(n-k-1)R_{xy}^2}{k(1-R_{xy}^2)}$$         (8)

4.     4. Decisions in the F-test can be made using Equations (9) and (10), considering that the test follows the F-Snedecor distribution with degrees of freedom (DF).

if $F_{count} \geq F_{table}$, then $H_0$ is rejected         (9)

if $F_{count} \leq F_{table}$, then $H_0$ is accepted         (10)

5.     5. Calculate the path coefficient individually (partially) using the T-test. The formula for conducting the T-test is shown in Equation (11).

$$T = \frac{Pxi}{se_{pk}}$$         (11)

6.     6. The testing procedure follows the T-distribution with degrees of freedom equal to (n-k-1). The test criteria are based on Equations (12) and (13).

if $T_{count} \geq T_{table}$, then $H_0$ is rejected         (12)

if $T_{count} \leq T_{table}$, then $H_0$ is accepted         (13)

### 3.3.4 Normality and Multicollinearity Test

The Normality Test checks if the residuals from the regression model follow a normal distribution (Mishra et al., 2019). The data must be transformed if it does not follow a normal distribution. In this study, the Kolmogorov-Smirnov normality test was employed (Anggraeni et al., 2022). The multicollinearity test checks the correlations between independent variables in a regression model (Daoud, 2017). If perfect multicollinearity exists, the regression coefficients cannot be determined, and the standard error value becomes infinite.

### 3.3.5 Determining Analysis Scenarios

Scenario analysis is conducted to understand how factors influencing dengue fever contribute to its incidence in different areas. Two scenarios are proposed based on the collected data: analysis in lowland areas (scenario 1) and highland areas (scenario 2).

### 3.3.6 Creating Analysis Stages According to the Conceptual Model

Based on the conceptual model that has been designed, the next step is to divide the model into several sub-structures to become an analysis stage. The following stages of analysis are designed according to the conceptual model:

- **1st Stage Analysis (Sub Structure-1).**

1st stage analysis examines how the causal factors influence the larvae-free rate. The analysis stage model can be seen in Figure 2. In 1st stage analysis, the climate factor becomes the independent variable, and the larvae-free index becomes the dependent variable. The regression equation can be seen in Equation (14).

*Figure 2. Sub structure-1*

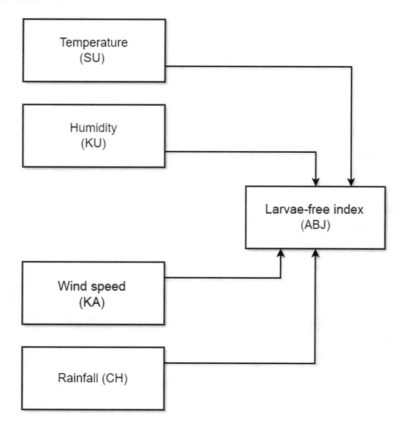

$$ABJ = a + b_1 SU + b_2 KU + b_3 KA + b_4 CH \qquad (14)$$

- **2nd Stage Analysis (Sub Structure-2).**

In 2nd stage analysis (Sub Structure-2), the goal is to understand how causal factors influence the incidence of dengue fever. The analysis model for this stage is depicted in Figure 3. In the previous Stage 1 analysis, the causal factors were considered independent variables, while the dengue fever incidence was the dependent variable. The regression equation is shown in Equation (15).

$$KDB = a + b_1 SU + b_2 KU + b_3 KA + b_4 CH + b_5 KP + b_5 ABJ \qquad (15)$$

## 3.4 Backpropagation-Artificial Neural Network (ANN) Forecasting

The analysis uses data on dengue fever incidents, larvae-free index, temperature, humidity, rainfall, wind speed, and population density. The dengue fever incidence and larvae-free index data were sourced from the Malang Health Service. The stage in ANN includes:

*Figure 3. Sub structure-2*

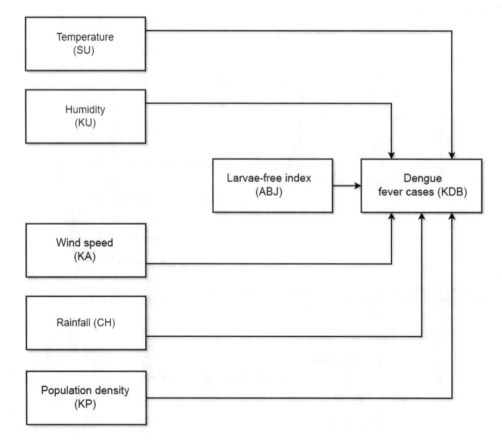

## 3.4.1 Data Normalization

We normalized the data due to the difference in ranges of the data, which have been normalized to a range of 0 to 1 using the Minmax function. The normalization process follows the formula from the min-max function, as shown in Equation (16).

$$X' = \frac{x - \min(x)}{\max(x) - \min(x)} \tag{16}$$

## 3.4.2 Determine ANN Architecture Design

The ANN structure comprises an input layer, hidden layer, and output layer, along with various parameters such as training function, adaptation learning function, transfer function, epoch, learning rate, and momentum, as displayed in Table 1. Table 1 shows the limits for each parameter in the initialization of the ANN.

## 3.4.3 Training and Testing Model

The training process utilizes 70% of the available data, while testing uses 30%. Both Regression and ANN models are employed to train and test the data.

## 3.4.4 Data Forecasting

Data forecasting utilizes the best ANN model derived from the training and testing process. The forecasting model uses independent variable data proven to directly affect the dependent variable, dengue fever incidence, in path analysis. For clarity, the forecasting data used is shown in Table 2. The best model from Table 2 is then applied to forecast data for other regions with similar direct influence models.

*Table 1. ANN design*

| Parameter | Value | Description |
|---|---|---|
| Input layer (n) | Independent variable | Independent variable |
| Hidden layer | n-3n node | Trial and error |
| Output layer | 1 node | Dengue fever cases variable (KDB) |
| Training function | 3 | Trial and error (Traingda, Traingdx, Trainlm) |
| Adaption learning function | 1 | Default (Learngdm) |
| Transfer function | 3 | Trial and error (Logsig, Tansig, Purelin) |
| Epoch | 500,1000,1500 | Trial and Error |
| Learning rate | 0.1 - 0.9 | Trial and Error |
| Momentum | 0.1 - 0.10 | Trial and Error |

*Table 2. Forecasting model data*

| Model | Independent Variable | Dependent Variable | Reference Area | Forecasting Area |
|-------|---------------------|-------------------|---------------|------------------|
| 1 | CH, KA, ABJ | KDB | Turen | Turen, Pakis |
| 2 | CH, ABJ | KDB | Dampit | Dampit, Wajak, Lawang |
| 3 | CH, KP, ABJ | KDB | Kepanjen | Kepanjen, Poncokusumo |
| 4 | ABJ | KDB | Pakisaji | Pakisaji |
| 5 | CH, KA, KP, ABJ | KDB | Sumbermanjing | Sumbermanjing |
| 6 | KU, CH, KP, ABJ | KDB | Jabung | Jabung |

## 4. EXPERIMENTAL

The experiment was conducted in the Malang Regency of Indonesia. The 33 regions in Malang Regency are distinguished based on their geographical conditions, namely lowlands and highlands. The following ten areas were chosen randomly through a simple random sampling method. The selected areas for the lowland group were Turen, Dampit, Kepanjen, Pakis, and Pakisaji. The selected areas for the highlands included Sumbermanjing Wetan, Wajak, Poncokusumo, Jabung, and Lawang. Two scenarios were used in the experiment. The scenario was used to see how dengue incidence's causative factors influenced dengue fever in different area groups. Then, forecasting is carried out using two approaches: Regression and Backpropagation.

### 4.1 Result

The results of the normality test from 10 regions in the sample area are shown in Table 3. A data normality test in Table 3 showed that four datasets were not normally distributed. Since four regions in Table 3 did not pass the normality test, data transformation is necessary to achieve a normal distribution. The transformation function used is $SQRT(X)$ for the Turen, Sumbermanjing Wetan, and Wajak areas. Meanwhile, the $SQRT(K–X)$ transformation is used for the Jabung area.

The results of the normalization test from the transformed data are displayed in Table 4. Besides, the results of the multicollinearity test from the 10 sample regions indicate that all regions passed the multicollinearity test. It allows the analysis to proceed to the path analysis stage. Relationship testing was carried out on scenario-1, which shows the lowland group, and scenario-2 for the highland group. Test results on Turen Region data in the lowland group are shown in Table 5.

Based on the results shown in Table 5, a path diagram can be constructed, as depicted in Figure 4.

Figure 4 illustrates the indirect influence of rainfall on dengue fever incidence and the direct influences of rainfall, larvae-free index, and wind speed on dengue fever incidence. The magnitude of each factor's influence is represented by the value "B" in Figure 4. It is evident from Figure 4 that the larvae-free index has the most significant influence on the incidence of dengue fever. Figure 5 visually represents the relationship between rainfall and larvae-free index. Besides, the relationship between CH, KA, ABJ, and KDB is present in Figure 6.

Figure 5 illustrates that the larvae-free index decreases as rainfall increases. From July to October 2015, when there was no rain, the larvae-free index was high, ranging from 89 to 95. Conversely, from November 2015 to January 2016, an increase in rainfall led to a decrease in the larvae-free index, as

*Table 3. Normality test result*

| Area | Sub Structure-1 | Sub Structure-2 | Description |
|---|---|---|---|
| Turen | 0.200 | 0.003 | Sub Structure-2 is abnormal |
| Dampit | 0.200 | 0.200 | Normal |
| Kepanjen | 0.200 | 0.200 | Normal |
| Pakis | 0.530 | 0.200 | Normal |
| Pakisaji | 0.530 | 0.200 | Normal |
| Sumbermanjing Wetan | 0.200 | 0.023 | Sub Structure-2 is abnormal |
| Poncokusumo | 0.174 | 0.200 | Normal |
| Wajak | 0.040 | 0.038 | Sub Structures-1 and 2 are abnormal |
| Jabung | 0.017 | 0.200 | Sub Structure-1 is abnormal |
| Lawang | 0.760 | 0.200 | Normal |

*Table 4. Normality test result in data transformation result*

| Area | Sub Structure-1 | Sub Structure-2 | Description |
|---|---|---|---|
| Turen | 0.200 | 0.200 | Normal |
| Sumbermanjing Wetan | 0.200 | 0.200 | Normal |
| Wajak | 0.200 | 0.200 | Normal |
| Jabung | 0.054 | 0.200 | Normal |

*Table 5. Results of relationship testing in the Turen region*

| Relation | Sig. Value | Test Result | Description |
|---|---|---|---|
| SU → ABJ | 0.623 | Ho accepted | Not Connected |
| KU → ABJ | 0.516 | Ho accepted | Not Connected |
| CH → ABJ | 0.001 | Ho rejected | Connected |
| KA → ABJ | 0.844 | Ho accepted | Not Connected |
| SU → KDB | 0.623 | Ho accepted | Not Connected |
| KU → KDB | 0.903 | Ho accepted | Not Connected |
| CH → KDB | 0.048 | Ho rejected | Connected |
| KA → KDB | 0.028 | Ho rejected | Connected |
| KP → KDB | 0.473 | Ho accepted | Not Connected |
| ABJ → KDB | 0.000 | Ho rejected | Connected |

shown in the graph. Figure 6 illustrates the relationship between rainfall, wind speed, larvae-free index, and dengue fever incidence in the Turen Region. Figure 6 demonstrates that the incidence of dengue fever tends to rise as rainfall and wind speed increase and the larvae-free index decreases. The opposite

*Figure 4. Path diagram of the Turen lowland region*

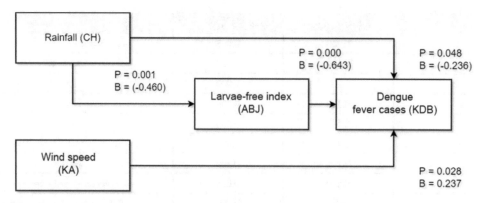

*Figure 5. Relationship of CH and CBJ in the Turen region*

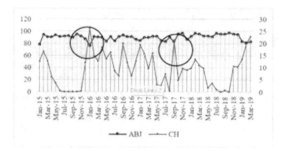

*Figure 6. Relationship between CH, KA, ABJ, and KDB in the Turen region*

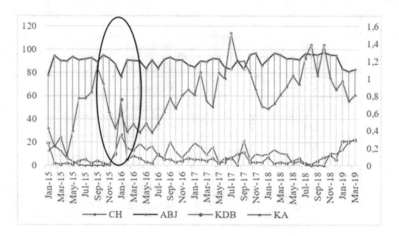

trend is also observed. For instance, in January 2016, there was an escalation in the incidence of dengue fever, corresponding to increased rainfall and wind speed, as well as a decrease in larvae-free indexes.

The analysis results for other areas in the lowland indicate the tested relationships for these sample areas displayed in Table 6. Additionally, the influence values between variables in lowland area displayed

*Table 6. Results of testing relationships between variables in the lowland sample region*

| Relation | Dampit | | Kepanjen | | Pakis | | Pakisaji | |
|---|---|---|---|---|---|---|---|---|
| | Sig. Value | Test Result | Sig. Value | Test Result | Sig. Value | Test Result | Sig. Value | Test Result |
| SU → ABJ | 0.920 | Not Connected | 0.451 | Not Connected | 0.531 | Not Connected | 0.043 | Connected |
| KU → ABJ | 0.489 | Not Connected | 0.377 | Not Connected | 0.781 | Not Connected | 0.660 | Not Connected |
| CH → ABJ | 0.000 | Connected | 0.011 | Connected | 5.000 | Connected | 0.028 | Connected |
| KA → ABJ | 0.243 | Not Connected | 0.231 | Not Connected | 0.002 | Connected | 0.411 | Not Connected |
| SU → KDB | 0.690 | Not Connected | 0.855 | Not Connected | 0.667 | Not Connected | 0.194 | Not Connected |
| KU → KDB | 0.125 | Not Connected | 0.228 | Not Connected | 0.255 | Not Connected | 0.232 | Not Connected |
| CH → KDB | 0.001 | Connected | 0.049 | Connected | 0.036 | Connected | 0.113 | Not Connected |
| KA → KDB | 0.854 | Not Connected | 0.489 | Not Connected | 0.029 | Connected | 0.650 | Not Connected |
| KP → KDB | 0.282 | Not Connected | 0.000 | Connected | 0.655 | Not Connected | 0.408 | Not Connected |
| ABJ → KDB | 0.004 | Connected | 0.000 | Connected | 0.000 | Connected | 0.000 | Connected |

*Table 7. Calculation of influence values between variables in lowland sample region*

| Independent Variable | Dampit | | Kepanjen | | Pakis | | Pakisaji | |
|---|---|---|---|---|---|---|---|---|
| | Direct | Indirect | Direct | Indirect | Direct | Indirect | Direct | Indirect |
| CH | 0.430 | 0.183 | 0.231 | 0.176 | 0.240 | 0.270 | - | 0.160 |
| ABJ | -0.363 | - | -0.542 | - | -0.660 | - | -0.523 | - |
| SU | - | - | - | - | - | - | - | 0.147 |
| KA | - | - | - | - | -0.254 | 0.292 | - | - |
| KP | - | - | 0.497 | - | - | - | - | - |

in Table 7. Table 7 illustrates the magnitude of the influence of the relationships between the interconnected variables. Based on the findings from Table 6 and Table 7, it is evident that rainfall has an indirect impact on dengue fever incidence in the Dampit and Kepanjen areas. In the Pakis area, both rainfall and wind speed have an indirect influence on the dengue fever incidence. Conversely, in Pakisaji, temperature and rainfall indirectly influence the incidence of dengue fever. Furthermore, the analysis reveals the direct influence of rainfall and larvae-free index on the occurrence of dengue fever. In Kepanjen, this influence includes rainfall, population density, and larvae-free index. Similarly, in the Pakis region, there is a direct influence of rainfall, wind speed, and larvae-free index on the occurrence of dengue fever. Conversely, in Pakisaji, the larvae-free index directly influences the dengue fever occurrence.

For the highland scenario, the results of the correlation analysis between independent variables in the Sumbermanjing area in the highlands are shown in Table 8. Meanwhile, the path diagram represents the information in Table 8, shown in Figure 7. Based on Figure 7, rainfall indirectly influences the occurrence of dengue fever. Additionally, wind speed, rainfall, population density, and larvae-free index directly impact the occurrence of dengue fever. The magnitude of these influences is depicted by the numbers attached to the relationship lines between variables. Among these factors, rainfall has the most

*Table 8. Results of relationship testing in the Sumbermanjing area*

| Relation | Sig. Value | Test Result | Conclusion |
|---|---|---|---|
| SU → ABJ | 0,726 | Ho accepted | Not Connected |
| KU → ABJ | 0,515 | Ho accepted | Not Connected |
| CH → ABJ | 0,000 | Ho rejected | Connected |
| KA → ABJ | 0,928 | Ho accepted | Not Connected |
| SU → KDB | 0,618 | Ho accepted | Not Connected |
| KU → KDB | 0,770 | Ho accepted | Not Connected |
| CH → KDB | 0,001 | Ho rejected | Connected |
| KA → KDB | 0,010 | Ho rejected | Connected |
| KP → KDB | 0,007 | Ho rejected | Connected |
| ABJ → KDB | 0,000 | Ho rejected | Connected |

*Figure 7. Relationship between CH, KA, ABJ, and KDB in the Turen region*

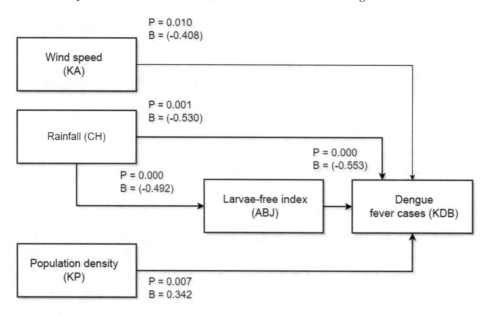

significant impact on the occurrence of dengue fever. The relationship between rainfall and larvae-free index is illustrated in Figure 8.

Figure 8 illustrates that the larvae-free index decreases as rainfall increases. Conversely, increased larvae-free index corresponds to decreased rainfall and air temperature. For instance, from October 2015 to January 2016, there was a decrease in the larvae-free index alongside increased rainfall. Figure 9 illustrates the relationship between wind speed, rainfall, population density, larvae-free index, and the occurrence of dengue fever in the Sumbermanjing area. Besides, Figure 9 indicates that the incidence of dengue fever tends to rise with increases in wind speed, rainfall, and population density, as well as a decrease in the larvae-free index and vice versa. For instance, there was an increase in the incidence

*Figure 8. Relationship between CH and ABJ in the Sumbermanjing region*

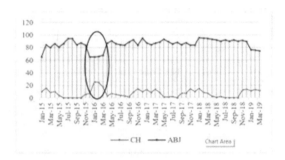

*Figure 9. Relationship between KA, CH, KP, and ABJ with KDB Sumbermanjing region*

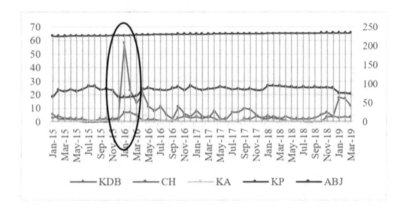

of dengue fever in January 2016, coinciding with an increase in wind speed, rainfall, and population density, as well as a decrease in the larvae-free index.

Additionally, the analysis of other areas in the highlands, including the testing of relationships for other sample areas, is presented in Table 9. Besides, the magnitude of the influence of the relationships between the interconnected variables is demonstrated in Table 10.

Based on the results from Table 9 and Table 10, in the Poncokusumo area, rainfall has an indirect impact on the occurrence of dengue fever. Additionally, rainfall, population density, and larvae-free index directly influence the incidence of dengue fever. In Wajak, rainfall also indirectly impacts the occurrence of dengue fever, which is a direct influence of rainfall and larvae-free index. In Jabung, air temperature and rainfall indirectly influence the incidence of dengue fever, while air humidity, rainfall, population density, and larvae-free index have a direct influence. Lastly, in Lawang, wind speed and rainfall indirectly influence the occurrence of dengue fever, and rainfall and larvae-free index are directly influenced.

The forecasting in this research is a way to leverage information on factors related to the causes of dengue fever. Factors directly proven to cause dengue fever are used as independent variables in forecasting, employing the Regression and Backpropagation methods. The regression forecasting utilizes the results of the previous regression equation, which identified the variables causing the incidence of dengue fever and their direct influence. The regression equation for the direct influence of these factors in each region is shown in Table 11. Besides the results of testing the regression model using training and testing data in each region are displayed in Table 12.

*Table 9. Results of testing relationships between variables in the highland sample region*

| Relation | Poncokusumo | | Wajak | | Jabung | | Lawang | |
|---|---|---|---|---|---|---|---|---|
| | Sig. Value | Test Result | Sig. Value | Test Result | Sig. Value | Test Result | Sig. Value | Test Result |
| SU → ABJ | 0.673 | Not Connected | 0.769 | Not Connected | 0.032 | Connected | 0.386 | Not Connected |
| KU → ABJ | 0.611 | Not Connected | 0.354 | Not Connected | 0.353 | Not Connected | 0.446 | Not Connected |
| CH → ABJ | 0.000 | Connected | 0.002 | Connected | 0.000 | Connected | 0.002 | Connected |
| KA → ABJ | 0.177 | Not Connected | 0.070 | Not Connected | 0.720 | Not Connected | 0.034 | Connected |
| SU → KDB | 0.122 | Not Connected | 0.789 | Not Connected | 0.150 | Not Connected | 0.256 | Not Connected |
| KU → KDB | 0.105 | Not Connected | 0.819 | Not Connected | 0.004 | Connected | 0.148 | Not Connected |
| CH → KDB | 0.048 | Connected | 0.002 | Connected | 0.000 | Connected | 0.000 | Connected |
| KA → KDB | 0.692 | Not Connected | 0.217 | Not Connected | 0.291 | Not Connected | 0.305 | Not Connected |
| KP → KDB | 0.000 | Connected | 0.209 | Not Connected | 0.003 | Connected | 0.105 | Not Connected |
| ABJ → KDB | 0.000 | Connected | 0.029 | Connected | 0.018 | Connected | 0.000 | Connected |

*Table 10. Calculation of influence values between variables in the highland sample region*

| Independent Variable | Poncokusumo | | Wajak | | Jabung | | Lawang | |
|---|---|---|---|---|---|---|---|---|
| | Direct | Indirect | Direct | Indirect | Direct | Indirect | Direct | Indirect |
| CH | 0.243 | 0.253 | 0.412 | 0.124 | 0.682 | 0.164 | 0.410 | 0.300 |
| ABJ | -0.539 | - | -0.289 | | -0.304 | - | -0.517 | - |
| SU | - | - | - | - | - | 0.076 | - | - |
| KU | - | - | - | - | -0.396 | - | - | - |
| KA | - | - | - | - | | | 0.198 | - |
| KP | 0.543 | - | - | - | 0.314 | - | - | - |

The comparison of the actual data with the forecasting results using training and testing data (total data from January 2015 to March 2019) in the Turen Region employing a regression model is shown in Figure 10.

Then, the forecasting process uses Backpropagation-ANN in lowland areas in Malang Regency, as stated in Table 13. Table 13 demonstrates the performance of forecasting results using ANN with independent variables that are proven to influence the incidence of dengue fever. The comparison between the actual data and the forecasting results using training and testing data (total data from January 2015 to March 2019) in the Turen Region using the ANN model is shown in Figure 11. Figure 11 illustrates that the forecasting results closely align with the actual pattern of dengue fever incidents. The ANN model utilizes independent variables such as rainfall, wind speed, and larvae-free rate to predict the incidence of dengue fever in the Turen Region.

*Table 11. Regression equations in each region*

| Region | Regression Model Equations |
|---|---|
| Turen | KDB = 27.309 + 0.186CH + 1.468KA - 2.820ABJ |
| Dampit | KDB = 24.731 + 0.352CH - 0.266ABJ |
| Kepanjen | KDB = -218.501 + 0.184CH + 0.112KA - 0.447ABJ |
| Pakis | KDB = 62.682 + 0.199CH - 4.787 KA - 0.614ABJ |
| Pakisaji | KDB = 52.809 - 0.532ABJ |
| Sumbermanjing Wetan | KDB = -63.782 + 0.530CH + 2.795KA + 4.932KP - 1.481ABJ |
| Poncokusumo | KDB = -109.413 + 0.133CH + 0.187KP - 0.679ABJ |
| Wajak | KDB = 12.430 + 0.269CH - 1.193ABJ |
| Jabung | KDB = 1.936 - 0.214KU + 0.355CH + 0.125KP - 0.150ABJ |
| Lawang | KDB = 39.812 + 0.264CH - 0.428ABJ |

*Table 12. SMAPE score results of regression model training and testing*

| Area | SMAPE of Training | SMAPE of Testing |
|---|---|---|
| Turen | 22.37% | 23.31% |
| Dampit | 35.58% | 43.46% |
| Kepanjen | 37.74% | 27.50% |
| Pakis | 34.15% | 34.43% |
| Pakisaji | 41.30% | 39.43% |
| Sumbermanjing Wetan | 32.14% | 15.59% |
| Poncokusumo | 44.73% | 35.27% |
| Wajak | 29.21% | 43.36% |
| Jabung | 34.23% | 16.60% |
| Lawang | 28.68% | 56.79% |

*Figure 10. Actual comparison with Turen forecasting results (regression model)*

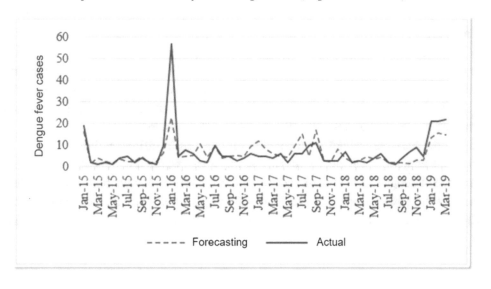

*Table 13. SMAPE score results of ANN model training and testing*

| Area | Model | SMAPE of Training | SMAPE of Testing |
|---|---|---|---|
| Turen | 1 | 26.98% | 19.03% |
| Pakis | 1 | 27.07% | 39.40% |
| Dampit | 2 | 30.60% | 19.31% |
| Wajak | 2 | 24.88% | 45.68% |
| Lawang | 2 | 25.23% | 41.01% |
| Kepanjen | 3 | 15.47% | 15.01% |
| Poncokusumo | 3 | 46.04% | 35.13% |
| Pakisaji | 4 | 46.79% | 26.80% |
| Sumbermanjing Wetan | 5 | 35.22% | 14.20% |
| Jabung | 6 | 41.07% | 16.32% |

*Figure 11. Actual comparison with Turen forecasting results (ANN model)*

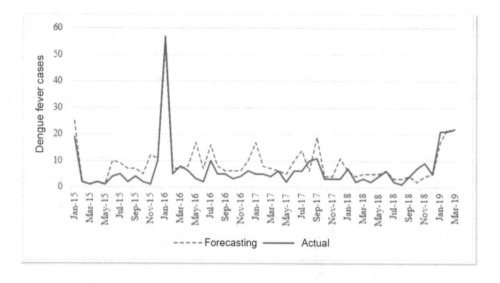

## 4.2 Discussion

Based on experiments conducted on data from 10 sample areas, it is evident that the factors influencing the occurrence of dengue fever vary in each region, including lowland and highland areas. The finding aligns with the findings of previous studies, as mentioned in reference (Adde et al., 2016), which indicate that the influence of various variables can differ across different regions.

The temperature variable has not been conclusively proven to influence the occurrence of dengue fever directly. This condition is evident across all sample areas, where no direct effect of air temperature on the occurrence of dengue fever is observed. However, it has been established that the air temperature variable does not directly influence the incidence of dengue fever. Only Pakisaji and Jabung show an indirect influence relationship with air temperature among the ten regions studied. These findings are consistent with research conducted by references (Adde et al., 2016; Atique et al., 2018; Chuang et al., 2017; Jain et al., 2019), which suggest that temperature plays a role in the occurrence of dengue fever outbreaks, albeit without specifying direct or indirect influences. The rainfall variable is proven to influence the occurrence of dengue fever directly. It is evidenced by 9 out of 10 regions showing a direct influence, including the Turen, Dampit, Kepanjen, Pakis, Sumbermanjing, Poncokusumo, Wajak, Jabung, and Lawang regions. Rainfall also exhibits an indirect influence, as observed in all studied areas. These findings are consistent with research conducted by references (Chuang et al., 2017; Jain et al., 2019; Xu et al., 2017). However, they contradict the notion presented by some studies that, based on correlation, rainfall generally does not affect dengue fever outbreaks (Anggraeni et al., 2020).

The humidity variable has not been conclusively proven to affect dengue fever incidence directly. This finding is consistent across all regions, where no direct effect of air humidity on the incidence of dengue fever is evident. However, it has been established that the air humidity variable does not directly influence the incidence of dengue fever. Only the Jabung region shows an indirect influence relationship with air humidity among the ten regions studied. These findings align with research conducted by references (Adde et al., 2016; Lai, 2018; Xu et al., 2017). The wind speed variable is proven to influence dengue fever incidence directly. It is demonstrated by 4 out of 10 regions, including the Turen, Pakis, Sumbermanjing, and Poncokusumo regions, showing a direct influence.

Additionally, the wind speed variable also exhibits an indirect influence, as observed in 2 out of 10 regions, namely the Pakis and Lawang regions. These findings align with research conducted by references (Anggraeni et al., 2021) and (Anggraeni et al., 2024). The population density variable directly influences the occurrence of dengue fever. It is supported by 4 out of the ten regions, including the Kepanjen, Sumbermanjing, Poncokusumo, and Jabung regions, showing a direct influence. This finding aligns with research conducted by (Anggraeni et al., 2020, 2024), which involved this variable in forecasting the number of dengue fever cases and demonstrated its effectiveness. The larvae-free index variable has been conclusively proven to influence dengue fever incidence directly. It is identified as the dominant factor influencing the incidence of dengue fever. This direct influence of larvae-free index on the incidence of dengue fever is evident in all areas studied, consistent with findings from (Anggraeni et al., 2020, 2024).

From the forecasting results, it can be observed that the performance of the regression method in predicting the incidence of dengue fever shows a level of accuracy in testing data with an average SMAPE value of 33.57%. This result indicates that the ANN forecasting performs better, with an average SMAPE value of 27.19%. The experimental results indicate that in 8 out of 10 regions in the Malang district, the Backpropagation model outperforms the Regression model in forecasting the occurrence of dengue fever based on influential variables. However, the Pakis and Wajak regions show better regression values compared to Backpropagation. This difference may be due to the reference parameters used in predicting the incidence of dengue fever in Pakis and Wajak, suggesting that the performance of these parameters may not lead to optimal forecasts in this dataset.

## 5. CONCLUSION

Research related to the analysis of the impact of climate on the spread of disease has been widely carried out in various countries. However, the results show that the influence of each variable, especially climate, can vary. This condition means that research related to influence analysis is still needed according to their respective regions. The results of experiments in lowlands and highlands at the selected regions show that the factors causing dengue fever to vary in each sub-district, both in lowland and highland areas. Their influence can also be direct or indirect. Environmental factors such as rainfall, free larvae index, wind speed, and geographic variability play an important role in the incidence of dengue fever. The limitation of this research only includes the influence of climate variables, the free larvae index, which shows mosquito density, and population density only. For future research, socioeconomic factors or healthcare infrastructure should be involved to better capture the dynamics of disease spread.

## REFERENCES

Adde, A., Roucou, P., Mangeas, M., Ardillon, V., Desenclos, J.-C., Rousset, D., Girod, R., Briolant, S., Quenel, P., & Flamand, C. (2016). Predicting Dengue Fever Outbreaks in French Guiana Using Climate Indicators. *{PLOS} Neglected Tropical Diseases, 10*(4), e0004681. doi:10.1371/journal.pntd.0004681

Altassan, K. K., Morin, C., Shocket, M. S., Ebi, K., & Hess, J. (2019). Dengue Fever in Saudi Arabia: A Review of Environmental and Population Factors impacting Emergence and Spread. *Travel Medicine and Infectious Disease, 30*, 46–53. doi:10.1016/j.tmaid.2019.04.006 PMID:30978417

Anggraeni, W., Pradani, H. N., Sumpeno, S., Yuniarno, E. M., Rachmadi, R. F., Purnomo, M. H., & Associates. (2021). Prediction of Dengue Fever Outbreak Based on Climate and Demographic Variables Using Extreme Gradient Boosting and Rule-Based Classification. *2021 IEEE 9th International Conference on Serious Games and Applications for Health (SeGAH)*, 1–8.

Anggraeni, W., Sumpeno, S., Yuniarno, E. M., Rachmadi, R. F., Gumelar, A. B., & Purnomo, M. H. (2020). Prediction of Dengue Fever Outbreak Based on Climate Factors Using Fuzzy-Logistic Regression. *2020 International Seminar on Intelligent Technology and Its Applications (ISITIA)*, (pp. 199–204). IEEE.

Anggraeni, W., Wicaksono, A. A., Yuniarno, E. M., Rachmadi, R. F., Sumpeno, S., & Purnomo, M. H. (2022). Multilevel Analysis of Temporal-Based Spatial Factors Impact in Dengue Fever Forecasting using RReliefF-Deep Learning. *2022 IEEE International Conference on Imaging Systems and Techniques (IST)*, (pp. 1–6). IEEE. 10.1109/IST55454.2022.9827717

Anggraeni, W., Yuniarno, E. M., Rachmadi, R. F., Sumpeno, S., Pujiadi, P., Sugiyanto, S., Santoso, J., & Purnomo, M. H. (2024). A Hybrid EMD-GRNN-PSO in Intermittent Time-Series Data for Dengue Fever Forecasting. *Expert Systems with Applications, 237*, 121438. doi:10.1016/j.eswa.2023.121438

Atique, S., Chan, T.-C., Chen, C.-C., Hsu, C.-Y., Iqtidar, S., Louis, V. R., Shabbir, S. A., & Chuang, T.-W. (2018). Investigating Spatio-Temporal Distribution and Diffusion Patterns of the Dengue Outbreak in Swat, Pakistan. *Journal of Infection and Public Health, 11*(4), 550–557. doi:10.1016/j.jiph.2017.12.003 PMID:29287804

Carvajal, T. M., Viacrusis, K. M., Hernandez, L. F. T., Ho, H. T., Amalin, D. M., & Watanabe, K. (2018). Machine Learning Methods Reveal the Temporal Pattern of Dengue Incidence using Meteorological Factors in Metropolitan Manila, Philippines. *BMC Infectious Diseases, 18*(1), 183. doi:10.1186/s12879-018-3066-0 PMID:29665781

Chuang, T.-W., Chaves, L. F., & Chen, P.-J. (2017). Effects of Local and Regional Climatic Fluctuations on Dengue Outbreaks in Southern Taiwan. *PLoS One*, *12*(6), e0178698. doi:10.1371/journal.pone.0178698 PMID:28575035

Daoud, J. I. (2017). Multicollinearity and Regression Analysis. *Journal of Physics: Conference Series*, *949*(1), 12009. doi:10.1088/1742-6596/949/1/012009

Ditjen P2P. (2019, February 1). Kesiapsiagaan Menghadapi Peningkatan Kejadian DBD Tahun 2019 [Preparedness to Face the Increase in DHF Incidents in 2019]. *Berita*. https://p2p.kemkes.go.id/kesiap-siagaan-menghadapi-peningkatan-kejadian-demam-berdarah-dengue-tahun-2019/

DuarteJ. L.Diaz-QuijanoF. A.BatistaA. C.GiattiL. L. (2019). Climatic Variables associated with Dengue Incidence in a City of the Western Brazilian Amazon Region. *Revista Da Sociedade Brasileira de Medicina Tropical, 52*. https://doi.org/ doi:10.1590/0037-8682-0429-2018

Jain, R., Sontisirikit, S., Iamsirithaworn, S., & Prendinger, H. (2019). Prediction of Dengue Outbreaks based on Disease Surveillance, Meteorological and Socioeconomic Data. *BMC Infectious Diseases*, *19*(1), 272. doi:10.1186/s12879-019-3874-x PMID:30898092

Jardiyanto, S. (2019). 72 Warga di Kabupaten Malang Terjangkit Demam Berdarah [72 Residents in Malang Regency Infected with Dengue Fever]. *Radar Malang Online*. https://radarmalang.id/januari-72-warga-di-kabupaten-malang-terjangkit-demam-berdarah/

Kementerian Kesehatan Republik Indonesia. (2016). *Wilayah dengan Kejadian Luar Biasa Demam Berdarah Dengue di 11 Provinsi Indonesia [Areas with Extraordinary Events of Dengue Hemorrhagic Fever in 11 Provinces of Indonesia]*. Depkes. http://www.depkes.go.id/article/print/16030700001/wilayah-klb-dbd-ada-di-11-provinsi.html

Kementerian Kesehatan Republik Indonesia. (2021). *Center for Data and Information*. Kemkes. https://pusdatin.kemkes.go.id/folder/view/01/structure-publikasi-data-pusat-data-dan-informasi.html

Labola, Y. A. (2020). *Daerah Rawan Kasus Demam Berdarah di Indonesia [Areas Prone to Dengue Fever Cases in Indonesia]*. Journalism Data. https://katadata.co.id/analisisdata/5e9a57b001ae9/daerah-rawan-kasus-demam-berdarah-di-indonesia

Lai, Y.-H. (2018). The Climatic Factors Affecting Dengue Fever Outbreaks in Southern Taiwan: An Application of Symbolic Data Analysis. *{BioMedical} Engineering {OnLine}, 17*(S2). doi:10.1186/s12938-018-0575-4

LaPorte, R. E. (1993). Needed: Universal Monitoring of All Serious Diseases of Global Importance. *American Journal of Public Health*, *83*(7), 941–943. doi:10.2105/AJPH.83.7.941 PMID:8328611

Mala, S., & Jat, M. K. (2019). Implications of Meteorological and Physiographical Parameters on Dengue Fever Occurrences in Delhi. *The Science of the Total Environment*, *650*, 2267–2283. doi:10.1016/j.scitotenv.2018.09.357 PMID:30292120

Mishra, P., Pandey, C. M., Singh, U., Gupta, A., Sahu, C., & Keshri, A. (2019). Descriptive Statistics and Normality Tests for Statistical Data. *Annals of Cardiac Anaesthesia*, *22*(1), 67. doi:10.4103/aca.ACA_157_18 PMID:30648682

Siriyasatien, P., Phumee, A., Ongruk, P., Jampachaisri, K., & Kesorn, K. (2016). Analysis of significant factors for dengue fever incidence prediction. *BMC Bioinformatics*, *17*(1), 166. doi:10.1186/s12859-016-1034-5 PMID:27083696

Souravlas, S., Sifaleras, A., & Katsavounis, S. (2019). A Parallel Algorithm for Community Detection in Social Networks, based on Path Analysis and threaded Binary Trees. *IEEE Access : Practical Innovations, Open Solutions*, *7*, 20499–20519. doi:10.1109/ACCESS.2019.2897783

Tanwar, S., Tyagi, S., & Kumar, N. (Eds.). (2019). Security and privacy of electronic healthcare records: Concepts, paradigms and solutions. Institution of Engineering and Technology.

Tsai, C. W., Yeh, T.-G., & Hsiao, Y.-R. (2018). Evaluation of Hydrologic and Meteorological impacts on Dengue Fever incidences in Southern Taiwan using Time-Frequency Analysis Methods. *Ecological Informatics*, *46*, 166–178. doi:10.1016/j.ecoinf.2018.05.002

Vekaria, D., Kumari, A., Tanwar, S., & Kumar, N. (2021). ξboost: An AI-Based Data Analytics Scheme for COVID-19 Prediction and Economy Boosting. IEEE Internet of Things Journal, 8(21). doi:10.1109/JIOT.2020.3047539

World Health Organization. (2017). *Dengue Guidelines for Diagnosis, Treatment, Prevention and Control: New Edition*. WHO. https://www.who.int/rpc/guidelines/9789241547871/en

World Health Organization. (2023). *Dengue and Severe Dengue*. Newsroom. https://www.who.int/newsroom/fact-sheets/detail/dengue-and-severe-dengue

Xiang, J., Hansen, A., Liu, Q., Liu, X., Tong, M. X., Sun, Y., Cameron, S., Hanson-Easey, S., Han, G.-S., Williams, C., Weinstein, P., & Bi, P. (2017). Association between Dengue Fever Incidence and Meteorological Factors in Guangzhou, China, 2005-2014. *Environmental Research*, *153*, 17–26. doi:10.1016/j.envres.2016.11.009 PMID:27883970

Xu, L., Stige, L. C., Chan, K.-S., Zhou, J., Yang, J., Sang, S., Wang, M., Yang, Z., Yan, Z., Jiang, T., Lu, L., Yue, Y., Liu, X., Lin, H., Xu, J., Liu, Q., & Stenseth, N. C. (2017). Climate Variation Drives Dengue Dynamics. *Proceedings of the National Academy of Sciences of the United States of America*, *114*(1), 113–118. doi:10.1073/pnas.1618558114 PMID:27940911

Yavari Nejad, F., & Varathan, K. D. (2021). Identification of Significant Climatic Risk Factors and Machine Learning Models in Dengue Outbreak Prediction. *BMC Medical Informatics and Decision Making*, *21*(1), 1–12. doi:10.1186/s12911-021-01493-y PMID:33931058

Yushananta, P., & Ahyanti, M. (2014). Pengaruh Faktor Iklim dan Kepadatan Jentik ae. Aegypti terhadap Kejadian DBD [The Influence of Climate Factors and Density of Aedes Aegypti Larvae on the Occurrence of Dengue Fever]. *Jurnal Kesehatan, 5*(1).

Zhu, G., Liu, T., Xiao, J., Zhang, B., Song, T., Zhang, Y., Lin, L., Peng, Z., Deng, A., Ma, W., & Hao, Y. (2019). Effects of Human Mobility, Temperature and Mosquito Control on the Spatiotemporal Transmission of Dengue. *The Science of the Total Environment, 651*, 969–978. doi:10.1016/j.scitotenv.2018.09.182 PMID:30360290

# Chapter 5
# Clustering and Unsupervised Learning

**Divyani Tirthyani**
*Manipal University Jaipur, India*

**Sunil Kumar**
*Manipal University Jaipur, India*

**Shally Vats**
*Manipal University Jaipur, India*

## ABSTRACT

*Machine learning (ML) is an approach driven by data, wherein computers acquire knowledge from information without requiring human interference. Artificial intelligence (AI) and machine learning (ML) have made significant contributions across diverse research domains, leading to enhanced outcomes. Clustering is defined as a fundamental challenge in various data-driven fields, representing an unsupervised learning model. Unsupervised learning methods and algorithms encompass the Apriori algorithm, ECLAT algorithm, frequent pattern growth algorithm, k-means clustering, and principal components analysis. Unsupervised learning methods have achieved notable success in fields such as machine vision, speech recognition, the development of autonomous vehicles, and natural language processing. This chapter provides a brief explanation of unsupervised clustering approaches. It also discusses literature review, intriguing challenges, and future prospects in the realm of unsupervised deep clustering.*

## 1. INTRODUCTION

Clustering serves as a valuable asset in the toolkit of data science. It helps find patterns in data where things are similar within groups but different between groups. Biologists and social scientists first used hierarchical clustering. It's a part of statistical multivariate analysis. Clustering is unsupervised, meaning it doesn't need labelled data. There are two main types: those based on probability models and those without specific assumptions. Probability model-based approaches assume that data comes from a mix

DOI: 10.4018/979-8-3693-3609-0.ch005

of probability models. They use a method called the expectation and maximisation (EM) algorithm to cluster the data. Nonparametric approaches use objective functions based on how similar or different data points are. These methods are often divided into hierarchical and partitional methods, with partitional methods being more commonly used (Sinaga & Yang, 2020). Unsupervised learning is important for making AI systems more like humans. That's because these systems need to figure things out on their own from lots of data without labels. Unsupervised learning is great for handling complicated tasks, unlike supervised learning, which is better at giving exact answers since programmers tell it what to learn from the data. Conversely, unsupervised learning can uncover surprises. It's what powers artificial neural networks, which are crucial for deep learning to happen. But even in neural networks, you can use supervised learning if you already know what results you want. Sometimes, learning without supervision is the aim itself. Unsupervised learning models, for example, can reveal hidden patterns in big sets of data and sort them into groups based on how similar or different they are (Naeem et al., 2023).

Below are several explanations highlighting the significance of unsupervised learning:

- Having lots of data without labels is a big chance for learning.
- Labelling data takes a lot of time and people.
- Machine learning can make this easier for everyone involved.
- Unsupervised learning is great for looking at new or messy data.
- It's especially good for dealing with huge amounts of data and finding patterns.

## 1.1 Motivation

Here's why we're dedicating a chapter to clustering and unsupervised learning in healthcare:

- A vast amount of healthcare information is being produced from diverse origins such as electronic health records, medical imaging, wearable technology, and genomic data. Using clustering and unsupervised learning helps make sense of all this data.
- Personalised medicine is becoming more important. Clustering algorithms help doctors group patients based on their similarities, making it easier to create treatment plans that fit each person.
- Healthcare organisations want to improve population health by identifying groups of people who are at risk for certain diseases. Clustering and unsupervised learning help with this, making it easier to target interventions and preventions.
- Healthcare organisations need to use their resources wisely. Clustering methods can help them see patterns in things like patient admissions and procedures, so they can plan better and be more efficient.
- Technology is getting better, making clustering and unsupervised learning more accessible and powerful. Using these techniques in healthcare can lead to new innovations and better care for patients.
- Healthcare and data science are coming together, so it's important for doctors, data scientists, and researchers to work together. This chapter will give them a good overview of how clustering and unsupervised learning can improve patient care and research in healthcare.

1.2 Chapter Contribution

- The main contributions of this survey include:
- Offering a comprehensive examination of clustering and unsupervised learning across different domains, including healthcare.
- Providing an overview of diverse clustering methodologies and unsupervised algorithms.
- Presenting a table summarising recent literature on clustering and unsupervised learning within the healthcare sector, emphasising their effects.
- Introducing a discourse on the limitations of current research and suggesting avenues for future investigation.
- Additionally, discussing the utility of Machine Learning in healthcare applications.

## 1.3 Organization of the Chapter

The rest of the chapter is structured as follows. In Section 2, we examine the fundamentals of unsupervised learning, its classifications, diverse algorithms, and provide an overview of clustering techniques. Section 3 presents a systematic literature survey and a literature review table with challenges/gaps and future directions. Section 4 presents a detailed description of various clustering types. Section 5 discusses the utilisation of machine learning, clustering, and unsupervised learning in healthcare applications. Section 6 describes the real world examples of clustering and unsupervised learning in healthcare. Section 7 describes the challenges of clustering and unsupervised learning in healthcare . In section 8 a case study on "Leveraging Clustering and Unsupervised Learning in Healthcare:" is presented and the paper is finally concluded in section 9.

## 2. BACKGROUND

In this section the overview of unsupervised learning, types of unsupervised learning, Unsupervised learning algorithm and description of clustering is presented.

## 2.1 Unsupervised Learning

In unsupervised learning, data scientists give the system images, and it's the system's job to figure out if they have pictures of cats. Unsupervised machine learning needs lots of data. Usually, supervised learning works the same way, getting better at its job as it sees more examples. In unsupervised learning, data scientists start by using datasets to teach algorithms. These datasets don't have labelled or categorised data points. The objective is for the algorithm to identify patterns within the dataset and assign scores to the data points accordingly. The difficulties in unsupervised learning include clustering, association, anomaly detection, and autoencoder problems, as shown in Figure 1.

When dealing with cat images, an unsupervised learning system could detect characteristics such as whiskers, lengthy tails, and retractable claws. Unsupervised learning operates akin to the way humans instinctively learn to identify and categorise objects. For instance, if you've never sampled ketchup or spicy sauce and are handed two unmarked bottles of each to taste, you could still tell the difference between them (one is sour, the other is spicy). After trying them multiple times, you'd get better at knowing their flavours and start sorting foods based on their sauce. By looking at the flavours, you could find out what makes the two sauces different and learn about their nutrition, even if you didn't know

*Figure 1. Types of unsupervised learning*

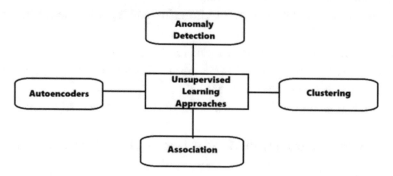

their names or tastes before. Alternatively, you could label one as "sweet sauce" and the other as "spicy sauce." Similarly, machines utilise unsupervised learning to identify patterns and organise data points, whereas supervised learning entails prior knowledge of labels and features.

## 2.2 Types of Unsupervised Learning

This section covers a range of unsupervised learning techniques, each with its own explanation.

### 2.2.1 Clustering

Clustering, also called cluster analysis, is about putting things into groups. There are different ways to do this, like splitting, organising hierarchically, overlapping, and using probabilities. In splitting, data is divided so that each piece is only in one group, known as exclusive pooling. An example of splitting is K-means clustering, where data points are put into groups step by step.Hierarchical clustering begins with each data point forming its individual cluster, then gradually merges similar clusters. Overlapping clustering groups data into fuzzy sets, where points can belong to multiple categories with different levels of belonging. For example, K-Means clustering gives each data point a suitable level of belonging to a group. Finally, probabilistic clustering employs probability distributions for cluster formation. Figure 2 illustrates an example of this clustering process.

### 2.2.2 Association

Association Rule Learning (ARL) is an unsupervised learning approach utilised to uncover relationships among variables within extensive datasets. Unlike certain other machine learning techniques, ARL accommodates non-numeric data. Essentially, ARL examines the associations between specific variables. For instance, if individuals purchase a motorcycle, they are able to purchase a helmet, highlighting the potential profitability of these associations. Therefore, if customers who acquire product X frequently also purchase product Y, an online retailer can recommend Y to those purchasing X, leveraging association rules to identify these correlations.These rules can help find connections between different sets of data, using measures like support and confidence to check how valid the patterns or relationships are. Support shows how often the "if/then" connection happens in the data, while confidence measures how

*Figure 2. Clustering example*

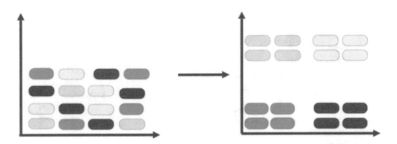

often that connection is true. Association rules help with tasks like analysing shopping carts and tracking online behaviour (Naeem et al., 2023).

## 2.2.3 Anomaly Detection

Anomaly detection is about finding unusual things in a dataset. These anomalies could show weird network behaviour, broken sensors, or data that needs cleaning before studying it. When data doesn't follow the usual patterns, it's called an anomaly. For example, strange network traffic might mean a hacked system is sending secret data to a wrong place. Anomaly detection spots these oddities by finding or predicting data points that don't fit the usual pattern. It's used in areas like spotting intrusions, insurance, catching fraud, and military monitoring.

## 2.2.4 Autoencoders

Autoencoders, a form of unsupervised learning, utilise neural networks to master the representation of data. These networks are designed with a narrow point in the middle, which forces them to make a compact version of the original data. It gets tricky when the input data doesn't have clear connections, but if there's some structure, like relationships between different parts of the data, the network can learn from it and use it to compress and then reconstruct the data. In network design, having an information bottleneck is really important. Without it, the network might just end up storing the input data without compressing it much. Figure 3 shows the different parts of the autoencoder algorithm (Naeem et al., 2023).

## 2.3 Unsupervised Learning Algorithms

Algorithms are really important for both clustering and association rule learning.In association rule learning, we employ techniques such as the a priori method, the ECLAT algorithm, and the frequent pattern

*Figure 3. Components of autoencoder*

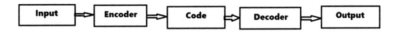

*Figure 4. Unsupervised learning algorithms*

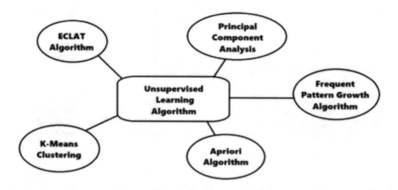

(FP) growth algorithm. In clustering, algorithms such as k-means clustering and principal component analysis (PCA) are commonly used. Figure 4 illustrates various unsupervised learning algorithms.

## 2.3.1 Apriori Algorithm

The Apriori algorithm is specifically designed for data mining, particularly suited for databases containing numerous transactions, like those tracking what people buy at supermarkets. Its main job is to find sets of items that are often bought together. This helps with analysing shopping carts and finding possible side effects of medicines.

## 2.3.2 ECLAT Algorithm

ECLAT (Equivalence Class Clustering and Bottom-up Lattice Traversal) is a data mining technique utilised to discover item sets and identify frequently occurring items. Unlike Apriori, which looks at data horizontally and needs to go through the database multiple times to find common items, ECLAT works differently. It uses a vertical approach, which means it's generally faster because It requires only a single scan of the database. Figure 5 illustrates the functioning of the ECLAT algorithm.

*Figure 5. Model of ECLAT algorithm*

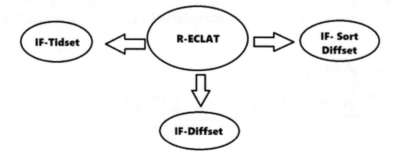

### 2.3.3 Frequent Pattern Growth Algorithm

The Apriori algorithm has seen enhancements with the development of the Frequent Pattern (FP) Growth algorithm. This updated method utilises a pattern or frequent tree (FT) structure to represent the database, enabling the discovery of the most prevalent patterns. Unlike the Apriori method, which requires searching the database n + 1 times (where n represents the length of the longest pattern), the FP growth approach only necessitates two scans.

### 2.3.4 Clustering Using K-Means

In data science, the k-means method is frequently employed iteratively. This algorithm divides things into clusters based on how similar they are. In the figure, you can see how the k-means process works visually. The letter "k" tells us how many clusters there will be, so if k is 3, there will be three groups. This approach organises data into distinct clusters, where each data point is grouped with others sharing similar characteristics. The objective is to determine cluster centroids, serving as focal points for the clusters, with each cluster having its centroid. When a new data point is introduced, the algorithm utilises metrics like Euclidean distance to assign it to the appropriate cluster. The iterative K-means clustering method is employed to compute centroids, continually refining them until optimal values are achieved. Typically, the number of clusters is predetermined, hence another term for this is the flat clustering algorithm. The "K" in K-means indicates the number of clusters present. The process of K-Means clustering is illustrated in Figure 6.

### 2.3.5 Principal Components Analysis (PCA)

PCA is a method utilised to simplify extensive datasets by reducing numerous variables into a smaller set while retaining most of the original data information. While cutting down on variables may mean losing some accuracy, it's worth it to simplify things. Smaller datasets are easier to work with and understand, making data analysis and machine learning more efficient. You can see how PCA works in Figure 7.

*Figure 6. Workflow of K-mean clustering*

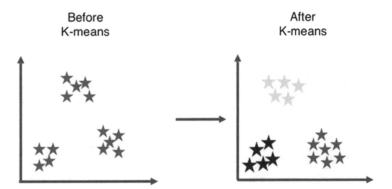

*Figure 7. Workflow of PCA*

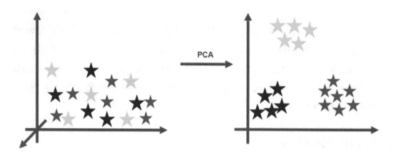

## 2.4 Clustering

A cluster is like a group of similar things within a dataset, making up a kind of invisible category.The objective of clustering is to create meaningful clusters of similar features within the available data. In clustering, you put similar things together and keep different ones apart. There are two main ways to cluster. Top-down clustering starts with the whole dataset as one group, based on something they have in common. Then it splits into smaller groups with less in common. Bottom-up clustering starts with each thing as its own group, then puts together things that are similar, gradually making bigger groups. Clustering falls into two main types: hard (non-overlapping), which groups based on exact values, and fuzzy (overlapping), which relies on probability. It's also called data segmentation or unsupervised automatic classification, because it splits big datasets into smaller groups based on similarities. Besides, clustering can spot outliers. There are various clustering methods like partitioning, density-based, model-based, and research-based techniques. Figure 8 shows how clustering works in unsupervised learning (Maurya et al., 2020).

## 3. RELATED WORK

Naeem et al. (2023) examine a variety of techniques, algorithms, and metrics employed in unsupervised learning. They assess the strengths and weaknesses of different studies within this domain, offering insights for researchers and proposing avenues for further research.

*Figure 8. Workflow of clustering in unsupervised ML*

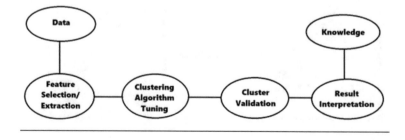

Cord et al. (2008) provide a summary of traditional clustering approaches like k-means and hierarchical clustering, alongside discussions on more recent clustering techniques such as kernel-based clustering and spectral clustering algorithms.

Satpathy et al. (2021) categorise retinal segmentation techniques into two primary categories: rule-based methods and machine learning-based methods. Rule-based methods adhere to predetermined rules, whereas machine learning methods utilise labelled data for model training.

Isaac Kofi Nti et al. (2022) conducted an extensive examination of employing machine learning (ML) in big data analytics (BDA). Initially identifying 1512 articles using specific keywords, they refined their selection to 140 articles based on a novel taxonomy they introduced. Their findings revealed that commonly utilised techniques in BDA include deep neural networks (15%), support vector machines (15%), artificial neural networks (14%), decision trees (12%), and ensemble learning techniques (11%).

Neeraj Maurya et al. (2020) did a survey on the theoretical basics of techniques used in feature selection(FS), clustering, and classification.

El-Alfy and Mohammed (2020) did a bibliometric analysis to look at the extensive literature and research performance in a growing research area that's getting more attention from businesses, industries, and academia. They used various measures and visual methods to look at things like research productivity, key contributors, publication patterns, growth rates, and how often research is cited or collaborated on. Mohammad Sultan Mahmud et al. (2020) thoroughly examine how data is divided and sampled for handling and analysing big data. They start by outlining the main big data frameworks used on Hadoop clusters. Pereira and Silveira (2019) present a framework designed to detect anomalies in time series data without requiring supervision. Their approach integrates representation learning and anomaly detection in a completely unsupervised manner. They employ a Variational Recurrent Autoencoder to initially understand the characteristics of time series data, followed by the application of clustering techniques and the Wasserstein distance to identify anomalies based on the learned information.

Madhavakanna (2018) conduct an extensive examination of the significance of Feature Selection techniques, Supervised Machine Learning techniques, Unsupervised Machine Learning techniques, and big data in healthcare.

Nonie Alexander et al. (2021) investigate various categories of Alzheimer's disease patients through the analysis of electronic health records (EHR). They use various clustering techniques to find groups of patients with similar characteristics. This research shows how outcomes can vary with different clustering methods and emphasises the need to carefully consider different approaches to find disease subtypes in complex EHR data. Wen-Chieh Yang et al. (2024) compare the groups of indigenous and non-indigenous patients based on diseases, timing, and amounts, pointing out potential health risks that could help hospitals plan better. These findings might help with personalised health education programs, tailored healthcare services, better distribution of resources in medical facilities, and understanding medical costs. Proposes an artificial neural network-driven federated learning approach to predict heart strokes in Healthcare 4.0 leveraging 5G connectivity (Bhatt, 2023). Introduces ρReveal, an AI-driven big data analytics scheme designed for predicting energy prices and reducing load (Kumari & Tanwar, 2021). Presents ArMor, a data analytics scheme tailored to detect malicious activities within Blockchain-based Smart Grid Systems (Kumari et al., 2020). Offers an AI-based peak load reduction strategy for residential buildings utilizing reinforcement learning techniques (Kumari & Tanwar, 2021). Introduces a multi-agent-based decentralized approach for residential energy management, employing deep reinforcement learning methods (Kumari et al., 2024).

*Table 1. Existing approaches of clustering and unsupervised learning in healthcare*

| Author | Year | Publisher | Short Description | Technique used |
|---|---|---|---|---|
| Tannu Chauhan et al. (2021) | 2021 | IEEE | This study aims to conduct a thorough examination of diabetes diagnosis utilising both supervised and unsupervised machine learning algorithms. | K-Mean Clustering SVM Decision Tree |
| Khalid and Prieto-Alhambra (2019) | 2019 | Springer | The aim of this research is to conduct an in-depth exploration of diabetes diagnosis using both supervised and unsupervised machine learning algorithms. | Cluster analysis Autoencoder |
| Md. Mehedi Hassan (2022) | 2022 | Elsevier | The objective of this study is to conduct an extensive analysis of diabetes diagnosis employing both supervised and unsupervised machine learning algorithms. | Predictive modelling Feature prioritisation Elbow technique Silhouette technique |
| Sinaga and Yang (2020) | 2020 | IEEE | This paper presents an unsupervised learning framework for the k-means algorithm, removing the requirement for initialization and parameter selection, while also facilitating the simultaneous determination of an optimal number of clusters. | K-means Unsupervised variant of k-means (U-k-means). |
| Javaid et al. (2022) | 2022 | Elsevier | This paper examines machine learning (ML) and its necessity in healthcare, followed by an exploration of the relevant characteristics and suitable foundations of ML for healthcare infrastructure. | Machine Learning Unsupervised learning |
| Wang et al. (2020) | 2020 | Elsevier | This paper investigates the use of unsupervised machine learning models to identify concealed disease clusters and patient subgroups through the analysis of electronic health records (EHRs). | Unsupervised learning Study of disease patterns in populations |
| Abdullah Alanazi (2022) | 2022 | Elsevier | This paper offers an overview of the challenges and opportunities in applying machine learning to healthcare. | Unsupervised Machine learning |
| Karesiddaiah and Savarimuthu (2021) | 2020 | Springer | This paper proposes a technique for filling in missing data, named CLUSTIMP, utilising an unsupervised neural network called Adaptive Resonance Theory 2 (ART2). | Unsupervised Machine learning Neural network |
| Hosny and Elhenawy (2021) | 2021 | IEEE | This paper thoroughly investigates the key clustering algorithms, provides a comparison of clustering methods suitable for handling large-scale data, and discusses the main challenges associated with each clustering approach. | Cluster analysis, self-organising learning, conventional clustering, concurrent clustering, real-time clustering |

## 4. CLUSTERING TYPES

Different types of clustering are methods to group data based on how similar or different they are from each other.

### 4.1 Basic Clustering Techniques

### 4.1.1 K-Means Clustering

K-means clustering is a partition clustering technique commonly employed for analysing medical data. Clustering techniques in medicine are used for tasks like classifying diseases, spotting diseases early, and predicting how diseases will progress. Studies have shown that K-means clustering is good at finding patients with heart failure. This could help healthcare workers improve their care, particularly when managing COVID-19 patients belonging to diverse ethnic backgrounds, by taking into account various important factors. Many studies have looked at specific diseases, and K-means is a popular clustering technique in analysing medical data. Clustering techniques fall into two primary categories: hierarchical clustering methods and partition clustering methods (Yang et al., 2024). Partitional clustering methods entail directly splitting a dataset into a flat partition consisting of k distinct clusters denoted as $C = \{C1, \ldots, Ck\}$. Typically, these methods strive to refine an initial solution through iterations to generate a local approximation of a global objective function. The widely employed partitional clustering approach is the standard k-means algorithm, which iteratively forms k clusters aiming to minimise the disparity between data objects and a set of k cluster centroids. Each centroid, termed a representative, is computed as the average of all objects allocated to a particular cluster (Cord et al., 2008).

## 4.1.2 Fuzzy Clustering

In clustering methods, fuzzy clustering stands out as a flexible and powerful technique, especially in healthcare settings. While conventional clustering methods allocate each data point to a single cluster, fuzzy clustering permits data points to be members of multiple clusters concurrently. This recognizes the uncertainty and overlap often seen in real-world datasets.In the healthcare field, where patient characteristics can be complex and overlapping, fuzzy clustering offers a deep understanding of patient groups. This helps in creating personalised treatment plans and assessing risks. By recognizing the inherent uncertainty in medical data, fuzzy clustering gives healthcare workers detailed insights into disease patterns, treatment results, and prognosis.

## 4.1.3 Hierarchical Clustering

In hierarchical clustering algorithms, data clusters are arranged in a series of nested groups, starting from individual clusters and moving towards one cluster containing all data points, or the other way around. Agglomerative techniques initiate from the individual object level, treating each object as a distinct cluster and subsequently merging them into larger clusters. Conversely, divisive methods operate oppositely, commencing from a single large cluster encompassing all objects and then dividing it into smaller clusters. Rather than creating a flat grouping of data, constructing a hierarchy of concepts through a series of nested clusters resembling a tree structure can be beneficial. While recent research has predominantly focused on partitional clustering methods, hierarchical clustering algorithms remain the preferred option for document clustering. This preference is particularly evident because text collections often exhibit prominent themes that naturally lend themselves to subdivision into smaller topics. Hierarchical algorithms typically fall into two primary categories:

**Agglomerative:** This method begins with each object having its own cluster. Then, it combines the most similar pairs of clusters in a bottom-up manner.

**Divisive:** On the other hand, this approach starts with one cluster containing all objects. Then, it splits the selected cluster into two sub-clusters in a top-down manner.

## 4.1.4 Partition-Based Clustering

Partitioning-based algorithms function by iteratively dividing the data of all clusters into partitions until a specific partitioning condition is met. Each partition corresponds to an individual cluster. Two well-known algorithms in this category are K-means and K-medoid. K-means continuously updates the centroid of each cluster until the desired data coverage objective is achieved (Hosny & Elhenawy, 2021).

## 4.1.5 Density-Based Clustering

Density clustering seeks to identify cluster arrangements by utilising numerical data and organising them according to dimensional distances. Initially, the data is segmented into three categories: core points, boundary points, and noise points. A point qualifies as a core point if it is encircled by at least m other points within a distance of n. A point is categorised as a boundary point if it is in proximity to at least one core point; otherwise, it is classified as noise (Hosny & Elhenawy, 2021).

## 4.1.6 Probabilistic and Generative Clustering

Model-based algorithms cluster data utilising diverse techniques, including statistical and conceptual methods. Within model-based algorithms, two prevalent approaches exist: the neural network approach and the analytical approach. While neural network approaches typically employ supervised techniques, Kohonen's SOM stands out as an exception, as it is a model specifically designed for clustering purposes (Hosny & Elhenawy, 2021).

## 4.1.7 Grid-Based Clustering

Grid-based clustering algorithms are receiving considerable attention due to their ability to detect clusters of various shapes and sizes. Within this category, two primary methods are prominent: the Fix-up method and the adaptive grid partition method. In the Fix-up grid partition method, each dimension of the data space is divided into uniform lengths, creating intersecting rectangular cells. Points located within the same cell are considered part of the same group and are treated collectively. All clustering tasks are performed using these grid cells. Conversely, the adaptive grid partition method divides the data space into non-overlapping grid cells of varying sizes, based on the distribution of the data. This results in a significant reduction in the total number of grid cells compared to the Fix-up partition method.

## 4.2 Modern Clustering Techniques

New clustering methods use fancy maths and computer tricks to group data together based on complex patterns and relationships.

## 4.2.1 Kernel Clustering

Kernel methods entail converting a dataset into a novel space, potentially with higher dimensions, to facilitate a deeper comprehension of nonlinear relationships among objects. Rather than directly computing the transformed representation $\varphi(x)$ for each data point x, we employ the "kernel trick" to assess the similarity between a pair of objects $(x_i, x_j)$ using a kernel function $\kappa$. This kernel function, formulated based on the dot product, $\kappa(x_i, x_j) = \varphi(x_i) \bullet \varphi(x_j)$ (Cord et al., 2008).

## 4.2.2 Spectral Clustering

Drawing inspiration from graph theory research, novel unsupervised feature extraction approaches have arisen. These methods employ linear algebra techniques to analyse the spectral characteristics of a graph representing a dataset. Typically, this entails generating a lower-dimensional space by decomposing a matrix derived from the graph using eigenvalue decomposition (EVD). Subsequently, established clustering algorithms can be applied in this reduced space to identify patterns within the data. Spectral clustering techniques have gained prominence due to their effectiveness and versatility across various applications such as image segmentation, gene expression analysis, and document clustering (Cord et al., 2008).

## 4.2.3 Self-Organising Maps

The self-organising map (SOM) is a popular and extensively utilised neural network model. It facilitates the conversion of a high-dimensional input space into a lower-dimensional output space while maintaining the underlying topology. Often, this output space is structured as a two-dimensional grid, commonly rectangular or hexagonal, simplifying comprehension. Alternatively, arrangements such as a three-dimensional output space are also feasible. Throughout the mapping process, the SOM accomplishes both vector projection, thereby reducing dimensionality, and vector quantization, identifying representative prototypes (Cord et al., 2008).

## 4.2.4 Cluster Validation

Assessing the outcomes of a clustering algorithm poses a fundamental hurdle in unsupervised learning. Unlike classification tasks where predetermined labels aid in evaluation, clustering methods lack such reference points in practical situations. Consequently, there's no definitive criterion for determining the correctness of a clustering solution for a given dataset. This ambiguity complicates the differentiation between a solution that effectively captures data patterns and one that fails to offer meaningful insights. While manual evaluation by an expert may work for some cases, it's impractical for larger datasets and risks introducing bias.

## 4.3 Scalable Clustering Techniques

Scalable clustering methods help manage big data better, ensuring groups are made well without slowing things down.

## 4.3.1 Sampling Based

This approach stands out as one of the most efficient means to manage extensive datasets and enhance operational speed. Its primary objective is to cluster data samples rather than the entire dataset. Following processing, the clustering outcomes are applied to the entire dataset, offering a broad overview. These methods have significantly contributed to accelerating techniques by downsizing data, thereby saving time and simplifying operations. Nonetheless, it's essential to acknowledge that these techniques introduce additional time and complexity during the preprocessing phase required for sampling operations. Additionally, clustering a subset of data may not yield the same level of accuracy as utilising the entire dataset.

## 4.3.2 Reduction and Projection Based

The growing complexity of data presents additional hurdles for numerous clustering algorithms, including difficulties with noisy features or sparse data. Although sampling methods can assist in diminishing data size, they may not always be optimal for addressing high-dimensional datasets. Projection techniques also target data size reduction but in a distinct manner. Presently, approaches such as feature selection, feature extraction, approximation, and random reduction are employed to address these challenges. Like sampling methods, these techniques require preprocessing of data. Feature selection involves reducing dimensionality by changing data attributes according to data dependencies, while feature extraction creates new useful features.

## 4.3.3 Subspace Clustering

Subspace clustering seeks to identify clusters within various subsets of dimensions, focusing on finding clusters using only specific dimensions. Generally, there are two types of subspace clustering distinguished by their search strategy: bottom-up and top-down. In bottom-up clustering, clusters are first identified in lower dimensions and then merged to explore higher dimension spaces. On the other hand, top-down clustering starts by finding clusters in all dimensions and then examining each cluster's subset of dimensions. In summary, subspace clustering tackles the challenges of high-dimensional datasets often faced by grid-based methods.

## 4.3.4 Map-Reduce Based

With processors encountering constraints in power and memory, there is a demand for algorithms capable of utilising multiple devices concurrently. The Map-Reduce framework has helped with this by solving issues like network connections, sharing data, and balancing workloads. This has made it easier for many researchers to use and improve algorithms in parallel processing systems.

## 4.3.5 Parallel and Distribution Based

The Data-Driven Path Identification (DDPI) approach combines k-means with neural network batch training concurrently. Instead of relying on a distributed system, the author introduced a method to parallelize the k-means algorithm using a neural network, coupled with a supervised step. The algorithm involves three parallelization steps: partitioning and distributing data, processing data across multiple systems, and merging the outcomes. This technique aids in alleviating the computational burden of neural techniques (Hosny & Elhenawy, 2021).

## 5. APPLICATIONS

Machine learning applications in healthcare are extensive and impactful:

- Efficiently gather patient histories
- Enhance healthcare service experiences
- Streamline treatment processes
- Enable robotic surgeries and image-guided therapies
- Automatically issue alerts
- Streamline decision-making processes
- Detect health concerns
- Coordinate online appointment bookings
- Analyse patient information
- Facilitate initial medication research
- Administer clinical trials
- Help address psychological issues
- Support patient diagnosis and treatment
- Contribute to pharmaceutical discovery
- Forecast disease onset
- Enhance radiology practices
- Detect minute abnormalities
- Innovate medical procedures
- Contribute to blood cancer treatment
- Enhance result accuracy
- Improve healthcare system efficiency
- Manage risks effectively
- Enhance clinical study accuracy
- Digitise healthcare records and informatics
- Elevate healthcare quality
- Enhance diagnostic precision
- Optimise operational efficiency
- Provide valuable family medical history (Javaid et al., 2022).

## 6. REAL-WORLD EXAMPLES OF CLUSTERING AND UNSUPERVISED LEARNING

Clustering and unsupervised learning are widely used in healthcare for different reasons. Here are some real-life examples:

- **Sorting Patients:** Hospitals use clustering to group patients with similar backgrounds or medical histories. This helps doctors plan treatments better and allocate resources where needed. For example, it can help identify groups of patients at high risk for diseases like diabetes or heart problems.

- **Understanding Diseases:** Scientists use unsupervised learning to find different types of diseases based on genes, molecules, or how they affect patients. For instance, in cancer research, this helps identify different kinds of tumours and how they respond to treatments, leading to better therapies.
- **Spotting Problems:** Healthcare systems use unsupervised learning to find unusual things in medical data. This could be a sign of a health issue or a mistake in diagnosis. For example, it can help catch strange patterns in patient vital signs that might mean they're getting worse or have an infection.
- **Finding New Medicines:** Scientists use clustering to organise different compounds based on their properties. This helps them find new drugs or new uses for existing ones.
- **Using Resources Wisely:** Hospitals use clustering to manage their resources better, like staff schedules or patient appointments. By grouping patients based on how long they're expected to stay or what they'll need, hospitals can use their resources more efficiently and reduce wait times.
- **Looking at Pictures:** Doctors use unsupervised learning to analyse medical images, like MRIs or CT scans. This helps them see important parts of the body more clearly and make better decisions about treatment. For example, it can help find tumours in the brain or heart.

# 7. CHALLENGES

## 7.1 Challenges for Implementing Machine Learning Models in Healthcare

Professionals must carefully examine and address the challenges associated with employing machine learning algorithms in healthcare. The success of any machine learning model relies on access to high-quality data that precisely reflects the served population. Therefore, it's crucial to establish strong data management practices at all levels when integrating machine learning models into healthcare. Additionally, it's important to create pipelines for data processing and machine learning, as well as user-friendly interfaces for the end products. These pipelines have the capability to transform raw data into datasets appropriate for training a variety of machine learning models.

It's crucial for pertinent stakeholders to establish a strong data governance strategy to efficiently utilise the generated data. Another notable obstacle is that machine learning-driven predictions frequently lack explanations unless interpretable models such as decision trees are employed. In cases where machine learning models are used to predict health outcomes, legal protocols may not be optimised if there's a potential error. This aspect can present significant practical challenges, given the complex nature of legal procedures across different jurisdictions (Alanazi, 2022).

## 7.2 Solutions or Mitigation Strategies for the Challenges Mentioned Above

Addressing the challenges of using machine learning (ML) in healthcare requires a comprehensive approach. Here are some ways to tackle these challenges:

High-Quality Data Management:

- Standardise data formats and protocols for collecting, storing, and sharing healthcare data.
- Regularly check data quality to correct errors and ensure accuracy.
- Protect patient information using encryption and access controls.

Data Processing and ML Pipeline Development:

- Develop automated pipelines to clean and prepare healthcare data for ML model training.
- Invest in scalable computing resources to handle large healthcare datasets.
- Monitor ML model performance to maintain accuracy over time.

Data Governance and Regulatory Compliance:

- Form teams with diverse expertise to oversee data governance and compliance efforts.
- Follow ethical guidelines and protocols for handling patient data to ensure privacy and autonomy.
- Stay informed about legal requirements and communicate with regulatory authorities.

Interpretability and Explainability of ML Models:

- Use ML algorithms and model architectures that provide clear explanations for predictions.
- Employ techniques to explain model decisions, such as feature importance analysis and Shape values.

Legal and Liability Considerations:

- Assess and mitigate legal and liability risks associated with ML-based healthcare predictions.
- Ensure transparency and obtain patient consent for using their data in ML applications.

By implementing these strategies, stakeholders can overcome the challenges of using ML in healthcare and effectively integrate these technologies into clinical practice responsibly.

## 8. CASE STUDY

### 8.1 Leveraging Clustering and Unsupervised Learning in Healthcare: A Case Study

**Introduction:** In the healthcare sector, the substantial volumes of data originating from electronic health records, medical imaging, wearable devices, and genetic testing present both challenges and opportunities. Clustering and unsupervised learning methods offer a strong way to extract useful insights from these vast datasets. This helps healthcare providers improve patient care, allocate resources better, and make operations more efficient. This case study explores how a fictional healthcare company, "HealthCare Innovations (HCI)," uses clustering and unsupervised learning to address key challenges and drive innovation in healthcare delivery.

Problem Statement:

HCI, a large healthcare network comprising hospitals, clinics, and research centres, faces several important challenges, including:

- Identifying groups of patients with similar clinical characteristics and risk profiles to customise treatment plans and interventions.
- Optimising resource allocation and scheduling across different healthcare facilities to ensure efficient use of resources.
- Discovering patterns and trends in population health records to strengthen preventive care initiatives and strategies for managing diseases.
- Improving the accuracy and effectiveness of interpreting medical images for diagnosing and planning treatments.

Solution:

HCI implements a comprehensive data-driven approach by using clustering and unsupervised learning methods to address the challenges mentioned earlier:

- Patient Segmentation: HCI uses clustering techniques like k-means or hierarchical clustering on electronic health record (EHR) data to identify distinct groups of patients based on factors such as demographics, medical histories, lab results, and lifestyle. This helps HCI tailor treatment plans, predict disease progression, and assess risks more effectively by grouping patients with similar characteristics.
- Resource Allocation and Capacity Planning: HCI analyses patient admission trends, bed occupancy rates, and procedure scheduling data across its facilities using clustering algorithms. By clustering healthcare facilities based on patient demographics, disease prevalence, and service usage patterns, HCI optimises resource allocation, staffing levels, and facility expansion plans to meet the diverse healthcare needs of the population.
- Population Health Management: HCI uncovers hidden patterns and connections in population health data from sources like health surveys, environmental factors, and Utilising unsupervised learning techniques like principal component analysis (PCA) and t-distributed stochastic neighbour embedding (t-SNE) to analyse socioeconomic indicators.By clustering individuals based on health habits, genetic factors, and environmental exposures, HCI gains insights into disease origins, identifies at-risk populations, and develops targeted interventions to promote well-being and prevent chronic diseases.
- Medical Image Analysis: HCI applies unsupervised learning techniques like clustering and dimensionality reduction to analyse medical imaging data, including MRI scans, CT scans, and histopathology images. By grouping similar image patterns and extracting key features, HCI enhances the accuracy of image interpretation, facilitates automated diagnosis, and assists radiologists and pathologists in decision-making processes.

## 8.2 Results and Benefits

By using clustering and unsupervised learning in healthcare, HCI achieves the following outcomes:

- Personalised patient care: Creating customised treatment plans and interventions by segmenting patients based on their characteristics.
- Improved operations: Efficiently distributing resources and planning capacities across healthcare facilities.

- Proactive healthcare: Early detection of disease risks and implementation of targeted preventive measures.
- Enhanced diagnosis: Improved analysis of medical images and decision support for diagnostic processes.
- Financial savings: Reduced healthcare costs through better resource management and preventive healthcare measures.

## 8.3 Conclusion

Using clustering and unsupervised learning techniques gives healthcare organisations like HCI valuable tools to extract important insights from complex healthcare data, leading to better patient outcomes and operational effectiveness. By employing these methods, HCI demonstrates its commitment to innovation, data-driven decision-making, and providing high-quality, personalised healthcare to its patients.

## 9. CONCLUSION

In conclusion, this assessment highlights the important impact and promising potential of clustering and unsupervised learning in healthcare. These methods, which include patient grouping, population health analysis, and medical image interpretation, offer vital insights for customising care, maximising resources, and treating diseases. Despite facing challenges, the ongoing advancement and adoption of these approaches are crucial for transforming healthcare delivery, leading to improved patient outcomes and operational efficiency.

## REFERENCES

Alanazi, A. (2022). Using machine learning for healthcare challenges and opportunities. *Informatics in Medicine Unlocked, 30*. doi:10.1016/j.imu.2022.100924

Alexander, N., Alexander, D. C., Barkhof, F., & Denaxas, S. (2021, December 8). Identifying and evaluating clinical subtypes of Alzheimer's disease in care electronic health records using unsupervised machine learning. *BMC Medical Informatics and Decision Making, 21*(1), 343. doi:10.1186/s12911-021-01693-6 PMID:34879829

Behura, A. (2021). The Cluster Analysis and Feature Selection: Perspective of Machine Learning and Image Processing. In R. Satpathy, T. Choudhury, S. Satpathy, S. N. Mohanty, & X. Zhang (Eds.), *Data Analytics in Bioinformatics*. doi:10.1002/9781119785620.ch10

Bhatt, H. (2023). *Artificial neural network-driven federated learning for heart stroke prediction in healthcare 4.0 underlying 5G*. IEEE. doi:10.1002/cpe.7911

Chauhan, T., Rawat, S., Malik, S., & Singh, P. (2021). *Supervised and Unsupervised Machine Learning based Review on Diabetes Care*. 2021 7th International Conference on Advanced Computing and Communication Systems (ICACCS), Coimbatore, India. 10.1109/ICACCS51430.2021.9442021

El-Alfy, E.-S. M., & Mohammed, S. A. (2020). A review of machine learning for big data analytics: Bibliometric approach. *Technology Analysis and Strategic Management, 32*(8), 984–1005. doi:10.1080/09537325.2020.1732912

Greene, D., Cunningham, P., & Mayer, R. (2008). Unsupervised Learning and Clustering. In M. Cord & P. Cunningham (Eds.), *Machine Learning Techniques for Multimedia. Cognitive Technologies*. Springer. doi:10.1007/978-3-540-75171-7_3

Hosny, M. , & Elhenawy, I. (2021). Scalable Clustering Algorithms for Big Data: A Review. *IEEE Access : Practical Innovations, Open Solutions, 9*, 80015–80027. doi:10.1109/ACCESS.2021.3084057

Javaid, M., Haleem, A., Singh, R. P., Suman, R., & Rab, S. (2022). Significance of machine learning in healthcare: Features, pillars and applications. *International Journal of Intelligent Networks, 3*. doi:10.1016/j.ijin.2022.05.002

Karesiddaiah, K & Savarimuthu, N. (2021). Clustering based imputation algorithm using unsupervised neural network for enhancing the quality of healthcare data. *Journal of Ambient Intelligence and Humanized Computing, 12*. . doi:10.1007/s12652-020-02250-1

Khalid, S. & Prieto-Alhambra, D. (2019). Machine Learning for Feature Selection and Cluster Analysis in Drug Utilisation Research. *Current Epidemiology Reports, 6*. . doi:10.1007/s40471-019-00211-7

Kumari, A., Kakkar, R., Tanwar, S., Garg, D., Polkowski, Z., Alqahtani, F., & Tolba, A. (2024). Multi-agent-based decentralized residential energy management using Deep Reinforcement Learning. *Journal of Building Engineering*. doi:10.1016/j.jobe.2024.109031

Kumari, A., Patel, M. M., Shukla, A., Tanwar, S., Kumar, N., & Rodrigues, J. J. P. C. (2020). *ArMor: A Data Analytics Scheme to identify malicious behaviors on Blockchain-based Smart Grid System*. GLOBECOM 2020 - 2020 IEEE Global Communications Conference, Taipei, Taiwan. 10.1109/GLOBECOM42002.2020.9348061

Kumari, A., & Tanwar, S. (2021). *Reveal: An AI-based Big Data Analytics Scheme for Energy Price Prediction and Load Reduction*. 2021 11th International Conference on Cloud Computing, Data Science & Engineering (Confluence), Noida, India. 10.1109/Confluence51648.2021.9377144

Kumari, A., & Tanwar, S. (2021). Al-based Peak Load Reduction Approach for Residential Buildings using Reinforcement Learning. *2021 International Conference on Computing, Communication, and Intelligent Systems (ICCCIS)*, Greater Noida, India. 10.1109/ICCCIS51004.2021.9397241

Madhavakanna, S. (2018). Application Of Machine Learning Techniques, Big Data Analytics In *Health-Care Sector – A Literature Survey*. IEEE. . doi:10.1109/I-SMAC.2018.8653654

Mahmud, M., Huang, J., Salloum, S., Emara, T., & Sadatdiynov, K. (2020). A survey of data partitioning and sampling methods to support big data analysis. *Big Data Mining and Analytics, 3*(2). . doi:10.26599/BDMA.2019.9020015

Maurya, N., Kumar, N., & Maurya, V. (2020). A review on machine learning (feature selection, classification and clustering) approaches of big data mining in different area of research. *Journal of Critical Reviews., 7*, 2610–2626. doi:10.31838/jcr.07.19.322

Mehedi Hassan, M. (2022). An unsupervised cluster-based feature grouping model for early diabetes detection. *Healthcare Analytics*, (2). doi:10.1016/j.health.2022.100112

Naeem, S., Ali, A., Anam, S., & Ahmed, M. (2023). An Unsupervised Machine Learning Algorithms: Comprehensive Review. *IJCDS Journal.*, *13*(1), 911–921. doi:10.12785/ijcds/130172

Nti, I., Quarcoo, J., Aning, J., & Fosu, G. (2022). A mini-review of machine learning in big data analytics: Applications, challenges, and prospects. *Big Data Mining and Analytics, 5*(2). doi:10.26599/BDMA.2021.9020028

Pereira, J., & Silveira, M. (2019). Learning Representations from Healthcare Time Series Data for Unsupervised Anomaly Detection. *2019 IEEE International Conference on Big Data and Smart Computing (BigComp)*, Kyoto, Japan. 10.1109/BIGCOMP.2019.8679157

Sinaga, K. P., & Yang, M.-S. (2020). Unsupervised K-Means Clustering Algorithm. *IEEE Access : Practical Innovations, Open Solutions*, 8, 80716–80727. doi:10.1109/ACCESS.2020.2988796

Wang, Y., Zhao, Y., & Terry, M. (2020). Unsupervised machine learning for the discovery of latent disease clusters and patient subgroups using electronic health records. *Journal of Biomedical Informatics, 102*. doi:10.1016/j.jbi.2019.103364

Yang, W.-C., Lai, J.-P., Liu, Y.-H., Lin, Y.-L., Hou, H.-P., & Pai, P.-F. (2024). Using Medical Data and Clustering Techniques for a Smart Healthcare System. *Electronics (Basel), 13*(1), 140. doi:10.3390/electronics13010140

# Chapter 6
# AI in Healthcare:
## Transformative Predictive Analytics With ML and DL

**Upinder Kaur**

ⓘD https://orcid.org/0000-0003-4560-8370
*Akal University, India*

**Harsh Kumar**
*Akal University, India*

**Ranbir Kaur**
*Akal University, India*

## ABSTRACT

*The emerging technologies are revolutionizing predictive analytics in HealthCare domain. The research in this sector has made great strides in managing disease management, which has eventually resulted in the saving of lives. The report significantly provides the progress of sophisticated learning methods capable of deciphering complex data relationships, thereby transforming broad datasets into actionable insights for disease diagnosis and prognosis. This goal is to assess the scope of ML and DL in healthcare predictions, focusing on the urgent need for reliable, accurate, and timely predictions while addressing ethical challenges. The authors provide a summary of the approaches worked under predictive analytics in healthcare, emphasizing its lifesaving potential through better decision-making through identifying barriers, suggestions, and future pathways.*

## 1. INTRODUCTION

The healthcare system shows continuous development for human beings, reflected in the progressive or regressive development of health. That reflects the present unpredictability, and regrettably, many people suffer from significant health complications as a result of delayed disease discovery. There are chronic diseases in the liver, kidney, and cardiovascular systems, which impact over 50 million people

DOI: 10.4018/979-8-3693-3609-0.ch006

worldwide. The early diagnosis of these can prevent them from progressing. Thus, timely disease detection is of the utmost significance.

The trends studied currently seem to have a substantial rise in complete consideration for the deployment of algorithms using these for the prediction of several diseases. Through examination of diverse data sources, these approaches can learn patterns and gather early signs of disease for prediction. This will support future healthcare, where financial limitations or hectic schedules may prevent individuals from easily accessing healthcare. This becomes even more critical. With healthcare data being created every day from all sorts of different sources, predictive analytics models have become increasingly important in the medical field. Although there is a growing amount of complicated data accessible, conventional techniques of storing and evaluating it are becoming more and more insufficient.

To generate a solution that can be used to predict diagnosis in medicine, evidence-based categorization of diseases needs to be synthesized into useful conclusions. Further in-depth review of every individual patient's data with characteristics must be conducted for identifying diseases and minimal errors in potential serious diseases. The current research reveals about the significant changes in the healthcare industry 4.0 w.r.t. the precision medicine, early diagnostic, accuracy in disease predication, robotic surgery, promote health and personal well-being. The availability computerized based system to integrate all Electronic Health Records (HER) to maintain, which digitizes medical records and maintain patient history. Patient data may now be efficiently captured, stored, retrieved, and analyzed, which improves healthcare delivery and decision-making.It's evident from the ML and DL based approaches(Saber et al., 2019)that it will be emerged as powerful tools for analyzing healthcare records. The data sources such as genomics, environment, social media, and patient medical records data are available to enhance various aspects of healthcare with precise prediction, diagnostics, treatment, and clinical workflow. Figure 1 highlights the different aspects of AI in healthcare

## 1.1 Motivation

The emergence of artificial intelligence (AI) in all domains of healthcare will revolutionise the healthcare 4.0. AI is now an indispensable tool in this, as it has more data can be analyzed, trends can be found, and competent judgments can be made. Through the field of predictive analysis, multiple aspects of AI use ML and DL approaches for predicting medical consequences and take pre-emptive actions during inpatient treatment. Further, accurate prediction is significant for early disease prediction; prompt action has a great impact on treatment outcomes and enhances patient prognosis. Thus, AI-driven prediction models play a crucial role in precision-based treatment plans for patients.

## 1.2 Chapter Contributions

- Our chapter covers the thorough work of literature available from 2019 to 2024 that examines all innovative research, current development, and deployment of ML and DL in healthcare predictive analysis.
- Further, deep analysis provides a comparative study with significant improvements using machine learning to overcome challenges in the existing healthcare domain. In a similar vein, our analysis of deep learning methodologies illuminates their sophisticated potential in analyzing intricate medical data and revealing complex patterns.

*Figure 1. Extensive factors influencing healthcare data*

- Notwithstanding the advancements made, the pathway of predictive analysis in the healthcare sector is replete with a variety of challenges. Some critical concerns linked to attention include data privacy, model transparency, and the necessity for rigorous validation mechanisms.
- This chapter presents an exhaustive examination of the methods and obstacles involved with healthcare prediction.

## 1.3 Chapter Organisation

Our chapter concludes with a comprehensive summary of AI and its achievements in the healthcare domain, challenges, and prospects as they have transformed predictive analysis in healthcare. Section 2 covers the background part; Next Sectionexplores all applications of AI based approaches in predictive healthcare, highlights capacity of these technologies to revolutionize the healthcare system, and also helps in enabling the development of precise predictive methods and individualized remediation approaches. Section 4 provides predictive healthcare analytics with recent research in this domain; Section 5 covers the open issues and challenges; and the last section concludes.

## 2. LITERATURE REVIEW

The substantial financial commitment towards research and the creation of cutting-edge technologies was concentrated on the domains of ML and DL-based techniques (Yoon & Li, 2019)Individual health impact forecasting reflects a growing interest in leveraging predictive analytics to enhance health coverage. Systems for clinical prognosis have proven useful in helping clinicians identify and treat patients who are more likely to acquire serious diseases. These models assess a variety of parameters specific to each patient to deliver individualized insights and aid therapeutic decision-making.

*Figure 2. AI, ML, DL*

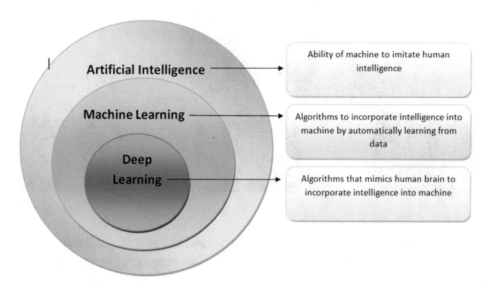

Although artificial intelligence (AI) is a system's ability to comprehend information and use computers and technology to help humans make decisions, solve problems, and innovate. Deep learning is concerned with artificial neural networks based on the structure and function of human brains, whereas machine learning is concerned with methods that allow computers that have not been explicitly programmed to make predictions or judgments to learn from data.Figure 2 shows that AI encompasses both deep learning and machine learning, emphasizing their critical role in leveraging data to produce insights and breakthroughs in healthcare. These strategies let healthcare practitioners use large volumes of data to create more accurate prediction models, resulting in better patient outcomes and more effective treatments. Figure 2. Shows the different domain of AI.

## 3. MACHINE LEARNING APPROACHES

ML approaches such as in (Uspenskaya-Cadoz et al., 2019)(Fung et al., 2021)(Miller, 2020),develop algorithms and models that enable computers to make predictions and learn from data., as in (Boudreaux et al., 2021) or decisions without being explicitly programmed. Essentially, techniques for machine learning empower systems to discover patterns in data and utilize those patterns to make educated judgments or predictions(Vimont et al., 2022). Figure 3 shows the different ML approaches.

The machine learning process generally comprises the subsequent stages:

1.  **Data Gathering-** Gathering pertinent data that imparts an understanding of the problem domain or task at hand constitutes the first step in machine learning. The aforementioned data may be derived from an assortment of origins, such as written documents, databases, and sensors.

*Figure 3. Different techniques in ML*

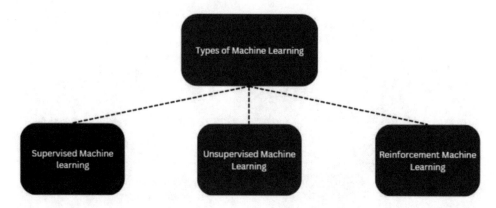

2. **Data Cleaning/Pre-processing:** After information is obtained, it must usually be compiled to ensure that it is in an adequate organization of data. This entails procedures like data cleansing, handling missing information, and formatting the data to be compatible with learning algorithms.

3. **Feature Selection/Engineering:** Frequently, the learning job does not require the examination of every feature (or variable) in the dataset. Feature selection is the process of determining which qualities are most relevant to improving the model's prediction capacity. To improve the model's performance, new features may need to be created from existing ones as part of feature engineering.

4. **Model Making/Evaluation:** The model to predict gets familiarized with the information being processed at this phase. Through the period of training, the computerized model attains knowledge about the patterns and correlations in the dataset, allowing it to create predictions or draw conclusions. Further, the training and evaluation phase will be conducted to assess the performance. The evaluation matrices measure will confirm the correctness of any model.

5. **Model Deployment:** Once the model passes the evaluation phase, the model may be used to generate predictions or judgments using novel, unknown data if its performance is deemed satisfactory. To identify the goal of generating information as well as automating the process of making decisions, the model may require to be seamlessly integrated with pre-existing systems or applications during deployment.

The ML approaches are categorized into following:

## 3.1 Supervised Machine Learning

This approach supports that each data point in the dataset has a label or result that is used to train the algorithm. Excellently it helps in mapping between input and output labels to learn the features, that supervised learning aims to discover so that the model can generate predictions on fresh, unseen data.

### 3.1.1 Linear Regression

As presented in (Oyeleye et al., 2022)(Mullie et al., 2024), this approach is a statistical method to focus on predictive analyses. Determining all the dependent variables (Y) with a limit by utilizing the inde-

*Figure 4. Linear regression*

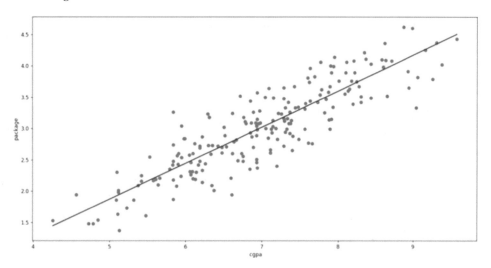

pendent variable (X). Y is termed as mX + c, here c provides the intercept and m for the slope and helps in generating a connection between X and Y. Any change in the dependent parameter (X) is reflected with this equation, providing the correlation between the two (Y). Employing certain regularization techniques can also aid in preventing overfitting. For conducting linear regression analysis on datasets of diverse sizes and intricacies, these tools provide adaptability and usefulness. Further in Figure 4, an presented the instance between the X and Ycorrelation variables, respectively, with green representing arbitrary deviations and red representing the real data.

### 3.1.2 Logistic Regression

The authors in (Johnston et al., 2019)(Bae et al., 2022)(Munjal et al., 2023), presented the statistical method for the examination of the coordination between these variables. This logistic curve is fitted on the data to determine the occurrence of an event. This uses dependent variables with binary values of 0 or 1, having variables like true or false or yes or no, respectively. To Predict categorical variables and resolve classification difficulties frequently employ this technique.Although logistic regression has advantages such as elucidating linear associations between dependent and independent variables and a comprehensive method to predict, it is not without its constraints. The results patterns shows in Figure 5.

### 3.1.3 Decision Tree Approach (DT)

The DT approaches presented in articles (Ed-daoudy&Maalmi, 2020)(Toth et al., 2021)(M. Hung et al., 2019) are predominantly employed for classification objectives as a supervised learning approach. The operational mechanism involves the evaluation of attribute values in ascending or descending order. Functioning as a tree-based strategy, the DT(Ed-daoudy&Maalmi, 2020)establishes a logical decision at the leaf node after delineating each pathway beginning by employing a data-separating sequence at the root. DT provides a fundamentally hierarchical depiction of information exchanges through the use of links and nodes. Figure 6 presents an instance of a DT.Although DTs are useful, they are not without

*Figure 5. Logistic regression*

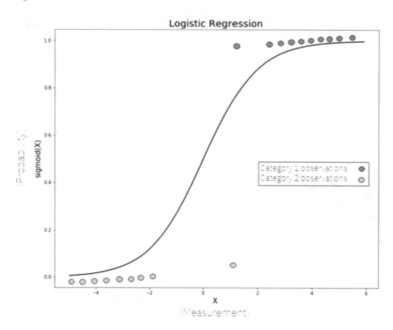

their limitations. These encompass a heightened level of intricacy with the expansion of the category count, vulnerability to minor adjustments resulting in changes to the architecture, and an extended duration of processing time needed for the training data. Python (Scikit-Learn), Weka, RStudio, Orange, and KNIME are often employed as implementation tools for DT.

### 3.1.4 Random Forest Approaches (RF)

RF(Alshakhs et al., 2020)(Alajmani& Jambi, 2020)(M. Hung et al., 2019) is suited for both regression and classification based problems, renowned for its dependably precise outcomes. An ensemble of decision trees (DTs) is constructed and their outputs are aggregated in this procedure. Utilizing the aggregate predictions of a forest of DTs, the RF classifier improves accuracy through the generation of a collection of DTs. Each DT in the RF(Iqbal et al., 2023)supports the best decision-making process by being trained using estimates and a subset of the dataset. RF creates numerous random trees from each group of features extracted at random from the input; the final output is the result of combining the outputs of all DTs.FINE-TAITING RF models require the employment of two critical parameters: "ntree," which sets the number of trees constituting the model, and "mtry," which governs theoverall quantity ofrandomly picked features included in each split. A trade-off is there with the "mtry" parameter: as its value increases, so does the correlation between trees; but, this also improves the accuracy of individual trees. Figure 7 presented example of Random Forest.RF(Irshad et al., 2023)generates predictions and constructs models using annotated datasets, which are subsequently applied to unannotated data for classification. A variance-controlled DT is constructed by combining bagging and random feature selection. In addition, overfitting issues that are frequently seen with single DTs are mitigated, and missing values are handled. Roughly (RF) processes extensive datasets; yet, its ensemble architecture necessitates substantial processing resources and training work.

*Figure 6. Decision tree*

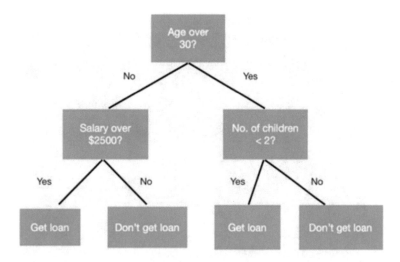

## 3.1.5 Support Vector Machines (SVMs)

In SVM machines, the go-to method for classification and regression is used (Sambyal et al., 2020)(Se-lya et al., 2021). As seen in Figure 8, SVM is a linear model that can handle both linear and nonlinear problems. Its basic idea is based on margin calculation, which involves segmenting the information to find correlations between different parts. Support vector machines (SVMs) try to find decision boundaries, or hyperplanes, that efficiently divide the data into classes. They do this by focusing on reducing structural risk. You can see the decision boundary that the support vectors represent at the intersections of the two classes.

*Figure 7. Random forest*

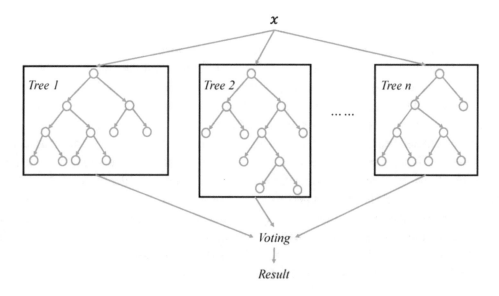

*Figure 8. Example of support vector machine approach*

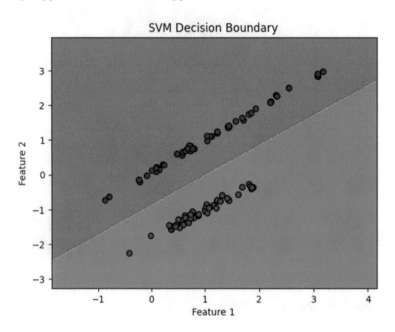

Support vector machines (SVMs) provide a range of benefits, including being able to process both structured and unstructured input and being able to handle complicated issues with the right functionality. Furthermore, SVM shows reduced allocation risk when generalizing and does an excellent job with high-dimensional data. Choosing the right kernel function isn't always easy, and training time goes up dramatically with big datasets. Furthermore, noisy data might impair SVM's performance.Popular support vector machine implementations include frameworks like SVMlight for C and LibSVM for Python, as well as SAS, Weka, Kernlab, Scikit-Learn, MATLAB, and Ruby.

### 3.1.6 K-Nearest Neighbour Approach (KNN)

In article (Sambyal et al., 2020)a "lazy learning" method called KNN presented falls under the category of non-parametric learning. It applies to the resolution of categorization issues. Figure 9 shows how K-Nearest Neighbors (KNN) calculates the distances between new test data points and nearby training data points to forecast the target label of a dataset, with a user-defined parameter K taken into account. Employing all labels of the training points in the problem, this approach specifies the classification label of the examined data point. Figure 9 presented the instance of KNN

Kis usually calculated from the dataset size using the formula k=n, where n is the dataset size. KNN has several benefits. When working with big training datasets, it shines. Users may provide properties and distance functions, making it both versatile and easy to implement. Identifying the ideal value for K could significantly impact the model's performance. Furthermore, it might be a difficult endeavor to ascertain the most effective distance function for a given dataset. In addition, because distances between every training data point must be computed, the computational expense of KNN may be rather large.In addition to software packages like WEKA, R, KNIME, and Orange, well-known implementation tools for KNN consist of Python libraries like Scikit-Learn.

*Figure 9. K-nearest neighbour*

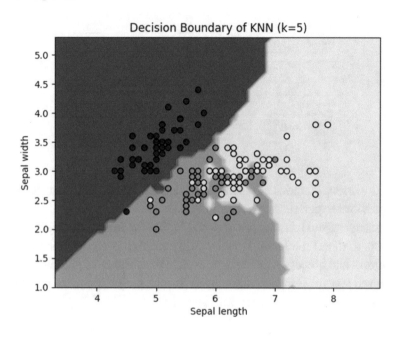

### 3.1.7 Naive Bayes

Naive Bayes (NB)(Sambyal et al., 2020)(Venkatesh et al., 2019)is established with minimal parameter estimation, which renders it especially well-suited for processing huge datasets, and is based on the probabilistic model of Bayes' theorem. NB executes classification in a solitary iteration through the data, promoting ease of implementation, and evaluating the extent of class membership due to defined class assignments. The foundational principle behind the NB classifier is feature independence, which asserts that adding one feature to a class does not affect adding any other features to the class. Text categorization jobs frequently implement this approach.

Notably, NB is suitable for addressing multi-class prediction problems without introducing the impact of extraneous features, is simple to implement, and may produce excellent results with minimal training data. Furthermore, it is capable of processing both continuous and discrete data types. NB, meanwhile, possesses several disadvantages. The implementation may face challenges related to zero-frequency difficulties and may not consistently adhere to the assumption of feature independence in real-world situations. Furthermore, NB does not regularly exhibit a high level of predictive accuracy.Python based as implementation tools used for NB.

## 3.2 Unsupervised Machine Learning

Supervised learning is dependent on accurate responses and external instructors to propel the learning process, but unsupervised learning occurs distinctly. Conversely, this capability allows robots to independently identify intricate patterns and processes inside data, devoid of predetermined goals or annotated instances. In circumstances where preset categories or labels are absent from the data and specialists lack prior information regarding which insights to derive, this methodology proves advanta-

*Figure 10. A sample of the systematic flow of Learning by unsupervised machines*

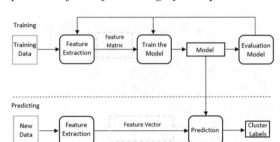

geous. Unsupervised learning empowers machines to deduce real-valued patterns and forecast events by capitalizing on previous experiences, as seen in Figure 10.

Supervised and unsupervised learning are opposed in that the former depends on accurate responses or external instructors to direct the latter. However, this capability empowers robots to independently identify intricate patterns and processes inside data, even in the absence of predetermined goals or labeled instances. Unsupervised learning empowers robots to deduce pragmatic patterns and forecast events by capitalizing on previous experiences, as seen in Figure 10.

### 3.2.1 K-Means Clustering Algorithm

In this algorithm, the most extensive adoption of unlabelled data experience and expertise to address clustering constraints. A predetermined number of clusters, commonly represented as k-sets, is utilized to classify a given dataset using this method. Precondition 1 delineates the pseudocode of the K-means method in Figure 11.

When dealing with scenarios involving huge datasets, K-means is particularly advantageous because of its processing efficiency. When employing a lower value of k, it often generates clusters that are more compact when compared to hierarchical techniques. Moreover, the ease of implementing and interpreting assembly results is a notable attribute of K-means.

*Figure 11. Pseudocode1: K-Means pseudocode*

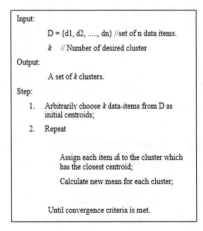

*Figure 12. Pre-processing and post-PCA data visualization*

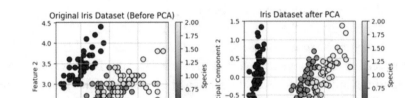

Despite this, K-means is not without its limitations. Determining the best value of k is a significant obstacle. Additionally, it should be noted that the performance of the method may be influenced by the variety of final cluster configurations that result from certain initializations. Local point optimization is a forte of K-means; yet, convergence to the globally optimal solution may not be guaranteed. The obtained results with the lowest J values will be chosen after the algorithm executed various epochs with varying initializations of k values (typically 20 to 100 times) to resolve this.

## 3.2.2 Principal Component Analysis Approach (PCA)

In this PCA, a significant approach for data analysis and providing direction for extracting patterns from dataset with reduce dimensionality. This handles data sizes through the preservation of useful features while minimizing loss of featured data, and generates streamlining summary from this datasets. Before the use of classification models, PCA is typically used to decrease data dimensionality. Furthermore, in the realm of data visualization, trend or behavior identification, and data quantity reduction, regularly deployed unsupervised procedures like clustering and dimensionality reduction strategies.

Primary Component Analysis (PCA) functions by reducing the dimension of multidimensional data, usually by converting two-dimensional data to one-dimensional space. As a result of this transformation, principal components (PC) are produced as new orthogonal variables. Data dimension reduction (PCA) enables computations to be executed more efficiently and effortlessly. An instance of PCA in action is a two-axis graph depicting a two-dimensional dataset. This graph serves to explain the functioning of PCA. This data is effectively reduced in dimension by the use of PCA, which converts it to a one-dimensional representation. Figure 12 provides a graphic representation of this process.

## 3.2.3 Apriori

Influential in the field of data mining is the Apriori approach, proposed by R. Agrawal et al. The operational mechanism of this system is predicated on the production of filters from repeated sets of components. This technique leverages an iterative process known as level-wise search to generate a collection of filter element dimensions (k+1) from prevalent k-item sets.The Apriori algorithm's initial scan of the dataset for frequently occurring single items yields items that satisfy a minimal support threshold, which make up the set L1. The process continues until no further frequent k-item sets are identified, after which L1 is utilized to produce L2, which is then utilized to locate L3. Each iteration identifies the common item sets through a comprehensive scan of the whole dataset.

The Apriori algorithm optimizes the utilization of the Apriori property. Efficiency can be enhanced by guaranteeing that every quasi-subset of a collection of categorical variables is also frequent. In the iterative process, this feature is employed to decrease the search space. To effectively find common element groups, the algorithm utilizes a two-step methodology that incorporates join and prune operations. Although the Apriori algorithm is uncomplicated, it is not without its constraints. Substantially wasting time is a consequence of the inefficiencies that may ensue from the development of a multitude of candidate sets that comprise duplicated item sets. Furthermore, the method has difficulties when confronted with sizable item sets or low minimum support criteria; it frequently requires several iterations of data mining, which results in the incorporation of extraneous items.

## 3.3 Reinforcement Machine Learning

Reinforcement learning (RL)(Jayasimha et al., 2020), the objective model differentiates it from supervised and unsupervised learning. Agents choose behaviors that change the environment and receive positive or negative numerical rewards. It is the agent's objective to maximize accumulated payouts. RL tasks are detailed environment specifications that create rewards.The Q learning and Monte Carlo Tree approach (MCT) methods are popular reinforcement learning techniques. They create a learning environment with repeated interaction and earn reward and penalty feedback, which helps in further strategy refinement. When agents learn from experience and work better afterwards in instances of robotics, gaming, finance, and autonomous vehicle control using RL,.

### 3.3.1 Q-Learning

Q-learning is a dynamic approach to asynchronous model-free reinforcement learning (RL). The actions were refined by iteratively examining the outcomes without domain maps, which allows multiple agents to learn optimum behaviour with Markovian domains. Q-learning is a low-computational incremental dynamic programming approach.. Iterative improvements are made to the evaluation of certain activities in particular states to maximize performance.Technological discoveries have integrated Q-learning with information theory to support applications in image classification, pattern recognition, anomaly detection, and natural language processing. Users' interaction with voice-based systems has also been enhanced through the development of RL frameworks.Q-learning may find reward values in multi-agent contexts because agents interact iteratively. Q-learning might become caught in local minima because agents may take the shortest path without considering other choices.

### 3.3.2 Monte Carlo Tree Approach (MCT)

As presented in (Rasjid, 2021), MCT is a strong sequential selection strategy that balances all exploration and exploitation using a complex tree search strategy. MCTS uses simulations and activity analytics to make wiser judgments in subsequent rounds. The decision-making method is particularly good at examining complicated, tree-like structures where nodes reflect issue configurations and edges indicate state changes.MCTS is linked to discrete-time random control tasks called Markov decision processes (MDP). Markov decision processes with partial observability can be implemented using an extension

*Figure 13. Basic MCTS process*

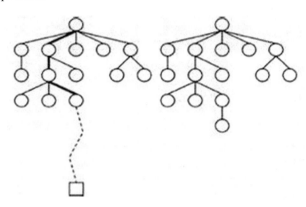

of MCTS (POMDP). By combining MCTS and deep reinforcement learning (RL), Google DeepMind produced AlphaGo.

A simple notion underpins MCTS. Figure 13 shows Tree 1's gradual and uneven construction. In each iteration, the tree policy identifies the important node of the current tree to keep an even keel between fully exploiting. The search tree is supplemented with child nodes and ancestor statistics after a simulation of the selected node. These simulations use a preset strategy, usually uniform random motions. MCTS reduces field knowledge by minimizing intermediate-state evaluation. This capability improves its applicability and efficiency across issue domains.

Table 1, presented a comparative summary of all ML based approaches in healthcare. There are a bunch of MLtechniques for predictive analytics in diagnose several disease issues with different levels of accuracy, model complexity, and data requirements. Naive Bayes and Logistic Regression have low complexity but high interpretability, making them good for heart disease and asthma. It's 99.5% accurate. Support Vector Machines (SVMs) and decision trees are both complex and interpretable. Their accuracy ranges from 65.70% to 89.36% when used to diagnose diabetes and breast cancer. A broader range of diseases has been predicted by high-complexity models, including Random Forest and Neural Networks (NN), with accuracies up to 99.52% but with limited interpretability. 80%–90 percent of the time, linear regression and KnearestNeighbor (KNN) models are accurate for predicting heart disease and blood pressure. In healthcare, balancing accuracy, interpretability, and data availability is key.

## 3.4 Deep Learning

Machine learning (ML) has transformed computer vision, online search, and optical character recognition over the past few decades. ML methods have also advanced human-level AI (AI). Model-based approaches fail to replicate human processing of information, notably in audio and visual.In (Thong Tran et al., 2022), The DL approach is presented, and this hierarchical representation solves the reconfiguration of human speech and production systems. A crucial phase transpired in 2006 when Hinton unveiled the deep belief network, an architecture for deep learning (DBN). Deep learning (DL) has seen significant advancements in classifier performance, especially when confronted with intricate datasets, beyond the capability of traditional learning approaches.

Deep learning, which is built of several nonlinear transformations and consists of algorithms designed for high-level abstractions of data via complicated models. Further feature extraction in unsupervised

*Table 1. Summary of the machine learning approaches in predictive healthcare*

| Approaches | Accuracy | Data Requirement | Interpretability | Diseases | References |
|---|---|---|---|---|---|
| Logistic Regression | 77.8%,74%,99.5% | Low | High | Asthmatic cases, Laparoscopic metabolic surgery,Acute neurological cases, etc. | (Johnston et al., 2019) (Bae et al., 2022) (Munjal et al., 2023) |
| Naive Bayes | 97.12% | Low | Medium | Heart | (Venkatesh et al., 2019) |
| Decision Tree | 84%,89.36% | Medium | High | Dental Care, Diabetes | (M. Hung et al., 2019) (Toth et al., 2021) |
| Random Forest | 92%,81%,91.6%,93.8%,99.52% | High | Low | Heart-related, Dental Care, Diabetes, In child mortality Ratio, HIV cases, Cancer diseases, Lyme, TB, etc. | (M. Hung et al., 2019) (Alshakhs et al., 2020) (Alajmani& Jambi, 2020) (Iqbal et al., 2023) (Irshad et al., 2023) |
| NN | 95% | High | Low | COVID-19 | (Fung et al., 2021) |
| SVM | 65.70% | Medium | Low | Diabetes, Breast Cancer | (Selya et al., 2021) |
| Linear Regression | 80% | Low | High | Heart, BP | (Oyeleye et al., 2022) |

surpasses previous algorithms and its ability to substitute handmade features.Diverse technologies, including machine translation, voice and visual object identification, test automation, and natural language processing (NLP), are spurred ahead by developments facilitated by DL as in (Hasan, 2020). These have surfaced in the last twenty years, each with enormous potential in fields like, natural language processing, Image processing, bioinformatics and speech recognition. DNNs and convolutional neural networks (CNNs) are prevalent DL designs (C.-Y. Hung et al., 2019), models of a convolutional neural network using recurrent convolutional layers and long short-term memory (LSTM) (RCNNs). Figure 14 presented the graph for comparison of ML and DL approaches

## 3.4.1 Convolutional Neural Network (CNN)

The CNN models presented in (Gurupur et al., 2019)(Nair, 2020)(An et al., 2021)are predominantly utilized in computer vision applications and represent a specific sort of neural network design that draws inspiration from the structure of the human visual cortex. CNNs function only as forward-moving information transmission mechanisms, functioning as automated feed-forward neural networks. Face identification, the location of human organs, language analysis, and biological picture recognition are a few of the several sectors in which their value extends.As seen in Figure 15, the fundamental structure of a CNN consists of pattern-accelerated classifiers. In extracting feature levels, each phase of the system receives as input the output from one level and passes it on to the next. A typical CNN(Elbagoury et

*Figure 14. Deep learning effectiveness for data complexity*

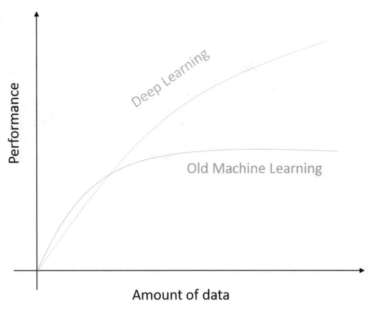

al., 2023)architecture has convolutional, pooling, and classification layers. Each successive layer level is commonly the consequence of the fusion of one or more prior layers.

Convolutional neural networks (CNNs) provide a multitude of benefits, including the integration of abstract information from 2D data, optimization of 2D and 3D image processing structures, and emulation of the human visual processing system. Shape anisotropy is effectively absorbed by CNNs with the incorporation of a max-pooling layer. CNNs that have undergone training using gradient-based learning algorithms are more resistant to the diminishing gradient problem. This is because the gradient-based approach directly optimizes the network weights to minimize the error criterion, thus guaranteeing weights that are highly optimized.

### 3.4.2 Long Short-Term Memory Approach (LSTM)

In the (Nancy, Ravindran, Vincent, et al., 2022)[33], the LSTM approach presented a multiplicative gate architecture and an internal memory that distinguish it as a unique recurrent neural network variation. Since Sepp Hochreiter and Jürgen Schmidhuber first introduced LSTM in 1997, it has undergone numerous configurations and experienced significant development.Several software applications, such as Google Translate, Alexa, Siri, Cortana, and Google Voice Assistant, have been significantly propelled by LSTM. Input, output, and forget gates make the network an RNN implementation with specified node connections. Figure 16 and 17 presented the instance of the LSTM.

The part of the LSTM cell includes:

- xt: This stores the input in vector form at time t.
- ht_1: Hidden state beforext.
- Ct_1: The prior state of memory.

*Figure 15. Architecture of CNN*

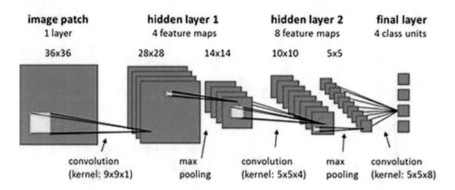

- ht:The present concealed state.
- ct: State of present memory.
- [x]: multiplication.
- [+]: addition.

By efficiently controlling error propagation across numerous time steps, LSTM circumvents the gradient loss issue that plagues conventional RNNs. Comparable to a computer's memory, this is accomplished by including cells with the ability to retain information beyond the recurrent network. A wide range of network topologies utilize LSTM, such as those based on attention and hierarchy, bidirectional, convolutional, grid, cross-modal, and associative processing.

- Bidirectional LSTM(Hong et al., 2020)(Nancy, Ravindran, Raj Vincent, et al., 2022)(Elbagoury et al., 2023) networks enable forward and backward movement of the state vector, allowing the consideration of dependencies in both temporal directions.
- Hierarchical LSTM networks address multidimensional issues through a process of subproblem decomposition, hierarchical organization, and weight adjustment to concentrate on certain subproblems.

*Figure 16. LSTM units*

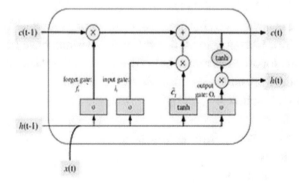

*Figure 17. LSTM*

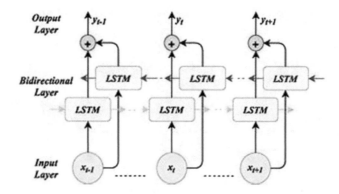

- By incorporating convolutional operations directly into LSTM networks, convolutional LSTM models connections that are both geographically and temporally dispersed with ease.
- By combining encoder and decoder components into the LSTM cell design and compressing and extending the network architecture, LSTM Autoencoder tackles the challenge of high-dimensional parameter prediction.
- Matrixes based on Grid of Long Short-Term Memory (LSTM) units are ideal for storing sequences, vectors, and images. By establishing connections across multiple dimensions, LSTM cells facilitate the extension of information flow.
- Without adding parameter space or computing time, Cross-Modal and Associative LSTMs utilize multiple conventional LSTMs to describe distinct variables, communicating via recursive connections to compute dependencies and generate multimodal predictions.

### 3.4.3 Recurrent Convolution Neural Network

Convolutional Neural Networks (CNNs)(Mayya et al., 2021)have become an essential instrument for tackling a multitude of obstacles in the field of computer vision. In recent years, a significant progression has occurred with the emergence of recurrent convolution neural networks, which are a novel generation of CNNs (RCNNs)(Shashikumar et al., 2021)(Ramkumar et al., 2023). The extensive connections for RCNNs are identified as the inspiration for these RCNNs, composed mostly of recurrent convolutional layers (RCLs), which enable the integration of recurring connections between neurons inside the traditional convolutional layer.Ming Liang and Xiaolin Hu originally introduced the notion of RCNNs, and Figure 18 illustrates its architecture. Local connectivity is demonstrated in this architectural design for both forward and redundant connections, where weights are distributed among single sites. The recurrent multilayer perceptron (RMLP), a technology used in dynamic control, has parallels to the design technique that is discussed here.

The pivotal component of RCNNs is the RCL, which evolved in separate time increments. RCNNs[39] provide major primary benefits. To begin with, these units possess the capability to include background information across a sufficiently vast region inside the present layer. Furthermore, by using weight sharing, recursive connections increase network depth while preserving an equivalent number of modifiable parameters. This is consistent with the current architectural style in CNN, which prioritizes structural

*Figure 18. Architectures of MLP, RNN, and CNN (left to right)*

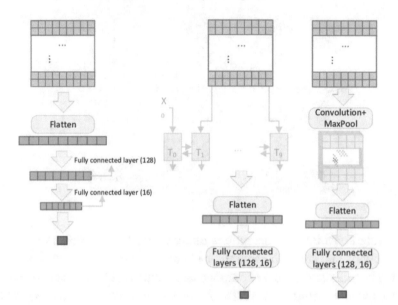

depths with a limited number of parameters. In essence, RCNNs simplify learning processes by introducing the concept of time and converting a CNN into a model with several routes connecting the input and output layers.By integrating longer pathways into RCNNs, it becomes possible to get exceptionally complex features, while shorter paths have the potential to improve gradient backpropagation during the training process.

Table 2, provides details of all existing ML approaches in healthcare. DLmethods have been used to address medical challenges with remarkable accuracy. With 99% accuracy, convolutional neural networks (CNNs) can diagnose retinal diseases, analyze chest X-rays, and interpret biomedical signals. Several RNN variants can process sequential data, like biomedical signals or predicting heart disease, including long-short-term Short-Term Memory (LSTM) and Bidirectional LSTM (Bi-LSTM). Stack ensembles are less common, but they have shown promise. Additionally, ANNs and DNNs have been used to find drugs and detect COVID-19, with ANNs hitting 99.90% accuracy. In fetal imaging during pregnancy, deep convolutional generation adversarial networks (DCGANs) achieved 97.50% accuracy. They're powerful tools for advancing healthcare diagnosis and treatment because of their complexity, data requirements, and generally low interpretability.

## 4. PREDICTIVE HEALTHCARE ANALYTICS

This study is based on scholarly articles and presentations sourced from esteemed academic platforms including IEEE, Springer, Elsevier, Hindawi, Frontiers, Taylor, and MDPI, as well as utilizing search tools like Google Scholar, Scopus, and Science Direct to find pertinent literature. From 2019 to 2024, the study spans Ml, DL, surgery, hepatology, radiology, cardiology, and nephrology. The primary emphasis of our analysis is the based-onML and DL techniques for forecasting in healthcare sector. This includes

*Table 2. Summary of the DL approaches in predictive healthcare*

| Approaches | Accuracy | Data Requirement | Interpretability | Diseases | References |
|---|---|---|---|---|---|
| Stacked Ensemble | 90.17% | High | Low | | (Nambiar Jyothi & Prakash, 2019) |
| CNN | 98.33%, 96.6%, 98%, 99% | High | Low | Retinal disease, chest x-ray, biomedical signal, Chronic diseases | (Gurupur et al., 2019) (Nair, 2020)(An et al., 2021)(Elbagoury et al., 2023) |
| DNN | 87.60% | Medium | Low | drugs | (C.-Y. Hung et al., 2019) |
| ANN | 99.90% | High | Low | COVID-19 | (Hasan, 2020) |
| LSTM | 99%,99% | High | Low | biomedical signal, Chronic diseases | (Elbagoury et al., 2023) (Ramkumar et al., 2023) |
| RNN | 90%,99% | High | Low | dysregulated immune system, Chronic diseases | (Shashikumar et al., 2021)(Yousuff et al., 2024) |
| DCGAN | 97.50% | High | Low | fetus during pregnancy | (Venkatasubramanian, 2022) |
| Bi-LSTM | 98.86% | High | Low | Heart | (Nancy, Ravindran, Vincent, et al., 2022) |

both empirical studies and review articles related to this area. The document provides a summary of the current research initiatives in healthcare forecasting, examining different methodologies, algorithms, evaluation metrics, and tools used in ML and DL applications. We have analyzed the results based on publication types and years, distributed approaches used, and a complete analysis of existing literature in healthcare. The detailed synopsis of the articles is provided in Table 3. The analysis findings are displayed in Figure 19 and 20. This comprehensive overview synthesizes significant advancements in various ML and DL-based techniques within healthcare analytics across a span from 2019 to 2024, emphasizing the evolution of methodologies and their impact on predictive accuracy and healthcare delivery.

Various machine learning methodologies were used in 2019, including stacked ensemble methods, logistic regression, Naive Bayes, and decision trees, including Random Forests. This demonstrated the early commitment to improving predictive modeling for healthcare applications. The efficacy of a stacked ensemble technique in identifying high-risk patients with an increased specificity of 94.90 percent and prediction accuracy of 90.17 percent while utilizing fewer data was emphasized (Nambiar Jyothi & Prakash, 2019). This demonstrates the potential of DL for efficiently managing complex healthcare data. Simultaneously, the investigation into logistic regression and Naive Bayes provided more evidence of machine learning's potential to improve illness prediction rates; the BPA-NB algorithm achieved an impressive 97.12% accuracy (Johnston et al., 2019; Venkatesh et al., 2019). During this time, there was also progress in the creation of healthcare delivery models, including an oral care recommender system that included machine learning. This underscored the importance of policy changes that would lead to enhanced health services (Hung et al., 2019).

As the year 2020 approached, there was a marginal change in attention towards an examination of the extensive ramifications of AI and ML in the healthcare sector, with a specific emphasis on dedicated domains like cardiovascular medicine and ECG modeling. The relevance of data quality, prediction results, and the interpretation of medical imagery (Miller, 2020) has been emphasized in studies that emphasized the need for healthcare practitioners to consult on AI development. A considerable improvement in the accuracy of retinal disease diagnosis (Nair, 2020; Hasan, 2020) marked the beginning of deep learning methods, namely CNN and ANN models, surpassing the performance of conventional approaches. Further demonstrating DL's expanding impact on delivering timely healthcare solutions (Alam et al., 2020) was the use of LSTM networks for early sepsis prediction. Evaluation studies highlighting DL's efficacy in enhancing classification precision and facilitating automated diagnostic procedures (Liu et al., 2020; Mayya et al., 2021) began to strengthen the significance of DL in healthcare analytics by 2021. Deep learning is more accurate and performs better in crucial domains such as sepsis diagnosis (An et al., 2021; Shashikumar et al., 2021), as evidenced by novel methodologies that employ CNN and RNN models. Research has demonstrated the ongoing development and practicality of machine learning approaches in this sector, as seen by the substantial progress made in illness categorization and prediction (Toth et al., 2021; Rasjid, 2021).

The year 2022 witnessed a significant turning point in the expansion of DL and ML applications to encompass more novel domains, such as health economics and mobile health monitoring (Kshirsagar et al., 2021; Thong Tran et al., 2022). The incorporation of technology into routine health management was underscored by the creation of operational systems for mobile monitoring and predictive models for healthcare analytics. Furthermore, the application of ARIMA in the prediction of heart rate and healthcare, costs demonstrated the adaptability and resilience of machine learning models when confronted with a wide range of healthcare issues (Oyeleye et al., 2022; Bae et al., 2022). In 2023 and 2024, the focus on DL applications in healthcare analytics increased, with research looking at the usage of advanced models like CNN, LSTM, and RNN for illness prediction and management. The use of these models to forecast heart disease and control diabetes demonstrated DL's potential for managing complicated health data and supporting proactive healthcare interventions (Ramkumar et al., 2023; Yousuff et al., 2024). During these years, review studies underlined the theoretical implications of ML and DL in healthcare, indicating that these technologies should be explored further to improve healthcare delivery and patient outcomes (Morid et al., 2023; Kim et al., 2023). The shift from core ML approaches to sophisticated DL models demonstrates a rising dependence on AI to handle complex healthcare concerns, with the potential for considerable improvements in patient care and health outcomes.

## Data Analysis and Findings

A) What is the distribution of publication years in the dataset?

B) What are the predominant approaches adopted in the dataset, and how do they contribute to the overall research landscape?

## 5. OPEN ISSUES AND CHALLENGES

- **Data Quality and Availability**: Deep learning models need tons of high-quality, annotated data to work. The sensitive nature of medical information, data silos, and privacy concerns can make it hard to get these datasets in healthcare. Further, different healthcare institutions have different data acquisition methods, which can affect data quality.
- **Model Interpretability:** Many deep learning models, especially complex architectures like CNNs and RNNs, work like "black boxes," making it tough to figure out how they make predic-

*Figure 19. Distribution as per year*

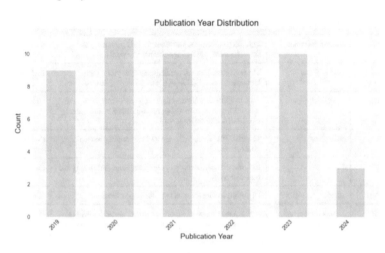

tions. Healthcare is one of the most important industries that lack interpretability since trust and accountability rely heavily on understanding the reasoning behind a diagnosis or treatment.

- **Generalized and Transferability of Dataset:** We have disease-specific datasets and area-specific datasets, the existing models trained on these datasets may not work well for global populations due to differences in demographics, prevalence related to several diseases, and other imaging techniques.Creating a more generated model and applying a transferability approach is difficult in the healthcare domain.

- **Complex Computation**: The data relating to medical and disease-specificand inferring from machine /deep learning models need excellent computational resources. These can be a great concern for deploying in resource-constrained environments, like rural hospitals or developing countries.

- **Ethical Issues:** As in healthcare, the patient data is under privacy concern, topublicize the patient healthcare for learning purposes needs to take careof lots of things, including patient consent, data

*Figure 20. Distribution as per the different approaches*

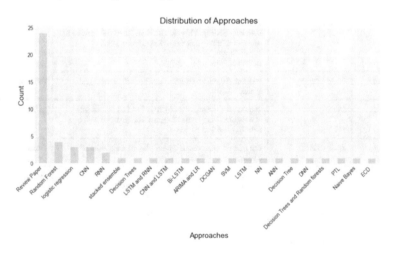

*Table 3. Summary of the research approaches in predictive healthcare analytics*

| Publication Year | Model | Approaches | Finding | References |
|---|---|---|---|---|
| 2019 | DL | stacked ensemble | This method enhances predicting 90.17% (accuracy) and 94.90%(specificity) for high-risk based patients. | (Nambiar Jyothi & Prakash, 2019) |
| 2019 | ML | Review Paper | The review outlines key predictive analytics tools and techniques, analyzing recent trends in their application. | (Saber et al., 2019) |
| 2019 | ML | logistic regression | Applying ML in healthcare data for predictive modeling and supporting patient monitoring, requires future technological infrastructure for real-world use. | (Johnston et al., 2019) |
| 2019 | ML | Naive Bayes | The BPA-NB scheme achieves 97.12% accuracy in predicting disease rates. | (Venkatesh et al., 2019) |
| 2019 | TL | PTL | PTL shows superior accuracy compared to single learning and generic models. | (Yoon & Li, 2019) |
| 2019 | DL | CNN | DLT is 40% more accurate than other approaches | (Gurupur et al., 2019) |
| 2019 | ML | Decision Trees and Random forests | A machine learning-based oral care recommender model is developed, emphasizing policy changes for better oral health delivery. | (M. Hung et al., 2019) |
| 2019 | DL | DNN | Deep multimodal NNs with early fusion achieve superior GI bleeding predictive power over conventional scores. | (C.-Y. Hung et al., 2019) |
| 2019 | ML | Review Paper | The GBT model identifies prodromal AD patients with 80% precision. | (Uspenskaya-Cadoz et al., 2019) |
| 2020 | ML | Review Paper | The study explores AI's impact on cardiovascular medicine, focusing on data quality, predictive outcomes, and medical image interpretation. It stresses the need for healthcare professionals to guide AI development and calls for regulatory standards in clinical AI use. Top of Form Bottom of Form | (Miller, 2020) |
| 2020 | DL | Review Paper | AUPRC, and MCC, the presented study surpasses the existing studies. | (Jayasimha et al., 2020) |
| 2020 | ML | Decision Tree | Results are stored in a Distributed mannerfor real-time analysis, enhancing distributed machine learning. | (Ed-daoudy&Maalmi, 2020) |
| 2020 | DL | Review Paper | Deep learning methods generally outperform traditional approaches in ECG modeling. | (Hong et al., 2020) |
| 2020 | ML | Random Forest | Random Forest with "Both" resampling and cross-validation is deemed the best fit for predictive modeling. | (Alshakhs et al., 2020) |
| 2020 | ML | Review Paper | Statistical and machine learning models for complications like retinopathy are critically reviewed. | (Sambyal et al., 2020) |
| 2020 | DL | CNN | RetoNet, a CNN architecture, excels in detecting retinal ailments from fundus images. | (Nair, 2020) |
| 2020 | DL | ANN | The proposed model surpasses traditional statistical analysis in performance. | (Hasan, 2020) |
| 2020 | ML | Random Forest | The authors compare five methods and prove the probability in diabetic patients. They find Random Forest performs best, while linear discriminant analysis performs worst. Top of Form Bottom of Form | (Alajmani& Jambi, 2020) |
| 2020 | ML | Review Paper | Risk associations and factors identified offer meaningful clinical insights. | (Liu et al., 2020) |
| 2020 | DL | LSTM | The study investigates the efficacy of an LSTM network in early predicting sepsis in a general hospital population following Sepsis-3 criteria. | (Alam et al., 2020) |
| 2021 | DL | Review Paper | The research enhances healthcare classification accuracy to 0.96%. | (Masud et al., 2021) |
| 2021 | DL | Review Paper | The author found that their context-attentive network significantly improves automatic diagnostic code assignment by effectively extracting clinical information from patient discharge summaries. | (Mayya et al., 2021) |
| 2021 | DL | CNN | The simple CNN model achieves high accuracy and performance metrics. | (An et al., 2021) |

| Publication Year | Model | Approaches | Finding | References |
|---|---|---|---|---|
| 2021 | DL | RNN | Automated methods aid in early sepsis detection for timely intervention. | (Shashikumar et al., 2021) |
| 2021 | ML | Review Paper | Different diseases show over 80% accuracy with specific diseases like lung and breast cancer achieving higher accuracy. | (Rasjid, 2021) |
| 2021 | ML | NN | The solution requires minimal training data, beneficial for healthcare where data acquisition is costly. | (Fung et al., 2021) |
| 2021 | ML | Decision Trees | Decision trees effectively classify diabetes with 89.36% accuracy. | (Toth et al., 2021) |
| 2021 | ML | Review Paper | An overview of machine learning in healthcare is provided, along with research directions. | (Boudreaux et al., 2021) |
| 2021 | ML | SVM | Linear-basis SVM outperforms logistic regression in predicting HR. | (Selya et al., 2021) |
| 2021 | ML | Review Paper | XAI ML models exceed actuarial models in predictive accuracy. | (Kshirsagar et al., 2021) |
| 2022 | DL | DCGAN | A practical system for mobile monitoring between MFH is developed. | (Venkatasubramanian, 2022) |
| 2022 | ML | ARIMA and LR | Data analytics techniques improve HR prediction using accelerometers. | (Oyeleye et al., 2022) |
| 2022 | ML | logistic regression | Improved logistic regression models show higher classification accuracy. | (Bae et al., 2022) |
| 2022 | ML | Review Paper | RF model outperforms GLM and NN in predicting healthcare costs. | (Vimont et al., 2022) |
| 2022 | DL | Review Paper | The Edge prediction accuracy is good with the provided method. | (Gutierrez-Torre et al., 2022) |
| 2022 | ML | Review Paper | The model provides educational content and enhances healthcare practices. | (Anandi & Ramesh, 2022) |
| 2022 | ML | Review Paper | The study achieves high accuracy in predicting readmission. | (Mohamed et al., 2022) |
| 2022 | ML | Review Paper | The authors investigate how machine learning (ML) can enhance health economics and outcomes research (HEOR). They identify five areas where ML could improve HEOR and emphasize the importance of transparent ML methods for decision-makers. They develop the PAL-ISADE Checklist to guide transparent ML applications in healthcare analytics. | (Padula et al., 2022) |
| 2022 | DL | Bi-LSTM | A Bi-LSTM intelligent health system reliably forecasts heart disease risk. | (Nancy, Ravindran, Raj Vincent, et al., 2022) |
| 2022 | DL | Review Paper | Deep learning-based techniques aid healthcare analytics. | (Thong Tran et al., 2022) |
| 2023 | ML | logistic regression | Ensemble regressor predicts mortality and morbidity effectively. | (Munjal et al., 2023) |
| 2023 | DL | CNN and LSTM | Extending the GMDH model improves prediction results significantly. | (Elbagoury et al., 2023) |
| 2023 | DL | LSTM and RNN | LSTM and RNN-based smart healthcare systems predict heart diseases accurately. | (Ramkumar et al., 2023) |
| 2023 | ML | Review Paper | The CODA platform is deployed successfully across multiple sites. | (Mullie et al., 2024) |
| 2023 | DL | ECD | Predictive analytics revolutionizes healthcare with improved accuracy. | (Sachdeva, 2023) |
| 2023 | DL | Review Paper | Research on deep learning (DL) implementations using patient time series data is reviewed, research gaps are identified, and prospects are proposed. | (Morid et al., 2023) |
| 2023 | ML | Random Forest | RF classifier efficiently predicts under 5 child mortality. | (Iqbal et al., 2023) |
| 2023 | DL | Review Paper | Future evaluation of the method may involve diagnostics on healthcare big data. | (Shafqat et al., 2023) |
| 2023 | ML | Random Forest | High accuracy and minimal execution time are achieved compared to cutting-edge algorithms. | (Irshad et al., 2023) |
| 2023 | ML | Review Paper | The study discusses theoretical implications in healthcare and big data. | (Kim et al., 2023) |

| Publication Year | Model | Approaches | Finding | References |
|---|---|---|---|---|
| 2024 | ML | Review Paper | The proposed scheduling approach improves profit and patient attendance. | (Kim et al., 2023) |
| 2024 | ML | Review Paper | Preceding affiliations or commercial interests that would have an influence upon that research topic or materials discussed in the article are therefore prohibited. | (Lee, 2024) |
| 2024 | DL | RNN | A novel approach using deep learning algorithms is proposed for diabetes management. | (Yousuff et al., 2024) |

privacy, and algorithmic bias. In some countries like the US and Europe, it's really hard to make sure models are fair, transparent, and compliant with regulations.

- **Data and Workflow:**Further integrating of deep/machine learning approaches into existing healthcare system workflows without disrupting them can be tough.Because technologies need more user-friendly interfaces and seamless integration from professionals in this domain, which means carefully looking at the design and considering the real environment.

- **Cases of rare diseases**: Some rare disease having only 1 to 2 percent of the global population suffers from the dataset availability issues.So, address thisless data availability in rare diseases, NLP techniques will help to analyze and generate meaningful data from unstructuredsources, such as medical literature or patient testimonials. Further, it requires a strategy to establish collaborations with other researchers or healthcare organizations that have similar datasets, allowing for the pooling of data and increased model accuracy.

This is a multidisciplinary approach to solving the above problems, including computer scientists, health care professionals, ethicists, and policymakers. To overcome we need research collaborations and adaptive regulatory frameworks to manage these obstacles and realize the potential of machine/deep learning in healthcare.

## 6. CONCLUSION

This chapter mainly highlights the intense impact of ML and DL techniques for stabilizing predictive analytics in the healthcare industry. Further, the utilization of complex algorithms and computational approaches, ML, and DL have substantially bolstered the ability to accurately forecast and control several diseases, hence indispensable contributions in the progression of healthcare. We highlight the comparative summary of different machine/deep learning approaches in this domain. Further tackles the need for accurate, dependable, and prompt healthcare forecasts while also addressing the ethical dilemmas that are intrinsic to the use of such technology. Moreover, by conducting an extensive analysis of issues and understanding possible future developments, this article argues about the ongoing incorporation of ML and DL in the healthcare sector. We underscore the significance of these technologies in enabling enhanced clinical decision-making in patient care, therefore establishing a foundation for a future in which predictive analytics is heavily utilized to promote public health outcomes. We analyzed and presented the potential issues and gaps in the existing research.

# REFERENCES

Alajmani, S., & Jambi, K. (2020). Assessing Advanced Machine Learning Techniques for Predicting Hospital Readmission. *International Journal of Advanced Computer Science and Applications*, *11*(2), 377–384. doi:10.14569/IJACSA.2020.0110249

Alam, M., Henriksson, A., Valik, J., Ward, L., Naucler, P., & Dalianis, H. (2020). Deep Learning from Heterogeneous Sequences of Sparse Medical Data for Early Prediction of Sepsis. *Proceedings of the 13th International Joint Conference on Biomedical Engineering Systems and Technologies*, (pp. 45–55). ACM. 10.5220/0008911400002513

Alshakhs, F., Alharthi, H., Aslam, N., Khan, I. U., & Elasheri, M. (2020). Predicting Postoperative Length of Stay for Isolated Coronary Artery Bypass Graft Patients Using Machine Learning. *International Journal of General Medicine*, *13*, 751–762. doi:10.2147/IJGM.S250334 PMID:33061545

An, J. Y., Seo, H., Kim, Y.-G., Lee, K. E., Kim, S., & Kong, H.-J. (2021). Codeless Deep Learning of COVID-19 Chest X-Ray Image Dataset with KNIME Analytics Platform. *Healthcare Informatics Research*, *27*(1), 82–91. doi:10.4258/hir.2021.27.1.82 PMID:33611880

Anandi, V., & Ramesh, M. (2022). Descriptive and Predictive Analytics on Electronic Health Records using Machine Learning. *2022 Second International Conference on Advances in Electrical, Computing, Communication and Sustainable Technologies (ICAECT)*, (pp. 1–6). ScitePress. 10.1109/ICAECT54875.2022.9808019

Bae, W. D., Alkobaisi, S., Horak, M., Park, C. S., Kim, S., & Davidson, J. (2022). Predicting Health Risks of Adult Asthmatics Susceptible to Indoor Air Quality Using Improved Logistic and Quantile Regression Models. *Life (Basel, Switzerland)*, *12*(10), 1631. doi:10.3390/life12101631 PMID:36295066

Boudreaux, E. D., Rundensteiner, E., Liu, F. F., Wang, B., Larkin, C., Agu, E., Ghosh, S., Semeter, J., Simon, G., & Davis-Martin, R. E. (2021). Applying Machine Learning Approaches to Suicide Prediction Using Healthcare Data: Overview and Future Directions. *Frontiers in Psychiatry*, *12*, 707916. doi:10.3389/fpsyt.2021.707916 PMID:34413800

Ed-daoudy, A., & Maalmi, K. (2020). Real-time heart disease detection and monitoring system based on fast machine learning using Spark. *Health and Technology*, *10*(5), 1145–1154. doi:10.1007/s12553-020-00460-3

Elbagoury, B. M., Vladareanu, L., Vlădăreanu, V., Salem, A. B., Travediu, A.-M., & Roushdy, M. I. (2023). A Hybrid Stacked CNN and Residual Feedback GMDH-LSTM Deep Learning Model for Stroke Prediction Applied on Mobile AI Smart Hospital Platform. *Sensors (Basel)*, *23*(7), 3500. doi:10.3390/s23073500 PMID:37050561

Fung, D. L. X., Hoi, C. S. H., Leung, C. K., & Zhang, C. Y. (2021). Predictive Analytics of COVID-19 with Neural Networks. *2021 International Joint Conference on Neural Networks (IJCNN)*, 1–8. 10.1109/IJCNN52387.2021.9534188

Gurupur, V. P., Kulkarni, S. A., Liu, X. L., Desai, U., & Nasir, A. (2019). Analysing the power of deep learning techniques over the traditional methods using medicare utilisation and provider data. *Journal of Experimental & Theoretical Artificial Intelligence*, *31*(1), 99–115. doi:10.1080/0952813X.2018.1518999

Gutierrez-Torre, A., Bahadori, K., Baig, S. U. R., Iqbal, W., Vardanega, T., Berral, J. L., & Carrera, D. (2022). Automatic Distributed Deep Learning Using Resource-Constrained Edge Devices. *IEEE Internet of Things Journal, 9*(16), 15018–15029. doi:10.1109/JIOT.2021.3098973

Hasan, N. (2020). A Methodological Approach for Predicting COVID-19 Epidemic Using EEMD-ANN Hybrid Model. *Internet of Things : Engineering Cyber Physical Human Systems, 11*, 100228. doi:10.1016/j.iot.2020.100228 PMID:38620369

Hung, C.-Y., Lin, C.-H., Chang, C.-S., Li, J.-L., & Lee, C.-C. (2019). Predicting Gastrointestinal Bleeding Events from Multimodal In-Hospital Electronic Health Records Using Deep Fusion Networks. *2019 41st Annual International Conference of the IEEE Engineering in Medicine and Biology Society (EMBC),* (pp. 2447–2450). IEEE. 10.1109/EMBC.2019.8857244

Hung, M., Xu, J., Lauren, E., Voss, M. W., Rosales, M. N., Su, W., Ruiz-Negrón, B., He, Y., Li, W., & Licari, F. W. (2019). Development of a recommender system for dental care using machine learning. *SN Applied Sciences, 1*(7), 785. doi:10.1007/s42452-019-0795-7

Jayasimha, A., Gangavarapu, T., Kamath, S. S., & Krishnan, G. S. (2020). Deep Neural Learning for Automated Diagnostic Code Group Prediction Using Unstructured Nursing Notes. *Proceedings of the 7th ACM IKDD CoDS and 25th COMAD,* (pp. 152–160). ACM. 10.1145/3371158.3371176

Johnston, S. S., Morton, J. M., Kalsekar, I., Ammann, E. M., Hsiao, C. W., & Reps, J. (2019). Using Machine Learning Applied to Real-World Healthcare Data for Predictive Analytics: An Applied Example in Bariatric Surgery. *Value in Health, 22*(5), 580–586. doi:10.1016/j.jval.2019.01.011 PMID:31104738

Kim, B., Srinivasan, K., Kong, S. H., Kim, J. H., Shin, C. S., & Ram, S. (2023). ROLEX: A NOVEL METHOD FOR INTERPRETABLE MACHINE LEARNING USING ROBUST LOCAL EXPLANA-TIONS. *Management Information Systems Quarterly, 47*(3), 1303–1332. doi:10.25300/MISQ/2022/17141

Kshirsagar, R., Hsu, L.-Y., Greenberg, C. H., McClelland, M., Mohan, A., Shende, W., Tilmans, N. P., Guo, M., Chheda, A., Trotter, M., Ray, S., & Alvarado, M. (2021). Accurate and Interpretable Machine Learning for Transparent Pricing of Health Insurance Plans. *Proceedings of the AAAI Conference on Artificial Intelligence, 35*(17), 15127–15136. doi:10.1609/aaai.v35i17.17776

Kumari, A., Tanwar, S., Tyagi, S., & Kumar, N. (2018). Fog computing for Healthcare 4.0 environment: Opportunities and challenges. *Computers & Electrical Engineering, 72.* doi:10.1016/j.compeleceng.2018.08.015

Lee, W. C. (2024). Seeing the whole elephant: Integrated advanced data analytics in support of RWE for the development and use of innovative pharmaceuticals. *Expert Review of Pharmacoeconomics & Outcomes Research, 24*(1), 57–62. doi:10.1080/14737167.2023.2275674 PMID:37902993

Liu, B., Li, Y., Ghosh, S., Sun, Z. N., Ng, K., & Hu, J. Y. (2020). Complication Risk Profiling in Diabetes Care: A Bayesian Multi-Task and Feature Relationship Learning Approach. *IEEE Transactions on Knowledge and Data Engineering, 32*(7), 1276–1289. doi:10.1109/TKDE.2019.2904060

Masud, M., Singh, P., Gaba, G. S., Kaur, A., Alroobaea, R., Alrashoud, M., & Alqahtani, S. A. (2021). CROWD: Crow Search and Deep Learning based Feature Extractor for Classification of Parkinson's Disease. *ACM Transactions on Internet Technology, 21*(3), 1–18. doi:10.1145/3418500

Mayya, V., S., S. K., Krishnan, G. S., & Gangavarapu, T. (2021). Multi-channel, convolutional attention based neural model for automated diagnostic coding of unstructured patient discharge summaries. *Future Generation Computer Systems, 118*, 374–391. doi:10.1016/j.future.2021.01.013

Miller, D. D. (2020). Machine Intelligence in Cardiovascular Medicine. *Cardiology, 28*(2), 53–64. doi:10.1097/CRD.0000000000000294 PMID:32022759

Mohamed, I., Fouda, M. M., & Hosny, K. M. (2022). Machine Learning Algorithms for COPD Patients Readmission Prediction: A Data Analytics Approach. *IEEE Access : Practical Innovations, Open Solutions, 10*, 15279–15287. doi:10.1109/ACCESS.2022.3148600

Morid, M. A., Sheng, O. R. L., & Dunbar, J. (2023). Time Series Prediction Using Deep Learning Methods in Healthcare. *ACM Transactions on Management Information Systems, 14*(1), 1–29. Advance online publication. doi:10.1145/3531326

Mullie, L., Afilalo, J., Archambault, P., Bouchakri, R., Brown, K., Buckeridge, D. L., Cavayas, Y. A., Turgeon, A. F., Martineau, D., Lamontagne, F., Lebrasseur, M., Lemieux, R., Li, J., Sauthier, M., St-Onge, P., Tang, A., Witteman, W., & Chassé, M. (2024). CODA: An open-source platform for federated analysis and machine learning on distributed healthcare data. *Journal of the American Medical Informatics Association : JAMIA, 31*(3), 651–665. doi:10.1093/jamia/ocad235 PMID:38128123

Munjal, N. K., Clark, R. S. B., Simon, D. W., Kochanek, P. M., & Horvat, C. M. (2023). Interoperable and explainable machine learning models to predict morbidity and mortality in acute neurological injury in the pediatric intensive care unit: Secondary analysis of the TOPICC study. *Frontiers in Pediatrics, 11*, 1177470. doi:10.3389/fped.2023.1177470 PMID:37456559

Nair, L. R. (2020). RetoNet: A deep learning architecture for automated retinal ailment detection. *Multimedia Tools and Applications, 79*(21–22), 15319–15328. doi:10.1007/s11042-018-7114-y

Nambiar Jyothi, R., & Prakash, G. (2019). *A Deep Learning-Based Stacked Generalization Method to Design Smart Healthcare Solution.*, doi:10.1007/978-981-13-5802-9_20

Nancy, A. A., Ravindran, D., Raj Vincent, P. M. D., Srinivasan, K., & Gutierrez Reina, D. (2022). IoT-Cloud-Based Smart Healthcare Monitoring System for Heart Disease Prediction via Deep Learning. *Electronics (Basel), 11*(15), 2292. doi:10.3390/electronics11152292

Nancy, A. A., Ravindran, D., Vincent, P., Srinivasan, K., & Reina, D. G. (2022). IoT-Cloud-Based Smart Healthcare Monitoring System for Heart Disease Prediction via Deep Learning. *Electronics (Basel), 11*(15), 2292. doi:10.3390/electronics11152292

Oyeleye, M., Chen, T. H., Titarenko, S., & Antoniou, G. (2022). A Predictive Analysis of Heart Rates Using Machine Learning Techniques. *International Journal of Environmental Research and Public Health, 19*(4), 2417. doi:10.3390/ijerph19042417 PMID:35206603

Padula, W. V., Kreif, N., Vanness, D. J., Adamson, B., Rueda, J. D., Felizzi, F., Jonsson, P., IJzerman, M. J., Butte, A., & Crown, W. (2022). Machine Learning Methods in Health Economics and Outcomes Research-The PALISADE Checklist: A Good Practices Report of an ISPOR Task Force. *Value in Health, 25*(7), 1063–1080. doi:10.1016/j.jval.2022.03.022 PMID:35779937

Ramkumar, G., Seetha, J., Priyadarshini, R., Gopila, M., & Saranya, G. (2023). IoT-based patient monitoring system for predicting heart disease using deep learning. *Measurement*, *218*, 113235. doi:10.1016/j.measurement.2023.113235

Rasjid, Z. E. (2021). Predictive Analytics in Healthcare: The Use of Machine Learning for Diagnoses. *2021 International Conference on Electrical, Computer and Energy Technologies (ICECET)*, (pp. 1–6). IEEE. 10.1109/ICECET52533.2021.9698508

Saber, H., Somai, M., Rajah, G. B., Scalzo, F., & Liebeskind, D. S. (2019). Predictive analytics and machine learning in stroke and neurovascular medicine. *Neurological Research*, *41*(8), 681–690. doi:10.1080/01616412.2019.1609159 PMID:31038007

Sachdeva, S. (2023). Standard-based personalized healthcare delivery for kidney illness using deep learning. *Physiological Measurement*, *44*(8), 084001. doi:10.1088/1361-6579/ace09f PMID:37343580

Sambyal, N., Saini, P., & Syal, R. (2020). Microvascular Complications in Type-2 Diabetes: A Review of Statistical Techniques and Machine Learning Models. *Wireless Personal Communications*, *115*(1), 1–26. doi:10.1007/s11277-020-07552-3

Selya, A., Anshutz, D., Griese, E., Weber, T. L., Hsu, B. N., & Ward, C. (2021). Predicting unplanned medical visits among patients with diabetes: Translation from machine learning to clinical implementation. *BMC Medical Informatics and Decision Making*, *21*(1), 111. doi:10.1186/s12911-021-01474-1 PMID:33789660

Shafqat, S., Fayyaz, M., Khattak, H. A., Bilal, M., Khan, S., Ishtiaq, O., Abbasi, A., Shafqat, F., Al-numay, W. S., & Chatterjee, P. (2023). Leveraging Deep Learning for Designing Healthcare Analytics Heuristic for Diagnostics. *Neural Processing Letters*, *55*(1), 53–79. doi:10.1007/s11063-021-10425-w PMID:33551665

Shashikumar, S. P., Josef, C. S., Sharma, A., & Nemati, S. (2021). DeepAISE? An interpretable and recurrent neural survival model for early prediction of sepsis. *Artificial Intelligence in Medicine*, *113*, 102036. Advance online publication. doi:10.1016/j.artmed.2021.102036 PMID:33685592

Tanwar, S., Tyagi, S., & Kumar, N. (Eds.). (2019). Security and privacy of electronic healthcare records: Concepts, paradigms and solutions. Institution of Engineering and Technology

Thong Tran, N. D., Leung, C. K., Madill, E. W. R., & Binh, P. T. (2022). A Deep Learning Based Predictive Model for Healthcare Analytics. *2022 IEEE 10th International Conference on Healthcare Informatics (ICHI)*, 547–549. 10.1109/ICHI54592.2022.00106

Toth, E. G., Gibbs, D., Moczygemba, J., & McLeod, A. (2021). Decision tree modeling in R software to aid clinical decision making. *Health and Technology*, *11*(3), 535–545. doi:10.1007/s12553-021-00542-w

Uspenskaya-Cadoz, O., Alamuri, C., Wang, L., Yang, M., Khinda, S., Nigmatullina, Y., Cao, T., Kayal, N., O'Keefe, M., & Rubel, C. (2019). Machine Learning Algorithm Helps Identify Non-Diagnosed Prodromal Alzheimer's Disease Patients in the General Population. *The Journal of Prevention of Alzheimer's Disease*, *6*(3), 185–191. doi:10.14283/jpad.2019.10 PMID:31062833

Venkatasubramanian, S. (2022). Ambulatory Monitoring of Maternal and Fetal using Deep Convolution Generative Adversarial Network for Smart Health Care IoT System. *International Journal of Advanced Computer Science and Applications*, *13*(1). Advance online publication. doi:10.14569/IJACSA.2022.0130126

Venkatesh, R., Balasubramanian, C., & Kahappan, M. (2019). Development of Big Data Predictive Analytics Model for Disease Prediction using Machine learning Technique. *Journal of Medical Systems*, *43*(8), 272. doi:10.1007/s10916-019-1398-y PMID:31278468

Vimont, A., Leleu, H., & Durand-Zaleski, I. (2022). Machine learning versus regression modelling in predicting individual healthcare costs from a representative sample of the nationwide claims database in France. *The European Journal of Health Economics*, *23*(2), 211–223. doi:10.1007/s10198-021-01363-4 PMID:34373958

Yoon, H., & Li, J. (2019). A Novel Positive Transfer Learning Approach for Telemonitoring of Parkinson's Disease. *IEEE Transactions on Automation Science and Engineering*, *16*(1), 180–191. doi:10.1109/TASE.2018.2874233

Yousuff, A. R. M., Hasan, M. Z., Anand, R., & Babu, M. R. (2024). *Leveraging deep learning models for continuous glucose monitoring and prediction in diabetes management: towards enhanced blood sugar control*. International Journal Of System Assurance Engineering And Management. doi:10.1007/s13198-023-02200-y

# Chapter 7

# Beyond Supervision:
## Exploring Unsupervised Learning Through Clustering

**Asif Iqbal Hajamydeen**
*Management and Science University, Malaysia*

**Warusia Yassin**
 https://orcid.org/0000-0001-9601-2572
*Universiti Teknikal Malaysia Melaka, Malaysia*

## ABSTRACT

*This chapter investigates the domain of unsupervised learning algorithms, delivering a detailed outline of its classifications and essential characteristics. Each algorithm is examined, assessing its appropriateness for different types of data. A systematic assessment is conducted with each algorithm and is checked using datasets that complement its strengths. The evaluation presents insights on how well these algorithms perform in comparison with contextually relevant datasets. It also provides the foundation for a systematic investigation into the details of unsupervised learning by matching each algorithm with an appropriate class of data. The knowledge gap between theory and practice was explored by clustering algorithms with prominent tools like Weka and goes beyond the clustering concept by establishing essential principles for unsupervised learning. Through the explanation of clustering algorithms with real world datasets, practical approaches were provided to employ unsupervised learning in real-world data.*

## 1. INTRODUCTION

Around fifty years ago, when research on artificial intelligence (AI) and robotics started in the 1960s, intelligence was conceived of as a computational method. Improvements in computer and engineering applications emerged from the classical and computational approach's evolution into a broader subject with numerous aspects in the 1980s. AI's principal objectives are to identify natural intelligence, interact with everyday events, and create intelligent algorithms. The creation of systems with advanced consciousness, knowledge, and thought processes is the ultimate idea of real intelligence.

DOI: 10.4018/979-8-3693-3609-0.ch007

The origins of AI can be found in Philosophy, Psychology, and Linguistics—especially Linguistics. AI is especially useful in situations where traditional methods would take a considerable amount of time. It is essential to understand that even though computers are capable of performing intelligent tasks, they lack real intellect demonstrated by humans. Ineffective methods in AI can resolve various difficulties with no real knowledge or intelligence of the difficulty, while strong methods use existing knowledge and a methodology to handle it. At the moment, AI technologies are constrained to limited disciplines like image recognition, speech recognition, and dialogue response. Detecting, reasoning, and developing are domains in which AI has not yet made substantial progress.

The explosion of large data and expanded computer processing capacity have led to a major expansion of AI technology. Even with these developments, these technologies are still confined to particular academic disciplines. It is true that cognitive functions like self-control, self-awareness, and self-understanding are difficult for AI to assist with (Lu et al., 2018). However rather than creating intelligent algorithms, the core goal of artificial intelligence is to comprehend natural forms of intelligence to interact with the real world (Pfiefer and Iida, 2004). This is a step towards giving machines the capacity to carry out activities without exact instructions or directions (Yadav et al., 2017). Most of the advancements in AI have been driven by machine learning, which relies on the availability of computing resources. Current AI systems are built on Deep Learning methods, which can function as black boxes that are difficult to interpret (Phan et al., 2020). Moving forward, it is important to address the limitations of these black box models and evolve towards interpretable models (Samek et al., 2017). This will enable future AI systems to be both intelligent and explainable, rather than simply labelled.

ML acts as a link between statistics, computer science, and other areas that involve automated enhancement over time for decision-making (Jordan and Mitchell, 2015). The primary technical purpose of all learning algorithms is their ability to accurately learn from data regardless of volume and handle data errors. Predictive models are built to serve as controllers for future action and decision-making (Domingos, 2012). Initially, there were two types of learning: supervised and unsupervised learning. Supervised algorithms learn from labelled data, where each instance has a related decision, while unsupervised algorithms act on unlabelled data, where decisions are not provided for each instance. Semi-supervised learning, which builds the model using a big amount of unlabelled data and a small amount of labelled data, bridged these two learning paradigms. Aside from supervised and unsupervised learning, Reinforcement Learning (RL) is another significant machine learning method that enables an agent to learn via experience and trial-and-error.

Predict a future in which computers are able to evaluate information and acquire from it, becoming progressively intelligent and constructive over time. The world of machine learning is an innovative wing of artificial intelligence that is changing markets and stimulating creativity at a rate never seen before. Clustering is a fundamental technique in machine learning that allows computers to classify and arrange large volumes of data, uncovering previously undiscovered patterns and insights. These algorithms are the unseen heroes behind many commonplace comforts and ground-breaking discoveries, from optimising supply chains in manufacturing to suggesting tailored content on streaming platforms. The field of data analysis aims to discover significant patterns in large datasets. One effective approach to achieve this is through the use of clustering algorithms. These methods help identify underlying structures and related objects, providing interpretation in complex data environments. However, labelling data can be time-consuming and labour-intensive, making labelled data expensive and not readily available. As a result, there is a need for algorithms that can build models with minimal labelled or unlabelled data.

Clustering algorithms play a critical role in an era where many industries rely on data-driven decision-making. These algorithms automatically identify patterns within data, allowing for evaluation without labels, and can extract valuable information from both structured and unstructured data. Depending on similarities, the algorithm can group data based on characteristics or features into relevant clusters. However, the performance of clustering algorithms can deteriorate when dealing with large volumes of noisy or incomplete data. To address this, various programming implementations have introduced variations and optimizations, resulting in improved versions compared to the original algorithms.

One industry greatly impacted by clustering algorithms is healthcare. For instance, in a hospital setting, the use of clustering can reduce patient waiting times and streamline processes. By assigning patients to appropriate treatment programs based on their medical needs, hospitals can improve patient satisfaction and provide timely care. Online retailers that employ clustering techniques to segment consumers have seen improved conversion rates, ultimately increasing revenue. Additionally, by tailoring marketing campaigns to specific client groups, these retailers can strengthen customer loyalty.Banks also rely on clustering algorithms to detect and prevent fraudulent transactions, thereby enhancing security procedures. Moreover, clustering algorithms have revolutionized supply chain operations in the production sector by streamlining manufacturing processes. This has led to a significant reduction in production interruptions and more efficient resource utilization, resulting in increased productivity and decreased operational expenses. In the context of smart cities, clustering is used to analyse energy usage and traffic patterns, ultimately improving traffic flow, and reducing energy consumption. By strategically planning infrastructure development based on insights gained from clustered data, cities can enhance their sustainability and environmental responsiveness.

The following are the fundamental concepts of Machine learning and Clustering to better understand the algorithms used, experiments conducted, and the result presented:

**Data:** The foundation of machine learning is data. It includes a range of formats, including text, photos, numbers, and more, and is used as the basis for machine learning model training.

**Algorithms:** The instruments that energise learning from data are machine learning algorithms. These algorithms can be segregated into groups that adopt distinct learning scenarios, such as reinforcement learning, supervised learning, and unsupervised learning.

**Training and Testing:** The two main stages of machine learning are training and testing. Training is used to educate the process, while testing is used to assess the prototype that has been learned. Two separate collections of data are required: one to train and another to test, in order to support this learning process. Testing data is new data used for prediction, whereas training data are samples of data that help the learning algorithm create models. Furthermore, throughout the learning process, an additional piece of data—referred to as validation data—is used to guarantee the correctness of the model. As such, it is essential to generate several data sets in order to confirm the validity of the model for every learning algorithm.

**Cross-validation:** This methodology is designed to obtain a reliable assessment of model performance using only the training data. It can also be used to assess a model when data is limited. This is achieved through a process called k-fold cross validation, where a single parameter (k) determines the number of divisions/folds that the data is split into. For example, if k is set to 10 and there are 100 instances in the dataset, 90 instances are used for training and 10 instances are used for testing. This process is repeated till each part of the data has been tested (10 instances) and trained on (90 instances). This ensures a thoroughgoing evaluation of the dataset for training and testing. Figure 1 below illustrates the step-by-step

*Figure 1. Cross validation*

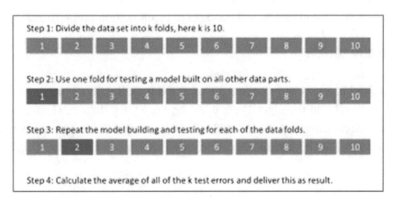

method of cross-validation. The number of folds determines the extent to which the dataset is verified, ensuring the accuracy of decisions made on new data over time.

**Model Evaluation:** The efficacy of machine learning models is valued using metrics including accuracy, precision, recall, and F1-score. These measures illustrate on how well the model applies to new, untested data.

**Deployment:** Following extensive training and assessment, machine learning models are employed in practical applications to generate predictions, categorizations, or judgements on new data.

## 1.1 Motivation

Clustering algorithms are unique tools in the large field of data analysis and machine learning that are essential for segmenting, comprehending, and identifying patterns in complex datasets. Irrespective of the intensity of prior knowledge, using clustering algorithms is motivated by their capacity to reveal latent structures in data, which can result in useful insights and well-informed decision-making. In order to separate and group data points according to commonalities, clustering algorithms are essential to ease with pattern recognition and data comprehension. Decision-making procedures in a variety of fields can benefit from the insights gathered via clustering, assisting stakeholders in making well-informed decisions based on a thorough comprehension of the data.

## 1.2 Contributions

The chapter makes the following contributions with respect to the topics detailed:

- Connects abstract ideas to real-world applications by thoroughly outlining each data analysis technique.
- Readers are given insights into which algorithms are appropriate for particular scenarios by evaluating applicability for different forms of data.
- Performance of each algorithm is evaluated through methodical assessments using contextually relevant information, providing readers with a clear grasp of the algorithms' applicability in real-world circumstances.

- Extends academic concepts to offer practical methods for unsupervised learning, making use of popular tools like Weka and real-world datasets to promote comprehension.

## 1.3 Chapter Organization

The chapter is organized in a way to provide a pleasant reading. Section 2 provides related work on the various clustering methods and the algorithms with the necessary details. Methodology by which the experiments were conducted together with details of the dataset is discussed in Section 3. Section 4 illustrates the accuracy achieved by various algorithms with diverse datasets and the chapter is concluded in section 5.

## 2. RELATED WORK

A cluster is a collection of similar instances which are in some way similar among each other inside the cluster and different from the instances of other clusters. Clustering is an unsupervised learning process having the ability to group similar instances together in a cluster. A dataset apt for clustering is a collection of data points that are objects belonging to some space, where a space is a universal set of data points from which the dataset is drawn (Rajaraman and Ullman, 2011). Clustering algorithms produces clusters on the data provided irrespective of cluster availability and non-availability in that data. If the provided data contain clusters, a clustering algorithm may generate better clusters than the other (Jain et.al., 1999).

Cluster analysis is an investigative data analysis to discover apparently unseen patterns. All spaces that can be subjected to clustering have a distance measure giving a distance between any two points in the space (Rajaraman and Ullman, 2011). Measuring the similarity between two patterns from the same feature space is essential for clustering process (Jain et.al., 1999, Kumari A. et.al., 2020). The clusters were generated using a similarity measure based on Euclidean or probabilistic distance and is one of the most widely used distance measure (Omran et.al., 2007, Kumari A. et.al., 2021).Clustering can be subdivided as hard and soft clustering. In hard clustering, an instance belongs to only one cluster, e.g., K-Means, whereas soft clustering allows an instance to co-exist in multiple clusters, e.g., Fuzzy C Means (FCM) as represented in Figure 2.

Datapoints requiring a binary response like yes or no and, normal or abnormal and true or lie are hard clustered, and these datapoints cannot logically exist in multiple clusters or categories. On the other hand, those datapoints which may possibly belong in multiple clusters are termed as soft clusters. For example, an individual having several choices of favourite food, and therefore a person considered according to their favourite food may exist inside several categories. Basically, there are two strategies in dividing the datapoints in a dataset that are (1) Closeness and (2) Point assignments. In 'Closeness', the clustering starts by considering each data point as a separate cluster, and the clusters were combined incrementally depending on the closeness (utilizing one of the existing descriptions for closeness) between each other. Combining clusters as such were stopped, when it leads to undesirable clusters, or the number of clusters were predetermined. Using point assignment, every data point is assigned to a cluster that can fits the best and this is usually preceded by an initial cluster estimation. Alternatively, depending on the variations among data points, clusters were combined and those data point which were different from the all the cluster members remains unassigned to any clusters and were called as outliers.

*Figure 2. Hard vs. soft clusters*

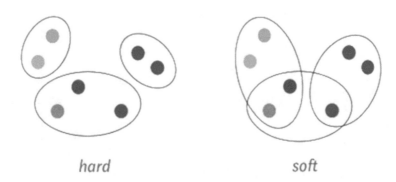

## 2.1 Clustering Methods

Clustering methods groups or clusters datapoints based on regulation(s)signifying the similarity or dissimilarity between the datapoints. There were many clustering methodologies which includes Centroid-based, Density-based, Distribution-based and Hierarchical Clustering. These methods are explained with examples in detail.

### 2.1.1 Density Based

Density based clusters were formed or generated by separating several concentration areas based on different density in the datapoints. The dense region has some similarity in between the datapoints that are different from the datapoints in a lower dense region. Density based methods are reasonably accurate and able to combine clusters. The notable illustrations on this policy are DBSCAN (Density-Based Spatial Clustering of Applications with Noise) and OPTICS (Ordering Points to Identify Clustering Structure) etc. Figure 3 presents various shapes of density-based clusters.

Density-based clustering techniques are used in the analysis of urban mobility to identify areas with high traffic and congestion patterns. Investigators utilize GPS or mobile phone data to cluster spatial-temporal data points based on density, effectively detecting congested areas, traffic bottlenecks, and peak

*Figure 3. Spherical vs. arbitrary*

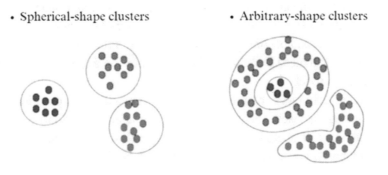

*Figure 4. Agglomerative vs. divisive*

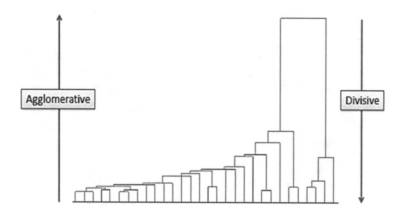

traffic hours. This information facilitates urban planners optimize transportation infrastructure, improve traffic flow, and reduce travel time.

## 2.1.2 Hierarchical Based

Hierarchical clusters are generated in a tree like structure called as dendrogram, where new clusters are formed by combining or dividing the existing clusters. Basically, the generated clusters are a composition or decomposition of datapoints based on similarities or dissimilarities. Depending on the approach of algorithm takes to complete the hierarchy, the algorithm is classified as Hierarchical Agglomerative Clustering (HAC) and Hierarchical Divisive Clustering (HDC). Figure 4 presents the way these approaches work.

Hierarchical Agglomerative Clustering (HAC) is a bottom-up approach, where each data point is considered as a separate cluster at first. All such clusters were merged consecutively based on the similarity, until all the data points come under the same cluster. For example, *W, X, Y* and *Z* do not have any friends and they are alone, means that they are initially separate clusters (Four Clusters). Later X and Y become friends; the cluster becomes three, after a while *W* friend with *Z*, where the cluster reduces to two. Gradually, *Y* establishes friendship with *Z* that eventually brings *W* and *X* together in the same cluster, which results in one cluster. Hierarchical Divisive Clustering (HDC) follows a top-down approach, all the data points were placed in one cluster initially. Consequently, the division of clusters continues based on the dissimilarity until the cluster number equals the number of datapoints. For example, all the living beings are in one cluster, which can be further classified as animals and plants forming two clusters. Depending on criteria every cluster can be further subdivided until the required cluster is reached or else every datapoint is singled out and becomes the only datapoint in the cluster. CURE (Clustering Using Representatives), BIRCH (Balanced Iterative Reducing Clustering and using Hierarchies) are notable examples following this approach.

Hierarchical clustering techniques are utilized in image segmentation to partition images into regions or objects that share analogous visual characteristics. In computer vision applications, algorithms such as agglomerative clustering with spatial constraints group pixels or image patches based on similarities in colour, texture, or intensity. By iteratively merging visually similar regions or segments, hierarchical

*Figure 5. Partitioning process*

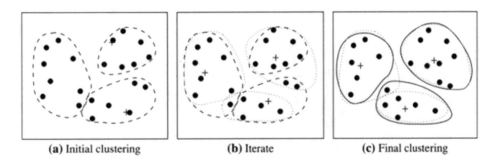

| (a) Initial clustering | (b) Iterate | (c) Final clustering |

segmentation trees are created, which capture the hierarchical structure of image content. This benefits in image understanding, object recognition, and scene analysis in various fields, including medical imaging, remote sensing, and autonomous driving.

## 2.1.3 Partition Based

A given set of datapoints are divided into $k$ partitions where every datapoint is assigned to one of the partitions initially. Partitions is improved by moving datapoints from one partition to another iteratively as shown in Figure 5.

The elementary requirement of partitioning method is that each partition must have at least one datapoint and no datapoints can exist in multiple partition or cluster. All partitions are represented with a centroid or a medoid where centroid is the average of all datapoints in a partition and a medoid is the most descriptive point of a cluster. Partition-based clustering techniques are used in bioinformatics to analyse gene expression data obtained from microarray or RNA-sequencing experiments. The Partitioning Around Medoids (PAM) algorithm helps researchers identify biologically relevant gene modules. It also enables researchers to infer regulatory networks and gain insights into the molecular mechanisms underlying complex biological processes, such as disease progression, drug response, and developmental pathways. This technique is particularly valuable for analysing gene expression patterns across different conditions or tissues.

## 2.1.4 Centroid Based

Different from hierarchical clustering, centroid based clustering arranges datapoints in non-hierarchical clusters. It is an iterative clustering where the similarity is derived by the proximity of a datapoint towards the cluster centroid, where a centroid is the most illustrative datapoint in a cluster or the middle of a cluster. Centroid also can be assumed as a multi-dimensional average or mean of the values in datapoints of a cluster. Centroid-based algorithms are competent although they are delicate to initial conditions and outliers. Figure 6 shows clusters with centroids. The most common centroid based clustering algorithm is K-Means.

Centroid-based clustering methods are exploited in healthcare management for the purpose of patient segmentation and resource allocation. These methods, including k-means clustering, categorize patients corresponding to their demographics, medical history, and patterns of healthcare utilization. This enables

*Figure 6. Clusters with centroids*

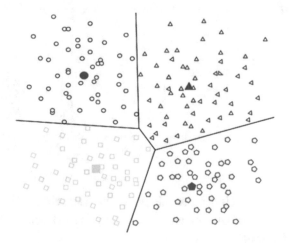

the more efficient allocation of resources by healthcare providers, permitting to optimize care delivery and improve patient outcomes. Moreover, this approach assists in the implementation of personalized care management strategies, ultimately leading to improved healthcare quality and efficiency.

## 2.1.5 Distribution Based

Distribution based model is conceptualized on the probability that all the data points in a dataset may fit into the same distribution or cluster. The grouping can be Normal or Gaussian. In a Gaussian distribution, all the data points were fitted to a fixed number of distributions (Figure 7) to avoid overfitting and the parameters were iteratively optimized (local optimum) to provide the best fit for a dataset. This may produce different results with multiple executions. Distribution based clustering generates complicated models for capturing the correlation and dependence between attributes.

The likelihood of a data point in a distribution is decided by the distance of a data point from the distribution centre. Therefore, the increase in distance from the distribution centre for a data point will move the data point to a different distribution. The widespread example of the distribution model is

*Figure 7. Distributed clusters*

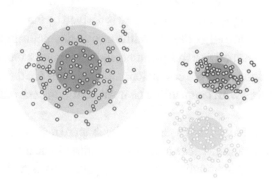

*Figure 8. Grid cells*

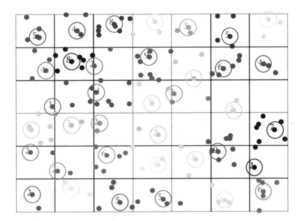

Expectation-Maximization (EM), an iterative learning method for unlabelled data points. The algorithm has a two-step procedure Expectation (E) and Maximization (M) where the existing parameters were utilised to recreate the unseen structure and this unseen structure is used to re-evaluate the parameters until convergence. Marketing professionals often use distribution-based clustering techniques to categorize their clientele based on their preferences and purchase histories. By analysing consumer attribute distributions, such as spending patterns, purchasing frequency, and demographics, marketers can identify distinct client segments that exhibit similar purchasing behaviours.

## 2.1.6 Grid-Based

Grid based method intends to divide all the data points into fixed number of cells forming a grid structure, and consequently combines the cells to build clusters as presented in Figure 8.Every nonempty cell in the grid is measured by a weight based on the number of data points contained in that grid. Clusters are generated by accumulating the neighbouring dense cells in the grid. Unlike density-based clustering, the density of a cell and the relationship with the adjacent cells were measured to form clusters rather than considering individual data points. Grid-based methods has less processing time naturally relying on the size of the grid and not the data points.

Grid-based clustering techniques are utilized in environmental monitoring to analyse the spatial distribution patterns of pollutants and natural resources. These techniques involve dividing a geographic area into grids, aggregating air quality measurements, and identifying regions with high pollution levels or similar characteristics. This process aids in identifying pollution hotspots, evaluating risks, and developing focused mitigation strategies to improve air quality and safeguard public health. As such, this method plays a vital role in assessing environmental risks and enhancing public health.

## 2.2 Clustering Algorithms

Clustering algorithms spontaneously distinguish the patterns within the data enabling the evaluation of data without labels, and it can extract values from large volume of structured and unstructured data. Depending on the similarities, the algorithm can segregate data based on the characteristics or features

*Figure 9. Class similarity*

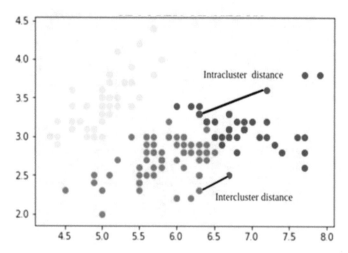

into relevant clusters. Typically, noise and outliers can negatively impact the effectiveness of clustering algorithms, making them less effective (Sharma and Seal, 2021).When clustered, all algorithms exhibit some degree of uncertainty in certain (noisy) data (Ahmad and Dang, 2015).The performance of clustering deteriorates with the increase in noise (Nguyen, 2023, Kumari A. et.al., 2021), volume and incompleteness of the data supplied for learning; consequently, reduced the quality of the dataset, which decreased the clustering performance (Budach et.al., 2022, Kumari A. et.al., 2024).Collectively, these findings establish how sensitive clustering algorithms are to the nature and quality of the input data, highlighting the need of robustness when dealing with challenging data circumstances.

Clustering has been implemented in numerous programming to apply variations and optimizations, enabling improved versions than the original. A good clustering algorithm is one which generates clusters with high intraclass similarity and low inter class similarity (Figure 9). Intraclass similarity refers to the similarity between the data points in the same cluster and inter class similarity refers to dissimilarity between a datapoint in one cluster with a data point in any of the clusters generated for a dataset. The clustering algorithms depends on a set of adjustable parameters by which the performance is decided. Adjusting the cluster parameters the measure performance can be done through one of the following three ways: (a) Using the default parameters of a particular algorithm (b) Changing one of the significant parameters keeping the rest as default (c) Adjusting all the parameters to achieve the required performance.

Clustering is one of the earliest like human needs, to designate the relevant features of human beings and things to be identified with a category making it applicable for several scientific disciplines. The objective of clustering is to determine a novel class that are of interest and their assessment is essential (Rokach and Maimon, 2005). Although huge number of clustering algorithms are existing and utilised successfully in various application domains (Hajamydeen & Udzir, 2016; Hajamydeen & Udzir, 2019), yet clustering remains difficult to be accomplished (Jain, 2010), as there was no single algorithm serves a variety of datasets in general. The performance of the clustering algorithm is affected by the data representation (Jain, 2010), i.e., the way the data is presented in a dataset that needs to be clustered.

## 2.2.1 Expectation–Maximization (EM) Clustering

The EM algorithm's basic idea is to use the dataset's current data to approximate any missing data, and then use the completed data to update the parametric values (Dempster et al., 1977; McLachlan and Krishnan, 2007). The goal of the EM algorithm is able to predict the number of clusters for a given dataset. It does this by using a statistical model known as Gaussian finite mixtures, which is divided into two recursive steps: expectation and maximisation. For each cluster, the model incorporates a set of K probability distributions to represent the data. Parameters such as the number of iterations and the log likelihood difference between consecutive iterations define each K distribution. These parameters are first determined by the algorithm from the input data; the likelihood that an instance for a given set of data belongs to a certain cluster is then calculated using the inferred parameters. The process of adjusting the parameter distribution is carried out until either the maximum number of iterations is reached, or the created clusters exhibit a particular degree of overall cluster goodness.

The algorithm has the following steps:

**Step 1:** Consider a set of initial parameters for any given set of incomplete data.

**Step 2:** Expectation (E): Utilizing the existing studied data of the dataset, assess (presume) the values of the missing data.

**Step 3:** Maximization (M): Update the parameters based on the complete data generated in Expectation (E) step.

**Step 4:** Iterate step 2 and step 3 till convergence.

EM is a clustering method to discover the maximum-likelihood estimations for model parameters, when data is incomplete, has missing data points and unobserved latent variables. The algorithm can detect model parameters despite missing data whereby it performs by taking arbitrary values for missing data points and uses those estimates to construct the new set of data. This new dataset is employed to generate a better guess from the previous set, and the process resumes until the algorithm converges. The restriction of EM is that it performs well with small amount of missing data and a moderate data dimensionality. The speed of Expectation (E) step is slower when the data dimensionality increases, and the process move towards a local maximum. EM has the capability to identify the number of clusters that are appropriate for a dataset based on the varying patterns present in that dataset, and consequently cluster the dataset based on its decision on the number of clusters for that dataset. It also can divide a dataset to a prescribed number of clusters provided the number of clusters are specified before clustering.

EM clustering is used in document clustering and topic modelling in Natural Language Processing (NLP). It enables the identification of hidden thematic frameworks within large text collections, thereby facilitating tasks such as sentiment analysis, information retrieval, and document summarization. Additionally, EM clustering improves the coherence and interpretability of generated topics by incorporating priors or restrictions on topic distributions. This enhancement makes topic modelling more valuable in practical applications.

## 2.2.2 Canopy clustering

Canopy clustering (McCallum and Nigam, 1999; McCallum et.al., 2000) requires single pass over the data and can run in batch or incremental mode. Has a heuristic to be used in batch mode for setting the T2 distance which determines the number of canopies (clusters) generated. Based on the request for a specific number of clusters (N), the algorithm generates and returns the top N canopies, when N <

number of canopies (batch and incremental learning). On the other hand, when N > number of canopies, the excess or difference in cluster (N) requested is supplied by choosing training instances arbitrarily (applicable for batch training only).

Canopy can predict the number of clusters appropriate for a particular dataset, but then it did not perform well with very smaller datasets, and with the data that is too homogeneous. Based the datasets considered for evaluation, the dataset Country has 167 instances and Text Similarity dataset has homogenous data. Canopy did not predict the number of clusters leaving all the instances un clustered. Hence, canopy is not viable choice to predict clusters if the instances are too homogeneous and are lesser. Therefore, the cluster numbers predicted by EM has been considered as benchmark and is utilized by canopy to generate the number of clusters.

Canopy clustering is a technique used in environmental research to pre-cluster environmental sensor data gathered from Internet of Things (IoT) devices placed in natural settings. It helps discover zones of interest and anomalies for further inquiry by grouping sensor observations based on spatial proximity and similarity in environmental characteristics such as temperature, humidity, and air quality. By using canopy clustering, researchers can identify spatial patterns, trends, and anomalies in environmental variables, thus aiding in the efficient processing of large-scale environmental sensor data. Additionally, this approach provides insights into ecosystem dynamics, habitat appropriateness, and environmental health indicators, making it valuable for ecosystem modelling, climate change research, and environmental monitoring.

## 2.2.3 K-Means Clustering

K-means (MacQueen, 1967) is a straightforward and common clustering technique that splits instances into K disjoint clusters based to the attribute values. Similar attribute values are shared by the instances that form the cluster, and K determines how many clusters could be produced. The K-means algorithm's steps are as follows:

1. State how many clusters can be found (K).
2. Divide all instances into K clusters at random, compute each cluster's centroids, and confirm that each centroid is distinct from the others to initialise the K cluster centroids.
3. Calculate the centroids' distances for each cluster by repeating the process on every instance. Assign every item to the cluster whose centroid is closest to it.
4. Recalculate both changed clusters' centroids.
5. Until the centroids shift, repeat step 3 again.

Furthermore, in order to determine the distance (or similarity) between two instances, a distance function is required. The most used distance function is the Euclidean distance, which considers all attributes equally in determining this value. The algorithm can accurately separate the events' features into clusters based on likelihood and treats each feature equally. Its ability to handle bigger datasets in a shorter amount of time further supports the use of it in the clustering strategy's second stage.

As K-Means is sensitive to noise and outliers, KMOR (K-Means with outlier removal) (Gan and Ng, 2017) was implemented by extending the basic algorithm to collect all the outliers in a separate cluster thereby generating usual clusters and outlier clusters simultaneously. The outliers were controlled using two parameters namely $n_0$ and $\gamma$. Efficiency of the algorithm is demonstrated by testing with real and synthetic data and compared with several similar algorithms. As the number of outliers were controlled by parameters, alternative ways of controlling outliers need to be explored. The Calinski-Harabasz criterion (Caliński and Harabasz,1974) is employed by the CascadeSimpleKMeans class in WEKA, an implementation of the K-means clustering algorithm, to calculate the ideal number of clusters. The algorithm can determine the best number of clusters automatically, provided the minimum and maximum number of clusters required is specified. There are two variants of K-Means available in the Weka tool, and both were tested with the datasets to verify which of this variant is superior.

K-means clustering is generally used in healthcare analytics to stratify patients and manage population health based on patient data. By clustering patients according to clinical characteristics such as medical history, diagnostic tests, and treatment outcomes, healthcare professionals can detect subclasses with similar healthcare needs and risk profiles. K-means clustering eases healthcare organizations to optimize service delivery, resource allocation, and collaboration. By utilizing personalized care management plans, pre-emptive interventions, and intensive preventive measures, patient outcomes can be improved, hospital readmission rates can be reduced, and healthcare costs can be lowered. It can also be used to identify high-risk patient groups for chronic care management, disease management programs, and community health initiatives, thus addressing healthcare inequalities and improving health outcomes.

## 2.2.4 Farthest First (FF) Clustering

Farthest First clustering (Hochbaum and Shmoys, 1985; Dasgupta and Long, 2005) clusters instances according to their maximum distance from previous cluster centres. In contrast to K-Means, which decides cluster centres by averaging, FF selects the element that is farthest from the existing cluster centres to be the new centre. In certain cases, this method increases performance and speeds up merging, exclusively for datasets with nonuniform density distributions. As a partitional method, farthest first clustering divides the dataset into clusters without taking hierarchical relationships into account. Large datasets can be handled by it because of its processing efficiency and relative simplicity.

The FF algorithm proceeds as follows:

1.  Select an arbitrary starting position to act as the initial cluster centre.
2.  Pick the point that is the distant from each of the earlier cluster centres as the next point.
3.  The freshly selected point should be assigned to the nearest cluster centre.
4.  In accordance, revise the cluster centres.
5.  Continue until the required number of clusters is reached.

Farthest First clustering is a valuable technique in the deployment of sensor networks. It aids in the selection of optimal sensor locations, maximizing coverage and minimizing redundancy. By initially selecting sensor nodes that are the farthest apart as initial centroids, this technique guarantees sufficient coverage of the entire monitoring region. The application of Farthest First clustering is highly beneficial in the strategic deployment of sensor networks for various purposes such as surveillance, infrastructure monitoring, and environmental monitoring. It significantly enhances situational awareness, enables early event detection, and facilitates prompt emergency response in domains such as disaster management, homeland security, and industrial monitoring.

## 2.2.5 Learning Vector Quantization (LVQ) Clustering

Learning Vector Quantization (LVQ) (Kohonen, 2003) is used in unsupervised clustering to gather data into distinct clusters without the necessity for labelled instances. Initially, a collection of prototype vectors (otherwise called as group representatives), usually selected at random, are initialised in the unsupervised version of LVQ, also known as SOM-U (Self-Organizing Map Unsupervised). A distance metric, such as Euclidean distance is applied to compare each data point to the prototype vectors during the training phase, and the closest prototype vector is located. Next, adjustments are made to the succeeding prototype vector so that it accurately captures the features of the current data point. The degree of the adjustments made depends on the neighbourhood function and learning rate, which both increasingly shorten the neighbourhood during training as the learning rate improves. The training process continues until a predetermined threshold., i.e., Predetermined number of iterations, is reached.

Unsupervised LVQ is used in fields like pattern recognition, data compression, and exploratory data analysis and is flexible because of its ability to adapt to different datasets. LVQ clustering has been extensively utilized in the manufacturing industry for tasks such as anomaly detection and quality control. This technique involves training the LVQ model using labelled sensor data from industrial processes. By doing so, the algorithm becomes adept at distinguishing between abnormal occurrences and normal operating circumstances. Consequently, LVQ can effectively detect malfunctioning parts or machinery, identify deviations from typical process behaviour, and promptly raise an alarm for preventive maintenance. The implementation of LVQ clustering in manufacturing processes enhances various aspects including product quality, production efficiency, and manufacturing process variability. Manufacturers can significantly reduce scrap rates and rework expenses, pinpoint the underlying causes of faults, and optimize process parameters by effectively grouping sensor data from the manufacturing lines. As a result, LVQ enables proactive quality control, predictive maintenance, and continuous improvement in manufacturing processes, ultimately leading to heightened customer satisfaction and product reliability.

## 2.2.6 Self-Organizing Maps (SOM)

Self-Organizing Maps (SOM) (Kohonen 1990, Kohonen, 2012) is a remarkable unsupervised learning method applied in a variety of fields. An array of neurons arranged in a topology that reflects the spatial relationships found in the data constitutes the basis of a SOM. Weight vectors are primarily assigned to the neurons arbitrarily, but through the training phase, these vectors are reformed to reflect significant aspects of the input data. Topology preservation is facilitated by competitive learning, whereby every input is linked to the neuron whose weight vector is nearest. SOMs are distinctive in organising high-dimensional, complicated data while maintaining its essential structure in a lower-dimensional representation.

SOM clustering has been used in neuroscience to analyse neural activity patterns and map the human brain. The SOM model is an algorithm that learns to depict spatial and temporal patterns of brain activity on a 2D, or 3D map by training it with neuroimaging data, such as fMRI or EEG signals. SOM enables the identification of functional connection patterns, the localization of brain regions associated with specific cognitive tasks or sensory stimuli, and the identification of neurological disease biomarkers. It provides insights into the brain's structure, the functional relationships between neurons, and how neural information is processed. By visualizing neural activity patterns on a topological map, neuroscientists can explore the neurological basis of cognitive behaviours and processes, uncover brain networks, and gain knowledge about brain plasticity. SOM facilitates data-driven analysis of brain imaging data, hypothesis generation, and identification of important patterns and relationships.

## 2.3 Advantages and Disadvantages of Unsupervised Learning

Although, unsupervised is considered ideal for most real time and dynamic contexts wherefrom the data is supplied, it has its own difficulties. The most significant advantage is its ability to handle unlabelled data. The disadvantage is that the output of clustering provides labels in the form of clusters and not known, which needs additional effort of the user to provide appropriate labels for each group.

The advantages are:

- Automatically divides the data points into groups based on the similarities faster as no previous knowledge required.
- Realises unusual data points for anomalies and potential hidden patterns which human eyes cannot sense.

Disadvantages are:

- Less accuracy and usefulness of results comparatively as the input data is not known (fresh) and not labelled in advance.
- Expensive as it needs human expertise to review the results and to provide appropriate labels for the generated groups.

## 3. PROPOSED METHODOLOGY

This section provides the information of the datasets used for the experiments together with the tools used to run the experiments. Additionally, it elaborates on the choice of datasets and the preprocessing of data before using it for the experiments.

## 3.1 Datasets and Tools

The datasets utilised are described in detail in this section, with particular attention paid to the selection of datasets and the characteristics included within them. Six publicly accessible real-world datasets (https://www.kaggle.com/datasets) with a range of occurrences and features were selected to evaluate the clustering algorithms' performance. **Table 1** lists the specifics of the datasets used for the experiments, including the quantity of features, the number of categories for which each dataset's examples have been marked, and the type of data.

## 3.2 Dataset Description and Treatment

The datasets deliver a variety of features and instances to facilitate the assessment of an algorithm's performance. The datasets have been handled cautiously, so as not to compromise their integrity. There are six distinct datasets, as indicated in **Table 1,** where four of the datasets were used as it is.

*Table 1. Dataset details*

| Datasets | Features | Instances | Remarks |
|---|---|---|---|
| Country | 10 | 167 | Nominal (1) Numeric (9) |
| Spine | 12 | 310 | Numeric (12) |
| Text Similarity | 3 | 4021 | Nominal (2) Numeric (1) |
| NIDS | 41 | 5000 | Nominal (3) Numeric (38) |
| Customer | 18 | 8950 | Nominal (1) Numeric (17) |
| Taxi Trip Fare | 8 | 20000 | Numeric (8) |

**Allocating Strategic Aid for Impact -** *Country (167 Instances)*: A non-profitable organisation have raised funds to assist countries based on socio-economic and health factors for strategic aid allocation. The dataset includes key indicators like GDP per capita, life expectancy, and literacy rates, and clustering analysis is employed to prioritize countries in critical need. This data-driven approach guarantees the effective utilization of funds, supporting the mission to reduce poverty and grant help in the weakest zones.

**Analysis of Back Pain -***Spine (310 Instances)***:** Thirty-one observations and thirteen columns make up the data. The back/spine's numerical properties are displayed in 12 columns. The objective of clustering is to group the data to decide whether all these numbers denote the existence of back pain or not., i.e., Normal (No back pain) or abnormal (Presence of back pain).

**Prediction of Text Similarity-** *Text Similarity (4021 Instances):* Quantifying the semantic similarity between text paragraph pairings in a dataset the task at hand. Predicting a similarity score between 0 and 1, where 0 symbolizes high dissimilarity and 1 implies high similarity, is the aim. In spite of the absence of labels in the dataset, this semantic textual similarity challenge can be tackled by candidates using any technique, as an unsupervised learning problem.

**Detection of Network Intrusion -** *NIDS (5000 Instances):* The dataset simulates a widespread variation of intrusions in a military network setting, simulating a local area network. By exposing the LAN to different attacks and establishing connections represented by a series of TCP packets between source and target IP addresses, this scenario produced raw TCP/IP dump data. Each link has 41 variables (three qualitative, 38 quantitative) which can be clustered and be labelled as "*Normal*" or "*Anomalous*" for recognizing and analysing network activities. There were 25,192 instances in the NIDS dataset; but then a subset of the first 5000 instances which can also serve as the representative of the dataset were considered for evaluation.

**Financial Services with a Focus -***Customer (8950 Instances):* This dataset focuses on market segmentation, which attempts to separate a large consumer market into smaller groups based on shared traits including current and potential customers. The goal of clustering is to create customer fragments based on eighteen behavioural characteristics, including balance, purchases, cash advances, and payment patterns. By splitting/categorising according to credit card usage patterns over the last six months, certain consumer cluster scan be provided with suggestions for loans, wealth management services, and savings plans.

**Optimizing Taxi Pricing Strategies -***Taxi Trip Fare (20000 Instances):* This dataset entails analysing taxicab journeys using a Public Dataset. Furthermore, clustering techniques are proposed as a way to envision fare trip pricing and upgrade the efficiency of ride-hailing services. Appropriate features such as trip duration, distance travelled, number of passengers, fare, tips, additional fees, total fare, and information on surge pricing are included in the dataset. On the other hand, Taxi Trip Fare dataset has 209673 instances, where the first 20000 instances were chosen for evaluation. The purpose of this subset construction is to assess how well the algorithms handle comparable datasets of different sizes.

## 3.3 Tool Description and Evaluation Factors

Weka (Waikato Environment for Knowledge Analysis) (Hall et.al., 2009), an active machine learning tool, was used to conduct the experiments. Weka is a recognised collection of Java machine learning algorithms that may be used to design innovative machine learning schemes. It can be used from your own Java code or applied directly to a dataset. It offers pre-processing, classification, regression, clustering, feature selection, and visualisation among other data mining activities. Weka was used to conduct the experiments with different datasets since the algorithms that were being tested are built with this tool. A total of six algorithms were evaluated with the six datasets which belongs to several categories and variations, however an additional of four clustering algorithms (Density-Based Spatial Clustering of Applications with Noise (DBSCAN), Spectral clustering, Hierarchical clustering, Cobweb clustering) were explained to get the understanding of various categories.

All the datasets were evaluated using Weka, and the accuracy of each algorithm in creating the model were calculated based on the measurements recorded for True Positives (TP), True Negatives (TN), False Positives (FP) and False Negatives (FN). A TN decision places two dissimilar instances in separate classes, a TP decision places two similar instances in the same class. FP and FN metrics are used to quantify the inaccuracy of classifying the events in the correct category. The accuracy of classification is determined by these four measurements, and as a result, the formula *Accuracy = (TP + TN) / (FP + FN + TP + TN)* is used to calculate the accuracy of clustering. To assess the algorithm's efficacy, Weka experimenter was used in the experiments, along with a 10-fold cross-validation. 10-fold makes the model less biased and assures that each instance from the original dataset has an equal likelihood of being included in the test and training sets.

## 4. RESULTS AND DISCUSSIONS

The performance of the algorithm with different dataset, especially the accuracy achieved by various clustering algorithms with different datasets were discussed in this section. Insights on the application of algorithm with various datasets were presented.

## 4.1 Expectation-Maximization

Majority of the clustering algorithms available can group the instances to specific number of clusters provided, the number of clusters are stated and do not have the ability to deduce the number of clusters by itself. Although, the algorithms like canopy can predict clusters, it did not work well with different types and sizes of data. Therefore, the number of clusters identified by EM has been utilized to specify the number of clusters for all other algorithms. **Table 2** specifies the number of clusters identified by EM for each of the datasets utilized for evaluation.

The accuracy achieved by EM is presented in Figure 10. The number of features and datatype of the feature did not have any influence on the accuracy of the clusters, however, the number of instances

*Table 2. Automatic cluster identification using EM*

| Datasets | Automatic Cluster Identification using EM |
|---|---|
| Country | 5 |
| Spine | 5 |
| Text Similarity | 15 |
| NIDS | 4 |
| Customer | 3 |
| Taxi Trip Fare | 3 |

being clustered has affected the accuracy. The graph presented demonstrates a gradual increase in the accuracy with the number of instances, but then it started to decline, when it crossed a certain limit.

The NIDS dataset's 99.50% accuracy rate demonstrates the effectiveness of EM in accurately identifying and categorizing network intrusions, suggesting that EM could enhance cybersecurity defences by enabling prompt detection and elimination of potential network security risks. The text similarity analysis achieved a 97.00% accuracy rate, demonstrating the efficiency of EM in detecting semantic similarities between textual material, which is crucial for applications like plagiarism detection, document clustering, and information retrieval.

## 4.2 Canopy

**Figure 11** represents the accuracy obtained with canopy clustering. Canopy clustering's 100.00% accuracy rate in estimating taxi trip fares makes it a valuable tool in fare estimate systems, enabling efficient location of related trip groups and precise pricing forecasts based on trip characteristics and historical data.

In customer segmentation and analysis, canopy clustering demonstrates its practical significance with an accuracy rate of 89.50% in the Customer dataset. This suggests that companies can use canopy

*Figure 10. Clustering accuracy of EM*

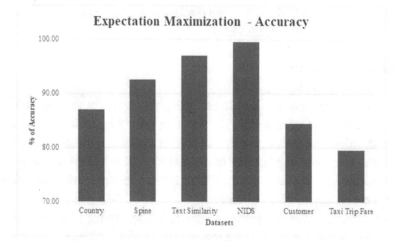

*Figure 11. Clustering accuracy of canopy*

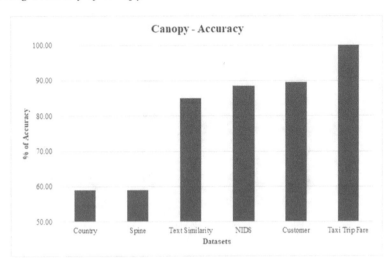

clustering to create client groups based on shared demographics, behaviours, and interests. This allows for more personalised customer experiences and more focused marketing campaigns.

## 4.3 K-Means and Cascading-Simple K-Means

The accuracy achieved by SimpleKMeans clustering is represented in Figure 12.Despite the very low accuracy ratings of 65.50% and 64.00% achieved while using SimpleKMeans to categorise countries and spinal disorders, there are still useful implications. SimpleKMeans may be used as an exploration tool to find possible patterns or clusters in the data, but further optimisation could be required for precise classification jobs. K-Means principally depend on the Euclidean distance, which performs best with numerical features, the success of K-Means clustering naturally associates optimistically with the number of numeric features in a dataset.

CascadeSimpleKMeans has two parameters (minimum and maximum clusters required) to be specify the range of the clusters to be divided for a dataset. Both parameters were set to same number to get the required clusters, i.e., Five for both minimum and maximum clusters. Figure 13displays the accuracy obtained with CascadeSimpleKMeans.

There are a lot of examples in some datasets, such as Text Similarity and Taxi Trip Fare (4,021 and 20,000, respectively). Given the great accuracy attained on these datasets, it appears that the CascadeSimpleKMeans algorithm is capable of handling enormous amounts of data, which qualifies it for use in big data situations and applications using large datasets.

## 4.4 Farthest First

Accuracy of FF presented in Figure 14 shows that, Certain datasets, such as Customer and NIDS, include a lot of features (41 and 18, respectively) and a lot of occurrences (5,000 and 8,950, respectively). The Farthest First technique is appropriate for big data applications and situations involving high-dimensional

*Figure 12. Clustering accuracy of SimpleKMeans*

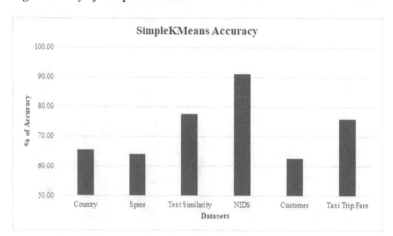

datasets because of the respectable accuracy attained on these datasets, which indicates that the algorithm can handle large-scale data successfully.

## 4.5 Learning Vector Quantization

The accuracy of the clusters generated were presented in Figure 15. The LVQ algorithm, with high accuracy scores (86% and 84%) on datasets like Text Similarity and NIDS, is deemed capable of handling complex, high-dimensional data, a common issue in real-world applications due to its ability to handle numerous features and instances.

*Figure 13. Clustering accuracy of CascadeSimpleKMeans*

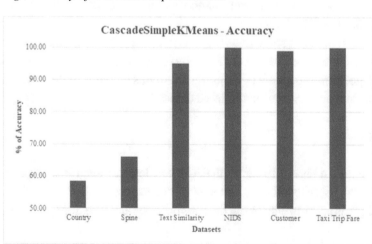

*Figure 14. Clustering accuracy of farthest first*

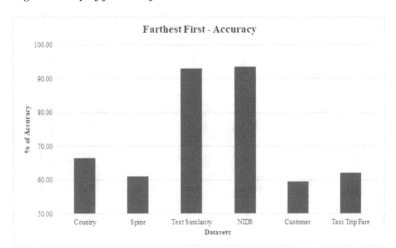

## 4.6 Self-Organizing Maps

Self-Organizing Maps exhibit higher accuracy with a variety of datasets (Figure 16), demonstrating its competence to effectively organize and represent complex data structures.

SOM's practical utility in fare estimate systems is highlighted by the perfect accuracy rate of 100.00% that was observed while forecasting taxi trip fares using this method. This implies that SOM can efficiently locate groups of related trips, allowing precise fare estimations based on trip attributes and historical data.

## 4.8 Performance Comparison of Various Clustering Algorithms

The accuracy of the algorithms with various datasets is presented in Figure 17. In conclusion, the characteristics of the datasets decide which clustering algorithm is best to apply for a particular case. In cases, tuning of the parameters to be set for an algorithm decides on the performance achieved. Self-

*Figure 15. Clustering accuracy of LVQ*

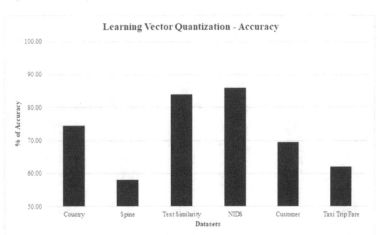

*Figure 16. Clustering accuracy of SOM*

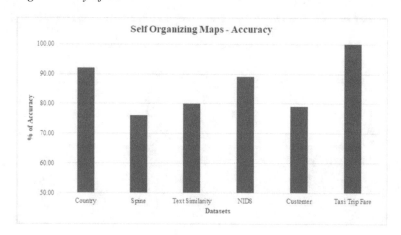

organizing maps and CascadeSimpleKMeans performed well on a variety of datasets, while expectation maximization works well in some circumstances. It is essential to comprehend the nature of the dataset to opt the best clustering algorithm.

Our investigation recognizes that accuracy may possibly not provide an extensive depiction of the intricacies related to cluster quality on its own. In order to acquire a meaningful understanding, scrutinising false positives and false negatives to verify their effect on the performance of clustering model becomes necessary. By exercising this, the limitations and challenges present in the clustering process are acknowledged and admitted, permitting further detailed assessment of the model's abilities.

*Figure 17. Clustering accuracy: Comparison*

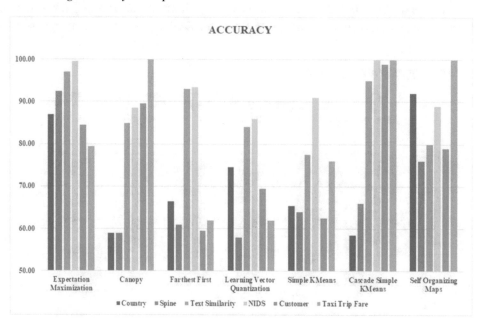

## 4.9 Limitations of the Experimental Design

Experimental designs are critical for revealing patterns and perceptions in data-driven investigation, particularly in the topic of clustering. However, it is important to consider the natural limitations of using clustering techniques. The rationale behind the limitations in experimental design for clustering is inspected in this study, especially on voluminous sample sizes, the sensitivity of algorithms to initial settings, and the importance of selecting methods and parameters with attention.

**Sample Bias:** We did not use the complete dataset; instead, we took the necessary examples out of the first part of the dataset, instead of using a particular sampling strategy that considers more examples or more attributes. Resource constraints and the requirements to streamline computational procedures guided to the choice not using the entire dataset. To speed up the evaluation and lower computational cost, the required instances were obtained from the starting of the dataset. It's critical to recognise, nevertheless, that this strategy might introduce biases as it disregards the probability of an organized or random sampling that takes a broader range of incidents or qualities into account. The justification is based on achieving a balance between the reasonable limitations and computing effectiveness.

**Parameter Sensitivity and Algorithm:** Bias may be introduced in clustering algorithm as the choice of number of clusters were based on those algorithms i.e. EM, which has the capability and efficiency in predicting the number of clusters for any given dataset. The predicted clusters by EM have been take as benchmark on the number of predicted clusters and were specified as the default cluster required for the other algorithms tested. The stability of outcome across diverse methods and parameter settings could be examined in future study to offer a more systematic comprehension of the essential patterns in the data.

## 4.10 Realistic Perspectives on Overcoming Obstacles

The following are the insights on overcoming the challenges in the clustering methods used for evaluation:

1. To moderate selection bias, future studies should consider utilizing more varied and representative samples. Sampling techniques based on key variables can augment the inclusivity of the dataset, improving the external validity of clustering models. Furthermore, sensitivity assessments should be directed to measure the strength of scores to different sampling schemes.
2. Perform sensitivity analysis to improve the robustness of clustering algorithms through various parameter selections. Stability and generalizability can be improved by utilizing collaborative approaches that incorporates the outcome of various clustering algorithms.
3. A better understanding of cluster quality can be obtained by adding metrics like silhouette analysis, external validation indices like Adjusted Rand Index in addition to standard accuracy measures. It is proposed to select metrics that corresponds to the specific objectives and features of clustering.

## 5. CONCLUSION

This chapter investigates into the interesting domain of unsupervised learning algorithms, analysing their properties and classifications. It demonstrates the performance and applicability of each algorithm by evaluating its performance with various datasets. The chapter bonds the knowledge gap between theory and practice by examining various datasets. It also showcases real-world uses of clustering algorithms using tools like Weka, providing practical approaches for implementing unsupervised learning in real-world settings. This comprehensive approach not only enhances the understanding of unsupervised learning but also equips us with the skills and resources to tackle complex data problems across diverse industries. The knowledge gained from this exploration will serve as a foundation for further research and innovation in unsupervised learning.

# REFERENCES

Ahmad, H. P., & Dang, S. (2015). Performance Evaluation of Clustering Algorithm Using different dataset. *International Journal of Advance Research in Computer Science and Management Studies, 8.*

Budach, L., Feuerpfeil, M., Ihde, N., Nathansen, A., Noack, N., Patzlaff, H., & Harmouch, H. (2022). *The effects of data quality on machine learning performance.* arXiv preprint arXiv:2207.14529.

Caliński, T., & Harabasz, J. (1974). A dendrite method for cluster analysis. *Communications in Statistics. Theory and Methods, 3*(1), 1–27. doi:10.1080/03610927408827101

Dasgupta, S., & Long, P. M. (2005). Performance guarantees for hierarchical clustering. *Journal of Computer and System Sciences, 70*(4), 555–569. doi:10.1016/j.jcss.2004.10.006

Dempster, A. P., Laird, N. M., & Rubin, D. B. (1977). Maximum likelihood from incomplete data via the EM algorithm. *Journal of the Royal Statistical Society. Series B, Statistical Methodology, 39*(1), 1–22. doi:10.1111/j.2517-6161.1977.tb01600.x

Domingos, P. (2012). A few useful things to know about machine learning. *Communications of the ACM, 55*(10), 78–87. doi:10.1145/2347736.2347755

Fisher, D. H. (1987). Knowledge acquisition via incremental conceptual clustering. *Machine Learning, 2*(2), 139–172. doi:10.1007/BF00114265

Gan, G., & Ng, M. K. P. (2017). K-means clustering with outlier removal. *Pattern Recognition Letters, 90*, 8–14. doi:10.1016/j.patrec.2017.03.008

Hajamydeen, A. I., & Udzir, N. I. (2016). A refined filter for UHAD to improve anomaly detection. *Security and Communication Networks, 9*(14), 2434–2447. doi:10.1002/sec.1514

Hajamydeen, A. I., & Udzir, N. I. (2019). A detailed description on unsupervised heterogeneous anomaly based intrusion detection framework. Scalable Computing. *Practice and Experience, 20*(1), 113–160.

Hall, M., Frank, E., Holmes, G., Pfahringer, B., Reutemann, P., & Witten, I. H. (2009). The Weka data mining software: An update. *SIGKDD Explorations, 11*(1), 1, 10–18. doi:10.1145/1656274.1656278

Hall, M., Frank, E., Holmes, G., Pfahringer, B., Reutemann, P., & Witten, I. H. (2009). The Weka data mining software: An update. *SIGKDD Explorations, 11*(1), 1, 10–18. doi:10.1145/1656274.1656278

Hochbaum, D. S., & Shmoys, D. B. (1985). A best possible heuristic for the k-center problem. *Mathematics of Operations Research, 10*(2), 180–184. doi:10.1287/moor.10.2.180

Jain, A. K. (2010). Data clustering: 50 years beyond K-means. *Pattern Recognition Letters, 31*(8), 651–666. doi:10.1016/j.patrec.2009.09.011

Jain, A. K., Murty, M. N., & Flynn, P. J. (1999). Data clustering: A review. *ACM Computing Surveys, 31*(3), 264–323. doi:10.1145/331499.331504

Johnson, S. C. (1967). Hierarchical clustering schemes. *Psychometrika, 32*(3), 241–254. doi:10.1007/BF02289588 PMID:5234703

Jordan, M. I., & Mitchell, T. M. (2015). Machine learning: Trends, perspectives, and prospects. *Science, 349*(6245), 255–260. doi:10.1126/science.aaa8415 PMID:26185243

Kohonen, T. (1990). The self-organizing map. *Proceedings of the IEEE, 78*(9), 1464–1480. doi:10.1109/5.58325

Kohonen, T. (2003). Learning vector quantization. In M. A. Arbib (Ed.), *The handbook of brain theory and neural networks* (2nd ed., pp. 631–634). MIT Press.

Kohonen, T. (2012). *Self-organization and associative memory* (Vol. 8). Springer Science & Business Media.

Kumari, A., Kakkar, R., Tanwar, S., Garg, D., Polkowski, Z., Alqahtani, F., & Tolba, A. (2024). Multi-agent-based decentralized residential energy management using Deep Reinforcement Learning. *Journal of Building Engineering*. doi:10.1016/j.jobe.2024.109031

Kumari, A., Patel, M. M., Shukla, A., Tanwar, S., Kumar, N., & Rodrigues, J. J. P. C. (2020). *ArMor: A Data Analytics Scheme to identify malicious behaviors on Blockchain-based Smart Grid System*. GLOBECOM 2020 - 2020 IEEE Global Communications Conference, Taipei, Taiwan. 10.1109/GLOBECOM42002.2020.9348061

Kumari, A., & Tanwar, S. (2021). *Reveal: An AI-based Big Data Analytics Scheme for Energy Price Prediction and Load Reduction*. 2021 11th International Conference on Cloud Computing, Data Science & Engineering (Confluence), Noida, India. 10.1109/Confluence51648.2021.9377144

Kumari, A., & Tanwar, S. (2021). AI-based Peak Load Reduction Approach for Residential Buildings using Reinforcement Learning. *2021 International Conference on Computing, Communication, and Intelligent Systems (ICCCIS)*, Greater Noida, India. 10.1109/ICCCIS51004.2021.9397241

Lu, H., Li, Y., Chen, M., Kim, H., & Serikawa, S. (2018). Brain intelligence: Go beyond artificial intelligence. *Mobile Networks and Applications, 23*(2), 368–375. doi:10.1007/s11036-017-0932-8

MacQueen, J. (1967). Some methods for classification and analysis of multivariate observations. In *Proceedings of the fifth Berkeley symposium on mathematical statistics and probability* (Vol. 1, No. 14, pp. 281-297).

McCallum, A., & Nigam, K. (1999). Text classification by bootstrapping with keywords, EM and shrinkage. In Unsupervised learning in natural language processing.

McCallum, A., Nigam, K., & Ungar, L. H. (2000). Efficient clustering of high-dimensional data sets with application to reference matching. In *Proceedings of the sixth ACM SIGKDD international conference on Knowledge discovery and data mining* (pp. 169-178). ACM. 10.1145/347090.347123

McLachlan, G. J., & Krishnan, T. (2007). *The EM algorithm and extensions*. John Wiley & Sons.

Murtagh, F., & Legendre, P. (2014). Ward's hierarchical agglomerative clustering method: Which algorithms implement Ward's criterion? *Journal of Classification, 31*(3), 274–295. doi:10.1007/s00357-014-9161-z

Ng, A., Jordan, M., & Weiss, Y. (2001). On spectral clustering: Analysis and an algorithm. *Advances in Neural Information Processing Systems*, 14.

Nguyen, T., Ibrahim, S., & Fu, X. (2023). *Deep Clustering with Incomplete Noisy Pairwise Annotations: A Geometric Regularization Approach*. arXiv preprint arXiv:2305.19391.

Omran, M. G., Engelbrecht, A. P., & Salman, A. (2007). An overview of clustering methods. *Intelligent Data Analysis, 11*(6), 583–605. doi:10.3233/IDA-2007-11602

Pfeifer, R., & Iida, F. (2004). Embodied artificial intelligence: Trends and challenges. In *Embodied artificial intelligence* (pp. 1–26). Springer. doi:10.1007/978-3-540-27833-7_1

Phan, T., Feld, S., & Linnhoff-Popien, C. (2020). *Artificial Intelligence—the new Revolutionary Evolution*.

Rajaraman, Á., & Ullman, J. D. (2011). *Mining of massive datasets*. Cambridge University Press. doi:10.1017/CBO9781139058452

Rokach, L., & Maimon, O. (2005). Clustering methods. In *Data mining and knowledge discovery handbook* (pp. 321–352). Springer. doi:10.1007/0-387-25465-X_15

Samek, W., Wiegand, T., & Müller, K. R. (2017). Explainable artificial intelligence: Understanding, visualizing and interpreting deep learning models. *arXiv preprint arXiv:1708.08296*.

Sharma, K. K., & Seal, A. (2021). Outlier-robust multi-view clustering for uncertain data. *Knowledge-Based Systems, 211*, 106567. doi:10.1016/j.knosys.2020.106567

Shi, J., & Malik, J. (2000). Normalized cuts and image segmentation. *IEEE Transactions on Pattern Analysis and Machine Intelligence, 22*(8), 888–905. doi:10.1109/34.868688

Yadav, A., Gupta, V., Sahu, H., & Shrimal, S. (2017). Artificial Intelligence-New Era. *International Journal of New Technology and Research, 3*(3).

# Chapter 8
# Understanding the Concepts of Tools and Techniques for Data Analysis Using RStudio

**Lalit Kumar**
*IILM University, India*

**Vivek Tyagi**
 https://orcid.org/0009-0002-4189-9174
*NAS College, Meerut, India*

## ABSTRACT

*Enormous research papers are floating in the journals market to get published. But now as per the quality standards and norms of publication, some guidelines have been formulated by the prominent authorities to eradicate the pandemic issue of plagiarism. Moreover, it has also been considered whether genuine or licensed software has been utilized to analyze the research data or not. Hence, it is the time to explore some avenues so that mass researchers can be benefitted. R-software, designed by Robert Gentleman and Ross Ihaka from R core team, and R Studio, an open-source integrated development environment (IDE) for R, founded by J.J. Allaire, have emerged as the best platforms for the upcoming researchers which are not bounded with any constraints of licensing. In this article, few packages of R- Software, their significance and implementation have been discussed and summarized. Furthermore some data analysis techniques like t-test, linear regression technique, etc. have also been illustrated using R Studio.*

## 1. INTRODUCTION

Data analysis is one of the most integrated parts of most of the research studies. Scholars, researchers and project organization analyze the situations of associations of variables and their interdependencies to determine the consensus and market trends. The use of R is integrated into examples and exercises to illustrate the concepts discussed, Gareth et al. (2013). Researchers use a wide range of statistical methods to analyze the data. R is utilized for data science tasks, covering data import, cleaning (tidying),

DOI: 10.4018/979-8-3693-3609-0.ch008

transformation, visualization, and modeling. It is known for its practical and hands-on approach to data analysis using R, Hadley et al. (2017). Various statistical software packages are utilized, designed for research studies that include SAS, SPSS and STATA.

## 1.1 R Software and R-Studio

R is a high level language which has been especially designed for statistical data analysis. It is free and can be downloaded with: http://www.cran.r-project.org. R is an extremely bendable and faster high-level programming language and environment which is an Open Source for all established operating systems like for Linux, Windows, and Mac and no licensing compliances are required.

The "user-contributed software" is one of the most idiosyncratic and instrumental characteristics of R, as numerous users have accorded code for administering paramount up-to-date techniques of statistical analysis, in extension to R implementing instinctively all established statistical analyses. Currently, Core Development Team of R maintains it. There is a base system in R with optional add-on packages for various variety of techniques being contributed by users from different parts of the world (currently, more than 1,200 packages are available on the Comprehensive R Archival Network, http://cran.r-project. org/). There is a collection of functions and corresponding documentation that work seamlessly with R. R is having the significant advantages over various other statistical softwares due to its philosophy. Statistical analyses are usually carried out as a series of steps, with transitional results being stored in objects, where these objects are later "cross-examined" for the intelligence of interest (R Development Core Team, 2007b). This is in dissimilarity to other extensively used programs (e.g., SAS and SPSS), which reproduce an ample output to the display. Information, stored in objects, can be recovered at some other times facilitates for easily maneuvering the outcomes of one analysis as raw data for different analysis. Furthermore, model tempering can be executed by devising of the objects as because all appropriate and applicable information is stored in the objects, which is of significant usages in many cases. New breakthroughs in statistical computing also typically make their way into R packages sooner than they do in other statistical software packages.

Besides R, R Studio, written in C++ programming language, is an open-source integrated development environment (IDE) for R. Founder of the programming language, Cold Fusion, J.J. Allaire, created the R studio.

## 1.2 Statistical Concepts

Parametric statistical analysis requires the following two fundamental prerequisites:

- The sample group's means are assumed to be normally distributed, according to the assumption of normality.
- The sample group's variances are assumed to be equal in relation to the corresponding population. Multiple Linear Regression

## 1.3 Multiple Linear Regression

In linear regression analysis, multiple linear regression is the most widely used type. Multiple linear regression is a predictive analysis that explains the link between one continuous dependent variable and two or more independent variables. Either continuous or categorical independent variables (dummy coded as necessary) are possible.

The term "multiple regression analysis" describes a group of methods used to examine the linear relationships between two or more variables. The $y_j$ in the equation is estimated by multiple regression.

$$y_j = \beta_0 + \beta_1 x_{1j} + \beta_2 x_{2j} + \; + \beta_p x_{pj} + \varepsilon_j$$

The independent variables (IVs) are the Xs. The dependent variable is Y. The number of observations (rows) is indicated by the subscript j. The unknown regression coefficients are denoted by the $\beta$'s. The b's stand for their estimates. Every $\beta$ denotes the initial unknown parameter (population), and b is an approximation of this $\beta$. The error (residual) of observation j is denoted by $\varepsilon j$.

Assumptions:

- The residuals from regression need to be regularly distributed.
- It is assumed that the dependent and independent variables have a linear relationship.
- The residuals have a roughly rectangular shape and are homoscedastic.
- The model assumes that there is no multi-collinearity, which means that there is little to no correlation between the independent variables.

## 1.4 Student's *t*-test

The null hypothesis, according to which there is no difference between the means of the two groups, is tested using the Student's t-test. It is applied in three situations:

1.  To test if a sample mean (as an estimate of a population mean) differs significantly from a given population mean (this is a one- sample *t*-test)

The formula for one sample *t*-test is

$$t = \frac{X - \mu}{SE}$$

where $X$ =sample mean, $\mu$ = population mean and SE=standard error

2.  To determine if there is a significant difference between the population means estimated by two independent samples (the unpaired t-test). The unpaired t-test formula is:

Where $X_1 - X_2$ denotes the difference of two groups' means and SE signifies the difference's standard error

3.  To determine if there is a significant difference between the population means estimated by the two dependent samples (paired t-test). When measurements are taken on the same subjects both before and after a treatment, this is a common setting for paired t-tests.

The formula for paired *t*-test is:

$$t = \frac{d}{SE}$$

Where *d* shows the difference of means and SE depicts the difference's standard error

*F*-test is utilized to compare the group variances, which is the ratio of variances ($\sigma_1/\sigma_2$). It is deduced that the group variances are significantly different, if F deviates from 1.0 significantly.

## 1.5 Chi-Square test ($\chi2$)

The chi-square test, a non-parametric test, is based on the chi square distribution. The developed hypothesis states that this test is intended to quantify the discrepancies between the observed and expected frequencies. Chi-square test can be applied to test:
- Good of fit of distributions
- Test of independence of attributes. The chi square statistic is defined as

$$\chi^2 = \sum (Oi - Ei)^2/Ei$$

where, Oi is the observed number of units in category i, and Ei is the expected number of units in category i.

## 1.6 One Way ANOVA

The purpose of the one-way ANOVA is to compare the means of two or more groups and ascertain whether there are any statistically significant differences between the means. It examines the following specific null hypothesis:

$$H_0: \mu_1 = \mu_2 = \mu_3 = \dots = \mu_k$$

Where, 'μ' depicts the group mean and 'k' are no. of groups.

The alternative hypothesis (HA), however, which states that there are at least two group means that are statistically significantly different from one another, is accepted if the one-way ANOVA yields a statistically significant result.

ANOVA can be utilized when there is one categorical independent variable and one quantitative dependent variable.

For example, three groups: green tea, black tea, and no tea—to investigate how tea affects weight loss. Additionally to determine whether crop yields across the three fertilizer categories differ from one another.

## 1.7 Assumptions of ANOVA

- Independence of observations.
- Normally-distributed response variable

- Homogeneity of variance

## 2. LITERATURE REVIEW

Garrett and Hadley (2011) introduced the lubridate package for R, which facilitates working with dates and times. It offers practical examples and guidance on handling temporal data in R. Norman Matloff's book (2011) is a guide to programming in R, covering both basic and advanced topics. It emphasizes the design aspects of R programming and how to write efficient and effective code for statistical analysis. Crawley's book (2012) is a comprehensive guide to the R programming language. It covers a wide range of topics, including data manipulation, statistical analysis, and graphics. Faraway's book (2014) is a comprehensive guide to the R programming language. It covers a wide range of topics, including data manipulation, statistical analysis, and graphics.

Robert I. Kabacoff's book (2015) is a practical guide to data analysis and visualization using R. It covers a wide range of topics, from basic statistical analysis to advanced data visualization techniques. Sanford Weisberg's book (2015) focuses on the application of linear models in statistical analysis using the R programming language. It covers the theory and practical aspects of linear modeling. Begum and Ahmed (2015) highlighted the significance of statistical tools in research work. It emphasizes how these tools can be used to collect, analyze, and interpret data, and draw meaningful conclusions from research findings. Ali and Bhaskar (2016) discussed the importance of basic statistical tools in research and data analysis. It covers topics such as descriptive statistics, hypothesis testing, and regression analysis.

Roger Peng's book (2016) focuses on the essential concepts and techniques of exploratory data analysis (EDA) using the R programming language. It is designed to help readers gain insights into their data through graphical and statistical methods. Grolemund and Wickham's book (2017) served as a practical guide for beginners and intermediate learners interested in diving into data science with R. It follows a data science workflow encompassing the following key steps, viz. Importing data, Tidying data, Transforming data, Visualizing data, Modeling data.

## 3. SOME BASICS OF R

As stated, R is an object-oriented programming language and environment in which objects are stored inside of R sessions or workspaces. These objects can be single numbers, datasets, or model outputs. Successively, you can use these objects inside of functions, use them to create other objects, or remove them wherever necessary.

Indeed, an object is a function in and of itself. Like $->$ (assign what is on the right to the object or on the left), the expression $<-$ is the assignment operator (assign what is on the right to the object on the left). At the prompt, expressions are plunged directly into a R session and are typically showcased by $>$.

To understand a figured out example, simply type the name of function (linear models, lm, in this case):

example (lm)

and you will find the graphical and printed output generated by "lm" function.

You just need to write the library function's name in brackets along with the library's name to utilize it. Thus to load the "MASS" library type:

library(MASS)

Other libraries are "MATRIX" and "ggplot2".
Fo having the view library's contents, "objects" with search() can be utilized, as:

Objects (grep ("MASS", search()))

The screen prompt > is an enticement to put R to work. Here you can use built-in functions or do simple calculations.

>log(42/7.3)

1.749795                                                                 [1]

As a line can only contain 128 characters, you can end a line at a position where it is clearly incomplete, so if you wish to offer a long directive, you can persevere in one or more additional lines.

>5+6+3+6+4+

+ 3+3+4

34                                                                       [1]

If semicolons are used to separate two or more expressions, they can appear on a single line:

>2+3;5*7;3-7

5                                                                        [1]

35                                                                       [1]

-4                                                                       [1]

Several built-in functions in R are given below:

- log(x):log to base e of x
- log10(x):log to base10 of x
- log(x,n):log to base n of x
- sqrt(x):square root of x

- choose(n,x):
  binomialcoefficients n!/(x!(n-x)!)
- floor(x):greatestinteger<x
- ceiling(x):smallestinteger>x
- round(x,digits=0):round x to an integer

The notations % / % (percent, divide, percent) and % % (percent, percent) are used to produce integer quotients and remainders, respectively. For example,

119% / %13 returns the integer quotient as

[1] 9 and

119%% 13 returns the remainder (known as modulo)

## 4. LOADING/ IMPORTING THE EXCEL FILE

The datasets (excel file) can be imported in R by loading "readxl" package. It can import both .xlsx and .xls files. This package is pre-installed in R studio.

Now, to load the file, as depicted in Table 1, go to:

```
File<ImportDataset<FromExcel OR
Type the following command in R console:
> library(readxl)
> CONSUMER_PREF_DATA<-
read_excel("D:/PatanjaliData/CONSUMER PREF DATA.xlsx",
range="A1:F10")
> View(CONSUMER_PREF_DATA)
[1] 2
```

Modulo is a helpful tool for determining if a number is even or odd, as well as if it is an explicit multiple of another integer. For example,15421%%7

```
==0
returns [1]True
```

One or more values of the same type, such as complex, real, integer, logical, string (or character), or raw, can be found in a vector. Although a single-valued variable, like 4.3, is commonly referred to as a scalar, in R, a scalar is actually a vector with length 1.

```
y<-1:5or
y<-c(1, 2, 3, 4,5)
```

Vector multiplication: Suppose x<-c(1, 2, 3, 4, 5) then x*y yields

```
[1]1491625
```

*Table 1. Consumer preference data*

| | age | edu | occU | income | Q1 | Q2 |
|---|---|---|---|---|---|---|
| **1** | 1 | 2 | 2 | 4 | 4 | 4 |
| **2** | 1 | 3 | 2 | 3 | 5 | 4 |
| **3** | 1 | 2 | 4 | 1 | 3 | 2 |
| **4** | 1 | 2 | 1 | 2 | 2 | 3 |
| **5** | 1 | 1 | 4 | 1 | 3 | 2 |
| **6** | 1 | 3 | 5 | 3 | 4 | 5 |
| **7** | 1 | 2 | 3 | 2 | 4 | 3 |
| **8** | 1 | 4 | 1 | 1 | 4 | 3 |
| **9** | 2 | 2 | 2 | 4 | 4 | 3 |

## 5. LOADING/IMPORTING THE DATAFRAMES(*.txt or*.dat)

An object containing rows and columns is called a data frame. Various study observations and experiment measurements are displayed in the rows. The values of the various variables are listed in the columns. (Note: A matrix's body values can only consist of numbers.; tin data frames they can be numbers or text).

The "read.table" imports the file in R. Following the file's import into R, we typically wish to conduct the following two tasks:

1)    Use attach to frame the variable reachable and usable by name within the R session
2)    Use names to retrieve a list of the variables names

To do so, following commands are to use:

```
data<-read.table("Path of .txt file", header=T)
attach(data) names(data)
```

To get the contents of dataframe, just type file name. Figure 1 represents the contents.

Now, the entity known as "data" possesses every feature of a dataframe. With summary, we are able to condense it, as depicted in Fig2.

```
summary(data)
```

It is always advisable or useful to have data with no null values in variables as far as statistical modelling is concerned. Using the 'no.omit' function, we can have a shorter and logical data frame

```
data1<-read.table("Path of .txt file ", header=T)
data1 na.omit(data1)
```

The above syntax will remove the rows, having missing values, from the original dataset.

*Figure 1. An example of dataframe*

|    | Field.Name | Area | Slope | Vegetation | Soil.pH | Damp | Worm.density |
|----|-----------|------|-------|-----------|---------|-------|-------------|
| 1 | Nashs.Field | 3.6 | 11 | Grassland | 4.1 | FALSE | 4 |
| 2 | Silwood.Bottom | 5.1 | 2 | Arable | 5.2 | FALSE | 7 |
| 3 | Nursery.Field | 2.8 | 3 | Grassland | 4.3 | FALSE | 2 |
| 4 | Rush.Meadow | 2.4 | 5 | Meadow | 4.9 | TRUE | 5 |
| 5 | Gunness.Thicket | 3.8 | 0 | Scrub | 4.2 | FALSE | 6 |
| 6 | Oak.Mead | 3.1 | 2 | Grassland | 3.9 | FALSE | 2 |
| 7 | Church.Field | 3.5 | 3 | Grassland | 4.2 | FALSE | 3 |
| 8 | Ashurst | 2.1 | 0 | Arable | 4.8 | FALSE | 4 |
| 9 | The.Orchard | 1.9 | 0 | Orchard | 5.7 | FALSE | 9 |
| 10 | Rookery.Slope | 1.5 | 4 | Grassland | 5.0 | TRUE | 7 |

*Figure 2. View of summary*

```
Field.Name          Area              Slope             Vegetation
Ashurst     : 1     Min.    :0.800    Min.    : 0.00    Arable    :3
Cheapside   : 1     1st Qu.:2.175     1st Qu.: 0.75     Grassland:9
Church.Field: 1     Median :3.000     Median : 2.00     Meadow    :3
Farm.Wood   : 1     Mean    :2.990    Mean    : 3.50    Orchard   :1
Garden.Wood : 1     3rd Qu.:3.725     3rd Qu.: 5.25     Scrub     :4
Gravel.Pit  : 1     Max.    :5.100    Max.    :11.00
(Other)     :14

Soil.pH              Damp              Worm.density
Min.    :3.500      Mode :logical     Min.    :0.00
1st Qu.:4.100      FALSE:14           1st Qu.:2.00
Median :4.600      TRUE :6            Median :4.00
Mean    :4.555     NA's :0            Mean    :4.35
3rd Qu.:5.000                         3rd Qu.:6.25
Max.    :5.700                        Max.    :9.00
```

## LOADING/ IMPORTING THE EXCEL FILE

The datasets (spss file) can be imported in R by loading "haven"package. It can import spss, sas and stata files. This package is pre-installed in R studio.

```
Now,toloadthefile,go to:
File<ImportDataset<FromSPSS OR
Type the following command in R console:
library(haven)
Mobile_Data <- read_sav("D:/MOBILE DATA ANALYSIS/Mobile Data.sav") View(Mobile_
Data)
```

*Figure 3. Matrix scatterplot*

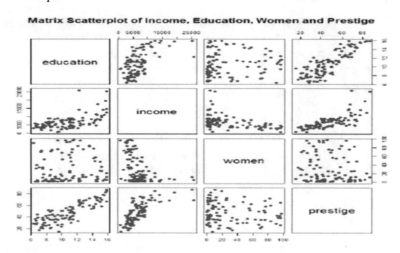

## 6. DATA ANALYSIS TECHNIQUES IN 'R' ENVIRONMENT

### 6.1 Multiple Linear Regression

A regression model can be developed for income as a function of number of years of education, prestige and proportion of working women. This technique can be applied on any type of datasets like .txt, .sav,.dat and.xlsx,etc. Here, the modelling is performed for .txt dataset, 'Prestige' which is available in 'library(car)'.

We will install several other packages to better represent the results from multiple linear regression.

```
library(car)
library(corrplot) # Corrplot will also be used in the example later on..
library(visreg) # With the help of this library, we may display multivariate
graphs.
library(rgl) library(knitr) library(scatterplot3d)
```

In multiple linear regression, '*income*' is the response variable and the independent variables or covariates are '*women*', '*prestige*' and '*education*'. The average number of years of school required for each profession is referred to as education. The percentage of women in the profession is referred to as the "women" variable, and the prestige score for each occupation—which is determined by a metric known as the "Pineo-Porter"—comes from a mid-1960s social survey.

Since the dataset 'Prestige' consists various variables, but we require only first four relevant variables, so we can create a new data frame and can have the summary using the following command:

```
newPdata=Prestige[,c(1:4)] summary(newPdata)
```

Fig3 reveals the following facts:

*Figure 4. Prestige data summary (rescaled)*

```
   education          income          women            prestige
 Min.   : 6.380   Min.   :  611   Min.   : 0.000   Min.   :14.80
 1st Qu.: 8.445   1st Qu.: 4106   1st Qu.: 3.592   1st Qu.:35.23
 Median :10.540   Median : 5930   Median :13.600   Median :43.60
 Mean   :10.738   Mean   : 6798   Mean   :28.979   Mean   :46.83
 3rd Qu.:12.648   3rd Qu.: 8187   3rd Qu.:52.203   3rd Qu.:59.27
 Max.   :15.970   Max.   :25879   Max.   :97.510   Max.   :87.20

  education.c        prestige.c        women.c
 Min.   :-4.358   Min.   :-32.033   Min.   :-28.98
 1st Qu.:-2.293   1st Qu.:-11.608   1st Qu.:-25.39
 Median :-0.198   Median : -3.233   Median :-15.38
 Mean   : 0.000   Mean   :  0.000   Mean   :  0.00
 3rd Qu.: 1.909   3rd Qu.: 12.442   3rd Qu.: 23.22
 Max.   : 5.232   Max.   : 40.367   Max.   : 68.53
```

1)  Income and education are positively associated.
2)  Average income in profession declines as the percentage of women increases.
3)  Plotting 'prestige' against 'income' appears to follow a similar trend in relation to education.

The following multiple linear regression model:

$$yi_{=\beta}1+_x2i\beta_{2+x}3_i\beta3+_{x4i}\beta_4+\varepsilon i$$

w$_h$er$_e$,

$x2 = $ Average no. of years of education in each profession
$x3=$Prestige score for each profession
$x4 = $ Percentage of women in the occupation

Next, we scale (de-mean) the independent variables using the following syntax and present a summary of the data. Centering is done to have a insightful and value-added interpretation of the intercept estimate.

```
education.c = scale(newPdata$education, center=TRUE, scale=FALSE)
prestige.c = scale(newPdata$prestige, center=TRUE, scale=FALSE)
women.c = scale(newPdata$women, center=TRUE, scale=FALSE)
#Bind all these new variables into newPdata1 and display a summary.
new.c.vars = cbind(education.c, prestige.c, women.c)
newPdata1=cbind(newPdata,new.c.vars)
names(newPdata1)[5:7] = c("education.c", "prestige.c", "women.c")
summary(newPdata1)
```

Figure 4 depicts the rescaled data summary. Further, the model and a summary of the results can be estimated as shown in Figure 5:

*Figure 5. Estimated model and its results*

```
Call:
lm(formula = income ~ education.c + prestige.c + women.c, data = newPdata1)

Residuals:
    Min      1Q  Median      3Q     Max
-7715.3  -929.7  -231.2   689.7 14391.8

Coefficients:
             Estimate Std. Error t value Pr(>|t|)
(Intercept) 6797.902    254.934  26.665  < 2e-16 ***
education.c  177.199    187.632   0.944    0.347
prestige.c   141.435     29.910   4.729 7.58e-06 ***
women.c      -50.896      8.556  -5.948 4.19e-08 ***
---
Signif. codes:  0 '***' 0.001 '**' 0.01 '*' 0.05 '.' 0.1 ' ' 1

Residual standard error: 2575 on 98 degrees of freedom
Multiple R-squared:  0.6432,  Adjusted R-squared:  0.6323
F-statistic: 58.89 on 3 and 98 DF,  p-value: < 2.2e-16
```

```
mod1 = lm(income ~ education.c + prestige.c + women.c, data=newPdata1)
summary(mod1)
```

## 6.2 t- TEST

When the population mean is considerably different from the sample mean, to test the same one-sample t-test is utilized.

To carry the same in R studio, we consider a sample of a data file "Marks.txt". To investigate the hypothesis that there is insignificant difference between the sample mean and population mean (Known), proceed in the following manner. To load the file,

```
File<ImportDataset<FromText(readr)
```

OR

Type the following command in R console:

```
Marks<-read.table("Path of .txt file", header=T)
attach(Marks) View(Marks)
```

By default, t.test function arguments: t.test(x1, x2= NULL, alternative = c("two.sided","less","greater"),mu=0, paired=FALSE,var.equal=FALSE, conf.level = 0.95)

Now, to execute the one-sample t-test with population mean, 85 in R Studio, type the command as:

```
t.test(x1,mu=85,alternative="greater")
```

Populated results will be:

```
OneSamplet-test
data:x1
```

```
t=-2.6841,df=14,p-value= 0.9911
alternative hypothesis: true mean is greater than 85
95percentconfidenceinterval: 77.82317 Inf
Sample estimates:
Mean of x 80.66667
```

The interpretation of the results confirms that the null hypothesis gets accepted since the p-value is greater than 0.05 and the sample and population means do not differ significantly.

To illustrate 2-independent samples t-test, we consider the data file "Marks.txt", consists two independent datasets of marks of a subject of Boys($x1$) and Girls($x2$), with an assumption of normal distribution and unequal variances.

To investigate the hypothesis that the average score of boys and girls is not significantly different from one another, following steps are to be carried out in R Studio.

Further to execute the "2-sample t-test, proceed with the below given command in R:

```
t.test(x₁,x₂)
```

Derived results will be as:

```
Welch Two Sample t-test

data:x₁ and x₂
t=-0.033773,df=25.132,p-
value=0.9733
alternative hypothesis: true difference in means is not equal to 0
95percentconfidenceinterval:
-4.1310223.997689
Sample estimates:
meanofx1meanofx2 80.6666780.73333
```

Here, the results reveal that there is no discernible difference in the means of the marks earned by boys and girls because the p-value is greater than 0.05, which prevents the null hypothesis from being rejected.

Further, the importance of a treatment can be evaluated using the paired t-test (before and after case) with the assumption, having sample from the normal population. To look at the hypothesis that the sample means do not significantly differ from one another i.e. before and after the treatment there is no effect on the sample, following steps can be executed in R Studio:

```
Treatment<-read.table("Pathof.txtfile", header=T)
attach(Treatment) View(Treatment)
t.test(Before,After,paired=TRUE)
```

where, "Before" and "After" are the two samples and the result will be as:

```
Paired t-test

data: Before and After
t=3.0864, df=19, p-value= 0.006077
alternative hypothesis: true difference in means is not equal to 0
95percentconfidenceinterval: 2.832321 14.767679
sample estimates:
mean of the differences 8.8
```

There is a significant change in the sample means, indicating that the treatment had an impact on the sample, because the p-value is less than 0.05, which rules out the acceptance of the null hypothesis.

## 6.3 Chi-Square TEST ($\chi 2$)

This test is utilized to test the goodness of fit and independence of characteristics.

As far as "Goodness of Fit" is concerned, let us take an example, no. of jobs available in four different categories. Now we want to test the variation in these categories are significant in real or just by randomness (insignificant). The command in R studio will be as:

```
jobs<-c(780,624,865,420)
names(jobs)<- c("Marketing", "Operations", "Sales", "HR")
jobs
Result:
Marketing    Operations   Sales HR
780 624 865    420
jobs/sum(jobs) Result:
Marketing Operations Sales 0.2900707 0.2320565 0.3216809

HR 0.1561919
```

As we assume that each category has an equal probability, so $H_0$ will be proportion of jobs in each category is 0.25 and $H_1$ will be proportion of jobs in each category is not equal.

```
probability<-c(0.25,0.25,0.25,0.25) chisq.test(jobs, p=probability)
```

Output:

```
Chi-squared test for given probabilities

data: jobs
X-squared=170.65,df=3,p- value < 2.2e-16
```

We can reject $H_0$ and come to the 95% confidence level conclusion that the proportion of jobs in each group is not equal because the p-value is 0.00, less than 0.05.

Further, sometimes we have two variables to study; chi-square test can be implemented to verify the interdependence of the two attributes. Here, in the below given example,

$H_0$: Intelligence is independent of Status

$H_1$: Intelligence and Status are dependent.

Suppose we have some data as:

```
candidates<- rbind(c(2890,3547),c(1675,1932))
dimnames(candidates)<-list(Intelligence
=c("Intelligent","Notintelligent"), Status=c("Rich","Poor"))
```

candidates

Result:

```
     Status
Intelligence      Rich      Poor
  Intelligent              2890       3547
 Notintelligent   16751932
```

Now, to conduct the chi-square test, type the following command in R terminal,

```
chisq.test(candidates) Output:
Pearson's Chi-squared test with Yates' continuity correction
data:candidates
X-squared=2.1518, df=1,p- value = 0.1424
```

Here, result reveals that Since the p value is higher than 0.05, the null hypothesis—that intelligence is independent of status—cannot be rejected. The above statistic of chi-square has been estimated with Yates' correction which is needed to reduce the error of approximation when sample size is small.

## 6.4 One Way ANOVA

Analysis of variance (ANOVA) is a technique to compare two or more groups' means. aov() function is used in R for fitting an ANOVA model. When summary() is used to present the model summary, aov() objects return an ANOVA table. To retrieve an object's ANOVA table or a comparison of nested models, utilize the anova() function (not to be distracted with aov()).

Now, to illustrate One Way ANOVA, we take an example of Marks of students of three different sections. Since there is no discernible difference in the marks of students from different sections, $H_0$ can be adjusted, however $H_1$ will indicate that there is a discernible difference in the grades of students from different parts. Here, "Marks" is the quantitative dependent variable while "Sections" is the categorical independent variable.

To conduct the test of ANOVA in R Studio, following are the commands:

```
one.way<-aov(Marks~Section, data=SectionsMarks)
summary(one.way)
```

```
Result willbe:
    Df  SumSq  MeanSq  Fvalue   Pr(>F)
Section      1      71 70.53 0.435 0.513
Residuals    43      6966 162.01
```

We can also have the same result using function anova() for an existing object (one.way), using:

```
anova(one.way) Output:
Analysis of Variance Table

Response: Marks
            Df   SumSq    MeanSq   Fvalue Pr(>F)
Section            1        70.5    70.533   0.4354 0.5129
Residuals    43  6966.3 162.006
```

We are unable to reject the null hypothesis and come to the conclusion that there is insignificant difference between the marks of students in different sections because the p-value is bigger than 0.05.

## 7. CONCLUSION

Bad statistics may lead to wrong conclusions, and hence it may enhance the unethical practices. A sufficient knowledge about the basic statistical concepts will help to improve and produce the research designs and quality research respectively which can be practiced for developing the testament-based guidelines. Furthermore, usage of non-licensed software to analyze the data will also lead to the rejection of a quality research. So, in this article, some data analysis techniques have been discussed along with their illustrations using R Studio, an open source integrated development environment. R software has shown to be an effective instrument for carrying out a wide range of statistical analyses, though with certain limitations for some techniques.

## REFERENCES

Ali, Z., & Bhaskar, S. B. (2016). Basic Statistical tools in research and data analysis. *Indian Journal of Anaesthesia*, *60*(9), 662–669. doi:10.4103/0019-5049.190623 PMID:27729694

Begum, K. J., & Ahmed, A. (2015). The Importance of Statistical Tools in Research Work. [IJSIMR]. *International Journal of Scientific and Innovative Mathematical Research*, *3*(12), 50–58.

Crawley, M. J. (2012). *The R Book* (2nd ed.). John Wiley and Sons Ltd. doi:10.1002/9781118448908

Faraway, J. J. (2014). *Linearmodels with R*. CRC Press.

Grolemund, G., & Wickham, H. (2011). Dates and Times Made Easy with lubridate. *Journal of Statistical Software*, *40*(3), 1–25. doi:10.18637/jss.v040.i03

Grolemund, G., & Wickham, H. (2017). *R for Data Science: Import, Tidy, Transform, Visualize, and Model Data*. O'Reilly Media.

Inani, S. (2016). *Two sample t test in R Studio*. [Video]. YouTube.

James, G., Witten, D., Hastie, T., & Tibshirani, R. (2013). *An Introduction to Statistical Learning with Applications in R*. Springer.

Kabacoff, R. I. (2015). *R in Action: Data Analysis and Graphics with R*. Manning Publications.

Kelley, K., Lai, K., & Wu, P. J. (2008). *Chapter: Using R For Data Analysis: A Best Practice For Research. Best Practices in Quantitative Methods*. SAGE Publications, Inc.

Matloff, N. (2011). *The Art of R Programming: A Tour of Statistical Software Design*. No Starch Press.

Peng, R. D. (2016). *Exploratory Data Analysis with R*. Springer.

Rai, B. (2020). *Goodness of Fit and Test of Independence with RExamples Using Chi-Square* Test. [Video]. YouTube..

Sherratt, T. (2015). *One Way ANOVA in R Studio*. [Video]. YouTube.

Weisberg, S. (2015). *Applied Linear Models with R*. CRC Press.

# Section 3
# Specialized Topics and Applications

*In the section titled "Specialized Topics and Applications," readers delve into advanced concepts and practical applications within the field of data analytics. This section explores specialized topics such as predictive modeling, clustering, natural language processing, and big data analytics. Readers gain insights into how these techniques are applied across various industries, including finance, healthcare, marketing, and supply chain management. Each chapter provides in-depth discussions and real-world case studies, offering readers a deeper understanding of how data analytics can be tailored to address specific challenges and opportunities within different domains.*

# Chapter 9

# Optimal Configuration of Solar–Based Combined Hydrogen, Heat, and Power (S–CHHP) to Minimize Harmonic in Point of Common Coupling (PCC)

**Hamed Hosseinnia**
*Tabriz University, Iran*

**Rana Rostami**
*Tabriz University, Iran*

## ABSTRACT

*The growth of the load makes the need to build a new power plant inevitable. According to the type of load, the type of DGs is selected. In loads that need both electricity and heat, simultaneous production units are used. Improving system technical criteria's such as: voltage stability, total harmonic distortion (THD), power loss are main aims of researchers. Harmonics are one of the stressful factors in the system. Harmonics are created both by the load and by the DGs themselves. In this chapter, the goal is to reduce the harmonics at the point of common coupling (PCC). For this purpose, solar-based combined hydrogen, heat, and power (S-CHHP) is used. Artificial intelligence (AI) is the one of strong tools in define and solve of optimization problems. Due to importance of data gathering, process and send/receive in this study, the system to manage information data with minimum error, is inevitable. Natural language process (NLP) is the best choice to utilize in this system.*

## 1. INTRODUCTION

In this section brief introduction according to solar based- combined hydrogen, heat and power (S-CHHP) and natural language process (NLP) are presented.

DOI: 10.4018/979-8-3693-3609-0.ch009

## 1.1. Motivation

Passing from traditional power system to the smart power system is known as restructuring. Restructuring needs some special infrastructure, such as: communication, bilateral power flow capability and converting new loads (electrical vehicles) from passive load to the active generation units (by integrating them as a virtual power plant). To evaluate several aspects of smart power system and its requirements, more of literatures are done. In Jafari et al. (2020), authors to postpone needs to the install a new power plants, make a new arrangement in the reconfiguration of distribution system(DS). Due to constraints in the plant capacity and reserve and need to other kinds of sources, in Hosseinnia et al. (2018a), authors studied sitting and sizing of DGs in the distribution network. In Vincent et al. (2020), authors analyzed electrical vehicles (EVs) impacts on daily load curve(DLC). To effectivity of EVs by employing demand response (DR) programs, several kinds of time-based and incentive-based DR programs are studied (Hosseinnia, Talavat, & Nazarpour, 2021). In Moghaddam et al. (2024), Monte Carlo method (MCM) is used to model system uncertainties. Artificial intelligent is utilized to predict the uncertainties in generation and demand side (Nasiri et al., 2023). In Rostami and Hosseinnia (2021), authors consider impacts of optimal sitting and sizing of remote terminal units (RTUs) on data gathering in the smart DS. Power quality, or more precisely, power quality disturbances, is generally defined as any change in power, i.e., change in voltage, current, or frequency, that interferes with normal operating conditions. The study of power quality and its control methods is an important issue for power generation companies, large industrial companies, and even home users. Studies have increased when the sensitivity of equipment to small changes in voltage, current, and frequency of the power supply is increased. Unfortunately, different terms are used to describe many system disturbances, which further confuses the definition of power quality problems today. The classification of disturbance phenomena by the IEEE standard is divided into the following 7 categories: 1- transient states 2- short-term changes 3- long-term changes 4- unbalance 5- waveform distortion 6- voltage fluctuations 7- frequency changes (Hosseinnia et al., 2020). Since the goal of smart grids is to provide higher reliability and create an environmentally friendly grid, the development of diverse renewable energy is one of the most important topics of smart grids. Due to the instability of these energies and the increase of power electronics in smart networks, power quality disturbances happen more easily and more often than in previous networks. In order to reduce the economic costs caused by poor power quality, it is necessary to monitor the power quality in smart networks. The method of identifying power quality phenomena in traditional networks is generally done with a power analyzer device, in such a way that the current and voltage ports are connected at the desired location and the device, after storing the information with the software designed for it, identifies the desired parameters. The transfer of traditional power grids to the smart grid creates a new field of data collection (Hosseinnia & Tousi, 2019). Advanced Metering Structure or AMI is one of the latest data collection mechanisms that emerged after the modernization of old power grids. In AMIs, there are smart meters (SM) to sense, collect and analyze the energy used through various communication structures. A variety of AMIs have replaced manual readings and provide more accurate real-time energy information for billing purposes. In addition, AMI is able to collect and analyze information that was very difficult to do in the past (Omri et al., 2024). Therefore, it is obvious to use AMI to detect power quality disturbances in smart grids. For this purpose, there are several meters with limited communication capabilities for AMIs. Generally, decisions are made locally and decentralized by surveyors. Then the local control center receives the local decisions and makes the final decision. In Hosseinnia et al. (2022), the classes of power quality disturbances are categorized as the factors that cause them, so that at the same time, in addition to detecting the type of disturbance, it also has the ability to detect the factor that causes it. Although the shortcoming of this reference is that the classes are limited and all power quality disturbances are not included in it, in this reference, the combination of two features of the effective value and also according to the previous reference the energy of the wavelet coefficients are used for classification. The wavelet transform is calculated separately for each of the phases and continues up to 9 levels, and at the end, the calculation of approximation coefficients is used in the last level to obtain the feature vector. In this reference, it is mentioned that the feature vector obtained from the energy of the coefficients is the best type of feature for the classification of power quality disturbance signals. Hosseinnia, Mohammadi-Ivatloo, and Mohammadpourfard (2021) has been used to identify the factors causing disturbances using wavelet. The factors causing disturbances are limited to such things as the energization of the transformer, the energization of the capacitor bank, as well as the operation of the converters. Daub4 wavelet is used as the mother wavelet and the square of the wavelet coefficients up to 4 levels is calculated and considered as a feature. Since a small transient occurs at the moment of energizing the transformer, as a result, by finding the highest value of the ripple coefficient, the moment of the beginning of this phenomenon can be found. Also, due to the creation of the second and fifth harmonics in the transformer startup, Fourier transform has been used to calculate these harmonics. In this reference, the wavelet coefficients in the first level are also used to find the number of voltage gaps. In Kabiri-Renani et al. (2024), wavelet is also used as a feature extraction tool. In such a way that the signal up to l level is decomposed by discrete wavelet transform and the energy of the detail coefficients forms the l+1 dimensional feature vector. It is also stated that parsing from level 7 and above does not provide more information and therefore the value of l is considered to be 7. It is mentioned in this reference that this feature is not enough and it does not have the ability to distinguish some classes, especially the voltage reduction class and the interruption class. In Pourghaderi et al. (2023), the db4 mother wavelet is used and the decomposition continues up to the third level. Then, the detail coefficients of the first to third level and the approximation coefficients of the last level are used to extract the features. Then, the eight characteristics of average, standard deviation, shape coefficient, skewness, peak coefficient in the graph, effective value, coefficient of the highest order and Fourier transformation are used to extract the characteristic. In Modarresi and Hosseinnia (2023), 5 classes of disturbances are considered and the harmonic classes of frequency changes and waveform gaps are ignored and sixteen cycles of voltage information are used. In this reference, only one feature vector is used and that is the effective value of the wavelet coefficients. Different mother wavelets have been used to decompose the signal and their output accuracy has been compared using the classifier. Also, the number of signal analysis levels has been checked and the signal has been analyzed from level one to ten, and different accuracy has been obtained for each level, and finally it has been concluded that analysis beyond the seventh level does not provide much information. In Ghasemi et al. (2023) and Taheri, Abedini, and Aminifar (2023), the signal has been decomposed into thirteen and ten levels, respectively, using the wavelet, and the energy of the coefficients and its normalized value have been used as features. Taheri, Abedini, and Aminifar (2023) used the db8 mother wavelet unlike other references. It also used packet wavelet to extract features. In this reference, the number of decomposition levels is not mentioned, but the feature vector is considered to be the absolute value of the extrema of the wavelet coefficients. In Solat et al. (2023), Daubechies family wavelets are examined and it is mentioned that this family, especially db4, db6, db8 and db10, has been widely used in the identification and classification of power quality disturbance signals. It is also stated in the selection of the mother wavelet type that disturbance signals can be divided into two categories. The first category with fast transient mode and the second category with slow transient mode. In the fast transient category, the waveform has sharp edges and rapid changes in a short period of time. For this category, db4 and db6 can be better options. In the second category with slow transients that have slow changes over a longer period of time, db4 and db6 are not able to follow and capture these disturbances. Hence db8 and db10 are used. In this reference, four classes of disturbances have been mentioned and their categories have been discussed. Also, for different disturbances, the wavelet decomposition level has been used up to different levels, and a specific decomposition level has not been used for all classes. Two feature vectors are used in this reference. which are the energy vector and the total harmonic distortion, respectively. In Al-Ja'afreh et al. (2023), only six classes of disturbances are considered. No feature has been extracted in this reference. In fact, the disturbance signal is decomposed by the wavelet, but the number of its levels is not mentioned, and the wavelet coefficients themselves are presented to the classifier for classification. In fact, in this reference, it is assumed that the coefficients themselves are sufficient to distinguish between the classes, and no mathematical and statistical operations have been performed on them. In Marquez and Mohammad (2023), the db4 mother wavelet is also used for feature extraction. The reasons for using this mother wavelet are shorter filter length, shorter computing time, and more density in real-time applications. In this reference, 9 classes of disturbances, which include mixed disturbances, are used for classification. To extract the feature, the signal is decomposed up to ten levels and the energy of the wavelet coefficients is calculated up to the tenth level. Also, the wavelet conversion of the sine signal is also done and its energy is also received. The difference of these two vector values along with features such as sum of squares of wavelet coefficients, average square of wavelet coefficients in ten levels and average entropy are considered for feature extraction. The last three years have ushered in the golden age of natural language processing (NLP), one of the most useful and visible forms of machine learning (ML) (Shariatkhah et al., 2023). NLP is a branch of machine learning that gives computers human-like abilities to understand text and speech. Thanks to increasing computing power, the amount of raw data available on the Internet, and the popularity of deep learning, natural language processing has gone from a hypothesis in the 1950s Turing test to an everyday reality. More than fifty years old, NLP is rooted in linguistics. Natural language processing is used in various fields such as medical research, search engines and business intelligence (Khalilzadeh & Haghifam, 2023). NLP enables computers to understand natural language like humans. Whether it is a spoken or written language, natural language processing uses artificial intelligence to receive input from the real world and, by processing it, presents it in a form that computers can understand. NLP or natural language processing is one of the main trends in technology because most of the information that is produced all over the world is in natural human language. In fact, all this information is produced in formats such as email, WhatsApp messages, Twitter updates, new articles, books and colloquial languages, etc. (Efstratiadi et al., 2023).

## 1.2. Chapter Contribution

NLP enables machines to decode all this information and extract meaning from them. The main advantage of natural language processing is that it improves the way humans and computers communicate. In fact, the closest way to make changes in computers is through codes, which is the language of computers. By enabling computers to understand human language, it will become much easier for humans to interact with computers. Other advantages of NLP are classified as follows:

- Improving the accuracy and efficiency of documents.

*Figure 1. NLL and S-CHHP and MG connected via PCC*

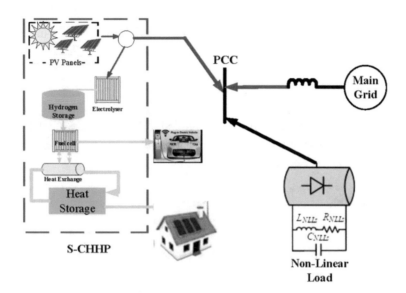

- It provides detailed insights that cannot be accessed by other means due to the large volume of data.
- Ease of use for sentiment analysis It enables organizations to use chat-bots to better interact with customers.
- Personal assistants like Alexa can interact in human language using this feature.
- The ability to automatically create a readable summary of a long and complex text.

## 1.3. Organization

In this paper, to identify and categorize power quality disturbances, data received by AMI needs to be analyzed. Since with the presence of new devices in the microgrid that were not common in traditional networks, voltage and current signals and their sampled data will undergo changes that will make the act of identifying and classifying signals different from what was in traditional networks. In the identification and classification of signals, existing methods will be used to transfer the signal from the time domain to other domains, such as Fourier transform, wavelet, S, etc. Since the data received from AMI is voluminous, in order not to lose information and delay in data processing, it is necessary to identify and classify signals with less computational load and faster. Figure 1 illustrates the connection of S-CHHP and NLL and MG via PCC.

The other parts of work are classified as follows:

In section 2 main aims of this work are formulated and demonstrated in detail. Section 3 describes the proposed identification algorithm. In section 4 all of obtained results are evaluated in detail. Section 5 concludes the work.

## 2. PROBLEM DEFINITION

This work involves harmonic study in presence of S-CHHP and MG and NLL. Functions and parameters are defined as follows.

### 2.1. Objective Function

Eliminating or reducing total harmonic which are generated by NLL or S-CHHP or MG is the main function of this study. One of important criteria to analyze system harmonic is known as total harmonic distortion (THD). This parameter is formulated as follows:

$$OF = \min(\sum_{i=3}^{n} THD_i^{current})$$

(1)

To identify the system harmonic, recursive least square method is proposed. The regression least squares method is a powerful mathematical tool for real-time estimation of the parameters of a signal. In this method, we assume that the estimation has already been done up to the moment t. Now enter the signal information received from AMI at the moment t+1 and the previous estimate is modified based on the new information received. In other words, there is real-time communication between the received signal and the estimator, and the estimate is updated with each new sample of received signal information. Therefore, assuming the received signal in the form of equation (2), this algorithm performs the estimation operation using equation (3) (estimation relation) and equation (4) (updating relation).

$$y(t) = \phi^t(t)\theta(t)$$

(2)

$$\hat{\theta}(t+1) = \hat{\theta}(t) + P(t+1)\phi(t+1)\left[y(t+1) - \hat{\phi}(t+1)\hat{\theta}(t)\right]$$

(3)

$$P(t+1) = \frac{1}{\lambda}\left[P(t) - \frac{P(t)\phi(t+1)\hat{\phi}(t+1)P(t)}{1 + \hat{\phi}(t+1)P(t)\phi(t+1)}\right]$$

(4)

In these relations, $\theta$ is the matrix of signal parameters, $\hat{\theta}$ estimation matrix of signal parameters, $\Phi^T$ is the matrix of coefficients of signal parameters or matrix of regressors, P is the covariance matrix and $\lambda$ is the forgetting coefficient.

### 2.2. S-CHHP Formulation

In this section, operational constraints of S-CHHP have been defined.

The output power of the PV depends on the three factors: ambient temperature, panels efficiency and the amount of absorbed sun irradiation and determined as follows (Hosseinnia & Farsadi, 2017; Hosseinnia et al., 2018b; Ntafalias et al., 2022):

$$P_{out,t}^{PV} = \eta^{PV} \times A \times (25 - T_{amb}) \times Ir_t \tag{5}$$

The process of decomposing $H_2$ and $O_2$ from the water is done by electrolyzer. This process is carried out by passing an electrical current between two separated electrodes. The output power of electrolyzer is determined as follows (Zhou et al., 2023):

$$P_t^{Out\_EL} = P_t^{Out\_SPL} \times \eta^{EL} \tag{6}$$

The fuel cell is an instrument to generate electricity from the chemical energy off $H_2$ and $O_2$. The output power of fuel cell has been calculated as follows (Bo et al., 2023):

$$P_t^{FuelCell} = P_t^{HSS\_Fuelcell} \times \eta^{fuelcell} \tag{7}$$

Hydrogen storage is used to intermittence electrolyzer and fuel cells. The hydrogen flow of hydrogen storage is defined as follows (Zhang et al., 2023):

$$HSS_t = HSS_{t-1} + \eta^{PH} \times P_t^{PH} - \frac{P_t^{HP}}{\eta^{HP}} \tag{8}$$

Heat flow in the thermal storage unit is defined as follows (Cai et al., 2023):

$$Heat_t^{HS} = \eta^{HS} \times Heat_{t-1}^{HS} + Heat_{t-1}^{HS-in} - Heat_{t-1}^{HS-out} \tag{9}$$

## 2.2.1 Power, Heat, and Hydrogen Balance Equation

The constraints related to power, heat and hydrogen balance are defined as follows (Hemmati et al., 2023):

$$P_t^{S-CHHP} + P_t^{Grid-Sell} - P_t^{Grid-buy} = P_t^{Load} \tag{10}$$

$$Heat_t^{S-CHHP} = Heat_t^{Storage} + Heat_t^{Load} \tag{11}$$

$$Hyd_t^{S-CHHP} = Hyd_t^{Storage} + Hyd_t^{Load} \tag{12}$$

## 3. PROPOSED IDENTIFICATION ALGORITHM

This section demonstrates the proposed solution methods.

### 3.1. Signal Estimation

Frequency response is one of traditional tools to identify system harmonic. If this method's performance wouldn't satisfied, the other methods such as recursive least squares method is a proper alternative.

Using the theory of symmetric components, for each harmonic component identified by the VFF-RLS estimator, positive, negative and zero sequences can be estimated by another VFF-RLS estimator. Therefore, similar to the harmonic identification algorithm described in the previous section, to identify the unbalanced signal of the currents measured and sent by AMIs, the matrix of regressors should be formed. Equation (13) shows the relationship between a three-phase harmonic current component and the sequences of that harmonic component (Hosseinnia & Farsadi, 2015; Rezaeeian et al., 2022).

$$\begin{bmatrix} I_0 \\ I_+ \\ I_- \end{bmatrix} = T^{-1} \begin{bmatrix} I_{ah} \\ I_{bh} \\ I_{ch} \end{bmatrix} \tag{13}$$

In this regard, h is the order of the harmonic component and T is the matrix of symmetric sequences for the harmonic component of the h order and is defined as relation (14).

$$T = \begin{bmatrix} \sin(h\omega t) & \sin(h\omega t) & \sin(h\omega t) \\ \sin(h\omega t) & \sin(h\omega t - 120) & \sin(h\omega t + 120) \\ \sin(h\omega t) & \sin(h\omega t + 120) & \sin(h\omega t - 120) \end{bmatrix} \tag{14}$$

The dimensions of the T matrix are known using PLL. On the other hand, the harmonic components of the current have been estimated from the previous step, so using relations (2) and (3), symmetrical sequences are estimated for each harmonic component. Sources of generation of harmonics and imbalance in power systems have the characteristic of changeability with time. In other words, the amplitude of each of the harmonic components of the current and the sequences related to that harmonic order can change at any moment of time. The methods of identifying power quality phenomena should be able to perform the identification process with high accuracy and speed in addition to identifying in normal conditions, in abnormal conditions and the presence of changes in the signal sent by AMIs. In the algorithm proposed in this article, the forgetting factor $\lambda$ is considered for this purpose. In fact, this parameter gives a weight factor to the measured data. If the signal is in normal conditions, the value of the forgetting coefficient is considered equal to one. With this choice, according to equation (2) and (3), the effect of old received data from AMIs in the recognition process is more than new data, and as a result, the value of covariance matrix is lower and the accuracy of the proposed algorithm is increased. In the conditions where the signal is accompanied by changes, the value of the forgetting coefficient is reduced to less than one, and as a result, according to the equation (2) and (3), the value of the coefficients

*Figure 2. Block diagram of the proposed algorithm for identifying harmonic components and current sequences*

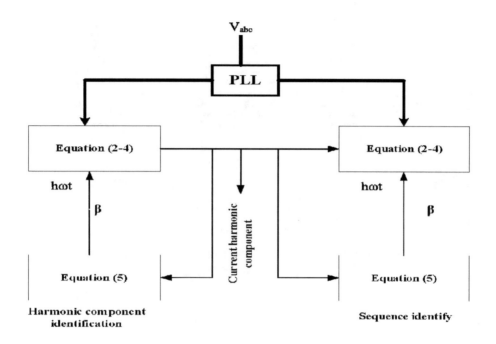

of the covariance matrix is increased and the effect of new data received from AMIs in the recognition process is greater than the data of It will be old. In such conditions, the recognition accuracy is reduced for a short period of time and the convergence speed of the algorithm is increased. In other words, the reduction of the forgetting coefficient leads to the resetting of the covariance matrix, and as a result, the convergence speed of the recognition algorithm increases. As long as the estimated parameters are accurately estimated, the value of the forgetting coefficient is kept less than one so that the convergence speed of the proposed algorithm is high. As soon as the estimation is done accurately, according to the equation (5), the estimation error is close to zero, and as a result, according to the equation (4), the value of the forgetting coefficient is equal to one, so that the estimation can be carried out with great accuracy in the new normal conditions of the signal. Figure 3 shows the block diagram of harmonics and unbalance detection by the proposed algorithm using voltage and current signals received from AMI. Figure 2 shows the mentioned algorithm to identify harmonic component and current sequence.

After identifying harmonics and current imbalance, in the next step, the contribution of each of the microgrids in producing these disturbances should be determined. The tree diagram in Figure (3) is proposed for this purpose. Based on the results obtained by this chart, it is possible to calculate and apply fines to each of the microgrids or to compensate them.

## 3.2. Natural Language Processing (NLP)

NLP tools process data in real-time, 24-hour and 7day and apply the same indicators to all your data. Therefore, it can be ensured that the obtained results are accurate and free of contradictions. Once NLP

*Figure 3. A tree diagram to determine the contribution of each system to the distortions created in the PCC*

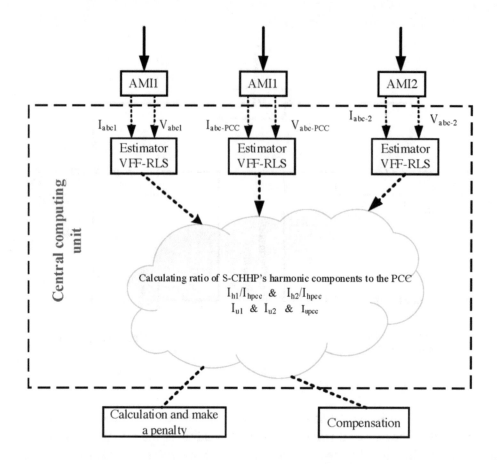

tools can understand what a piece of text is about, and even measure things like sentiment, businesses can begin to prioritize and organize their data to fit their needs (Daryani et al., 2024; Jodeiri-Seyedian et al., 2023; López et al., 2024; Toghranegar et al., 2022).

Some specific applications of NLP in the field of speech recognition are:

- Answering phone calls: NLP can be used to answer phone calls. For example, NLP can be used to identify the caller, determine the purpose of the call, and answer the caller's questions.
- Control of electronic devices: NLP can be used to control electronic devices such as televisions, refrigerators and air conditioners. For example, NLP can be used to receive voice commands from the user and execute them.
- Subtitle generation: NLP can be used to generate subtitles for movies, TV shows, and speeches. For example, NLP can be used to recognize speech in video and convert it to text.

Natural language processing is a growing and promising area of artificial intelligence that plays a role in applications as diverse as chatbots and search engines. This technology allows companies to automate some of their daily processes and benefit from unstructured data. This data gives company's actionable

*Figure 4. NLP schematic*

*Table 1. System parameters*

| Parameter | Description | Value |
|---|---|---|
| V | AC voltage | 150 v |
| f | Frequency | 60 Hz |
| $P^{pv}$ | Capacity of solar cell | 10kW |
| $P^{CHHP}$ | Capacity of CHHP | 50 kW |
| Z | Constant load | 4 Ω, 10 Ω, 1 mH |
| $P^{battery}$ | Batteries capacity | 4450Ah |
| Z1 | Non-linear load | 0.3 Ω, 0.5 Ω, 0.5 mH |
| Zt | Transmission line impedance | 10 μΩ, 1 μH |
| $\rho_1, \rho_2$ | Control constant of the forgetting factor | $3.2 \times 10^{-5}$ |

information that is used to improve customer satisfaction and provide a better experience. Conception schematic of NLP is illustrated in figure (4).

## 4. RESULTS

In this paper, set of powerful tools (recursive least square (RLS), NLP) are used to optimal configuration of S-CHHP and minimize THD in PCC.

### 4.1. Input Data

To analyze all of claims, S-CHHP, MG and NLL, in the system with parameters in the table (1) is used.

### 4.2. Simulation Results

In this work identification of harmonic and recognize contribution of S-CHHP, MG and NLL in harmonic creating is a main aim. Beside of utilizing RLS-based method to harmonic identification, some

*Figure 5. Presented power system*

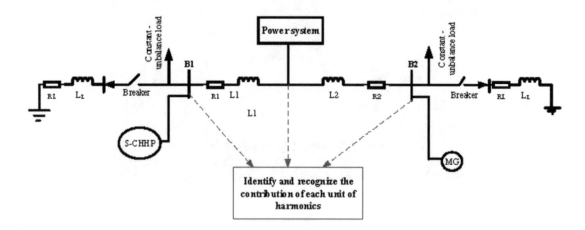

features of NLP, such as: remaindering, removal of stop-words and analyzing are used. Figure (5) shows the studied power syste. Wi-Fi –based local area network (LAN) is used in the proposed system. by considering specific LAN to each unit, the interference problem has been solved. By using web app over LAN, S-CHHP, MG and NLL are controlled. By setting charbot, controlling rules are sent.

In the presented system, breakers of S-CHHP and MG are operated at t=0.5 and t=0.6, respectively. By this work, existing load is separated from the MG and S-CHHP. Current waveform of B1, B2 and $B^{PCC}$ are figured in 6(a-c), respectively. Based on these waveforms and the operation of the keys, the current of bus B1 at the moment t=0.6 s, bus B2 at the moment t=0.5 s and bus $B^{pcc}$ has decreased at both moments. Therefore, identification of harmonics and current imbalance in all buses can be investigated in two working conditions. The first is the moments when the currents are unchanged, and the second working conditions are the moments when the current changes its status and goes from one flow level to another flow level. Due to the presence of non-linear and unbalanced loads, the waveforms of the B1 and B2 currents include harmonic and unbalanced current components. So that the average amount of harmonic distortion of current in B1 and B2 basses is equal to 10% and 8%, respectively. $B^{pcc}$ bass current is the result of summing B1 and B2 bass currents and the average amount of harmonic distortion of its current is equal to 10%.

The current waveforms in Figures 6(a-c) contain different harmonic components as well as positive, negative and zero sequences. In order to identify the harmonic components and its imbalances, the current of B1, B2 and $B^{pcc}$ buses is analyzed by the proposed VFF-RLS estimator. Waveforms 7(a), (b), (c) and (d) respectively show the main component of the current, the harmonic content of the current, the positive sequence of the main component and the negative and zero sequence of the B1 bass current.

Similar to bus B1, for buses B2 and $B^{pcc}$, the current signal is analyzed using the VFF-RLS estimator and the parameters of the main current component, harmonic components of the current, positive sequence of the main current component, and negative and zero sequences of the main current component are shown in Figures 8, respectively. A), (b), (c) and (d) are estimated for B2 bus and Figures 9 (a), (b), (c) and (d) are estimated for $B^{pcc}$ bus.

*Figure 6. Current waveform of B1, B2, and B$^{PCC}$*

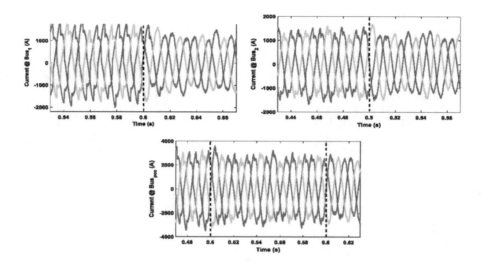

Table 2, gives all amount of harmonic sequences in each order of harmonic. Since zero-sequence of load current wouldn't have considered in any of loads, its values in table (2) is equal to zero. Negative and positive sequence value in each order of harmonic are shown, clearly.

*Figure 7. Harmonic components and its imbalances, the current of B1*

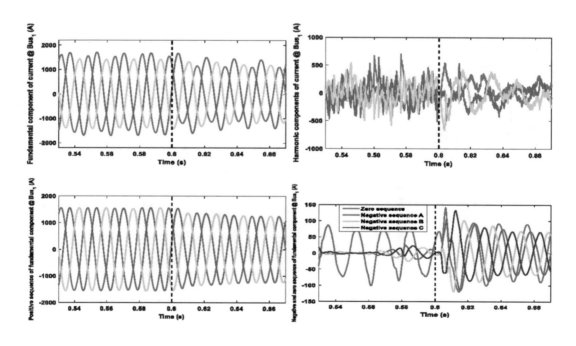

*Figure 8. Harmonic components and its imbalances, the current of B2*

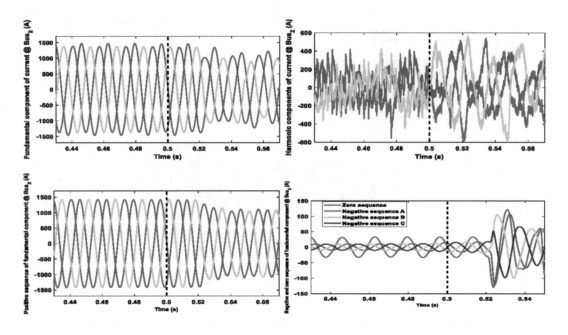

## 5. CONCLUSION

*Figure 9. harmonic components and its imbalances, the current of $B^{PCC}$*

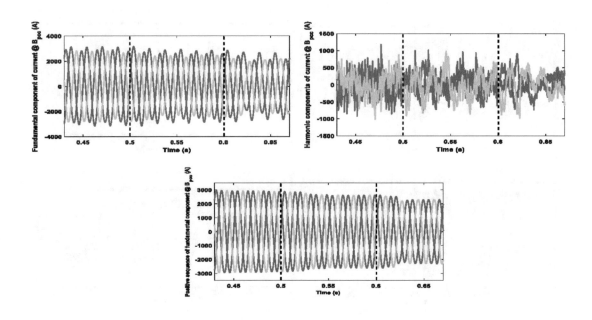

*Table 2. Zero, negative, and positive sequences in each harmonic order*

| harmonic Order | loads Current Content | | | |
|---|---|---|---|---|
| | Before t=0.7 s | | After t=0.7 s | |
| fundamental | + | 100% | + | 100% |
| | - | 10.72% | - | 8.04% |
| | 0 | 0.00% | 0 | 0.00% |
| third | + | 4.10% | + | 6.95% |
| | - | 1.77% | - | 2.53% |
| | 0 | 0.00% | 0 | 0.00% |
| fifth | + | 0.54% | + | 1.02% |
| | - | 6.47% | - | 10.25% |
| | 0 | 0.00% | 0 | 0.00% |
| seventh | + | 0.56% | + | 1.01% |
| | - | 0.82% | - | 3.03% |
| | 0 | 0.00% | 0 | 0.00% |
| ninth | + | 1.25% | + | 0.71% |
| | - | 0.73% | - | 0.71% |
| | 0 | 0.00% | 0 | 0.00% |
| eleventh | + | 0.54% | + | 1.08% |
| | - | 1.59% | - | 1.68% |
| | 0 | 0.00% | 0 | 0.00% |
| thirteen | + | 0.32% | + | 0.27% |
| | - | 0.95% | - | 0.42% |
| | 0 | 0.00% | 0 | 0.00% |

One of the important indicators in the system is the minimal harmonics (voltage and current). Dispersed production sources, while helping to produce energy, can also be a source of harmonic production. Other causes of harmonic production in the system are non-linear loads. At the common connection point where the distributed generation source and the upstream network and the non-linear load are connected, current and voltage harmonics can be created. Harmonic identification and recognize contribution of each part (S-CHHP, MG or NLL) are the main aims of this study. To gather and process and send/receive of harmonics (which are determined by the measuring systems) with minimum error natural language process (NLP) is used. On the other hand, measuring units that transmit and collect data through AMI and LAN, need NLP to reduce errors in exchange large volume of information. Results verify the performance of proposed approach in harmonic identification and NLP positive role in information management.

# REFERENCES

Al-Ja'afreh, M. A. A., Mokryani, G., & Amjad, B. (2023). An enhanced CNN-LSTM based multi-stage framework for PV and load short-term forecasting: DSO scenarios. *Energy Reports*, *10*, 1387–1408. doi:10.1016/j.egyr.2023.08.003

Bo, R., Bai, L., Conejo, A. J., Wu, J., Jiang, T., Ding, F., & Enayati, B. (2023). Special section on local and distributed electricity markets. *IEEE Transactions on Smart Grid*, *14*(2), 1347–1352. doi:10.1109/TSG.2022.3228852

Cai, Y., Xu, X., Liu, J., Yu, X., & Jia, H. (2023). Coordinative Control of Hydropower Plant and Industrial Thermostatically Controlled Loads for Frequency Response. In 2023 IEEE Power & Energy Society General Meeting (PESGM) (pp. 1-5). IEEE. doi:10.1109/PESGM52003.2023.10252287

Daryani, N., Zare, K., Tohidi, S., Guerrero, J. M., & Bazmohammadi, N. (2024). Optimal construction of microgrids in a radial distribution system considering system reliability via proposing dominated group search optimization algorithm. *Sustainable Energy Technologies and Assessments*, *63*, 103622. doi:10.1016/j.seta.2024.103622

EfstratiadiM.TsakanikasS.PapadopoulosP.SalinasD. (2023). A novel holistic energy management system incorporating PV generation and battery storage for commercial customers. Authorea Preprints.

Ghasemi, H., Farahani, E. S., Fotuhi-Firuzabad, M., Dehghanian, P., Ghasemi, A., & Wang, F. (2023). Equipment failure rate in electric power distribution networks: An overview of concepts, estimation, and modeling methods. *Engineering Failure Analysis*, *145*, 107034. doi:10.1016/j.engfailanal.2022.107034

Hemmati, M., Amjady, N., & Ehsan, M. (2023). Islanded Micro-Grid Modeling and Optimization of its Operation Considering Cost of Energy not Served by an Enhanced Differential Search Algorithm. *Energy Engineering and Management*, *3*(4), 2–13.

Hosseinnia, H., & Farsadi, M. (2015). Utlization Cat Swarm Optimization Algorithm for Selected Harmonic Elemination in Current Source Inverter. *International Journal of Power Electronics and Drive Systems*, *6*(4), 888. doi:10.11591/ijpeds.v6.i4.pp888-896

Hosseinnia, H., & Farsadi, M. (2017). Effect of Reconfiguration and Capacitor Placement on Power Loss Reduction and Voltage Profile Improvement. *Transactions on Electrical and Electronic Materials*, *18*(6), 345–349.

Hosseinnia, H., Modarresi, J., & Nazarpour, D. (2020). Optimal eco-emission scheduling of distribution network operator and distributed generator owner under employing demand response program. *Energy*, *191*(C), 116553. doi:10.1016/j.energy.2019.116553

Hosseinnia, H., Mohammadi-Ivatloo, B., & Mohammadpourfard, M. (2021). Optimal Techno-Economic Planning of a Smart Parking Lot—Combined Heat, Hydrogen, and Power (SPL-CHHP)-Based Microgrid in the Active Distribution Network. *Applied Sciences (Basel, Switzerland)*, *11*(17), 8043. doi:10.3390/app11178043

Hosseinnia, H., Mohammadi-Ivatloo, B., & Mohammadpourfard, M. (2022). Multi-objective configuration of an intelligent parking lot and combined hydrogen, heat and power (IPL-CHHP) based microgrid. *Sustainable Cities and Society, 76*, 76. doi:10.1016/j.scs.2021.103433

Hosseinnia, H., Nazarpour, D., & Talavat, V. (2018a). Utilising reliability-constrained optimisation approach to model microgrid operator and private investor participation in a planning horizon. *IET Generation, Transmission & Distribution, 12*(21), 5798–5810. doi:10.1049/iet-gtd.2018.5930

Hosseinnia, H., Nazarpour, D., & Talavat, V. (2018b). Benefit maximization of demand side management operator (DSMO) and private investor in a distribution network. *Sustainable Cities and Society, 40*, 625–637. doi:10.1016/j.scs.2018.04.022

Hosseinnia, H., Talavat, V., & Nazarpour, D. (2021). Effect of considering demand response program (DRP) in optimal configuration of combined heat and power (CHP). *International Journal of Ambient Energy, 42*(6), 612–617. doi:10.1080/01430750.2018.1562974

Hosseinnia, H., & Tousi, B. (2019). Optimal operation of DG-based micro grid (MG) by considering demand response program (DRP). *Electric Power Systems Research, 167*, 252–260. doi:10.1016/j.epsr.2018.10.026

Jafari, A., Ganjeh Ganjehlou, H., Khalili, T., & Bidram, A. (2020). A fair electricity market strategy for energy management and reliability enhancement of islanded multi-microgrids. *Applied Energy, 270*, 115170. doi:10.1016/j.apenergy.2020.115170

Jodeiri-Seyedian, S.-S., Fakour, A., Nourollahi, R., Zare, K., & Mohammadi-Ivatloo, B. (2023). Eco-environmental Impacts of x-to-x energy conversion on interconnected multi-energy microgrids: A multi-objective optimization. *Sustainable Cities and Society, 99*, 104947. doi:10.1016/j.scs.2023.104947

Kabiri-Renani, Y., Arjomandi-Nezhad, A., Fotuhi-Firuzabad, M., & Shahidehpour, M. (2024). Trans-active-Based Day-Ahead Electric Vehicles Charging Scheduling. *IEEE Transactions on Transportation Electrification, 1*. doi:10.1109/TTE.2023.3348490

Khalilzadeh, R., & Haghifam, M. R. (2023). Planning and comparing a pure AC or a hybrid AC/DC distribution network: A case study for an urban zone and an industrial park. *Journal of Iranian Association of Electrical and Electronics Engineers, 20*(2), 77–86. doi:10.52547/jiaeee.20.2.77

López, M. Z., Zareipour, H., & Quashie, M. (2024). Forecasting the Occurrence of Electricity Price Spikes: A Statistical-Economic Investigation Study. *Forecasting, 6*(1), 1–23.

Marquez, J. A., & Mohammad, A. A. (2023). Optimal planning and operation of distribution systems using network reconfiguration and flexibility services. *Energy Reports, 9*, 3910–3919. doi:10.1016/j.egyr.2023.02.082

Modarresi, J., & Hosseinnia, H. (2023). Worldwide Daily Optimum Tilt Angle Model to Obtain Maximum Solar Energy. *Journal of the Institution of Electronics and Telecommunication Engineers, 69*(1), 549–557. doi:10.1080/03772063.2020.1831412

Moghaddam, A., Ayub, S. B., Zare, K., & Golpîra, H. (2024). Modeling the power trading strategies of a retailer with multi-microgrids: A robust bi-level optimization approach. *Energy Sources. Part B, Economics, Planning, and Policy, 19*(1), 2288952. doi:10.1080/15567249.2023.2288952

Nasiri, N., Saatloo, A. M., Mirzaei, M. A., Ravadanegh, S. N., Zare, K., Mohammadi-ivatloo, B., & Marzband, M. (2023). A robust bi-level optimization framework for participation of multi-energy service providers in integrated power and natural gas markets. *Applied Energy, 340*(C), 121047. doi:10.1016/j.apenergy.2023.121047

Ntafalias, A., Tsakanikas, S., Skarvelis-Kazakos, S., Papadopoulos, P., Skarmeta-Gómez, A. F., González-Vidal, A., Tomat, V., Ramallo-González, A. P., Marin-Perez, R., & Vlachou, M. C. (2022). Design and Implementation of an Interoperable Architecture for Integrating Building Legacy Systems into Scalable Energy Management Systems. *Smart Cities, 5*(4), 1421–1440. doi:10.3390/smartcities5040073

Omri, M., Jooshaki, M., Abbaspour, A., & Fotuhi-Firuzabad, M. (2024). Modeling Microgrids for Analytical Distribution System Reliability Evaluation. *IEEE Transactions on Power Systems*, 1–12. doi:10.1109/TPWRS.2024.3354299

Pourghaderi, N., Fotuhi-Firuzabad, M., Moeini-Aghtaie, M., Kabirifar, M., & Dehghanian, P. (2023). A local flexibility market framework for exploiting DERs' flexibility capabilities by a technical virtual power plant. *IET Renewable Power Generation, 17*(3), 681–695. doi:10.1049/rpg2.12624

Rezaeeian, S., Bayat, N., Rabiee, A., Nikkhah, S., & Soroudi, A. (2022). Optimal Scheduling of Reconfigurable Microgrids in Both Grid-Connected and Isolated Modes Considering the Uncertainty of DERs. *Energies, 15*(15), 5369. doi:10.3390/en15155369

Rostami, R., & Hosseinnia, H. (2021). Energy Management of Reconfigurable Distribution System in Presence of Wind Turbines by Considering Several Kinds of Demands. *Energy, 2*(2), 199–203.

Shariatkhah, M. H., Haghifam, M. R., & Paqaleh, M. A. (2023). Simultaneous placement of DGs and capacitors in distribution networks-determining the optimum configuration. *Energy Engineering and Management, 1*(1), 11–18.

Solat, S., Aminifar, F., Safdarian, A., & Shayanfar, H. (2023). An expansion planning model for strategic visioning of active distribution network in the presence of local electricity market. *IET Generation, Transmission & Distribution, 17*(24), 5410–5429. doi:10.1049/gtd2.13053

Taheri, M., Abedini, M., & Aminifar, F. (2023). A Novel Centralized Load Shedding Approach to Assess Short-Term Voltage Stability: A Model-Free Using Time Series Forecasting. *IEEE Transactions on Power Delivery, 38*(5), 3076–3083. doi:10.1109/TPWRD.2023.3266265

Toghranegar, S., Rabiee, A., & Soroudi, A. (2022). Enhancing the unbalanced distribution network's hosting capacity for DERs via optimal load re-phasing. *Sustainable Cities and Society, 87*, 87. doi:10.1016/j.scs.2022.104243

Vincent, R., Ait-Ahmed, M., Houari, A., & Benkhoris, M. F. (2020). Residential microgrid energy management considering flexibility services opportunities and forecast uncertainties. *International Journal of Electrical Power & Energy Systems, 120*, 105981. doi:10.1016/j.ijepes.2020.105981

Zhang, L., Li, J., Xu, X., Liu, F., Guo, Y., Yang, Z., & Hu, T. (2023). High spatial granularity residential heating load forecast based on Dendrite net model. *Energy, 269*(C), 126787. doi:10.1016/j.energy.2023.126787

Zhou, Y., Wu, J., & Gan, W. (2023). P2P energy trading via public power networks: Practical challenges, emerging solutions, and the way forward. *Frontiers in Energy, 17*(2), 189–197. doi:10.1007/s11708-023-0873-9

# Chapter 10
# Innovative Advancements in Big Data Analytics:
## Navigating Future Trends With Hadoop Integration

**Tarun Kumar Vashishth**

https://orcid.org/0000-0001-9916-9575

*IIMT University, India*

**Vikas Sharma**

https://orcid.org/0000-0001-8173-4548

*IIMT University, India*

**Asheesh Pandey**

*ABES Engineering College, Ghaziabad, India*

**Tanuja Tomer**

*Nimbus Academy of Management, India*

## ABSTRACT

*This research looks at the changing face of big data analytics with a special focus on Hadoop incorporation by examining new developments and potential future directions. Over the years, the field of data analytics has gone through tremendous expansion due to the large amount of complex data generated from various sectors. In this light, Hadoop is identified as a highly adaptive and distributed computing system that serves as a powerful resource to extract valuable information from big datasets. This chapter analyzes advanced artificial intelligence techniques, real-time data analysis methodologies, emerging research directions, and ethics of big data. It highlights their implementation within the Hadoop platform. In an attempt to explore the mutual influence that exists between studies using Hadoop and evolving paradigms of analytics, it can be concluded that this study endeavors to provide an exhaustive navigation manual to scholars, practitioners, and industry observers who are interested in exploring the frontiers of big data analytics through Hadoop and its analytic evolution.*

DOI: 10.4018/979-8-3693-3609-0.ch010

## 1. INTRODUCTION

Big Data Analytics have played an important role in identifying tomorrow's trends and directions by guiding the future technological innovation landscape in light of the quickly changing face of information technology. Hadoop, one of these pivotal technologies spearheading this paradigm shift, is a potent and scalable open-source framework. With the exponential growth rate of data today, distributed computing architecture enables organizations to store and process large datasets across clusters of commodity hardware. This seamless integration not only streamlines data management but also unleashes opportunities for companies to extract meaningful knowledge from their own resources with parallel processing and fault tolerance capabilities.An analysis of the link between Big Data Analytics and Hadoop (Dhavapriya & Yasodha, 2016) presents an effective mechanism for data type identification, enabling predictive analytics (Basha et al., 2019), while supporting a culture that relies on data for decision-making.This article delves into the transformative potential of these technologies, exploring how their integration shapes the future of data analytics, enhances business intelligence (Minelli, Chambers & Dhiraj, 2013), and contributes to the evolution of a more efficient and informed digital landscape (Dubuc, Stahl & Roesch, 2020).

## 1.1 Background and Rationale

The introduction of Hadoop in Big Data Analytics is an important advancement in the design of the data processing and analytics domain. An enriching description about the background and rationale of the introduction of Hadoop in Big Data Analytics can be understood as follows: The explosion of data sources in different forms across different domains has made data processing and analytics even more challenging. Relational database management systems are constrained by their limited capabilities to deal with numbers on a constant rise with their hardware-bound storage and processing mechanisms. The rationale of Hadoop in big data analytics is to provide an open source framework to overcome the arising challenges of data volume and velocity in storage and processing. The capability of this framework is to handle large amounts of data by the distributed storage and processing, and such an approach offers numerous benefits over traditional databases, including parallel computing, fault tolerance, and scalability.The background of this integration is rooted in the desire to unlock actionable insights from massive and complex datasets that conventional systems found daunting. Moreover, as businesses increasingly recognize the strategic importance of data-driven decision-making, the background of Hadoop's integration into Big Data Analytics aligns with the industry's pursuit of innovation and competitiveness. Organizations seek to derive meaningful patterns, trends, and correlations from vast datasets, ultimately transforming raw data into actionable intelligence. The rationale behind Hadoop's inclusion lies in its ability to distribute data across clusters, allowing for parallel processing and ensuring reliability even in the face of hardware failures. This background underscores a fundamental shift in data management paradigms, emphasizing the necessity of scalable and flexible solutions to navigate the intricacies of modern data analytics. As we delve into the exploration of these innovative advancements, understanding the background and rationale for Hadoop integration becomes pivotal in comprehending the transformative (Vashishth et al., 2023) impact it has on shaping the future trends and directions in Big Data Analytics.

## 1.2 Objectives of the Study

The study on "Innovative Advancements in Big Data Analytics: Navigating Future Trends and Direction with Hadoop Integration" aims to explore and understand the dynamic landscape of big data analytics, focusing on the background and rationale for the integration of Hadoop (Dhyani & Barthwal, 2014). In recent years, the exponential growth of digital data has necessitated a shift in analytical approaches, prompting organizations to seek innovative solutions for effective data management and analysis. Against this backdrop, Hadoop (Podeschi & DeBo, 2019) has emerged as a pivotal technology due to its scalability, fault tolerance, and distributed computing capabilities. The background of this study encompasses the evolution of big data analytics, highlighting the challenges posed by the sheer volume, variety, and velocity of data. The rationale for integrating Hadoop (Oancea & Dragoescu, 2014) lies in its ability to address these challenges, offering a robust framework that can efficiently process and analyze large datasets across distributed environments. Furthermore, the study aims to provide insights into the key drivers behind the adoption of Hadoop in the context of big data analytics. It will explore how organizations stand to benefit from the integration of Hadoop, including enhanced data processing speed, cost-effective scalability, and the ability to derive valuable insights for informed decision-making. By delving into the background and rationale, the study seeks to establish a foundation for comprehending the significance of Hadoop integration in navigating the future trends and directions of big data analytics. This understanding is crucial for organizations and researchers alike, as they strive to harness the full potential of big data while mitigating the associated challenges.

## 1.3 Scope and Significance of Big Data Analytics and Hadoop Integration

The scope and significance of integrating Big Data Analytics with Hadoop are vast and transformative, shaping the landscape of data-driven decision-making across various domains. The scope encompasses the ability to process and analyze massive volumes of structured and unstructured data, enabling organizations to extract meaningful insights that were previously unattainable. Hadoop's distributed computing architecture extends this scope by providing a scalable and cost-effective solution to handle the ever-increasing data deluge. In terms of significance, the integration of Big Data Analytics with Hadoop (Bhosale & Gadekar, 2014) holds immense strategic value for organizations. Firstly, it facilitates real-time data processing (Cha & Wachowicz, 2015), allowing businesses to make informed decisions promptly. This is particularly crucial in industries such as finance, healthcare, and e-commerce, where timely insights can drive competitive (Vashishth et al., 2024) advantage. Secondly, the integration enables the storage and analysis of diverse data types, including text, images, and videos, providing a comprehensive view of information. Thirdly, Hadoop's fault-tolerant design enhances data reliability, ensuring that organizations can trust the accuracy and consistency of their analytical results.

Moreover, the significance extends to cost-effectiveness, as Hadoop's open-source nature and ability to scale horizontally make it a more economical option for large-scale data storage and processing compared to traditional databases. The integration also empowers organizations to implement advanced analytics, including machine learning and predictive modeling, fostering a deeper understanding of trends and patterns within their datasets.

*Figure 1. Big data analytics and Hadoop integration*

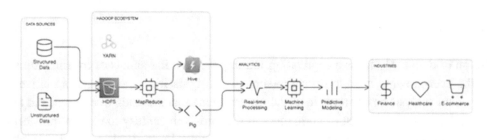

## 1.4 Motivation of the Chapter

The motivation behind the chapter "Innovative Advancements in Big Data Analytics: Navigating Future Trends and Direction with Hadoop Integration" stems from the recognition of the transformative potential of big data analytics and the importance of staying abreast of emerging trends in the field. The exponential growth of data across various industries necessitates innovative solutions to effectively harness and derive actionable insights from this wealth of information. The integration of Hadoop, a leading big data framework, offers unprecedented capabilities for processing and analyzing vast datasets, but navigating the evolving landscape of big data analytics requires a deep understanding of emerging trends, challenges, and best practices. Therefore, this chapter seeks to provide readers with a comprehensive exploration of the latest advancements in big data analytics, particularly focusing on the integration of Hadoop, while also offering insights into future directions and strategies for leveraging these advancements to drive business success. By elucidating the evolving trends and potential implications of Hadoop integration, the chapter aims to empower practitioners, researchers, and decision-makers with the knowledge and tools needed to navigate the complex terrain of big data analytics and stay ahead in an increasingly data-driven world.

## 1.5 Organization of Chapter

The rest of the chapter is organized as: Section 2 (Related work) elaborates Evolution of Data Analytics. Section 3 (Methodology) presents a methodology focused on Big Data Analytics with Hadoop Integration. Section 4 (Discussion) explores the Hadoop as a Catalyst for Scalable Analytics, Emerging Trends in Big Data Analytics, Symbiotic Relationship: Hadoop and Analytics Paradigms, Navigating the Future: Roadmap for Researchers and Practitioners and Future Scope. Section 5 (conclusion) explores the conclusion of the chapter Innovative Advancements in Big Data Analytics: Navigating Future Trends and Direction with Hadoop Integration.

## 2. EVOLUTION OF DATA ANALYTICS

### 2.1 Historical Overview

The evolution of data analytics is a captivating journey through the annals of information technology, reflecting the ever-growing need to derive meaningful insights from the expanding universe of data. Historically, data analysis has its roots in statistics, where manual methods were employed to scrutinize and interpret datasets. The advent of computers in the mid-20th century marked a transformative era, allowing for more systematic and automated data processing. Early databases and data management systems emerged, laying the groundwork for structured data analysis (Naganathan V., 2018)(A. Kumari et. al.,2021). The 1990s witnessed the rise of data warehouses, enabling organizations to consolidate and store vast amounts of data for analysis. The concept of data mining gained prominence, focusing on discovering patterns and relationships within datasets.

As the internet era dawned, the volume and variety of data exploded, necessitating more advanced analytical approaches. The 2000s saw the emergence of Business Intelligence (BI) tools (Ajah & Nweke, 2019)(A. Kumari et. al., 2021,2021), providing interactive dashboards and reports for decision-makers. Apache Hadoop (Nandimath et al., 2013) (Azeroual & Fabre, 2021), introduced in the mid-2000s, played a pivotal role by providing a scalable, distributed framework for processing and storing Big Data.

The evolution continues into the present era, characterized by the integration of artificial intelligence and machine learning into data analytics. These technologies enable predictive analytics and automated decision-making, ushering in a new era of data-driven insights. The journey from manual statistical analysis to the current era of sophisticated data analytics reflects not only technological advancements but also the increasing recognition of data as a strategic asset for businesses and organizations across diverse industries.

### 2.2 Unprecedented Growth in Data Generation

The 21st century has witnessed an unprecedented surge in data generation, characterized by an exponential increase in the volume, variety, velocity, and complexity of information. This phenomenal growth can be attributed to various factors, including the widespread adoption of digital technologies, the proliferation of internet-connected devices, and the digitization of industries and services. Social media platforms, e-commerce transactions, IoT devices, sensors, and mobile applications contribute significantly to this data deluge, generating vast amounts of structured and unstructured data in real-time.

The proliferation of data-generating sources has not only transformed the way individuals and businesses operate but have also presented both challenges and opportunities. On one hand, the sheer magnitude of data poses challenges related to storage, processing, and analysis. On the other hand, this wealth of information holds immense potential for extracting valuable insights, driving innovation, and informing decision-making across various sectors.

The advent of Big Data technologies, such as Hadoop and Apache Spark, has provided scalable and distributed solutions to process and analyze massive datasets efficiently. Cloud computing has also played a crucial role, offering scalable storage and computing resources on-demand.

As we navigate through this era of unprecedented data growth, organizations are increasingly recognizing the strategic importance of harnessing data analytics, artificial intelligence, and machine learning to derive actionable insights. Effectively managing and making sense of the vast amounts of data generated daily has become a critical aspect of innovation, competitiveness, and informed decision-making in the digital age.

## 2.3 Role of Quantitative Mining in Various Industries

A key factor in the transformation and optimization of many sectors is quantitative mining, leveraging the power of insights derived from vast datasets. Here's a glimpse into how data analytics contributes across different sectors:

I. Healthcare:
   a. Predictive Analysis: Predictive analytics in healthcare helps forecast disease outbreaks, patient admission rates, and treatment outcomes, improving resource allocation.
   b. Patient Care: Analyzing patient data enhances personalized treatment plans, monitors patient outcomes, and improves overall healthcare delivery.
II. Finance:
   a. Risk Management: Financial institutions use analytics to assess and manage risks, detect fraudulent activities, and ensure compliance with regulations.
   b. Customer Insights: Analyzing customer data helps in personalized financial services, targeted marketing, and improving customer satisfaction.
III. Retail:
   a. Demand Forecasting: Retailers leverage analytics for inventory management, demand forecasting, and optimizing supply chain logistics.
   b. Customer Behavior: Understanding customer preferences through data analytics enables personalized marketing, product recommendations, and improved customer experience.
IV. Manufacturing:
   a. Predictive Maintenance: Analytics aids in predicting equipment failures, minimizing downtime, and optimizing maintenance schedules.
   b. Supply Chain Optimization: Data analytics optimizes supply chain processes, reducing costs, improving efficiency, and ensuring timely production.
V. Telecommunications:
   a. Network Optimization: Analytics helps telecom companies optimize network performance, identify and resolve issues, and plan for capacity upgrades.
   b. Customer Churn Prediction: Analyzing customer behavior assists in predicting and reducing churn by offering targeted services and promotions.
VI. Education:
   a. Student Performance: Analytics in education helps track student performance, identify learning gaps, and customize teaching strategies.
   b. Institutional Efficiency: Data analytics is used to improve administrative processes, resource allocation, and strategic decision-making in educational institutions.
VII. Energy:
   a. Smart Grids: Data analytics optimizes energy distribution, improves grid efficiency (Wu et al., 2028), and enhances renewable energy integration.
   b. Predictive Maintenance: Analyzing data from sensors and devices helps predict and prevent equipment failures in the energy sector.

VIII.  Transportation:
  a.  Route Optimization: Data analytics is used for optimizing transportation (Ma, Zhao & Zhao 2023) routes, reducing fuel consumption, and improving overall logistics efficiency.
  b.  Predictive Analytics: Predicting maintenance needs and monitoring vehicle performance enhances the reliability and safety of transportation systems.

IX.  In essence, quantitative mining empowers industries to make informed decisions, enhance operational efficiency, and uncover valuable insights, ultimately driving innovation and competitiveness in today's data-driven world.

The methodology employed in "Innovative Advancements in Big Data Analytics: Navigating Future Trends and Direction with Hadoop Integration" encompasses a multifaceted approach aimed at providing a comprehensive understanding of the subject matter. Firstly, a thorough review of existing literature on big data analytics, Hadoop integration, and related topics is conducted to establish a foundational knowledge base and identify key trends, challenges, and emerging directions in the field. This literature review serves as the cornerstone for subsequent analyses and discussions within the chapter.

Furthermore, primary research methods such as interviews, surveys, and case studies may be employed to gather insights from industry experts, practitioners, and organizations actively involved in big data analytics and Hadoop integration. These primary research efforts offer valuable firsthand perspectives, real-world experiences, and practical insights that complement the findings from the literature review. Moreover, data analysis techniques may be utilized to examine trends, patterns, and correlations within datasets relevant to big data analytics and Hadoop integration. Statistical analysis, data visualization, and other analytical methods help uncover valuable insights and support the chapter's assertions and recommendations. Additionally, a comparative analysis of different Hadoop-based solutions, frameworks, and approaches may be conducted to evaluate their strengths, weaknesses, and suitability for various use cases and industries. This comparative analysis aids in providing a nuanced understanding of the diverse landscape of Hadoop integration and informs readers about the potential benefits and trade-offs associated with different approaches.

Overall, the methodology employed in "Innovative Advancements in Big Data Analytics: Navigating Future Trends and Direction with Hadoop Integration" is characterized by a rigorous and comprehensive approach that combines literature review, primary research, data analysis, and comparative analysis to offer valuable insights and guidance to readers interested in leveraging Hadoop for advanced big data analytics.

# 3. HADOOP AS A CATALYST FOR SCALABLE ANALYTICS

## 3.1 Overview of Hadoop Framework

Large amounts of data may be handled and processed via Hadoop, a powerful open-source framework that runs on dispersed clusters of commodity hardware. One of the main components of the Big Data ecosystem is Hadoop, created by the Apache Software Foundation. It provides a scalable and affordable way to store, process, and analyze large amounts of data. The Hadoop Distributed File System (HDFS) for distributed storage and Map Reduce for distributed processing are the two primary parts of the framework. Large files are divided into smaller blocks by HDFS and then distributed among cluster nodes to

*Figure 2. Hadoop framework architecture*

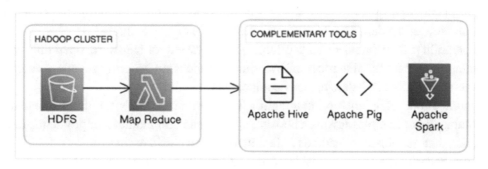

provide high availability and fault tolerance. Inspired on ideas from functional programming, Map Reduce divides jobs into smaller subtasks and distributes them across the nodes to enable parallel processing.

The ability of Hadoop to extend horizontally, which enables businesses to add additional nodes to the cluster as data quantities increase, is one of its main advantages. Hadoop's fault tolerance and scalability allow it to handle the large and varied datasets that characterize the modern data environment. Furthermore, Hadoop has developed into a crucial component of the data processing pipeline, supporting a wide range of data types and facilitating the integration of structured and unstructured data. Hadoop's capabilities are extended beyond its initial Map Reduce paradigm by its ecosystem, which includes complementing tools like Apache Hive for SQL-based querying, Apache Pig for high-level data flow scripting, and Apache Spark for in-memory processing.

Hadoop has found widespread adoption across industries, including finance, healthcare, retail, and telecommunications, offering organizations a powerful framework to harness the potential of Big Data. As the digital era continues to generate unprecedented amounts of data, Hadoop remains a cornerstone technology for organizations seeking to extract actionable insights and drive innovation from their data assets.

## 3.2 Distributed Computing Principles

Distributed computing principles revolve around the concept of leveraging multiple interconnected computers to work together as a unified system. These principles are fundamental for designing, implementing, and managing distributed systems, which distribute processing tasks across a network of computers to improve performance, reliability, and scalability. Some key principles of distributed computing include:

a) Concurrency: Distributed systems often involve multiple components or nodes working simultaneously. Concurrency principles ensure effective coordination and synchronization of tasks to avoid conflicts and inconsistencies in the shared data.

b) Fault Tolerance: Distributed systems must be resilient to failures, which can occur in network connections, hardware, or software components. Principles of fault tolerance involve redundancy, error detection, and recovery mechanisms to ensure continuous operation despite failures.

c) Scalability: Distributed computing systems should be scalable, allowing them to handle increased workload by adding more resources. This involves designing architectures that can efficiently distribute and balance the workload across multiple nodes.

d) Consistency: Maintaining consistency across distributed systems, where data is stored and processed on multiple nodes is crucial. Consistency principles ensure that all nodes in the system provide a coherent view of the data despite the distributed nature of processing.

e) Interoperability: Distributed systems often involve a variety of hardware, operating systems, and programming languages. Interoperability principles focus on ensuring seamless communication and interaction between heterogeneous components.

f) Communication: Efficient communication between nodes is vital in distributed systems. Communication principles involve choosing appropriate communication protocols, message formats, and data serialization methods to facilitate effective data exchange.

g) Security: Security is a critical consideration in distributed systems. Principles of security involve implementing encryption, authentication, and authorization mechanisms to protect data and ensure the integrity of communication between nodes.

h) Load Balancing: Effective load balancing is essential to distribute processing tasks evenly across nodes, preventing bottlenecks and maximizing resource utilization. Load balancing principles ensure optimal performance (Raj et al., 2015) and resource efficiency in distributed systems.

i) Decentralization: Distributed systems often favour decentralization to avoid single points of failure and enhance scalability. Principles of decentralization involve distributing control and decision-making across multiple nodes.

j) Resource Management: Efficiently managing resources such as memory, processing power and storage across distributed nodes is crucial. Resource management principles involve dynamic allocation, monitoring, and optimization of resources in response to changing workloads.

Understanding and applying these distributed computing principles is key to designing resilient, scalable, and efficient systems capable of handling the challenges posed by distributed environments.

## 3.3 Scalability and Processing Large-Scale Datasets

Scalability in the context of distributed computing refers to the ability of a system to handle an increasing amount of work or data by adding resources without compromising performance (Sardi et al., 2023). When it comes to processing large-scale datasets, scalability becomes a critical factor in ensuring efficient and timely data analysis. Several key principles and strategies contribute to achieving scalability in processing large-scale datasets:

a) Parallelization: Distributing the workload across multiple processing units or nodes allows for parallel execution of tasks. This approach enables the system to process data faster as each node works on a portion of the dataset simultaneously, enhancing overall throughput.

b) Horizontal Scaling: Instead of relying on a single powerful machine, horizontally scaling involves adding more machines or nodes to the system. This approach ensures that the processing capability of the system grows as the dataset size increases.

c) Distributed File Systems: Scalable processing often requires scalable storage. Distributed file systems, such as Hadoop Distributed File System (HDFS), provide a means to store and access large datasets across multiple nodes, facilitating parallel processing.

d) Data Partitioning: Breaking down large datasets into smaller partitions allows for more efficient parallel processing. Each partition can be processed independently on different nodes, enhancing the system's ability to handle large volumes of data.

e) MapReduce Programming Model: MapReduce is a programming model that simplifies large-scale data processing by dividing tasks into two phases - Map and Reduce. This model facilitates parallel execution and scalability, as different nodes can perform the Map and Reduce tasks independently.

f) In-Memory Processing: Utilizing the system's memory for data processing, as opposed to relying solely on disk (Mukherjeeet et al., 2012) storage, can significantly improve processing speed. Technologies like Apache Spark leverage in-memory processing for efficient large-scale data analytics.

g) Load Balancing: Distributing the workload evenly across all available resources prevents bottlenecks and ensures that each node contributes to the processing tasks proportionally. Load balancing is crucial for maintaining optimal performance as the system scales.

h) Data Compression and Storage Optimization: Minimizing the storage footprint of large datasets through compression and optimization techniques can enhance scalability. It reduces the amount of data that needs to be processed and transferred across the network.

i) Asynchronous Processing: Adopting asynchronous processing, where tasks can be executed independently and results are combined later, improves overall system efficiency and responsiveness, especially in scenarios with diverse processing times for different data subsets.

j) Dynamic Resource Allocation: Scalable systems should be able to adapt to varying workloads by dynamically allocating resources based on demand. This ensures efficient resource utilization while processing large-scale datasets.

By incorporating these principles and strategies, scalable systems can effectively handle the challenges associated with processing large-scale datasets, providing organizations with the agility and capability to derive valuable insights from their expansive data resources.

## 4. EMERGING TRENDS IN BIG DATA ANALYTICS

### 4.1 Advanced Machine Learning Techniques

Advanced machine learning techniques represent a sophisticated and evolving set of methodologies that go beyond traditional approaches, enabling more nuanced, accurate, and versatile modeling. Some notable advanced machine learning techniques include:
Deep Learning:

- Neural Networks: Deep neural networks with multiple layers (deep learning) are instrumental in problems including complicated pattern identification, audio and picture recognition, and linguistic processing.
- Convolutional Neural Networks (CNNs): Specialized neural networks designed for image processing, CNNs excel at feature extraction and are widely used in computer vision applications.
- Persistent Neural Networks (PNNs): Particularly effective for sequence data, PNNs are commonly applied in tasks like language modeling, speech recognition, and time-series analysis.

Transfer Learning: Transfer learning is pre-training a model on a huge dataset and then optimizing it for a particular task. This method makes use of the expertise from one area to enhance performance in another, particularly in situations when the amount of labeled data is restricted.

Ensemble Learning:Ensemble techniques combine predictions from multiple models to achieve better accuracy and robustness. Methods such as Random Forests and Gradient Boosting are widely used for classification and regression tasks.

Generative Adversarial Networks (GANs): A generator and a discriminator, two neural networks playing a game together, make up a GAN. GANs have applications in picture synthesis, style transfer, and realistic content creation. They are skilled at producing synthetic data.

Reinforcement learning: Through interaction with an environment, an agent is trained to make successive decisions. This method has proven effective in fields including autonomous systems, robotics, and gaming.

Semi-Supervised and Unsupervised Learning: Semi-supervised learning utilizes a combination of labeled and unlabeled data, making it useful when acquiring labeled data is expensive. Unsupervised learning techniques, like clustering and dimensionality reduction, extract patterns from unlabeled data.

AutoML (Automated Machine Learning): AutoML involves automating the process of model selection, hyper parameter tuning, and feature engineering. This streamlines the machine learning pipeline, making it more accessible to users with varying levels of expertise.

Explainable AI (XAI): With the increasing complexity of models, explainability becomes crucial. XAI predictions, making machine learning models more interpretable and trustworthy.

Bayesian Methods: Bayesian approaches incorporate probability distributions to model uncertainty, making them valuable in scenarios where uncertainty quantification is essential. Bayesian methods are often used in optimization, hyper parameter tuning, and Bayesian neural networks.

Meta-Learning: Training models to learn how to learn is known as meta-learning. These models are well suited for situations with sparse labeled data since they swiftly adjust to new jobs.

These advanced techniques reflect the continuous evolution of machine learning, addressing challenges in diverse domains and pushing the boundaries of what is achievable in terms of accuracy, efficiency, and interpretability.

## 4.2 Real-Time Data Processing Paradigms

Real-time data processing paradigms have become increasingly crucial in the contemporary digital landscape, where the demand for instant insights and quick decision-making is paramount. One prominent paradigm is Stream Processing, which focuses on handling and analyzing data in motion. Stream processing systems enable the continuous processing of data as it arrives, allowing organizations to gain insights and take actions in near real-time. Apache Kafka and Apache Flink are examples of stream processing frameworks widely used for ingesting, processing, and analyzing streaming data. Another paradigm is Complex Event Processing (CEP), which identifies patterns and relationships within streams of events. CEP systems excel at recognizing and responding to complex events or combinations of events in real time (Cha & Wachowicz, 2015), making them valuable for applications like fraud detection, monitoring, and IoT data analysis (Banerjee et al., 2020).

Additionally, In-Memory Data Grids (IMDGs) leverage the power of distributed, in-memory computing to process and analyze data rapidly. IMDGs reduce latency by storing and accessing data in RAM, making them suitable for applications requiring instant access to the most up-to-date information. These

*Figure 3. Real-time processing paradigms*

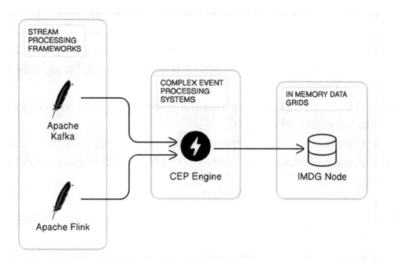

paradigms collectively empower organizations to harness the potential of real-time data, facilitating quick responses to dynamic situations, enhancing operational efficiency, and supporting a wide range of applications across industries.

## 4.3 Ethical Considerations in Analytics

The ethical considerations in data analytics are paramount, given the profound impact that analytics can have on privacy, fairness, and broader societal issues. As organizations leverage data to extract insights and make informed decisions, it becomes crucial to navigate ethical dilemmas responsibly. Here is a more comprehensive exploration of the ethical considerations in analytics and potential solutions:

1. Privacy Concerns:
   ◦ Dilemma: Data analytics often involves processing personal information, raising concerns about privacy infringement and the potential misuse of sensitive data.
   ◦ Solution: Implement robust privacy policies, anonymize or pseudonymize data wherever possible, and ensure transparent communication with individuals about data collection, usage, and protection.
2. Bias and Fairness:
   ◦ Dilemma: Biases in data, algorithms, or model training can lead to unfair or discriminatory outcomes, perpetuating existing societal inequalities.
   ◦ Solution: Regularly audit algorithms for bias, strive for diverse and representative datasets, and incorporate fairness considerations into the design and evaluation of models.
3. Informed Consent:
   ◦ Dilemma: Obtaining genuine and informed consent from individuals for data collection and analysis can be challenging, leading to potential ethical concerns.
   ◦ Solution: Prioritize transparency, educate individuals about the purpose and implications of data analytics, and provide clear options for opting in or out of data collection.

4. Data Security:
   ◦ Dilemma: The security of data is crucial, and breaches can lead to significant ethical concerns, including unauthorized access and potential harm to individuals.
   ◦ Solution: Implement robust cybersecurity measures, encrypt sensitive data, conduct regular security audits, and establish protocols for responding to and mitigating data breaches.

5. Accountability and Transparency:
   ◦ Dilemma: Lack of accountability and transparency in data analytics processes can erode trust and create ethical challenges.
   ◦ Solution: Clearly communicate the methods and processes used in analytics, establish accountability frameworks, and be transparent about the limitations and uncertainties associated with the analysis.

6. Social Impact:
   ◦ Dilemma: Data analytics can have far-reaching consequences on society, impacting employment, public policy, and social structures.
   ◦ Solution: Conduct thorough impact assessments, involve diverse stakeholders in decision-making, and actively engage with the broader community to understand and address potential societal implications.

7. Algorithmic Decision-Making:
   ◦ Dilemma: Relying solely on algorithmic decision-making without human oversight can lead to unintended consequences and ethical concerns.
   ◦ Solution: Introduce human oversight, ensure interpretability of algorithms, and establish mechanisms for challenging and correcting decisions made by automated systems.

8. Data Ownership and Access:
   ◦ Dilemma: Determining ownership of data and controlling access raises ethical questions, especially in collaborative or multi-stakeholder environments.
   ◦ Solution: Clearly define data ownership rights, establish access controls based on ethical principles, and ensure fair and responsible data sharing practices.

9. Long-Term Impact:
   ◦ Dilemma: The long-term impact of data analytics on society, including job displacement, economic inequality, and concentration of power, raises ethical considerations.
   ◦ Solution: Proactively assess and mitigate potential long-term consequences, engage in ongoing dialogue with stakeholders, and advocate for policies that address societal challenges arising from data analytics.

In addressing these ethical considerations, organizations and practitioners in data analytics must prioritize responsible practices, engage in continuous education, and actively contribute to the development of ethical guidelines and standards within the industry.

## 5. SYMBIOTIC RELATIONSHIP: HADOOP AND ANALYTICS PARADIGMS

### 5.1 Integration Challenges and Opportunities

Integration in the context of technology refers to the process of combining different systems, software, or components to work together as a cohesive whole. While integration offers numerous opportunities for improved efficiency and functionality, it also presents challenges that organizations must navigate.
Challenges:

a) **Data Silos:** One of the most common challenges is the existence of data silos, where information is trapped in isolated systems or departments, hindering collaboration and holistic decision-making.

b) **Compatibility Issues:** Integrating diverse technologies and systems may lead to compatibility issues, especially when dealing with legacy systems that were not designed to work seamlessly with newer solutions.

c) **Complexity:** As the number of integrated components increases, so does the complexity of the overall system. Managing and maintaining complex integrations can become challenging, impacting system performance and reliability.

d) **Security Concerns:** Integrating systems may expose vulnerabilities, and ensuring a secure flow of data between different components becomes crucial to prevent unauthorized access and data breaches.

e) **Costs:** Integration projects can incur significant costs, including software licenses, development efforts, and the need for specialized expertise. Budget constraints may hinder organizations from achieving comprehensive integration.

Opportunities:

a) **Improved Efficiency:** Integration streamlines processes by allowing seamless data flow between systems. This can lead to increased operational efficiency, reduced manual efforts, and faster decision-making.

b) **Enhanced Customer Experience:** Integration enables a more comprehensive view of customer data, allowing organizations to provide personalized and consistent experiences across various touch points.

c) **Innovation:** Integrated systems create a foundation for innovation by enabling the adoption of emerging technologies (Goyal et al., 2020) such as artificial intelligence, machine learning, and the Internet of Things (IoT).

d) **Business Agility:** Integrated systems can adapt to changing business requirements more effectively. This agility is crucial for organizations to stay competitive and responsive to market dynamics.

e) **Data-driven Insights:** Integration facilitates the aggregation of data from different sources, enabling organizations to derive meaningful insights and make informed decisions based on a holistic view of their information.

f) **Streamlined Communication:** Integration fosters better communication and collaboration between departments. Information sharing becomes more seamless, breaking down silos and promoting a unified organizational approach.

g) **Scalability:** Well-designed integrations support scalability, allowing organizations to expand their operations without significant disruptions.

h) **Competitive Advantage:** Organizations that successfully integrate their systems gain a competitive advantage by being more agile, innovative, and capable of delivering enhanced services to their customers.

In navigating integration challenges and leveraging opportunities, organizations need a strategic approach, considering factors such as the scalability of solutions, the security of data, and ongoing maintenance requirements. Successful integration initiatives align with business goals and contribute to a more interconnected and adaptable technological ecosystem.

## 5.2 Enhancing Analytical Capabilities With Hadoop

Enhancing analytical capabilities with Hadoop has become a strategic imperative for organizations seeking to harness the power of big data. Hadoop, an open-source framework, provides a scalable and distributed computing environment that enables the processing of vast datasets across clusters of commodity hardware. Its distributed file system, HDFS, allows for efficient storage and retrieval of large volumes of structured and unstructured data. The integration of Hadoop significantly enhances analytical capabilities by enabling parallel processing and distributed computing, making it well-suited for handling diverse data types and massive datasets. With tools like Apache Hive and Apache Pig, organizations can leverage Hadoop's processing power for querying and analyzing data using SQL-like queries and high-level data flow scripting. Additionally, Hadoop's ecosystem includes Apache Spark, a powerful in-memory processing engine, which further accelerates data processing and analytics. This integration empowers businesses to derive actionable insights, perform complex analytics, and support advanced machine learning applications. Furthermore, Hadoop facilitates the integration of data from various sources, providing a holistic view for comprehensive analysis. By enhancing analytical capabilities with Hadoop, organizations can unlock the potential of their data, fostering innovation, improving decision-making processes, and gaining a competitive edge in the dynamic landscape of data analytics.

## 5.3 Case Studies and Success Stories

a. Retail - Amazon: Amazon utilizes data analytics extensively for personalized recommendations, inventory management, and pricing optimization. Their success lies in leveraging customer data to enhance the shopping experience, increase customer satisfaction, and drive sales.

b. Healthcare - Memorial Sloan Kettering Cancer Center: The Memorial Sloan Kettering Cancer Center employs data analytics to analyze patient data, pathology reports, and treatment outcomes. They can anticipate how patients will react to various therapies by using machine learning algorithms, which will result in more individualized and efficient cancer care.

c. Finance - Capital One: Capital One is a notable example of a financial institution using data analytics for risk management, fraud detection, and customer insights. They leverage analytics to offer personalized financial products, detect fraudulent transactions, and make data-driven decisions for credit risk assessments.

d. Manufacturing - General Electric: General Electric utilizes Industrial Internet of Things (IIoT) data analytics in its manufacturing processes. They employ predictive maintenance algorithms to

*Figure 4. Enhancing analytical capabilities with Hadoop*

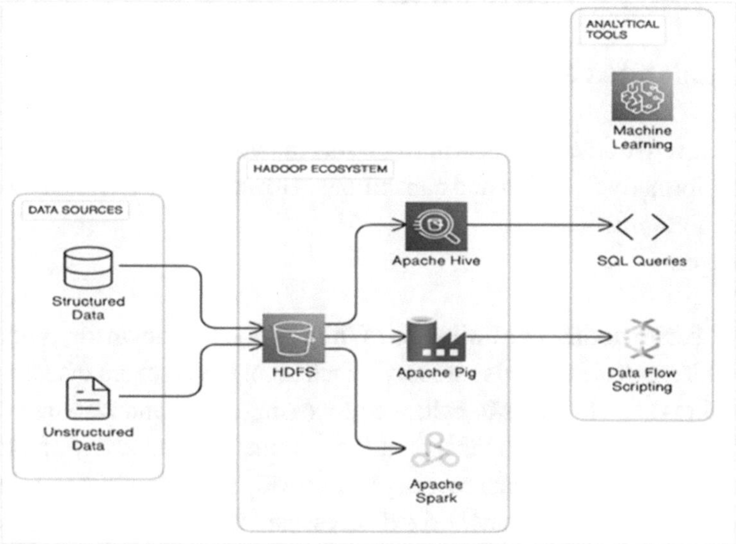

anticipate equipment failures, optimize production efficiency, and reduce downtime, resulting in substantial cost savings.

e.  Technology - Google: Google's success is deeply rooted in its use of data analytics for search algorithms, targeted advertising, and user experience optimization. The company continuously analyzes user behavior and search patterns to refine its services, enhance relevance, and deliver a seamless user experience.

f.  Telecommunications - AT&T:AT&T applies data analytics to optimize network performance, predict maintenance needs, and improve customer service. By analyzing vast amounts of data from network operations, they can enhance the reliability and efficiency of their telecommunications infrastructure.

g.  Transportation - Uber: Uber relies on data analytics for real-time route optimization, surge pricing, and driver allocation. The company uses algorithms to analyze vast amounts of data to ensure efficient and cost-effective transportation services for both riders and drivers.

These success stories highlight the diverse applications of data analytics across industries, demonstrating how organizations leverage insights to enhance operations, improve decision-making, and deliver value to their customers.

# 6. NAVIGATING THE FUTURE: ROADMAP FOR RESEARCHERS AND PRACTITIONERS

## 6.1 Research Challenges and Opportunities

The exploration of innovative advancements in Big Data Analytics with Hadoop integration is a dynamic field, promising transformative insights and capabilities. However, this research domain is not without its challenges and opportunities.

Research Challenges:

a) **Scalability and Performance Optimization:** While Hadoop is known for its scalability, optimizing performance on large-scale datasets remains a challenge. Researchers face the task of developing efficient algorithms and strategies to enhance processing speed and resource utilization.

b) **Data Security and Privacy:** With the increasing volume and sensitivity of data processed by Big Data Analytics, ensuring robust data security and privacy protection poses a significant challenge. Addressing concerns related to unauthorized access and data breaches is crucial.

c) **Complexity in Hadoop Ecosystem:** The Hadoop ecosystem is expansive, comprising various tools and frameworks. Navigating the complexity of these components and ensuring seamless integration while maintaining coherence in the analytics pipeline is a research challenge.

d) **Real-time Processing:** Big Data Analytics is moving towards real-time processing for instant insights. Integrating Hadoop with technologies that support real-time data processing, such as Apache Flink or Apache Kafka, poses a research challenge in terms of system architecture and efficiency.

Research Opportunities:

a) **Optimizing Hadoop for Machine Learning:** Expanding the integration of Hadoop with machine learning frameworks presents a significant opportunity. Researchers can explore ways to enhance Hadoop's capabilities for large-scale machine learning tasks, fostering advancements in predictive analytics.

b) **Enhanced Data Governance:** Innovations in data governance within the Hadoop ecosystem can provide researchers with opportunities to improve data quality, metadata management, and access controls. Developing robust governance frameworks aligning with evolving industry standards is an avenue for research.

c) **Dynamic Resource Management:** Research can focus on creating intelligent resource management mechanisms within Hadoop clusters. This includes dynamic allocation of resources based on workload, optimizing resource utilization, and improving overall cluster efficiency.

d) **Integration with Cloud Services:** The integration of Hadoop with cloud computing services is a burgeoning area. Researchers can explore ways to seamlessly integrate Hadoop with cloud platforms, leveraging the scalability and flexibility offered by cloud infrastructure.

e) **Explainable AI in Hadoop:** With the growing importance of ethical AI, integrating explainable AI techniques within Hadoop can be a valuable research opportunity. Enhancing transparency in analytics models and decision-making processes contributes to responsible AI adoption.

f) **Cybersecurity in Big Data:** Research can address cybersecurity challenges in Big Data Analytics, especially when integrating Hadoop. This involves developing robust security measures, encryption techniques, and anomaly detection mechanisms to safeguard sensitive data.

g) **Edge Computing Integration:** Investigating the integration of Hadoop with edge computing architectures provides opportunities for enhancing data processing capabilities at the edge of the network, enabling more efficient and responsive analytics.

Navigating these challenges and embracing these opportunities requires interdisciplinary collaboration, leveraging expertise in computer science, data management, machine learning, and cybersecurity. Researchers in this domain play a pivotal role in shaping the future trends and directions of Big Data Analytics with Hadoop integration, contributing to the advancement of data-driven decision-making across various industries.

## 6.2 Industry Best Practices

Industry best practices refer to the most effective and efficient methods, processes, and approaches that are widely recognized and adopted within a particular industry. These practices are developed based on successful experiences, lessons learned, and the evolving standards in a given field. Here are some common industry best practices applicable across various sectors:

a) **Quality Management Systems (ISO Standards):** Implementing quality management systems based on international standards, such as ISO 9001, helps organizations enhance customer satisfaction, improve processes, and maintain high-quality products and services.

b) **Agile Project Management:** Agile methodologies, like Scrum or Kanban, are widely adopted in software development and increasingly in other industries. These iterative and collaborative approaches enhance project flexibility, adaptability, and responsiveness to changing requirements.

c) **Cybersecurity Measures:** Robust cybersecurity practices, including regular audits, employee training, encryption, and intrusion detection systems, are crucial for protecting sensitive data and preventing cyber threats in an increasingly digital environment.

d) **Supply Chain Visibility:** Achieving transparency and visibility throughout the supply chain helps organizations optimize logistics, reduce risks, and enhance collaboration with suppliers, ensuring a more efficient and resilient supply chain.

e) **Environmental Sustainability:** Sustainable practices are being adopted by several companies in an effort to reduce their environmental effect. This entails cutting back on waste, making the most use of energy, and using eco-friendly components in goods.

f) **Employee Training and Development:** Investing in ongoing training and development programs for employees ensures that they stay updated on industry trends, technologies, and best practices, contributing to enhanced productivity and innovation.

g) **Customer Relationship Management (CRM):** Implementing CRM systems helps businesses manage and analyze customer interactions, streamline communication, and improve customer satisfaction, loyalty, and retention.

h) **Data Encryption and Privacy Policies:** Protecting sensitive data through encryption and adhering to strict privacy policies are critical best practices, particularly in industries dealing with personal or confidential information.

i) **Continuous Improvement (Kaizen):** Adopting a culture of continuous improvement, inspired by Kaizen principles, encourages organizations to regularly assess and refine processes, leading to increased efficiency and innovation.

j) **Health and Safety Protocols:** Implementing comprehensive health and safety protocols ensures a safe working environment, compliance with regulations, and the well-being of employees, contractors, and other stakeholders.

k) **Corporate Social Responsibility (CSR):** Organizations are increasingly integrating CSR practices into their operations, addressing social and environmental concerns, contributing to community development, and fostering a positive corporate image.

l) **Cloud Computing Adoption:** Embracing cloud computing services allows organizations to scale their IT infrastructure, improve flexibility, and enhance collaboration, while often reducing costs associated with traditional on-premise solutions.

m) **Strategic Planning and Risk Management:** Developing and regularly updating strategic plans, coupled with effective risk management practices, helps organizations navigate uncertainties, identify opportunities, and make informed decisions.

n) **Diversity and Inclusion Initiatives:** Encouraging diversity and inclusion in the workplace fosters creativity, innovation, and a more positive organizational culture. Companies are recognizing the benefits of diverse perspectives in decision-making processes.

o) These industry best practices are not one-size-fits-all and may vary based on the specific needs and characteristics of different sectors. Organizations often tailor these practices to align with their unique goals, challenges, and regulatory environments. Adhering to industry best practices is a key strategy for organizations to maintain competitiveness, achieve operational excellence, and adapt to a rapidly evolving business landscape.

## 6.3 Recommendations for Effective Hadoop Integration

Integrating Hadoop effectively into an organization's infrastructure requires careful planning, consideration of specific use cases, and adherence to best practices. Here are recommendations for ensuring successful Hadoop integration:

a. Clearly Define Objectives: Clearly define the objectives and goals of Hadoop integration. Identify specific use cases and business problems that Hadoop is intended to address, whether it's data storage, processing, analytics, or a combination of these.

b. Understand Data Requirements: Have a thorough understanding of the organization's data requirements. Analyze the types of data to be processed, the volume, velocity, and variety of data, as well as any specific compliance or security considerations.

c. Build a Skilled Team: Assemble a skilled team with expertise in Hadoop technologies and related tools. This may include data engineers, data scientists, and administrators who are well-versed in Hadoop ecosystem components.

d. Choose the Right Distribution: Select the appropriate Hadoop distribution based on organizational needs. Popular distributions include Cloudera, Hortonworks (now part of Cloudera), and MapR. Evaluate features, support, and community contributions before making a decision.

e. Plan for Scalability: Design the Hadoop cluster with scalability in mind. Consider the potential growth in data volume and processing requirements. Plan for adding nodes to the cluster as needed and ensure scalability aligns with organizational growth.

f. Integration with Existing Systems: Ensure seamless integration with existing systems and technologies. This may involve integrating Hadoop with relational databases, enterprise data warehouses, or other data storage and processing systems.

g. Effective Data Ingestion: Implement efficient data ingestion processes to bring data into the Hadoop ecosystem. Consider tools like Apache NiFi, Apache Kafka, or Sqoop for reliable and scalable data ingestion.

h. Optimize Data Storage: Optimize data storage using Hadoop Distributed File System (HDFS) and appropriate compression techniques. Consider the storage format (e.g., Parquet, Avro) based on query and processing requirements.

i. Performance Tuning: Perform regular performance tuning to optimize the Hadoop cluster. This includes tuning configurations, adjusting resource allocations, and optimizing queries to enhance overall system performance.

j. Monitoring and Logging: Implement comprehensive monitoring and logging tools to track the health, performance, and usage of the Hadoop cluster. This facilitates proactive issue identification and resolution.

k. Training and Documentation: Provide training for the team members involved in Hadoop integration. Create comprehensive documentation for configurations, processes, and best practices to ensure knowledge transfer and continuity.

l. Stay Informed About Updates: Stay informed about updates and advancements in the Hadoop ecosystem. Regularly review and update the Hadoop distribution and related tools to leverage new features and improvements.

m. Plan for Disaster Recovery: Develop a robust disaster recovery plan, including data backup and restoration processes. Ensure that critical data and configurations are backed up regularly to prevent data loss.

n. Evaluate Cloud Options: Consider cloud-based Hadoop solutions for flexibility and scalability. Cloud platforms such as Amazon EMR, Microsoft Azure HDInsight, and Google Cloud Dataproc provide managed Hadoop services.

By following these recommendations, organizations can navigate the complexities of Hadoop integration, optimize their data processing capabilities, and derive valuable insights from large-scale data analytics.

## 7. FUTURE SCOPE

The future scope of Hadoop integration holds tremendous potential for addressing emerging challenges and leveraging evolving technologies. As we look ahead, several trends and considerations shape the trajectory of Hadoop integration, but it's important to acknowledge potential limitations and drawbacks.

- Enhanced Scalability and Performance: Future developments in Hadoop integration are likely to focus on enhancing scalability and performance. This includes optimizing resource utilization,

*Figure 5. Use cases of ensuring successful Hadoop integration*

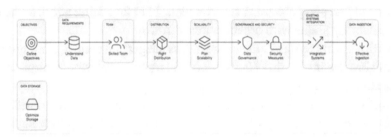

improving parallel processing capabilities, and accommodating the growing demands of large-scale data processing.

- Real-time and Stream Processing: The future scope emphasizes the integration of real-time and stream processing capabilities within the Hadoop ecosystem. This evolution addresses the need for instant insights and responsiveness, making Hadoop more adaptable to dynamic data scenarios.

- Convergence with Cloud Technologies: Hadoop's integration with cloud technologies is poised to expand, providing organizations with scalable and flexible cloud-native solutions. This convergence allows for better resource management, cost-efficiency, and the ability to leverage cloud-based analytics services.

- Simplified Ecosystem and User-Friendly Interfaces: To make Hadoop more accessible, future developments may focus on simplifying the ecosystem and introducing user-friendly interfaces. This addresses the complexity often associated with Hadoop, making it more inclusive for a broader range of users.

- Integration with Advanced Analytics and AI: Hadoop's future lies in seamless integration with advanced analytics, artificial intelligence (AI), and machine learning (ML). This integration empowers organizations to derive deeper insights, automate decision-making processes, and unlock the full potential of their data.

- Improved Data Governance and Security: The future scope emphasizes strengthening data governance and security within Hadoop. This includes advancements in encryption techniques, access controls, and auditing mechanisms to address evolving compliance requirements and privacy concerns.

- Hybrid and Multi-Cloud Deployments: Organizations are likely to adopt hybrid and multi-cloud strategies for Hadoop integration. This approach allows them to leverage on-premise and cloud resources, providing flexibility, redundancy, and improved disaster recovery capabilities.

- Cross-Platform Compatibility: Future developments aim to ensure cross-platform compatibility within the Hadoop ecosystem. This enables seamless integration with diverse data processing and analytics tools, fostering a more interconnected data environment.

### 7.1 Acknowledging Potential Limitations

- Complexity and Skill Requirements: Despite future efforts to simplify the ecosystem, Hadoop integration may still pose challenges related to complexity, requiring organizations to invest in skilled personnel and ongoing training.

- Resource Intensiveness: Hadoop's resource-intensive nature may remain a consideration. Organizations need to carefully manage hardware resources, especially as data volumes continue to grow, to avoid potential bottlenecks.
- Data Security and Compliance: As Hadoop evolves, ensuring robust data security and compliance measures becomes critical. Organizations must navigate potential vulnerabilities and stay vigilant in addressing emerging threats to safeguard sensitive information.
- Integration Costs: The initial costs associated with Hadoop integration, including hardware, software, and skilled personnel, can be significant. Organizations need to weigh these costs against the expected benefits and long-term value.
- Evolution of Alternative Technologies:The landscape of big data technologies is dynamic, and alternative solutions may emerge that challenge the dominance of Hadoop. Organizations should stay abreast of industry trends and evaluate the evolving technology landscape.

In embracing the future scope of Hadoop integration, organizations must approach these advancements with a comprehensive understanding of potential limitations and drawbacks. Proactive management, continuous assessment, and strategic planning will be essential to derive maximum value from Hadoop in the evolving landscape of big data analytics.

## 8. CONCLUSION

In conclusion, the integration of Hadoop represents a powerful and transformative journey for organizations seeking to harness the potential of big data analytics. Hadoop, with its distributed computing framework, offers the scalability and processing capabilities required to tackle vast and diverse datasets. However, successful Hadoop integration is not a one-size-fits-all endeavor; it demands careful planning, strategic considerations, and adherence to best practices.Clear objectives and a deep understanding of data requirements lay the foundation for effective Hadoop integration. Building a skilled and knowledgeable team, choosing the right Hadoop distribution, and planning for scalability are critical steps in this process. Attention to data governance, security, and seamless integration with existing systems ensures that Hadoop becomes an integral part of the organization's data ecosystem.Effective data ingestion, optimization of data storage, and continuous performance tuning contribute to the efficiency of the Hadoop cluster. Monitoring, logging, and proactive disaster recovery planning are essential elements for maintaining the health and reliability of the integrated Hadoop environment. Furthermore, staying informed about updates and advancements in the Hadoop ecosystem ensures organizations can leverage the latest features and improvements.The journey toward effective Hadoop integration goes beyond technical considerations. It requires organizational commitment, a culture of continuous improvement, and a strategic approach to align Hadoop capabilities with business goals. As the organization evolves in its data analytics journey, Hadoop becomes a catalyst for innovation, enabling advanced analytics, machine learning, and real-time processing.In a rapidly changing technological landscape, organizations must remain agile and adaptable. The integration of Hadoop provides a solid foundation for navigating the complexities of big data analytics, unlocking insights that drive informed decision-making, enhance operational efficiency, and foster a competitive edge in the digital era. With a thoughtful and well-executed Hadoop integration strategy, organizations are poised to navigate future trends and directions in the ever-expanding realm of big data analytics.

## REFERENCES

Ajah, I. A., & Nweke, H. F. (2019). Big data and business analytics: Trends, platforms, success factors and applications. *Big Data and Cognitive Computing*, *3*(2), 32. doi:10.3390/bdcc3020032

Anuradha, J. (2015). A brief introduction on Big Data 5Vs characteristics and Hadoop technology. *Procedia Computer Science*, *48*, 319–324. doi:10.1016/j.procs.2015.04.188

Azeroual, O., & Fabre, R. (2021). Processing big data with apachehadoop in the current challenging era of COVID-19. *Big Data and Cognitive Computing*, *5*(1), 12. doi:10.3390/bdcc5010012

Banerjee, A., Chakraborty, C., Kumar, A., & Biswas, D. (2020). Emerging trends in IoT and big data analytics for biomedical and health care technologies. Handbook of data science approaches for biomedical engineering, 121-152. doi:10.1016/B978-0-12-818318-2.00005-2

Basha, S. M., Rajput, D. S., Bhushan, S. B., Poluru, R. K., Patan, R., Manikandan, R., & Manikandan, R. (2019). Recent Trends in Sustainable Big Data Predictive Analytics: Past Contributions and Future Roadmap. *International Journal on Emerging Technologies*, *10*(2), 50–59.

Bhosale, H. S., & Gadekar, D. P. (2014). A review paper on big data and hadoop. *International Journal of Scientific and Research Publications*, *4*(10), 1–7.

Cha, S., & Wachowicz, M. (2015, June). Developing a real-time data analytics framework using Hadoop. In *2015 IEEE International Congress on Big Data* (pp. 657-660). IEEE. 10.1109/BigDataCongress.2015.102

Dhavapriya, M., & Yasodha, N. (2016). Big data analytics: Challenges and solutions using Hadoop, map reduce and big table. [IJCST]. *International Journal of Computer Science Trends and Technology*, *4*(1), 5–14.

Dhyani, B., & Barthwal, A. (2014). Big data analytics using Hadoop. *International Journal of Computer Applications, 108*(12), 0975-8887.

Dubuc, T., Stahl, F., & Roesch, E. B. (2020). Mapping the big data landscape: Technologies, platforms and paradigms for real-time analytics of data streams. *IEEE Access : Practical Innovations, Open Solutions*, *9*, 15351–15374. doi:10.1109/ACCESS.2020.3046132

Erraissi, A., Belangour, A., & Tragha, A. (2017). A Comparative Study of Hadoop-based Big Data Architectures. *Int. J. Web Appl.*, *9*(4), 129–137.

Goyal, D., Goyal, R., Rekha, G., Malik, S., & Tyagi, A. K. (2020, February). Emerging trends and challenges in data science and big data analytics. In *2020 International conference on emerging trends in information technology and engineering (ic-ETITE)* (pp. 1-8). IEEE. 10.1109/ic-ETITE47903.2020.316

Kumari, A., Patel, M. M., Shukla, A., Tanwar, S., Kumar, N., & Rodrigues, J. J. P. C. (2020). *ArMor: A Data Analytics Scheme to identify malicious behaviors on Blockchain-based Smart Grid System*. GLOBECOM 2020 - 2020 IEEE Global Communications Conference, Taipei, Taiwan. 10.1109/GLOBECOM42002.2020.9348061

Kumari, A., & Tanwar, S. (2021). *Reveal: An AI-based Big Data Analytics Scheme for Energy Price Prediction and Load Reduction.* 2021 11th International Conference on Cloud Computing, Data Science & Engineering (Confluence), Noida, India. 10.1109/Confluence51648.2021.9377144

Kumari, A., & Tanwar, S. (2021). Al-based Peak Load Reduction Approach for Residential Buildings using Reinforcement Learning. *2021 International Conference on Computing, Communication, and Intelligent Systems (ICCCIS)*, Greater Noida, India. 10.1109/ICCCIS51004.2021.9397241

Ma, C., Zhao, M., & Zhao, Y. (2023). An overview of Hadoop applications in transportation big data. [English Edition]. *Journal of Traffic and Transportation Engineering*, *10*(5), 900–917. doi:10.1016/j.jtte.2023.05.003

Mazumdar, S., & Dhar, S. (2015, March). Hadoop as Big Data Operating System—The Emerging Approach for Managing Challenges of Enterprise Big Data Platform. In *2015 IEEE First International Conference on Big Data Computing Service and Applications* (pp. 499-505). IEEE. 10.1109/BigDataService.2015.72

Minelli, M., Chambers, M., & Dhiraj, A. (2013). *Big data, big analytics: emerging business intelligence and analytic trends for today's businesses* (Vol. 578). John Wiley & Sons. doi:10.1002/9781118562260

Mukherjee, A., Datta, J., Jorapur, R., Singhvi, R., Haloi, S., & Akram, W. (2012, December). Shared disk big data analytics with apachehadoop. In *2012 19th International Conference on High Performance Computing* (pp. 1-6). IEEE.

Naganathan, V. (2018). Comparative analysis of Big data, Big data analytics: Challenges and trends. [IRJET]. *International Research Journal of Engineering and Technology*, *5*(05), 1948–1964.

Nandimath, J., Banerjee, E., Patil, A., Kakade, P., Vaidya, S., & Chaturvedi, D. (2013, August). Big data analysis using Apache Hadoop. In *2013 IEEE 14th International Conference on Information Reuse & Integration (IRI)* (pp. 700-703). IEEE. 10.1109/IRI.2013.6642536

Oancea, B., & Dragoescu, R. M. (2014). *Integrating R and hadoop for big data analysis.* arXiv preprint arXiv:1407.4908.

Podeschi, R. J., & DeBo, J. (2019). Integrating big data analytics into an undergraduate information systems program using Hadoop. *Information Systems Education Journal*, *17*(4), 42.

Raj, P., Raman, A., Nagaraj, D., & Duggirala, S. (2015). High-performance big-data analytics. Computing Systems and Approaches. Springer. doi:10.1007/978-3-319-20744-5

Sardi, A., Sorano, E., Cantino, V., & Garengo, P. (2023). Big data and performance measurement research: Trends, evolution and future opportunities. *Measuring Business Excellence*, *27*(4), 531–548. doi:10.1108/MBE-06-2019-0053

Singh, D., & Garg, R. (2021). R and Hadoop Integration for Big Data Analytics. In *Proceedings of 3rd International Conference on Computing Informatics and Networks: ICCIN 2020* (pp. 13-22). Springer Singapore. 10.1007/978-981-15-9712-1_2

Vashishth, T. K., Kumar, B., Sharma, V., Chaudhary, S., Kumar, S., & Sharma, K. K. (2023). The Evolution of AI and Its Transformative Effects on Computing: A Comparative Analysis. In B. Mishra (Ed.), *Intelligent Engineering Applications and Applied Sciences for Sustainability* (pp. 425–442). IGI Global. doi:10.4018/979-8-3693-0044-2.ch022

Vashishth, T. K., Sharma, V., Sharma, K. K., Kumar, B., Chaudhary, S., & Panwar, R. (2024). AI and Data Analytics for Market Research and Competitive Intelligence. In AI and Data Analytics Applications in Organizational Management (pp. 155-180). IGI Global. doi:10.4018/979-8-3693-1058-8.ch008

Wu, W., Lin, W., Hsu, C. H., & He, L. (2018). Energy-efficient hadoop for big data analytics and computing: A systematic review and research insights. *Future Generation Computer Systems*, *86*, 1351–1367. doi:10.1016/j.future.2017.11.010

## KEY TERMS AND DEFINITIONS

**Artificial Intelligence (AI):** A branch of computer science that aims to create machines and systems capable of performing tasks that typically require human intelligence. These tasks include learning, reasoning, problem-solving, perception, speech recognition, and language understanding. AI systems leverage algorithms, data, and computational power to simulate cognitive functions, enabling them to adapt, improve, and execute tasks without explicit programming.

**Big Data:** This refers to extremely large and complex datasets that exceed the capabilities of traditional data processing methods. Characterized by the three Vs—volume, velocity, and variety—Big Data encompasses massive volumes of information generated at high speeds from diverse sources, including structured and unstructured data. The goal is to analyze and extract valuable insights from these extensive datasets to inform decision-making, discover patterns, and gain a deeper understanding of various phenomena.

**Hadoop:** An open-source framework designed for the distributed storage and processing of large volumes of data. It provides a scalable and fault-tolerant ecosystem that includes the Hadoop Distributed File System (HDFS) for storage and Map Reduce for parallel processing. Hadoop enables organizations to efficiently handle massive datasets across clusters of commodity hardware, facilitating advanced analytics, machine learning, and the extraction of valuable insights from diverse sources of information.

**Internet of Things (IoT):** The network of interconnected devices embedded with sensors, software, and connectivity features that enable them to collect, exchange, and act upon data. This network allows everyday objects, from household appliances to industrial machines, to communicate and share information over the internet, leading to increased automation, efficiency, and the potential for smarter decision-making.

**Machine Learning (ML):** A subset of artificial intelligence (AI) that focuses on the development of algorithms and statistical models enabling computer systems to improve their performance on tasks without explicit programming. ML involves the automatic learning of patterns and insights from data, allowing systems to make predictions, classifications, or decisions based on experience and training rather than explicit programming.

# Chapter 11
# Data Ethics and Privacy

**Alka Golyan**
*Dayanand College, India*

**Shikhar Panchal**
*Nirma University, India*

**Dhruvesh Vaghasiya**
*Nirma University, India*

**Harsh Parekh**
*Nirma University, India*

## ABSTRACT

*The ethical issues surrounding data acquisition, use, and management have gained prominence in the quickly changing field of data analytics. In the framework of contemporary data analytics, this chapter examines the complex issues of data ethics and privacy. It looks at the moral dilemmas brought on by gathering and using enormous volumes of data, such as those involving permission, openness, and justice. It also explores the effects of data analytics methods on society's values and individual privacy rights, including machine learning and artificial intelligence. The chapter also covers new rules and frameworks being developed to address ethical issues with data analytics procedures. This chapter offers insights into best practices for managing the ethical complexity inherent in data-driven decision-making through the analysis of case studies and ethical problems. Ultimately, it emphasizes how crucial it is to embrace moral standards and privacy-protecting methods to guarantee ethical and long-lasting data analytics procedures in the future.*

## 1. INTRODUCTION

The quick development of data analytics has brought a new era of unparalleled data collecting, analysis, and decision-making skills. However, these technical developments have also given rise to complicated moral dilemmas and privacy concerns, which calls for carefully studying data-driven behaviours' social and ethical ramifications (Duan, Y. et. al., 2019; Wang, H. et. al., 2016; Minell,. M., et. al., 2013). This

DOI: 10.4018/979-8-3693-3609-0.ch011

*Figure 1. Cost of a data breach by industry in millions*

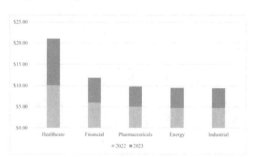

chapter delves into the complex world of data ethics and privacy, examining the various problems and issues resulting from gathering, utilizing, and handling enormous amounts of data (Rajasegar, R. et. al., 2024; Braun, A. et. al., 2017; Aparna Kumari, et. al., 2019). With the integration of artificial intelligence and machine learning, data analytics techniques are becoming more complex, and it is essential to carefully assess the potential effects on individual privacy rights and social values.The idea of consent is at the heart of one of the most important ethical conundrums: How can we ensure that people are fully informed and have given their meaningful approval for their data to be collected and used? Organizations must be open and honest about their data practices so that people are aware of how and why their data is being used. This makes transparency a crucial principle (Stahl, B. et. al., 2018; Mullins, M. et. al., 2021; Martin, K. 2022). Fairness and justice are vital issues since data analytics models and algorithms can reinforce preexisting prejudices and discriminatory practices. The possibility of unforeseen effects must be carefully considered, and we must seek to create moral frameworks that uphold justice, responsibility, and respect for human rights (Mühlhoff, R., 2021; Aparna, K. et. al., 2018).

Figure 1 shows the average cost of a data breach varied across industries in both 2022 and 2023. In the healthcare sector, the average cost increased slightly from $10.10 million in 2022 to $10.93 million in 2023. Similarly, the financial sector saw a slight decrease from $5.97 million in 2022 to $5.90 million in 2023. The pharmaceutical industry also experienced a decrease from $5.01 million in 2022 to $4.82 million in 2023. Notably, the energy sector, which was combined with technology in 2023, saw a slight increase to $4.78 million compared to $4.72 million in 2022. Meanwhile, the industrial sector maintained a relatively stable average cost of $4.72 million in both years (Cost of a Data Breach Report 2023).

These figures underscore the significant financial impact of data breaches across various industries and emphasize the importance of adhering to ethics and privacy standards to mitigate such risks. Regardless of the sector, organizations must prioritize ethical data practices and robust privacy measures to safeguard sensitive information and mitigate the financial and reputational consequences associated with data breaches.

Furthermore, new frameworks and rules are being created as the area of data analytics develops to address the ethical challenges these techniques bring. This chapter will examine the latest legal and regulatory environments, understanding the different strategies and policies designed to protect people's right to privacy and encourage responsible data handling. This chapter thoroughly examines best practices for managing the ethical complexity inherent in data-driven decision-making by investigating real-world case studies and ethical problems. We'll look at ways to apply moral principles—like data minimization, anonymization, and robust data governance frameworks—to ensure that the advantages of data analytics are achieved while respecting core ethical principles and human rights. In the end, this chapter highlights how crucial it is to adopt moral principles and privacy-preserving techniques to guarantee moral and long-lasting data analytics practices in the future. We must proactively address these ethical and privacy issues as data analytics continues to change our society to create a trustworthy and accountable atmosphere for data-driven innovation.

## 1.1 Motivation

This chapter was inspired by the growing importance and necessity of resolving privacy and ethical issues in the quickly developing field of data analytics. The necessity to closely consider the moral and societal ramifications of an organization's use of large data sets and sophisticated analytical tools is increasing. Ethical frameworks, best practices, and legal requirements are essential to ensuring responsible and reliable data-driven decision-making because data analytics can affect individual privacy rights, reinforce prejudices, and change social norms. This chapter seeks to provide readers with the information and resources they need to navigate data ethics and privacy issues, advocating for sustainable and moral data analytics practices that strike a balance between innovation and the defence of core human rights and values.

## 1.2 Research Contribution

- This chapter explores the moral problems and privacy issues brought on by contemporary data analytics techniques, which require collecting and utilizing massive amounts of data.
- We examine how modern analytical methods, affect individual privacy rights, fairness, and societal values.
- It provides information on new laws, guidelines, and best practices that can be used to preserve morality and safeguard privacy while negotiating the moral challenges of data-driven decision-making.

## 1.3 Organization of Chapter

The chapter is organized into several sections. Section 2 provides a literature review to contextualize critical concepts and emerging trends. Section 3 focuses on challenges. Section 4 focuses on Ethics and Privacy Models, exploring theoretical frameworks and practical approaches. Section 5 presents case studies, illustrating ethical decision-making in a practical context. Finally, the Conclusion section synthesizes findings and offers insights from the chapter's discussions, emphasizing the importance of ethical considerations and privacy protection in data analytics practices.

## 2. LITERATURE REVIEW

Ethical considerations and privacy concerns in data analytics have garnered significant attention in recent years, reflecting the growing recognition of the need to balance innovation with ethical responsibility in the digital age. A comprehensive review of existing literature reveals many research efforts aimed at understanding and addressing the moral challenges and privacy implications associated with data-driven decision-making processes.

Numerous scholars have emphasized the importance of ethical frameworks and guidelines for responsible data analytics practices. For instance, (Jones and Kamvar) advocate adopting ethical principles such as transparency, accountability, and fairness to mitigate risks and promote trust in data-driven decision-making (Von Radecki et. al.). Similarly, (Eger, C., Miller, G., & Scarles, C.) highlight the role of organizational culture and leadership in fostering a commitment to ethical conduct and privacy protection within data analytics initiatives. Privacy preservation techniques have emerged as a research focus, with scholars exploring various methods to balance data utility with individual privacy rights. Differential privacy, a widely studied approach, aims to enable the analysis of sensitive data while preserving the privacy of individuals by introducing noise or perturbation to query responses (Dwork et al.). Other techniques, such as homomorphic encryption and secure multi-party computation, offer alternative solutions for privacy-preserving data analytics (Iezzi, M. 2020). The ethical implications of machine learning algorithms in data analytics have also received considerable attention. Researchers have identified algorithmic bias, fairness, and interpretability challenges, which can profoundly impact decision-making processes and societal outcomes (Barocas & Selbst; Selbst & Barocas). Efforts to address these challenges include the development of fairness-aware machine learning techniques and algorithmic auditing frameworks (Kamiran & Calders). In addition to technical considerations, regulatory frameworks play a crucial role in shaping ethical practices and safeguarding privacy in data analytics. Scholars have conducted comparative analyses of existing regulations, such as the European Union's General Data Protection Regulation (GDPR) and the California Consumer Privacy Act (CCPA), to evaluate their effectiveness in protecting individual privacy rights and promoting ethical data handling practices (Cate). Furthermore, ethical decision-making frameworks and tools have been proposed to assist organizations and practitioners in navigating the complex ethical landscape of data analytics. Models such as the Ethical Matrix (Macnaghten et al.) and the Ethical Systems Engineering Framework (Van de Poel & Robaey) offer structured approaches to identifying and evaluating ethical considerations in data analytics projects, facilitating informed decision-making and risk assessment.

Overall, the literature review underscores the multidimensional nature of ethical considerations and privacy concerns in data analytics. By synthesizing insights from diverse disciplinary perspectives, researchers aim to advance understanding and promote responsible and ethical practices in the increasingly data-driven societies of the future.

## 3. CHALLENGES ON DATA ETHICS AND PRIVACY

- Rapid Technological Advancements: Keeping pace with rapid technological advancements presents a significant challenge. New technologies, such as artificial intelligence and big data analytics, constantly emerge, introducing novel ethical dilemmas and privacy concerns that require ongoing exploration and analysis.
- Evolving Regulatory Landscape: The legal and regulatory environment surrounding data ethics and privacy is constantly evolving. Adapting to new regulations, such as the General Data Protection Regulation (GDPR) or the California Consumer Privacy Act (CCPA) and staying compliant with evolving legal requirements can be challenging for organizations.
- Data Complexity and Volume: The sheer volume and complexity of data collected and processed pose challenges in ensuring ethical data practices and protecting individuals' privacy rights.

Handling vast amounts of data while maintaining ethical standards and privacy protections requires robust data governance frameworks and sophisticated technological solutions.

- Ethical Decision-Making: Ethical decision-making in data analytics can be complex and subjective, particularly when balancing competing interests, such as maximizing business profits and protecting individual privacy rights. Organizations may struggle to navigate ethical dilemmas effectively and may lack clear guidelines or frameworks for ethical decision-making.

- Privacy Risks and Security Threats: The proliferation of privacy risks and security threats, including data breaches, hacking incidents, and malicious attacks, poses significant challenges to data ethics and privacy. Organizations must implement robust security measures and privacy-enhancing technologies to mitigate these risks effectively.

- Cultural and Organizational Change: Promoting a culture of ethical awareness and accountability within organizations can be challenging, particularly in industries where data-driven decision-making is prioritized over ethical considerations. Encouraging cultural and organizational change to prioritize ethical values and privacy protection requires leadership commitment and ongoing education and training initiatives.

- Stakeholder Trust and Perception: Building and maintaining trust with stakeholders, including customers, employees, regulators, and the public, is essential for the success of data ethics and privacy initiatives. Addressing concerns about data misuse, privacy breaches, and ethical lapses requires transparent communication, accountability, and proactive measures to address stakeholder feedback and concerns.

## 4. ETHICS AND PRIVACY MODELS

- **Ethical Principles**
- Transparency: Businesses should be open and honest about gathering, using, and processing data. People should be given clear and easily accessible information about how and why their data is used.

- Consent: People ought to be allowed to give their meaningful and informed permission before having their personal information collected and used. The consent procedure must be unambiguous, transparent, and simple to withdraw.

- Fairness and Non-discrimination: Relative design and implementation of data analytics procedures are necessary to avoid maintaining or enhancing preexisting prejudices or discriminatory practices.

- Privacy and Data Minimization: Organizations should gather and handle the minimal personal information needed for the intended use. To safeguard individuals' rights to privacy, they should put strong privacy-preserving measures in place.

- Accountability and Ethical Governance: Organizations should set up explicit governance structures, policies, and procedures throughout the data analytics lifecycle to guarantee accountability and moral decision-making.

- Purpose Limitation: Only specific legal purposes should be identified for the collection and use of data, and those purposes should not be compromised by additional processing. This rule ensures that information isn't utilized for unauthorized or unexpected reasons.

- Data Minimization: Companies should gather and keep the minimum data required to fulfil their objectives. Data reduction lowers the possibility of illegal access and privacy violations.
- Accuracy: Businesses should strive to guarantee the integrity and quality of the data they gather and keep. Accurate data is necessary for people to make educated decisions and avoid harm.
- Security: It is recommended that organizations implement suitable security measures to safeguard data against unwanted access, disclosure, change, or destruction. The level of security should match the severity of the data being handled.
- **Privacy-Preserving Techniques**
- Differential privacy: safeguarding personal information while allowing for statistical analysis of sensitive data by adding controlled noise or disturbance to query responses.
- Homomorphic Encryption: This method maintains data privacy and secrecy by allowing calculations to be made on encrypted data without the need for decryption.
- Secure Multi-Party Computation: Enabling several parties to collaboratively calculate a function over their respective inputs while maintaining the privacy of those inputs.
- Data Anonymization and Pseudonymization: obfuscating or removing personally identifiable information from data to preserve data utility while protecting individual privacy.
- **Ethical Frameworks and Tools**
- Ethical Matrix: A structured approach to identifying and evaluating ethical considerations in data analytics projects, considering different stakeholder perspectives and moral principles.
- Ethical Systems Engineering Framework: A systematic framework incorporating ethical considerations throughout the data analytics system development lifecycle, from requirements analysis to deployment and monitoring.
- Algorithmic Auditing: Conduct regular audits and assessments of machine learning algorithms and decision-making models to detect and mitigate potential biases, fairness issues, and ethical violations.
- **Regulatory Compliance**
- Adhere to relevant data protection and privacy regulations, such as the General Data Protection Regulation (GDPR), the California Consumer Privacy Act (CCPA), and any other applicable local or industry-specific regulations.
- Establish robust data governance frameworks and processes to ensure Compliance with regulatory requirements and ethical standards.
- **Ethical Awareness and Training**
- Foster an organizational culture that values ethical conduct and privacy protection by providing regular training and awareness programs for employees and stakeholders involved in data analytics initiatives.
- Encourage open dialogue and collaboration with relevant stakeholders, including data subjects, policymakers, and ethical advisory boards, to continuously refine and improve ethical practices.

## 5. FUTURE DIRECTION

The chapter on data ethics and privacy is expected to take a dynamic and revolutionary turn in the future. The relevance of ethical considerations and privacy protection in data analytics methods is becoming more widely acknowledged due to rapid technological improvements and the rise of data-driven decision-making. Future paths will probably entail accepting new developments in algorithmic accountability and ethical AI trends and advances, emphasising creating transparent, understandable, and accountable AI systems. Adopting frameworks and technologies that protect privacy will also continue to be prioritized to protect people's right to privacy and reduce the possibility of data misuse. Organizations must prioritize strong data governance and compliance procedures as privacy legislation becomes more complex and demanding to guarantee that legal requirements and moral principles are followed. In addition, future paths will include encouraging stakeholder participation, openness, and initiatives that establish trust to cultivate an ethically conscious and accountable culture within firms. In the increasingly data-centric digital landscape, the chapter hopes to promote confidence, fairness, and societal well-being by embracing these future trends and helping to improve responsible and ethical data practices.

## 6. CASE STUDIES

1.  In a particular situation, customer data was being used to make marketing strategies better using advanced computer programs. These programs, called algorithms, could analyze customer information and make predictions about what they might buy next. But there was a problem: the predictions were more accurate when they used personal information like health conditions. This raised some big questions about ethics, or what's right and wrong. People were worried that using this personal data without asking might hurt customers' privacy and trust. To figure out what to do, a thorough examination, called a risk assessment, was done to see what might happen if personal data was used without permission. The results were concerning: it could lead to serious problems like private information getting into the wrong hands and customers being harmed. To solve this, it was suggested to create strict rules about privacy and always ask customers if it's okay to use their sensitive data before doing anything with it. Even though this might make the predictions a bit less accurate, it was decided that protecting customer trust and privacy was more important. After these decisions, the company changed its policies about collecting and using data. Now, customers have a say in whether their information can be used for marketing purposes. Plus, the employees got trained on how to handle data properly and respect customers' privacy. This was all done to make sure the company was doing the right thing and keeping customers safe and happy. By taking these steps, the company aimed to prevent any ethical problems and make sure they were doing things the right way, according to their values and what society expects.

An iterative method for making ethical decisions is depicted in the Figure 2. It starts with determining whether a situation raises any potential ethical concerns. Next, information is acquired to develop a thorough understanding, considering all parties affected and participating. When core values clash, they are identified. Ethical guiding concepts such as virtues, rights, and obligations are used to assess the problem. Using moral imagination, potential solutions are found, and their implications are imagined. The optimal solution is put into practice, and the results are tracked. This circular process emphasizes the continual nature of ethical reasoning and the necessity of thoroughly examining ethical quandaries from numerous viewpoints before acting. It also fosters continuous re-evaluation when new information becomes available, or circumstances change (Case Study Accessed on March 2024).

*Figure 2. Ethical decision-making process*

2.    In one incident, the popular trading app Robinhood faced a data breach in November 2021, impacting more than five million users. Hackers accessed a customer support system, getting hold of users' email addresses, names, phone numbers, and other personal details. Thankfully, sensitive information like Social Security numbers, bank accounts, and debit card details remained safe. However, this breach highlights the importance of data ethics and privacy in safeguarding personal information. Data ethics and privacy are vital for protecting sensitive data from unauthorized access and misuse. In this case, the breach occurred due to security flaws in data storage, emphasizing the need for robust measures to prevent such incidents. By prioritizing data ethics and privacy, organizations can implement stronger security protocols, encryption techniques, and access controls to safeguard user data. It's essential for companies like Robinhood to take proactive steps to prevent data breaches and uphold the trust of their users (Ethics in Data Science and Proper Privacy and Usage of Data. Accessed on March 2024).

## 7. CONCLUSION

In this chapter, we've examined the complex terrain of ethics and privacy in data analytics. Recognizing how critical it is to protect individual privacy rights and ethical standards in the digital age, we have conducted an extensive analysis based on a wide range of previously published works and real-world case studies. Our investigation has shown companies' and practitioners' intricate moral difficulties when utilizing data for business insights, ranging from the moral challenges of algorithmic decision-making to the subtle privacy implications of data collecting and analysis. Essential ethical requirements, including responsibility, openness, and fairness, have been emphasized, highlighting the necessity for businesses to prioritize ethical principles and implement appropriate data practices. We have also underlined the critical role privacy preservation strategies like data anonymization, encryption, and differential privacy play in safeguarding confidential data and reducing privacy threats associated with data analytics procedures. Organizations can protect privacy rights and support important data analysis projects by combining these privacy-enhancing technologies with solid data governance systems. We have emphasized the significance of carefully identifying ethical challenges, acquiring relevant information, and evaluating alternative solutions against ethical benchmarks through the ethical decision-making process illustrated in the case study. In an increasingly data-centric world, firms may build customer trust, reduce risks, and protect their brand by putting ethical values first and promoting an ethically conscious culture.

# REFERENCES

Barocas, S., & Selbst, A. D. (2016). Big data's disparate impact. *California Law Review, 104*, 671.

Duan, Y., Edwards, J. S., & Dwivedi, Y. K. (2019). Artificial intelligence for decision making in the era of Big Data–evolution, challenges and research agenda. *International Journal of Information Management, 48*, 63–71. doi:10.1016/j.ijinfomgt.2019.01.021

Dwork, C., Naor, M., Pitassi, T., & Rothblum, G. N. (2010, June). Differential privacy under continual observation. In *Proceedings of the forty-second ACM symposium on Theory of computing* (pp. 715-724). ACM. 10.1145/1806689.1806787

Eger, C., Miller, G., & Scarles, C. (2019). Corporate philanthropy through the lens of ethical subjectivity. *Journal of Business Ethics, 156*(1), 141–153. doi:10.1007/s10551-017-3551-1

Iezzi, M. (2020, December). Practical privacy-preserving data science with homomorphic encryption: an overview. In *2020 IEEE International Conference on Big Data (Big Data)* (pp. 3979-3988). IEEE. 10.1109/BigData50022.2020.9377989

Kamiran, F., & Calders, T. (2012). Data preprocessing techniques for classification without discrimination. *Knowledge and Information Systems, 33*(1), 1–33. doi:10.1007/s10115-011-0463-8

Kumari, A. (2018). *Verification and validation techniques for streaming big data analytics in internet of things environment.* . doi:10.1049/iet-net.2018.5187

Kumari, A., Tanwar, S., Tyagi, S., Kumar, N., Parizi, R. M., & Choo, K.-K. R. (2019). Fog data analytics: A taxonomy and process model. *Journal of Network and Computer Applications, 128*. doi:10.1016/j.jnca.2018.12.013

Macnaghten, P., Kearnes, M. B., & Wynne, B. (2005). Nanotechnology, governance, and public deliberation: What role for the social sciences? *Science Communication, 27*(2), 268–291. doi:10.1177/1075547005281531

Martin, K. (2022). *Ethics of data and analytics: Concepts and cases.* Auerbach Publications. doi:10.1201/9781003278290

Minelli, M., Chambers, M., & Dhiraj, A. (2013). *Big data, big analytics: emerging business intelligence and analytic trends for today's businesses* (Vol. 578). John Wiley & Sons. doi:10.1002/9781118562260

Mühlhoff, R. (2021). Predictive privacy: Towards an applied ethics of data analytics. *Ethics and Information Technology*, *23*(4), 675–690. doi:10.1007/s10676-021-09606-x

Mullins, M., Holland, C. P., & Cunneen, M. (2021). Creating ethics guidelines for artificial intelligence and big data analytics customers: The case of the consumer European insurance market. *Patterns (New York, N.Y.)*, *2*(10), 100362. doi:10.1016/j.patter.2021.100362 PMID:34693379

Rajasegar, R. S., Gouthaman, P., Ponnusamy, V., Arivazhagan, N., & Nallarasan, V. (2024). Data Privacy and Ethics in Data Analytics. In Data Analytics and Machine Learning: Navigating the Big Data Landscape (pp. 195-213). Singapore: Springer Nature Singapore. doi:10.1007/978-981-97-0448-4_10

Selbst, A. D., & Barocas, S. (2018). The intuitive appeal of explainable machines. *Fordham Law Review*, *87*, 1085.

Stahl, B. C., & Wright, D. (2018). Ethics and privacy in AI and big data: Implementing responsible research and innovation. *IEEE Security and Privacy*, *16*(3), 26–33. doi:10.1109/MSP.2018.2701164

Ten Cate, O., Dahdal, S., Lambert, T., Neubauer, F., Pless, A., Pohlmann, P. F., van Rijen, H., & Gurtner, C. (2020). Ten caveats of learning analytics in health professions education: A consumer's perspective. *Medical Teacher*, *42*(6), 673–678. doi:10.1080/0142159X.2020.1733505 PMID:32150499

Van de Poel, I., & Robaey, Z. (2017). Safe-by-design: From safety to responsibility. *NanoEthics*, *11*(3), 297–306. doi:10.1007/s11569-017-0301-x PMID:29238409

von Radecki, A., Tcholtchev, N., Lämmel, P., & Schaj, G. (). *Building Data Ecosystems to Unlock the Value of Urban (Big) Data: A Good Practices Reference Guide.*

Wang, H., Xu, Z., Fujita, H., & Liu, S. (2016). Towards felicitous decision making: An overview on challenges and trends of Big Data. *Information Sciences*, *367*, 747–765. doi:10.1016/j.ins.2016.07.007

# Section 4

# Applications Across Industries and Future Trends

*In the section titled "Applications Across Industries and Future Trends," readers are introduced to the diverse real-world applications of data analytics spanning various sectors such as finance, healthcare, marketing, and supply chain management. Through a series of case studies and discussions, readers gain insights into how data analytics is utilized to address specific challenges and drive innovation within each industry. Additionally, the section explores emerging trends and future directions in data analytics, offering a glimpse into the evolving landscape of the field and preparing readers for the challenges and opportunities that lie ahead.*

# Chapter 12
# Enhancing Learner Motivation and Academic Achievement:
## The Impact of the ARCS Model of Motivational Design on Technology–Enhanced Learning Environments

**Ahgalya Subbiah**
 https://orcid.org/0009-0006-4427-0872
*Management and Science University, Malaysia*

## ABSTRACT

*This study examines the impact of technology on education, specifically focusing on motivation and learning principles for instructional enhancement. For 84 junior students from both computer science and computer forensics, ARCS-based instruction showed improved motivation and academic performance. CS students experienced a 50% increase in success opportunities, while CF students had a 70% higher satisfaction rate with rewards. Statistical analysis confirmed the differences (p &lt; 0.05), indicating tailored educational approaches; CS students adapt well; CF students prefer intrinsic reinforcement. However, academic achievement varied significantly, emphasizing the need for refined motivational strategies, particularly for CF students. The findings suggest that ARCS-based instruction benefits motivation and academic achievement, necessitating tailored approaches across subject areas. Integrating motivation science and technology can create captivating learning experiences that promote lifelong learning and academic success.*

## 1. INTRODUCTION

In recent times, the integration of technology into educational settings has seen a significant rise, with the pace of adoption and innovation continuing to escalate. Each new technological advancement brings about a surge of excitement and literature spotlighting its advantages and potential applications. However, this initial excitement often fades, leaving researchers and educators faced with the ongoing challenge of

DOI: 10.4018/979-8-3693-3609-0.ch012

devising motivating and effective instructional learning encounters. While adjustments specific to technology may require further exploration, there exist fundamental principles of motivation and learning that endure across various technologies and delivery methods (McClelland, D. C., 1988). By understanding and implementing these principles, educators can craft learning experiences that are both motivating and instructional, regardless of the technology employed. The timeless principles of motivation and learning serve as a bedrock for constructing captivating and meaningful learning encounters, even amidst the swiftly evolving technological landscape (Dong & Li, 2022).

In the domain of personal growth and intellectual progress, the core lies in the acquisition of knowledge, yet enthusiasm for exploration and the pursuit of wisdom may diminish for individuals over time. Factors such as rigid educational frameworks, lack of autonomy, and an exaggerated emphasis on academic performance can hinder a person's inherent curiosity and innate drive to gain knowledge. Understanding the complex dynamics of motivation holds paramount importance in nurturing a lasting passion for learning (Durrani, U., & Kamal, M., 2020). By fostering fervent enthusiasm for acquiring knowledge, learners can delve into a sustained level of motivation that will prove beneficial both academically and personally. Motivation presents itself in two distinct forms: intrinsic and extrinsic, each carrying its own significance in the realm of learning. Intrinsic motivation arises when an activity is pursued for its inherent worth, while extrinsic motivation occurs when an activity is undertaken with the expectation of a reward or to avoid punishment. Both types of motivation play a pivotal role in the educational journey; extrinsic motivation may provide an initial push, while intrinsic motivation fosters deep self-propulsion. When these essential conditions are fulfilled, learners are more likely to be deeply engaged, driven, and successful in their academic pursuits (Chuang, et al., 2023). Determination is a key part of the educational journey, exerting substantial influence over the learning process. Delving into the science behind motivation and employing methodologies that cater to both intrinsic and extrinsic motivators can enrich the educational voyage. External stimuli have the power to instigate self-evolution among learners, precipitating shifts in mindset and conduct conducive to nurturing intrinsic motivation. Principles entrenched in the realm of motivation, including autonomy, ability, interconnectedness, pertinence, setting challenging yet attainable aims, acknowledgment, and incentives, as well as constructive feedback, can be seamlessly integrated into pedagogical approaches to elevate the calibre of learning. By cultivating an educational milieu that attends to the motivational requisites of learners, educators can sow the seeds of an enduring passion for learning, propelling learners towards realizing their utmost potential.

This study examines the impact of the ARCS Model of Motivational Design on motivation and learning outcomes in a technology-enhanced learning environment. The focus of this research is to investigate the relationship between motivation to learn and technology use, specifically in the context of a Computer System Design course for junior Computer Science and Computer Forensics students. The study spanned an entire semester, from 2023 to January 2024, and involved a cohort of eighty-four students. Data were collected using quantitative research methods, including questionnaires, and written final exam results. The ARCS model was implemented in an experimental group, while a comparison group received instruction using traditional lecture methods. The effectiveness of the ARCS Model of Motivational Design was evaluated by comparing the outcomes of the two groups, with the aim of identifying any potential advantages or disadvantages of each instructional approach. The study employed a rigorous research design, using valid and reliable measurement tools to ensure the accuracy and reliability of the findings. The use of Google Forms allowed for the collection of student feedback throughout the semester. The findings of this study contribute to the growing body of literature on the application of motivational design principles in educational contexts, particularly in relation to technology-enhanced learning environments. By focusing on the motivational aspects of technology-integrated education, this research aims to provide insights into how to design engaging and effective learning experiences in contemporary educational settings. In summary, this study investigates the impact of the ARCS Model of Motivational Design on student motivation and learning outcomes in a technology-enhanced learning environment. By comparing the outcomes of an experimental group taught using the ARCS model and a comparison group taught using traditional lecture methods, the study aims to contribute to a better understanding of how to design engaging and effective learning experiences in contemporary educational settings.

## 1.2 Motivation of the Study

The integration of technology into educational settings has rapidly increased in recent years, presenting both opportunities and challenges for educators. While initial enthusiasm for new technological advancements may be high, sustaining motivation and engagement over time remains a significant concern. This chapter aims to explore the enduring principles of motivation and learning that underpin effective instructional design, regardless of the technology employed. By understanding and implementing these principles, educators can create learning experiences that are both motivating and instructional, ultimately enhancing student engagement and academic success.

## 1.3 Chapter Contribution

This chapter delves into the literature surrounding motivational design principles in education, with a particular focus on technology-enhanced learning environments. Chapter contributions are as follows:

- It underscores the crucial role of incorporating motivational strategies into instructional design to create engaging and effective learning experiences.
- In addition, the chapter lays the groundwork for the study's exploration of the ARCS Model of Motivational Design's impact on student motivation and learning outcomes in a technology-enhanced learning environment.
- The study aims to compare the outcomes of different instructional approaches, providing insights for educators on how to design more engaging and effective learning experiences in today's modern educational settings.
- The study seeks to contribute to the ongoing conversation about the best ways to leverage technology to enhance learning outcomes and motivation for students.

## 1.4 Chapter Organization

The chapter initiates by exploring the reasons for examining the enduring principles of motivation and learning in the context of technology-integrated education. It then highlights the chapter's contributions to the existing literature on motivational design principles and sets the stage for the study's investigation of the ARCS Model of Motivational Design's impact. Additionally, the chapter provides a roadmap of the subsequent sections, which include a review of relevant literature, a detailed description of the research methodology, a presentation of study findings, and a discussion of the implications and future directions. The chapter aims to offer a comprehensive understanding of the study's objectives and structure, providing a clear and concise guide for readers as they delve into the exploration of motivational design principles

*Figure 1. Keller's instructional model of motivation*

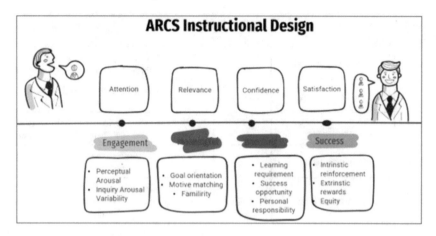

in technology-enhanced learning environments. The chapter's organization and content are designed to be accessible and engaging, appealing to both scholars and practitioners in the field of education.

## 2. THE MOTIVATIONAL DESIGN MODEL: ARCS MODEL

The ARCS Model of Motivational Design, conceptualized by John Keller in 1987, offers a systematic framework for enhancing motivation in the learning process. According to Keller, motivation is a product of individual value satisfaction and the anticipation of success (Keller & Kopp, 1987). Keller defines motivation as 'the purposeful desire to do, select, and persist in an activity' (Keller, 1987). The ARCS Model includes four main categories: Attention, Relevance, Confidence, and Satisfaction. These categories encompass a series of subcategories that delve deeper into specific aspects of motivation. Each of these aspects is segmented into three subcategories, yet all can merge into a unified motivational process as illustrated in Figure 1.

The ARCS Model offers a comprehensive framework for designing instructional materials that foster motivation and engagement in the learning process (Keller, J. M., 2006, 2010). The above illustration can be simplified as follows:

a)  Attention: The learning material must effectively capture the learners' attention, thereby generating interest and curiosity.

b)  Relevance: The learning material should be meaningful and significant to learners, showing its applicability to their personal goals and real-world scenarios.

c)  Confidence: Learners must have confidence in their ability to succeed, supported by clear learning expectations, structured tasks, and constructive feedback.

d)  Satisfaction: Learners should experience a sense of reward or reinforcement upon completing the learning experience, derived from a combination of intrinsic motivation and external incentives.

By considering each of these sub-components, educators can create a more dynamic and supportive learning environment that empowers learners to achieve their full potential. Consequently, building

*Table 1. Keller's motivational model determinants and procedures*

| Keller's ARCS Model Components | Instructional Design Sub-Components | Model Niche | Propositions and Procedures |
|---|---|---|---|
| Attention | Perceptual Arousal | Engagement | How can I effectively keep learners' engagement and attention throughout the learning experience?(1) |
| | Inquiry Arousal | | How can I effectively promote and encourage a sense of curiosity in learners?(2) |
| | Variability | | How can I employ diverse techniques to effectively sustain learners' focus and concentration?(3) |
| Relevance | Goal orientation | Meaningful | What is the most effective way to address and fulfil my learners' needs and preferences?(4) |
| | Motive matching | | When and how should I offer my learners suitable choices, responsibilities, and opportunities for influence to perfect their learning experience?(5) |
| | Familiarity | | What are the strategies for relating the lesson content to the lives and familiar contexts of my students?(6) |
| Confidence | Learning Requirements | Boosting | What are the known ways to promote a growth mindset and optimistic outlook for success in my learners?(7) |
| | Success Opportunity | | In what ways will the learning experience bolster learners' beliefs in their own capabilities and skills?(8) |
| | Personal Responsibility | | What strategies can I use to help learners recognize that their success earned through their hard work and innate abilities?(9) |
| Satisfaction | Intrinsic Reinforcement | Success | What are the effective ways to ease learners' application and practice of their newfound knowledge and abilities?(10) |
| | Extrinsic Rewards | | How can we give our learners recognition and encouragement for their achievements and successes?(11) |
| | Enquiry | | How can we show our learners appreciation and support for their accomplishments and victories?(12) |

upon the ARCS model and its perspectives, this framework extends to encompass related motivational factors within the learning environment. This is consistent with the crucial need for satisfaction in the learning experience. Table 1 presents the determinants of ARCS motivational factors aimed at capturing a learner's motivation.

The above representation of the design model conceptualizes motivational processes, highlighting the functional similarities in these processes across different levels of analysis. This relates to learners' ability to become proactive and take initiative in their learning journey.

## 2.2 Previous Research

Investigations have been conducted with the aim of applying the ARCS model to learners of different age groups and subjects. Among these studies, there is a focus on examining earlier research related to the use of the ARCS model in the Computer System Design subject for junior learners. These investigations have explored the effectiveness of the ARCS model in enhancing learner motivation and engagement in the Computer System Design subject learning process. By analysing the findings of these studies, valuable insights have been gained into the application of the ARCS model in Computer System Design subject instruction and how to promote learner motivation and engagement. The ARCS model has been integrated into robot-assisted teaching to improve sustainable learning efficiency and motivation in programming classes, with interactive robots interacting with students using the ARCS motivation model. This approach has helped students develop motivation, relevance, and confidence in learning (Hsieh, Y. et al., 2020, & Tanwar, S. et al., 2019). In control engineering and image processing, a motivation system based on the ARCS model was designed using a drone as the control object. This system allowed students to tune the parameters of a PID controller and see the drone's responses, significantly increasing their interest in learning these techniques (Rahok, S. et al., 2019 & Tanwar, S. et al., 2029).

The ARCS model has also been applied in engineering subjects to increase student interest and reduce the number of backlogs. Implementing the ARCS model in lectures has developed a positive expectation for success and satisfaction in students' work (Usmadi, U. et al., 2018). An ARCS-based e-book used in a Mathematics-I course resulted in improved student achievement and motivation, as well as reduced mathematics anxiety levels compared to traditional printed books or static PDFs (Alekhya, N., & Kishore, N., 2018). The ARCSI (ARCS with Islamic values) learning model, which incorporates Islamic values and a scientific approach, has been successfully applied in junior high school mathematics classes, creating a pleasant learning environment and encouraging critical thinking (Türel, Y., & Sanal, S., 2018).

Furthermore, the ARCS model has been used in integrated thematic learning in elementary schools, showing improvements in both the learning process and student learning outcomes (Efriyenef, F., & Fitria, Y., 2021). The ARCS model has also been combined with STAD and NHT cooperative learning strategies in mathematics classes, leading to enhanced teacher and student activities, as well as student motivation and learning outcomes (Chang, Y. et al., 2018). Similarly, a study by Ucar, H. and Kumtepe, A.T. (2019) found that the ARCS Model was effective in promoting student motivation and academic achievement in a blended learning environment. The researchers used a quasi-experimental design to evaluate the impact of the ARCS Model on student motivation and learning outcomes and found that students who received instruction using the ARCS Model had higher levels of motivation and academic achievement compared to a control group. However, not all studies have found positive results for the ARCS Model. For example, a study by Lee and Kim (2023) found that the ARCS Model was not effective in promoting student motivation and academic achievement in a mobile learning environment. The researchers used a randomized controlled trial to evaluate the impact of the ARCS Model on student motivation and learning outcomes and found that there was no significant difference between the experimental group and the control group.

In programming language learning, the ARCS model combined with the flipped classroom approach significantly promoted learning outcomes for learners. The effectiveness of the ARCSI learning model with a scientific approach was shown in junior high school mathematics classes, where it was found to be effective in improving student learning outcomes (Nurjannah, U., 2019). A literature review on the use of the ARCS model in education highlighted its application in various countries and educational settings, including computer-based learning approaches. The review suggested future research directions, such as applying design-based research to educational problems that the ARCS model might address. The outcome of this review showed that integration of the motivational model tremendously increased student affective domain, cognitive domain, learning behaviours, and psychological traits (Kun Li, J. Keller, 2018 & Kumari A. et al., 2020). In the study, the researchers developed a challenge-based gamified program called Educhall and investigated its impact on students' motivation, flow, and academic success in a mobile learning environment. The study found that the application of challenge-based gamified learning method increased the level of academic performance and overall motivation of the students. However, the study did not find a significant increase in the flow level of learners. The study concludes that challenge-based gamified learning can be an effective approach to increase students' motivation and academic success in a mobile learning environment (Baah, C. et al., 2023).Moreover, a study conducted by Chuang and Wu (2023) on Integrating Chatbot and Augmented Reality Technology into Biology Learning during COVID-19 also results that the AR-based chatbot system significantly influenced student motivation and learning outcomes in biology during COVID-19, offering new online learning tools for home use. A study on designing blended teaching using ARCS model by (Durrani, U., & Kamal, M., 2020) showed that blended teaching methodologies based on the ARCS model, process, and strategies effectively enhance and sustain students' motivation and interest in online learning during the COVID-19 outbreak. The ARCS model is a model that widely researched and recognized for its potential to enhance motivation, engagement, and learning outcomes in various educational contexts. Its versatility and adaptability have been demonstrated in various instructional approaches, such as robot-assisted teaching, e-books, and blended learning. The model has been successful in addressing key motivational factors like attention, relevance, confidence, and satisfaction. However, the effectiveness of the ARCS model influenced by contextual factors, such as instructional design, learner characteristics, and environmental factors. While certain studies have reported significant improvements in motivation and learning outcomes, others have found mixed or inconclusive results. Therefore, it is essential to consider these factors when implementing motivational strategies like the ARCS model.

The methodological approaches used in previous studies can also impact the interpretation of their findings. Future research should aim to employ rigorous research designs and standardized measurement tools to ensure the validity and reliability of findings. The integration of technology in education can enhance student engagement and motivation. However, it is essential to continually assess the effectiveness of these approaches and adapt them to meet the evolving needs of learners in a digital age In conclusion, while the ARCS model shows promise as a framework for enhancing motivation and engagement in educational settings, its effectiveness depends on various contextual factors and methodological considerations. By critically analysing previous research and addressing these factors, educators can leverage the ARCS model to design engaging and effective learning experiences that empower students to reach their full potential.

## 2.3 Integrating the ARCS Model to Enhance the Learning Experience and Outcomes in Instructional Design

When creating instructional materials, it is essential to consider learners' motivation to learn. The ARCS model serves as a helpful framework for designing and delivering instruction that fosters motivation. This model consists of four categories of general process questions and motivational strategies. Table 2 outlines the process of generating instructional deliverables.

## 3. USE OF ARCS DESIGN IN INSTRUCTIONAL DESIGN

The Computer System Design subject, designed for second-semester bachelor-level students from the Computer Science and Computer Forensics faculty, aims to introduce them to key concepts while familiarizing them with the intricacies of a solid foundation in computer architecture. The core of the subject is to encourage peer interaction, enhance efficient system designing skills, and promote collaborative and independent learning. The Computer System Design course includes multiple modules, each de-

*Table 2. Procedure on creating instructional material using ARCS model*

| Process | Procedure |
|---|---|
| Step 1 | In instructional design, conducting a student analysis is a crucial step in developing a motivational profile that can inform the design of motivational objectives. This analysis helps in identifying the initial motivational goals of students and detecting any gaps in these objectives. For example, when a student selects a course like Computer System Design, the instructor may be interested in understanding the reasons behind this choice. By gathering this information, the instructor can make informed judgments about the initial motivations of the student, which can be confirmed through interviewing a focus group of students during the first session of the semester. The student analysis can provide valuable insights into the motivational objectives that need to be developed to meet the unique needs of the students, based on their prior knowledge and experiences. |
| Step 2 | When developing motivational aims based on the motivational profiles of students, it is essential to align these aims with the four categories of the ARCS model. These motivational goals should encompass cognitive, affective, or psychomotor skills and be specified based on the student's perspective. To evaluate the effectiveness of the motivational strategies used, techniques such as direct observations, interviews, and self-reported questionnaires can be employed. It is crucial to design suitable motivational aims based on the motivational profiles of students, considering their prior knowledge and experiences. Furthermore, evaluating the effectiveness of the motivational strategies used is essential, as this can offer valuable insights into the students' motivation and engagement in the learning process. By monitoring and assessing the motivational aims, the course coordinator can make informed judgments about the success of the motivational strategies used and make necessary adjustments to ensure that the learning outcomes are achieved. |
| Step 3 | The third step in the ARCS model involves integrating the designed motivational strategies for each motivational goal into the instruction. This can include techniques such as question-based openings, open discussions to develop a concept, or encouraging students to share their views on an open issue to arrive at a specific topic. These strategies can help enhance the confidence of students and engage them in the lecture room. When selecting proper motivational strategies, it is important to keep a few factors in mind. Firstly, the strategies should not consume too much time, as this can detract from the learning aims. Secondly, the strategies should be compatible with the instructional method, including the educator's teaching style. Thirdly, the strategies should be acceptable to the students and fall within the time and budget constraints of the development and implementation phases of the instruction. Moreover, it is essential to ensure that the motivational strategies do not detract from the learning aims. Instead, they should complement the learning outcomes and help students achieve their full potential. |
| Step 4 | The decisive step in the ARCS model involves implementing the motivational strategies that have been designed and integrated into the instruction. This can include pilot runs or small group-based try-outs to assess the appeal of each strategy from the perspective of the students. This step is crucial in determining the effectiveness of the suggested strategies and whether they are achieving the intended results. By gathering feedback from students and assessing the impact of the strategies, the subject lecturer can make informed decisions about which strategies are working and which ones need adjustments. |

signed to delve into specific aspects of computer systems, offering a comprehensive understanding of the subject matter. These modules are appropriately designed to offer a comprehensive understanding of the subject matter. The course features a blend of engaging lectures, enriching readings, and interactive online assessments, ensuring that students are actively engaged in their learning journey and can apply the concepts they learn in real-world scenarios (Chang et al., 2018). The course is conducted in a traditional classroom setting where the instructors and students are physically present in a lecture room for each module. The subject is purposely planned to delve into specific aspects of computer systems, and the interactive online assessments for exercises and tests are designed to evaluate the students' understanding of the course material, their ability to apply the concepts in real-world scenarios, and their ability to communicate their ideas effectively. During the September 2023 semester, both the Computer Science and Computer Forensics programs were taught by the same researcher, following the same structure for each course. However, the teaching methods used for each program differed.

For the Computer Science program, a traditional lecture-teaching approach was employed, where the instructor delivered lectures on the course material, and the students took notes and asked questions. On the other hand, for the Computer Forensics program, the instructor utilized the ARCS model approach.

*Figure 2. Summary of process and procedure*

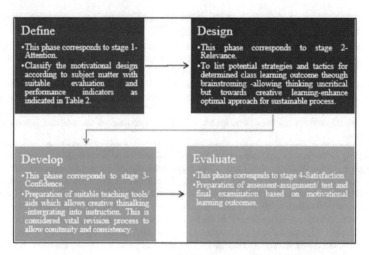

The ARCS model is a well-established instructional design model that focuses on creating motivation to learn by enhancing attention, relevance, confidence, and satisfaction. The instructor employed this model to craft engaging and interactive learning experiences that motivated students to learn and apply the course material. Overall, both the Computer Science and Computer Forensics programs were taught by the same researcher and followed the same structure. However, the teaching methods used for each program were tailored to the specific needs and learning styles of the students. The ARCS model approach used in the Computer Forensics program was designed to create an engaging and interactive learning experience that motivated students to learn and apply the course material.

## 3.1 Strategies Approached Using ARCS Model

The Computer Science class adopted a different approach to motivation compared to the Computer Forensics class. Specifically, they implemented the ARCS motivation model, drawing on motivational strategies grounded in the factors identified by Keller (1983) and other relevant studies. In contrast to the Computer Science class, which may not have utilized these motivational strategies, the Computer Forensics class intentionally applied the ARCS model to enhance student engagement and motivation. By using this model, the Computer Forensics class aimed to create a learning environment that fostered attention, relevance, confidence, and satisfaction, as shown in Table 2. The design of motivation follows a systematic process based on the ARCS model, which consists of four stages: defining, designing, developing, and evaluating (Dinser, S., 2020). During the defining stage, researchers identify specific learning aims and the needs of the learners. The designing stage involves selecting the most appropriate motivational strategies based on the defined aims and learner needs. The developing stage focuses on creating the actual class-based strategies using various instructional design techniques. Finally, during the evaluating stage, the effectiveness of the motivational strategies in achieving the learning aims and engaging the learners is assessed. These processes are summarized and illustrated in Figure 2.

Based on the motivational design framework, the researcher has integrated learning goals and prerequisites to create an engaging and self-directed learning experience for students. To achieve this, various tools such as visual aids, primarily PowerPoint presentations, have been used to stimulate students' inter-

*Table 3. The motivational design strategies and approach*

| SDP | Preparation and Anticipation | ARCS Subcategories | Proposed design | Motivation Strategy | Facilitation Methods |
|---|---|---|---|---|---|
| Define | Attention | Perceptual arousal | • Prepare the classroom setup, ensuring it is conducive to learning.<br>• Check the class schedule and prepare for any blended learning sessions.<br>• Ensure the lecture room temperature is comfortable and that all electrical equipment is ready to use. | • Share the Google Classroom link through the group WhatsApp for easy access.<br>• Send messages or emails regarding Zoom meetings, including meeting links, dates, and times to join.<br>• Select a class leader as the resource person to communicate regarding synchronous Zoom meetings.<br>• Facilitate communication between the resource person and peers during synchronous Zoom meetings.<br>• Encourage communication on the synchronous Google Classroom platform for collaborative learning.<br>• Share messages with links to access the feedback forms for gathering input from students.<br>• | Visual and YouTube teaching materials, greet students with smile and make enquiry and whereabout to show concern |
| | | Inquiry arousal | • Set up Google Classroom and upload individual activities for online self-learning and sessions.<br>• Greet students warmly and inquire about their background and expectations for the class.<br>• Form groups and select a leader to lead each group.<br>• Conduct in-class individual activities and group activities to promote engagement.<br>• Facilitate asynchronous communications to encourage student interaction outside of class.<br>• Request students to submit online surveys or feedback forms to gather their input and improve the learning experience. | | Q&A sessions, group assignment |
| | | Variability | | | Class exercises and activities |
| Design | Relevance | Goal orientation | • Clearly define student learning outcomes for the course.<br>• Deliver the subject content primarily in English language, with translation available, when necessary, in Malay language.<br>• Utilize both face-to-face (F2F) and online platform-based delivery methods to cater to different learning preferences and circumstances.<br>• Accommodate students' needs and availability by offering flexibility in scheduling and access to course materials and resources. | • Make announcements in the WhatsApp Group and Google Classroom to inform students about important updates and reminders.<br>• Upload the Subject Planning for the September 2023 semester on Google Classroom to provide students with an overview of the course structure and topics.<br>• Encourage English language communication (both verbal and written) to support students' language proficiency and communication skills.<br>• Utilize Google Classroom as a companion for students by providing related reading materials and learning resources to familiarize them with the online platform.<br>• Schedule classes to occur on weekdays, with two-hour lectures followed by a one-hour tutorial session, to ensure structured and consistent learning experiences for students. | Online video lecture |
| | | Motive matching | | | Personal coaching, addressing students personally by name. group discussion, classroom setup in groups. |
| | | Familiarity | | | Check on recent updates on latest hardware in computer hardware shop-class assignment |
| Develop | Confidence | Learning requirements | • Implement student-cantered learning concepts where students engage in self-study on assigned topics and participate in class discussions to enhance comprehension. Incorporate various activities to cater to different learning styles.<br>• Offer both individual and group activities, facilitating face-to-face and online interactions to accommodate diverse student preferences and needs.<br>• Include oral and written activities to promote communication skills development and reinforce learning objectives.<br>• Utilize Google Classroom as an interactive platform for communication, collaboration, and resource sharing among students and instructors. | • Enable students to revise and resubmit their work multiple times to encourage continuous improvement and mastery of concepts.<br>• Require students to submit their planned activities via Google Classroom to ensure transparency and organization.<br>• Facilitate open communication between lecturers and students, fostering a supportive learning environment where questions and concerns can be freely addressed.<br>• Remain flexible and adaptable to accommodate students' learning preferences and needs, adjusting instructional methods and materials as necessary.<br>• Utilize a variety of ICT tools to facilitate blended learning, integrating technology seamlessly into the learning process to enhance engagement and interaction. | Provide the explanation of the subject requirement and rubrics as evaluation criteria. |
| | | Success opportunities | | | Explain rubric and difficulty for the class in assignment, immediate feedback. |
| | | Personal control | | | Personal mentoring & coaching Be good listener |

| SDP | Preparation and Anticipation | ARCS Subcategories | Proposed design | Motivation Strategy | Facilitation Methods |
|---|---|---|---|---|---|
| Evaluate | Satisfaction | Intrinsic reinforcement | • Feedback on submissions<br>• Discussions | • Provide written feedback based on the outcomes of the activities to share insights and comments with students.<br>• Encourage verbal communication for direct access to students' opinions and thoughts, fostering open dialogue and discussion during class sessions. | Praise in class, select as mentor of the subject/ student-teacher |
| | | Extrinsic rewards | | | Bonus marks based on achievement |
| | | Equity | | | Consistency on assessment, ability to check results and assignment. |

est in computer system design. Creative aids have also been employed to supplement the presentations, and students' names are occasionally called out during sessions to support their attention (Afjar et al., 2020). Additionally, complementary strategies such as question-and-answer sessions and collaborative problem-solving tasks have been utilized to further enhance student engagement. Students are grouped and tasked with selecting a topic covered during the semester for in-depth exploration and presentation, serving as an evaluative component (Alekhya, N., & Kishore, N., 2018). By doing so, students are encouraged to take ownership of their learning and develop critical thinking skills. Overall, the researcher has synthesized learning outcomes and preparatory measures to create a motivational and engaging learning environment for students as presented in Table 3.

## 4. VALIDATING ARCS MODEL DESIGN AND DEVELOPMENT

To uphold the integrity of ARCS Model Design and Development, the researcher diligently adhered to ethical guidelines and secured informed consent from all participants prior to study commencement.

### 4.1 Research Participants

In the pursuit of academic excellence, the researcher embarked on a study aimed at evaluating the impact of the ARCS motivation model on student motivation and academic achievement. The researcher specifically targeted two cohorts of eighty-four students enrolled in Computer Science and Computer Forensics in the semester starting in September 2023. The primary aim of the study was to conduct an experimental investigation to compare the level of motivation induction and academic achievement between the two groups. Two sets of classes were conducted, one without the application of the ARCS model (for Computer Science students) and the other with its implementation (for Computer Forensics students). The study utilized a pre-test/post-test control group design, with the control group consisting of forty-nine students enrolled in Computer System Design without the ARCS model. The experimental group, comprising thirty-five students, was enrolled in the same course with the ARCS model. The ARCS motivation model is a theoretical framework consisting of four components: Attention, Relevance, Confidence, and Satisfaction. These components aim to stimulate and support students' motivation, ultimately leading to improved academic achievement. The researcher implemented motivational design strategies and approach strategies detailed in Table 3. The researcher assessed the level of motivation induction in both groups by evaluating the extent to which the ARCS components were incorporated into the classes.

*Table 4. Analysis of motivational learning design of two groups*

| Preparation and Anticipation | ARCS Subcategories | Indicator | Group | Likert Scale Rate | | | | | Mean | Standard Deviation |
|---|---|---|---|---|---|---|---|---|---|---|
| | | | | Strongly agree | Agree | Neutral | Disagree | Strongly Disagree | | |
| Attention | Perceptual arousal | 1 | CS | 3 | 8 | 0 | 0 | 0 | 3.67 | 3.30 |
| | | | CF | 2 | 5 | 1 | 3 | 7 | 3.60 | 2.15 |
| | Inquiry arousal | 2 | CS | 0 | 1 | 5 | 7 | 2 | 3.75 | 2.38 |
| | | | CF | 3 | 8 | 0 | 0 | 0 | 5.50 | 2.50 |
| | Variability | 3 | CS | 4 | 8 | 0 | 0 | 0 | 6.00 | 2.00 |
| | | | CF | 0 | 0 | 3 | 5 | 3 | 3.67 | 0.94 |
| Relevance | Goal orientation | 4 | CS | 7 | 4 | 5 | 0 | 0 | 5.33 | 1.25 |
| | | | CF | 6 | 8 | 2 | 0 | 0 | 5.33 | 2.49 |
| | Motive matching | 5 | CS | 3 | 2 | 2 | 0 | 0 | 2.33 | 0.47 |
| | | | CF | 0 | 5 | 2 | 3 | 3 | 3.25 | 1.09 |
| | Familiarity | 6 | CS | 5 | 2 | 7 | 8 | 0 | 4.40 | 2.97 |
| | | | CF | 5 | 4 | 1 | 7 | 0 | 3.40 | 2.58 |
| Confidence | Learning requirements | 7 | CS | 2 | 6 | 4 | 1 | 0 | 2.60 | 2.15 |
| | | | CF | 0 | 6 | 3 | 1 | 6 | 3.20 | 2.48 |
| | Success opportunities | 8 | CS | 1 | 6 | 4 | 3 | 2 | 3.20 | 1.72 |
| | | | CF | 0 | 2 | 7 | 2 | 1 | 2.40 | 2.42 |
| | Personal control | 9 | CS | 4 | 7 | 2 | 2 | 0 | 3.00 | 2.37 |
| | | | CF | 2 | 1 | 4 | 6 | 1 | 2.80 | 1.94 |
| Satisfaction | Intrinsic reinforcement | 10 | CS | 8 | 9 | 0 | 0 | 0 | 3.40 | 4.18 |
| | | | CF | 0 | 0 | 11 | 3 | 15 | 5.80 | 6.11 |
| | Extrinsic rewards | 11 | CS | 10 | 2 | 5 | 0 | 0 | 3.40 | 3.78 |
| | | | CF | 6 | 7 | 5 | 8 | 0 | 5.20 | 2.79 |
| | Equity | 12 | CS | 0 | 2 | 5 | 1 | 3 | 2.20 | 1.72 |
| | | | CF | 0 | 8 | 2 | 5 | 3 | 3.60 | 2.73 |

Lagend:

CS: Computer Science

CF: Computer Forensics

To evaluate academic achievement, the researcher collected data on students' mid-semester exam scores in both the control and experimental groups. A quantitative analysis was then conducted to compare the mean mid-semester exam scores between the two groups, allowing the researcher to determine the effectiveness of the ARCS motivation model on student motivation and academic achievement.

## 4.2 Research Instruments

To assess the efficiency of the ARCS motivation model, the researcher analysed survey data collected at the conclusion of the fourteen-week September 2023 semester, alongside mid-term exam results. The

*Table 5. Results of T-test of motivational design*

| Preparation and Anticipation | ARCS Subcategories | Group | F Value | P Value |
|---|---|---|---|---|
| Attention | Perceptual arousal | CS | 0.0126 | 0.009 |
| | | CF | | |
| | Inquiry arousal | CS | 1.0027 | 0.032 |
| | | CF | | |
| | Variability | CS | 4.446 | 0.005 |
| | | CF | | |
| Relevance | Goal orientation | CS | 0 | 1.000 |
| | | CF | | |
| | Motive matching | CS | 1.0202 | 0.003 |
| | | CF | | |
| | Familiarity | CS | 0.0258 | 0.062 |
| | | CF | | |
| Confidence | Learning requirements | CS | 0.6668 | 0.008 |
| | | CF | | |
| | Success opportunities | CS | 0.2901 | 0.006 |
| | | CF | | |
| | Personal control | CS | 0.0085 | 0.009 |
| | | CF | | |
| Satisfaction | Intrinsic reinforcement | CS | 0.0835 | 0.004 |
| | | CF | | |
| | Extrinsic rewards | CS | 0.2922 | 0.006 |
| | | CF | | |
| | Equity | CS | 0.0539 | 0.005 |
| | | CF | | |

survey aimed to gauge students' levels of engagement in the course, including twelve categories derived from Keller's (1983) sub-factors of motivational design. Each survey item used a 5-point Likert scale, ranging from "Strongly Agree" to "Strongly Disagree," to bolster statistical reliability (see Appendix 1). Mid-term exam scores served as a metric for academic performance. The study's focus was to enhance students' comprehension of Computer System Design; thus, mid-term exams were divided into two sections, each assessing content knowledge with the largest score of 25, amounting to one hundred points for each exam. The aggregate mid-term exam score accounted for 20% of the final grade.

## 4.3 Survey Results and Analysis

In a comprehensive analysis of survey results, the researcher investigated the influence of motivational factors on learning preferences and design strategies, discovering notable differences between Computer

Science (CS) and Computer Forensics (CF) groups. These findings emphasize the importance of customized motivational strategies to effectively enhance learning motivation for each group.

## 4.3.1 Learning Motivation Design

To evaluate the extent of motivation induction in both cohorts, the researcher analysed the responses to the motivation factors derived from the survey conducted. The findings presented in Table 4, which offers a clear and comprehensive overview of the motivation levels in both groups.

The Computer Science (CS) and Computer Forensics (CF) groups were analyzed, revealing notable differences in engagement, relevance, confidence, and satisfaction. CS participants exhibited higher engagement in learning requirements, while CF participants preferred personal control. CS students reported 50% more success opportunities. Additionally, CF participants showed a 70% higher satisfaction rate with intrinsic and extrinsic rewards compared to CS students. These results underscore the necessity for tailored educational approaches that consider the distinct learning preferences of CS and CF students. CS students may benefit from a more structured learning environment, whereas CF students may thrive with a more personalized approach. By adapting educational strategies to accommodate the needs of both groups, educators can enhance learning outcomes and satisfaction. A two-sample t-test was conducted to compare the mean values of a scale between the two groups, as presented in Table 5. This statistical test assesses whether there is a significant difference between the means of two independent groups. It assumes equal variances for the two groups, with the null hypothesis being that the population means are equal. The calculated t-value is compared to a critical value from the t-distribution table. If the calculated t-value exceeds the critical value, the null hypothesis is rejected, indicating a significant difference between the two means.

The data analysis examined the influence of twelve motivational factors on learning preferences and motivational design strategies in the Computer Science (CS) and Computer Forensics (CF) groups. The findings revealed significant differences between the two groups in factors such as variability, motive matching, learning requirements, success opportunities, personal control, intrinsic reinforcement, and extrinsic rewards ($p < 0.05$). These results underscore the importance of tailored motivational strategies in enhancing learning motivation. Specifically, the CS group exhibited higher mean scores in variability (CS: 6.00) compared to the CF group (CF: 3.67), suggesting a stronger engagement with diverse learning methods. This finding indicates that CS students may benefit from a more varied and dynamic learning environment. Conversely, the CF group displayed higher mean scores in intrinsic reinforcement (CF: 5.80) compared to CS (CS: 3.40), indicating a greater appreciation for internal rewards. This result suggests that CF students may be more motivated by factors such as self-fulfilment and personal development. These insights underscore the nuanced impact of motivational factors on learning experiences and highlight the importance of a tailored approach to motivational design strategies. By considering the unique needs and preferences of each group, educators can create a more engaging and effective learning environment that promotes motivation and success.

## 4.3.2 Academic Excellence

The midterm test results as presented in Table 6, reveal a significant difference in academic achievement between the Computer Science (CS) and Computer Forensics (CF) groups. While CS students scored higher on average, CF students' scores, which were lower, showed comparable variability. Interestingly,

*Table 6. Results of T-test for midterm test*

| Midterm Test | Group | Mean | Standard Deviation | F | Critical F Value | P value |
|---|---|---|---|---|---|---|
| Sec A | CS | 41.0 | 8.20 | 49.44 | 4.12 | 0.0001 |
| | CF | 28.2 | 8.387 | | | |
| Sec B | CS | 29.8 | 8.068 | 0.009 | 4.14 | 0.0009 |
| | CF | 31.4 | 8.781 | | | |

CF students' mean scores increased from 28.2 to 31.4 in Sec A to Sec B, while CS students' scores remained stable. This suggests that there may be room for refining motivational strategies for CF students to further bridge the gap with their CS counterparts. Furthermore, the observed differences in critical F values and p-values between the CS and CF groups imply varying degrees of impact from motivational design strategies. The highly significant F value and p-value for CS students suggest robust motivational effects, while CF's values suggest a more nuanced response. This highlights the need for tailored motivational interventions in CF, potentially addressing unique challenges or preferences to perfect learning outcomes and promote academic success. Overall, the midterm results emphasize the importance of tailored motivational approaches for both CS and CF students. By implementing motivational strategies that address individual differences and contextual factors, educators can enhance students' motivation and academic achievement. However, it is important to use proper statistical analysis techniques and validation methods to ensure the accuracy and reliability of the findings. Additionally, it is essential to consider the ethical implications of the analysis and to use transparent and interpretable machine learning algorithms or statistical analysis tools to minimize the potential for bias or discrimination. By following these recommendations, educators can create a fair, and effective learning environment that caters to the diverse needs and preferences of their students.

## 5. CONCLUSION AND RECOMMENDATIONS

This study utilized Keller's ARCS motivational model to improve learners' motivation in Computer System Design, with the aim of imparting content knowledge. Instructional strategies based on the ARCS model were designed and implemented, and two groups of students enrolled in the course in September 2023 were compared: a Computer Forensics group exposed to ARCS-based instruction and a Computer Science group receiving traditional-style teaching without ARCS application. Data were collected via surveys and mid-term results. The findings suggest that ARCS-based instruction positively impacted learners' motivation and academic achievement. The experimental group exhibited higher levels of attention, relevance, confidence, and satisfaction than the control group, indicating the effectiveness of the ARCS model in enhancing motivation and engagement, ultimately leading to improved academic performance.

Moreover, the ARCS motivational model is a valuable tool for educators designing instructional methods tailored to learners' needs and preferences. By incorporating principles of attention, relevance, confidence, and satisfaction into their teaching practices, educators can promote academic success and enhance the overall learning experience for students.

However, it is essential to acknowledge that individual differences and contextual factors may influence learners' motivation and academic achievement. Therefore, a tailored approach to motivational design strategies may be necessary to optimize learning outcomes for diverse learners. Educators should consider factors such as prior knowledge, learning styles, and cultural backgrounds when implementing motivational interventions. Despite the promising findings, the study has certain limitations that warrant consideration. These include reliance on self-reported measures, potentially limited sample size, and the possibility of unaccounted confounding variables influencing results. Future research should aim to address these limitations by employing more robust research designs, utilizing larger and more diverse samples, and incorporating objective measures of motivation and academic achievement.

Furthermore, while this study provides valuable insights into the short-term effects of ARCS model implementation, future research should also explore the long-term impact on learner motivation and academic success. Longitudinal studies could shed light on the sustainability of motivation-enhancing interventions over time and provide a more comprehensive understanding of their effectiveness. In conclusion, this research underscores the potential of the ARCS motivational model to enhance learners' motivation and academic achievement in Computer System Design courses. Educators and instructional designers can leverage these findings to create more engaging and effective learning experiences tailored to the needs of diverse learners, ultimately fostering a culture of academic success and lifelong learning

## REFERENCES

Afjar, A. M., & Syukri, M. (2020, September 14-15). Attention, relevance, confidence, satisfaction (ARCS) model on students' motivation and learning outcomes in learning physics. *Journal of Physics, 1460*. Kota Banda Aceh, Indonesia. https://doi.org/10.1088/1742-6596/1460/1/012119

Alekhya, N., & Kishore, N. (2018). Application of ARCS Model and Motivational Design in Engineering Subjects - A Case Study [IJMPERD]. *International Journal of Mechanical and Production Engineering Research and Development, 8*(1), 27–34. doi:10.24247/ijmperdfeb20184

Baah, C. (2023). Exploring the role of gamification in motivating students to learn. *Cogent Education, 10*(1), Exploring the role of gamification in motivating students to learn, *Cogent Education*. doi:10.10 80/2331186X.2023.2210045

Chang, Y.-H., Song, A., & Fang, R. (2018, July 1). The Study of Programming Language Learning by Applying Flipped Classroom. *IEEE International Conference on Knowledge Innovation and Invention (ICKII).* IEEE. https://doi.org/10.1109/ICKII.2018.8569171

Chuang, C.-H., Lo, J. H.-L., & Wu, Y.-K. (2023). Integrating Chatbot and Augmented Reality Technology into Biology Learning during COVID-19. *Electronics (Basel), 12*(1), 222. doi:10.3390/electronics12010222

Dinçer, S. (2020). The effects of materials based on ARCS Model on motivation: A meta-analysis. *İlköğretim 19(2)*, 016-104219. . doi:10.17051/ilkonline.2020.695847

Dong, L. (2022). Psychological Emotion and Behavior Analysis in Music Teaching Based on the Attention, Relevance, Confidence, and Satisfaction Motivation Model. *Frontiers in Psychology, 13*, 917476. doi:10.3389/fpsyg.2022.917476 PMID:35837625

Durrani, U., & Kamal, M. (2020). Penerapan Model ARCS Untuk Meningkatkan Hasil Belajar Siswa Pada Pembelajaran Tematik Terpadu Di Sekolah Dasar. MENDIDIK: *Jurnal Kajian Pendidikan dan Pengajaran, 7(2)*.151-156. . doi:10.30653/003.202172.189

Durrani, U., & Kamal, M. M. (2021). Towards Applying ARCS Model for a Blended Teaching Methodologies: A Quantitative Research on Students' Motivation Amid the COVID-19. In E. I. Brooks, A. Brooks, C. Sylla, & A. K. Møller (Eds.), *Design, Learning, and Innovation. DLI 2020. Lecture Notes of the Institute for Computer Sciences, Social Informatics and Telecommunications Engineering* (Vol. 366). Springer. doi:10.1007/978-3-030-78448-5_14

Hsieh, Y., Lin, S., Luo, Y., Jeng, Y., Tan, S., Chen, C., & Chiang, P. (2020). ARCS-Assisted Teaching Robots Based on Anticipatory Computing and Emotional Big Data for Improving Sustainable Learning Efficiency and Motivation. *Sustainability (Basel), 12*(14), 5605. doi:10.3390/su12145605

Keller, J. M. (1987). Development and use of the ARCS model of instructional design. *Journal of instructional development, 10(3)*, 2-10.

Keller, J. M. (2006). *Part I: Development of a Concept Inventory Addressing Students' Beliefs and Reasoning Difficulties Regarding the Greenhouse Effect; Part II: Distribution of Chlorine Measured by the Mars Odyssey Gamma Ray Spectrometer.* [Doctoral dissertation, The University of Arizona]. https://repository.arizona.edu/handle/10150/193632

Keller, J. M. (2010). The Arcs model of motivational design. In *Motivational design for learning and performance* (pp. 43–74). Springer. doi:10.1007/978-1-4419-1250-3_3

Keller, J. M., & Kopp, T. (1987). Application of the ARCS model of motivational design. In C. M. Reigeluth (Ed.), *Instructional theories in action: Lessons illustrating selected theories and models* (pp. 289–320). LawrenceErlbaum Associates, Inc.

Kim, B. (2018). A Study on the Application and the Effect of Business Culture Class Using Keller's ARCS Motivational Model. *Journal of Digital Convergence, 16*, 73–82.

Kumari, A., Patel, M. M., Shukla, A., Tanwar, S., Kumar, N., & Rodrigues, J. J. P. C. (2020). ArMor: A Data Analytics Scheme to identify malicious behaviors on Blockchain-based Smart Grid System. *GLOBECOM 2020 - 2020 IEEE Global Communications Conference.* IEEE. 10.1109/GLOBECOM42002.2020.9348061

Li, K., & Keller, J. M. (2018). Use of the ARCS model in education: A literature review. *Computers & Education, 122*, 54–62. doi:10.1016/j.compedu.2018.03.019

McClelland, D. C. (1988). *Human Motivation.* Cambridge University Press. doi:10.1017/CBO9781139878289

Nurjannah, U. (2019). *PENERAPAN ARCS PADA PEMBELAJARAN MATEMATIKA MENGGUNAKAN MODEL STAD DAN NHT DI SMP NEGERI 3 AMPELGADING MALANG.* Jurnal Ilmu Kependidikan. doi:10.33506/jq.v7i1.350

Rahok, S., Oneda, H., Osawa, S., & Ozaki, K. (2019). Motivation System for Students to Learn Control Engineering and Image Processing. *Journal of Robotics Mechatronics*, *31*(3), 405–411. doi:10.20965/jrm.2019.p0405

Tanwar, S., Bhatia, Q., Patel, P., Kumari, A., Singh, P. K., & Hong, W.-C. (2020). Machine Learning Adoption in Blockchain-Based Smart Applications: The Challenges, and a Way Forward. *IEEE Access : Practical Innovations, Open Solutions*, *8*, 474–488. doi:10.1109/ACCESS.2019.2961372

Tanwar, S., Tyagi, S., & Kumar, N. (Eds.). (2019). Security and privacy of electronic healthcare records: Concepts, paradigms and solutions. Institution of Engineering and Technology.

Türel, Y., & Sanal, S. (2018). The effects of an ARCS based e-book on student's achievement, motivation, and anxiety. *Computers & Education*, *127*, 130–140. doi:10.1016/j.compedu.2018.08.006

Ucar, H., & Kumtepe, A. T. (2019). Effects of the ARCS-V-based motivational strategies on online learners' academic performance, motivation, volition, and course interest. *Journal of Computer Assisted Learning*, *36*(3), 335–349. doi:10.1111/jcal.12404

Usmadi, U., & Ergusni, E. (2018). Design of ARCSI Learning Model with Scientific Approach for Teaching Mathematics in School. *International Journal of Trends in Mathematics Education Research*. . doi:10.33122/ijtmer.v1i1.28

# APPENDIX

## Semester September 2023

## Computer System and Design

You are presented with a list of statements about the student class engagement environment. Please state to what extent you agree or disagree with them by checking the appropriate option statement.

Indicate your group:

| Computer Science | | | | | | : | |
|---|---|---|---|---|---|---|---|
| Computer Forensics | | | | | | : | |
| **ARCS Model** | **Indicator** | **ARCS Question** | **Strongly agree** | **Agree** | **Neutral** | **Disagree** | **Strongly Disagree** |
| Attention | 1 | The class setup is well-designed and conducive to learning. | | | | | |
| | 2 | The environment stimulates my curiosity and need for inquiry. | | | | | |
| | 3 | The class activities and exercises were enjoyable and engaging. | | | | | |
| Relevance | 4 | The class provided valuable insights and knowledge on the topics covered, which I found to be useful. | | | | | |
| | 5 | he class has fostered a sense of belonging in me, making me feel comfortable and committed to the learning process. | | | | | |
| | 6 | The examples provided in the class helped me relate the topics to real-world scenarios, creating a sense of familiarity and making the learning experience more engaging. | | | | | |
| Confidence | 7 | I have the capacity to grasp complex subjects that fall within my skill set." | | | | | |
| | 8 | Solving challenging problems during class activities is something I can still accomplish, and it brings me joy in the learning process. | | | | | |
| | 9 | I experienced a feeling of triumph in the classroom setting with my friends." | | | | | |
| Satisfaction | 10 | I feel content when I receive effective treatment and valuable feedback | | | | | |
| | 11 | Receiving recognition for my work makes me feel respected and esteemed. | | | | | |
| | 12 | The assessment made is transparent and fair | | | | | |

Upon completion, please submit this form to you class leader. Thank you for your support and participation. Your comments treated confidential and only use for analysis and subject improvement purposes. Thank you.

# Chapter 13
# Future Trends in Data Analytics

**S. Thangamani**

*Nandha Engineering College, India*

**R. Saranya**

*Nandha Engineering College, India*

## ABSTRACT

*Data analytics stands at the precipice of an unprecedented transformation, driven by technological breakthroughs, shifting user demands, and evolving industry landscapes. This abstract delineates forthcoming trends poised to redefine the fabric of data analytics in the foreseeable future. The future of data analytics is characterized by a convergence of cognitive computing, ethical AI, hybrid cloud architectures, augmented data management, blockchain technology, edge intelligence, and continuous intelligence. By embracing these transformative trends, organizations can unlock the full potential of data analytics, foster innovation, and drive sustainable growth in an increasingly data-driven world. AI-Powered Automation and machine learning algorithms are set to revolutionize data analytics by automating repetitive tasks, uncovering hidden patterns, and delivering actionable insights at scale. Ethical data governance with growing concerns about privacy, security, and algorithmic bias, ethical data governance emerges as a cornerstone of responsible data practices.*

## 1. INTRODUCTION

Data analytics, once confined to retrospective analysis and descriptive reporting, has evolved into a dynamic discipline characterized by predictive insights, prescriptive recommendations, and real-time decision-making capabilities. The advent of artificial intelligence (AI), machine learning (ML), and advanced analytics techniques has propelled the field into uncharted territory, enabling organizations to extract actionable intelligence from vast and disparate datasets with unprecedented speed and accuracy (Delen, D. 2019; Chem, W. et. al., 2015; Kumari, A. et. al. 2022; Jubi, R, 2024). At the forefront of this evolution is the inexorable rise of AI-powered analytics, which promises to revolutionize the way organizations derive value from their data assets (Kumari, A. et. al. 2020). By harnessing the cognitive capabilities of AI and ML algorithms, organizations can automate mundane tasks, uncover hidden pat-

DOI: 10.4018/979-8-3693-3609-0.ch013

terns, and unearth insights that elude human intuition alone (Jarrahi, M. 2019; Raisch, S., & Krakowski, S. 2021). From predictive maintenance and demand forecasting to personalized customer experiences and fraud detection, AI-powered analytics is poised to drive innovation, efficiency, and competitive advantage across a myriad of industries as shown in Fig 1.

However, as organizations increasingly rely on AI-driven analytics to inform critical decisions, ethical considerations and responsible data governance emerge as pressing concerns Kumari A & Tanwar S. 2020. The proliferation of data privacy regulations, heightened awareness of algorithmic bias, and growing calls for transparency and accountability underscore the importance of establishing robust frameworks that prioritize fairness, privacy, and trust in data-driven decision-making processes (Janssen, M., & Kuk, G.,2016; Abiteboul, S., & Stoyanovich, J. 2019). Furthermore, the convergence of edge computing, IoT devices and real-time analytics capabilities is reshaping the way organizations process, analyze, and act upon data. Edge analytics, which enables real-time data processing and decision-making at the network periphery, holds the promise of unlocking actionable insights from distributed data sources, revolutionizing industries such as manufacturing, healthcare, and transportation (Qiu, T. et.al., 2020; Wang, X. et. al., 2020; Lea, P. 2018).

In parallel, the democratization of data analytics is empowering users of all skill levels to access, analyze, and derive insights from data independently. Self-service analytics platforms, intuitive visualization tools, and natural language processing interfaces are democratizing access to data-driven insights, fostering a culture of data-driven decision-making and innovation at all levels of the organization (Vemulapalli, G. 2023; Fischli, R. 2024).

## 1.1 Motivation

The motivation to explore future trends in data analytics is driven by the need to anticipate and prepare for transformative shifts reshaping the data analytics landscape, and to harness the full potential of emerging technologies and methodologies to drive innovation, foster collaboration, and address pressing societal challenges. By embracing future trends in data analytics with foresight, intentionality, and a commitment to ethical and socially responsible practices, organizations can unlock the full potential of data to drive positive change and create a better future for all. By exploring future trends in data analytics through an ethical and socially responsible lens, organizations can proactively address the ethical implications of their data practices, mitigate risks, and build trust among stakeholders. Whether it's adopting privacy-preserving technologies to protect user data, implementing transparent and accountable AI algorithms to mitigate bias, or promoting data literacy and digital inclusion to empower marginalized communities, understanding and embracing the ethical dimensions of data analytics is essential for organizations seeking to leverage data for the public good.

## 1.2 Research Contribution

By identifying and analyzing emerging technologies, methodologies, and best practices, researchers can make several valuable contributions to the field of data analytics:

1.  Anticipating Technological Advancements: Research on future trends in data analytics enables academics and practitioners to anticipate and prepare for upcoming technological advancements that have the potential to reshape the field. By staying ahead of the curve, researchers can guide

*Figure 1. Modern technology trends in data analytics*

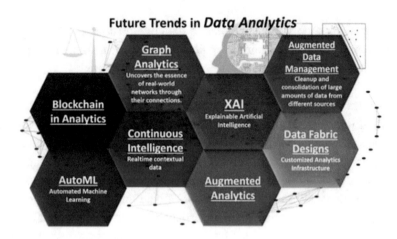

the development of new tools, techniques, and methodologies that unlock new opportunities for innovation and efficiency.

2. Informing Strategic Decision-Making: Understanding future trends in data analytics provides valuable insights that inform strategic decision-making within organizations. By identifying emerging technologies and methodologies with the greatest potential for impact, researchers can help organizations allocate resources, prioritize initiatives, and position themselves for success in an increasingly data-driven world.

3. Driving Innovation and Competitiveness: Research on future trends in data analytics fuels innovation and drives competitiveness across industries. By uncovering new ways to leverage data for business insights, process optimization, and customer engagement, researchers empower organizations to differentiate themselves in the market, seize new opportunities, and stay ahead of competitors.

4. Addressing Societal Challenges: The societal implications of data analytics cannot be overstated, and research on future trends plays a crucial role in addressing pressing societal challenges. By exploring ethical considerations, responsible data governance practices, and strategies for leveraging data for the public good, researchers contribute to the development of frameworks and guidelines that promote fairness, transparency, and accountability in data-driven decision-making.

5. Fostering Collaboration and Knowledge Sharing: Research on future trends in data analytics fosters collaboration and knowledge sharing within the academic and industry communities. By disseminating insights, best practices, and case studies, researchers facilitate cross-disciplinary collaboration, encourage the exchange of ideas, and accelerate the adoption of innovative approaches to data analytics.

6. Promoting Education and Skill Development: As data analytics becomes increasingly pervasive across industries, research on future trends plays a critical role in promoting education and skill development in the field. By identifying emerging technologies and methodologies, researchers inform curriculum development, training programs, and professional certifications that equip students and professionals with the knowledge and skills needed to succeed in a rapidly evolving data-driven landscape.

## 2. EMERGING TRENDS IN DATA ANALYTICS

Analytics is the systematic computational analysis of data or statistics. It is used for the discovery, interpretation, and communication of meaningful patterns in data. It also entails applying data patterns toward effective decision-making in fig 2.

1.  Cognitive Analytics: Cognitive analytics integrates artificial intelligence (AI), machine learning (ML), and natural language processing (NLP) to enable systems to understand, learn, and derive insights from data in a manner akin to human cognition. By simulating human thought processes, cognitive analytics can handle unstructured data sources, detect complex patterns, and provide deeper contextual understanding, thus facilitating more informed decision-making.

2.  Ethical Data Governance: With the proliferation of data and increasing concerns about privacy, security, and algorithmic bias, ethical data governance is becoming a crucial aspect of data analytics. Organizations are developing robust frameworks to ensure transparent, fair, and accountable data practices, thereby earning trust, complying with regulations, and mitigating risks associated with data misuse.

3.  Edge Analytics: The rise of edge computing and the Internet of Things (IoT) has led to the emergence of edge analytics, enabling real-time data processing and analysis at the network edge. By processing data closer to its source, edge analytics reduces latency, conserves bandwidth, and enables rapid decision-making, making it ideal for applications such as IoT devices, autonomous vehicles, and industrial automation.

4.  Augmented Analytics: Augmented analytics leverages AI and ML algorithms to enhance human decision-making by automating data preparation, pattern recognition, and insights generation. By augmenting human capabilities with machine intelligence, augmented analytics enables users to derive actionable insights from complex datasets more efficiently, thus fostering a culture of data-driven decision-making across organizations.

5.  Privacy-Preserving Technologies: As data privacy regulations become more stringent, organizations are turning to privacy-preserving technologies such as federated learning, homomorphic encryption, and differential privacy to enable collaborative analytics while protecting sensitive data. These technologies allow organizations to extract insights from distributed datasets without compromising individual privacy rights or data security.

6.  Real-Time and Continuous Intelligence: The demand for real-time insights is driving the adoption of real-time and continuous intelligence solutions. By analyzing streaming data in motion, organizations can gain actionable insights in near real-time, enabling proactive decision-making, predictive analytics, and automated responses to events as they occur.

7.  Explainable AI and Transparency: As AI algorithms increasingly influence decision-making processes, there is a growing need for transparency and explain ability. Explainable AI techniques elucidate the inner workings of AI models, enabling users to understand, trust, and validate algorithmic decisions, thereby promoting accountability, reducing bias, and building trust in AI-driven analytics solutions.

*Figure 2. Recent emerging trends in data analytics*

## 2.1 Cognitive Analytics

Emerging trends in cognitive analytics represent the cutting edge of innovation in the field, offering exciting opportunities to leverage AI and ML technologies for extracting actionable insights from complex and unstructured data sources. By staying abreast of these trends, researchers and practitioners can harness the full potential of cognitive analytics to drive innovation, inform decision-making, and create value in diverse domains and industries. One recent technique that has gained significant attention in the realm of Cognitive Analytics is Transformer-based architectures, particularly in the context of natural language processing (NLP).

Transformers in fig 3, introduced in the groundbreaking paper "Attention is All You Need" by Vaswani Et al. in 2017, have revolutionized the field of NLP. These models rely on self-attention mechanisms to capture contextual relationships between words in a sequence, enabling them to process and generate text with remarkable fluency and accuracy. Cognitive analytics represents a powerful approach to data analysis that combines advanced analytics technologies with human-like cognitive capabilities to unlock insights, drive decision-making, and create value in an increasingly data-driven world. Unlike traditional analytics, which primarily focuses on descriptive and diagnostic analysis, cognitive analytics aims to emulate human thought processes to perform more sophisticated forms of analysis, including predictive and prescriptive analytics.

## 2.2 Ethical Data Governance

Ethical data governance is a critical aspect of emerging trends in data analytics, as organizations grapple with the growing importance of privacy, fairness, transparency, and accountability in their data practices. Here are some key considerations and practices within ethical data governance:

- Privacy Protection

*Figure 3. Transformer-based architectures*

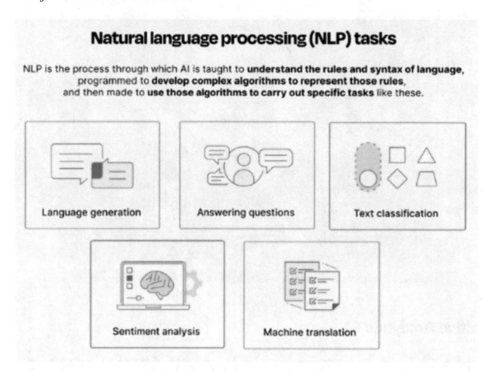

- Fairness and Bias Mitigation
- Transparency and Accountability
- Data Governance Frameworks
- User Empowerment and Consent Management
- Cross-Organizational Collaboration

By embracing these emerging trends in ethical data governance, organizations can demonstrate their commitment to responsible data practices, mitigate risks associated with data misuse, and build trust and confidence among customers, partners, regulators, and society at large. Ethical data governance is not only a legal and regulatory imperative but also a strategic imperative that enables organizations to unlock the full potential of data analytics while safeguarding individual rights and societal values.

## 2.3 Privacy-Preserving Technologies

Privacy-preserving technologies encompass a range of techniques and methodologies aimed at enabling useful analysis and insights from data while protecting the privacy and confidentiality of sensitive information. These privacy-preserving technologies enable organizations to derive insights from sensitive data while protecting individual privacy rights and complying with data protection regulations. By incorporating these techniques into their data analytics workflows, organizations can harness the power of data analytics while mitigating the risks associated with data privacy and confidentiality. With the increasing volume of sensitive data being collected and analyzed, ensuring privacy has become a paramount concern for organizations, governments, and individuals. Privacy-preserving technologies help address this concern by allowing data to be analyzed in a way that minimizes the risk of privacy breaches or unauthorized disclosures.

## 2.4 Real-Time and Continuous Intelligence

Real-time and continuous intelligence refers to the process of analyzing data streams and generating insights in near real-time, allowing organizations to make timely decisions, detect anomalies, and respond rapidly to changing conditions.

- In today's fast-paced business environment, organizations need to react quickly to emerging trends, threats, and opportunities.
- Real-time and continuous intelligence enables organizations to monitor key metrics, detect patterns, and identify outliers as they occur, facilitating agile decision-making and proactive risk management.

Key Components of Real-Time and Continuous Intelligence are:

- Data Streams: Real-time and continuous intelligence relies on data streams, which consist of a continuous flow of data generated by various sources such as sensors, devices, applications, and social media.
- Data Processing: Data streams are processed in real-time using streaming analytics platforms, which perform tasks such as data ingestion, transformation, aggregation, and analysis.
- Analytics: Advanced analytics techniques such as machine learning, statistical analysis, and complex event processing (CEP) are applied to data streams to derive insights, detect patterns, and predict future outcomes.
- Visualization and Actionable Insights: Insights derived from real-time and continuous intelligence are presented to users in a visually intuitive manner, enabling them to take immediate action based on the analysis results.

## 3. THE EVOLVING ROLE OF DATA ANALYSTS

In this evolving role, data analysts are expected to possess a broader skill set beyond technical proficiency. This includes domain expertise, business acumen, communication skills, and the ability to translate data insights into actionable recommendations for stakeholders across various departments within organizations. Analytical thinking, critical problem-solving skills, and the ability to ask the right questions to derive meaningful insights from data are also crucial aspects of the evolving role. Furthermore, the integration of advanced technologies such as artificial intelligence (AI), machine learning (ML), and big data analytics has reshaped the role of data analysts as shown in Figure 4.

They now leverage these tools and techniques to extract deeper insights, predict trends, and automate analytical processes, requiring continuous learning and adaptation to stay competitive in the field. Collaboration with cross-functional teams, including data scientists, engineers, and business stakeholders, has become essential for data analysts. They work closely with these teams to develop data-driven solutions, integrate analytics into business processes, and optimize data infrastructure. Effective communication

*Figure 4. The evolving role of data analysts*

skills are vital for data analysts to convey complex technical concepts to non-technical stakeholders and influence decision-making. Moreover, data analysts play a significant role in ensuring data governance, including data quality, security, and compliance with regulatory requirements. Ethical considerations such as data privacy and responsible data practices are also paramount in the evolving role.

## 3.1 Historical Context

While historical context typically refers to past events and developments, in the context of the evolving role of data analysts, "recent advanced content about Historical Context" could refer to contemporary discussions or analyses of how historical trends and developments have shaped the present state of data analysis. Here are some points that could constitute advanced content regarding the historical context of data analysis:

- Technological Advancements and Data Collection:
  - Exploration of how recent technological advancements, such as the proliferation of internet-connected devices, social media platforms, and sensor networks, have led to unprecedented volumes of data being generated.
- Evolution of Analytical Methods:
  - Discussion of how historical developments in statistical and computational methods have paved the way for modern data analysis techniques.
  - Exploration of how traditional statistical methods have been augmented or replaced by advanced machine learning algorithms, deep learning models, and other data-driven approaches.
- Impact of Data Analytics on Industries:
  - Analysis of how historical trends in data analysis have impacted various industries, such as finance, healthcare, marketing, and retail.

    ◦   Examination of case studies or examples illustrating how organizations have leveraged historical data analysis to drive innovation, improve decision-making, and gain competitive advantage.

- Role of Data Analysts in Historical Context:
  - ◦ Evaluation of the evolving role of data analysts within organizations over time, from basic data processing tasks to strategic decision-making roles.
  - ◦ Examination of how data analysts have adapted to changes in technology, methodologies, and organizational structures to meet evolving business needs.
- Lessons Learned from Historical Data Analysis:
  - ◦ Reflection on key lessons learned from historical data analysis projects, including successes, failures, and best practices.
  - ◦ Discussion of how historical data analysis experiences can inform future strategies and approaches in the field of data analytics.

## 3.2 Integration of Advanced Technologies

Integration of advanced technologies refers to the incorporation of cutting-edge tools, algorithms, and platforms into data analysis workflows to enhance analytical capabilities and derive deeper insights from data. Data analysts can uncover valuable insights, drive innovation, and make data-driven decisions that lead to business success. However, it's crucial for data analysts to remain vigilant about ethical considerations and continuously update their skills to keep pace with rapid technological advancements. These are the some advanced technologies over the Integration of Advanced Technologies.

- Artificial Intelligence and Machine Learning (AI/ML)
- Big Data Analytics
- Advanced Data Visualization
- Natural Language Processing (NLP)
- Edge Computing and IoT Analytics
- Ethical and Responsible AI
- Continuous Learning and Adaptation

## 3.3 Career Development and Continuous Learning

In the evolving role of data analysts, there's a growing emphasis on continuous learning and skill development to keep pace with rapidly changing technologies and methodologies. Organizations that foster a culture of continuous learning provide resources such as training programs, online courses, workshops, and professional certifications to support the professional growth of data analysts. By prioritizing career development and continuous learning, data analysts can position themselves for long-term success and make meaningful contributions to organizations in the ever-evolving field of data analytics.

Professional Development Resources:

- Professionals can access a variety of resources for continuous learning, including online courses, webinars, workshops, conferences, and professional certifications.

- Organizations may provide training programs and learning opportunities to support the professional development of their employees.

Skill Diversification:

- Data analysts are encouraged to diversify their skill set beyond technical expertise to include domain knowledge, business acumen, communication skills, and problem-solving abilities.
- Diversified skills enable professionals to tackle complex challenges, collaborate effectively with interdisciplinary teams, and drive impactful results.

Adaptability to Emerging Technologies:

- Data analysts must stay updated with emerging technologies such as artificial intelligence, machine learning, big data analytics, and cloud computing.
- Continuous learning enables professionals to acquire new skills, experiment with cutting-edge tools and techniques, and leverage innovative solutions to solve real-world problems.

Career Advancement Opportunities:

- Continuous learning opens up opportunities for career advancement, including promotions, salary increases, and transitions to more senior roles.
- Professionals can explore diverse career pathways within the field of data analytics, such as data scientist, business analyst, data engineer, or analytics manager, based on their interests and aspirations.

Networking and Mentorship:

- Networking with peers, industry experts, and mentors provides valuable insights, guidance, and opportunities for collaboration.
- Engaging in professional communities, attending industry events, and seeking mentorship relationships facilitate knowledge sharing and career development.

Personal Growth and Fulfillment:

- Continuous learning contributes to personal growth, satisfaction, and fulfillment by fostering a sense of achievement, curiosity, and lifelong curiosity.
- Professionals who prioritize continuous learning are more resilient, adaptable, and empowered to navigate their career paths and achieve their goals.

## 4. FUTURE WITH DATA ANALYTICS

The scope of data analytics is growing. This growth supports the data analytics industry with a great increase in the collected data, which can be used to tap into several market sectors. The future with data

*Figure 5. Future trends in data analytics*

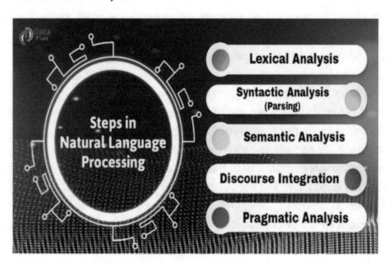

analytics holds immense promise and potential across various domains and industries and also data analytics in shaping the future of various industries and sectors as shown in Figure 5.

Recent advanced content on the future with data analytics explores cutting-edge trends, emerging technologies, and innovative applications that are reshaping the landscape of data-driven decision-making. Here's an overview of some key themes and topics:

1.  AI-Powered Predictive Analytics:
    ◦   Advanced machine learning algorithms and deep learning models are being deployed to develop predictive analytics solutions that can forecast future trends, behaviors, and outcomes with unprecedented accuracy.
    ◦   Techniques such as time series forecasting, predictive modeling, and anomaly detection are being applied across various industries, from finance and healthcare to retail and manufacturing.
2.  Explainable AI and Interpretability:
    ◦   There's a growing emphasis on developing explainable AI models that provide transparent and interpretable insights into the decision-making process.
    ◦   Techniques such as model explainability, feature importance analysis, and causal inference are enabling stakeholders to understand how AI models arrive at their predictions and recommendations, enhancing trust and accountability.
3.  Edge Analytics and IoT Integration:
    ◦   Edge analytics is gaining traction as organizations seek to process and analyze data closer to the source, enabling real-time insights and faster decision-making.
    ◦   With the proliferation of IoT devices and sensors, edge analytics platforms are being deployed to analyze streaming data from connected devices, enabling applications such as predictive maintenance, remote monitoring, and smart cities.
4.  Ethical AI and Responsible Data Practices:

- There's increasing awareness of the ethical implications of AI and data analytics, leading to the development of frameworks, guidelines, and best practices for responsible data use.
- Initiatives such as fairness, accountability, and transparency in AI (FAT AI) are promoting ethical AI development and implementation, addressing concerns related to bias, privacy, and algorithmic fairness.

5. Augmented Analytics and Natural Language Processing (NLP):
   - Augmented analytics platforms are integrating natural language processing (NLP) capabilities to enable conversational analytics and intuitive data exploration.
   - By leveraging NLP techniques such as sentiment analysis, topic modeling, and entity recognition, users can interact with data using natural language queries, enabling broader access to insights and democratizing data analytics.

6. DataOps and Agile Analytics:
   - DataOps practices are being adopted to streamline and automate data analytics workflows, enabling organizations to deliver insights faster and more efficiently.
   - Agile analytics methodologies, such as iterative development, rapid prototyping, and cross-functional collaboration, are helping teams adapt to changing requirements and deliver value incrementally.

7. Blockchain and Data Security:
   - Blockchain technology is being explored for its potential to enhance data security, integrity, and transparency in data analytics.
   - Applications such as decentralized data marketplaces, secure data sharing, and tamper-proof audit trails are leveraging blockchain to address cybersecurity concerns and establish trust in data exchange processes.

## 4.1 Natural Language Processing (NLP) Integration

Natural Language Processing (NLP) in Fig 6 integration refers to the incorporation of NLP techniques and technologies into various applications and systems to enable them to understand, interpret, and generate human language. NLP integration plays a critical role in enabling computers to understand and process human language, powering a wide range of applications and systems across industries such as healthcare, finance, e-commerce, and customer service.

Steps in Natural Language Processing:

a.  Lexical Analysis

We have to analyze the structure of words. The collection of words and phrases in a language is a lexicon of a language.

b.  Syntactic Analysis (Parsing)

We use parsing for the analysis of the word. Although, have to arrange words in a particular manner. That shows the relationship between words.

*Figure 6. Natural language processing*

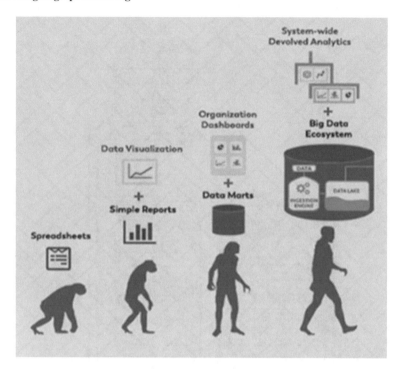

c.   Semantic Analysis

It describes a dictionary meaning which is meaningful. In the task domain, mapping syntactic structures and objects.

d.   Discourse Integration

In this step, the meaning of any sentence depends upon the meaning of the previous sentence. In addition. Also brings the meaning to immediately succeeding sentence.

e.   Pragmatic Analysis

In this step, data is interpreted on what it actually meant. Although, we have to derive aspects of language which require real-world knowledge.
Examples of NLP Systems:

a.   Customer Review
   ◦   As it's a most important factor that helps companies to discover relevant information for their business. Further, helps in improving customer satisfaction.
   ◦   As more suggestion comes, it's more relevant services are better. Also, helps in understanding the customer's needs.
b.   Virtual digital assistants

*Figure 7. Steps in natural language processing*

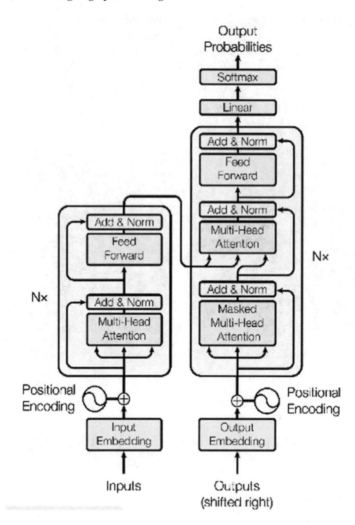

Virtual digital assistant technologies are currently the most well-known type of artificial intelligence in Figure 7.

## 4.2 Conversational Analytics

Conversational analytics refers to the use of data analytics techniques to analyze and derive insights from conversations between humans and computer systems, such as chatbots, virtual assistants, and other conversational interfaces. Conversational analytics empowers organizations to leverage the wealth of data generated by conversational interfaces to gain actionable insights, optimize user experiences, and drive business success in an increasingly conversational world.

## 4.3 Democratization of Insight

The democratization of insight refers to the process of making data-driven insights and analytics capabilities accessible to a broader audience within an organization, beyond traditional data analysts or data scientists. By democratizing insight, organizations can unlock the full potential of their data assets, empower employees to make data-driven decisions, and drive innovation and growth in an increasingly data-driven world. The democratization of insight refers to the process of making data-driven insights and analytics accessible and understandable to a broader range of users within an organization, regardless of their technical expertise or role. The democratization of insight empowers organizations to leverage the full potential of data by enabling a wider range of users to access, analyze, and derive insights from data. By democratizing access to data and analytics tools, organizations can foster a data-driven culture, promote innovation, and drive business success.

## 4.4 Challenges and Considerations

In envisioning the future with data analytics, several challenges and considerations emerge:

1. Data Privacy and Ethics:
   - As data analytics becomes more pervasive, maintaining data privacy and ethical standards becomes increasingly challenging. Organizations must navigate regulations such as GDPR and CCPA while ensuring ethical use of data to build trust with users.
2. Data Quality and Governance:
   - With the proliferation of data sources and types, ensuring data quality and governance becomes crucial. Organizations need robust processes for data cleansing, integration, and governance to derive reliable insights from diverse datasets.
3. Complexity and Scalability:
   - The increasing complexity and scale of data analytics pose challenges in terms of infrastructure, tooling, and talent. Organizations must invest in scalable infrastructure, advanced analytics platforms, and skilled personnel to handle the growing volume and complexity of data.
4. Interdisciplinary Collaboration:
   - Data analytics often requires collaboration across diverse disciplines, including data science, domain expertise, and business strategy. Organizations must foster interdisciplinary collaboration and communication to leverage diverse perspectives and expertise effectively.
5. Bias and Fairness:
   - Addressing bias and ensuring fairness in data analytics algorithms and models is crucial for responsible decision-making. Organizations must proactively identify and mitigate bias in data, algorithms, and decision processes to avoid unintended consequences and discriminatory outcomes.
6. Adaptability and Agility:
   - The pace of technological innovation and market dynamics requires organizations to be agile and adaptable in their data analytics initiatives. Flexibility in tool selection, methodology, and strategy is essential to respond effectively to evolving trends and challenges.

7. Talent Acquisition and Retention:
   ◦ The demand for skilled data analysts, data scientists, and other data professionals continues to outstrip supply. Organizations must invest in talent acquisition, training, and retention strategies to build and maintain a skilled workforce capable of driving innovation and value creation through data analytics.
8. Security and Cyber security:
   ◦ With the increasing value of data assets, cyber security threats pose significant risks to data analytics initiatives. Organizations must prioritize data security and implement robust cyber security measures to protect against data breaches, cyber attacks, and unauthorized access.
9. Cultural Transformation:
   ◦ Embracing a data-driven culture requires a shift in mindset, behavior, and organizational practices. Leaders must champion a culture of data literacy, experimentation, and evidence-based decision-making to foster innovation and drive organizational success in the future with data analytics.

Addressing these challenges and considerations is essential for organizations to realize the full potential of data analytics and capitalize on the opportunities presented by the future of data-driven decision-making.

## 4.5 Preparing for the Future

Preparing for the future with data analytics involves several key steps and strategies. These key steps and strategies helps organizations can effectively prepare for the future with data analytics and position themselves for success in an increasingly data-driven world.

1. Data Privacy and Ethics
2. Data Quality and Governance
3. Complexity and Scalability
4. Interdisciplinary Collaboration
5. Bias and Fairness
6. Adaptability and Agility
7. Talent Acquisition and Retention
8. Security and Cyber security
9. Cultural Transformation

By adopting these strategies and considerations, organizations can effectively prepare for the future with data analytics, unlock the full potential of their data assets, and drive sustainable growth and innovation in the digital age.

## 5. CONCLUSION

The future with data analytics holds immense promise and potential for organizations across industries. As technology continues to advance and data becomes increasingly abundant, organizations must strategically prepare to leverage data analytics to drive innovation, enhance decision-making, and gain competitive advantage. Key trends such as the proliferation of big data, advancements in artificial intelligence and machine learning, and the rise of predictive analytics are reshaping the landscape of data-driven insights. However, navigating the future with data analytics requires careful consideration of challenges such as data privacy, ethical concerns, and talent acquisition.

To thrive in this data-driven future, organizations must invest in advanced technologies, develop data science capabilities, and prioritize data governance and security. Fostering a culture of collaboration, experimentation, and continuous learning will be essential for driving innovation and adapting to evolving trends and challenges. Ultimately, success in the future with data analytics will hinge on organizations' ability to harness the power of data to solve complex problems, drive informed decision-making, and create value for customers, employees, and stakeholders. By embracBing a data-driven mindset and adopting a strategic approach to data analytics, organizations can unlock new opportunities, drive growth, and achieve sustainable success in the digital age.

## REFERENCES

Abiteboul, S., & Stoyanovich, J. (2019). Transparency, fairness, data protection, neutrality: Data management challenges in the face of new regulation. [JDIQ]. *ACM Journal of Data and Information Quality*, *11*(3), 1–9. doi:10.1145/3310231

Chen, W. J., Kamath, R., Kelly, A., Lopez, H. H. D., Roberts, M., & Yheng, Y. P. (2015). *Systems of insight for digital transformation: Using IBM operational decision manager advanced and predictive analytics*. IBM Redbooks.

Brown, D. (2020). The Future of Data Analytics: A Roadmap. Future Technologies Journal. . doi:10.2345/ftj.2020.004

Delen, D. (2019). *Prescriptive analytics: The final frontier for evidence-based management and optimal decision making*. FT Press.

Doe, J. (2017). Future Trends in Data Analytics: A Perspective. *Data Analytics Trends Journal*. DOI: . doi:10.1234/dat.2017.123456

Wilson, E. (2021). *Emerging Trends in Data Analytics and Business Intelligence*. Business Analytics Review. doi:10.6789/bar.2021.005

Fischli, R. (2024). Data-owning democracy: Citizen empowerment through data ownership. *European Journal of Political Theory*, *23*(2), 204–223. doi:10.1177/14748851221110316

Janssen, M., & Kuk, G. (2016). The challenges and limits of big data algorithms in technocratic governance. *Government Information Quarterly*, *33*(3), 371–377. doi:10.1016/j.giq.2016.08.011

Jarrahi, M. H. (2019). In the age of the smart artificial intelligence: AI's dual capacities for automating and informating work. *Business Information Review*, *36*(4), 178–187. doi:10.1177/0266382119883999

JohnsonA. (2019) "Trends and Challenges in Big Data Analytics", Publisher: Big Data Insights, DOI: doi:10.7890/bdi.2019.135790

Kumari, A., & Tanwar, S. (2020). Secure data analytics for smart grid systems in a sustainable smart city: Challenges, solutions, and future directions. *Sustainable Computing : Informatics and Systems*, *28*, 100427. Advance online publication. doi:10.1016/j.suscom.2020.100427

Kumari, A., & Tanwar, S. (2022). A secure data analytics scheme for multimedia communication in a decentralized smart grid. *Multimedia Tools and Applications*, *81*(24), 34797–34822. doi:10.1007/s11042-021-10512-z

Kumari. (2020). *A Data Analytics Scheme for Security-aware Demand Response Management in Smart Grid System*. 2020 IEEE 7th Uttar Pradesh Section International Conference on Electrical, Electronics and Computer Engineering (UPCON), Prayagraj, India. 10.1109/UPCON50219.2020.9376458

Lea, P. (2018). *Internet of Things for Architects: Architecting IoT solutions by implementing sensors, communication infrastructure, edge computing, analytics, and security*. Packt Publishing Ltd.

Liu, X. (2024). Research on dimension reduction for visualization of simplified security region of integrated energy system considering renewable energy access. *International Journal of Electrical Power & Energy Systems*, *156*, 109777. doi:10.1016/j.ijepes.2023.109777

Anderson, M. (2022). Future Directions in Data Analytics: Challenges and Opportunities. Journal of Data Innovation.

Oussous, A., Benjelloun, F.-Z., Ait Lahcen, A., & Belfkih, S. (2018). Big Data technologies: A survey. *Journal of King Saud University. Computer and Information Sciences*, *30*(4), 431–448. doi:10.1016/j.jksuci.2017.06.001

Qiu, T., Chi, J., Zhou, X., Ning, Z., Atiquzzaman, M., & Wu, D. O. (2020). Edge computing in industrial internet of things: Architecture, advances and challenges. *IEEE Communications Surveys and Tutorials*, *22*(4), 2462–2488. doi:10.1109/COMST.2020.3009103

Ragazou, K., Passas, I., Garefalakis, A., Galariotis, E., & Zopounidis, C. (2023). Big Data Analytics Applications in Information Management Driving Operational Efficiencies and Decision-Making: Mapping the Field of Knowledge with Bibliometric Analysis Using R. *Big Data Cogn. Comput.*, *7*(1), 13. doi:10.3390/bdcc7010013

Raisch, S., & Krakowski, S. (2021). Artificial intelligence and management: The automation–augmentation paradox. *Academy of Management Review*, *46*(1), 192–210. doi:10.5465/amr.2018.0072

Sarker, I. H. (2021). *Data Science and Analytics: An Overview from Data-Driven Smart Computing*. Decision-Making and Applications Perspective. doi:10.1007/s42979-021-00765-8

Smith, J. (2018). Advanced Analytics: The Next Big Thing. *International Conference on Data Science*. IEEE. DOI: 10.5678/icds.2018.987654

Vemulapalli, G. (2023). Self-Service Analytics Implementation Strategies for Empowering Data Analysts. *International Journal of Machine Learning and Artificial Intelligence*, *4*(4), 1–14.

Wang, X., Han, Y., Leung, V. C., Niyato, D., Yan, X., & Chen, X. (2020). Convergence of edge computing and deep learning: A comprehensive survey. *IEEE Communications Surveys and Tutorials*, *22*(2), 869–904. doi:10.1109/COMST.2020.2970550

# Chapter 14
# Conclusion and Practical Takeaways

**Aparna Kumari**

(iD) https://orcid.org/0000-0001-5991-6193

*Department of Computer Science and Engineering, Institute of Technology, Nirma University, Ahmedabad, India*

## ABSTRACT

*Data analytics, which includes fundamental ideas, cutting-edge techniques, and practical applications, is essential for directing well-informed decision-making in various industries. Starting with the importance of data preparation and integrity, the trip proceeds via exploratory data analysis and large-scale data-set analysis made possible by state-of-the-art tools such as Hadoop. Practical examples of data-driven decision-making's real-world advantages in various businesses are highlighted with ethical issues and privacy ramifications. Future trends are examined, including the merging of artificial intelligence and the changing function of data analysts. In light of data analytics' revolutionary potential in creating a data-centric landscape, creating a culture that supports real-world application, lifelong learning, and ongoing skill development is advocated.*

## 1. SUMMARIZING KEY INSIGHTS

Throughout this comprehensive exploration of data analytics, we have covered many topics, from the foundational concepts to cutting-edge techniques and applications. The journey has been enlightening, providing a holistic understanding of the data analytics landscape and its pivotal role in driving informed decision-making across various domains. In the introductory chapters, we established a strong foundation by understanding the essence of data analytics and its significance in today's data-driven world. We recognized the crucial role of data in shaping business strategies and gaining a competitive edge, underscoring the importance of leveraging data-driven insights for informed decision-making. The data preparation and cleaning phase emerged as a critical step, emphasizing the importance of collecting high-quality data from diverse sources, ensuring data integrity through rigorous cleaning and preprocessing techniques, and engineering meaningful features to enhance analytical capabilities. This phase laid the

DOI: 10.4018/979-8-3693-3609-0.ch014

groundwork for accurate and insightful analyses. Exploratory data analysis (EDA) proved invaluable for uncovering patterns, relationships, and insights hidden within complex datasets. We learned to summarize and communicate data effectively through descriptive statistics and data visualisation techniques, enabling better understanding and interpretation of the underlying information.

We delved into various analytical techniques, including predictive analytics, regression models, classification algorithms, decision trees, and unsupervised learning methods like clustering. These powerful tools enabled us to build predictive models, classify data into distinct groups, and uncover hidden patterns and structures within complex datasets, unlocking a wealth of actionable insights for decision-making. Time series analysis and forecasting techniques allow us to analyze and predict patterns in data that evolve over time, while natural language processing (NLP) opens new avenues for extracting insights from unstructured text data, enabling applications like sentiment analysis and text classification. As we ventured into big data analytics and Hadoop, we learned how to handle and analyze massive datasets that traditional techniques and systems could not process efficiently. This capability enabled us to uncover valuable insights from complex, high-volume data sources, such as IoT sensor data, social media streams, and large-scale transactional data.

Throughout our journey, we recognized the critical importance of data ethics and privacy, exploring ethical considerations, privacy concerns, and responsible data handling practices. We learned how to ensure that our analytical endeavours respect individual rights, maintain data integrity, and comply with relevant regulations, fostering trust and transparency in the use of data. Through numerous case studies across industries, we witnessed the practical applications of data analytics in finance, healthcare, marketing, supply chain management, and beyond. These real-world examples demonstrated the tangible impact of data-driven decision-making, showcasing how organizations can gain valuable insights, optimize operations, and drive innovation by harnessing the power of data.

As we looked toward the future, we will explore emerging trends in data analytics, such as the integration of Gen AI, Federated learning, and other decentralized computing techniques. We will also examine the evolving role of data analysts as strategic decision-makers and storytellers capable of translating complex data into actionable insights that drive business growth.

## 2. ENCOURAGEMENT FOR PRACTICAL APPLICATION

The knowledge and skills acquired throughout this book are not merely theoretical constructs but powerful tools that can transform how you approach decision-making processes and drive tangible results. Embrace the opportunities data analytics presents and dare to challenge traditional methods and assumptions. Encourage a data-driven culture within your organization, fostering an environment where data-driven insights are valued and leveraged for informed decision-making. Collaborate with cross-functional teams to translate analytical insights into actionable strategies that drive business growth and success, bridging the gap between technical expertise and domain knowledge.

Continuously seek out real-world datasets and challenging problems to apply your analytical skills. Engage in hands-on projects, participate in data analytics competitions, or propose data-driven initiatives within your organization. Practice is the key to mastering the art of data analytics and gaining practical experience in tackling complex, real-world challenges.

## 3. PRACTICAL TAKEAWAYS IN DATA ANALYTICS

Data analytics is a dynamic and rapidly evolving field, and embracing a mindset of lifelong learning and continuous skill development is crucial. Stay updated on the latest trends, attend industry conferences and workshops, and cultivate a network of professionals who can share their experiences and insights. Invest in professional development by pursuing advanced certifications, enrolling in online courses, or engaging in self-guided learning through online resources and communities. Continuously expand your knowledge and skills in machine learning, deep learning, data visualization, and emerging analytical tools and platforms. Foster a culture of curiosity and experimentation within your team or organization. Encourage the exploration of new techniques, the adoption of innovative tools, and the willingness to take calculated risks. Celebrate failures as learning opportunities and embrace the iterative nature of data analytics, where continuous improvement and adaptation are essential for success.

In conclusion, the data analytics journey is exciting and transformative, filled with countless opportunities to uncover valuable insights, drive innovation, and shape the future of data-driven decision-making. Embrace the knowledge and skills you have acquired, apply them with passion and dedication, and continue to grow and adapt as the field evolves. By doing so, you can contribute to your organisation's success and play a vital role in shaping a data-driven world where informed decisions lead to remarkable achievements and positive impact.

# Compilation of References

Abedjan, Z., Chu, X., Deng, D., Fernandez, R. C., Ilyas, I. F., Ouzzani, M., Papotti, P., Stonebraker, M., & Tang, N. (2016). Detecting data errors: Where are we and what needs to be done? *Proceedings of the VLDB Endowment International Conference on Very Large Data Bases*, *9*(12), 993–1004. doi:10.14778/2994509.2994518

Abiteboul, S., & Stoyanovich, J. (2019). Transparency, fairness, data protection, neutrality: Data management challenges in the face of new regulation. [JDIQ]. *ACM Journal of Data and Information Quality*, *11*(3), 1–9. doi:10.1145/3310231

Acito, F. (2023). Data Preparation. In *Predictive Analytics with KNIME: Analytics for Citizen Data Scientists* (pp. 53–83). Springer Nature Switzerland. doi:10.1007/978-3-031-45630-5_4

Adde, A., Roucou, P., Mangeas, M., Ardillon, V., Desenclos, J.-C., Rousset, D., Girod, R., Briolant, S., Quenel, P., & Flamand, C. (2016). Predicting Dengue Fever Outbreaks in French Guiana Using Climate Indicators. *{PLOS} Neglected Tropical Diseases, 10*(4), e0004681. doi:10.1371/journal.pntd.0004681

Afanasiev, M., & Lysenkova, M. (2019). How University Acts in the Development of "Smart Cities." *SHS Web of Conferences, 71*, 05011. 10.1051/shsconf/20197105011

Afjar, A. M., & Syukri, M. (2020, September 14-15). Attention, relevance, confidence, satisfaction (ARCS) model on students' motivation and learning outcomes in learning physics. *Journal of Physics, 1460*. Kota Banda Aceh, Indonesia. https://doi.org/10.1088/1742-6596/1460/1/012119

Ahmad, H. P., & Dang, S. (2015). Performance Evaluation of Clustering Algorithm Using different dataset. *International Journal of Advance Research in Computer Science and Management Studies, 8*.

Ahmadi, I., Abou Nabout, N., Skiera, B., Maleki, E., & Fladenhofer, J. (2024). Overwhelming targeting options: Selecting audience segments for online advertising. *International Journal of Research in Marketing*, *41*(1), 24–40. doi:10.1016/j.ijresmar.2023.08.004

Ahmad, M. L., & Kaur, N. (2017). Smart health hospitals in smart city perspective. *International Journal of Civil Engineering and Technology*, *8*(5), 1271–1279.

Ahsan, M. M., Ali, M. S., & Siddique, Z. (2024). Enhancing and improving the performance of imbalanced class data using novel GBO and SSG: A comparative analysis. *Neural Networks*, *173*, 106157. doi:10.1016/j.neunet.2024.106157 PMID:38335796

Ajah, I. A., & Nweke, H. F. (2019). Big data and business analytics: Trends, platforms, success factors and applications. *Big Data and Cognitive Computing*, *3*(2), 32. doi:10.3390/bdcc3020032

Ajakwe, S. O., Ihekoronye, V. U., Ajakwe, I. U., Jun, T., Kim, D. S., & Lee, J. M. (2022c). Connected Intelligence for Smart Water Quality Monitoring System in IIoT. *In 2022 13th International Conference on Information and Communication Technology Convergence (ICTC)* (pp. 2386-2391). IEEE.

Ajakwe, S. O., Ihekoronye, V. U., Kim, D. S., & Lee, J. M. (2022a). SimNet: UAV-integrated sensor nodes localization for communication intelligence in 6G networks. In *2022 27th Asia Pacific Conference on Communications (APCC)* (pp. 344-347). IEEE.

Ajakwe, S. O., Ihekoronye, V. U., Kim, D. S., & Lee, J. M. (2022b). Tractable minacious drones aerial recognition and safe-channel neutralization scheme for mission critical operations. In *2022 IEEE 27th International Conference on Emerging Technologies and Factory Automation (ETFA)* (pp. 1-8). IEEE. 10.1109/ETFA52439.2022.9921494

Ajakwe, S. O., Ihekoronye, V. U., Mohtasin, G., Akter, R., Aouto, A., Kim, D. S., & Lee, J. (2022). VisioDECT Dataset: An Aerial Dataset for Scenario-Based Multi-Drone Detection and Identification. https://dx.doi.org/10.21227/n27q-7e06

Ajakwe, S. O., Nwakanma, C. I., Kim, D. S., & Lee, J. M. (2021, June). Intelligent and Real-Time Smart Card Fraud Detection for Optimized Industrial Decision Process. In *2021 Korean Institute of Communication and Sciences Summer Conference* (Vol. 75, pp. 1368-1370).

Ajakwe, S. O., Ajakwe, I. U., Jun, T., Kim, D. S., & Lee, J. M. (2023b). CIS-WQMS: Connected intelligence smart water quality monitoring scheme. *Internet of Things : Engineering Cyber Physical Human Systems*, 23, 100800. doi:10.1016/j. iot.2023.100800

Ajakwe, S. O., Arkter, R., Ahakonye, L. A. C., Kim, D. S., & Lee, J. M. (2021, October). Real-time monitoring of COVID-19 vaccination compliance: a ubiquitous IT convergence approach. In *2021 International Conference on Information and Communication Technology Convergence (ICTC)* (pp. 440-445). IEEE. 10.1109/ICTC52510.2021.9620806

Ajakwe, S. O., Ihekoronye, V. U., Kim, D. S., & Lee, J. M. (2022a). DRONET: Multi-tasking framework for real-time industrial facility aerial surveillance and safety. *Drones (Basel)*, 6(2), 46. doi:10.3390/drones6020046

Ajakwe, S. O., Ihekoronye, V. U., Kim, D. S., & Lee, J. M. (2023). ALIEN: Assisted Learning Invasive Encroachment Neutralization for Secured Drone Transportation System. *Sensors (Basel)*, 23(3), 1233. doi:10.3390/s23031233 PMID:36772272

Ajakwe, S. O., Nwakanma, C. I., Lee, J. M., & Kim, D. S. (2020, October). Machine learning algorithm for intelligent prediction for military logistics and planning. In *2020 International Conference on Information and Communication Technology Convergence (ICTC)* (pp. 417-419). IEEE. 10.1109/ICTC49870.2020.9289286

Ajakwe, S. O., Saviour, I. I., Kim, J. H., Kim, D. S., & Lee, J. M. (2023a). BANDA: A Novel Blockchain-Assisted Network for Drone Authentication. In *2023 Fourteenth International Conference on Ubiquitous and Future Networks (ICUFN)* (pp. 120-125). IEEE. 10.1109/ICUFN57995.2023.10201012

Akter, S., Wamba, S. F., Gunasekaran, A., Dubey, R., & Childe, S. J. (2016). How to improve firm performance using big data analytics capability and business strategy alignment? *International Journal of Production Economics*, 182, 113–131. doi:10.1016/j.ijpe.2016.08.018

Alajmani, S., & Jambi, K. (2020). Assessing Advanced Machine Learning Techniques for Predicting Hospital Readmission. *International Journal of Advanced Computer Science and Applications*, 11(2), 377–384. doi:10.14569/ IJACSA.2020.0110249

Alam, M. K. (2021). A systematic qualitative case study: Questions, data collection, NVivo analysis and saturation. *Qualitative Research in Organizations and Management*, 16(1), 1–31. doi:10.1108/QROM-09-2019-1825

Alam, M., Henriksson, A., Valik, J., Ward, L., Naucler, P., & Dalianis, H. (2020). Deep Learning from Heterogeneous Sequences of Sparse Medical Data for Early Prediction of Sepsis. *Proceedings of the 13th International Joint Conference on Biomedical Engineering Systems and Technologies*, (pp. 45–55). ACM. 10.5220/0008911400002513

Alanazi, A. (2022). Using machine learning for healthcare challenges and opportunities. *Informatics in Medicine Unlocked, 30*. doi:10.1016/j.imu.2022.100924

Al-Azzam, M. K., & Alazzam, M. B. (2019). Smart city and Smart-Health framework, challenges and opportunities. *International Journal of Advanced Computer Science and Applications, 10*(2), 171–176. doi:10.14569/IJACSA.2019.0100223

Alekhya, N., & Kishore, N. (2018). Application of ARCS Model and Motivational Design in Engineering Subjects - A Case Study [IJMPERD]. *International Journal of Mechanical and Production Engineering Research and Development, 8*(1), 27–34. doi:10.24247/ijmperdfeb20184

Alexander, N., Alexander, D. C., Barkhof, F., & Denaxas, S. (2021, December 8). Identifying and evaluating clinical subtypes of Alzheimer's disease in care electronic health records using unsupervised machine learning. *BMC Medical Informatics and Decision Making, 21*(1), 343. doi:10.1186/s12911-021-01693-6 PMID:34879829

Ali, Z., & Bhaskar, S. B. (2016). Basic Statistical tools in research and data analysis. *Indian Journal of Anaesthesia, 60*(9), 662–669. doi:10.4103/0019-5049.190623 PMID:27729694

Al-Ja'afreh, M. A. A., Mokryani, G., & Amjad, B. (2023). An enhanced CNN-LSTM based multi-stage framework for PV and load short-term forecasting: DSO scenarios. *Energy Reports, 10*, 1387–1408. doi:10.1016/j.egyr.2023.08.003

Aljumah, A. I., Nuseir, M. T., & Alam, M. M. (2021). Traditional marketing analytics, big data analytics and big data system quality and the success of new product development. *Business Process Management Journal, 27*(4), 1108–1125. doi:10.1108/BPMJ-11-2020-0527

Almihat, M. G. M., Kahn, M. T. E., Aboalez, K., & Almaktoof, A. M. (2022). Energy and Sustainable Development in Smart Cities: An Overview. *Smart Cities, 5*(4), 1389–1408. doi:10.3390/smartcities5040071

Alrawashdeh, G. S., Fyffe, S., Azevedo, R. F., & Castillo, N. M. (2023). Exploring the impact of personalized and adaptive learning technologies on reading literacy: A global meta-analysis. *Educational Research Review*, 100587.

Alshakhs, F., Alharthi, H., Aslam, N., Khan, I. U., & Elasheri, M. (2020). Predicting Postoperative Length of Stay for Isolated Coronary Artery Bypass Graft Patients Using Machine Learning. *International Journal of General Medicine, 13*, 751–762. doi:10.2147/IJGM.S250334 PMID:33061545

Altassan, K. K., Morin, C., Shocket, M. S., Ebi, K., & Hess, J. (2019). Dengue Fever in Saudi Arabia: A Review of Environmental and Population Factors impacting Emergence and Spread. *Travel Medicine and Infectious Disease, 30*, 46–53. doi:10.1016/j.tmaid.2019.04.006 PMID:30978417

Anandi, V., & Ramesh, M. (2022). Descriptive and Predictive Analytics on Electronic Health Records using Machine Learning. *2022 Second International Conference on Advances in Electrical, Computing, Communication and Sustainable Technologies (ICAECT)*, (pp. 1–6). ScitePress. 10.1109/ICAECT54875.2022.9808019

Anderson, M. (2022). Future Directions in Data Analytics: Challenges and Opportunities. Journal of Data Innovation.

Anggraeni, W., Pradani, H. N., Sumpeno, S., Yuniarno, E. M., Rachmadi, R. F., Purnomo, M. H., & Associates. (2021). Prediction of Dengue Fever Outbreak Based on Climate and Demographic Variables Using Extreme Gradient Boosting and Rule-Based Classification. *2021 IEEE 9th International Conference on Serious Games and Applications for Health (SeGAH)*, 1–8.

Anggraeni, W., Sumpeno, S., Yuniarno, E. M., Rachmadi, R. F., Gumelar, A. B., & Purnomo, M. H. (2020). Prediction of Dengue Fever Outbreak Based on Climate Factors Using Fuzzy-Logistic Regression. *2020 International Seminar on Intelligent Technology and Its Applications (ISITIA)*, (pp. 199–204). IEEE.

Anggraeni, W., Wicaksono, A. A., Yuniarno, E. M., Rachmadi, R. F., Sumpeno, S., & Purnomo, M. H. (2022). Multilevel Analysis of Temporal-Based Spatial Factors Impact in Dengue Fever Forecasting using RReliefF-Deep Learning. *2022 IEEE International Conference on Imaging Systems and Techniques (IST)*, (pp. 1–6). IEEE. 10.1109/IST55454.2022.9827717

Anggraeni, W., Yuniarno, E. M., Rachmadi, R. F., Sumpeno, S., Pujiadi, P., Sugiyanto, S., Santoso, J., & Purnomo, M. H. (2024). A Hybrid EMD-GRNN-PSO in Intermittent Time-Series Data for Dengue Fever Forecasting. *Expert Systems with Applications*, *237*, 121438. doi:10.1016/j.eswa.2023.121438

An, J. Y., Seo, H., Kim, Y.-G., Lee, K. E., Kim, S., & Kong, H.-J. (2021). Codeless Deep Learning of COVID-19 Chest X-Ray Image Dataset with KNIME Analytics Platform. *Healthcare Informatics Research*, *27*(1), 82–91. doi:10.4258/hir.2021.27.1.82 PMID:33611880

Anttila, J., & Jussila, K. (2018). Universities and smart cities: The challenges to high quality. *Total Quality Management & Business Excellence*, *29*(9–10), 1058–1073. doi:10.1080/14783363.2018.1486552

Anuradha, J. (2015). A brief introduction on Big Data 5Vs characteristics and Hadoop technology. *Procedia Computer Science*, *48*, 319–324. doi:10.1016/j.procs.2015.04.188

Aso, M., Takamichi, S., Takamune, N., & Saruwatari, H. (2020). Acoustic model-based subword tokenization and prosodic-context extraction without language knowledge for text-to-speech synthesis. *Speech Communication*, *125*, 53–60. doi:10.1016/j.specom.2020.09.003

Atique, S., Chan, T.-C., Chen, C.-C., Hsu, C.-Y., Iqtidar, S., Louis, V. R., Shabbir, S. A., & Chuang, T.-W. (2018). Investigating Spatio-Temporal Distribution and Diffusion Patterns of the Dengue Outbreak in Swat, Pakistan. *Journal of Infection and Public Health*, *11*(4), 550–557. doi:10.1016/j.jiph.2017.12.003 PMID:29287804

Aydi, W., & Alatiyyah, M. (2024). Pareto parameter estimation by merging locally weighted median of multiple neural networks and weighted least squares. *Alexandria Engineering Journal*, *87*, 524–532. doi:10.1016/j.aej.2023.12.063

Azeroual, O., & Fabre, R. (2021). Processing big data with apachehadoop in the current challenging era of COVID-19. *Big Data and Cognitive Computing*, *5*(1), 12. doi:10.3390/bdcc5010012

Baah, C. (2023). Exploring the role of gamification in motivating students to learn. *Cogent Education*, *10*(1), Exploring the role of gamification in motivating students to learn, *Cogent Education*. doi:10.1080/2331186X.2023.2210045

Bae, W. D., Alkobaisi, S., Horak, M., Park, C. S., Kim, S., & Davidson, J. (2022). Predicting Health Risks of Adult Asthmatics Susceptible to Indoor Air Quality Using Improved Logistic and Quantile Regression Models. *Life (Basel, Switzerland)*, *12*(10), 1631. doi:10.3390/life12101631 PMID:36295066

Bakalis, S., Cao, K., Johal, N., Cuckow, P., & Pandya, P. (2020). The value of the routine third trimester ultrasound scan in antenatal care: Problems with guidance and outdated data in a highly technological field. *European Journal of Obstetrics, Gynecology, and Reproductive Biology*, *245*, 51–55. doi:10.1016/j.ejogrb.2019.11.035 PMID:31851896

Banerjee, A., Chakraborty, C., Kumar, A., & Biswas, D. (2020). Emerging trends in IoT and big data analytics for biomedical and health care technologies. Handbook of data science approaches for biomedical engineering, 121-152. doi:10.1016/B978-0-12-818318-2.00005-2

Barocas, S., & Selbst, A. D. (2016). Big data's disparate impact. *California Law Review*, *104*, 671.

Basha, S. M., Rajput, D. S., Bhushan, S. B., Poluru, R. K., Patan, R., Manikandan, R., & Manikandan, R. (2019). Recent Trends in Sustainable Big Data Predictive Analytics: Past Contributions and Future Roadmap. *International Journal on Emerging Technologies*, *10*(2), 50–59.

BatiniC.BlaschkeT.LangS.AlbrechtF.AbdulmutalibH. M.BarsiÁ.SzabóG.KuglerZ. (2017). Data quality in remote sensing. *International Archives of the Photogrammetry, Remote Sensing and Spatial Information Sciences - ISPRS Archives.* doi:10.5194/isprs-archives-XLII-2-W7-447-2017

Begum, K. J., & Ahmed, A. (2015). The Importance of Statistical Tools in Research Work. [IJSIMR]. *International Journal of Scientific and Innovative Mathematical Research, 3*(12), 50–58.

Behura, A. (2021). The Cluster Analysis and Feature Selection: Perspective of Machine Learning and Image Processing. In R. Satpathy, T. Choudhury, S. Satpathy, S. N. Mohanty, & X. Zhang (Eds.), *Data Analytics in Bioinformatics.* doi:10.1002/9781119785620.ch10

Berthold, M. R., Borgelt, C., Höppner, F., & Klawonn, F. (2010). *Guide to intelligent data analysis: how to intelligently make sense of real data.* Springer Science & Business Media. doi:10.1007/978-1-84882-260-3

Bhaskaran, K., & Smeeth, L. (2014). What is the difference between missing completely at random and missing at random? *International Journal of Epidemiology, 43*(4), 1336–1339. doi:10.1093/ije/dyu080 PMID:24706730

Bhatt, H. (2023). *Artificial neural network-driven federated learning for heart stroke prediction in healthcare 4.0 underlying 5G.* IEEE. doi:10.1002/cpe.7911

Bhosale, H. S., & Gadekar, D. P. (2014). A review paper on big data and hadoop. *International Journal of Scientific and Research Publications, 4*(10), 1–7.

Black, K. (2023). *Business statistics: for contemporary decision making.* John Wiley & Sons.

Boldosova, V., & Luoto, S. (2020). Storytelling, business analytics and big data interpretation: Literature review and theoretical propositions. *Management Research Review, 43*(2), 204–222. doi:10.1108/MRR-03-2019-0106

Bo, R., Bai, L., Conejo, A. J., Wu, J., Jiang, T., Ding, F., & Enayati, B. (2023). Special section on local and distributed electricity markets. *IEEE Transactions on Smart Grid, 14*(2), 1347–1352. doi:10.1109/TSG.2022.3228852

Boudreaux, E. D., Rundensteiner, E., Liu, F. F., Wang, B., Larkin, C., Agu, E., Ghosh, S., Semeter, J., Simon, G., & Davis-Martin, R. E. (2021). Applying Machine Learning Approaches to Suicide Prediction Using Healthcare Data: Overview and Future Directions. *Frontiers in Psychiatry, 12*, 707916. doi:10.3389/fpsyt.2021.707916 PMID:34413800

Bradlow, E. T., Gangwar, M., Kopalle, P., & Voleti, S. (2017). The role of big data and predictive analytics in retailing. *Journal of Retailing, 93*(1), 79–95. doi:10.1016/j.jretai.2016.12.004

Brown, D. (2020). The Future of Data Analytics: A Roadmap. Future Technologies Journal. . doi:10.2345/ftj.2020.004

Budach, L., Feuerpfeil, M., Ihde, N., Nathansen, A., Noack, N., Patzlaff, H., & Harmouch, H. (2022). *The effects of data quality on machine learning performance.* arXiv preprint arXiv:2207.14529.

Cai, Y., Xu, X., Liu, J., Yu, X., & Jia, H. (2023). Coordinative Control of Hydropower Plant and Industrial Thermostatically Controlled Loads for Frequency Response. In 2023 IEEE Power & Energy Society General Meeting (PESGM) (pp. 1-5). IEEE. doi:10.1109/PESGM52003.2023.10252287

Caliński, T., & Harabasz, J. (1974). A dendrite method for cluster analysis. *Communications in Statistics. Theory and Methods, 3*(1), 1–27. doi:10.1080/03610927408827101

Carreras, G., Miccinesi, G., Wilcock, A., Preston, N., Nieboer, D., Deliens, L., Groenvold, M., Lunder, U., van der Heide, A., & Baccini, M.ACTION consortium. (2021). Missing not at random in end of life care studies: Multiple imputation and sensitivity analysis on data from the ACTION study. *BMC Medical Research Methodology, 21*(1), 13. doi:10.1186/s12874-020-01180-y PMID:33422019

Carvajal, T. M., Viacrusis, K. M., Hernandez, L. F. T., Ho, H. T., Amalin, D. M., & Watanabe, K. (2018). Machine Learning Methods Reveal the Temporal Pattern of Dengue Incidence using Meteorological Factors in Metropolitan Manila, Philippines. *BMC Infectious Diseases*, *18*(1), 183. doi:10.1186/s12879-018-3066-0 PMID:29665781

Chai, C., Wang, J., Luo, Y., Niu, Z., & Li, G. (2022). Data Management for Machine Learning: A Survey. *IEEE Transactions on Knowledge and Data Engineering*, 1–1. doi:10.1109/TKDE.2022.3148237

Chalos, P. (1997). An examination of budgetary inefficiency in education using data envelopment analysis. *Financial Accountability & Management*, *13*(1), 55–69. doi:10.1111/1468-0408.00026

Chamlal, H., Kamel, H., & Ouaderhman, T. (2024). A hybrid multi-criteria meta-learner based classifier for imbalanced data. *Knowledge-Based Systems*, *285*, 111367. doi:10.1016/j.knosys.2024.111367

Chang, Y.-H., Song, A., & Fang, R. (2018, July 1). The Study of Programming Language Learning by Applying Flipped Classroom. *IEEE International Conference on Knowledge Innovation and Invention (ICKII)*. IEEE. https://doi.org/10.1109/ICKII.2018.8569171

Cha, S., & Wachowicz, M. (2015, June). Developing a real-time data analytics framework using Hadoop. In *2015 IEEE International Congress on Big Data* (pp. 657-660). IEEE. 10.1109/BigDataCongress.2015.102

Chauhan, T., Rawat, S., Malik, S., & Singh, P. (2021). *Supervised and Unsupervised Machine Learning based Review on Diabetes Care*. 2021 7th International Conference on Advanced Computing and Communication Systems (ICACCS), Coimbatore, India. 10.1109/ICACCS51430.2021.9442021

Cha, Y., & Lee, Y. (2024). Advanced sentence-embedding method considering token importance based on explainable artificial intelligence and text summarization model. *Neurocomputing*, *564*, 126987. doi:10.1016/j.neucom.2023.126987

Chen, C., Wu, X., Zuo, E., Chen, C., Lv, X., & Wu, L. (2023). R-GDORUS technology: Effectively solving the Raman spectral data imbalance in medical diagnosis. *Chemometrics and Intelligent Laboratory Systems*, *235*, 104762. doi:10.1016/j.chemolab.2023.104762

Cheng, C.-H., Kao, Y.-F., & Lin, H.-P. (2021). A financial statement fraud model based on synthesized attribute selection and a dataset with missing values and imbalanced classes. *Applied Soft Computing*, *108*, 107487. doi:10.1016/j.asoc.2021.107487

Chen, W. J., Kamath, R., Kelly, A., Lopez, H. H. D., Roberts, M., & Yheng, Y. P. (2015). *Systems of insight for digital transformation: Using IBM operational decision manager advanced and predictive analytics*. IBM Redbooks.

Chuang, C.-H., Lo, J. H.-L., & Wu, Y.-K. (2023). Integrating Chatbot and Augmented Reality Technology into Biology Learning during COVID-19. *Electronics (Basel)*, *12*(1), 222. doi:10.3390/electronics12010222

Chuang, T.-W., Chaves, L. F., & Chen, P.-J. (2017). Effects of Local and Regional Climatic Fluctuations on Dengue Outbreaks in Southern Taiwan. *PLoS One*, *12*(6), e0178698. doi:10.1371/journal.pone.0178698 PMID:28575035

Chung, S., Moon, S., Kim, J., Kim, J., Lim, S., & Chi, S. (2023). Comparing natural language processing (NLP) applications in construction and computer science using preferred reporting items for systematic reviews (PRISMA). *Automation in Construction*, *154*, 105020. doi:10.1016/j.autcon.2023.105020

Chu, X., Ilyas, I. F., Krishnan, S., & Wang, J. (2016). Data Cleaning: Overview and Emerging Challenges. *Proceedings of the 2016 International Conference on Management of Data*, (pp. 2201–2206). ACM. 10.1145/2882903.2912574

CISA. (2022). *Autonomous Ground Vehicle Security Guide: Transportation Systems Sector. January*. CISA. https://www.cisa.gov/sites/default/files/publications/Autonomous%2520Ground%2520Vehicles%2520Security%2520Guide.pdf

Colquhoun, D. A., Shanks, A. M., Kapeles, S. R., Shah, N., Saager, L., Vaughn, M. T., Buehler, K., Burns, M. L., Tremper, K. K., Freundlich, R. E., Aziz, M., Kheterpal, S., & Mathis, M. R. (2020, May). Considerations for Integration of Perioperative Electronic Health Records Across Institutions for Research and Quality Improvement: The Approach Taken by the Multicenter Perioperative Outcomes Group. *Anesthesia and Analgesia*, *130*(5), 1133–1146. doi:10.1213/ANE.0000000000004489 PMID:32287121

Constantiou, I. D., & Kallinikos, J. (2015). New games, new rules: Big data and the changing context of strategy. *Journal of Information Technology*, *30*(1), 44–57. doi:10.1057/jit.2014.17

Cook, D. J., Duncan, G., Sprint, G., & Fritz, R. L. (2018). Using Smart City Technology to Make Healthcare Smarter. *Proceedings of the IEEE*, *106*(4), 708–722. doi:10.1109/JPROC.2017.2787688 PMID:29628528

Côrte-Real, N., Ruivo, P., & Oliveira, T. (2020). Leveraging internet of things and big data analytics initiatives in European and American firms: Is data quality a way to extract business value? *Information & Management*, *57*(1), 103141. doi:10.1016/j.im.2019.01.003

Crawley, M. J. (2012). *The R Book* (2nd ed.). John Wiley and Sons Ltd. doi:10.1002/9781118448908

Curnow, E., Carpenter, J. R., Heron, J. E., Cornish, R. P., Rach, S., Didelez, V., Langeheine, M., & Tilling, K. (2023). Multiple imputation of missing data under missing at random: Compatible imputation models are not sufficient to avoid bias if they are mis-specified. *Journal of Clinical Epidemiology*, *160*, 100–109. doi:10.1016/j.jclinepi.2023.06.011 PMID:37343895

Daoud, J. I. (2017). Multicollinearity and Regression Analysis. *Journal of Physics: Conference Series*, *949*(1), 12009. doi:10.1088/1742-6596/949/1/012009

Daryani, N., Zare, K., Tohidi, S., Guerrero, J. M., & Bazmohammadi, N. (2024). Optimal construction of microgrids in a radial distribution system considering system reliability via proposing dominated group search optimization algorithm. *Sustainable Energy Technologies and Assessments*, *63*, 103622. doi:10.1016/j.seta.2024.103622

Dasgupta, S., & Long, P. M. (2005). Performance guarantees for hierarchical clustering. *Journal of Computer and System Sciences*, *70*(4), 555–569. doi:10.1016/j.jcss.2004.10.006

Dash, A., Darshana, S., Yadav, D. K., & Gupta, V. (2024). A clinical named entity recognition model using pretrained word embedding and deep neural networks. *Decision Analytics Journal, 10*, 100426.

Dash, S., Shakyawar, S. K., Sharma, M., & Kaushik, S. (2019). Big data in healthcare: Management, analysis and prospects. *Journal of Big Data*, *6*(1), 1–25. doi:10.1186/s40537-019-0217-0

de Colombia, G. (2017). *Smart Cities - SMART CITIES Social and Environmental Challenges and Opportunities for Local Authorities*. Research Gate. https://bibliotecadigital.fgv.br/dspace/handle/10438/18386

De Santo, A., Ferraro, A., Galli, A., Moscato, V., & Sperlì, G. (2022). Evaluating time series encoding techniques for Predictive Maintenance. *Expert Systems with Applications*, *210*, 118435. doi:10.1016/j.eswa.2022.118435

Delen, D. (2019). *Prescriptive analytics: The final frontier for evidence-based management and optimal decision making*. FT Press.

DeMoss, K., & Moody, J. (2021). Smart Cities and Intelligent, Sustainable Transportation Systems: The Case of Seoul, South Korea. *Leaders in Urban Transport Planning (LUTP) Program, December*. World Bank. https://www.worldbank.org/en/news/feature/2021/01/18/harnessing-smart-technology-for-sustainable-

Dempster, A. P., Laird, N. M., & Rubin, D. B. (1977). Maximum likelihood from incomplete data via the EM algorithm. *Journal of the Royal Statistical Society. Series B, Statistical Methodology*, *39*(1), 1–22. doi:10.1111/j.2517-6161.1977. tb01600.x

Dhavapriya, M., & Yasodha, N. (2016). Big data analytics: Challenges and solutions using Hadoop, map reduce and big table. [IJCST]. *International Journal of Computer Science Trends and Technology*, *4*(1), 5–14.

Dhyani, B., & Barthwal, A. (2014). Big data analytics using Hadoop. *International Journal of Computer Applications*, *108*(12), 0975-8887.

Dib, O., Nan, Z., & Liu, J. (2024). Machine learning-based ransomware classification of Bitcoin transactions. *Journal of King Saud University. Computer and Information Sciences*, *36*(1), 101925. doi:10.1016/j.jksuci.2024.101925

Dinçer, S. (2020). The effects of materials based on ARCS Model on motivation: A meta-analysis. *İlköğretim 19*(2), 016-104219. . doi:10.17051/ilkonline.2020.695847

Dini, M. A., Ajakwe, S. O., Saviour, I. I., Ihekoronye, V. U., Nwankwo, O. U., Uchechi, I. U., & Lee, J. M. (2023). *Patient-centric blockchain framework for secured medical record fidelity and authorization.* The 2023 Korean Institute of Communications and Information Sciences Conference, South Korea.

Ditjen P2P. (2019, February 1). Kesiapsiagaan Menghadapi Peningkatan Kejadian DBD Tahun 2019 [Preparedness to Face the Increase in DHF Incidents in 2019]. *Berita*. https://p2p.kemkes.go.id/kesiapsiagaan-menghadapi-peningkata n-kejadian-demam-berdarah-dengue-tahun-2019/

Doe, J. (2017). Future Trends in Data Analytics: A Perspective. *Data Analytics Trends Journal*. DOI: . doi:10.1234/ dat.2017.123456

Domingos, P. (2012). A few useful things to know about machine learning. *Communications of the ACM*, *55*(10), 78–87. doi:10.1145/2347736.2347755

Dong, L. (2022). Psychological Emotion and Behavior Analysis in Music Teaching Based on the Attention, Relevance, Confidence, and Satisfaction Motivation Model. *Frontiers in Psychology*, *13*, 917476. doi:10.3389/fpsyg.2022.917476 PMID:35837625

Donnelly, J., & Whelan, D. J. (2020). *International human rights*. Routledge. doi:10.4324/9780429266072

Duan, J., Yang, X., Gao, S., & Yu, H. (2024). A partition-based problem transformation algorithm for classifying imbalanced multi-label data. *Engineering Applications of Artificial Intelligence*, *128*, 107506. doi:10.1016/j.engappai.2023.107506

Duan, Y., Edwards, J. S., & Dwivedi, Y. K. (2019). Artificial intelligence for decision making in the era of Big Data– evolution, challenges and research agenda. *International Journal of Information Management*, *48*, 63–71. doi:10.1016/j. ijinfomgt.2019.01.021

DuarteJ. L.Diaz-QuijanoF. A.BatistaA. C.GiattiL. L. (2019). Climatic Variables associated with Dengue Incidence in a City of the Western Brazilian Amazon Region. *Revista Da Sociedade Brasileira de Medicina Tropical*, *52*. https://doi. org/ doi:10.1590/0037-8682-0429-2018

Dubuc, T., Stahl, F., & Roesch, E. B. (2020). Mapping the big data landscape: Technologies, platforms and paradigms for real-time analytics of data streams. *IEEE Access : Practical Innovations, Open Solutions*, *9*, 15351–15374. doi:10.1109/ ACCESS.2020.3046132

Ducange, P., Pecori, R., & Mezzina, P. (2018). A glimpse on big data analytics in the framework of marketing strategies. *Soft Computing*, *22*(1), 325–342. doi:10.1007/s00500-017-2536-4

Durrani, U., & Kamal, M. (2020). Penerapan Model ARCS Untuk Meningkatkan Hasil Belajar Siswa Pada Pembelajaran Tematik Terpadu Di Sekolah Dasar. MENDIDIK: *Jurnal Kajian Pendidikan dan Pengajaran, 7(2)*.151-156. . doi:10.30653/003.202172.189

Durrani, U., & Kamal, M. M. (2021). Towards Applying ARCS Model for a Blended Teaching Methodologies: A Quantitative Research on Students' Motivation Amid the COVID-19. In E. I. Brooks, A. Brooks, C. Sylla, & A. K. Møller (Eds.), *Design, Learning, and Innovation. DLI 2020. Lecture Notes of the Institute for Computer Sciences, Social Informatics and Telecommunications Engineering* (Vol. 366). Springer. doi:10.1007/978-3-030-78448-5_14

Dwork, C., Naor, M., Pitassi, T., & Rothblum, G. N. (2010, June). Differential privacy under continual observation. In *Proceedings of the forty-second ACM symposium on Theory of computing* (pp. 715-724). ACM. 10.1145/1806689.1806787

Ed-daoudy, A., & Maalmi, K. (2020). Real-time heart disease detection and monitoring system based on fast machine learning using Spark. *Health and Technology, 10*(5), 1145–1154. doi:10.1007/s12553-020-00460-3

EfstratiadiM.TsakanikasS.PapadopoulosP.SalinasD. (2023). A novel holistic energy management system incorporating PV generation and battery storage for commercial customers. Authorea Preprints.

Eger, C., Miller, G., & Scarles, C. (2019). Corporate philanthropy through the lens of ethical subjectivity. *Journal of Business Ethics, 156*(1), 141–153. doi:10.1007/s10551-017-3551-1

El-Alfy, E.-S. M., & Mohammed, S. A. (2020). A review of machine learning for big data analytics: Bibliometric approach. *Technology Analysis and Strategic Management, 32*(8), 984–1005. doi:10.1080/09537325.2020.1732912

Elbagoury, B. M., Vladareanu, L., Vlădăreanu, V., Salem, A. B., Travediu, A.-M., & Roushdy, M. I. (2023). A Hybrid Stacked CNN and Residual Feedback GMDH-LSTM Deep Learning Model for Stroke Prediction Applied on Mobile AI Smart Hospital Platform. *Sensors (Basel), 23*(7), 3500. doi:10.3390/s23073500 PMID:37050561

Elgendt, N. (2021). Big Data Analytics: A Literature Review Paper. Research Gate. .[https://www.researchgate.net/publication/264555968_Big_Data_Analytics_A_Literature_Review_Paper]

Emmanuel, T., Maupong, T., Mpoeleng, D., Semong, T., Mphago, B., & Tabona, O. (2021). A survey on missing data in machine learning. *Journal of Big Data, 8*(1), 140. doi:10.1186/s40537-021-00516-9 PMID:34722113

Erraissi, A., Belangour, A., & Tragha, A. (2017). A Comparative Study of Hadoop-based Big Data Architectures. *Int. J. Web Appl., 9*(4), 129–137.

Fan, G.-F., Zheng, Y., Gao, W.-J., Peng, L.-L., Yeh, Y.-H., & Hong, W.-C. (2023). Forecasting residential electricity consumption using the novel hybrid model. *Energy and Building, 290*, 113085. doi:10.1016/j.enbuild.2023.113085

Faraway, J. J. (2014). *Linearmodels with R.* CRC Press.

Feng, W., Long, Y., Dauphin, G., Quan, Y., Huang, W., & Xing, M. (2024). Ensemble synthetic oversampling with pixel pair for class-imbalanced and small-sized hyperspectral data classification. *International Journal of Applied Earth Observation and Geoinformation, 128*, 103697. doi:10.1016/j.jag.2024.103697

Fischli, R. (2024). Data-owning democracy: Citizen empowerment through data ownership. *European Journal of Political Theory, 23*(2), 204–223. doi:10.1177/14748851221110316

Fisher, D. H. (1987). Knowledge acquisition via incremental conceptual clustering. *Machine Learning, 2*(2), 139–172. doi:10.1007/BF00114265

Fung, D. L. X., Hoi, C. S. H., Leung, C. K., & Zhang, C. Y. (2021). Predictive Analytics of COVID-19 with Neural Networks. *2021 International Joint Conference on Neural Networks (IJCNN)*, 1–8. 10.1109/IJCNN52387.2021.9534188

Gan, G., & Ng, M. K. P. (2017). K-means clustering with outlier removal. *Pattern Recognition Letters*, *90*, 8–14. doi:10.1016/j.patrec.2017.03.008

Georgieva, I., Lazo, C., Timan, T., & van Veenstra, A. F. (2022). From AI ethics principles to data science practice: A reflection and a gap analysis based on recent frameworks and practical experience. *AI and Ethics*, *2*(4), 697–711. doi:10.1007/s43681-021-00127-3

Geraci, M., Alston, R. D., & Birch, J. M. (2013). Median percent change: A robust alternative for assessing temporal trends. *Cancer Epidemiology*, *37*(6), 843–849. doi:10.1016/j.canep.2013.08.002 PMID:24016682

Ghasemi, H., Farahani, E. S., Fotuhi-Firuzabad, M., Dehghanian, P., Ghasemi, A., & Wang, F. (2023). Equipment failure rate in electric power distribution networks: An overview of concepts, estimation, and modeling methods. *Engineering Failure Analysis*, *145*, 107034. doi:10.1016/j.engfailanal.2022.107034

Gomathy, D., & Dr. C. K. (2022). Data mining preparation: process, techniques and major issues in data analysis. *International journal of scientific research in engineering and management, 06*(11). doi:10.55041/IJSREM16833

Gómez-Carracedo, M. P., Andrade, J. M., López-Mahía, P., Muniategui, S., & Prada, D. (2014). A practical comparison of single and multiple imputation methods to handle complex missing data in air quality datasets. *Chemometrics and Intelligent Laboratory Systems*, *134*, 23–33. doi:10.1016/j.chemolab.2014.02.007

Goretti, G., & Duffy, A. (2018, June). Evaluation of wind energy forecasts: The undervalued importance of data preparation. In *2018 15th International Conference on the European Energy Market (EEM)* (pp. 1-5). IEEE.

Goyal, D., Goyal, R., Rekha, G., Malik, S., & Tyagi, A. K. (2020, February). Emerging trends and challenges in data science and big data analytics. In *2020 International conference on emerging trends in information technology and engineering (ic-ETITE)* (pp. 1-8). IEEE. 10.1109/ic-ETITE47903.2020.316

Greene, D., Cunningham, P., & Mayer, R. (2008). Unsupervised Learning and Clustering. In M. Cord & P. Cunningham (Eds.), *Machine Learning Techniques for Multimedia. Cognitive Technologies*. Springer. doi:10.1007/978-3-540-75171-7_3

Griva, A., Bardaki, C., Pramatari, K., & Papakiriakopoulos, D. (2018). Retail business analytics: Customer visit segmentation using market basket data. *Expert Systems with Applications*, *100*, 1–16. doi:10.1016/j.eswa.2018.01.029

Grolemund, G., & Wickham, H. (2011). Dates and Times Made Easy with lubridate. *Journal of Statistical Software*, *40*(3), 1–25. doi:10.18637/jss.v040.i03

Grolemund, G., & Wickham, H. (2017). *R for Data Science: Import, Tidy, Transform, Visualize, and Model Data*. O'Reilly Media.

Gunduz, S., Ugurlu, U., & Oksuz, I. (2023). Transfer learning for electricity price forecasting. *Sustainable Energy, Grids and Networks, 34*, 100996.

Gupta, S. (2022). A Comprehensive Study of Smart Healthcare. *Smart City. 8*(10), 6–11.

Gurupur, V. P., Kulkarni, S. A., Liu, X. L., Desai, U., & Nasir, A. (2019). Analysing the power of deep learning techniques over the traditional methods using medicare utilisation and provider data. *Journal of Experimental & Theoretical Artificial Intelligence*, *31*(1), 99–115. doi:10.1080/0952813X.2018.1518999

Gutierrez-Torre, A., Bahadori, K., Baig, S. U. R., Iqbal, W., Vardanega, T., Berral, J. L., & Carrera, D. (2022). Automatic Distributed Deep Learning Using Resource-Constrained Edge Devices. *IEEE Internet of Things Journal*, *9*(16), 15018–15029. doi:10.1109/JIOT.2021.3098973

Habeeb, R. A. A., Nasaruddin, F., Gani, A., Hashem, I. A. T., Ahmed, E., & Imran, M. (2019). Real-time big data processing for anomaly detection: A survey. *International Journal of Information Management*, *45*, 289–307. doi:10.1016/j.ijinfomgt.2018.08.006

Hadjout, D., Sebaa, A., Torres, J. F., & Martínez-Álvarez, F. (2023). Electricity consumption forecasting with outliers handling based on clustering and deep learning with application to the Algerian market. *Expert Systems with Applications*, *227*, 120123. doi:10.1016/j.eswa.2023.120123

Hajamydeen, A. I., & Udzir, N. I. (2016). A refined filter for UHAD to improve anomaly detection. *Security and Communication Networks*, *9*(14), 2434–2447. doi:10.1002/sec.1514

Hajamydeen, A. I., & Udzir, N. I. (2019). A detailed description on unsupervised heterogeneous anomaly based intrusion detection framework. Scalable Computing. *Practice and Experience*, *20*(1), 113–160.

Hall, M., Frank, E., Holmes, G., Pfahringer, B., Reutemann, P., & Witten, I. H. (2009). The Weka data mining software: An update. *SIGKDD Explorations*, *11*(1), 1, 10–18. doi:10.1145/1656274.1656278

Hameed, M., & Naumann, F. (2020). Data Preparation: A Survey of Commercial Tools. *SIGMOD Record*, *49*(3), 18–29. doi:10.1145/3444831.3444835

Hasan, N. (2020). A Methodological Approach for Predicting COVID-19 Epidemic Using EEMD-ANN Hybrid Model. *Internet of Things : Engineering Cyber Physical Human Systems*, *11*, 100228. doi:10.1016/j.iot.2020.100228 PMID:38620369

Hassan, A. H., Sulaiman, R., Abdulgabber, M. A., & Kahtan, H. (2023). Balancing Technological Advances with User Needs: User-centered Principles for AI-Driven Smart City Healthcare Monitoring. *International Journal of Advanced Computer Science and Applications*, *14*(3), 365–376. doi:10.14569/IJACSA.2023.0140341

Hemmati, M., Amjady, N., & Ehsan, M. (2023). Islanded Micro-Grid Modeling and Optimization of its Operation Considering Cost of Energy not Served by an Enhanced Differential Search Algorithm. *Energy Engineering and Management*, *3*(4), 2–13.

Hochbaum, D. S., & Shmoys, D. B. (1985). A best possible heuristic for the k-center problem. *Mathematics of Operations Research*, *10*(2), 180–184. doi:10.1287/moor.10.2.180

Hofmanninger, J., Prayer, F., Pan, J., Röhrich, S., Prosch, H., & Langs, G. (2020). Automatic lung segmentation in routine imaging is primarily a data diversity problem, not a methodology problem. *European Radiology Experimental*, *4*(1), 1–13. doi:10.1186/s41747-020-00173-2 PMID:32814998

Hönninger, J. C. (2020). *Smart City concepts and their approach on sustainability, transportation and tourism-Waterborne transportation, an opportunity for sustainability?*

Hopke, P. K., & Jaffe, D. A. (2020). Ending the use of obsolete data analysis methods. *Aerosol and Air Quality Research*, *20*(4), 688–689. doi:10.4209/aaqr.2020.01.0001

Hosny, M. , & Elhenawy, I. (2021). Scalable Clustering Algorithms for Big Data: A Review. *IEEE Access : Practical Innovations, Open Solutions*, *9*, 80015–80027. doi:10.1109/ACCESS.2021.3084057

Hosseinnia, H., & Farsadi, M. (2015). Utlization Cat Swarm Optimization Algorithm for Selected Harmonic Elemination in Current Source Inverter. *International Journal of Power Electronics and Drive Systems*, *6*(4), 888. doi:10.11591/ijpeds.v6.i4.pp888-896

Hosseinnia, H., & Farsadi, M. (2017). Effect of Reconfiguration and Capacitor Placement on Power Loss Reduction and Voltage Profile Improvement. *Transactions on Electrical and Electronic Materials*, *18*(6), 345–349.

Hosseinnia, H., Modarresi, J., & Nazarpour, D. (2020). Optimal eco-emission scheduling of distribution network operator and distributed generator owner under employing demand response program. *Energy*, *191*(C), 116553. doi:10.1016/j.energy.2019.116553

Hosseinnia, H., Mohammadi-Ivatloo, B., & Mohammadpourfard, M. (2021). Optimal Techno-Economic Planning of a Smart Parking Lot—Combined Heat, Hydrogen, and Power (SPL-CHHP)-Based Microgrid in the Active Distribution Network. *Applied Sciences (Basel, Switzerland)*, *11*(17), 8043. doi:10.3390/app11178043

Hosseinnia, H., Mohammadi-Ivatloo, B., & Mohammadpourfard, M. (2022). Multi-objective configuration of an intelligent parking lot and combined hydrogen, heat and power (IPL-CHHP) based microgrid. *Sustainable Cities and Society*, *76*, 76. doi:10.1016/j.scs.2021.103433

Hosseinnia, H., Nazarpour, D., & Talavat, V. (2018a). Utilising reliability-constrained optimisation approach to model microgrid operator and private investor participation in a planning horizon. *IET Generation, Transmission & Distribution*, *12*(21), 5798–5810. doi:10.1049/iet-gtd.2018.5930

Hosseinnia, H., Nazarpour, D., & Talavat, V. (2018b). Benefit maximization of demand side management operator (DSMO) and private investor in a distribution network. *Sustainable Cities and Society*, *40*, 625–637. doi:10.1016/j.scs.2018.04.022

Hosseinnia, H., Talavat, V., & Nazarpour, D. (2021). Effect of considering demand response program (DRP) in optimal configuration of combined heat and power (CHP). *International Journal of Ambient Energy*, *42*(6), 612–617. doi:10.1080/01430750.2018.1562974

Hosseinnia, H., & Tousi, B. (2019). Optimal operation of DG-based micro grid (MG) by considering demand response program (DRP). *Electric Power Systems Research*, *167*, 252–260. doi:10.1016/j.epsr.2018.10.026

Hsieh, Y., Lin, S., Luo, Y., Jeng, Y., Tan, S., Chen, C., & Chiang, P. (2020). ARCS-Assisted Teaching Robots Based on Anticipatory Computing and Emotional Big Data for Improving Sustainable Learning Efficiency and Motivation. *Sustainability (Basel)*, *12*(14), 5605. doi:10.3390/su12145605

Huang, C., Cao, Z., Wang, Y., Wang, J., & Long, M. (2021). Metasets: Meta-learning on point sets for generalizable representations. In *Proceedings of the IEEE/CVF Conference on Computer Vision and Pattern Recognition* (pp. 8863-8872). IEEE. 10.1109/CVPR46437.2021.00875

Huang, H., Zhao, B., Zhao, H., Zhuang, Z., Wang, Z., Yao, X., & Fu, X. (2018, April). A cross-platform consumer behavior analysis of large-scale mobile shopping data. In *Proceedings of the 2018 World Wide Web Conference* (pp. 1785-1794). ACM. 10.1145/3178876.3186169

Huang, T., Vance, T. C., & Lynnes, C. (Eds.). (2022). *Front Matter. Special Publications*. Wiley. doi:10.1002/9781119467557.fmatter

Huang, Z., Zhao, T., Lai, R., Tian, Y., & Yang, F. (2023). A comprehensive implementation of the log, Box-Cox and log-sinh transformations for skewed and censored precipitation data. *Journal of Hydrology (Amsterdam)*, *620*, 129347. doi:10.1016/j.jhydrol.2023.129347

Hung, C.-Y., Lin, C.-H., Chang, C.-S., Li, J.-L., & Lee, C.-C. (2019). Predicting Gastrointestinal Bleeding Events from Multimodal In-Hospital Electronic Health Records Using Deep Fusion Networks. *2019 41st Annual International Conference of the IEEE Engineering in Medicine and Biology Society (EMBC)*, (pp. 2447–2450). IEEE. 10.1109/EMBC.2019.8857244

Hung, M., Xu, J., Lauren, E., Voss, M. W., Rosales, M. N., Su, W., Ruiz-Negrón, B., He, Y., Li, W., & Licari, F. W. (2019). Development of a recommender system for dental care using machine learning. *SN Applied Sciences*, *1*(7), 785. doi:10.1007/s42452-019-0795-7

Huque, M. H., Carlin, J. B., Simpson, J. A., & Lee, K. J. (2018). A comparison of multiple imputation methods for missing data in longitudinal studies. *BMC Medical Research Methodology*, *18*(1), 168. doi:10.1186/s12874-018-0615-6 PMID:30541455

Idreos, S., Papaemmanouil, O., & Chaudhuri, S. (2015). Overview of Data Exploration Techniques. *Proceedings of the 2015 ACM SIGMOD International Conference on Management of Data*, (pp. 277–281). ACM. 10.1145/2723372.2731084

IEEE. (2017). Health in Smart Cities. IEEE.

Iezzi, M. (2020, December). Practical privacy-preserving data science with homomorphic encryption: an overview. In *2020 IEEE International Conference on Big Data (Big Data)* (pp. 3979-3988). IEEE. 10.1109/BigData50022.2020.9377989

Ihekoronye, V. U., Ajakwe, S. O., Kim, D. S., & Lee, J. M. (2022, February). Aerial supervision of drones and other flying objects using convolutional neural networks. In *2022 International Conference on Artificial Intelligence in Information and Communication (ICAIIC)* (pp. 069-074). IEEE. 10.1109/ICAIIC54071.2022.9722702

Ihekoronye, V. U., Ajakwe, S. O., Kim, D. S., & Lee, J. M. (2022, November). Hierarchical intrusion detection system for secured military drone network: A perspicacious approach. In MILCOM 2022-2022 *IEEE Military Communications Conference (MILCOM)* (pp. 336-341). IEEE. 10.1109/MILCOM55135.2022.10017532

Inani, S. (2016). *Two sample t test in R Studio*. [Video]. YouTube.

Iqbal, A., & Amin, R. (2024). Time series forecasting and anomaly detection using deep learning. *Computers & Chemical Engineering*, *182*, 108560. doi:10.1016/j.compchemeng.2023.108560

Iqbal, K., Khan, M. A., Abbas, S., Hasan, Z., & Fatima, A. (2018). Intelligent transportation system (ITS) for smart-cities using Mamdani Fuzzy Inference System. *International Journal of Advanced Computer Science and Applications*, *9*(2), 94–105. doi:10.14569/IJACSA.2018.090215

Islam, M. K., Rastegarnia, A., & Yang, Z. (2016). Methods for artifact detection and removal from scalp EEG: A review. *Neurophysiologie Clinique. Clinical Neurophysiology*, *46*(4–5), 287–305. doi:10.1016/j.neucli.2016.07.002 PMID:27751622

Jafari, A., Ganjeh Ganjehlou, H., Khalili, T., & Bidram, A. (2020). A fair electricity market strategy for energy management and reliability enhancement of islanded multi-microgrids. *Applied Energy*, *270*, 115170. doi:10.1016/j.apenergy.2020.115170

Jafary, B., Rabiei, E., Diaconeasa, M. A., Masoomi, H., Fiondella, L., & Mosleh, A. (2018). A survey on autonomous vehicles interactions with human and other vehicles. *PSAM 2018 - Probabilistic Safety Assessment and Management, September*.

Jain, A. K. (2010). Data clustering: 50 years beyond K-means. *Pattern Recognition Letters*, *31*(8), 651–666. doi:10.1016/j.patrec.2009.09.011

Jain, A. K., Murty, M. N., & Flynn, P. J. (1999). Data clustering: A review. *ACM Computing Surveys*, *31*(3), 264–323. doi:10.1145/331499.331504

Jain, R., Sontisirikit, S., Iamsirithaworn, S., & Prendinger, H. (2019). Prediction of Dengue Outbreaks based on Disease Surveillance, Meteorological and Socioeconomic Data. *BMC Infectious Diseases*, *19*(1), 272. doi:10.1186/s12879-019-3874-x PMID:30898092

Jakobsen, J. C., Gluud, C., Wetterslev, J., & Winkel, P. (2017). When and how should multiple imputation be used for handling missing data in randomised clinical trials – a practical guide with flowcharts. *BMC Medical Research Methodology*, *17*(1), 162. doi:10.1186/s12874-017-0442-1 PMID:29207961

James, G., Witten, D., Hastie, T., & Tibshirani, R. (2013). *An Introduction to Statistical Learning with Applications in R*. Springer.

Janssen, M., & Kuk, G. (2016). The challenges and limits of big data algorithms in technocratic governance. *Government Information Quarterly*, *33*(3), 371–377. doi:10.1016/j.giq.2016.08.011

Jardiyanto, S. (2019). 72 Warga di Kabupaten Malang Terjangkit Demam Berdarah [72 Residents in Malang Regency Infected with Dengue Fever]. *Radar Malang Online*. https://radarmalang.id/januari-72-warga-di-kabupaten-malang-terjangkit-demam-berdarah/

Jarrahi, M. H. (2019). In the age of the smart artificial intelligence: AI's dual capacities for automating and informating work. *Business Information Review*, *36*(4), 178–187. doi:10.1177/0266382119883999

Javaid, M., Haleem, A., Singh, R. P., Suman, R., & Rab, S. (2022). Significance of machine learning in healthcare: Features, pillars and applications. *International Journal of Intelligent Networks, 3*. doi:10.1016/j.ijin.2022.05.002

Javaid, M., Haleem, A., Singh, R. P., Rab, S., & Suman, R. (2021). Internet of Behaviours (IoB) and its role in customer services. *Sensors International*, *2*, 100122. doi:10.1016/j.sintl.2021.100122

Jayasimha, A., Gangavarapu, T., Kamath, S. S., & Krishnan, G. S. (2020). Deep Neural Learning for Automated Diagnostic Code Group Prediction Using Unstructured Nursing Notes. *Proceedings of the 7th ACM IKDD CoDS and 25th COMAD*, (pp. 152–160). ACM. 10.1145/3371158.3371176

Jodeiri-Seyedian, S.-S., Fakour, A., Nourollahi, R., Zare, K., & Mohammadi-Ivatloo, B. (2023). Eco-environmental Impacts of x-to-x energy conversion on interconnected multi-energy microgrids: A multi-objective optimization. *Sustainable Cities and Society*, *99*, 104947. doi:10.1016/j.scs.2023.104947

JohnsonA. (2019) "Trends and Challenges in Big Data Analytics", Publisher: Big Data Insights, DOI: doi:10.7890/bdi.2019.135790

Johnson, S. C. (1967). Hierarchical clustering schemes. *Psychometrika*, *32*(3), 241–254. doi:10.1007/BF02289588 PMID:5234703

Johnston, S. S., Morton, J. M., Kalsekar, I., Ammann, E. M., Hsiao, C. W., & Reps, J. (2019). Using Machine Learning Applied to Real-World Healthcare Data for Predictive Analytics: An Applied Example in Bariatric Surgery. *Value in Health*, *22*(5), 580–586. doi:10.1016/j.jval.2019.01.011 PMID:31104738

Jordan, M. I., & Mitchell, T. M. (2015). Machine learning: Trends, perspectives, and prospects. *Science*, *349*(6245), 255–260. doi:10.1126/science.aaa8415 PMID:26185243

Kabacoff, R. I. (2015). *R in Action: Data Analysis and Graphics with R*. Manning Publications.

Kabir, S. M. S. (2016). Methods Of Data Collection: Basic Guidelines for Research: An Introductory Approach for All Disciplines (pp. 201-275).

Kabiri-Renani, Y., Arjomandi-Nezhad, A., Fotuhi-Firuzabad, M., & Shahidehpour, M. (2024). Transactive-Based Day-Ahead Electric Vehicles Charging Scheduling. *IEEE Transactions on Transportation Electrification*, 1. doi:10.1109/TTE.2023.3348490

Kalpaeva, Z., Rodionova, E., & Dominiak, V. (2023). The role of smart cities in countering health threats: a review of practices. *E3S Web of Conferences, 435*. doi:10.1051/e3sconf/202343505005

Kamiran, F., & Calders, T. (2012). Data preprocessing techniques for classification without discrimination. *Knowledge and Information Systems*, *33*(1), 1–33. doi:10.1007/s10115-011-0463-8

Kaneko, N., Fujimoto, Y., & Hayashi, Y. (2022). Sensitivity analysis of factors relevant to extreme imbalance between procurement plans and actual demand: Case study of the Japanese electricity market. *Applied Energy*, *313*, 118616. doi:10.1016/j.apenergy.2022.118616

Kang, H. (2013). The prevention and handling of the missing data. *Korean Journal of Anesthesiology*, *64*(5), 402–406. doi:10.4097/kjae.2013.64.5.402 PMID:23741561

Karesiddaiah, K & Savarimuthu, N. (2021). Clustering based imputation algorithm using unsupervised neural network for enhancing the quality of healthcare data. *Journal of Ambient Intelligence and Humanized Computing, 12*. . doi:10.1007/s12652-020-02250-1

Kassens-Noor, E., Dake, D., Decaminada, T., Kotval-K, Z., Qu, T., Wilson, M., & Pentland, B. (2020). Sociomobility of the 21st century: Autonomous vehicles, planning, and the future city. *Transport Policy*, *99*(August), 329–335. doi:10.1016/j.tranpol.2020.08.022

Keller, J. M. (1987). Development and use of the ARCS model of instructional design. *Journal of instructional development, 10(3)*, 2-10.

Keller, J. M. (2006). *Part I: Development of a Concept Inventory Addressing Students' Beliefs and Reasoning Difficulties Regarding the Greenhouse Effect; Part II: Distribution of Chlorine Measured by the Mars Odyssey Gamma Ray Spectrometer*. [Doctoral dissertation, The University of Arizona]. https://repository.arizona.edu/handle/10150/193632

Keller, J. M. (2010). The Arcs model of motivational design. In *Motivational design for learning and performance* (pp. 43–74). Springer. doi:10.1007/978-1-4419-1250-3_3

Keller, J. M., & Kopp, T. (1987). Application of the ARCS model of motivational design. In C. M. Reigeluth (Ed.), *Instructional theories in action: Lessons illustrating selected theories and models* (pp. 289–320). LawrenceErlbaum Associates, Inc.

Kelley, K., Lai, K., & Wu, P. J. (2008). *Chapter: Using R For Data Analysis: A Best Practice For Research. Best Practices in Quantitative Methods*. SAGE Publications, Inc.

Kementerian Kesehatan Republik Indonesia. (2016). *Wilayah dengan Kejadian Luar Biasa Demam Berdarah Dengue di 11 Provinsi Indonesia [Areas with Extraordinary Events of Dengue Hemorrhagic Fever in 11 Provinces of Indonesia]*. Depkes. http://www.depkes.go.id/article/print/16030700001/wilayah-klb-dbd-ada-di-11-provinsi.html

Kementerian Kesehatan Republik Indonesia. (2021). *Center for Data and Information*. Kemkes. https://pusdatin.kemkes.go.id/folder/view/01/structure-publikasi-data-pusat-data-dan-informasi.html

Khalid, S. & Prieto-Alhambra, D. (2019). Machine Learning for Feature Selection and Cluster Analysis in Drug Utilisation Research. *Current Epidemiology Reports, 6*. . doi:10.1007/s40471-019-00211-7

Khalilzadeh, R., & Haghifam, M. R. (2023). Planning and comparing a pure AC or a hybrid AC/DC distribution network: A case study for an urban zone and an industrial park. *Journal of Iranian Association of Electrical and Electronics Engineers*, *20*(2), 77–86. doi:10.52547/jiaeee.20.2.77

Khan, A. A., Chaudhari, O., & Chandra, R. (2024). A review of ensemble learning and data augmentation models for class imbalanced problems: Combination, implementation and evaluation. *Expert Systems with Applications*, *244*, 122778. doi:10.1016/j.eswa.2023.122778

Khan, S. I., & Hoque, A. S. M. L. (2020). SICE: An improved missing data imputation technique. *Journal of Big Data*, *7*(1), 37. doi:10.1186/s40537-020-00313-w PMID:32547903

Khan, U. T., & Zia, M. F. (2021). Smart city technologies, key components, and its aspects. *4th International Conference on Innovative Computing, ICIC 2021,* November 2021. IEEE. 10.1109/ICIC53490.2021.9692989

Kim, B. (2018). A Study on the Application and the Effect of Business Culture Class Using Keller's ARCS Motivational Model. *Journal of Digital Convergence*, *16*, 73–82.

Kim, B., Srinivasan, K., Kong, S. H., Kim, J. H., Shin, C. S., & Ram, S. (2023). ROLEX: A NOVEL METHOD FOR INTERPRETABLE MACHINE LEARNING USING ROBUST LOCAL EXPLANATIONS. *Management Information Systems Quarterly*, *47*(3), 1303–1332. doi:10.25300/MISQ/2022/17141

Kim, J., Kwak, Y., Mun, S.-H., & Huh, J.-H. (2023). Imputation of missing values in residential building monitored data: Energy consumption, behavior, and environment information. *Building and Environment*, *245*, 110919. doi:10.1016/j.buildenv.2023.110919

Kohonen, T. (1990). The self-organizing map. *Proceedings of the IEEE*, *78*(9), 1464–1480. doi:10.1109/5.58325

Kohonen, T. (2003). Learning vector quantization. In M. A. Arbib (Ed.), *The handbook of brain theory and neural networks* (2nd ed., pp. 631–634). MIT Press.

Kohonen, T. (2012). *Self-organization and associative memory* (Vol. 8). Springer Science & Business Media.

Kshirsagar, R., Hsu, L.-Y., Greenberg, C. H., McClelland, M., Mohan, A., Shende, W., Tilmans, N. P., Guo, M., Chheda, A., Trotter, M., Ray, S., & Alvarado, M. (2021). Accurate and Interpretable Machine Learning for Transparent Pricing of Health Insurance Plans. *Proceedings of the AAAI Conference on Artificial Intelligence*, *35*(17), 15127–15136. doi:10.1609/aaai.v35i17.17776

Kumari, A. (2018). *Verification and validation techniques for streaming big data analytics in internet of things environment.* . doi:10.1049/iet-net.2018.5187

Kumari, A., & Tanwar, S. (2020). *A Data Analytics Scheme for Security-aware Demand Response Management in Smart Grid System.* 2020 IEEE 7th Uttar Pradesh Section International Conference on Electrical, Electronics and Computer Engineering (UPCON), Prayagraj, India. 10.1109/UPCON50219.2020.9376458

Kumari, A., & Tanwar, S. (2021). *Reveal: An AI-based Big Data Analytics Scheme for Energy Price Prediction and Load Reduction.* 2021 11th International Conference on Cloud Computing, Data Science & Engineering (Confluence), Noida, India. 10.1109/Confluence51648.2021.9377144

Kumari, A., Kakkar, R., Tanwar, S., Garg, D., Polkowski, Z., Alqahtani, F., & Tolba, A. (2024). Multi-agent-based decentralized residential energy management using Deep Reinforcement Learning. *Journal of Building Engineering*. doi:10.1016/j.jobe.2024.109031

Kumari, A., Tanwar, S., Tyagi, S., & Kumar, N. (2018). Fog computing for Healthcare 4.0 environment: Opportunities and challenges. *Computers & Electrical Engineering, 72*. doi:10.1016/j.compeleceng.2018.08.015

Kumari, A., Tanwar, S., Tyagi, S., Kumar, N., Parizi, R. M., & Choo, K.-K. R. (2019). Fog data analytics: A taxonomy and process model. *Journal of Network and Computer Applications, 128.* doi:10.1016/j.jnca.2018.12.013

Kumari, D. (2020). *Redills: Deep Learning-Based Secure Data Analytic Framework for Smart Grid Systems.* 2020 IEEE International Conference on Communications Workshops (ICC Workshops), Dublin, Ireland. 10.1109/ICCWorkshops49005.2020.9145448

Kumari, M. M. (2020). *ArMor: A Data Analytics Scheme to identify malicious behaviors on Blockchain-based Smart Grid System.* GLOBECOM 2020 - 2020 IEEE Global Communications Conference, Taipei, Taiwan. 10.1109/GLOBECOM42002.2020.9348061

Kumari, A., & Tanwar, S. (2020). Secure data analytics for smart grid systems in a sustainable smart city: Challenges, solutions, and future directions. *Sustainable Computing : Informatics and Systems, 28,* 100427. doi:10.1016/j.suscom.2020.100427

Kumari, A., & Tanwar, S. (2021). AI-based Peak Load Reduction Approach for Residential Buildings using Reinforcement Learning. *2021 International Conference on Computing, Communication, and Intelligent Systems (ICCCIS),* Greater Noida, India. 10.1109/ICCCIS51004.2021.9397241

Kumari, A., & Tanwar, S. (2022). A secure data analytics scheme for multimedia communication in a decentralized smart grid. *Multimedia Tools and Applications, 81*(24), 34797–34822. doi:10.1007/s11042-021-10512-z

Kwak, S. K., & Kim, J. H. (2017). Statistical data preparation: Management of missing values and outliers. *Korean Journal of Anesthesiology, 70*(4), 407. doi:10.4097/kjae.2017.70.4.407 PMID:28794835

Kwon, O., Lee, N., & Shin, B. (2014). Data quality management, data usage experience and acquisition intention of big data analytics. *International Journal of Information Management, 34*(3), 387–394. doi:10.1016/j.ijinfomgt.2014.02.002

Kyriazopoulou, C. (2015). Smart city technologies and architectures: A literature review. *SMARTGREENS 2015 - 4th International Conference on Smart Cities and Green ICT Systems, Proceedings,* 5–16. 10.5220/0005407000050016

Labola, Y. A. (2020). *Daerah Rawan Kasus Demam Berdarah di Indonesia [Areas Prone to Dengue Fever Cases in Indonesia].* Journalism Data. https://katadata.co.id/analisisdata/5e9a57b001ae9/daerah-rawan-kasus-demam-berdarah-di-indonesia

Lai, Y.-H. (2018). The Climatic Factors Affecting Dengue Fever Outbreaks in Southern Taiwan: An Application of Symbolic Data Analysis. *{BioMedical} Engineering {OnLine}, 17*(S2). doi:10.1186/s12938-018-0575-4

Lake, S. E., & Tsai, C. W. (2022). An exploration of how training set composition bias in machine learning affects identifying rare objects. *Astronomy and Computing, 40,* 100617. doi:10.1016/j.ascom.2022.100617

LaPorte, R. E. (1993). Needed: Universal Monitoring of All Serious Diseases of Global Importance. *American Journal of Public Health, 83*(7), 941–943. doi:10.2105/AJPH.83.7.941 PMID:8328611

Lavanya, P. M., & Sasikala, E. (2024). 6 - Enhanced performance of drug review classification from social networks by improved ADASYN training and Natural Language Processing techniques. In D. J. Hemanth (Ed.), *Computational Intelligence Methods for Sentiment Analysis in Natural Language Processing Applications* (pp. 111–127). Morgan Kaufmann. doi:10.1016/B978-0-443-22009-8.00004-5

Lea, P. (2018). *Internet of Things for Architects: Architecting IoT solutions by implementing sensors, communication infrastructure, edge computing, analytics, and security.* Packt Publishing Ltd.

Lea, R. (2017). Smart Cities: An Overview of the Technology Trends Driving Smart Cities. *IEEE Advancing Technology for Humanity, 3*(March), 1–16.

Lee, W. C. (2024). Seeing the whole elephant: Integrated advanced data analytics in support of RWE for the development and use of innovative pharmaceuticals. *Expert Review of Pharmacoeconomics & Outcomes Research*, *24*(1), 57–62. doi:10.1080/14737167.2023.2275674 PMID:37902993

Legaspi, J., Bhada, S. V., Mathisen, P., & Dewinter, J. (2020). Smart City Transportation: A Multidisciplinary Literature Review. *Conference Proceedings - IEEE International Conference on Systems, Man and Cybernetics, 2020-October*(January), (pp. 957–964). IEEE. 10.1109/SMC42975.2020.9283471

Li, K., & Keller, J. M. (2018). Use of the ARCS model in education: A literature review. *Computers & Education*, *122*, 54–62. doi:10.1016/j.compedu.2018.03.019

Lim, S. J. (2023). E-Healthcare System in Smart Cities using Ai-Enabled Internet of Things: Applications and Challenges. *International Journal of Intelligent Systems and Applications in Engineering*, *11*(7s), 655–660.

Li, S., Marsaglia, N., Garth, C., Woodring, J., Clyne, J., & Childs, H. (2018, September). Data reduction techniques for simulation, visualization, and data analysis. *Computer Graphics Forum*, *37*(6), 422–447. doi:10.1111/cgf.13336

Liu, B., Li, Y., Ghosh, S., Sun, Z. N., Ng, K., & Hu, J. Y. (2020). Complication Risk Profiling in Diabetes Care: A Bayesian Multi-Task and Feature Relationship Learning Approach. *IEEE Transactions on Knowledge and Data Engineering*, *32*(7), 1276–1289. doi:10.1109/TKDE.2019.2904060

Liu, D., Zhong, S., Lin, L., Zhao, M., Fu, X., & Liu, X. (2024). Feature-level SMOTE: Augmenting fault samples in learnable feature space for imbalanced fault diagnosis of gas turbines. *Expert Systems with Applications*, *238*, 122023. doi:10.1016/j.eswa.2023.122023

Liu, X. (2024). Research on dimension reduction for visualization of simplified security region of integrated energy system considering renewable energy access. *International Journal of Electrical Power & Energy Systems*, *156*, 109777. doi:10.1016/j.ijepes.2023.109777

Li, X., Zhong, Y., Shang, W., Zhang, X., Shan, B., & Wang, X. (2022). Total electricity consumption forecasting based on Transformer time series models. *Procedia Computer Science*, *214*, 312–320. doi:10.1016/j.procs.2022.11.180

Li, Y., Sun, H., Dong, B., & Wang, H. W. (2018). Cost-efficient data acquisition on online data marketplaces for correlation analysis. *Proceedings of the VLDB Endowment International Conference on Very Large Data Bases*, *12*(4), 362–375. doi:10.14778/3297753.3297757

Li, Y., Zhou, Q., Fan, Y., Pan, G., Dai, Z., & Lei, B. (2024). A novel machine learning-based imputation strategy for missing data in step-stress accelerated degradation test. *Heliyon*, *10*(4), e26429. doi:10.1016/j.heliyon.2024.e26429 PMID:38434061

Lógó, J. M., Krausz, N., Potó, V., & Barsi, A. (2021). Quality Aspects of High-Definition Maps. *The International Archives of the Photogrammetry, Remote Sensing and Spatial Information Sciences*, *43*, 389–394. doi:10.5194/isprs-archives-XLIII-B4-2021-389-2021

López, M. Z., Zareipour, H., & Quashie, M. (2024). Forecasting the Occurrence of Electricity Price Spikes: A Statistical-Economic Investigation Study. *Forecasting*, *6*(1), 1–23.

Lu, H., Li, Y., Chen, M., Kim, H., & Serikawa, S. (2018). Brain intelligence: Go beyond artificial intelligence. *Mobile Networks and Applications*, *23*(2), 368–375. doi:10.1007/s11036-017-0932-8

Łukawska, M., Cazor, L., Paulsen, M., Rasmussen, T. K., & Nielsen, O. A. (2024). Revealing and reducing bias when modelling choice behaviour on imbalanced panel datasets. *Journal of Choice Modelling*, *50*, 100471. doi:10.1016/j.jocm.2024.100471

M. (2022). VisioDECT Dataset: An Aerial Dataset for Scenario-Based Multi-Drone Detection and Identification. *IEEE Dataport*.

Ma, C., Zhao, M., & Zhao, Y. (2023). An overview of Hadoop applications in transportation big data. [English Edition]. *Journal of Traffic and Transportation Engineering*, *10*(5), 900–917. doi:10.1016/j.jtte.2023.05.003

Macnaghten, P., Kearnes, M. B., & Wynne, B. (2005). Nanotechnology, governance, and public deliberation: What role for the social sciences? *Science Communication*, *27*(2), 268–291. doi:10.1177/1075547005281531

MacQueen, J. (1967). Some methods for classification and analysis of multivariate observations. In *Proceedings of the fifth Berkeley symposium on mathematical statistics and probability* (Vol. 1, No. 14, pp. 281-297).

Madhavakanna, S. (2018). Application Of Machine Learning Techniques, Big Data Analytics In *HealthCare Sector – A Literature Survey*. IEEE. . doi:10.1109/I-SMAC.2018.8653654

Madley-Dowd, P., Hughes, R., Tilling, K., & Heron, J. (2019). The proportion of missing data should not be used to guide decision on multiple imputation. *Journal of Clinical Epidemiology*, *10*, 63–73. doi:10.1016/j.jclinepi.2019.02.016 PMID:30878639

Mahdavinejad, M. S., Rezvan, M., Barekatain, M., Adibi, P., Barnaghi, P., & Sheth, A. P. (2018). Machine learning for Internet of Things data analysis: A survey. *Digital Communications and Networks*, *4*(3), 161–175. doi:10.1016/j.dcan.2017.10.002

Mahmud, M., Huang, J., Salloum, S., Emara, T., & Sadatdiynov, K. (2020). A survey of data partitioning and sampling methods to support big data analysis. *Big Data Mining and Analytics, 3*(2). . doi:10.26599/BDMA.2019.9020015

Makarova, I., Buyvol, P., Fatikhova, L., & Parsin, G. (2021). Influence of smart education on characteristics of urban lands' transport systems. *MATEC Web of Conferences, 334*, 01001. 10.1051/matecconf/202133401001

Mala, S., & Jat, M. K. (2019). Implications of Meteorological and Physiographical Parameters on Dengue Fever Occurrences in Delhi. *The Science of the Total Environment*, *650*, 2267–2283. doi:10.1016/j.scitotenv.2018.09.357 PMID:30292120

Malhotra, D., & Rishi, O. (2021). An intelligent approach to design of E-Commerce metasearch and ranking system using next-generation big data analytics. *Journal of King Saud University. Computer and Information Sciences*, *33*(2), 183–194. doi:10.1016/j.jksuci.2018.02.015

Mandžuka, S. (2015). *Intelligent Transport Systems: Selected Lectures*.

Mariani, S., De Piero, M. E., & Haverich, A. (2023). Future noninvasive monitoring. In *Cardiopulmonary Bypass* (pp. 65–83). Elsevier. doi:10.1016/B978-0-443-18918-0.00005-X

Marquez, J. A., & Mohammad, A. A. (2023). Optimal planning and operation of distribution systems using network reconfiguration and flexibility services. *Energy Reports*, *9*, 3910–3919. doi:10.1016/j.egyr.2023.02.082

Martin, K. (2022). *Ethics of data and analytics: Concepts and cases*. Auerbach Publications. doi:10.1201/9781003278290

Masud, M., Singh, P., Gaba, G. S., Kaur, A., Alroobaea, R., Alrashoud, M., & Alqahtani, S. A. (2021). CROWD: Crow Search and Deep Learning based Feature Extractor for Classification of Parkinson's Disease. *ACM Transactions on Internet Technology*, *21*(3), 1–18. doi:10.1145/3418500

Mateo, J., Torres, A. M., Soria, C., & Santos, J. L. (2013). A method for removing noise from continuous brain signal recordings. *Computers & Electrical Engineering*, *39*(5), 1561–1570. doi:10.1016/j.compeleceng.2012.11.006

Matloff, N. (2011). *The Art of R Programming: A Tour of Statistical Software Design*. No Starch Press.

Matta, A., Fritz, K., Kim, B., Kim, S., & Akhmouch, A. (2020). Smart Cities and Inclusive Growth. *Smart Cities and Inclusive Growth, per year*, 1–59.

Maurya, N., Kumar, N., & Maurya, V. (2020). A review on machine learning (feature selection, classification and clustering) approaches of big data mining in different area of research. *Journal of Critical Reviews.*, 7, 2610–2626. doi:10.31838/jcr.07.19.322

Mayya, V., S., S. K., Krishnan, G. S., & Gangavarapu, T. (2021). Multi-channel, convolutional attention based neural model for automated diagnostic coding of unstructured patient discharge summaries. *Future Generation Computer Systems, 118*, 374–391. doi:10.1016/j.future.2021.01.013

Mazumdar, S., & Dhar, S. (2015, March). Hadoop as Big Data Operating System—The Emerging Approach for Managing Challenges of Enterprise Big Data Platform. In *2015 IEEE First International Conference on Big Data Computing Service and Applications* (pp. 499-505). IEEE. 10.1109/BigDataService.2015.72

Mazumder, S. B. (2017). *Distributed Computing in Big Data Analytics: Concepts, Technologies and Applications*. Springer. doi:10.1007/978-3-319-59834-5

Mazza, P. I. (2021). Education & Smart Cities: The Role of the Goals of Agenda 2030 for Sustainable Development of Smart Cities Patricia. *International Journal of Innovative Studies in Sociology and Humanities, 6*(2), 24–31.

McCallum, A., & Nigam, K. (1999). Text classification by bootstrapping with keywords, EM and shrinkage. In Unsupervised learning in natural language processing.

McCallum, A., Nigam, K., & Ungar, L. H. (2000). Efficient clustering of high-dimensional data sets with application to reference matching. In *Proceedings of the sixth ACM SIGKDD international conference on Knowledge discovery and data mining* (pp. 169-178). ACM. 10.1145/347090.347123

McClelland, D. C. (1988). *Human Motivation*. Cambridge University Press. doi:10.1017/CBO9781139878289

McGilvray, D. (2021). *Executing data quality projects: Ten steps to quality data and trusted information*. Academic Press.

McLachlan, G. J., & Krishnan, T. (2007). *The EM algorithm and extensions*. John Wiley & Sons.

Mehedi Hassan, M. (2022). An unsupervised cluster-based feature grouping model for early diabetes detection. *Healthcare Analytics*, (2). doi:10.1016/j.health.2022.100112

Memon, S. M. Z., Wamala, R., & Kabano, I. H. (2023). A comparison of imputation methods for categorical data. *Informatics in Medicine Unlocked, 42*, 101382. doi:10.1016/j.imu.2023.101382

Mensah, J. A., Ocran, E., & Asiedu, L. (2023). On multiple imputation-based reconstruction of degraded faces and recognition in multiple constrained environments. *Scientific African, 22*, e01964.. doi:10.1016/j.sciaf.2023.e01964

Miller, D. D. (2020). Machine Intelligence in Cardiovascular Medicine. *Cardiology, 28*(2), 53–64. doi:10.1097/CRD.0000000000000294 PMID:32022759

Minelli, M., Chambers, M., & Dhiraj, A. (2013). *Big data, big analytics: emerging business intelligence and analytic trends for today's businesses* (Vol. 578). John Wiley & Sons. doi:10.1002/9781118562260

Mishra, P., Pandey, C. M., Singh, U., Gupta, A., Sahu, C., & Keshri, A. (2019). Descriptive Statistics and Normality Tests for Statistical Data. *Annals of Cardiac Anaesthesia, 22*(1), 67. doi:10.4103/aca.ACA_157_18 PMID:30648682

Modarresi, J., & Hosseinnia, H. (2023). Worldwide Daily Optimum Tilt Angle Model to Obtain Maximum Solar Energy. *Journal of the Institution of Electronics and Telecommunication Engineers, 69*(1), 549–557. doi:10.1080/03772063.2020.1831412

Moghaddam, A., Ayub, S. B., Zare, K., & Golpîra, H. (2024). Modeling the power trading strategies of a retailer with multi-microgrids: A robust bi-level optimization approach. *Energy Sources. Part B, Economics, Planning, and Policy*, *19*(1), 2288952. doi:10.1080/15567249.2023.2288952

Mohamed, I., Fouda, M. M., & Hosny, K. M. (2022). Machine Learning Algorithms for COPD Patients Readmission Prediction: A Data Analytics Approach. *IEEE Access : Practical Innovations, Open Solutions*, *10*, 15279–15287. doi:10.1109/ACCESS.2022.3148600

Mohammadzadeh, Z., Saeidnia, H. R., Lotfata, A., Hassanzadeh, M., & Ghiasi, N. (2023). Smart city healthcare delivery innovations: A systematic review of essential technologies and indicators for developing nations. *BMC Health Services Research*, *23*(1), 1–14. doi:10.1186/s12913-023-10200-8 PMID:37904181

Molenberghs, G., Fitzmaurice, G., Kenward, M. G., Tsiatis, A., & Verbeke, G. (Eds.). (2014). *Handbook of Missing Data Methodology* (0 ed.). Chapman and Hall/CRC. doi:10.1201/b17622

Morid, M. A., Sheng, O. R. L., & Dunbar, J. (2023). Time Series Prediction Using Deep Learning Methods in Healthcare. *ACM Transactions on Management Information Systems*, *14*(1), 1–29. Advance online publication. doi:10.1145/3531326

Mühlhoff, R. (2021). Predictive privacy: Towards an applied ethics of data analytics. *Ethics and Information Technology*, *23*(4), 675–690. doi:10.1007/s10676-021-09606-x

Mukherjee, A., Datta, J., Jorapur, R., Singhvi, R., Haloi, S., & Akram, W. (2012, December). Shared disk big data analytics with apachehadoop. In *2012 19th International Conference on High Performance Computing* (pp. 1-6). IEEE.

Müller-Eie, D., & Kosmidis, I. (2023). Sustainable mobility in smart cities: A document study of mobility initiatives of mid-sized Nordic smart cities. *European Transport Research Review*, *15*(1), 36. Advance online publication. doi:10.1186/s12544-023-00610-4

Mullie, L., Afilalo, J., Archambault, P., Bouchakri, R., Brown, K., Buckeridge, D. L., Cavayas, Y. A., Turgeon, A. F., Martineau, D., Lamontagne, F., Lebrasseur, M., Lemieux, R., Li, J., Sauthier, M., St-Onge, P., Tang, A., Witteman, W., & Chassé, M. (2024). CODA: An open-source platform for federated analysis and machine learning on distributed healthcare data. *Journal of the American Medical Informatics Association : JAMIA*, *31*(3), 651–665. doi:10.1093/jamia/ocad235 PMID:38128123

Mullins, M., Holland, C. P., & Cunneen, M. (2021). Creating ethics guidelines for artificial intelligence and big data analytics customers: The case of the consumer European insurance market. *Patterns (New York, N.Y.)*, *2*(10), 100362. doi:10.1016/j.patter.2021.100362 PMID:34693379

Munjal, N. K., Clark, R. S. B., Simon, D. W., Kochanek, P. M., & Horvat, C. M. (2023). Interoperable and explainable machine learning models to predict morbidity and mortality in acute neurological injury in the pediatric intensive care unit: Secondary analysis of the TOPICC study. *Frontiers in Pediatrics*, *11*, 1177470. doi:10.3389/fped.2023.1177470 PMID:37456559

Murakami, M., Takebayashi, Y., Harigane, M., Mizuki, R., Suzuki, Y., Ohira, T., Maeda, M., & Yasumura, S. (2020). Analysis of direction of association between radiation risk perception and relocation using a random-intercept and cross lagged panel model: The Fukushima Health Management Survey. *SSM - Population Health*, *12*, 100706. doi:10.1016/j.ssmph.2020.100706 PMID:33344746

Murtagh, F., & Legendre, P. (2014). Ward's hierarchical agglomerative clustering method: Which algorithms implement Ward's criterion? *Journal of Classification*, *31*(3), 274–295. doi:10.1007/s00357-014-9161-z

Nabi, F., & Zhou, X. (2024). Enhancing intrusion detection systems through dimensionality reduction: A comparative study of machine learning techniques for cyber security. *Cyber Security and Applications, 2*, 100033.

Naeem, S., Ali, A., Anam, S., & Ahmed, M. (2023). An Unsupervised Machine Learning Algorithms: Comprehensive Review. *IJCDS Journal.*, *13*(1), 911–921. doi:10.12785/ijcds/130172

Naganathan, V. (2018). Comparative analysis of Big data, Big data analytics: Challenges and trends. [IRJET]. *International Research Journal of Engineering and Technology*, *5*(05), 1948–1964.

Nair, L. R. (2020). RetoNet: A deep learning architecture for automated retinal ailment detection. *Multimedia Tools and Applications*, *79*(21–22), 15319–15328. doi:10.1007/s11042-018-7114-y

Naiseh, M., & Shukla, P. (2023). The well-being of Autonomous Vehicles (AVs) users under uncertain situations. *ACM International Conference Proceeding Series*. ACM. 10.1145/3597512.3603150

Nambiar Jyothi, R., & Prakash, G. (2019). *A Deep Learning-Based Stacked Generalization Method to Design Smart Healthcare Solution.*, doi:10.1007/978-981-13-5802-9_20

Nancy, A. A., Ravindran, D., Raj Vincent, P. M. D., Srinivasan, K., & Gutierrez Reina, D. (2022). IoT-Cloud-Based Smart Healthcare Monitoring System for Heart Disease Prediction via Deep Learning. *Electronics (Basel)*, *11*(15), 2292. doi:10.3390/electronics11152292

Nandimath, J., Banerjee, E., Patil, A., Kakade, P., Vaidya, S., & Chaturvedi, D. (2013, August). Big data analysis using Apache Hadoop. In *2013 IEEE 14th International Conference on Information Reuse & Integration (IRI)* (pp. 700-703). IEEE. 10.1109/IRI.2013.6642536

Nasiri, N., Saatloo, A. M., Mirzaei, M. A., Ravadanegh, S. N., Zare, K., Mohammadi-ivatloo, B., & Marzband, M. (2023). A robust bi-level optimization framework for participation of multi-energy service providers in integrated power and natural gas markets. *Applied Energy*, *340*(C), 121047. doi:10.1016/j.apenergy.2023.121047

Ng, A., Jordan, M., & Weiss, Y. (2001). On spectral clustering: Analysis and an algorithm. *Advances in Neural Information Processing Systems*, 14.

Ngueilbaye, A., Wang, H., Mahamat, D. A., & Junaidu, S. B. (2021). Modulo 9 model-based learning for missing data imputation. *Applied Soft Computing*, *103*, 107167. doi:10.1016/j.asoc.2021.107167

Nguyen, T., Ibrahim, S., & Fu, X. (2023). *Deep Clustering with Incomplete Noisy Pairwise Annotations: A Geometric Regularization Approach*. arXiv preprint arXiv:2305.19391.

Nguyen, H. V., Ha, D. H., Dao, A. T. M., Golley, R. K., Scott, J. A., Spencer, J., Bell, L., Devenish-Coleman, G., & Do, L. G. (2023). Pairwise approach for analysis and reporting of child's free sugars intake from a birth cohort study. *Community Dentistry and Oral Epidemiology*, *51*(5), 820–828. doi:10.1111/cdoe.12770 PMID:35815733

Nikolov, R., Shoikova, E., Krumova, M., Kovatcheva, E., Dimitrov, V., & Shikalanov, A. (2016). Learning in a Smart City Environment. *Journal of Communication and Computer*, *13*(7), 338–350. doi:10.17265/1548-7709/2016.07.003

Nissen, J. M., & Shemwell, J. T. (2016). Gender, experience, and self-efficacy in introductory physics. *Physical Review. Physics Education Research*, *12*(2), 020105. doi:10.1103/PhysRevPhysEducRes.12.020105

Noor, N. M., Al Bakri Abdullah, M. M., Yahaya, A. S., & Ramli, N. A. (2014). Comparison of Linear Interpolation Method and Mean Method to Replace the Missing Values in Environmental Data Set. *Materials Science Forum*, *803*, 278–281. . doi:10.4028/www.scientific.net/MSF.803.278

Ntafalias, A., Tsakanikas, S., Skarvelis-Kazakos, S., Papadopoulos, P., Skarmeta-Gómez, A. F., González-Vidal, A., Tomat, V., Ramallo-González, A. P., Marin-Perez, R., & Vlachou, M. C. (2022). Design and Implementation of an Interoperable Architecture for Integrating Building Legacy Systems into Scalable Energy Management Systems. *Smart Cities*, *5*(4), 1421–1440. doi:10.3390/smartcities5040073

Nti, I., Quarcoo, J., Aning, J., & Fosu, G. (2022). A mini-review of machine learning in big data analytics: Applications, challenges, and prospects. *Big Data Mining and Analytics, 5*(2). doi:10.26599/BDMA.2021.9020028

Nurjannah, U. (2019). *PENERAPAN ARCS PADA PEMBELAJARAN MATEMATIKA MENGGUNAKAN MODEL STAD DAN NHT DI SMP NEGERI 3 AMPELGADING MALANG.* Jurnal Ilmu Kependidikan. doi:10.33506/jq.v7i1.350

Oancea, B., & Dragoescu, R. M. (2014). *Integrating R and hadoop for big data analysis.* arXiv preprint arXiv:1407.4908.

OECD. (2015). *Enhancing the Contribution of Export.* OECD. https://www.oecd.org/regional/regionaldevelopment/Smart-Cities-FINAL.pdf

Oh, C., Chung, J.-Y., & Han, Y. (2024). Domain transformation learning for MR image reconstruction from dual domain input. *Computers in Biology and Medicine, 170*, 108098. doi:10.1016/j.compbiomed.2024.108098 PMID:38330825

Oladimeji, D., Gupta, K., Kose, N. A., Gundogan, K., Ge, L., & Liang, F. (2023). Smart Transportation: An Overview of Technologies and Applications. *Sensors (Basel), 23*(8), 1–32. doi:10.3390/s23083880 PMID:37112221

Olatunbosun, S. and Min-Koo, Kim. (2022). *Measuring Construction Workers' Cognitive Status Using Physiological Signals: A Systematic Review.* The 22nd International Conference on Construction Applications of Virtual Reality, South Korea.

Omidlou, N., & Kaufmann, H. R. (2023). reviewed paper The Role of Smart Cities on Smart Healthcare Management Neda Omidlou. *Hans Rüdiger Kaufmann.*, (September), 807–815.

Omran, M. G., Engelbrecht, A. P., & Salman, A. (2007). An overview of clustering methods. *Intelligent Data Analysis, 11*(6), 583–605. doi:10.3233/IDA-2007-11602

Omri, M., Jooshaki, M., Abbaspour, A., & Fotuhi-Firuzabad, M. (2024). Modeling Microgrids for Analytical Distribution System Reliability Evaluation. *IEEE Transactions on Power Systems*, 1–12. doi:10.1109/TPWRS.2024.3354299

Ortega, A., Frossard, P., Kovačević, J., Moura, J. M., & Vandergheynst, P. (2018). Graph signal processing: Overview, challenges, and applications. *Proceedings of the IEEE, 106*(5), 808–828. doi:10.1109/JPROC.2018.2820126

Oussous, A., Benjelloun, F.-Z., Ait Lahcen, A., & Belfkih, S. (2018). Big Data technologies: A survey. *Journal of King Saud University. Computer and Information Sciences, 30*(4), 431–448. doi:10.1016/j.jksuci.2017.06.001

Oyeleye, M., Chen, T. H., Titarenko, S., & Antoniou, G. (2022). A Predictive Analysis of Heart Rates Using Machine Learning Techniques. *International Journal of Environmental Research and Public Health, 19*(4), 2417. doi:10.3390/ijerph19042417 PMID:35206603

Pacheco Rocha, N., Dias, A., Santinha, G., Rodrigues, M., Queirós, A., & Rodrigues, C. (2019). Smart Cities and Healthcare: A Systematic Review. *Technologies, 7*(3), 1–15. doi:10.3390/technologies7030058

Padula, W. V., Kreif, N., Vanness, D. J., Adamson, B., Rueda, J. D., Felizzi, F., Jonsson, P., IJzerman, M. J., Butte, A., & Crown, W. (2022). Machine Learning Methods in Health Economics and Outcomes Research-The PALISADE Checklist: A Good Practices Report of an ISPOR Task Force. *Value in Health, 25*(7), 1063–1080. doi:10.1016/j.jval.2022.03.022 PMID:35779937

Pallavi, P. (2017). Smart Education Leads To a Smart City. *International Journal of Advance Research in Science and Engineering, 6*(01), 129–132.

Pawlikowska-Piechotka, A., Łukasik, N., Ostrowska-Tryzno, A., & Sawicka, K. (2017). *A Smart City Initiative.* 561–583. doi:10.4018/978-1-5225-1978-2.ch024

Peer, E., Rothschild, D., Gordon, A., Evernden, Z., & Damer, E. (2022, August). Data quality of platforms and panels for online behavioral research. *Behavior Research Methods*, *54*(4), 1643–1662. doi:10.3758/s13428-021-01694-3 PMID:34590289

Peng, R. D. (2016). *Exploratory Data Analysis with R*. Springer.

Pereira, J., & Silveira, M. (2019). Learning Representations from Healthcare Time Series Data for Unsupervised Anomaly Detection. *2019 IEEE International Conference on Big Data and Smart Computing (BigComp)*, Kyoto, Japan. 10.1109/BIGCOMP.2019.8679157

Pereira, R. M., Costa, Y. M. G., & Silla, C. N. Jr. (2020). MLTL: A multi-label approach for the Tomek Link undersampling algorithm. *Neurocomputing*, *383*, 95–105. doi:10.1016/j.neucom.2019.11.076

Pfeifer, R., & Iida, F. (2004). Embodied artificial intelligence: Trends and challenges. In *Embodied artificial intelligence* (pp. 1–26). Springer. doi:10.1007/978-3-540-27833-7_1

Phan, T., Feld, S., & Linnhoff-Popien, C. (2020). *Artificial Intelligence—the new Revolutionary Evolution*.

Plummer, J., Rappaport, S. D., Hall, T., & Barocci, R. (2007). *The online advertising playbook: Proven strategies and tested tactics from the advertising research foundation*. John Wiley & Sons.

Podeschi, R. J., & DeBo, J. (2019). Integrating big data analytics into an undergraduate information systems program using Hadoop. *Information Systems Education Journal*, *17*(4), 42.

Pourghaderi, N., Fotuhi-Firuzabad, M., Moeini-Aghtaie, M., Kabirifar, M., & Dehghanian, P. (2023). A local flexibility market framework for exploiting DERs' flexibility capabilities by a technical virtual power plant. *IET Renewable Power Generation*, *17*(3), 681–695. doi:10.1049/rpg2.12624

Qiu, T., Chi, J., Zhou, X., Ning, Z., Atiquzzaman, M., & Wu, D. O. (2020). Edge computing in industrial internet of things: Architecture, advances and challenges. *IEEE Communications Surveys and Tutorials*, *22*(4), 2462–2488. doi:10.1109/COMST.2020.3009103

R., S., S., S. R., R., H., S., A., & C., R. K. (2022). Artificial Intelligence in Smart cities and Healthcare. *EAI Endorsed Transactions on Smart Cities, 6*(3), e5. doi:10.4108/eetsc.v6i3.2275

Rabe-Hesketh, S., & Skrondal, A. (2023). Ignoring Non-ignorable Missingness. *Psychometrika, 88*(1), 31–50. doi:10.1007/s11336-022-09895-1 PMID:36539650

Radwan, A. H., & Morsi, A. A. G. (2023). Autonomous vehicles and changing the future of cities: Technical and urban perspectives. *Journal of Urban Regeneration and Renewal*, *16*(1), 85–108.

Raebel, M. A., Shetterly, S., Lu, C. Y., Flory, J., Gagne, J. J., Harrell, F. E., Haynes, K., Herrinton, L. J., Patorno, E., Popovic, J., Selvan, M., Shoaibi, A., Wang, X., & Roy, J. (2016). Methods for using clinical laboratory test results as baseline confounders in multi-site observational database studies when missing data are expected. *Pharmacoepidemiology and Drug Safety*, *25*(7), 798–814. doi:10.1002/pds.4015 PMID:27146273

Ragazou, K., Passas, I., Garefalakis, A., Galariotis, E., & Zopounidis, C. (2023). Big Data Analytics Applications in Information Management Driving Operational Efficiencies and Decision-Making: Mapping the Field of Knowledge with Bibliometric Analysis Using R. *Big Data Cogn. Comput., 7*(1), 13. doi:10.3390/bdcc7010013

Raghupathi, W., & Raghupathi, V. (2014). Big data analytics in healthcare: Promise and potential. *Health Information Science and Systems*, *2*(1), 1–10. doi:10.1186/2047-2501-2-3 PMID:25825667

Rahok, S., Oneda, H., Osawa, S., & Ozaki, K. (2019). Motivation System for Students to Learn Control Engineering and Image Processing. *Journal of Robotics Mechatronics, 31*(3), 405–411. doi:10.20965/jrm.2019.p0405

Rai, B. (2020). *Goodness of Fit and Test of Independence with RExamples Using Chi-Square* Test. [Video]. YouTube..

Raisch, S., & Krakowski, S. (2021). Artificial intelligence and management: The automation–augmentation paradox. *Academy of Management Review, 46*(1), 192–210. doi:10.5465/amr.2018.0072

Raj, P., Raman, A., Nagaraj, D., & Duggirala, S. (2015). High-performance big-data analytics. Computing Systems and Approaches. Springer. doi:10.1007/978-3-319-20744-5

Rajaraman, A., & Ullman, J. D. (2011). *Mining of massive datasets.* Cambridge University Press. doi:10.1017/CBO9781139058452

Rajasegar, R. S., Gouthaman, P., Ponnusamy, V., Arivazhagan, N., & Nallarasan, V. (2024). Data Privacy and Ethics in Data Analytics. In Data Analytics and Machine Learning: Navigating the Big Data Landscape (pp. 195-213). Singapore: Springer Nature Singapore. doi:10.1007/978-981-97-0448-4_10

Ramkumar, G., Seetha, J., Priyadarshini, R., Gopila, M., & Saranya, G. (2023). IoT-based patient monitoring system for predicting heart disease using deep learning. *Measurement, 218,* 113235. doi:10.1016/j.measurement.2023.113235

Ramos Rojas, J. A., Beth Kery, M., Rosenthal, S., & Dey, A. (2017). Sampling techniques to improve big data exploration. *2017 IEEE 7th Symposium on Large Data Analysis and Visualization (LDAV),* (pp. 26–35). IEEE. 10.1109/LDAV.2017.8231848

Rao, S., Verma, A. K., & Bhatia, T. (2023). Hybrid ensemble framework with self-attention mechanism for social spam detection on imbalanced data. *Expert Systems with Applications, 217,* 119594. doi:10.1016/j.eswa.2023.119594

Raschka, S. (2018). Model evaluation, model selection, and algorithm selection in machine learning. *arXiv preprint arXiv:1811.12808.*

Rasjid, Z. E. (2021). Predictive Analytics in Healthcare: The Use of Machine Learning for Diagnoses. *2021 International Conference on Electrical, Computer and Energy Technologies (ICECET),* (pp. 1–6). IEEE. 10.1109/ICECET52533.2021.9698508

Renard, F., Guedria, S., Palma, N. D., & Vuillerme, N. (2020). Variability and reproducibility in deep learning for medical image segmentation. *Scientific Reports, 10*(1), 13724. doi:10.1038/s41598-020-69920-0 PMID:32792540

Rezaeeian, S., Bayat, N., Rabiee, A., Nikkhah, S., & Soroudi, A. (2022). Optimal Scheduling of Reconfigurable Microgrids in Both Grid-Connected and Isolated Modes Considering the Uncertainty of DERs. *Energies, 15*(15), 5369. doi:10.3390/en15155369

Rezvani, S., & Wang, X. (2023). A broad review on class imbalance learning techniques. *Applied Soft Computing, 143,* 110415. doi:10.1016/j.asoc.2023.110415

Ribeiro, P., Dias, G., & Pereira, P. (2021). Transport systems and mobility for smart cities. *Applied System Innovation, 4*(3), 61. doi:10.3390/asi4030061

Rizk, D. K. A. A. (2020). Proposed Framework for Smart Healthcare Services. *Future Computing and Informatics Journal, 4*(2), 90–97. doi:10.54623/fue.fcij.4.2.4

Rocha, N. P., Dias, A., Santinha, G., Rodrigues, M., Queirós, A., & Rodrigues, C. (2019). Smart Cities and Public Health: A Systematic Review. *Procedia Computer Science, 164,* 516–523. doi:10.1016/j.procs.2019.12.214

Rokach, L., & Maimon, O. (2005). Clustering methods. In *Data mining and knowledge discovery handbook* (pp. 321–352). Springer. doi:10.1007/0-387-25465-X_15

Rostami, R., & Hosseinnia, H. (2021). Energy Management of Reconfigurable Distribution System in Presence of Wind Turbines by Considering Several Kinds of Demands. *Energy, 2*(2), 199–203.

Sa'adi, Z., Yusop, Z., Alias, N. E., Chow, M. F., Muhammad, M. K. I., Ramli, M. W. A., Iqbal, Z., Shiru, M. S., Rohmat, F. I. W., Mohamad, N. A., & Ahmad, M. F. (2023). Evaluating Imputation Methods for rainfall data under high variability in Johor River Basin, Malaysia. *Applied Computing and Geosciences, 20*, 100145.

Saber, H., Somai, M., Rajah, G. B., Scalzo, F., & Liebeskind, D. S. (2019). Predictive analytics and machine learning in stroke and neurovascular medicine. *Neurological Research, 41*(8), 681–690. doi:10.1080/01616412.2019.1609159 PMID:31038007

Sachdeva, S. (2023). Standard-based personalized healthcare delivery for kidney illness using deep learning. *Physiological Measurement, 44*(8), 084001. doi:10.1088/1361-6579/ace09f PMID:37343580

Sadjati, I. M. (2017). Smart Education dan Smart City. *Optimalisasi Peran Sains Dan Teknologi Untuk Mewujudkan Smart City*, 11–34. https://repository.ut.ac.id/7070/1/UTFMIPA2017-01-ida.pdf

Sambyal, N., Saini, P., & Syal, R. (2020). Microvascular Complications in Type-2 Diabetes: A Review of Statistical Techniques and Machine Learning Models. *Wireless Personal Communications, 115*(1), 1–26. doi:10.1007/s11277-020-07552-3

Samek, W., Wiegand, T., & Müller, K. R. (2017). Explainable artificial intelligence: Understanding, visualizing and interpreting deep learning models. *arXiv preprint arXiv:1708.08296.*

Sardi, A., Sorano, E., Cantino, V., & Garengo, P. (2023). Big data and performance measurement research: Trends, evolution and future opportunities. *Measuring Business Excellence, 27*(4), 531–548. doi:10.1108/MBE-06-2019-0053

Sarker, I. H. (2021). *Data Science and Analytics: An Overview from Data-Driven Smart Computing*. Decision-Making and Applications Perspective. doi:10.1007/s42979-021-00765-8

Scala, D., Aguilar Cuesta, Á. I., Rodríguez-Domenech, M. Á., & Cañizares Ruiz, M. (2024). Bibliometric Study on the Conceptualisation of Smart City and Education. *Smart Cities, 7*(1), 597–614. doi:10.3390/smartcities7010024

Schafer, J. B., Konstan, J. A., & Riedl, J. (2001). E-commerce recommendation applications. *Data Mining and Knowledge Discovery, 5*(1/2), 115–153. doi:10.1023/A:1009804230409

Seifian, A., Bahrami, M., Shokouhyar, S., & Shokoohyar, S. (2023). Data-based drivers of big data analytics utilization: Moderating role of IT proactive climate. *Benchmarking, 30*(10), 4461–4486. doi:10.1108/BIJ-11-2021-0670

Selbst, A. D., & Barocas, S. (2018). The intuitive appeal of explainable machines. *Fordham Law Review, 87*, 1085.

Sellam, T., & Kersten, M. (2016). Ziggy: Characterizing query results for data explorers. *Proceedings of the VLDB Endowment International Conference on Very Large Data Bases, 9*(13), 1473–1476. doi:10.14778/3007263.3007287

Selya, A., Anshutz, D., Griese, E., Weber, T. L., Hsu, B. N., & Ward, C. (2021). Predicting unplanned medical visits among patients with diabetes: Translation from machine learning to clinical implementation. *BMC Medical Informatics and Decision Making, 21*(1), 111. doi:10.1186/s12911-021-01474-1 PMID:33789660

Senjaya, W. F., Yahya, B. N., & Lee, S.-L. (2023). Ergonomic risk level prediction framework for multiclass imbalanced data. *Computers & Industrial Engineering, 184*, 109556. doi:10.1016/j.cie.2023.109556

Shafqat, S., Fayyaz, M., Khattak, H. A., Bilal, M., Khan, S., Ishtiaq, O., Abbasi, A., Shafqat, F., Alnumay, W. S., & Chatterjee, P. (2023). Leveraging Deep Learning for Designing Healthcare Analytics Heuristic for Diagnostics. *Neural Processing Letters*, *55*(1), 53–79. doi:10.1007/s11063-021-10425-w PMID:33551665

Shaheen, S., Cohen, A., Dowd, M., & Davis, R. (2019). *A Framework for Integrating Transportation Into Smart Cities*. Issue October. doi:10.31979/mti.2019.1705

ShakahG. (2022). *Modeling of Healthcare Monitoring System of Smart Cities*. *11*(2), 926–931. https://doi.org/ doi:10.18421/TEM112

Shariatkhah, M. H., Haghifam, M. R., & Paqaleh, M. A. (2023). Simultaneous placement of DGs and capacitors in distribution networks-determining the optimum configuration. *Energy Engineering and Management*, *1*(1), 11–18.

Sharma, K. K., & Seal, A. (2021). Outlier-robust multi-view clustering for uncertain data. *Knowledge-Based Systems*, *211*, 106567. doi:10.1016/j.knosys.2020.106567

Sharma, R., Saghapour, E., & Chen, J. Y. (2024). An NLP-based Technique to Extract Meaningful Features from Drug SMILES. *iScience*, *109127*(3), 109127. doi:10.1016/j.isci.2024.109127 PMID:38455979

Shashikumar, S. P., Josef, C. S., Sharma, A., & Nemati, S. (2021). DeepAISE? An interpretable and recurrent neural survival model for early prediction of sepsis. *Artificial Intelligence in Medicine*, *113*, 102036. Advance online publication. doi:10.1016/j.artmed.2021.102036 PMID:33685592

Shen, C. (2018). A transdisciplinary review of deep learning research and its relevance for water resources scientists. *Water Resources Research*, *54*(11), 8558–8593. doi:10.1029/2018WR022643

Sherman, H. D., & Zhu, J. (2006). *Service productivity management: Improving service performance using data envelopment analysis (DEA)*. Springer science & business media. doi:10.1007/0-387-33231-6

Sherratt, T. (2015). *One Way ANOVA in R Studio*. [Video]. YouTube.

Shi, J., & Malik, J. (2000). Normalized cuts and image segmentation. *IEEE Transactions on Pattern Analysis and Machine Intelligence*, *22*(8), 888–905. doi:10.1109/34.868688

Shoba, V., Mahima, S., & Mahesh, P. (2023). Addressing the challenges of handling missing data in Data Science applications. *International Journal of Innovative Research in Information Security*, *10*(3), 76–78. doi:10.26562/ijiris.2023.v0903.05

Shukla, D. (2023). A narrative review on types of data and scales of measurement: An initial step in the statistical analysis of medical data. *Cancer Research, Statistics, and Treatment*, *6*(2), 279–283. doi:10.4103/crst.crst_1_23

Sinaga, K. P., & Yang, M.-S. (2020). Unsupervised K-Means Clustering Algorithm. *IEEE Access : Practical Innovations, Open Solutions*, *8*, 80716–80727. doi:10.1109/ACCESS.2020.2988796

Singh, D., & Garg, R. (2021). R and Hadoop Integration for Big Data Analytics. In *Proceedings of 3rd International Conference on Computing Informatics and Networks: ICCIN 2020* (pp. 13-22). Springer Singapore. 10.1007/978-981-15-9712-1_2

Singh, N. P., Gautam, A. K., & Sharan, T. (2022). An insight into the hardware and software aspects of a BCI system with focus on ultra-low power bulk driven OTA and Gm-C based filter design, and a detailed review of the recent AI/ML techniques. In *Artificial Intelligence-Based Brain-Computer Interface* (pp. 283–315). Elsevier. doi:10.1016/B978-0-323-91197-9.00015-1

Siripatana, B., Nopchanasuphap, K., & Chuai-Aree, S. (2021). Intelligent Traffic Light System Using Image Processing. *Proceedings - 2nd SEA-STEM International Conference, SEA-STEM 2021*, (pp. 14–18). IEEE. 10.1109/SEA-STEM53614.2021.9668057

Siriyasatien, P., Phumee, A., Ongruk, P., Jampachaisri, K., & Kesorn, K. (2016). Analysis of significant factors for dengue fever incidence prediction. *BMC Bioinformatics*, *17*(1), 166. doi:10.1186/s12859-016-1034-5 PMID:27083696

Smart Cities, E. U. Information System. (2017). The making of a smart city: best practices across Europe. *European Commission*, 256. www.smartcities-infosystem.eu

Smith, J. (2018). Advanced Analytics: The Next Big Thing. *International Conference on Data Science*. IEEE. DOI: 10.5678/icds.2018.987654

Solanas, A. (2015). *Smart Health : Improving Health services within Smart Cities. December.*

Solat, S., Aminifar, F., Safdarian, A., & Shayanfar, H. (2023). An expansion planning model for strategic visioning of active distribution network in the presence of local electricity market. *IET Generation, Transmission & Distribution*, *17*(24), 5410–5429. doi:10.1049/gtd2.13053

Souravlas, S., Sifaleras, A., & Katsavounis, S. (2019). A Parallel Algorithm for Community Detection in Social Networks, based on Path Analysis and threaded Binary Trees. *IEEE Access : Practical Innovations, Open Solutions*, *7*, 20499–20519. doi:10.1109/ACCESS.2019.2897783

Stahl, B. C., & Wright, D. (2018). Ethics and privacy in AI and big data: Implementing responsible research and innovation. *IEEE Security and Privacy*, *16*(3), 26–33. doi:10.1109/MSP.2018.2701164

Strong, C. (2015). *Humanizing big data: Marketing at the meeting of data, social science and consumer insight*. Kogan Page Publishers.

Sullivan, D., & Andridge, R. (2015). A hot deck imputation procedure for multiply imputing nonignorable missing data: The proxy pattern-mixture hot deck. *Computational Statistics & Data Analysis*, *82*, 173–185. doi:10.1016/j.csda.2014.09.008

Sun, Z., Ying, W., Zhang, W., & Gong, S. (2024). Undersampling method based on minority class density for imbalanced data. *Expert Systems with Applications*, *123328*, 123328. doi:10.1016/j.eswa.2024.123328

Swift, R. S. (2001). *Accelerating customer relationships: Using CRM and relationship technologies*. Prentice Hall Professional.

Tae, K. H., Roh, Y., Oh, Y. H., Kim, H., & Whang, S. E. (2019). Data Cleaning for Accurate, Fair, and Robust Models: A Big Data - AI Integration Approach. *Proceedings of the 3rd International Workshop on Data Management for End-to-End Machine Learning*, (pp. 1–4). IEEE. 10.1145/3329486.3329493

Taherdoost, H. (2021). *Data Collection Methods and Tools for Research; A Step-by-Step Guide to Choose Data Collection Technique for Academic and Business Research Projects.*

Taheri, M., Abedini, M., & Aminifar, F. (2023). A Novel Centralized Load Shedding Approach to Assess Short-Term Voltage Stability: A Model-Free Using Time Series Forecasting. *IEEE Transactions on Power Delivery*, *38*(5), 3076–3083. doi:10.1109/TPWRD.2023.3266265

Talamo, C., Pinto, M. R., Viola, S., & Atta, N. (2019). Smart cities and enabling technologies: Influences on urban Facility Management services. *IOP Conference Series. Earth and Environmental Science*, *296*(1), 012047. doi:10.1088/1755-1315/296/1/012047

Talosig, E. (2022). *Improving Digital Marketing for Attracting the Target Customer Segments.*

Tanwar, S., Tyagi, S., & Kumar, N. (Eds.). (2019). Security and privacy of electronic healthcare records: Concepts, paradigms and solutions. Institution of Engineering and Technology

Tanwar, S., Tyagi, S., & Kumar, N. (Eds.). (2019). Security and privacy of electronic healthcare records: Concepts, paradigms and solutions. Institution of Engineering and Technology.

Tanwar, S., Bhatia, Q., Patel, P., Kumari, A., Singh, P. K., & Hong, W.-C. (2020). Machine Learning Adoption in Blockchain-Based Smart Applications: The Challenges, and a Way Forward. *IEEE Access : Practical Innovations, Open Solutions*, *8*, 474–488. doi:10.1109/ACCESS.2019.2961372

Templeton, G. F., Kang, M., & Tahmasbi, N. (2021). Regression imputation optimizing sample size and emulation: Demonstrations and comparisons to prominent methods. *Decision Support Systems*, *151*, 113624. doi:10.1016/j.dss.2021.113624

Ten Cate, O., Dahdal, S., Lambert, T., Neubauer, F., Pless, A., Pohlmann, P. F., van Rijen, H., & Gurtner, C. (2020). Ten caveats of learning analytics in health professions education: A consumer's perspective. *Medical Teacher*, *42*(6), 673–678. doi:10.1080/0142159X.2020.1733505 PMID:32150499

*The use of Big Data Analytics in healthcare.* (2021). Springer. .[https://link.springer.com/article/10.1186/s40537-021-00553-4]

Thong Tran, N. D., Leung, C. K., Madill, E. W. R., & Binh, P. T. (2022). A Deep Learning Based Predictive Model for Healthcare Analytics. *2022 IEEE 10th International Conference on Healthcare Informatics (ICHI)*, 547–549. 10.1109/ICHI54592.2022.00106

Toghranegar, S., Rabiee, A., & Soroudi, A. (2022). Enhancing the unbalanced distribution network's hosting capacity for DERs via optimal load re-phasing. *Sustainable Cities and Society*, *87*, 87. doi:10.1016/j.scs.2022.104243

Toth, E. G., Gibbs, D., Moczygemba, J., & McLeod, A. (2021). Decision tree modeling in R software to aid clinical decision making. *Health and Technology*, *11*(3), 535–545. doi:10.1007/s12553-021-00542-w

Tsai, C. W., Yeh, T.-G., & Hsiao, Y.-R. (2018). Evaluation of Hydrologic and Meteorological impacts on Dengue Fever incidences in Southern Taiwan using Time-Frequency Analysis Methods. *Ecological Informatics*, *46*, 166–178. doi:10.1016/j.ecoinf.2018.05.002

Türel, Y., & Sanal, S. (2018). The effects of an ARCS based e-book on student's achievement, motivation, and anxiety. *Computers & Education*, *127*, 130–140. doi:10.1016/j.compedu.2018.08.006

Ucar, H., & Kumtepe, A. T. (2019). Effects of the ARCS-V-based motivational strategies on online learners' academic performance, motivation, volition, and course interest. *Journal of Computer Assisted Learning*, *36*(3), 335–349. doi:10.1111/jcal.12404

Usmadi, U., & Ergusni, E. (2018). Design of ARCSI Learning Model with Scientific Approach for Teaching Mathematics in School. *International Journal of Trends in Mathematics Education Research*. . doi:10.33122/ijtmer.v1i1.28

Uspenskaya-Cadoz, O., Alamuri, C., Wang, L., Yang, M., Khinda, S., Nigmatullina, Y., Cao, T., Kayal, N., O'Keefe, M., & Rubel, C. (2019). Machine Learning Algorithm Helps Identify Non-Diagnosed Prodromal Alzheimer's Disease Patients in the General Population. *The Journal of Prevention of Alzheimer's Disease*, *6*(3), 185–191. doi:10.14283/jpad.2019.10 PMID:31062833

Vairetti, C., Assadi, J. L., & Maldonado, S. (2024). Efficient hybrid oversampling and intelligent undersampling for imbalanced big data classification. *Expert Systems with Applications*, *246*, 123149. doi:10.1016/j.eswa.2024.123149

Van Buuren, S. (2018). *Flexible Imputation of Missing Data* (2nd ed.). Chapman and Hall/CRC., doi:10.1201/9780429492259

Van de Poel, I., & Robaey, Z. (2017). Safe-by-design: From safety to responsibility. *NanoEthics*, *11*(3), 297–306. doi:10.1007/s11569-017-0301-x PMID:29238409

Van Dusen, B., & Nissen, J. (2020). Associations between learning assistants, passing introductory physics, and equity: A quantitative critical race theory investigation. *Physical Review. Physics Education Research*, *16*(1), 010117. doi:10.1103/PhysRevPhysEducRes.16.010117

Vashishth, T. K., Sharma, V., Sharma, K. K., Kumar, B., Chaudhary, S., & Panwar, R. (2024). AI and Data Analytics for Market Research and Competitive Intelligence. In AI and Data Analytics Applications in Organizational Management (pp. 155-180). IGI Global. doi:10.4018/979-8-3693-1058-8.ch008

Vashishth, T. K., Kumar, B., Sharma, V., Chaudhary, S., Kumar, S., & Sharma, K. K. (2023). The Evolution of AI and Its Transformative Effects on Computing: A Comparative Analysis. In B. Mishra (Ed.), *Intelligent Engineering Applications and Applied Sciences for Sustainability* (pp. 425–442). IGI Global. doi:10.4018/979-8-3693-0044-2.ch022

Vekaria, D., Kumari, A., Tanwar, S., & Kumar, N. (2021). ξboost: An AI-Based Data Analytics Scheme for COVID-19 Prediction and Economy Boosting. IEEE Internet of Things Journal, 8(21). doi:10.1109/JIOT.2020.3047539

Vemulapalli, G. (2023). Self-Service Analytics Implementation Strategies for Empowering Data Analysts. *International Journal of Machine Learning and Artificial Intelligence*, *4*(4), 1–14.

Venkatasubramanian, S. (2022). Ambulatory Monitoring of Maternal and Fetal using Deep Convolution Generative Adversarial Network for Smart Health Care IoT System. *International Journal of Advanced Computer Science and Applications*, *13*(1). Advance online publication. doi:10.14569/IJACSA.2022.0130126

Venkatesh, R., Balasubramanian, C., & Kahappan, M. (2019). Development of Big Data Predictive Analytics Model for Disease Prediction using Machine learning Technique. *Journal of Medical Systems*, *43*(8), 272. doi:10.1007/s10916-019-1398-y PMID:31278468

Verbeke, G., & Molenberghs, G. (2024). *Hierarchical and incomplete data*. Elsevier.

Vimont, A., Leleu, H., & Durand-Zaleski, I. (2022). Machine learning versus regression modelling in predicting individual healthcare costs from a representative sample of the nationwide claims database in France. *The European Journal of Health Economics*, *23*(2), 211–223. doi:10.1007/s10198-021-01363-4 PMID:34373958

Vincent, R., Ait-Ahmed, M., Houari, A., & Benkhoris, M. F. (2020). Residential microgrid energy management considering flexibility services opportunities and forecast uncertainties. *International Journal of Electrical Power & Energy Systems*, *120*, 105981. doi:10.1016/j.ijepes.2020.105981

Visan, M., Negrea, S. L., & Mone, F. (2021). Towards intelligent public transport systems in Smart Cities; Collaborative decisions to be made. *Procedia Computer Science*, *199*, 1221–1228. doi:10.1016/j.procs.2022.01.155

Vodák, J., Šulyová, D., & Kubina, M. (2021). Advanced technologies and their use in smart city management. *Sustainability (Basel)*, *13*(10), 5746. doi:10.3390/su13105746

Vogel, A., Oremović, I., Šimić, R., & Ivanjko, E. (2018). Improving traffic light control by means of fuzzy logic. *Proceedings Elmar - International Symposium Electronics in Marine, 2018-Septe*(September). IEEE. 10.23919/ELMAR.2018.8534692

von Radecki, A., Tcholtchev, N., Lämmel, P., & Schaj, G. (). *Building Data Ecosystems to Unlock the Value of Urban (Big) Data: A Good Practices Reference Guide.*

Walkup, J. T., & Strawn, J. R. (2020). High-quality antidepressant prescribing: Please consider whether "perfection is the enemy of progress". *BMC Medicine*, *18*(1), 1–3. doi:10.1186/s12916-020-01621-x PMID:32438910

Wang, Y., Zhao, Y., & Terry, M. (2020). Unsupervised machine learning for the discovery of latent disease clusters and patient subgroups using electronic health records. *Journal of Biomedical Informatics, 102*. doi:10.1016/j.jbi.2019.103364

Wang, H., Xu, Z., Fujita, H., & Liu, S. (2016). Towards felicitous decision making: An overview on challenges and trends of Big Data. *Information Sciences, 367*, 747–765. doi:10.1016/j.ins.2016.07.007

Wang, S., Ren, J., Bai, R., Yao, Y., & Jiang, X. (2024). A Max-Relevance-Min-Divergence criterion for data discretization with applications on naive Bayes. *Pattern Recognition, 149*, 110236. doi:10.1016/j.patcog.2023.110236

Wang, X., Han, Y., Leung, V. C., Niyato, D., Yan, X., & Chen, X. (2020). Convergence of edge computing and deep learning: A comprehensive survey. *IEEE Communications Surveys and Tutorials, 22*(2), 869–904. doi:10.1109/COMST.2020.2970550

Wang, Y., Kung, L., & Byrd, T. A. (2018). Big data analytics: Understanding its capabilities and potential benefits for healthcare organizations. *Technological Forecasting and Social Change, 126*, 3–13. doi:10.1016/j.techfore.2015.12.019

Wedel, M., & Kannan, P. K. (2016). Marketing analytics for data-rich environments. *Journal of Marketing, 80*(6), 97–121. doi:10.1509/jm.15.0413

Weisberg, S. (2015). *Applied Linear Models with R*. CRC Press.

White, M. G. (2020). Why human subjects research protection is important. *The Ochsner Journal, 20*(1), 16–33. doi:10.31486/toj.20.5012 PMID:32284679

Williamson, B. (2015). Educating the smart city: Schooling smart citizens through computational urbanism. *Big Data & Society, 2*(2), 1–13. doi:10.1177/2053951715617783

Williams, R. (2015). *Missing data Part 1: overview, traditional methods*. University of Notre Dame.

Wilson, E. (2021). *Emerging Trends in Data Analytics and Business Intelligence*. Business Analytics Review. doi:10.6789/bar.2021.005

Wolff, A., Kortuem, G., & Cavero, J. (2015). Towards smart city education. *2015 Sustainable Internet and ICT for Sustainability. SustainIT, 2015*(May), 1–3. doi:10.1109/SustainIT.2015.7101381

World Health Organization. (2017). *Dengue Guidelines for Diagnosis, Treatment, Prevention and Control: New Edition*. WHO. https://www.who.int/rpc/guidelines/9789241547871/en

World Health Organization. (2023). *Dengue and Severe Dengue*. Newsroom. https://www.who.int/news-room/fact-sheets/detail/dengue-and-severe-dengue

Wu, W., Lin, W., Hsu, C. H., & He, L. (2018). Energy-efficient hadoop for big data analytics and computing: A systematic review and research insights. *Future Generation Computer Systems, 86*, 1351–1367. doi:10.1016/j.future.2017.11.010

Xiang, J., Hansen, A., Liu, Q., Liu, X., Tong, M. X., Sun, Y., Cameron, S., Hanson-Easey, S., Han, G.-S., Williams, C., Weinstein, P., & Bi, P. (2017). Association between Dengue Fever Incidence and Meteorological Factors in Guangzhou, China, 2005-2014. *Environmental Research, 153*, 17–26. doi:10.1016/j.envres.2016.11.009 PMID:27883970

Xie, Y., Huang, X., Qin, F., Li, F., & Ding, X. (2024). A majority affiliation based under-sampling method for class imbalance problem. *Information Sciences, 662*, 120263. doi:10.1016/j.ins.2024.120263

Xiong, Z., Sheng, H., Rong, W. G., & Cooper, D. E. (2012). Intelligent transportation systems for smart cities: A progress review. *Science China. Information Sciences, 55*(12), 2908–2914. doi:10.1007/s11432-012-4725-1

Xu, L., Stige, L. C., Chan, K.-S., Zhou, J., Yang, J., Sang, S., Wang, M., Yang, Z., Yan, Z., Jiang, T., Lu, L., Yue, Y., Liu, X., Lin, H., Xu, J., Liu, Q., & Stenseth, N. C. (2017). Climate Variation Drives Dengue Dynamics. *Proceedings of the National Academy of Sciences of the United States of America*, *114*(1), 113–118. doi:10.1073/pnas.1618558114 PMID:27940911

Yadav, A., Gupta, V., Sahu, H., & Shrimal, S. (2017). Artificial Intelligence-New Era. *International Journal of New Technology and Research*, *3*(3).

Yadav, M., Kakkar, M., & Kaushik, P. (2023). Harnessing Artificial Intelligence to Empower HR Processes and Drive Enhanced Efficiency in the Workplace to Boost Productivity. *International Journal on Recent and Innovation Trends in Computing and Communication*, *11*(8s), 381–390. doi:10.17762/ijritcc.v11i8s.7218

Yang, W.-C., Lai, J.-P., Liu, Y.-H., Lin, Y.-L., Hou, H.-P., & Pai, P.-F. (2024). Using Medical Data and Clustering Techniques for a Smart Healthcare System. *Electronics (Basel)*, *13*(1), 140. doi:10.3390/electronics13010140

Yan, H., Cui, Z., Luo, X., Wang, R., & Yao, Y. (2023). Emphasizing feature inter-class separability for improving highly imbalanced overlapped data classification. *Knowledge-Based Systems*, *276*, 110745. doi:10.1016/j.knosys.2023.110745

Yavari Nejad, F., & Varathan, K. D. (2021). Identification of Significant Climatic Risk Factors and Machine Learning Models in Dengue Outbreak Prediction. *BMC Medical Informatics and Decision Making*, *21*(1), 1–12. doi:10.1186/s12911-021-01493-y PMID:33931058

Yoon, S. Y., Zelt, T., & Narloch, U. (2021). *Smart City Pathways for Developing Asia: An Analytical Framework and Guidance*. ADB.. https://www.adb.org/publications/smart-city-pathways-developing-asia

Yoon, H., & Li, J. (2019). A Novel Positive Transfer Learning Approach for Telemonitoring of Parkinson's Disease. *IEEE Transactions on Automation Science and Engineering*, *16*(1), 180–191. doi:10.1109/TASE.2018.2874233

Yousuff, A. R. M., Hasan, M. Z., Anand, R., & Babu, M. R. (2024). *Leveraging deep learning models for continuous glucose monitoring and prediction in diabetes management: towards enhanced blood sugar control*. International Journal Of System Assurance Engineering And Management. doi:10.1007/s13198-023-02200-y

Yushananta, P., & Ahyanti, M. (2014). Pengaruh Faktor Iklim dan Kepadatan Jentik ae. Aegypti terhadap Kejadian DBD [The Influence of Climate Factors and Density of Aedes Aegypti Larvae on the Occurrence of Dengue Fever]. *Jurnal Kesehatan, 5*(1).

Zareapoor, M., Shamsolmoali, P., & Yang, J. (2021). Oversampling adversarial network for class-imbalanced fault diagnosis. *Mechanical Systems and Signal Processing, 149*, 107175. Eyuboglu, S., Varma, M., Saab, K., Delbrouck, J. B., Lee-Messer, C., Dunnmon, J., ... & Ré, C. (2022). Domino: Discovering systematic errors with cross-modal embeddings. *arXiv preprint arXiv:2203.14960*. Li, Q., Shen, C., Chen, L., & Zhu, Z. (2021). Knowledge mapping-based adversarial domain adaptation: A novel fault diagnosis method with high generalizability under variable working conditions. *Mechanical Systems and Signal Processing, 147*, 107095.

Zhang, H., & Zou, F. (2020). A Survey of the Dark Web and Dark Market Research. *2020 IEEE 6th International Conference on Computer and Communications, ICCC 2020*, (pp. 1694–1705). IEEE. 10.1109/ICCC51575.2020.9345271

Zhang, L., Li, J., Xu, X., Liu, F., Guo, Y., Yang, Z., & Hu, T. (2023). High spatial granularity residential heating load forecast based on Dendrite net model. *Energy*, *269*(C), 126787. doi:10.1016/j.energy.2023.126787

Zhao, C., & Shen, W. (2024). Imbalanced domain generalization via Semantic-Discriminative augmentation for intelligent fault diagnosis. *Advanced Engineering Informatics*, *59*, 102262. doi:10.1016/j.aei.2023.102262

Zhao, Y., Zhao, N., & Lyu, R. (2023). The dynamic coupling and spatio-temporal differentiation of green finance and industrial green transformation: Evidence from China regions. *Heliyon, 9*(12), e22726. doi:10.1016/j.heliyon.2023.e22726 PMID:38076129

Zhou, Y., Wu, J., & Gan, W. (2023). P2P energy trading via public power networks: Practical challenges, emerging solutions, and the way forward. *Frontiers in Energy, 17*(2), 189–197. doi:10.1007/s11708-023-0873-9

Zhuang, R., Fang, H., Zhang, Y., Lu, A., & Huang, R. (2017). Smart learning environments for a smart city: From the perspective of lifelong and lifewide learning. *Smart Learning Environments, 4*(1), 6. doi:10.1186/s40561-017-0044-8

Zhu, G., Liu, T., Xiao, J., Zhang, B., Song, T., Zhang, Y., Lin, L., Peng, Z., Deng, A., Ma, W., & Hao, Y. (2019). Effects of Human Mobility, Temperature and Mosquito Control on the Spatiotemporal Transmission of Dengue. *The Science of the Total Environment, 651*, 969–978. doi:10.1016/j.scitotenv.2018.09.182 PMID:30360290

Zhu, J., Ge, Z., Song, Z., & Gao, F. (2018). Review and big data perspectives on robust data mining approaches for industrial process modeling with outliers and missing data. *Annual Reviews in Control, 46*, 107–133. doi:10.1016/j.arcontrol.2018.09.003

Zimmer, M. (2020). "But the data is already public": on the research ethics in Facebook. In *The ethics of information technologies* (pp. 229–241). Routledge. doi:10.4324/9781003075011-17

Zuccalà, M., & Verga, E. S. (2017). Enabling Energy Smart Cities through Urban Sharing Ecosystems. *Energy Procedia, 111*(September 2016), 826–835. doi:10.1016/j.egypro.2017.03.245

# About the Contributors

**Aparna Kumari**, is associated with the Department of Computer Science and Engineering, Institute of Technology, Nirma University, Ahmedabad, Gujarat, India. She is having more than 12+ years of experience and focuses on cutting-edge research and teaching. Her broad research area includes Smart Grid Systems, Blockchain Technology, Electric Vehicles, and Renewable Energy Sources. Recently, She has won Shri P Prahlaad Chabaria Award-2023 for Best women Profession- as a Runner up from Hope foundation, IEEE India council, IEEE affinity group, IEEE pune section and WIE. She has been listed in the world's Top 2% Scientists as per the list published by Stanford University's USA in the years 2021,2022, and 2023. Two of her novel works on COVID-19 have been approved by the WHO and included in their "COVID-19 Global literature on coronavirus disease" database. She authored/co-authored 40 publications (28 in peer-reviewed SCI-indexed International journals, 10 papers presented in top-tier IEEE International conferences, and 02 book chapters in Springer and IET). She is an active member of IEEE and Women in Engineering (WIE) India. She strives to contribute to society through her outreach to societal projects. She aims to facilitate access to resources for underprivileged students.

\*\*\*

**Simeon Okechukwu Ajakwe** received his Ph.D. degree in IT-Convergence Engineering with distinction, Kumoh National Institute of Technology, Gumi, South Korea, in 2023. Prior to this, he received his Master of Science (MSc) degree in Information Technology (2016) with distinction from the Federal University of Technology, Owerri, Imo State, Nigeria, Bachelor of Science (2009), and a Diploma degree (2004) in Computer Science from Imo State University, Owerri; and the Institute of Management Technology, Enugu, respectively. Simeon is a Chartered Information Technology Professional (Citp) with many years of IT-related industrial and academic experience. He is a member of IEEE, the Association of Computing Machinery (ACM), the Computer Professionals of Nigeria (CPN), and the Nigeria Computer Society (NCS). He has received several awards, such as Best PhD Thesis Award, Best Paper Award, Research Excellence Award, etc. Simeon has served as an editor and reviewer for different reputable peer-reviewed journals as well as published several articles and conference papers. His research interest cut across wireless communications, UAV networks, localization and positioning system, AI, Drones surveillance

**Wiwik Anggraeni** completed her undergraduate studies in Mathematics at Institut Teknologi Sepuluh Nopember (ITS), Surabaya, Indonesia, in 1997. She pursued her master's degree in informatics at ITS, graduating in 2003. Then, she completed her doctoral education in Electrical Engineering at ITS in 2022. Following this, she began her career as a lecturer in the Department of Information Systems at ITS in 2001. Her research interests include predictive and business analytics, focusing on modeling and forecasting

**Israel Ayodamola Bayode** is a dedicated Ph.D. researcher in the Department of Applied Environmental Science and Engineering at Kyung Hee University, focusing primarily on the application of Artificial Intelligence (AI) to address global challenges within the energy sector. With a robust background in computational and mathematical skills, Bayode obtained both his Bachelor's and Master's degrees in Mathematics from the esteemed University of Ibadan in 2014 and 2018, respectively. His diverse professional experience encompasses project management, data analytics, data science, and DevOps engineering, showcasing versatility and proficiency across multiple technical domains. Driven by a profound passion for leveraging AI to address complexities in energy, environment, health, and finance, Bayode also maintains keen interests in cutting-edge technologies such as robotic process automation, blockchain technology, and clean energy. His commitment to advancing research and innovation is palpable through his academic journey and professional pursuits, establishing him as a valuable contributor to the fields of data science and artificial intelligence.

**Opeyemi Deji-Oloruntoba** received a Bachelor of Science in Biochemistry from the University of Ado-Ekiti Nigeria in 2003 and a Master of Technology from the Federal University of Technology Akure Nigeria with a distinction in Food Science and Technology, Akure Nigeria in 2012. She is currently pursuing a Ph.D. degree in Smart foods and Drug Biotechnology at Inje University, South Korea. She is a Part-time researcher with the Institute of Antioxidant and Antiaging. She is a member of the Nigerian Institute of Food Science and Technology (NIFST). Her research interests cut across Smart food solutions, Biotechnology, Antioxidants, and C.elegans models for biomedical research, and diabetic research. She is an ardent advocate for the sustainable development goals

**Duorinaah Francis Xavier** holds a Bachelor's degree in Quantity Surveying and Construction Economics from the Kwame Nkrumah University of Science and Technology, Ghana (2021). Currently, he is pursuing an interdisciplinary master's degree in Safety Engineering and Big Data while working as a research assistant in the Smart Construction and Systems Laboratory at Chungbuk National University, South Korea. His research focuses on the utilization of immersive technologies, machine learning, and physiological monitoring to enhance construction worker safety.

**Alka Golyan**, a dedicated educator and researcher in Computer Science, holds a master's in computer applications from Pune University and is multiple times NET qualified. With over 10 years of academic experience, including roles as an Assistant Professor at Dayanand College and Pranami Group of Colleges, she has demonstrated excellence in teaching and administration. Alka has also contributed to academia through conference papers.

**Rushi Shah** is a dedicated researcher in computer science, pioneering innovative solutions at the intersection of artificial intelligence and cybersecurity. With a passion for advancing technology, he strives to unravel complex challenges and drive progress in the digital realm.

**Asif Iqbal Hajamydeen** holds a Bachelor's degree in Computer Science from Bharathidasan University, India (1995) and an M.Sc in Computer Science from the same university (1998). He earned his Ph.D. in 2014 from Universiti Putra Malaysia with a thesis on "Unsupervised Anomaly-Based Intrusion Detection Framework for Heterogeneous Logs." Beginning his career as a Lecturer in 2000, he taught programming at Kolej TAFE Seremban, Malaysia. Over the years, he transitioned to Imperia Institute of Technology as a Software Development Trainer and later joined Management & Science University in 2007 as a Lecturer, where he now holds the position of Associate Professor (2022). Besides teaching, he supervises postgraduate students, obtained Professional Technologist recognition in 2022, and currently serves as the Manager of the Cyber Security Operation Centre at the Centre of Cyber Security and Big Data in the university.

**Mauridhi Hery Purnomo** earned his bachelor's degree from Institut Teknologi Sepuluh Nopember (ITS) Surabaya, Indonesia, in 1985, then his Master's in Engineering, as well as the Ph.D. degree from Osaka City University, Osaka, Japan, in 1995 and 1997 respectively. He joined Institut Teknologi Sepuluh Nopember, Surabaya, in 1985 and has been a Professor since 2004. His research interest currently pertains to intelligent applications, electric power systems operation, control, and management.

**Upinder Kaur** is working as an Assistant Professor in the Department of Computer Science and Engineering, Akal University, Bathinda, Punjab, India. She received her Ph. D. Degree at Department of Computer Science and Applications, Kurukshetra University, Kurukshetra. She is in teaching since October 2006. She holds Master of Technology (M. Tech.) degree in Computer Science and Engineering from MMEC,Mullana, Ambala, India .Her main research interests are in the areas of Distributed Computing, Distributed Data Structures, Cloud Computing, Data Science and Analytics, ML/DL. Currently working on the research issues in applications of deep learning in agriculture and health care. She has attended many National and International Conferences/workshops and she has more than 25 research papers in national / international journals and conferences. She has also a member of IEEE, ACM and supervising three Ph.D. Scholars and several graduate and undergraduate students in multi-cloud domain and data science in agriculture and deep learning in bio-signals.

**Sunil Kumar** is working as professor and head of the computer communication and engineering department in Manipal University Jaipur. He has completed his PhD in 2015. He has teaching experience of 20 years .He is guiding many research scholars. He has published many research papers in journals of repute. He is a senior member of many professional societies like IEEE.

**Nisrina Nur Mahmudha** has completed the undergraduate program at the Sepuluh Nopember Institute of Technology (ITS) Department of Information Systems and graduated in 2019. While studying, she was active in the Data Engineering and Business Intelligence laboratories. Currently, she works for a private company operating in the health sector. His research interests are data science, including forecasting.

**Samuel O. Olatunbosun** is a driven and innovative Architectural Engineering student at Chungbuk National University, South Korea. Passionate about revolutionizing construction safety, he dedicates his research to leveraging artificial intelligence solutions. He holds a Diploma and a Bachelor's degree in Quantity Surveying from The Polytechnic, Ibadan and Obafemi Awolowo University, Nigeria respectively. His research interests are construction safety, construction analytics, wearable sensing, Neuroergonomics, AI. Samuel has consistently demonstrated academic excellence. His outstanding achievements have been recognized through prestigious awards such as the Academic Excellence Award, Best Graduating Student Award, and the esteemed Glocal Hope Scholarship.

**Asheesh Pandey** has more than 19 years of teaching, research and industry experience. He has worked with various reputed institutions of Dr A. P. J. Abdul Kalam Technical University Lucknow. He has 2 years of industry experience as software developer in HCL Technology. Currently he is working as Senior Assistant Professor, Department of Computer Applications, ABES Engineering College Ghaziabad. He is MCA, MTech (CS), Pursuing PhD (CS). During his research, he has published many research papers in Scopus, SCI, WoS and UGC Care journals. He has written several books and refreshers for BCA, BSc CS/IT, BTech, MCA students on Python For Beginners- Learn Python In 21 Days, Digital Electronics & Computer Organization, Software Engineering, Computer Fundamental & Office Automation, Information System Analysis and Design. His area of interest is C/C++, Java, Python, Artificial Intelligence, Machine Learning, Data Structure, ANN and Software Engineering etc.

**Harsh Parekh** is a dedicated researcher in computer science, pioneering innovative solutions at the intersection of artificial intelligence and cybersecurity. With a passion for advancing technology, he strives to unravel complex challenges and drive progress in the digital realm.

**Pujiadi Pujiadi** has a master's degree in health engineering. He has worked in the Public Health Office of Malang Regency for more than 23 years. So far, he has dealt with infectious diseases, especially diseases caused by mosquitoes, such as dengue fever. Currently, he is the person in charge of the dengue fever prevention program

**Nikhil Raval** is a dedicated researcher in computer science, pioneering innovative solutions at the intersection of artificial intelligence and cybersecurity. With a passion for advancing technology, he strives to unravel complex challenges and drive progress in the digital realm.

**Vikas Sharma** completed his Graduation and Post Graduation from Chaudhary Charan Singh University, Meerut, U.P. Currently Pursuing his Ph.D. in Computer Science and Engineering from Govt. Recognized University. Presently, he is working as an Assistant Professor in the Department of Computer Science and Applications, IIMT University, Meerut, U.P. He has been awarded as Excellence in teaching award 2019. He is the reviewer member of some reputed journals. He has published several book chapters and research papers of national and international reputed journals.

**Ahgalya Subbiah** is currently a Senior Lecturer with the Faculty of Information Science and Engineering (FISE) at the Management and Science University (MSU). She has many years of experience teaching System and Data Science courses such as System Analysis and Design, Database System, Project Management, Software Engineering Design, and Strategic IS, IS Infrastructure and Data Mining, etc. She graduated from UTM with a PhD degree in Information System. Her research focuses on Service System Value, HCI, e-Government, Public Policy, Health Informatics, Gerontology and IoT. She worked in Citibank Singapore for six years and gained plenty of industry experience through different functions and been in education & training for the past twelve years and helped many young students to GOT. Her research in the last decade has revolved around the following theme: Service Innovation & Co-Creation of Value between the computational complexity of various computational problems, particularly lattice problems. Some of her recent research centers around improving construction of such extractors in various settings, and their applications.

**Divyani Tirthyani** is pursuing PhD from Manipal University Jaipur in Computer & Communication Department, working as Assistant Professor in a reputed Engineering College. Her research interest are AI and ML in Healthcare.

**Tanuja Tomer** is persuing Ph.D from Himgiri Zee University, Dehradun. Prior PhD has been working as MBA coordinator at Nimbus Academy of Management, Dehradun since 2017. I have teaching experience of around 09 years. My Academic qualification is MBA (Human Resource management &amp; International business). My area of interest is Human Resource management, Organizational Behavior, Strategic Management, Training and Development. I have participated in more than 10 FDPs of AICTE and have 4 research papers published in UGC journals.

**Dhruvesh Vaghasiya** is a dedicated researcher in computer science, pioneering innovative solutions at the intersection of artificial intelligence and cybersecurity. With a passion for advancing technology, he strives to unravel complex challenges and drive progress in the digital realm.

**Tarun Kumar Vashishth** is an active academician and researcher in the field of computer science with 22 years of experience. He earned Ph.D. Mathematics degree specialized in Operations Research; served several academic positions such as HoD, Dy. Director, Academic Coordinator, Member Secretary of Department Research Committee, Assistant Center superintendent and Head Examiner in university examinations. He is involved in academic development and scholarly activities. He is member of International Association of Engineers, The Society of Digital Information and Wireless Communications, Global Professors Welfare Association, International Association of Academic plus Corporate (IAAC), Computer Science Teachers Association and Internet Society. His research interest includes Cloud Computing, Artificial Intelligence, Machine Learning and Operations Research; published more than 25 research articles with 2 books and 20 book chapters in edited books. He is contributing as member of editorial and reviewers boards in conferences and various computer journals published by CRC Press, Taylor and Francis, Springer, IGI global and other universities.

**Shally Vats** is working as an assistant professor at Manipal University Jaipur. She has completed her PhD from Banasthali Vidyapith, Banasthali. She has a teaching experience of 12 years. She has published many journal and conference papers. She is a reviewer of many journals of repute. She is a member of many professional societies like IEEE.

**Warusia Mohamed Yassin** is a senior lecturer in Department of Computer Systems and Communication at the Faculty of Information Technology and Communication, Universiti Teknikal Malaysia Melaka (UTeM). He is a head of information security, digital forensic and computer networking (INSFORNET) research group. He completes his Bachelor Degree in Computer Science (2008), Master of Science (2011) and PhD (2015) at Universiti Putra Malaysia (UPM). His research interests include Security In Computing, Malware Analysis, Machine Learning, Deep Learning, and Deepfake.

# Index

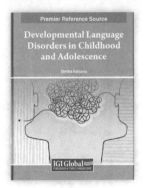

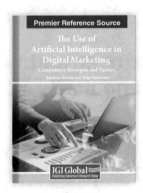

  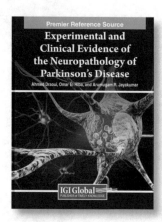 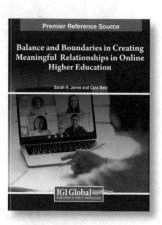

www.igi-global.com

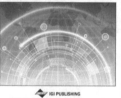

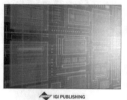

Printed in the United States
by Baker & Taylor Publisher Services